small arms survey 2007

guns and the city

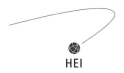

HEI

A Project of the Graduate
Institute of International Studies,
Geneva

CAMBRIDGE
UNIVERSITY PRESS

CAMBRIDGE UNIVERSITY PRESS
Cambridge, New York, Melbourne, Madrid, Cape Town, Singapore, São Paulo

Cambridge University Press
The Edinburgh Building, Cambridge CB2 8RU, UK

Published in the United States of America by Cambridge University Press, New York

www.cambridge.org
Information on this title: www.cambridge.org/9780521706544

First published 2007

Printed in the United Kingdom at the University Press, Cambridge

A catalogue record for this publication is available from the British Library

ISBN 978-0-521-88039-8 hardback
ISBN 978-0-521-70654-4 paperback

FOREWORD

Every year gun crime kills about 250,000 people and injures many more. The resources needed to tackle armed violence and deal with its aftermath divert funding from education, health care, and job creation. The fear of being assaulted with a firearm or being caught in crossfire confines people to living behind high walls and locked doors. Gun violence, in short, hurts all of us.

The problem is especially acute in cities, where violent criminal activity is most often concentrated. But cities also provide opportunities for addressing gun violence, especially when the resolve of residents is harnessed.

When I took office in Bogotá in the mid-1990s, armed violence was spiralling out of control and levels of confidence in public security provision had reached record lows. We introduced a programme called 'security for everyone' and, with the support of the Catholic Church and the police, we reduced the number of licences to carry firearms in the evening and at weekends throughout the city. We also searched for guns at police roadblocks and drew on individual support and private funding to launch a weapons buy-back programme in 1995 and 1996.

These efforts—aided by media coverage—achieved striking results: a 26 per cent decline in Bogotá's homicide rate over two years (1995 to 1996) and a gradual shift in the mindset of people who had previously thought it was important to carry a firearm for protection.

Bogotá was not alone in facing high levels of gun violence. During the same period the mayor of Cali introduced temporary restrictions on carrying firearms and other security guarantees such as road checks and an increased police presence. The homicide rate declined notably as a result.

With the support of national and international actors, such interventions can be usefully replicated elsewhere. In Bogotá we relied on individual and private-sector support because we lacked strong national backing. To be even more effective in confronting the perpetrators and facilitators of gun violence, politicians, justice departments, and law enforcement agencies at all levels must work together.

The *Small Arms Survey 2007: Guns and the City* connects the dots between the individuals and organizations whose inaction or actions affect levels of armed violence at the municipal, national, regional, and international levels. In so doing, and in reminding us that we have the means to improve security, this book is essential reading for anyone concerned with mitigating the suffering armed violence causes families and communities around the world.

Antanas Mockus

Former Mayor of Bogotá, Colombia (1995–97 and 2000–03)

June 2007

CONTENTS

ABOUT THE SMALL ARMS SURVEY

The Small Arms Survey is an independent research project located at the Graduate Institute of International Studies in Geneva, Switzerland. Established in 1999, the project is supported by the Swiss Federal Department of Foreign Affairs, and by sustained contributions from the governments of Belgium, Canada, Finland, the Netherlands, Norway, Sweden, and the United Kingdom. The Survey is also grateful for past and current project support received from the Governments of Australia, Denmark, France, Germany, New Zealand, and the United States, as well as from different United Nations agencies, programmes, and institutes.

The objectives of the Small Arms Survey are: to be the principal source of public information on all aspects of small arms and armed violence; to serve as a resource centre for governments, policy-makers, researchers, and activists; to monitor national and international initiatives (governmental and non-governmental) on small arms; to support efforts to address the effects of small arms proliferation and misuse; and to act as a clearinghouse for the sharing of information and the dissemination of best practices. The Survey also sponsors field research and information-gathering efforts, especially in affected states and regions. The project has an international staff with expertise in security studies, political science, law, economics, development studies, and sociology, and collaborates with a network of researchers, partner institutions, non-governmental organizations, and governments in more than 50 countries.

NOTES TO READERS

Abbreviations: Lists of abbreviations can be found at the end of each chapter.

Chapter cross-referencing: Chapter cross-references appear capitalized in brackets throughout the text. For example, in Chapter 5 on Urban Landscapes of Armed Violence: 'Conflict and post-conflict urban armed violence also heavily affects cities ranging from Bujumbura (BURUNDI) to Mogadishu and Kabul.'

Exchange rates: All monetary values are expressed in current US dollars (USD). When other currencies are also cited, unless otherwise indicated, they are converted to USD using the 365-day average exchange rate for the period 1 September 2005 to 31 August 2006.

Small Arms Survey: The plain text—Small Arms Survey—is used to indicate the overall project and its activities, while the italicized version—*Small Arms Survey*—refers to the publication. The *Survey,* appearing italicized, refers generally to past and future editions.

Web site: For more detailed information and current developments on small arms issues, readers are invited to visit the Small Arms Survey Web site at www.smallarmssurvey.org.

Small Arms Survey
Graduate Institute of International Studies
47, Avenue Blanc, 1202 Geneva, Switzerland

Tel.: +41 22 908 5777
Fax: +41 22 732 2738
Email: smallarm@hei.unige.ch
Web site: www.smallarmssurvey.org

ACKNOWLEDGEMENTS

In keeping with our tradition, the seventh edition of the *Small Arms Survey* is a collective product of the staff of the Small Arms Survey project, based at the Graduate Institute of International Studies in Geneva, Switzerland. A large number of researchers in Geneva and around the world have contributed to this volume, and it has benefited from the input and advice of numerous government officials, advocates, experts, and colleagues from the small arms research community and beyond.

The principal chapter authors were assisted by in-house and external contributors who are acknowledged in the relevant chapters. Special thanks go out to those individuals who generously shared their time and insights for our study of the 2006 UN Programme of Action Review Conference (TRANSFER CONTROLS).

In addition, detailed reviews on the chapters were provided by: Pete Abel, Philip Alpers, Holger Anders, Frida Berrigan, Jurgen Brauer, Jeremy Brickhill, Philip Cook, Ken Epps, William Godnick, Keith Hartley, William Hartung, Håvard Hegre, Mariam Jooma, Roger Keil, Nicholas Marsh, Jimmy McLure, Lisa Misol, Janvier Nkurunziza, Enrique Perez, Jorge Restrepo, Matt Schroeder, Luiz Eduardo Soares, Hilde Wallacher, Susan Waltz, Camilla Waszink, Siemon Wezeman, and Adrian Wilkinson.

Eric G. Berman, Keith Krause, and Glenn McDonald were responsible for the overall planning and organization of this edition. Tania Inowlocki managed the editing and production

Small Arms Survey 2007

Editors
Eric G. Berman, Keith Krause, Emile LeBrun, and Glenn McDonald

Publications Manager
Tania Inowlocki

Design and layout
Richard Jones, Exile: Design & Editorial Services

Cartography
Jillian Luff, MAP*grafix*

Copy-editors
Alex Potter with Tania Inowlocki

Proofreader
John Linnegar with Donald Strachan

Principal chapter authors

Introduction	Keith Krause
Chapter 1	Barbara Gimelli Sulashvili
Chapter 2	Aaron Karp
Chapter 3	Anne-Kathrin Glatz and Lora Lumpe
Chapter 4	Glenn McDonald, Sahar Hasan, and Chris Stevenson
Photo essay	Lucian Read
Chapter 5	Oliver Jütersonke, Keith Krause, and Robert Muggah
Chapter 6	Nicolas Florquin and Stéphanie Pézard
Chapter 7	Rubem César Fernandes and Marcelo de Sousa Nascimento
Chapter 8	Phillip Killicoat
Chapter 9	James Bevan and Pablo Dreyfus
Chapter 10	Claire Mc Evoy

of the *Survey* with the help of Diana Rodriguez. Alex Potter copy-edited the book with Tania Inowlocki; Jillie Luff produced the maps; Rick Jones provided the layout and design; John Linnegar proofread the *Survey* with Donald Strachan; and Lisa Kenwright of Indexing Specialists (UK) compiled the index. Ceri Thomas of Daly Design created the illustrations on page 121.

John Haslam and Carrie Cheek of Cambridge University Press provided support throughout the production of the *Survey*. Barbara Gimelli Sulashvili, Anne-Kathrin Glatz, Sahar Hasan, Jonah Leff, Tom O'Connell, Sarah Petrino, Chris Stevenson, and Savannah de Tessières assisted with fact-checking. David Olivier, Fridrich Štrba, Carole Touraine, and Guillemette Carlucci provided administrative support.

The project also benefited from the support of the Graduate Institute of International Studies, in particular Philippe Burrin, Andrea Bianchi, Andrew Clapham, Oliver Jütersonke, and Monique Nathoo.

We are extremely grateful to the Swiss government for its generous financial and overall support of the Small Arms Survey project, in particular Erwin Bollinger, Sascha Fuls, Thomas Greminger, Cristina Hoyos, Roman Hunger, Anna Ifkovits, Peter Maurer, Jürg Streuli, Anton Thalmann, and Othmar Wyss. Financial support for the project was also provided by the Governments of Belgium, Canada, Finland, Germany, the Netherlands, Norway, Sweden, the United Kingdom, and the United States. In addition, the project has received financial support for various projects from the Geneva International Academic Network, the Organisation for Economic Co-operation and Development, the UN Development Programme, the UN Institute for Disarmament Research, and the World Health Organization. The project further benefits from the support of international agencies, including the International Committee of the Red Cross, the UN Office for Disarmament Affairs, the UN High Commissioner for Refugees, and the UN Office on Drugs and Crime.

In Geneva, the project has received support and expert advice from: David Atwood, Peter Batchelor, Nicolas Florquin, Magnus Hellgren, Peter Herby, Kari Kahiluoto, Patricia Lewis, Merete Lundemo, Patrick McCarthy, David Meddings, Marc-Antoine Morel, Jennifer Milliken, and Daniël Prins.

Beyond Geneva, we also received support from a number of colleagues. In addition to those mentioned above, and in specific chapters, we would like to thank: Michael Ashkenazi, Michael Cassandra, Barbara Frey, Thomas Jackson, Guy Lamb, Edward Laurance, Yeshua Moser-Puangsuwan, and Alex Vines.

This year we lost a close friend and collaborator, Sarah Meek, who died in a car accident. She was present at the creation of the Small Arms Survey, served on our International Programme Council, and contributed to many projects and reports over the years. She remains an inspiration to those who had the privilege to know and work with her, and we dedicate this volume to her.

Our sincere thanks go out to many other individuals (who remain unnamed) for their continuing support of the project. Our apologies to anyone we have failed to mention.

Keith Krause, Programme Director
Eric G. Berman, Managing Director

A French policeman holds a shotgun shell recovered after his unit was shot upon in Grigny, south of Paris, on the 11th night of urban riots in November 2005. © Franck Prevel/Reuters

Introduction

The global small arms process spawned one disappointment, but also some good news, in 2006. The failure of the UN Programme of Action Review Conference to reach a substantive outcome was followed, within months, by agreement on initial steps towards the negotiation of a legally binding Arms Trade Treaty (ATT). The Review Conference undoubtedly represented a missed opportunity to examine the successes and failures of recent years, consolidate various strands of work, and chart a path forward. Nevertheless, it appears to have had little impact (positive or negative) on national, regional, or international efforts to stem the proliferation and misuse of small arms and light weapons.

Since 2001, an estimated USD 660 million has been invested in about 600 different activities in at least 94 states (Maze and Parker, 2006). These range from national capacity-building to stockpile management, post-conflict disarmament, surplus weapons destruction, and research and awareness-raising. In addition to the ATT resolution, significant initiatives of the past year included the following:

- a UN Group of Governmental Experts examined the prospects for enhanced regulation of international arms brokering to stem the illicit trafficking in arms;
- the Swiss government, together with the UN Development Programme, hosted a ministerial-level summit that saw 42 states endorse the Geneva Declaration on Armed Violence and Development, committing them to achieving measurable reductions in armed violence by 2015;
- large-scale post-conflict disarmament, demobilization, and reintegration (DDR) efforts involving more than 1.25 million ex-combatants in more than 22 countries were conducted in places as diverse as Angola, Colombia, Eritrea, and Indonesia (Caramés, Fisas, and Sanz, 2007);
- a large-scale NATO- and European-led programme was launched to destroy surplus weapons and ammunition stocks in Ukraine, estimated to have the world's third-largest arsenal (Griffiths, 2007);
- the Economic Community of West African States (ECOWAS) negotiated and signed a legally binding convention designed to strengthen regional initiatives to stem illicit weapons trafficking and misuse (Berkol, 2007).

These diverse initiatives, some diplomatic, some programmatic, testify to the continued high level of engagement with the issue of small arms and armed violence, and the recognition, at least in some regions, of the need for broad-based multilateral action, whether within or alongside the UN system.

New perspectives

Since 2007 has been declared (somewhat arbitrarily) the first year to see more than half of the world's population living in cities, it seems appropriate to focus on urban armed violence as a distinct problem requiring policies and programmes that engage local governments and actors around the world. A range of innovative initiatives have been launched by urban leaders in such places as Bogotá, Boston, Johannesburg, Rio de Janeiro, and St. Louis. Programmes tackling small arms and violence have also been initiated by networks of urban leaders, such as the anti-gang initiative led by Los Angeles officials or the bi-partisan Mayors Against Illegal Guns initiative that involves more than 200 mayors in more than 40 US states.

Urban settings pose particular challenges to armed violence prevention and reduction. They are sites of large-scale violent criminal activity, principally because of the opportunities and anonymity offered by modern cities. They are also zones of political unrest and instability, where violence is mobilized and manipulated for political ends. Even so, cities are often densely regulated and effectively governed spaces, providing many opportunities for policies and programmes that address the different risks and vulnerabilities to armed violence, beyond a focus on weapons alone.

Chapter highlights

The *Small Arms Survey 2007* follows the traditional structure, with the first section comprising chapters that update or extend our knowledge on the production, transfer, stockpiles and holdings of weapons, and measures to regulate or control them. The highlights in this section include a relatively comprehensive—if still tentative—map of the global distribution of weapons in civilian hands, a review of new initiatives and continuing debates relating to arms transfer controls, and an in-depth look at licensed (and unlicensed) production as a vector of proliferation.

The thematic section opens with a photo essay by award-winning combat photographer Lucian Read on the impact of small arms in the Philippines. It is followed by the lead chapter, 'Guns in the City', and two case studies: one on urban armed violence in Brazil, the other on armed violence in Bujumbura, Burundi.

The last section offers a study of the link between conflict and the cost of firearms, using a global database of Kalashnikov prices, and a chapter that draws on field research in Brazil and Uganda to document the diversion of ammunition to non-state actors. The final chapter presents initial findings from our large-scale project mapping arms, armed violence, and insecurity in South Sudan following the signing of the Comprehensive Peace Agreement in 2005. The full range of publications from this project can be found at: www.smallarmssurvey.org/sudan.

Update chapters

Chapter 1 (Production): Licensed and unlicensed production of small arms, light weapons, and their ammunition is the focus of this year's production chapter. It highlights the importance of this neglected, but quantitatively significant, aspect of the industry. Based on new research, it shows that 60–80 per cent of all current military small arms production is undertaken by firms that have acquired the production know-how from others.

Since this involves the transfer of technology from a restricted number of original owners to a larger number of producers, licensed and unlicensed production multiplies the sources of small arms. As small arms technology proliferates, the risk of irresponsible transfer and misuse also increases. This chapter presents major problem scenarios and the best practices that can remedy them. It concludes that the most effective counter-proliferation strategies target the initial export of production know-how.

Chapter 2 (Civilian firearms): Providing the most comprehensive portrait of civilian firearms distribution to date, this chapter analyses official registration data and various estimates and uses statistical modelling to estimate that there are about 650 million weapons in civilian hands worldwide, or roughly one gun for every seven people in the world. This implies that the previous Small Arms Survey estimate of 640 million total weapons will have to be revised upwards (to an estimated 875 million firearms worldwide), and further that civilians own roughly 75 per cent of all firearms, easily outnumbering military and law enforcement small arms.

Definition of small arms and light weapons

The Small Arms Survey uses the term 'small arms and light weapons' broadly to cover both military-style small arms and light weapons as well as commercial firearms (handguns and long guns). When possible, it follows the definition used in the United Nations' Report of the Panel of Governmental Experts on Small Arms (United Nations, 1997):

Small arms: revolvers and self-loading pistols, rifles and carbines, assault rifles, sub-machine guns, and light machine guns.

Light weapons: heavy machine guns, hand-held under-barrel and mounted grenade launchers, portable anti-tank and anti-aircraft guns, recoilless rifles, portable launchers of anti-tank and anti-aircraft missile systems, and mortars of less than 100 mm calibre.

The Survey uses the terms 'firearm' and 'gun' to mean hand-held weapons that fire a projectile through a tube by explosive charge. The terms 'small arms' and 'light weapons' are used more comprehensively to refer to all hand-held, man-portable, explosively or chemically propelled or detonated devices. Unless the context dictates otherwise, no distinction is intended between commercial firearms (such as hunting rifles) and small arms and light weapons designed for military use (such as assault rifles).

The UN definition was agreed through consensus by government officials. It was negotiated, in other words, to serve practical political goals that differ from the needs of research and analysis. While the UN definition is used in the *Survey* as a baseline, the analysis in this and subsequent chapters is broader, allowing consideration of weapons such as home-made (craft) firearms that might be overlooked using the UN definition. The term small arm is used in this chapter to refer both to small arms and light weapons (i.e. the small arms industry) unless otherwise stated, whereas light weapon refers specifically to light weapons.

The chapter also reveals changing patterns of civilian ownership. Civilians are acquiring more powerful firearms and in poorer areas sales of automatic rifles are increasing. There also appears to be a general link between per capita wealth and gun ownership: where gun ownership laws remain unchanged, greater national wealth leads to higher levels of gun ownership.

Chapter 3 (Transfers): Transfers of small arms, light weapons, and ammunition that are authorized by governments are not always legal or responsible. Some authorized transfers contravene international law, including norms relating to human rights and armed conflict. Other transfers can be considered irresponsible because they entail a high risk of diversion to unauthorized recipients. Building on analysis presented in the *Small Arms Survey 2004,* this chapter provides numerous examples of governments transferring weapons even though they knew, or should have known, of circumstances creating a significant risk of misuse.

The chapter also updates and fine-tunes the annual Small Arms Trade Transparency Barometer, revealing that transparency remains poor in many countries.

Chapter 4 (Transfer controls): This chapter takes stock of the latest developments in the global small arms process, with a specific focus on the issue of transfer controls. Key challenges in the area of transfer controls include unpacking relevant *Programme of Action* commitments, deciding whether and how to address the question of transfers to non-state actors, and developing means of effectively implementing transfer licensing criteria.

States have extensive existing responsibilities in relation to the transfer of weapons. Relevant legally binding norms include direct limitations on certain arms transfers, as well as the rule holding states 'complicit' in violations of international law committed with arms they transfer to others despite a known (or knowable) risk of misuse. Guidelines identifying factors to be considered when deciding whether to authorize a particular transfer can help states take a more systematic, rigorous, and objective approach to these decisions.

Urban violence section

Photo essay (Philippines): This year the *Small Arms Survey* showcases award-winning photographer Lucian Read's coverage of the impact of small arms in the Philippines. The photos reveal complex relationships between the firearms and the people who make, want, use, suffer from, and confront them. They capture the gunsmiths who depend on the arms trade for their livelihood, as well as those who buy the finished product. They show the coffined bodies and mourners of victims of gun violence, and the attempts to prosecute perpetrators. They also portray efforts to impose a firearm ban in the run-up to the May 2007 elections, while offering a glimpse of opponents of gun control.

Chapter 5 (Urban violence): For the first time in human history, most of the world's inhabitants live in cities rather than rural areas. In recognition of this global shift, the 2007 edition of the *Small Arms Survey* contributes to a growing literature that seeks to identify and develop responses to the particular dynamics of urban armed violence. This chapter observes that rapid and large-scale urbanization is strongly associated with escalating rates of armed violence, whether political or criminal in nature.

Individual and collective reactions are based on perceived as well as real insecurities, often involving strategies to contain violence or export it to the urban periphery. The chapter documents a host of municipal approaches to the prevention and reduction of urban armed violence. Ranging from coercive and top-down to compliance-oriented and voluntary approaches, they vary in effectiveness. Successful programmes often combine a variety of strategies.

Chapter 6 (Burundi): This chapter looks at conflict and post-conflict armed violence in Bujumbura, the capital of Burundi. During a drawn-out civil war, Bujumbura was a theatre of armed violence between increasingly segregated and heavily armed neighbourhoods. Since the 2003 ceasefire armed violence rates have declined, though at a slower pace in Bujumbura than in other regions of Burundi.

Recent field research in six of Burundi's 17 provinces finds that the DDR process and civilian disarmament initiatives have produced mixed results. Small arms that were previously used during the conflict are weapons of choice for those perpetrating post-conflict violence in Burundi. In Bujumbura pistols and revolvers are also commonly carried for protection. The persistence of armed violence in Bujumbura—both criminal and politically motivated—suggests that measures targeting small arms proliferation have been inadequate.

Chapter 7 (Brazil): The rate of armed violence in Brazil grew threefold from 1982 to 2002, from 7 to 21 deaths per 100,000. It continued to increase until 2004, when the first signs of a potential decline were noted.

This chapter analyses data on social demographics, public health, and firearms availability from 5,507 municipalities across Brazil. It identifies the risk and protection factors conditioning armed violence across the country. Being male, black, young, and out of school and work are among the variables associated with victimization by armed violence, while suicide is more common among higher-income groups. The chapter finds that social inequality is correlated with armed violence, while poverty is not.

Other topics

Chapter 8 (Economics): Using available information on global prices of various Kalashnikov assault rifles, the chapter examines whether a set of factors influences demand and supply in the small arms market and analyses the relationship between gun prices and civil war. In assessing the role of firearms demand, the chapter tests factors associated with the income and motivation of buyers, concluding that weapons prices do not appear to be associated with homicide rates, economic downturns, or young male demographics. Supply-side factors that affect gun prices include the effectiveness of a country's regulations, porosity of borders, the level of military spending in neighbouring countries, and recent experience of conflict. A critical finding is that cheaper weapons prices lead to an increased risk of civil war, independently of other conflict risk factors.

Chapter 9 (Ammunition diversion): This chapter presents findings from two pilot studies that are part of the Survey's Ammunition Tracing Project. Employing new methodologies and extensive field research, the chapter charts illicit flows of ammunition in Karamoja, northern Uganda, and Rio de Janeiro, Brazil. The chapter reveals evidence that much of the ammunition circulating among non-state actors in the two regions has been illicitly diverted from state security forces. By mapping and quantifying ammunition flows, the chapter provides solid evidence of the critical role that diverted arms and ammunition play in sustaining armed violence. It also provides further inputs for the expanding ammunition debate.

Chapter 10 (South Sudan): Drawing on field research undertaken as part of the Survey's Sudan Human Security Baseline Assessment project, this chapter maps out the numerous security threats facing South Sudan in the aftermath of the January 2005 Comprehensive Peace Agreement (CPA). It underscores the fragility of the peace deal and points to the need for sustained international attention to the region. Conflicts between those supporting the fledgling security framework provided by South Sudanese authorities pursuant to the CPA and various actors seeking to undermine the peace, combined with points of contention among the parties, raise the spectre of renewed North–South conflict.

Conclusion

This edition of the *Small Arms Survey* expands the potential scope of our policy interventions—from a narrow focus on supply-side control measures to a broader menu of instruments rooted in development, humanitarian, criminal justice, and (this year) urban planning perspectives. This does *not* mean that the problem of small arms proliferation and misuse is necessarily also expanding, but rather that our understanding of the different aspects of arms and armed violence—including the means to address their human, social, and economic costs—is deepening. In the long run, this will improve our ability to develop and deploy policies and programmes appropriate to the widely varied contexts associated with small arms proliferation and misuse.

Future editions of the *Survey* will tackle such themes as the public health approach to armed violence; post-conflict DDR; and the importance of small arms to security sector governance. In collaboration with old and new partners, we will continue to work to provide information and analysis that can underpin policies and programmes aimed at reducing and preventing armed violence. ✐

Keith Krause

Programme Director, Small Arms Survey

Bibliography

Berkol, Ilhan. 2007. *Analysis of the ECOWAS Convention on Small Arms and Light Weapons and recommendations for the development of a Plan of Action.* GRIP Analytical Note. Brussels: Groupe de recherche et d'information sur la paix et la sécurité.

Caramés, Albert, Vicenç Fisas, and Eneko Sanz. 2007. *Análisis de los programas de desarme, desmovilización y reintegración (DDR) existentes en el mundo durante 2006.* Barcelona: Escola de Cultura de Pau de la Universidad Autónoma de Barcelona.

Griffiths, Hugh. 2007. 'In the Interests of All: Negotiated Surplus Decision-Making in Ukraine.' Unpublished background paper. Geneva: Small Arms Survey. February.

Maze, Kerry and Sarah Parker. 2006. *International Assistance for Implementing the Programme of Action to Prevent, Combat and Eradicate the Illicit Trade in Small Arms and Light Weapons in All its Aspects: Findings of a Global Survey.* Geneva: UN Institute for Disarmament Research.

A mujahideen soldier squats with a Russian-type, though Chinese-made, machine gun in Kabul Province, Afghanistan, in November 1991. © Mervyn Patterson/Panos Pictures

that causes their injury or death.

t. New information presented in

assault rifles,[1] and carbines—the

ducers that acquired the necessary

...nology from others.[2]

Both licensed and unlicensed production involve the acquisition of production technology by an actor that did not previously possess it. While this need not lead to an overall increase in the number of weapons produced, it does involve the dissemination of weapons production know-how to a greater number of actors. As such, knowledge becomes more widespread, and the risk that small arms end up in the wrong hands increases. Simple solutions to this problem are not an option. Production know-how, once transferred, cannot be retrieved.

This chapter examines the impact of licensed and unlicensed production on the proliferation of small arms and light weapons, along with measures that reduce the risk of diversion and misuse. More specifically, it considers the following questions:

- Which states are the major original owners and which states the acquirers of small arms manufacturing technology?
- Which weapons are most frequently produced under licence or as unlicensed copies, and why?
- What is the relative proportion of licensed and unlicensed production?
- What commercial, national, and international measures can curb the uncontrolled proliferation of small arms produced under licence?

This study of licensed and unlicensed production sheds light on a much-neglected, but quantitatively important, aspect of the small arms industry. It also reveals that production arrangements tend to follow the logic of the arms trade and, accordingly, require similar control measures. The chapter's most important findings include the following:

- States that originally own technology are easily outnumbered by those that acquire it. Furthermore, most original owners are themselves acquirers of production technology.
- Only 57 per cent of weapons produced by technology acquirers are produced under licence.
- Man-portable air defence systems (MANPADS) technology is now quite strictly controlled, even though there is still some unlicensed production.
- Production based on former Soviet Union (USSR) technology represents a disproportionately high share of unlicensed production worldwide.

- Every year, 530,000 to 580,000 military rifles, assault rifles, and carbines are produced under licence or as unlicensed copies, representing 60 to 80 per cent of total annual production.
- An effective counter-proliferation strategy, among other things, targets the diversion and export of the manufacturing know-how needed for licensed and unlicensed production.

The first section of this chapter unpacks the issue of licensed weapons production. After a general description of the phenomenon, it takes a closer look at the costs and benefits associated with licensed production, along with accompanying risks. The following section outlines the key features of current licensed and unlicensed production of small arms. It also estimates the annual global production of military rifles, assault rifles, and carbines, including the proportion manufactured under licence or as unlicensed copies. The last section focuses on the problems that licensed and unlicensed production of small arms pose, before presenting a number of best practices and policy options.

Most small arms production licences are non-exclusive in nature.

LICENSED PRODUCTION: A PRIMER

Licensed production in general occurs in virtually all areas of the modern economy. The motives behind it are numerous, ranging from the anticipated increase of market share and returns on investment in research and development on the part of the licenser company, to the wish to develop domestic industry and create jobs on the part of the licensee country. Accordingly, licensed production agreements can involve many different juridical and organizational arrangements.

This section explores the phenomenon of licensed production of small arms, light weapons, and their ammunition. It discusses its forms and specificities, the motives behind it, and the problems surrounding it.

Characteristics of a partnership

In its most general sense, 'a license agreement is a partnership between an IP [intellectual property] owner (licensor) and another who is authorized to use such rights (licensee) under certain conditions' (WIPO, 2003, p. 11). Accordingly, in a licensed production agreement, the licensee (usually a company) is manufacturing a product for which it is granted production rights under certain conditions, while the licensor retains the ownership of the intellectual property necessary for production. In the case of small arms and light weapons, licensing agreements typically bring together a licensor company that supplies technical data, prototypes, and/or machine tools and a licensee company located in another country (Small Arms Survey, 2001, p. 9).

Most small arms production licences are *non-exclusive* in nature, i.e. the licensor retains the right to use the licensed property itself, and to attribute further licences to third parties (Small Arms Survey, 2002, p. 42). In fact, all of the largest small arms producers have production licensing agreements with several manufacturers for models they also produce themselves. Heckler & Koch, for example, used to produce its G3 assault rifle in its own production facilities in Germany. At the same time, it gave production licences to manufacturers in 15 countries between 1961 and the present (DAKS, n.d., pp. 8, 12; Jones and Cutshaw, 2004).[3] Much less frequent are *sole licences,* where the licensor retains the right to use the licensed property itself, but cannot grant further licences to third parties; and *exclusive licences,* where not even the licensor retains the right to use the licensed property (Small Arms Survey, 2002, p. 42).

As opposed to intellectual property rights *sales* or *assignments,* licence contracts subject the use of intellectual property to various conditions. Licence contracts may contain provisions restricting weapons production to a certain period of time or a quantity beyond which further production is illegal. Venezuela, for example, has recently acquired a production licence for AK-103 rifles and ammunition that is limited to ten years and allows the assembly of up to 900,000 rifles from kits supplied by Izhmash, with maximum annual production of 25,000 rifles (BBC, 2006b; 2006c; Pyadushkin, 2006; Vogel, 2006). Restrictions may also be imposed on the weapons' final end use or destination. The Russian Federation has granted a production licence for Kalashnikov rifles to India, whose stated purpose is the supply of the Indian Army and law enforcement bodies (RosBusinessConsulting, 2004). Other restrictions may relate to the licensed activity, e.g. whether small arms are fully produced or partially assembled, and whether entire weapons or only their components are produced. In addition, licence agreements may contain clauses specifying quality standards or addressing the situation where one of the partners makes improvements to the product (Small Arms Survey, 2002, p. 43). Finally, a licence agreement determines the form and scope of compensation given to the intellectual property holder. Usually, the licensor receives direct monetary benefits in the form of a flat fee (lump sum) or a running royalty, frequently a share of the licensee's revenue (WIPO, 2003, p. 11).

Besides these conditions, which are usually explicitly stated in the agreement, there are two basic, but largely implicit, conditions that necessarily underpin any licence agreement: 'the licensor must have ownership of the relevant IP', and 'the IP must be protected by law [e.g. covered by a patent] or at least eligible for protection' (WIPO, 2003,

Venezuelan President Hugo Chávez inspects a Kalashnikov assault rifle being assembled at the Izhmash plant in Izhevsk, Russia, July 2006. © AFP/Getty Images

p. 11). Although this might seem obvious, it cannot always be assumed. Izhmash, for example, cannot claim intellectual property rights for early Kalashnikov designs, because, until 1997, the product had not been patented (ITAR-TASS, 1998; *Petersburg Times,* 1999; Pyadushkin, 2006).

In the area of small arms production, licence agreements involve the voluntary and conscious transfer of technology. Such an agreement may involve several different types of technology transfer:

- **Know-how contract:** The owner of technology communicates its know-how to another person or legal entity, either in *tangible form* (e.g. documents, photographs, blueprints of machines or products, technical drawings, architectural plans, lists of spare parts, manuals, or instructions) or in *intangible form* (e.g. conversations between the engineers of the supplier and the recipient, the observation of a production line, or a training programme for the employees of the recipient).
- **Acquisition of equipment and other capital goods:** The technology owner transfers equipment and other capital goods (machinery, entire production lines, component parts for assembly, etc.) to another person or legal entity through *sale* or *gift.*
- **Joint venture agreements:** The technology owner enters into an alliance with another person or legal entity. In *equity joint ventures,* the supplier and recipient of technology agree on the creation of a separate legal entity, while in *contractual joint ventures* no such entity is created.
- **Turn-key project:** The technology owner hands over an entire industrial plant or production line operating according to agreed performance standards (WIPO, 2006, pp. 4–5).

The costs, benefits, and risks of licensed production

Small arms producers share a common aim, namely to maximize sales in order to increase returns on research, development, and production costs. Licensed manufacturing is one means of achieving this. Others include direct exports, joint ventures, and foreign direct investment. This section discusses why companies engage in licensed small arms production, in particular the associated economic and political benefits and costs.

Costs and benefits for the licensor

Licensing weapons production gives a licensor additional income (royalty payments) that can help recoup research and development costs. Along with direct exports, this may be vital for the small arms industry in countries where domestic demand is too small to sustain the industry (Poth, 2001; Small Arms Survey, 2004, pp. 118–23).

Licensing weapons production can help the licensor to recoup R&D costs.

By granting a licence, the original producer of small arms can indirectly access new markets in a cost-effective way, sometimes penetrating markets that are otherwise inaccessible. The technology owner benefits from the fact that the licensee company knows the local market much better and is able to make necessary changes, such as the translation of labels and instructions, and the adaptation of the product to local regulations. Moreover, owing to its knowledge of the local culture, the licensee may be able to market the product more successfully (WIPO, 2003, p. 12). To cite one example, the 9 x 19 mm Model 92FS self-loading pistol, initially produced by Armi Beretta in Italy, is produced under licence by the US company Beretta as the M9. It has been modified slightly in order to fit US requirements (Jones and Cutshaw, 2004, pp. 267, 311).

Finally, through indirect counter-trade and offset arrangements (see Box 1.1), the licensor country may see an increase in job opportunities in sectors other than the defence sector, or otherwise gain access to investment opportunities in the licensee country. In 2006 Russian Federation business interests gained new investment opportunities in the Venezuelan energy sector when the two countries agreed on defence deals of more than USD 1 billion, including licensed production of AK-103s (Anderson, 2006b). Yet, as small arms deals are usually relatively small compared to other defence deals, the role of counter-trade and offsets should not be overestimated. Moreover, the overall benefits of an indirect offset deal may be tempered by the loss of jobs in the licensor country's defence sector.

Costs and benefits for the licensee

Most of the countries producing small arms under licence are developing countries. They often seek to establish indigenous defence industries, reduce import dependence, and/or secure and retain jobs within the country. Malaysia's defence industry is too small and its research capabilities too limited to satisfy the government's goal of self-reliance in meeting domestic defence needs. Malaysia therefore tries to spur the transfer of foreign technology to the local defence industry through licensed production agreements (*New Straits Times,* 2003). Similarly, India has not achieved independence in defence production. In 2005, with an Indian manufacturing project lagging behind schedule (Lockwood, 2006a), India concluded a licence agreement with the Russian Federation for the transfer of equipment needed for the assembly of rifles (RosBusinessConsulting, 2004). Libya appears anxious to restore its defence industry after the lifting of the embargo against the country in October 2004. The country reportedly concluded a licensed production agreement with the Russian Federation for Kalashnikov assault rifles in late 2004 (Novichkov, 2004). Turkey shares similar objectives: 'to develop an indigenous high-technology industry in order to reduce Turkey's reliance on foreign companies and encourage the involvement of local companies in defence manufacture' (Sariibrahimoglu, 1999).

Through a licensing agreement, the licensee company gains access to superior technology without having to undertake its own research and development. Further, it avoids the risks inherent in the development of many new products by manufacturing weapons that have already proved their worth (WIPO, 2003). As a consequence, the company can quickly gain access to new domestic markets or even enter the export business. Colombia, for example, produces 5.56 mm Galil rifle ammunition under licence from Israel, which it then exports back to Israel. Reportedly, the aim is to make the Colombian armed forces self-sufficient in small arms and ammunition, and then to take on the regional export market (McDermott, 2004a; 2006). Yet, for non-US and non-European rifle-producing countries engaged in licensed production, export sales are only a secondary goal; their main concern is domestic. Only a handful of them—e.g. Israel Military Industries Ltd. (IMI), Singapore Technologies Kinetics, Denel Ltd. (South Africa), Australian Defence Industries, and China North Industries Corporation (NORINCO)—have a chance to become serious players in a competitive international market (Lockwood, 2006a).

Licensee countries often seek to establish indigenous defence industries or to reduce import dependence.

Whether licensed production is a cost-effective means of achieving the goals described above largely depends on the case-specific interaction of costs and benefits. Total royalty payments should not exceed the research and development costs necessary for domestic development. The potential licensee also needs to consider whether the direct imports of small arms would be cheaper than licensed production. Generally, a country will engage in licensed production only if such benefits as national self-reliance, security of supply, job creation, and/or additional export income outweigh the cost of the licensing arrangement.

Costs and benefits for both licensor and licensee

Through a licensed production agreement, the licensor and licensee countries can strengthen their political and military cooperation. This may benefit the licensor in that it enhances its political influence in the licensee state. This was the main motive behind the production licences the USSR granted to countries in its zones of influence (Pyadushkin,

Box 1.1 Offset policies in the arms trade

Offsets are often demanded as compensation for certain defence deals (Willet and Anthony, 2001, p. 3). *Direct* offsets are directly linked to the arms sale in question. Instead of simply buying weapons from the seller in another country, for example, the buyer country may take over the manufacture of a portion of the weapons that have been ordered, or may secure access to certain technology or know-how connected to the products it is buying. *Indirect* offsets occur when the compensation is unrelated to the actual purchase of arms or defence services. The buyer country, for example, might require the seller country to buy agricultural products or non-defensive industrial goods in return for its arms purchase (Brauer and Dunne, 2004; Willet and Anthony, 2001, p. 3; FAS, 2001).

Licensed production of small arms falls into the category of direct offsets. The recipient 'buys' a certain number of weapons, but in return has technology transferred to its domestic industry. The Greek government, for example, recently selected the Heckler & Koch G36 as its army's standard rifle. Yet the government arms company sought a licence to produce domestically at least 50 per cent of the 112,370 rifles needed (62 per cent of the contract value) (Lockwood, 2006b).

Over recent years, the value of defence offset agreements has been increasing. Whereas in 1998 the average offset require-ment was around 58 per cent of the value of the contract (FAS, 2001), offset investments of 100 per cent have become more common since then. Occasionally, compensations of up to 300 per cent have been reported. While offset deals for small arms and light weapons are relatively small compared to other defence contracts, they have followed the same upward trend. For instance, the contract for the licensed production in Turkey of 5.56 mm assault rifles as replacements for the H&K G3, finally won by Heckler & Koch with its HK33E, required a 100 per cent offset (*Jane's Defence Weekly,* 1995). The European Defence Agency's attempts to limit offset requirements to a maximum of 100 per cent reflect the extremes of current practice (Tigner, 2006a). Some purchasers have even requested a non-refundable 'pre-offset' of about 10 per cent from companies competing for a contract (FAS, 2001).

Small arms offset deals, especially those comprising a licensed production agreement, often result in a net loss of jobs in the seller country, as they technically result in the outsourcing of production (Lumpe, 1995). The arms industry claims, however, that without the granting of offsets, a deal would not be possible, and the net loss for the economy would be even bigger. It is difficult for the general public to assess the validity of such arguments, because publicly available information about offset deals remains scarce (FAS, 2001).

Offset arrangements may have a detrimental effect on competition. It is not without reason that the General Agreement on Tariffs and Trade prohibits offset deals in government procurement (WTO, 1994, annex 4b, art. 16). This rule, however, does not automatically cover defence procurements (art. 23) (Willett and Anthony, 2001, p. 22). Stricter regulation of offset deals is needed to limit their negative impacts. As it seeks to facilitate more liberal defence procurement practices, the European Defence Agency is trying to harmonize the elements of a typical offset contract. Despite the European Commission's release of an 'interpretive communication' (EU, 2006) on the subject, Europe's biggest arms-producing countries—Britain, France, Germany, Italy, Spain, and Sweden—are poised for confrontation over the issue with numerous smaller states, which are seeking to develop their domestic defence industries (Tigner, 2006a; 2006b; 2007).

2006). While such arrangements can increase the licensee's political and security dependence on the licensor, they can also confer important practical benefits on both parties, e.g. in the form of increased standardization of military equipment among allies, as is the case among North Atlantic Treaty Organisation (NATO) countries (*Jane's International Defence Review,* 2004).

The risks of licensed production

Various risks are involved in licensed production. For the licensor, it may prove difficult to control the quality of products produced under its licence. It is not always obvious to the consumer who produced a certain weapon, and a weapon produced under licence of lesser quality than the original can damage the reputations of the original licensor and original product. Furthermore, a licence may offer no guarantee of additional income for the licensor. If this is dependent on revenue, and little or no revenue is generated, the licensor will see no financial gain from the deal. Finally, a licensee sometimes becomes a direct competitor of the licensor, reducing overall benefits to the licensor if lost sales outweigh any royalties paid under the licensing agreement (WIPO, 2003, pp. 12–13).

Table 1.1	**Benefits, costs, and risks of licensed production**	
	For the licensor	**For the licensee**
Benefits	• Additional income through royalty payments • Increased return on research and development costs • Access to new markets • Access to investment opportunities in exchange for technology transfer • Strengthened political and military cooperation • Increased political influence on the licensee • Standardization of military equipment among allies • Rights to technological improvements developed by the licensee	• Establishment or strengthening of a domestic small arms industry • Cost-effective way of gaining self-sufficiency in small arms production • Fostering of the domestic high-tech sector • Reduced defence spending abroad • Economic growth • Increased gross domestic product • Job creation • Maintaining or expanding access to international markets • Gaining access to superior technology • Avoiding risks by producing tried and tested defence technology • Strengthened political and military cooperation • Standardization of military equipment among allies
Costs	• Loss of jobs in the small arms industry • Net financial loss as a result of exaggerated direct offsets	• Increased political and security dependence • Additional production expenses arising from royalty payments
Risks	• Creation of new competitors • Anticipated revenue gains may not materialize • Damaged reputation as a result of quality problems	• Dependence on foreign technology

For the licensee, the only significant risk of licensed production is its continued dependence on foreign technology and political will. This is also the case, however, if the country buys its armaments directly from another country. However, licensed production is preferable for the licensee country in this context in that technology and know-how, once transferred, cannot be taken back, so that even if the licensor country's attitude to the licensee country turns negative, the technology and know-how remain in the latter's possession.

As will be argued below, for the international community, the broader risk connected to licensed production is the irrevocable proliferation of the technology and know-how necessary for small arms production. Even though small arms manufacturing technology is relatively mature and therefore, in principle, accessible, licensed production greatly facilitates the multiplication of sources of small arms. This in turn increases the risk of potential misuse, diversion, and unauthorized transfer.

THE SCOPE OF LICENSED PRODUCTION[4]

This section will outline the scope of licensed production worldwide. The first part focuses on the geographical distribution of licensed small arms production. It provides an overview of major licensors and licensees, and discusses their particular characteristics. The second part of the section takes a closer look at the different kinds of weapons produced under licence, while the last part offers a global estimate of the annual production of the most common military small arms and light weapons. The cut-off date for data compilation was the end of August 2006.

So far, the chapter has not paid much attention to the distinction between licensed production and unlicensed production. This distinction is important, however, both for this section's global mapping exercise and the chapter's later exploration of proliferation risks. In both cases, technology and manufacturing know-how move from the original owner to a different producer. In the case of licensed production, this is done willingly, in exchange for compensation and subject to certain conditions. Unlicensed production, on the other hand, involves the acquisition and use of manufacturing technology without the consent of the original owner.

Information on the licensed production of small arms and light weapons is relatively scarce—even scarcer than for other aspects of the small arms industry. In most cases, information is available on the owner and acquirer country and company, as well as on the models produced. In many cases, however, it is unclear whether the weapons are being produced under proper licence or as unlicensed copies. It is also difficult to obtain data on quantities licensed and eventually produced, or the value of a licensing contract.

As a result, the chapter will distinguish the status of production using the following three categories: (i) licensed production, (ii) unlicensed production, and (iii) licensing situation unclear. The label 'licensed production' is applied only in cases when the sources explicitly refer to the terms 'licence' or 'licensed'. 'Unlicensed production' is applied where the sources mention explicit terms indicating the absence of a licence, such as 'unauthorized copy'. Cases for which no information is available or for which the situation is ambiguous are labelled 'licensing situation unclear'.[5]

For the purposes of this research, the term 'licensed' refers to cases where production takes place on the basis of a licensing agreement between two companies in different countries. The label 'unlicensed production', in turn, implies that production should be based on a licence—because the producer does not own the relevant technology—but is not. It excludes production by the original holder of technology, as well as cases where the right of production is 'inherited' by another legal entity, as with the successor states of the former USSR. The labels 'licensed' and 'unlicensed' merely indicate whether or not production is based on a licence agreement. They say nothing about whether a company is authorized by its government to produce the weapons in question.

> Seventeen states own small arms manufacturing technology while 52 have acquired it.

Countries and companies

Worldwide, there are currently 17 original owner states of small arms manufacturing technology whose products are produced in other countries either under licence or as unlicensed copies. In contrast to this relatively small number of original owners, there are 52 acquirer countries. The numbers of licences acquired or products copied without licence vary considerably by country. This study has identified 212 cases of licensed or unlicensed production (see Table 1.2). In the two cases where a consortium of several states grants a licence (for the production of Euromissiles Milan-2 anti-tank guided weapons) and where a group of states produces under licence together (in the Stinger Project Group), the study counted original owner and acquirer states individually.

The geographic distribution of licensed and unlicensed production of small arms is relatively concentrated (see Map 1.1). On the one hand, a small number of producer countries possess the original technology and manufacturing know-how and can therefore grant licences to others. On the other hand, a large number of countries acquire technology and know-how from others. All but five original owners are also acquirers, the exceptions being Austria, Belgium, the Russian Federation, South Africa, and Switzerland (marked with an asterisk in Table 1.2). Thus, while most acquirer states do not develop any production technology themselves, most original owners of technology acquire certain technology from others. Evidently, even the countries that can afford the research and development costs of some types of weapon prefer to reduce expenses where possible by purchasing licences for other products.

Table 1.2 **Current cases of technology transfer and/or acquisition (licensed or unlicensed) by country, to August 2006**[6]				
	More than 15 cases	**5–15 cases**	**Fewer than 5 cases**	**Total**
Group 1 Technology owners (17 countries)	Russian Federation (82)* Germany (34) Belgium (27)*	United States (13) Israel (8) Italy (8) China (7) France (7) Switzerland (6)*	Austria (4)* Sweden (4) United Kingdom (4) Czech Republic (3) Norway (2) Egypt (1) Serbia & Montenegro (1) South Africa (1)*	212
Group 2 Technology acquirers (52 countries)	China (24) Bulgaria (17)	Egypt (11) Iran (10) Greece (10) Pakistan (10) India (9) Romania (9) Turkey (9) Poland (8)	Czech Republic (4) Hungary (4) Italy (4) Nigeria (4) Saudi Arabia (4) Serbia & Montenegro (4) Vietnam (4) Argentina (3) Australia (3) Canada (3) Chile (3) Indonesia (3) Malaysia (3) North Korea (3) Singapore (3) South Korea (3) Spain (3) United States (3) Brazil (2) Colombia (2) Iraq (2) Libya (2) Philippines (2) Portugal (2) Sweden (2) Thailand (2) United Kingdom (2) Venezuela (2) Albania (1) Bangladesh (1) Croatia (1) Denmark (1) Estonia (1) France (1) Germany (1) Israel (1) Japan (1) Mexico (1) Morocco (1) Netherlands (1) Norway (1) Slovakia (1)	212

Note: Numbers in brackets indicate total cases of technology transfer and/or acquisition (licensed or unlicensed).

* These countries are not acquirers of technology. The other countries in Group 1 are owners of some technology but are acquirers of other technology and therefore also appear in Group 2.

Source: Gimelli Sulashvili (2006)

Map 1.1 **Original owners and acquirers of small arms manufacturing technology, to August 2006**

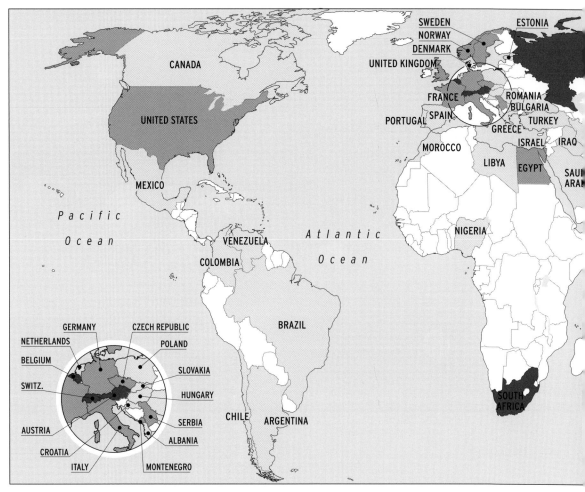

Source: Gimelli Sulashvili (2006)

Technology owners are concentrated not only in a limited number of countries, but also in a small number of companies. Many of these companies have a large range of products whose production is licensed or which are copied without licence worldwide. Examples include Izhmash in the Russian Federation, Heckler & Koch in Germany, and FN Herstal in Belgium. Table 1.3 lists 27 cases of licensed and unlicensed manufacture of FN Herstal products by 20 different countries.

Out of the 212 total cases identified by this study, 121, or 57 per cent, are based on a licensing agreement. In 51 cases (24 per cent), weapons are produced without any licence, while for 40 cases (19 per cent) the licensing situation is unclear (see Figure 1.1).

Strikingly, in 17 of the 51 unlicensed cases, China is the acquiring country. Also, out of the 24 cases in which China has acquired manufacturing know-how, only one case is clearly based on a licence, whereas in six cases the licensing status of production is unclear. Production may occur without a licence for several different reasons. In

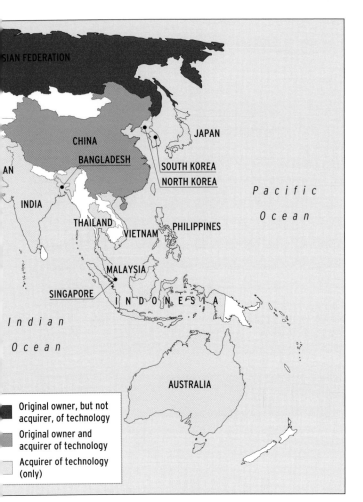

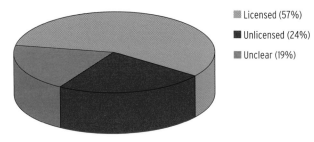

Figure 1.1 **Proportion of licensed production, unlicensed production, and unclear licensing situations for military small arms and light weapons, to August 2006**

■ Licensed (57%)
■ Unlicensed (24%)
■ Unclear (19%)

Source: Gimelli Sulashvili (2006)

some cases, the original licence has expired, but production continues none the less. In others, the producer never obtains a licence, acquiring the technology through other—often illicit—means (see next section). Both scenarios may be applicable to China. Given this country's known violation of intellectual property rights in other sectors, it is plausible that the state is sanctioning—or at least turning a blind eye to—such practices. Other states that frequently produce unlicensed copies of weapons and ammunition include Bulgaria, Iran, Poland, and Romania, though all to a lesser extent than China.

The three former Eastern Bloc countries on this list (Bulgaria, Poland, and Romania) produce weapons whose technology they acquired from the USSR several decades ago. Box 1.2 explains the reasons for this. Not surprisingly, then, the Russian Federation is today the original owner of technology whose products are most subject to unlicensed production. Of the 82 cases where the Russian Federation is the original owner of technology, production is based on a proper licence in only slightly more than a quarter of the cases (22 cases). In 33 cases, manufacture takes place without licence, while the licensing situation is unclear for 27 cases. German weapons, in contrast, are mostly produced abroad under licence. Overall, 27 of the 52 acquiring countries produce only under licence.

In some cases, acquirers sub-license a third party with the agreement of the original owner of the production technology. Bulgaria, for example, retransferred production licences for Kalashnikov rifles to Algeria and Tanzania with the permission of the USSR. Hungary did the same with regard to

Table 1.3 Licensed and unlicensed production of FN Herstal products, to August 2006

Acquiring country	Acquiring company	Original designation	Licensing situation
Rifles, assault rifles, carbines			
Argentina	Fábrica Militar Fray Luis Beltrán	FN FAL 7.62 mm rifle	Licensed
Brazil	Imbel	FN FAL 7.62 mm rifle	Licensed
Indonesia	PT Pindad	FNC 5.56 mm assault rifle	Licensed
Nigeria	DICON	FN FAL 7.62 mm rifle	Licensed
Sweden	N/A	FNC 5.56 mm assault rifle	Licensed
United States	DSA	FN FAL 7.62 mm rifle	Licensed
Machine guns, light machine guns, sub-machine guns			
Argentina	Direccion General de Fabricaciones Militares	MAG 7.62 mm general-purpose machine gun	Unclear
Australia	Australian Defence Industries (ADI)	Minimi 5.56 mm light machine gun	Licensed
Canada	Diemaco	Minimi 5.56 mm light machine gun	Licensed
Egypt	Maadi Company for Engineering Industries	MAG 7.62 mm general-purpose machine gun	Licensed
Greece	EBO	Minimi 5.56 mm light machine gun	Licensed
India	OFB	MAG 7.62 mm general-purpose machine gun	Licensed
Singapore	Ordnance Development and Engineering Company of Singapore	MAG 7.62 mm general-purpose machine gun	Unlicensed
Sweden	Bofors Carl Gustav	Browning M2 HB 0.50 machine gun	Licensed
United Kingdom	Manroy Engineering	MAG 7.62 mm general-purpose machine gun	Unclear
Side-arms			
Argentina	Fábrica Militar Fray Luis Beltrán	9 mm High-Power pistol	Licensed
China	NORINCO	9 mm High-Power pistol	Unlicensed
China	NORINCO	9 mm High-Power Mark 2 pistol	Unclear
China	NORINCO	9 mm High-Power Mark 3 pistol	Unlicensed
Hungary	Fegyver es Gaykeszuelekgyara	9 mm High-Power M1935GP	Unclear
India	Rifle Factory	9 mm High-Power pistol	Unclear
Indonesia	PT Pindad	9 mm High-Power pistol	Unclear
Israel	KSN Industries Ltd.	9 mm High-Power pistol	Unclear
Ammunition			
Italy	Fiocchi Munizioni	5.7 mm x 28 mm	Licensed
Philippines	Government Arsenal	5.56 mm x 45 mm	Licensed
United States	Winchester Olin	5.7 mm x 28 mm	Licensed
Vietnam	N/A	7.62 mm x 51 mm	Licensed

Source: Gimelli Sulashvili (2006)

Table 1.4 Selected cases of sub-licensing or unlicensed recopying, to August 2006

Original owner of technology	Original model	Acquirer	Licence produced/ copied model	Reacquirer(s)	Means of transmission
USSR/Russian Federation (Izhmash)	Various Kalashnikov rifles	Bulgaria (JSC Arsenal)	Various Kalashnikov rifles	Algeria Tanzania	Sub-licensing with permission of the original owner of technology
United States (Colt)	M16 assault rifle	China (NORINCO)	Type CQ assault rifle	Iran (DIO)	Unlicensed recopying of a product produced without a licence
USSR/Russian Federation (Izhmash)	Kalashnikov assault rifle	China (NORINCO)	Type 81 assault rifle	Bangladesh (BOF)	Licensed production of a product that had previously been copied without a licence
USSR/Russian Federation	12.7 mm DShK 38/46 heavy machine gun	China (NORINCO)	Type 54	Pakistan (POF)	Licensed production of a product that had previously been copied without a licence

Source: Gimelli Sulashvili (2006); Pyadushkin (2006)

Malta and Mozambique, while Romania sub-licensed Zimbabwe (Pyadushkin, 2006). In other instances, products copied without licence are recopied in the same way by a third country. For example, Iran produces unlicensed copies of the Chinese Type CQ assault rifle, which is itself an unlicensed copy of the M16. There are even cases where a licence has been sold for manufacturing technology that had previously been acquired without a licence. Bangladesh and Pakistan are producing weapons under licence from China. China, however, earlier copied the product without licence from the USSR/Russian Federation (Gimelli Sulashvili, 2006). Table 1.4 provides details of some of these cases.

Licensed and unlicensed products

The Russian Federation is the champion among original owners of arms production technology, with its light weapons being produced elsewhere in 36 cases; its rifles, assault rifles, and carbines in 21 cases; and its machine guns in 20 cases. Belgium is the second most important original holder of technology, with its side-arms being produced elsewhere in eight cases and small arms ammunition in four cases. On the side of the acquirers, China is the most important country in the area of side-arms (nine cases); machine guns (seven cases); and rifles, assault rifles, and carbines (four cases), while Bulgaria is the most frequent acquirer of technology for the production of light weapons (nine cases).

As mentioned above, the USSR/Russian Federation represents a special case, since many of its products are manufactured abroad without a licence (see Box 1.2). Therefore, as Figure 1.2 shows, the USSR/Russian Federation cases disproportionately contribute to unlicensed production.

If the USSR/Russian Federation is excluded from the analysis, unlicensed production becomes somewhat less common. This may well be the trend of the future. The Russian Federation has stepped up its efforts to conclude

Figure 1.2 **Proportion of licensed and unlicensed production per weapon type, including/excluding the USSR/ Russian Federation, to August 2006**

NUMBER OF CASES

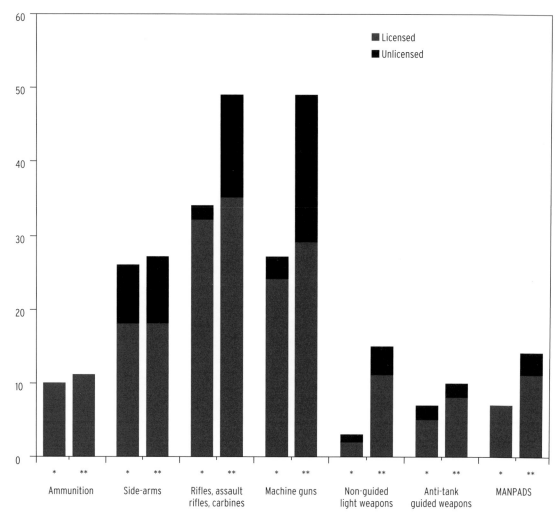

WEAPON TYPE

* Excluding the USSR/Russian Federation
** Including the USSR/Russian Federation
Source: Gimelli Sulashvili (2006)

licensing agreements with a number of countries and to secure greater control over the use of its production tech-nology (Pyadushkin, 2006).

The 96 non-USSR/Russian Federation cases of licensed production identified in this study are unevenly distrib-uted across different weapons categories. Licence agreements are most frequently concluded for the production of military rifles, assault rifles, carbines, side-arms, and machine guns. Licensed production of ammunition and light weapons is relatively rare (Figure 1.3). The reasons for this difference are explored below.

Figure 1.3 Proportion of weapons types among the 96 current cases of licensed production, excluding the USSR/Russian Federation, to August 2006

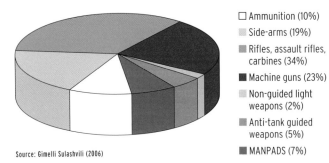

- ☐ Ammunition (10%)
- ▨ Side-arms (19%)
- ▉ Rifles, assault rifles, carbines (34%)
- ▉ Machine guns (23%)
- ▨ Non-guided light weapons (2%)
- ▉ Anti-tank guided weapons (5%)
- ▉ MANPADS (7%)

Source: Gimelli Sulashvili (2006)

Small arms ammunition

Forecast International (2006[7]) notes that '[d]ue to the unique nature of this market, players rarely, if ever, make licensing arrangements' in relation to small arms ammunition. The product is of very limited complexity, and research and development costs are therefore low (Anders and Weidacher, 2006, p. 55), so that royalties and the price for a licence may easily exceed them. Moreover, economies of scale can be reached in a short time. As a consequence, licensed production is not very attractive for producers, especially as major ammunition manufacturers are willing to transfer production machinery without connecting this transfer to a licence agreement (Anders, 2005). Accordingly, there is no incentive for companies to engage in unlicensed production of ammunition either (see Figure 1.2).

Anti-tank guided weapons and MANPADS

The technology of anti-tank guided weapons (ATGWs) and MANPADS is highly complex. To develop such weapons, enormous research and development costs are necessary, development takes a long time, and economies of scale are not easily reached. For most countries, therefore, licensed or unlicensed production is the only way to access this technology, especially in the case of MANPADS. The few states that possess the technology have pledged, however, not to make it easily available to others (Small Arms Survey, 2005, pp. 123–41). Excluding the Russian Federation, there are only four original owners of MANPADS technology: China, France, Sweden, and the United States. These states have transferred this know-how to only six other countries—Germany, Greece, the Netherlands, Pakistan, South Korea, and Turkey. As it is difficult and costly to reproduce these complex weapon systems through copying or reverse engineering, states seeking to acquire the technology are dependent on technology owners. This is in line with the findings of this study, which found no cases of unlicensed MANPADS production if the cases involving the former USSR are excluded.[8]

To get the full picture on MANPADS, however, the case of the former USSR has to be included. Currently, all cases of unlicensed production and the majority of cases for which the licensing situation is unclear involve Soviet technology. The former USSR granted MANPADS production licences to other nations (Bulgaria, China, the Czech Republic, Egypt, North Korea, Pakistan, Poland, Romania, and Vietnam) at various times, and all but three of them (the Czech Republic, Pakistan, and Vietnam) continue production, even though the licence has expired (see Box 1.2). Moreover, it appears likely that China, which produces the Soviet 'Strela' without licence under the name HN-5, has granted a production licence for this technology to Pakistan (Small Arms Survey, 2004, p. 82; Pyadushkin with Haug and Mateeva, 2003). This gives reason for concern, as intensive efforts by the international community to control strictly the transfer of MANPADS technology are being undermined by unlicensed production based on Soviet technology.

Small arms and non-guided light weapons

In all the remaining weapons categories, which include side-arms, rifles, assault rifles, carbines, machine guns, and non-guided light weapons, the findings are mixed. The technology necessary for the production of these weapons is mature, so that it is possible for small arms and light weapons manufacturers to design and produce them on their own without extremely high research and development costs. Economies of scale can also be achieved without too much difficulty. The barriers to entry in the market are, however, somewhat higher than in the case of small arms ammunition. Depending on the circumstances, it may be more efficient to acquire a production licence. In fact, this is often the most cost-effective means of building up an indigenous defence industry.

The proportion of unlicensed production is relatively high in these weapons categories. Even excluding the USSR/Russian Federation, production status is unclear or production takes place without a licence in 29 per cent of the 101 cases identified in this study. For side-arms alone, unlicensed production makes up 47 per cent. If the USSR/Russian Federation is included in the analysis, the overall share of unlicensed or unclear production cases increases to 44 per cent overall (51 per cent for side-arms).

These findings suggest that additional counter-proliferation measures that target licensed production will be most effective for weapons categories other than ammunition, ATGWs, and MANPADS. Such measures will not be effective for ammunition, since there is too little licensed production overall. For ATGWs and MANPADS, the relevant technology is already relatively closely guarded, and many safeguards are in place. Additional measures would only increase effective control in this area if they specifically targeted production based on former Soviet technology.

Estimating global production

As mentioned above, data on the number of small arms produced under licence is rare. Referring to open source information, this section derives a global estimate for annual licensed and unlicensed production of military small arms, in particular military rifles, assault rifles, and carbines.

Based on the known volume of small arms production in ten selected licensee states, the average number of weapons produced each year under licence can be calculated. Assuming that the duration of a production cycle ranges from 15 to 20 years (Small Arms Survey, 2006, pp. 23–24), the annual average varies between 9,600 and 10,500 weapons for each licence agreement. This may be below the full production capacity of a factory located in an industrialized country, but these numbers seem realistic, as most of the acquirer countries identified in this study are not fully industrialized (Gimelli Sulashvili, 2006).

Currently, there are 55 cases of military rifle, assault rifle, and carbine production, out of which 64 per cent are licensed (35 cases) and 25 per cent unlicensed (14 cases), while in 11 per cent of the cases the licensing situation is unknown (6 cases). Because there is some doubt about the existence of a licence agreement, the last category is added to that of unlicensed production. Global annual production by acquirer countries can be estimated by multiplying the figure for average annual production, derived above, by the number of existing cases of licensed and unlicensed production. While this admittedly yields a rough estimate, in the absence of more specific data it does provide us with a sense of the overall scale of production.

Figure 1.4 **Proportion of military rifles, assault rifles, and carbines in total annual licensed and unlicensed production, to August 2006**

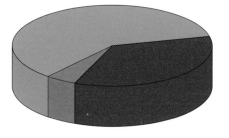

■ Assault rifles (60%)

■ Rifles (35%)

■ Carbines (5%)

Source: Gimelli Sulashvili (2006)

Figure 1.5 **Proportion of global licensed and unlicensed production of military rifles, assault rifles, and carbines by region, to August 2006**

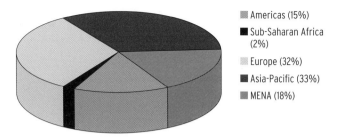

■ Americas (15%)

■ Sub-Saharan Africa
(2%)

■ Europe (32%)

■ Asia-Pacific (33%)

■ MENA (18%)

Source: Gimelli Sulashvili (2006)

Applying this methodology, the annual total of licensed and unlicensed production of military rifles, assault rifles, and carbines can be estimated at between 530,000 and 580,000 weapons. This is roughly equivalent to 320,000–350,000 assault rifles, 182,000–200,000 rifles, and 28,000–30,000 carbines (Figure 1.4). This estimate complements, and is coherent with, previous Survey findings on military small arms production. The 2002 and 2006 editions of the *Small Arms Survey,* though using different methodologies, concluded that between 700,000 and 900,000 military small arms are produced every year (815,000 in 2000) (Small Arms Survey, 2002, p. 13; 2006, pp. 7–35). The figure for licensed and unlicensed production presented here represents 60 to 80 per cent of this amount.

Europe and the Asia–Pacific region account for the greatest share of licensed and unlicensed production of military assault rifles, rifles, and carbines, followed by the Middle East and the Americas. The African continent accounts for only a very small part of such production. In Europe, unlicensed production of these weapons exceeds licensed production, since several former Eastern Bloc countries continue to manufacture weapons for which the licence has expired (see Figure 1.5).

CURBING PROLIFERATION: PROBLEMS AND SOLUTIONS

As indicated above, the licensed and unlicensed transfer of weapons production technology poses certain risks for technology owners and the international community as a whole. The following sections examine three problem scenarios, as well as the regulatory practices and policy options that can address these. The violation of intellectual property rights (i.e. unlicensed production), examined in the first section, is an obvious concern for technology owners. Yet, for the international community as a whole the key problems are the diversion of manufacturing technology and the irresponsible export of weapons produced under licence. Without adequate control measures, licensed production can easily fuel proliferation and increase the risk that small arms and light weapons end up in the wrong hands.

Unauthorized production

In over a quarter of the cases examined earlier, small arms production takes place without a licence. This is a huge problem for the original owners of technology, as it deprives them of the royalties and other fees they are entitled to.

One way of acquiring the necessary production knowledge without a licence is through reverse engineering—the process of taking a weapon apart and analysing its design in detail in order to construct a new weapon. In many instances, however, production is not unlicensed from the beginning. Often, a producer acquires a licence, produces under licence as long as it is valid, and then continues to produce the weapon beyond the licence expiry date. While Bulgaria was still part of the Soviet Eastern Bloc, Bulgarian State Arsenals acquired a production licence for

Box 1.2   Licensed and unlicensed Kalashnikov production: echoes from the cold war

Throughout the cold war, the USSR used military assistance, including the transfer of arms, as a means of enhancing the military power of its allies and promoting its political influence in various zones of strategic interest. It granted production licences and transferred manufacturing technology only to its closest allies—mostly for small arms and light weapons. In order to obtain a production licence, the acquirer first had to purchase directly a large number of the same weapons that were subsequently to be produced under licence. This continues to be the practice of the Russian Federation.

Much like the arms trade in general, licensed production arrangements were managed by governmental bodies through bilateral agreements with counterparts in allied countries. In such agreements, the transfer of a manufacturing licence was documented by an exchange of letters annexed to military cooperation agreements. Most licences were granted royalty-free, but contained a number of precise conditions.[9] The most important condition, included in every agreement, stipulated that licensed production could serve domestic needs only, and that export to third countries was strictly subject to the permission of the Soviet government.[10] The same condition applied to the technical modernization of weapons produced under licence. Furthermore, licensed production periods could be limited.

After the demise of the Soviet Union, the situation changed radically. Firstly, domestic military procurement decreased, and arms exports became the major source of revenue for the Russian Federation's defence industry. Secondly, the demand for new Russian Federation small arms diminished as the global market was flooded with surplus stocks from the old USSR and its allies. Thirdly, licensees started to export weapons produced under licence, thus offering serious competition to Russian Federation manufacturers in the global market. As a result, the issue of the licensed manufacture of small arms began to receive increased attention from the Russian Federation defence industry. Rosoboronexport, a merger of several previous governmental arms trade bodies, was established. It took stock of the numerous production licences previously granted to foreign countries and began to assert Russian Federation manufacturers' intellectual property rights.

The Russian Federation government claims that most of the licences formerly granted by the USSR have expired. This would mean that every year a large number of weapons based on the Kalashnikov design are produced as unlicensed copies by companies around the world. Russian Federation production accounts for only about 10–12 per cent of the world market in Kalashnikov rifles. Given that a production licence costs about USD 6–10 million, Kalashnikov's loss in terms of potential overseas licences is huge. The more important problem for the Russian Federation, however, is exporting by former licensees. Rosoboronexport mentions, for example, a tender organized by the US administration in Iraq in 2003 for small arms supplies for the new Iraqi Army. Bulgarian State Arsenals won the contract for 40,000 Kalashnikov rifles at a price of about USD 65 per weapon. From the Russian Federation standpoint, the export of weapons produced under licence to third countries without its approval represents a violation of bilateral agreements concluded with the former USSR. The granting of sub-licences by Soviet-era licensees is a further concern for the Russian Federation.

In order to counter such practices, the Russian Federation has initiated bilateral negotiations with former Soviet licensees, including all those in Eastern Europe. While the licensees generally agree to pay royalties, they balk at making the export of licensed products dependent on Russian Federation permission, as in their view this would give the Russian Federation an unfair commercial advantage.

At the same time, Russian small arms manufacturers are trying to protect their intellectual property rights by patenting their small arms technology. Izhmash has patented its design of the AK assault rifle, including components and technical innovations. Since 1997 it has received patents for AK rifles in 14 countries.[11] It applied for a patent in Bulgaria as well, but, according to Izhmash, approval is still pending. Izhmash has also patented the Dragunov SVD and SVDS sniper rifles, the Nikonov AN-94 assault rifle, the Bizon sub-machine gun, and the Saiga hunting rifle. Even though patents can help prevent future violations of the patent holder's intellectual property, they have limitations. Firstly, patents are not retroactive. Izhmash cannot patent the original AK-47, but only its own modifications to the original AK design introduced after the introduction of the patent. Secondly, a patent is not universal. It has to be recognized and enforced in each country where the patentee wants to protect its rights. Thirdly, a patent is of limited duration: patent protection is limited to a certain number of years, and thereafter the invention becomes a public good.

The Russian Federation government has supported the efforts of its arms manufacturers by putting the issue on the international agenda. It has defended its exclusive right to manufacture Kalashnikov rifles within the framework of the Wassenaar Arrangement, the Organization for Security and Co-operation in Europe (OSCE) Forum for Security Co-operation, and the United Nations. At the UN Programme of Action Review Conference in 2006, the Russian Federation argued that the term 'illicit small arms and light weapons manufacturing and transfer' should be understood as including 'unlicensed small arms and light weapons manufacturing or small arms and light weapons manufacturing under expired licences'. Mikhail Kalashnikov himself promoted this position. In addition to its diplomatic efforts, the Russian Federation regularly draws the attention of world media to problem cases of unlicensed production.

Sources: Pyadushkin (2006); Anderson (2006a); BBC (2006a); RIA Novosti (2006a; 2006b); Petersburg Times (1999); UNGA (2006)

Kalashnikovs. The licence expired around 1999, but Bulgaria, in irrevocable possession of the necessary technology, continued production beyond that date (*Dnevnik,* 2006). In other cases, production may exceed the number of units agreed upon in the licence agreement.

There are other, subtler ways of getting around a licence. One common method involves the introduction of slight modifications in the design or functioning of a weapon. It can thus be argued that the resulting weapon is not an unlicensed copy, but rather a new product, not subject to licence (Nassauer and Steinmetz, 2005, p. 14; *Dnevnik,* 2006). The classic example of minor modifications marketed as new weapons designs is the Kalashnikov (see Box 1.2). Croatia offers a further example: the country produces the APS95 assault rifle firing 5.56 mm NATO ammunition. Its design owes much to the Israeli Galil series, but reportedly includes some 'local revisions', e.g. an additional doubling of the optical sight. Furthermore, Croatia has developed a modified version of a 9 mm ERO sub-machine gun, which itself is a copy of the Israeli Uzi (Gander, 1997; Bazargan, 2003). In theory, the original owner of technology could benefit from technological improvements made by an acquirer (WIPO, 2003, p. 12). In practice, however, the acquirer often becomes a rival to the original technology owner in international markets.

The interests of technology owners can be addressed through the enforcement of intellectual property right laws. A well-developed body of national—and even international—norms allows companies and countries to assert their rights and protect their technology from unlicensed production. According to the Wassenaar Arrangement's *Best*

A gun dealer presents a Romanian-made AKM assault rifle in his gun shop in Dallas, Texas, 2004. © Jeff Mitchell/Reuters

Box 1.3   Mexico and the 'new' FX05 Xihuacóatl assault rifle

At the beginning of the 21st century, Mexico decided to replace approximately 146,000 Heckler & Koch G3 rifles, its standard combat rifle. The initial choice of the Mexican Secretariat of National Defence (SEDENA) for the replacement was the HK33 rifle. After an initial phase of experimental assembly with parts and components imported from Germany, however, it shifted its preference to the HK G36 (Dreyfus, 2006).

In May 2005 SEDENA announced that Mexico would launch a six-year programme for the production of the G36 rifle under licence. This programme provided for a USD 45 million investment from the Mexican government and the transfer of production technology from Heckler & Koch to Mexico's General Directorate of Military Industry in the form of a USD 27 million purchase of machinery from Germany. However, calculating that the costs for local research, development, and production would amount to USD 4.4 million, the Mexican Army instead opted for a weapon of indigenous design: the FX05 Fusil Xihuacóatl 2005. During 2006 Mexico intended to produce 10,000 weapons for its special forces, and then replace all the rifles of the Mexican Army over the following seven years (Dreyfus, 2006).

On the surface, the FX05 almost exactly resembles the G36 (the G36K or G36C in particular). There are, however, some significant external differences: there is a different flash suppressor, the cocking handle is on the left instead of on the top, the carrying handle is detachable, there is only one sight, and the butt stock is shaped differently. SEDENA officially argues that the FX05 is not a licensed version of the G36 (Dreyfus, 2006). Heckler & Koch has confirmed that there is no production licence in this case. Currently, the company is investigating whether elements of the firing mechanism have been copied, but has not indicated whether it will take any follow-up action should this be the case.[12]

Practice Guidelines for Exports of Small Arms and Light Weapons, for example, '[p]articipating States agree that unlicensed manufacture of foreign-origin [small arms and light weapons] is inconsistent with these Best Practice Guidelines' (Wassenaar Arrangement, 2002, para. I.4).

The successful implementation of such norms largely rests with the acquirer state. It is up to it to investigate and take legal action against unlicensed producers. Yet a lack of capacity and/or political will results in lacklustre implementation in many cases. In the face of this difficulty, technology owners sometimes try to limit their losses by concluding licensing agreements that provide for the payment of royalties, but do not otherwise reduce competition.

While certainly important, infringements on the intellectual property rights of technology owners are only part of the problem. The uncontrolled proliferation of production technology poses a threat to the international community as a whole. Enforcing intellectual property rights does little, on its own, to address this broader problem, notwithstanding Mikhail Kalashnikov's claim that this would also limit the number of guns landing up in the wrong hands (UNGA, 2006). The enforcement of intellectual property rights could help reduce the number of weapons produced, but would do little to curtail the transfer of technology and weapons to undesirable end users. Measures targeting diversion more directly, including export control measures, are far more effective.

Irresponsible transfer of manufacturing technology

As mentioned earlier, licensors and licensees may have economic or political motivations for licensed production. Very often, these go hand in hand. For example, by acquiring a production licence, a state may be able to reduce procurement costs, create jobs, and increase national self-reliance all at the same time.

Sometimes, however, economic and political goals are squarely opposed. Licensors, in particular, may face a choice between the economic benefits of a production licence and their political or legal commitments. Pursuant to several multilateral agreements, including the commitments outlined in the *OSCE Document on Small Arms and Light Weapons* (OSCE, 2000), as well as many national standards, production licences must be refused if there is a significant risk that the transferred technology or weapons to be produced under licence would be diverted or misused by the recipient (TRANSFER CONTROLS).

In a much-cited example from the 1990s, Heckler & Koch won a fierce competition for a contract from Turkey's Silahsan for the replacement of 350,000 G3 rifles (*Jane's Defence Weekly,* 1995; Jones and Cutshaw, 2004, pp. 28–29; Small Arms Survey, 2001, p. 40).[13] Germany apparently had great economic interest in the deal, otherwise Heckler & Koch would probably not have been willing to grant offsets of 100 per cent in order to secure it (*Jane's Defence Weekly,* 1995). According to Germany's political principles and commitments, however, this licence was problematic, as the Turkish state had a record of systematic human rights violations and was engaged in an armed conflict with the country's Kurdish minority. As a result, the German government temporarily held up its authorization (Sariibrahimoglu, 2005).

Other problematic technology transfers have also occurred in the past. For example, in the 1970s and 1980s, during the time of apartheid, South Africa received military technology from various states. Its R4 assault rifle was a copy of the Israeli Galil. It remains unclear, however, whether it was produced with or without a licence (*Jane's International Defence Review,* 1997b; Nairn, 1986; GlobalSecurity.org, 2005). In 1991, as the former Yugoslavia slid into civil war, France's Manufactures d'Armes Automatiques de Bayonne granted a licence for the manufacture of 9 mm MAB PA-15 pistols to the Serbian company Zastava Arms (Jones and Cutshaw, 2004, p. 250). Iraq under Saddam Hussein produced 9 x 19 mm Helwan pistols under an Egyptian licence (Forecast International, 2006).

Transfers of production technology and manufacturing know-how are irrevocable. Once transferred, such knowledge cannot be taken back. Even though many licence agreements contain safeguard clauses in theory prohibiting the retransfer of manufacturing technology, this is difficult to control in practice. There is always a risk that blueprints for production—as well as the weapons produced under licence—will fall into the wrong hands (Small Arms Survey, 2006, p. 223).

Various measures at the company, national, and international levels can address the problems outlined above.

It is in the licensor company's own interest to collect detailed information concerning the final destination, end user, and intended use of weapons that are going to be produced under its licence. It has a strong interest, moreover, in concluding a licensing agreement only if it can be as sure as possible that weapons produced with its technology will not end up in the wrong hands.

To this end, a licensor company can introduce internal guidelines governing the choice of potential partners in a licensing arrangement, including eligibility criteria. Both licensor and licensee companies can also develop minimum standards for the content of licensing agreements, including safeguards. Under the banner of 'corporate social responsibility', major international companies have subscribed to such standards in such fields as climate change and biodiversity. Numerous governments support initiatives of this kind.[14] There is no reason why such initiatives should not extend to the domain of small arms and light weapons production, but so far this has been quite rare. Saab Bofors Dynamics is an exception.[15]

It is, however, the licensor state that is responsible for authorizing (or refusing) the transfer of arms production technology in accordance with applicable international standards. Best practice in this area dictates that the licensor state treat exports of machinery, know-how, and technology in the same way as direct small arms exports. In this way, production licences are refused if the export to the same state of the weapons to be produced under licence would also be refused.

Many of the major original technology-owning states have relatively strict legal regulations excluding the granting of small arms production licences to problematic companies or states. Nevertheless, there is often a problem with the effective application of such laws.

Licensor states are expected to treat exports of technology as they would exports of small arms.

The German government allows the export of war weapons and other military equipment (including manufacturing technology) to NATO countries, European Union (EU) member states, and countries with NATO equivalent status (Germany, 2000, sec. II, para. 1).[16] As a general rule, such products cannot be transferred to countries that are involved in armed conflict or facing an imminent outbreak of conflict. Nor can weapons be exported if this would aggravate the threat of armed conflict (Germany, 2000, sec. III, para. 5). The situation in a licensee country can, however, change in the years following the conclusion of a licensing agreement. The withdrawal of licences in such cases would not usually make much difference, since manufacturing know-how, once transferred, cannot be taken back.

The UK government requires a licence for the export of technology necessary for the development, production, or use of military equipment (BASIC, International Alert, and Saferworld, 2002, p. 9). There is a potential loophole in such legislation, however. Depending on how the requirement of 'necessity' is interpreted, technology that is involved in small arms production, but not exclusively so, can slip past licensing authorities. For this reason, it is important that the licensing agreement as a whole, as well as the final use of exported technology, be considered before a licence is granted.

Few international instruments address the issue of licensed weapons production.

In the United States, licensing agreements have to be authorized by the US State Department under its Direct Commercial Sales Program (United States, 1997, arts. 120.9, 120.10, 124.1, 124.8). The US Congress must be notified before production licence agreements with a value higher than USD 50 million are approved (BASIC, International Alert, and Saferworld, 2002, p. 10). This threshold, however, excludes most licensing agreements for the production of small arms and/or light weapons, which typically are worth less than USD 50 million. Independent observers have argued that the US Congress—or other relevant legislative structures in other countries—should receive notification of small arms/light weapons licensing deals with any country, of any value, along with an explanation as to why the proposed agreement is in the national interest of the licensor country (Lumpe, 1995).

Given the transnational nature of licensed weapons production, there is a clear need for international regulation. Nevertheless, very few international instruments address this issue. One that does is the *European Union Code of Conduct for Arms Exports* (EU, 1998), which prescribes common EU criteria for the export of military equipment.[17] By extension, it has become very difficult for an EU member state to grant a production licence to a country previously denied such a licence by another EU state (EU, 1998, operative provision 3).

Among all small arms and light weapons, MANPADS have been singled out for especially stringent treatment. The *Elements for Export Controls of Man-Portable Air Defence Systems (MANPADS),* adopted by the Wassenaar Arrangement in December 2003, defines the term 'export' broadly so as to include co-production and licensed production. MANPADS are to be exported 'only to foreign governments or to agents specifically authorised to act on behalf of a government' (Wassenaar Arrangement, 2003, para. 2.1). Any decision to authorize the export of MANPADS is to take into account such things as the recipient government's capacity for and commitment to stockpile security (Wassenaar Arrangement, 2003, para. 2.7). The OSCE adopted the same MANPADS guidelines virtually verbatim in May 2004 (OSCE, 2004, paras. 2.1 and 2.7). Under the Asia–Pacific Economic Cooperation MANPADS guidelines, licensees are to protect transferred technology 'against unauthorized re-transfer, loss, theft and diversion' (APEC, 2003, para. 3).

Irresponsible transfer of weapons produced under licence

Re-export of small arms produced under licence might be deliberate state policy. Capital investment, the payment of royalties, and technical assistance fees make licensed production costly. In order to offset these expenses and thus lower the average cost per weapon for their own armed forces, some countries resort to exporting these weapons to third countries, even if pursuant to their national regulations or international commitments they are not authorized to do so (Lumpe, 1995). Many production licence agreements oblige the licensee to declare the final recipient of any arms produced under licence. In some cases, the export of such weapons is prohibited outright. Moreover, many agreements oblige both licensor and licensee to ensure that these provisions are upheld. Nevertheless, it is virtually impossible for the licensor to exercise *de facto* control over final recipients.

Governments have, on occasion, deliberately arranged or facilitated the irresponsible transfer of weapons produced under licence. For example, between 1991 and 1995 Argentinean President Menem signed three decrees authorizing the export of small arms and ammunition produced by Argentina under licence. The end-user certificates gave Panama and Venezuela as the final destinations, but the goods eventually ended up in Ecuador,[18] which at the time was involved in an armed border clash with its neighbour, Peru. These weapons also surfaced among belligerent parties in the Yugoslav conflict. Other small arms, such as FN FAL rifles produced under Belgian licence, made their way into the hands of organized criminals, such as the mafia of Rio de Janeiro (Vranckx, 2005, p. 14).

Yet, many irresponsible retransfers are not deliberate. Sometimes, a lack of capacity for effective arms control is the problem; in other cases, a government does not consider itself bound by an agreement brokered by a predecessor. This has been the case with licences for the production of small arms ammunition granted by France and Germany to other states. As a consequence, the two licensors have recently imposed significant restrictions on permissible destinations for ammunition production facilities. Yet not all licensors act with the same rigour. In recent years, independent observers have criticized Belgium for neglecting the question of likely licensee compliance before granting ammunition production licences (Anders, 2005). The controversy surrounding the New Lachaussée ammunition factory in Tanzania offers one prominent example of this problem (Small Arms Survey, 2005, p. 14).

At the end of the day, corruption, neglect, or theft seems to lie at the heart of most unauthorized exports of small arms produced under licence. In 2004 the Colombian

With his Israeli-designed Galil rifle, a Colombian soldier trains to combat leftist armed groups and the cocaine trade. Barrancominas, Colombia, 2001. © Reuters

secret police reported regular flows from Brazil into Colombia of Beretta pistols, as well as 9 mm Model 12 sub-machine guns, which the Brazilian company Imbel produces under licence. The Colombian authorities have also seized 400 rifles bearing the mark of the Venezuelan armed forces (McDermott, 2004b).

Even if small arms produced under licence are not re-exported to a third party, these weapons replace older stocks, which might in turn be transferred abroad. In July 2006 President Chávez stated that Venezuela could supply other countries in need of military equipment, in particular Bolivia. Even though so far there is no evidence for such plans by the Government of Venezuela, the Bush administration suspects that the AK-103s to be produced in Venezuela under a Russian licence might be diverted to armed groups throughout the continent. As Venezuela's production facilities have never operated at full capacity, it is unlikely that the country will even be able to arm all members of its armed forces with new Kalashnikovs.[19] It is possible, however, that Venezuela's surplus stocks of old rifles will 'cascade' to other countries, even though they do not seem to be in the best condition (Baranauskas, 2006a; 2006b; 2006c; Small Arms Survey, 2006, p. 87). Cascading may occur years after the licensed production arrangement is agreed on, and may not appear directly connected to the licence agreement (Nassauer and Steinmetz, 2005, p. 14; Small Arms Survey, 2006, pp. 25–26).

The responsibility of licensor states does not end with an initial transfer of production equipment or technology. It is equally important that they anticipate and act to prevent the illicit transfer of weapons produced under licence. German law provides one example of best practice in this area. The regulations 'Political Principles for the Export of War Weapons and Other Military Equipment' specify that:

> Cascading may occur years after the licensed production arrangement is agreed on.

> *Export licences for war weapons or other military equipment of a quantity and type relevant to war weapons may be granted only on presentation of governmental end-use certificates that preclude re-exports without prior authorization. This applies* mutatis mutandis *to any other military equipment related to war weapons exported in connection with a manufacturing licence.*[20] *For the export of such equipment used for the manu-facture of war weapons definitive end-use certificates must be furnished* (Germany, 2000, sec. IV, para. 2).

The same regulations state that 'stringent standards are to be applied in assessing whether the recipient country is capable of carrying out effective export controls' (Germany, 2000, sec. IV, para. 2). This provision would preclude a transfer of technology to states that have inadequate end-user controls or a record of violating international arms embargoes.

In order to address the problem of 'cascading' surpluses, Germany makes it a condition of new licensed production arrangements that old stocks be destroyed on a one-to-one basis:

> *In the export of technology and production equipment, there is the fundamental rule that no licences are issued in connection with the opening of new production lines for small arms and ammunition in third countries. For third countries, the 'new for old' principle is also applied wherever possible. This calls for sales contracts to be worded to ensure that the recipient destroys weapons that are to be replaced by the new consignment, rather than reselling them. Moreover, insofar as possible, the exporter is to require the consignee in a third country in new supply contracts to destroy the weapons supplied in the case of a later removal from use* (Germany, 2003, p. 17).

Best practice can achieve little if it constitutes the exception rather than the rule. International norms help raise standards across the board, yet remain rare. The *OSCE Document on Small Arms and Light Weapons* offers one example of international regulation in this area:

Participating States will make every effort within their competence to ensure that licensing agreements for small arms production concluded with manufacturers located outside their territory will contain, where appropriate, a clause applying the above criteria to any exports of small arms manufactured under license in that agreement (OSCE, 2000, sec. III.A.3).

The 'above criteria' that the provision mentions are the same as those applied by the *OSCE Document* to the direct export of small arms and light weapons (OSCE, 2000, sec. III.A.2). These provisions, though politically (but not legally) binding, are still significant: the 56 participating states of the OSCE include all of the world's major original technology owners.

The regulatory challenge

As noted above, there are relatively few norms governing licensed production at the regional or global levels. Only the *OSCE Document on Small Arms and Light Weapons* explicitly regulates both the initial transfer of arms manufacturing technology and the subsequent transfer of weapons produced under licence. Other instruments, such as the *EU Code,* cover only the initial technology transfer. While the *UN Programme of Action* makes reference to 'illegal' or 'illicit' manufacturing (UNGA, 2001, sec. II, paras. 2–4, 6), these provisions would, at most, apply only to unlicensed production. They do not address the broader proliferation problems outlined above. At present, there are no norms of universal application that explicitly govern licensed production. Existing international instruments on MANPADS could serve as a model in this regard.

> The enforcement of norms governing licensed production rests entirely with states.

Enhanced international cooperation could also bring much-needed transparency to licensed production—encouraging states to exchange information on such things as pending authorizations and the behaviour of licensees.[21] Improved transparency would help in particular to curb the irresponsible transfer of small arms and light weapons produced under licence.

Normative development is one challenge, effective enforcement another. The enforcement of norms governing licensed production rests entirely with states—both the original owners of technology and its acquirers. Key national-level action includes the following:

- enforcing intellectual property laws within the national territory;
- encouraging corporate social responsibility in the small arms industry;
- applying the criteria used for direct weapons exports to the authorization of production licensing agreements;
- addressing the issue of weapons superseded by new production when authorizing licensing agreements;
- strictly enforcing national laws governing the international transfer of manufacturing technology;
- ensuring consistent legislative oversight;
- collecting and updating information on production licensing agreements; and
- exchanging information on licensed production with other states.

These measures are often resource-intensive, yet the risks inherent in the transfer of weapons manufacturing technology justify concerted action. It is difficult to forecast the consequences of a particular technology transfer. Alliances may change. Countries that seem stable may suddenly lapse into conflict. Sustained vigilance is therefore necessary.

CONCLUSION

The licensed and unlicensed manufacture of small arms and light weapons is an often-neglected aspect of small arms production. Yet, new information presented in this chapter indicates that together they account for a large share of military small arms production—60 to 80 per cent. These are the weapons most often used in armed conflict: military rifles, assault rifles, and carbines. The chapter estimates that anywhere from 530,000 to 580,000 of these weapons are produced annually, either under licence or as unlicensed copies. These findings are consistent with earlier estimates of annual military small arms production (Small Arms Survey, 2002, p. 13; 2006, pp. 7–35).

With the exception of MANPADS, the know-how required to manufacture small arms and light weapons is no longer concentrated in a handful of technology *owners,* but is instead distributed over a large number of technology *acquirers*. While most manufacturing technology is transferred under licence, unlicensed production represents roughly one-quarter of all known cases of technology transfer.

The licensed production of small arms and light weapons offers many benefits to licensors and licensees, but it also poses certain risks, including proliferation risks that are of concern to the international community as a whole. Manufacturing technology can be diverted to irresponsible end users, and weapons produced under licence may end up being misused.

The chapter presents examples of best practice, especially at the national level, designed to strengthen control over the initial transfer of manufacturing technology, as well as the subsequent sale of weapons produced under licence. While any strategy designed to curb global small arms proliferation needs to address the issue of licensed production, only exceptionally do regional and international instruments explicitly regulate this activity.

The chapter outlines a range of options for the regulation of licensed production at the company, national, and multilateral levels. It also emphasizes that the measures that are most effective in curbing weapons proliferation are those that directly target diversion and strengthen control over the initial transfer of manufacturing technology. Initiatives designed to strengthen the enforcement of intellectual property rights, though potentially beneficial to the . technology owner, have only a limited impact on proliferation.

Existing instruments for the control of MANPADS offer a useful model for more concerted efforts to grapple with the problem of licensed production. New and existing measures must also be effectively applied and enforced, especially at the national level, where the main power of regulation resides.

The risks of licensed production are becoming clearer, yet international efforts to address these lag behind. Best practice has yet to proliferate. ■

LIST OF ABBREVIATIONS

ATGW	anti-tank guided weapon	OSCE	Organization for Security and Co-operation in Europe
EU	European Union		
IMI	Israel Military Industries Ltd.	SEDENA	Secretaría de la Defensa Nacionál (Secretariat of National Defence)
IP	intellectual property		
MANPADS	man-portable air defence system(s)	USD	United States dollar
NATO	North Atlantic Treaty Organisation	USSR	Union of Soviet Socialist Republics (Soviet Union)
NORINCO	China North Industries Corporation		

ENDNOTES

1   There is no clear distinction between rifles and assault rifles. All assault rifles have the capacity of fully automatic fire, but so do some rifles. In general, assault rifles tend to be shorter, lighter, and fire smaller ammunition, and are therefore more portable.

2   This chapter focuses on military weapons only, for a number of reasons. These are the weapons of 'main concern' for modern armed conflict, as reflected in the report of the UN Panel of Governmental Experts on Small Arms. Paragraph 24 of the report reads: 'The small arms and light weapons which are of main concern for the purpose of the present report are those which are manufactured to military specifications for use as lethal instruments of war'; while paragraph 27 holds that they 'are also of particular advantage for irregular warfare or terrorist and criminal action' (UN, 1997). While non-military weapons such as sporting and hunting rifles are also produced under licence, they do not pose the same proliferation dangers as do military arms. Handguns are a major problem, in particular because they are used in civilian violence worldwide, but the unavailability of production data makes their general inclusion in this study realistically impossible, and only those specifically manufactured for military use are included. Furthermore, this focus on military weapons allows comparison with the findings of the *Small Arms Survey 2006* on production for armed forces (Small Arms Survey, 2006, pp. 7–35).

3   Brazil, France, Greece, Iran, Malaysia, Mexico, Myanmar, Norway, Pakistan, the Philippines, Portugal, Saudi Arabia, Sweden, Thailand, Turkey.

4   If not stated otherwise, this section is based on Gimelli Sulashvili (2006).

5   In most cases, the status of production is known so that the catch-all category of 'licensing situation unclear' is not very frequent (only 19 per cent of all cases).

6   A detailed list of all 212 cases referred to in this table is available in Annexe 1 on the Small Arms Survey Web site: <http://www.smallarmssurvey.org/files/sas/publications/yearb2007.html>

7   On p. 1 of the sections entitled 'Small Arms Ammunition (Europe)', 'Small Arms Ammunition (International)', and 'Small Arms Ammunition (United States)'.

8   There is, however, one case where the licensing situation is unclear (Pakistan's production of a Swedish model).

9   Only in a few cases, such as Libya, did the licensee have to pay for the licence.

10 Warsaw Pact allies were allowed, however, to transfer the licensed weapons among one other in the framework of intra-pact industrial cooperation.

11 Azerbaijan, China, the Czech Republic, Finland, Georgia, Hungary, Poland, Romania, Slovenia, Turkey, and the Ukraine, while the Eurasian patent is valid in Belarus, the Russian Federation, and Tajikistan.

12 Interview with a spokesperson of Heckler & Koch, Oberndorf, Germany, January 2007.

13 Its rivals in the deal were FN Herstal (Belgium), Giat Industries (France), IMI (Israel), Chartered Industries (Singapore), and Colt (United States).

14 See, for example, Canada (2006) and United Kingdom (2006).

15 Pursuant to its basic principles on sustainability and citizenship, the company pledges to act in accordance with the law of the countries in which it conducts business and to help protect human rights. Moreover, the company points out that it is subject to Swedish law and administrative procedures (Saab Bofors Dynamics, 2006).

16 Countries with NATO equivalent status are Australia, Japan, New Zealand, and Switzerland.

17 Notwithstanding the lack of explicit reference to licensed production or production facilities, the term 'military equipment' can be interpreted as encompassing technology and know-how, as practice in the United Kingdom demonstrates (BASIC, International Alert, and Saferworld, 2002, p. 9).

18 Ten thousand small arms produced by Fabricaciones Militares under licence from the Belgian company FN Herstal, and ten million rounds of ammunition (Vranckx, 2005, p. 14).

19 Projections for the up-coming Kalashnikov production range from 250,000 to 500,000 units over the ten years covered by the production licence. Venezuela's forces amount to approximately 500,000 members (127,000 full-time army personnel, 172,000 part-time army personnel, 38,000 National Guard paramilitary personnel, and reservists). Under the cautious assumption that the production facilities would run at full capacity, and adding the 100,000 rifles that will be directly imported from the Russian Federation, not a lot of surplus weapons would remain for export (Baranauskas, 2006a).

20 '[O]ther military equipment related to war weapons' can be a 'plant or documentation for the manufacture of war weapons' (Germany, 2000, sec. III, para. 5).

21 EU (1998); Wassenaar Arrangement (2003); APEC (2003); OSCE (2004).

BIBLIOGRAPHY

Abel, Pete. 2000. 'Manufacturing Trends: Globalizing the Source.' In Lora Lumpe, ed. *Running Guns: The Global Black Market in Small Arms*. London: Zed Books, pp. 81–104.

Adeyemi, Seygun. 2004. 'Chinese Set to Run Nigerian Defence Group.' *Jane's Defence Weekly*. 29 September.

Anders, Holger. 2005. *Export of Production Equipment for Ammunition: Practices in Germany, France and Belgium*. Note d'analyse. Brussels: Groupe de recherche et d'information sur la paix et la sécurité. 26 May. <http://www.grip-publications.eu/bdg/g4577.html>

—— and Reinhilde Weidacher. 2006. 'The Production of Ammunition for Small Arms and Light Weapons.' In Stéphanie Pézard and Holger Anders, eds. *Targeting Ammunition*. Geneva: Small Arms Survey.

Anderson, Guy. 2006a. 'Russia Suffers from Failure to Patent Exported Military Equipment.' *Jane's Defence Industry*. 1 August.

——. 2006b. 'Russia Eyes Venezuela for Energy Investment.' *Jane's Defence Industry*. 1 September.

APEC (Asia–Pacific Economic Cooperation). 2003. *APEC Guidelines on Control and Security of Man-Portable Air Defense Systems (MANPADS)*.

Baranauskas, Tom. 2006a. 'Further Details Emerge on Venezuelan AK-103 Rifle Production Plans.' *Forecast International Government & Industry Group*. Newtown: Forecast International. 28 June.

——. 2006b. 'Venezuelan Arms Import Update.' *Forecast International*. Newtown: Forecast International. 19 July.

——. 2006c. 'Recent Developments in Venezuela Military Affairs.' *Forecast International Government & Industry Group*. Newtown: Forecast International. 31 July.

BASIC (British American Security Information Council), International Alert, and Saferworld. 2002. *Building Comprehensive Controls on Small Arms Manufacturing, Transfer and End-use*. London and Washington, DC: BASIC, International Alert, and Saferworld.

Bazargan, Darius. 2003. 'Balkan Gun Traffickers Target UK.' *BBC News*. 7 December.

BBC (British Broadcasting Corporation). 2006a. 'Russian Arms Maker Reports Estimate for Fake Kalashnikovs.' *BBC Monitoring Former Soviet Union*. 15 April.

——. 2006b. 'Venezuela May Build Kalashnikov Factory under Russian Licence.' *BBC Monitoring Former Soviet Union*. 10 June.

——. 2006c. 'Venezuela Could Sign Russian Rifle Plant Deal in July, Says Arms Firm Head.' *BBC Monitoring Latin America*. 21 June.

——. 2006d. 'UN Initiates Arms Trade Agreement.' *BBC News*. 27 October.

Brauer, Jurgen and J. Paul Dunne, eds. 2004. *Arms Trade and Economic Development, Theory, Policy, and Cases in Arms Trade Offsets*. London: Routledge.

Canada. 2006. *Corporate Social Responsibility*. <http://strategis.ic.gc.ca/epic/internet/incsr-rse.nsf/en/Home>

DAKS (Deutsches Aktionsnetz Kleinwaffen Stoppen). n.d. *Im Visier: Heckler & Koch*. Freiburg: RüstungsInformationsBüro, DAKS.

Delius, Ulrich. 2004a. *Der Tod aus Oberndorf*. Gesellschaft für bedrohte Völker. June. <http://www.gfbv.it/3dossier/africa/darfur-delius.html>

——. 2004b. *Völkermord mit deutschen Lizenzwaffen in Darfur?* Gesellschaft für bedrohte Völker. 28 September. <http://www.gfbv.de/inhaltsDok.php?id=460>

De Standaard (Groot Bijgaarden). 2002. 'Nigeria Manufactures War Guns Under License of Belgium's FN Herstal.' 29 March.

Dnevnik (Sofia). 2006. 'Russia Revives Dispute with Bulgarian Arms Makers over Production Licences.' 27 April.

Dreyfus, Pablo. 2006. *Mexico and the 'New' FX05 Xihuacóatl Assault Rifle: Saving Money and . . . Surplus*. Background paper. Geneva: Small Arms Survey. October.

Eastbusiness.org. 2006. 'Zastava Arms Sells Licence for Production of CZ99 and 357 Pistols.' 21 March.

EU (European Union). 1998. *European Union Code of Conduct on Arms Exports*. 8 June. Reproduced in UN document A/CONF.192/PC/3 of 13 March 2000. <http://www.smallarmssurvey.org/files/portal/issueareas/measures/Measur_pdf/r_%20measur_pdf/European%20Union/EUCodeof Conduct%20080698.pdf>

——. Commission of the European Communities. 2006. *Interpretative Communication on the Application of Article 296 of the Treaty in the Field of Defence Procurement*. COM(2006) 779 final. 7 December. <http://ec.europa.eu/internal_market/publicprocurement/dpp_en.htm>

Evening News (Edinburgh). 1999. 'Shot to Fame.' 18 June.

FAS (Federation of American Scientists). 2001. *Offsets: The Industrial, Employment and Security Costs of Arms Exports*. <http://fas.org/asmp/campaigns/offsets.html>

FN Herstal. 2005. '5.7 x 28 mm Ammunition, Part of an Agreement between FN Herstal and FIOCCHI.' <http://www.fnherstal.com/html/Index.htm>

Forecast International. 2005. *Ordnance & Munitions Forecast*. Newtown: Forecast International, Customer Service Department. October.

——. 2006. *Ordnance & Munitions Forecast*. Newtown: Forecast International, Customer Service Department. January.

Foss, Christoper F. and Ian Kemp. 2004. 'Anti-Armour Weapons—Making an Impact.' *Jane's Defence Weekly*. 9 June.

Gander, Terry J. 1997. 'Weapons and Equipment, Croatian Weapons Target the Small-arms Market.' *Jane's International Defence Review*. 1 June.

Germany. 2000. 'Political Principles for the Export of War Weapons and Other Military Equipment.' Decision of 19 January 2000. Reproduced in Germany, 2003, Annexe 1a.

——. 2003. *Report by the Government of the Federal Republic of Germany on Its Policy on Exports of Conventional Military Equipment in 2003 (2003 Military Equipment Export Report)*. Berlin: Federal Ministry of Economics and Technology. Official English translation from the German original. <http://www.smallarmssurvey.org/files/portal/issueareas/transfers/transfers_pdf/n_reports/ArmsExportsGermany2003e.pdf>

Gimelli Sulashvili, Barbara. 2006. *Small Arms and Light Weapons Licensed Production*. Background paper. Geneva: Small Arms Survey.

GlobalSecurity.org. 2005. *South African Defense Industry*. <http://www.globalsecurity.org/military/world/rsa/industry.htm>

Hagelin, Björn, Pieter D. Wezeman, and Siemon T. Wezeman. 1999. 'Register of the Transfers and Licensed Production of Major Conventional Weapons, 1998.' In Stockholm International Peace Research Institute. *SIPRI Yearbook 1999: Armaments, Disarmament and International Security*. Oxford: Oxford University Press, pp. 454–500.

Hughes, Robin. 2004. 'Iran Unveils Bullpup Assault Rifles.' *Jane's Defence Weekly*. 20 October.

Ing, David. 1998. 'Headlines, Germany Is Poised to Win Spanish Rifle Deal.' *Jane's Defence Weekly*. 22 July.

ITAR-TASS (Information Telegraph Agency of Russia). 1998. 'Russia Company Takes out Patent on Kalashnikov Gun.' 16 February.

Jane's Defence Weekly. 1995. 'Armed Forces Update. Turkey Close to 5.56 mm Choice.' 23 September.

——. 1999. 'Country Briefing—Saudi Arabia, on the Road to "Self-sufficiency".' 18 August.

——. 2000. 'In Brief—EADS Delivers 10,000th Stinger.' 18 October.

——. 2004. 'DAS 2004: AUG Rifle Assembly to Move East.' 21 April.

Jane's International Defence Review. 1997a. 'Weapons and Equipment, Brazil Exhibits Indigenous Developments.' 1 August.

——. 1997b. 'Quarterly Report, South Africa.' 1 September.

——. 2004. 'Hungary Moves to Adopt NATO Medium-calibre Munitions.' 1 March.

——. 2005. 'Belgian Defence Industry—FN Herstal: FN Herstal Plots Transatlantic Course.' 1 November.

Jones, Richard and Charles Cutshaw, eds. 2004. *Jane's Infantry Weapons 2004–2005*. Coulsdon: Jane's Information Group.

Karniol, Robert. 2002. 'Country Briefing: The Philippines—Battling the Home Front.' *Jane's Defence Weekly*. 6 November.

——. 2006a. 'Country Briefing: Vietnam—Off the Ground.' *Jane's Defence Weekly*. 4 January.

——. 2006b. 'Bangladesh and NORINCO Close to Rifle Production Agreement.' *Jane's Defence Weekly*. 1 March.

——. 2006c. 'Lieutenant General Moeen Ahmed—Bangladesh Chief of Army Staff.' *Jane's Defence Weekly*. 26 April.

Lockwood, David. 2005. 'Forecast International Report: Russia No Longer Controls RPG-7 Market.' *Forecast International/Ordnance & Munitions Forecast*. Newtown: Forecast International. 19 August.

——. 2006a. 'International Military Rifle Market Maintains Domestic Focus.' *Forecast International/Ordnance & Munitions Forecast*. Newtown: Forecast International. 1 January.

——. 2006b. 'Greece Selects Heckler & Koch G36.' *Forecast International/Ordnance & Munitions Forecast*. Newtown: Forecast International. 15 January.

——. 2006c. 'Russian 30 mm Automatic Grenade Launcher Production Thumping Along.' *Forecast International/Ordnance & Munitions Forecast*. Newtown: Forecast International. 19 June.

Lumpe, Lora. 1995. Testimony in front of the US Senate, Appropriations Committee, Subcommittee on Foreign Operations. *Federal Document Clearing House Congressional Testimony*. May 23.

Mahadzir, Dzirhan. 2006. 'Malaysia Seeks to Acquire Colt M4s.' *Jane's Defence Weekly*. 10 May.

McDermott, Jeremy. 2004a. 'Huge Expansion for Colombian Arms Industry.' *Jane's Defence Weekly*. 23 June.

——. 2004b. 'Colombia Struggles to Counter Arms Smuggling.' *Jane's Intelligence Review*. 1 December.

——. 2006. 'Country Briefing: Colombia—No End in Sight.' *Jane's Defence Weekly*. 26 July.

Moscow Times. 2002. 'Everybody's Favourite Gun Turns 55.' 21 November.

Nairn, Allan. 1986. 'South Africa's War Machine.' *Multinational Monitor*, Vol. 7, No. 7. 15 April.

Nassauer, Otfried and Christopher Steinmetz. 2005. *"Made in Germany" Inside: Komponenten—die vergessenen Rüstungsexporte*. Berlin: Oxfam (Germany) and Berliner Informationszentrum für Transatlantische Sicherheit. February.

New Straits Times (Kuala Lumpur). 2003. 'Enhancing Defence Capabilities.' 5 October.

Novichkov, Nikolai. 2004. 'Russia Resumes Military–Technical Co-production with Libya.' *Jane's Defence Weekly*. 27 October.

OSCE (Organization for Security and Co-operation in Europe). 2000. *OSCE Document on Small Arms and Light Weapons*. Forum for Security Co-operation. FSC.DOC/1/00 of 24 November.

——. 2004. *OSCE Principles for Export Controls of Man-Portable Air Defence Systems (MANPADS)*. Decision No. 3/04. FSC.DEC/3/04 of 26 May.

Petersburg Times, The. 1999. 'Russia's Defence Loses Big in Patent Sellouts.' 16 April.

Poth, Robert. 2001. *Was ich nicht weiss . . .* June. <http://rpoth.at/pastwork/kleinwaff_oest.shtml>

Pyadushkin, Maxim. 2006. *The Licensed Production of Soviet/Russian Small Arms and Light Weapons*. Background paper. Geneva: Small Arms Survey. October.

—— with Maria Haug and Anna Mateeva. 2003. *Beyond the Kalashnikov: Small Arms Production, Exports, and Stockpiles in the Russian Federation*. Occasional Paper No. 10. Geneva: Small Arms Survey.

RIA Novosti. 2006a. 'Russia Pushing Ban on Illegal Production of Kalashnikov Rifles.' 28 April.

——. 2006b. 'Rosoboronexport to Sue over Illegal Arms Production Abroad.' 27 June.

RosBusinessConsulting. 2004. 'Kalashnikov Automatic Rifles to be Produced in India.' *RosBusinessConsulting Database*. 15 October.

Saab Bofors Dynamics. 2006. *Sustainability*. <http://www.saabgroup.com/en/AboutSaab/saab_in_society/saab_in_society.htm>

Sariibrahimoglu, Lale. 1999. 'Briefing—Turkish Procurement, One Year On.' *Jane's Defence Weekly*. 22 September.

——. 2005. 'Turkey to License Produce M4 Rifles.' *Jane's Defence Weekly*. 26 October.

Schroeder, Matthew. 2004. *Small Arms, Terrorism, and the OAS Firearms Convention*. Occasional Paper No. 1. Washington, DC: Federation of American Scientists. March. <http://fas.org/asmp/library/OAS/FullReport.pdf>

Small Arms Survey. 2001. *Small Arms Survey 2001: Profiling the Problem*. Oxford: Oxford University Press.

——. 2002. *Small Arms Survey 2002: Counting the Human Cost*. Oxford: Oxford University Press.

——. 2004. *Small Arms Survey 2004: Rights at Risk*. Oxford: Oxford University Press.

——. 2005. *Small Arms Survey 2005: Weapons at War*. Oxford: Oxford University Press.

——. 2006. *Small Arms Survey 2006: Unfinished Business*. Oxford: Oxford University Press.

Tigner, Brooks. 2006a. 'EDA Strives to Rein in Offsets.' *DefenceNews.com*. 28 August.

——. 2006b. 'EU Girds to Enforce Competition Rules.' *DefenceNews.com*. 11 December.

——. 2007. 'EDA to Push for Borderless EU Defence Tech Base.' *Defence News.com*. 12 February.

Times of India. 2004. 'India Gets Nod to Make AK-47s.' 15 October.

UN (United Nations). 1997. *Report of the Panel of Governmental Experts on Small Arms*. A/52/298. New York: UN. 27 August.

UNGA (United Nations General Assembly). 2001. *United Nations Programme of Action to Prevent, Combat and Eradicate the Illicit Trade in Small Arms and Light Weapons in All Its Aspects*. July. Reproduced in UN document A/CONF.192/15.

——. 2006. '*Note verbale* dated 29 June 2006 from the Permanent Mission of the Russian Federation addressed to the Secretariat of the United Nations Conference to Review Progress made in the Implementation of the Programme of Action to Prevent, Combat and Eradicate the Illicit Trade in Small Arms and Light Weapons in All Its Aspects.' 29 June. Reproduced in UN document A/CONF.192/2006/RC/6. <http://www.un.org/events/smallarms2006/pdf/rc.6-e.pdf>

United Kingdom. 2006. *The UK Government Gateway to Corporate Social Responsibility*. <http://www.csr.gov.uk/>

United States. Department of State. 1997. *International Traffic in Arms Regulations*. <http://www.fas.org/spp/starwars/offdocs/itar/>

Vogel, Ben. 2006. 'Venezuela Signs Major Aircraft Contract with Russia.' *Jane's Defence Industry Review*. 1 September.

Vranckx, An. 2005. *European Arms Exports to Latin America: An Inventory*. Background report. International Peace Information Service. March.

Wassenaar Arrangement on Export Controls for Conventional Arms and Dual-Use Goods and Technologies. 2002. *Best Practice Guidelines for Exports of Small Arms and Light Weapons (SALW)*. 12 December. <http://www.wassenaar.org/docs/best_practice_salw.htm>

——. 2003. *Elements for Export Controls of Man-Portable Air Defence Systems (MANPADS)*. 12 December. <http://www.wassenaar.org/2003Plenary/MANPADS_2003.htm>

Willett, Susan and Ian Anthony. 2001. *Countertrade and Offsets Policies and Practices in the Arms Trade*. Copenhagen Peace Research Institute. <http://www.ciaonet.org/wps/wis01/>

WIPO (World Intellectual Property Organization). 2003. 'IP Licensing: Reaping the Benefits.' *WIPO Magazine*. May–June.

——. 2006. 'Overview of Contractual Agreements for the Transfer of Technology.'
    <http://www.wipo.int/sme/en/documents/pdf/technology_transfer.pdf>

WTO (World Trade Organization). 1994. General Agreement on Tariffs and Trade. Annexe 4b, 'Agreement on Government Procurement'.
    <http://www.wto.org/english/docs_e/legal_e/gpr-94_e.pdf>

ACKNOWLEDGEMENTS

Principal author

Barbara Gimelli Sulashvili

Contributors

Maxim Pyadushkin, Pablo Dreyfus, and William Thayer

Confiscated guns are hoisted by a magnet into a smelting pot, where they will be destroyed. Montevideo, Uruguay, August 2006. © Andres Stapff/Reuters

Completing the Count
CIVILIAN FIREARMS

2

INTRODUCTION

Separated by geography, culture, religion, education, and wealth, the people of Ireland and Yemen could hardly be more different. Superficially, their small arms problems are equally dissimilar: Ireland has a moderate level of civilian gun ownership and little gun violence; Yemen is one of the most heavily armed and most violent societies on earth.

But observers in both countries describe their national small arms problems in remarkably similar language. Two dramatically different societies are united by a common sense that the proliferation of firearms is a basic challenge to social cohesion and future prosperity. Both are affected by swift changes in domestic gun violence patterns and global small arms proliferation. Increasingly, authorities in both countries are turning to similar solutions: trying to restrain possession, encouraging citizens to get rid of their guns, and attempting to restore the ability of national institutions to reduce violence (see Boxes 2.2 and 2.3).

Compared to small arms proliferation elsewhere, Ireland's problems might seem quaint and Yemen's extreme, but they are united by the *universal challenge* posed by small arms to society. Like people in many other places, the Irish and Yemenis feel compelled to reconsider popular assumptions and official policies in order to catch up with social forces otherwise beyond their control. And like many other states, these countries are grappling with trends that are felt more than understood.

The relationship between society and small arms is changing the world over. Small arms are proliferating virtually everywhere. And it is civilian ownership, the focus of this chapter, that appears to be changing most rapidly. Among the major findings of this chapter are the following:

- Civilians own approximately 650 million firearms worldwide, roughly 75 per cent of the known total. Civilians in the United States own some 270 million of these.
- There are at least 875 million combined civilian, law enforcement, and military firearms in the world today.
- This is equal to roughly one gun for every seven people worldwide (without the United States, the figure drops to about one gun for every ten people).
- These figures do not include older, pre-automatic small arms still maintained by armed forces or craft-produced civilian guns.
- Nearly 79 million civilian firearms are known to be registered with authorities, roughly 9 per cent of the suspected civilian total.
- The rising availability of handguns has transformed urban weapons ownership, while semi- or fully automatic rifles have transformed possession in urban and rural settings.
- Organized destruction projects have eliminated at least 8.5 million small arms since 1991, three-quarters of which came from armed services. An unknown number are also lost through accidental wastage.

As the first detailed global assessment, this chapter offers the most complete outline so far of the global distribution of factory-made civilian firearms. Rather than a definitive statement, though, it should be regarded as part of a process of continuous investigation. The total of 650 million civilian firearms and 875 million in total is a significant increase over previous Small Arms Survey estimates. This does not represent a real increase in the number of firearms, rather it results from better global reporting, additional research and more effective research methods. More focused research is absolutely essential in order to transform the relatively crude map of global firearms into a more textured portrait. And research has only begun to explore relationships between weapons holdings and their destructive effects.

The analysis presented here relies mostly on *static* data, creating only a snapshot of the global firearms balance in the year 2006. There are not yet enough *dynamic,* time-series reports to permit a reliable sense of how civilian holdings are developing in most countries. The general global impression, though, leaves no doubt that civilians are continually acquiring more-powerful guns. There is a connection between per capita wealth and gun ownership, which is strong enough to suggest that so long as gun ownership laws are not changed, greater national wealth leads to greater gun ownership.

Recent improvements in reporting and research allow for more accurate gun ownership estimates.

The connection between gun availability and violence is one of the most controversial topics of gun policy debate. It is widely accepted that '"[g]un cultures" do not automatically translate into armed conflict' (Schwandner-Sievers, 2005, p. 206). Many of the examples explored in this chapter illustrate a strong connection between ownership levels and depravity. Others show that weapons proliferation does not always lead to social chaos. However, this chapter does not try to resolve debates over the connection between guns and violence. It is intended, rather, to facilitate investigation of broader enigmas: the forces that determine when small arms proliferation has a marginal effect and when it causes catastrophe.

By clarifying the global geography of small arms, the chapter helps to show where problems and solutions can be found. It adds support to the belief that in this field, as in others, the state is often not the dominant actor (Castles, 2007; Florini, 2000). In most of the world, the state is not the primary holder of guns; civilians are. Furthermore, state-owned weapons are often not the most likely to be used. Although the issue of the relative dangers of civilian and military small arms still requires systematic investigation, civilian-owned weapons appear to be increasingly prominent in global small arms phenomena. Regions with the highest rates of firearm killings, such as Brazil, Colombia, Darfur, Gaza, and Iraq, are also the centre of debates over who controls the most deadly weapons.

To be sure, state-controlled arsenals are more coherent than civilian holdings. Only military and some law enforcement small arms tend to be stockpiled and inventoried. As a result, state arsenals are much more amenable to policy. But the overwhelming quantitative dominance of civilian firearms makes state-owned arsenals less important. State-owned small arms tend to be more powerful, weapon for weapon, than civilian-owned firearms, but this too is changing. The data reported here points to the need for new ways of thinking about small arms pathologies, and the need for a paradigm that emphasizes the salience of society as much as, and possibly more than, the state.

A BRIEF HISTORY OF GUN NUMBERS

The emergence of small arms proliferation as a major international issue was accompanied by widespread frustration at ignorance over how many small arms existed and where they mattered most. Although it is usually clear enough where the worst damage is being done, a lack of understanding of the geography of small arms itself hindered policy-making and action. All too often, priorities have responded to crises and opportunities, without the strategic dimension that only broader insights permit.

Unable to pinpoint where the weapons are most common and where they are most dangerous, activists and policy-makers have been handicapped in their efforts to formulate priorities and articulate concrete agendas. The lack of hard data is the result of many forces. Sometimes it comes from weak official oversight; at other times from deliberate state secrecy, or ideological or political opposition to transparency (Small Arms Survey, 2004, p. 51; Tiahrt, 2004).

In the early days of international small arms research, scholars relied on indirect techniques to approximate the scale of global firearm numbers: for example, using firearm suicides as a proxy to assess civilian holdings is fairly effective for Western societies (Killias, 1993; Killias, Kesteren, and Rindlisbacher, 2001). The first efforts to articulate estimates for global firearm totals used nothing more than a sense of feel. Jasjit Singh and Owen Greene proposed separately in 1995 that there were roughly 500 million firearms of all sorts in the world (Singh, 1995, p. ix).[1] In 2001 small arms specialist Gregory Fetter maintained that the total was closer to 594 million, although his method of arriving at that figure does not appear to have been more sophisticated (Fetter, 2001). Such figures remain in widespread use, which explains how a recent US government report could conclude that

> estimates indicate that the overall number of small arms and light weapons in circulation globally range from 100 to 500 million and up. Efforts to obtain precise data on totals regarding these weapons and their sources, whether legal or illegal, is generally guesswork (Grimmit, 2006, p. 3).

In reality, research has gone far beyond such early approximations. The Small Arms Survey has consistently striven to elevate global estimation, initially through building-block methods. Relying on techniques designed to ensure reproducible results, this approach benefitted from the rapid growth of the field in the period just before and after the 2001 UN Conference on the Illicit Trade in Small Arms and Light Weapons in All Its Aspects. Through incremental accumulation of national reports and country research, a continuously more detailed picture of the global distribution of firearms began to emerge. This led to the conclusion in 2002 that there were more than 639 million firearms whose existence could be documented with sufficient certainty (Small Arms Survey, 2002, ch. 2). These findings were exclusively for firearms. The total number of other types of small arms and light weapons, especially, remains more elusive, with the partial exception of man-portable air defence missile systems (Bevan, 2004).

The subsequent five years have permitted the accumulation of evidence and the development of more sophisticated analytical techniques, creating a rich basis for extrapolation. Although these methods rely on estimation methods, their confidence levels have improved dramatically over the years. The 2006 edition of the *Small Arms Survey* concluded that there were 'at least 26.3 million law enforcement weapons' in the world and 'approximately 200 million modern, official military firearms worldwide' (Small Arms Survey, 2006, p. 37). The current edition establishes that, in addition to these weapons, civilians privately have approximately 650 million firearms, for a combined total of roughly 875 million firearms of all types worldwide.

There are at least 875 million civilian, law enforcement, and military firearms in the world.

NO NEUTRAL NUMBERS

Animated debates over data such as conflict fatalities leave no doubt that statistics have profound implications for policy-making and action (Burnham et al., 2006). Estimates of the *absolute size* of small arms holdings play a major role in focusing international attention on small arms issues. Cumulative data on small arms holdings is also an essential scientific tool and provides the basis for more conclusive insights into the role of small arms in human affairs. The *relative scale* of holdings in different countries and among different categories of actors—law enforcement, military, civilians, non-state groups—shapes priorities for specific action.

Perceptions of the scale of small arms proliferation colour all aspects of the issue. The 2001 *UN Programme of Action*, for example, stressed the illicit trade in small arms, suspected as the most serious aspect of small arms proliferation (Laurance and Stohl, 2002). The belief that the small arms of non-state actors are especially dangerous for regional stability justifies investments in the disarmament, demobilization, and reintegration of former combatants. Weapons destruction and stockpile security improvement emphasize military stockpiles, in the belief that these are an especially important target for efforts to control illegal trade. Destroying surplus military weapons today, in other words, reduces the risk that the same weapons will be used by terrorists, insurgents, or criminals tomorrow. Military stockpiles are also more amenable to destruction than civilian holdings, which usually are not so conveniently concentrated.

Only in recent years, however, has evidence accumulated to show that, almost everywhere, civilian holdings are significantly larger than law enforcement or military stockpiles (see Table 2.1). The cumulative data shows that most of the world's firearms are owned by civilians—roughly 75 per cent of the known total—greatly outnumbering the other two categories. As experts became aware that civilian-owned firearms play a major role in the illicit trade and regional violence, previously overlooked civilian holdings began to attract greater political attention. The *relative size* of civilian weapons holdings, the major theme of this chapter, is important for informing initiatives—national, regional, and international—to address firearm-related violence.

Growing awareness of the relative dominance of civilian guns has led some to call for civilian access to be better reflected in multilateral small arms policy-making (Cukier and Sidel, 2005; Karp, 2006a). A prominent report acknowledges that the *UN Programme of Action*, with its focus on illegal transfers and state-owned weapons, has been 'a useful guide for action' (CHD, 2005, p. 9), but also a barrier to dealing with some of the most serious problems. Instead of focusing exclusively on illegal transfers and official inventories, 'efforts to control guns and ammunition must address the fact that the bulk of the world's small arms arsenal are in the hands of civilians, and that civilian misuse is a primary source of firearm-related death and insecurity' (CHD, 2005, p. 9).

While basic data quality is improving considerably, none of our basic categories is comprehensive. Numerous small arms belong to unidentified *law enforcement* agencies, such as fish and wildlife pro-

A police officer carries guns seized from a house in Dartford, UK, in September 2006. The raid targeted the supply of US guns to London criminals. © Akira Suemori/AP Photo

Box 2.1 The attrition enigma

One of the great mysteries of weapons totals is the rate of attrition, whether through intentional destruction or accidental loss. Weapons are durable goods and can remain in useable condition for centuries with minimal care. Weapons also often have considerable market value and are therefore unlikely to be destroyed or abused frivolously. But like any human creation, firearms are subject to the principle of entropy, which ensures that all matter deteriorates over time. How long does it take for a typical gun to disappear? This is a vital question for any attempt to ascertain total firearm numbers, but one that cannot be resolved today.

A prominent example of this problem is the tens of millions of military bolt-action rifles and revolvers manufactured in the first half of the 20th century. Although largely replaced in military service by automatic rifles and semi-automatic pistols, vintage weapons are commonly seen in service in Africa, Asia, and Latin America. How many of these have been destroyed? And what is the overall rate of attrition among the approximately 875 million firearms believed to exist worldwide? At this point, we can only speculate.

The actual rate of loss from wastage and misuse can only be guessed. An attrition rate of one per cent (which assumes that typical weapons last 100 years) would result in the elimination of roughly eight million guns per year, independently of destruction programmes like those discussed above. This can be compared to the estimated seven million new weapons manufactured each year. If true, this difference would suggest that total global firearm numbers are declining. Yet, the overall attrition rate could be lower. Resolution of the *attrition enigma* requires further research.

tection agencies, prison authorities, and domestic security agencies. Of greater statistical importance are older, *pre-automatic military firearms* (mostly revolvers and bolt-action rifles), the generation of equipment acquired by the world's armed forces in the first half of the 20th century. Although they retain only limited military importance, they remain popular with civilian buyers. They probably number in the tens of millions, perhaps over a hundred million. *Civilian ownership* in much of the world is heavily influenced by local craft production. Although these typically crude firearms might look unimpressive, tens of millions exist, causing considerable destruction in much of the world. These three groups are seldom included in the statistics developed here.

The number of uncounted firearms is offset to some extent by the destruction of small arms from state-owned stockpiles and civilian holdings. There are currently no formulas for estimating such losses. Some, but not all, formal destruction programmes are publicized, as discussed below. Even less is known about the rate of routine attrition. Most firearms are designed to endure harsh treatment, and can remain serviceable for centuries. Even the definition of wastage is problematic, since firearms in bad condition can often be repaired. But an unknown number become permanently unusable through bad storage or are irreparably broken. Currently, the effect on global holdings can only be guessed (see Box 2.1).

Table 2.1 The division of global firearms (millions)

Category	Low total	Average	High total	Proportion
Law enforcement	26	26	26	2.5–3.5%
Military	150	200	250	20–25%
Civilian	570	650	730	73–77%
Global total	**745**	**875**	**1,000**	

Notes:

Law enforcement totals cover only known law enforcement agencies (see Small Arms Survey, 2006, ch. 2). Military totals do not include older, non-automatic weapons. Civilian totals do not include craft production. Global totals do not equal the totals of the three categories, due to rounding. Percentages do not equal 100, due to rounding.

Sources: Annexe 3; Small Arms Survey (2006, pp. 37, 56)

Box 2.2 Ireland: isolated no longer

Long an active participant in international small arms diplomacy, the Republic of Ireland used to act more out of a sense of international responsibility than domestic need (Ireland, 2005). Insulated by geography and culture, gun problems were assumed to be something that happened elsewhere. This sense is changing rapidly. By international standards, Ireland still has relatively little gun crime, but the country is acutely aware that old assumptions no longer hold true. No country, it seems, is isolated from global trends.

Previously, Irish small arms problems were associated exclusively with terrorism in Northern Ireland. This declined sharply following the Downing Street Declaration of 1993. With most Irish Republican Army (IRA) weapons reportedly 'decommissioned' under the terms of the April 1998 Belfast Agreement, the underlying small arms problem seemed to be resolved. In September 2005 the Independent International Commission on Decommissioning reported that 'the IRA has met its commitment to put all its arms beyond use in a manner called for by the legislation' (IICD, 2005, p. 2; see also BBC, 2005). Although scepticism about IRA decommissioning remains, an era of violence seems to be at an end.

Instead of Northern Ireland, now it is the Republic of Ireland that is feeling the effects of criminal gun violence. Historically, its gun laws were restrictive. Handguns were banned in the early 1970s. The Firearms and Wildlife Act of 1976 banned high-calibre rifles and repeating shotguns (Cusack, 1996). Despite these measures, in the early 2000s the Irish police (the Garda Síochána) were reporting steep increases in gun crime. Absolute numbers were low by international standards—from 450 firearm offences in 2001, increasing to 600 in 2002—but the change was a shock (Breslin, 2004). By 2006 the press were describing the phenomenon as an 'epidemic' of gun crime (*Emigrant Online,* 2006). Officials began to speak of an emerging 'gun culture' (Connolly, 2006).

The problem, as described by Justice Minister Michael McDowell, is

Drug dealing is dealing in death, firearms possession is dealing in death. And they are to be regarded in my view both by An Garda Síochána, by the legislature, by Government and by the judiciary as people who are potential or actual murderers. They are in the business of homicide, be it delayed or threatened or actual. They must be dealt with as that, they must be dealt with by the same severity and the same degree of energy as the paramilitaries were in the past (UTV, 2006).

Despite restrictions, Ireland is not unarmed: shotguns are relatively common. Garda spokespersons said that their 2006 amnesty was based on the assumption that the rate of public gun ownership in Ireland is roughly the same as in Britain (Connolly, 2006), but the number of licences suggests that legal ownership is considerably higher. In England and Wales there are 1.5 million licences for individual gun owners, one for every 28 residents (Ellis and Coleman, 2006). It has been reported that Ireland issued 209,000 firearm licences in 2004, one for every 19 residents (O'Keeffe and Hogan, 2004). Unregistered weapons are estimated to number at least 150,000, and this figure could be considerably higher, for a total of at least 360,000 firearms in civilian control.

Garda spokespersons maintain that the organization's most serious concern is not traditional shotgun ownership, but an invasion of handguns and automatics smuggled in from Europe. Of greatest concern are some 5,000 firearms in the hands of criminal gangs (McDonald, 2006). Many are semi-automatic pistols and sub-machine guns, previously unknown in public hands (Clonan, 2005). They have fueled unprecedented, murderous rivalries among drug gangs. Small arms proliferation appears to be an unexpected consequence of integration into a border-free Europe, leaving national leaders and law enforcement officials struggling to cope (Mulqueen, 2007).

The official reaction has been threefold: a police crackdown on smuggling, an amnesty for illegal firearms, and expansion and possible rearming of police. Under Operation Anvil, about 800 illegal firearms are seized annually and illegal firearm possession and misuse are kept down, with 715 seizures in 2005 (Garda Síochána, 2006, pp. 23, 80; Lally, 2006). An amnesty in 2006 was expected to net 3,000 guns, projected from the number received by English and Welsh police in a similar amnesty (Connolly, 2006). Instead, only 562 were received (McDonald, 2006). Finally, the Garda are increasing the number of officers and weighing demands that more be armed: currently 3,000 out of 12,265 officers are qualified to carry guns (Garda Síochána, 2006, p. 4; *Sunday Business Post,* 2006).

These steps will help Ireland deal with rising gun crime, but they have been tried elsewhere and found wanting. It is hard to avoid the conclusion that Ireland is becoming more like the rest of the world in terms of firearm-related problems.

Box 2.3 Yemen: deadly and elusive

Concerned that firearms undermine stability and discourage investment, the Government of Yemen has tried to reduce their visibility in the country, discouraging the carrying of firearms in public and restricting markets (Allen, 2000). There is no evidence that official efforts have significantly affected the country's exceptional gun culture. One result is chronic violence. For the first six months of 2005, official statistics report 614 homicides—80 per cent of which involved guns (Al-Qadhi, 2005b). These do not include most incidents of ethnic and tribal violence—rarely reported to official authorities—thought to kill another 2,000 annually (Brandon, 2006; IRIN 2006a; 2006b). UN studies also conclude that Yemen has become a major exporter of weapons and ammunition to conflicts in the region (UNSC, 2006, pp. 27–29).

Assertions that its 20–25 million people have 50, 60, or even 80 million guns are very popular in Yemen, where they have become a nationalist trope (see Table 2.2). Such figures are impossible to accept literally. For a start, most of the country's

guns appear to be AK-47 versions, of which no more than about 100 million are believed to exist worldwide (Karp, 2006b, p. 54). Rather, the meaning of these exaggerated figures is metaphorical.

Much lower figures come from more systematic estimates. An influential study, based on field research and analysis, concludes that Yemen has 6–9 million guns (Miller, 2003, p. 169). Another approach focuses on ownership among typical Yemeni adult men, who are believed to own 3–4 firearms each. This view is reaffirmed by Eiz Eddin al Asbahi, director of the Human Rights Information and Training Centre, a leading Yemeni gun control NGO (Madayash, 2007). Estimates of the size of the Yemeni population vary from the official figure of 19.7 in 2005 to demographic estimates of 24.5 million in 2006 (IRIN, 2005; CIA, 2006). With about half Yemen's people still children (WRI, 2007), adult men constitute roughly one-quarter of the population, or 5–6 million people. A similar conclusion comes from a survey of 2,083 respondents by Abdul Salam al Hakimi, showing that 60 per cent of all adults (both men and women) have a gun (Madayash, 2007). Asbahi's and Hakimi's perspectives support estimates of at least 17 million civilian firearms.

The Small Arms Survey concludes that Yemenis own between 6 million and 17 million firearms, averaged to an estimated total of 11 million civilian firearms for the country.

Yemenis demonstrate in September 2005 to demand the adoption of a proposed gun ban that was submitted to parliament more than a decade earlier.
© Khaled Fazaa/AFP/Getty Images

Table 2.2 Published estimates of Yemeni civilian firearm ownership (millions)

Estimate	Origin	Sources
6-9	Interviews and analysis	Miller (2003, p. 169)
9	'Estimates'	Arab News (2005)
9	Eiz Eddin al Asbahi	Madayash (2007)
17	'Unofficial estimates'	Al-Qadhi (2005b)
17	'NGO estimate'	Al-Qadhi (2005a)
17	'Unofficial estimates'	IRIN (2005; 2006b)
50-60	Former Interior Minister Yahia al-Mutawaki	Al-Qadhi (2005a)
60	N/A	Brandon (2006)
60	'Interior Ministry'	Yemen Observer (2005)
60	'Estimated'	Allen (2000)
60-80	'Government officials'	Willems (2004)
12	Estimate	Krott (2007, pp. 31-32)

INVISIBLE GIANT: THE WELL-ARMED CIVILIAN

If evenly distributed, there would be at least one civilian firearm for every nine people worldwide; one for every seven people when military and law enforcement weapons are included. But distribution is far from even. Gun ownership is highly concentrated among the largest and wealthiest societies. The ten largest gun-owning societies have roughly 380–480 million civilian firearms, 60–75 per cent of the global total (see Table 2.3). This is partially because the biggest gun-owning societies also tend to be the most populous, but this figure is also genuinely disproportionate, because such societies contain only about half the world's people. The same figure shows that the disproportion is even clearer when considering the top 30 gun-owning societies, which have about 450–590 million civilian firearms, or 70–90 per cent of the global total.

With less than 5 per cent of the world's population, the United States is home to roughly 35–50 per cent of the world's civilian-owned guns, heavily skewing the global geography of firearms and any relative comparison (see Table 2.3). Of some eight million new firearms manufactured annually around the world, roughly 4.5 million are bought by the people of the United States (US ATF, 2000, p. 1). With this sustained and unsurpassed level of routine gun-buying, American civilians will become even more dominant in global gun ownership. Therefore, any discussion of civilian gun ownership must devote disproportionate attention to the United States, if only because of the scale of its gun culture.

Exceptional civilian gun habits in the United States distort impressions of global trends. Without the US share, the global civilian total falls from 570–730 million to roughly 320–440 million civilian firearms, and instead of outnumbering military firearms by three or five to one, civilian weapons would outnumber their military counterparts by two

Table 2.3 **The 30 largest civilian firearm holdings (in descending order)**

Country	Averaged total firearms	Low total estimate	High total estimate	Population	Low est. firearms per 100 people	High est. firearms per 100 people
1. United States	270,000,000	250,000,000	290,000,000	300,000,000	83.0	97.0
2. India	46,000,000	32,000,000	60,000,000	1,064,000,000	3.0	5.6
3. China	40,000,000	30,000,000	50,000,000	1,288,400,000	2.3	3.9
4. Germany	25,000,000	20,000,000	30,000,000	82,551,000	24.0	36.0
5. France	19,000,000	18,000,000	20,000,000	59,725,000	30.0	34.0
6. Pakistan	18,000,000	18,000,000	18,000,000	148,400,000	12.0	12.0
7. Mexico	15,500,000	15,500,000	15,500,000	102,291,000	15.0	15.0
8. Brazil	15,300,000	15,300,000	15,300,000	174,471,000	8.8	8.8
9. Russian Federation	12,750,000	6,500,000	19,000,000	143,425,000	5.0	13.0
10. Yemen	11,500,000	6,000,000	17,000,000	19,000,000	32.0	90.0
11. Thailand	10,000,000	10,000,000	10,000,000	62,000,000	16.1	16.1
12. Canada	9,950,000	7,900,000	12,000,000	31,600,000	25.0	38.0
13. Iraq	9,750,000	7,000,000	12,500,000	25,000,000	28.0	50.0
14. Turkey	9,000,000	7,000,000	11,000,000	71,000,000	10.0	16.0
15. Italy	7,000,000	4,000,000	10,000,000	57,646,000	6.9	17.3
16. Saudi Arabia	6,000,000	4,500,000	7,600,000	23,000,000	19.6	33.0
17. South Africa	5,950,000	4,200,000	7,700,000	45,300,000	9.3	17.0
18. Argentina	4,850,000	4,100,000	5,600,000	38,377,000	10.7	14.6
19. Spain	4,500,000	4,500,000	4,500,000	41,101,000	11.0	11.0
20. Philippines	3,900,000	2,800,000	5,000,000	81,500,000	3.4	6.1
21. Iran	3,500,000	3,500,000	3,500,000	66,000,000	5.3	5.3
22. England and Wales	3,400,000	2,000,000	4,700,000	60,400,000	3.3	7.8
22. Switzerland	3,400,000	2,300,000	4,500,000	7,344,000	31.0	61.0
24. Ukraine	3,100,000	2,200,000	6,200,000	48,356,000	5.0	13.0
25. Colombia	3,100,000	2,300,000	3,900,000	42,954,279	5.4	9.1
26. Australia	3,050,000	2,900,000	3,200,000	19,900,000	15.0	16.0
27. Serbia	3,050,000	2,100,000	4,000,000	8,104,000	26.0	49.0
28. Finland	2,900,000	2,150,000	3,600,000	5,210,000	41.0	69.0
29. Sweden	2,800,000	2,100,000	3,600,000	8,956,000	23.0	40.0
30. Angola	2,800,000	1,500,000	4,000,000	13,500,000	11.0	30.0

Sources: See Annexe 4

Figure 2.1 **Total civilian firearms in 30 countries**

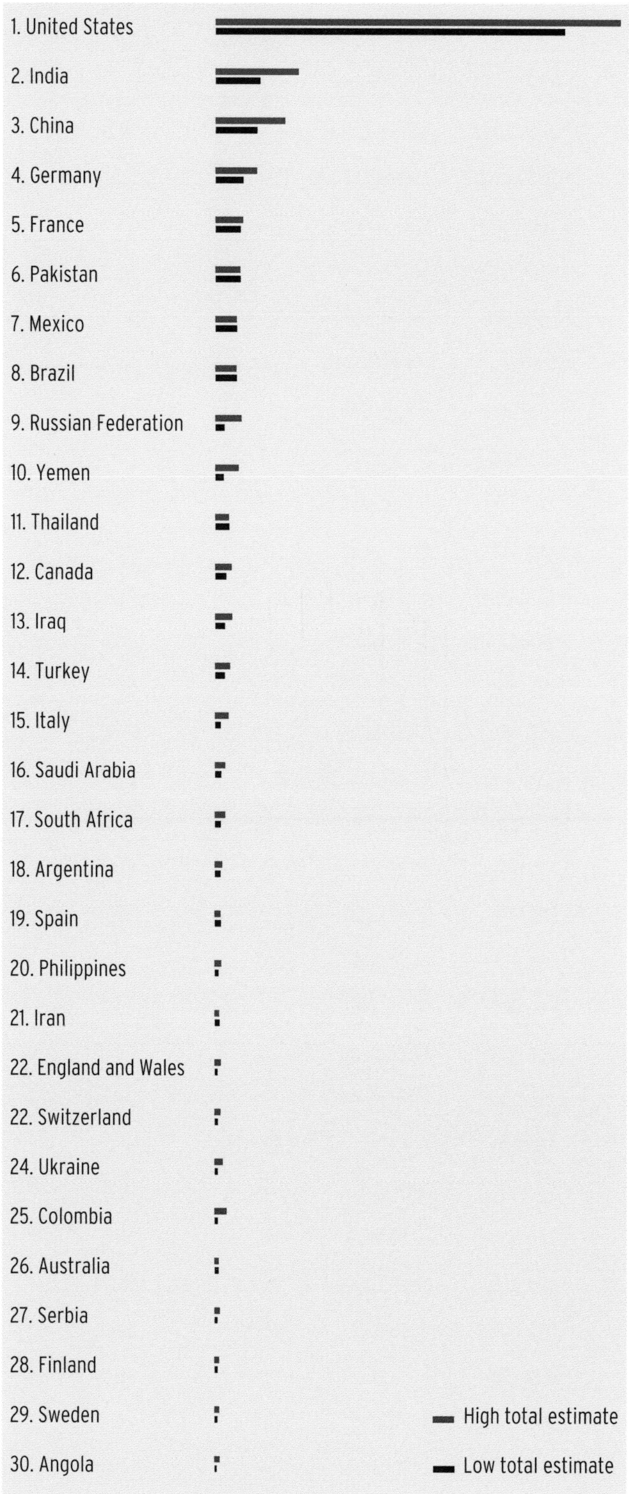

1. United States	
2. India	
3. China	
4. Germany	
5. France	
6. Pakistan	
7. Mexico	
8. Brazil	
9. Russian Federation	
10. Yemen	
11. Thailand	
12. Canada	
13. Iraq	
14. Turkey	
15. Italy	
16. Saudi Arabia	
17. South Africa	
18. Argentina	
19. Spain	
20. Philippines	
21. Iran	
22. England and Wales	
22. Switzerland	
24. Ukraine	
25. Colombia	
26. Australia	
27. Serbia	
28. Finland	
29. Sweden	■ High total estimate
30. Angola	■ Low total estimate

Source: Latest calculations as contained in Small Arms Survey 2007

or three to one. After the United States, a few disproportionately armed societies stand out. Only Switzerland and Yemen begin to approach American levels of gun ownership, and both of these cases are clouded by great doubt (see Boxes 2.3 and 2.5). Others also stand out, such as Germany, Finland, France, Iraq, and Serbia. But civilian ownership tends to be more even among other large gun-owning societies, where ownership rates of 5–15 per 100 residents are common.

Of course, these comparisons assume that the types of guns are equally powerful across national civilian holdings—a gross distortion. This chapter cannot elucidate the character of various civilian weapons, but only describes their relative scales. We can, however, identify certain trends. Prior to the 1960s, there was little difference in the destructive capabilities of civilian and military handguns and rifles. This changed when most military organizations switched to weapons capable of fully automatic operation, giving them much greater firepower. Many law enforcement agencies made a similar transition in the 1980s to semi-automatic pistols and smaller numbers of fully automatic weapons. The armed services and law enforcement agencies also have substantial quantities of specialized small arms and light weapons seldom seen in civilian hands in most countries, including grenades, grenade launchers, medium machine guns, and rocket launchers.

Other leading gun-owning societies tend either to be *large,* or *wealthy,* or have a recent history of intense *violent* conflict. Sheer national size accounts for the importance of societies such as China and India, where low levels of relative ownership nonetheless lead to large holdings in absolute terms (Table 2.3). The significance of wealth is revealed by the prominence of European countries, many of which have large civilian holdings, despite other factors militating against civilian gun acquisition. Countries such as Angola and Colombia, on the other hand, illustrate the way armed conflict permanently affects civilian gun possession.

WAYS OF KNOWING: REGISTERING, ESTIMATING, AND CORRELATIVE MODELLING

There is no single scientific technique that can ascertain the total number of firearms in civilian hands. Small Arms Survey country data has been assembled using numerous sources and methods, following an order of precedence (see Table 2.4). It relies when possible on official registration data, with independent estimates used to give greater comprehensiveness. The largest group of civilian weapons has been identified through such independent assessments alone, presented here as low to high estimates. When neither registration data nor independent assessments are available, estimates have been based on correlative statistical analysis by the Small Arms Survey, as described below. The latter includes a large group of countries—76 in all—but since most are small or poor, they have only 12–16 per cent of the civilian firearms identified. Greatest use is made, in other words, of the strongest data sources; less reliable methods are introduced progressively, when necessary, to ensure completeness.

NATIONAL REGISTRATION DATA: SOLID BUT PARTIAL

The most reliable data is official gun registration statistics, but they tell an incomplete story. The registration data made available to the Small Arms Survey establishes the existence of a total of 78 million firearms in civilian hands worldwide. Compared to the civilian firearms estimated using other techniques explained below, declared registration covers roughly 10–14 per cent of all civilian firearms believed to exist.

More registration data exists, but it has not been made available for research. Some countries have registration data, but do not make it available publicly. Others maintain registration records in ways that inhibit national accumu-

Table 2.4 **Sources of civilian firearm data (all firearms in millions)**				
Number of countries	**Registered firearms**	**Independent est. low**	**Independent est. high**	**Small Arms Survey est.**
52	74.3	106.9	188.7	0.0
25	3.7	0.0	0.0	8.9
25	0.0	301.4	377.8	0.0
76	0.0	0.0	0.0	76.4
178	**78.0**	**408.3**	**566.5**	**85.3**

Notes: Sources cover 178 countries with populations over 250,000. Complete country data appears in the annexes. Countries for which independent estimates only are given include Mozambique and Sudan, for which low-confidence registration data has been disregarded. The very low official registration figures of China and Tunisia have also been disregarded, and they have been treated as Small Arms Survey estimate countries. Their registration figures appear in Annexe 3.
Sources: Annexes 1, 2, and 3

lation. Germany illustrates this problem (see Box 2.4). In a few countries, such as China, Mozambique, Sudan, and Tunisia, registration laws are not consistently applied or are ignored. An egregious example is Sudan, where the Ministry of the Interior recently reported 6,724 registered firearms, out of some 2.2–3.6 million guns believed to be in civilian hands (Karp, 2006b).

The world's largest nation is affected by similar enigmas. China's firearms law of 1996 (China, 1996) forbids civilians to own guns unless specifically approved by law enforcement authorities. In practice, this has been interpreted to sharply limit ownership. According to a report from 2005, the country of 1.3 billion people had only 680,000 legally registered civilian firearms. But the same source noted that over five million military firearms were distributed to Chinese civilians in the 1950s and 1960s, and never recovered (*Courrier international,* 2005). Registration is not comprehensive anywhere, but China is typical of cases where relatively few of the guns in civilian hands are known to authorities. A completely different sense of scale comes from a series of police campaigns against illegal firearms since 1996. As of 2002, these campaigns reportedly seized 2.3 million guns (Small Arms Survey, 2005, p. 82). In 2005 total seizures were said to be five million guns (Hu, 2005). More recently, the chief Chinese public security official responsible for firearm issues maintained that 38 million firearms were seized by police in the period 1996–2006 (Xiao, 2006). While such figures test credulity, they convey a sense that civilian ownership in China is much more common than official registration data suggests.

Gun registration is a vital clue to the scale of civilian holdings.

A more typical example of the weaknesses of registration is Jordan, where some 126,000 firearms are registered, but at least 500,000 more are believed to be in civilian hands (Al-Fawz, 2002, p. 91). The situation is even more complicated in countries such as the Czech Republic, the Philippines, or South Africa, where registration is temporary. When owners fail to renew or surrender weapons as their registration expires, a growing pool of unregistered weapons emerges. Even in such cases, though, registration is a vital clue to the scale of civilian holdings. Some of the largest gun-owning societies—such as Iraq, the United States, and Yemen—simply do not have systematic registration.

Even where comprehensive registration is the long-standing law of the land, compliance is imperfect. One of the best-known examples is England and Wales (Scotland and Northern Ireland keep separate statistics). There were 1,742,300 legally registered firearms in England and Wales as of 31 March 2005 (Ellis and Coleman, 2006). The number of illegal, unregistered weapons there has been estimated by various observers at between 300,000 and 4,000,000 (Cramb, 2006; Goodchild and Lashmar, 2005). Some of these firearms were held back when comprehensive registration was introduced in the 1960s (Greenwood, 1972, pp. 17–38). Others have been smuggled into the country since then.

British uncertainty is exacerbated, though, by idiosyncrasies of categorization. Low estimates appear to refer only to guns in criminal hands. The high figures appear to include CO_2-powered air guns, starter pistols, and imitation guns, many of which can be converted to fire standard small arms ammunition. A recent study, sponsored by the British Home Office, described the country's illicit market cautiously. It noted that

[t]he market in illegal firearms appears fragmented with prices being sensitive to a number of variables, notably including the type, age and alleged provenance of any particular firearm. Supply is reinforced by a number of processes, including illegal importation, leakage from legitimate sources and the conversion of imitation firearms (Hales, Lewis, and Silverstone, 2006, p. 112).

Semi-automatic pistols and sub-machine guns also appear in the UK with increasing frequency (Hales, Lewis, and Silverstone, 2006, pp. 54–56, 111–12).

Box 2.4   Germany's very private arsenal

Germany illustrates typical problems of estimation. The country has a long history of civilian gun ownership, encouraged by militia-based armies in the 19th century, the side effects of two world wars, and interest in hunting and sport shooting. Although gun ownership is widespread, Germany has relatively little gun crime. Firearm murders amount to 150-300 annually and suicides total some 900 per year (Cukier and Sidel, 2005, p. 35). Gun ownership usually receives little attention, except in the wake of mass shootings. The most serious recent incident occurred in Erfurt in 2003. A similar, but much less deadly, incident occurred on 21 November 2006, when a high school student in Emsdetten, near Münster, shot and wounded five people before killing himself (Jüttner, 2006). Such incidents are instrumental in shaping German public attitudes toward gun ownership.

German gun laws are permissive. Current members of shooting and hunting clubs, the country's most visible, but a minority of all, owners number 1.6 million and 340,000, respectively (Graff, 2002). Sport shooters are allowed to own up to four handguns, three semi-automatic rifles or shotguns, and 'any reasonable number' of single-shot firearms. Hunters are limited to 'two handguns for final shots of wounded animals', but 'any reasonable number' of rifles and shotguns (IMC, 2006, p. 2). In practice, this allows the accumulation of large collections, illustrated in 2005 by the revelation of 120 unregistered firearms belonging to a collector in the Black Forest. He was prosecuted, but only for insecure storage (*Der Enztäler,* 2005, p. 6).

There are no reliable totals for German gun ownership. The country has no central registry. Records are maintained by the state (*Land*) or county (*Landkreis*). Even when made available, moreover, registration statistics appear highly incomplete. There is no agreement on when to include particular categories such as starter pistols or black-powder weapons, both of which are common. Confusion is most extreme in the five eastern states that made up the former East Germany—home to one-third Germany's population—where there has been little reporting on gun ownership.

The most comprehensive estimates come from police spokespersons and firearms specialists. Speaking immediately after the incident in Emsdetten (see above), Rainer Wendt, an official of the Germany police union (Gewerkschaft der Polizei, or GdP), said that the country has about 45 million civilian guns: about 10 million registered firearms; 20 million that should be registered, but apparently are not; and 15 million firearms—such as antiques, starter pistols, air guns, and black-powder weapons like those used at Emsdetten—that do not have to be registered (DDP, 2006; ZDF, 2006). Usually—but misleadingly—simplified to 30 million, this estimate has been repeated by police spokespersons since 1996 (Becker, 2001, p. 4; Hickisch, 2000).

A more detailed estimate comes from a report on the introduction of comprehensive registration in 1972, when the nation's civilian holdings reportedly totalled 17-20 million firearms, of which only 3.2 million were registered (Dobler, 1994, p. 27). The same data was used by the German Foreign Ministry to conclude that '[e]stimates in 1972 ranged from 15,000,000 to 25,000,000 firearms held among the civilian population of the old FRG [Federal Republic of Germany]' (UN, 1999). In the 35 years since then, roughly 8 million additional firearms were legally acquired, accounting for the rest of the *registered* guns thought to exist today; legal purchases of newly manufactured guns amount to 200,000-250,000 annually (Statistisches Bundesamt, 2003). This excludes the former East Germany before reunification and illegally acquired weapons.

Similar totals come from scaling up regional estimates. According to a Bavarian police spokesperson, the region, with a population of 11 million, has some 1.5 million legal and 3 million unregistered firearms (ČTK, 2002). Extrapolated to a nation of 82 million, this would equal 32 million total civilian firearms.

The Small Arms Survey concludes that German civilian holdings are probably more than 20 million and probably less than 30 million (see Table 2.5). The lowest estimates are based on a low figure of 15 million in 1972, plus subsequent purchases of about 8 million new guns. It assumes minimal foreign smuggling and very low ownership in the former East Germany. The high estimate assumes that there were 20 million total firearms in 1972, plus 8 million new guns, higher foreign smuggling, and growing ownership in the area of the former East Germany. Neither parameter includes air guns, black-powder weapons, etc.

Table 2.5 **Estimates of German civilian firearm ownership (millions)**				
Registered	**Unregistered**	**National total**	**Year(s)**	**Sources**
3.2	14.0–17.0	17.0–20.0	1972	Dobler (1994); UN (1999)
		15.0–25.0	1972	UN (1999)
1.5	3.0	32.0	2002	ČTK (2002)*
10.0	20.0–35.0	30.0–45.0	1996–2006	Becker (2001); Wendt (see Box 2.4); DDP (2006); ZDF (2006)
		20.0–30.0	2007	Small Arms Survey

*The ČTK estimate refers to Bavaria only. The national figure of 32 million is based on multiplying the estimate for Bavaria by 7.1 to match the national population.

More fundamentally, registration data cannot capture every civilian gun. Registration schemes miss firearms already in civilian hands before registration came into effect, weapons left over from wars, weapons smuggled into the country and acquired through informal markets, the trade in stolen weapons, and unregulated craft production. Firearm registration with owner licensing, if robustly enacted and enforced, will capture many of these weapons over the long term. But many of the world's registration schemes have been introduced or improved only recently.

Firearms pre-date the creation of the registration systems, which in most countries started in the 1930s or later. The creation of registration systems, mostly in Europe and European colonies, was a response to rapid increases in civilian firearm acquisition after the First World War. As has become commonplace elsewhere since, civilian ownership grew largely because of the effects of warfare, which acquainted a large swath of the population with gun handling and made firearms easier to acquire (Herman, 2001). Combined with the crime waves and political chaos that affected many countries during the inter-war years, concern over growing gun violence led to many responses, including gun licensing and registration reforms.

Although longitudinal data is lacking, this increase appears to have been fuelled by the combination of declining absolute prices after the First World War and rising personal incomes after the Great Depression. An unintended consequence of the First World War was industrial overcapacity in all areas of war production in Europe and North America, including small arms production (Cooling, 1981; Pearton, 1982). While other sectors of military industry struggled, small arms makers faced few additional costs in adapting production to civilian markets. Guns purchased in the early phases of this boom largely escaped subsequent registration. Surpluses from the Second World War also appear to have been largely unrecorded. Additional sources of unregistered firearms include failure to register purchases, a form of law evasion that was relatively easy even in countries with ostensibly mandatory registration requirements, before legal reform in the 1970s made evasion harder. Since then, the rise of informal markets—black markets, leakage from military stockpiles, smuggling, and small-scale private transactions—has become a problem virtually everywhere.

An alternative source of information is production and import–export data. After registration, such data is one of the most reliable indicators of the scale of civilian gun ownership in the United States, for example. This too, though, appears to be significantly incomplete. In the best-understood example, US international trade statistics usually do not include weapons imported as components for reassembling in the United States. The total scale of US imports of parts for reassembling is unknown, but may amount to hundreds of thousands of guns annually.

In countries where craft production is largely unregulated, small-scale manufacturers contribute directly to the total of unregistered and often unknown weapons. In countries such as China, Colombia, Ghana, Pakistan, and the Philippines, illicit or unregulated craft production is a major supplier to the informal gun market (Xiao, 2006; Small Arms Survey, 2003, pp. 26–35). Little, if any, of this production shows up in official data.

In sum, registration data is the best place to start an assessment of a country's civilian firearms holdings, but it also inherently incomplete. Under no circumstances should it be treated as the whole story.

INDEPENDENT ESTIMATES: ADDING AVAILABLE FIGURES

Because official data never tells the whole story and other techniques are unreliable or simply unavailable, comprehensive gun ownership figures routinely rely on estimation. Estimation techniques embrace everything from *coup d'oeil* guesses to peer-reviewed monographs, from informal expert opinions to systematic research. The best are studies appearing as published monographs, such as the series produced by Saferworld, the South Eastern and Eastern Europe Clearinghouse for the Control of Small Arms and Light Weapons (SEESAC), and the Small Arms Survey. Others are based on locally produced reports. Several are statements from local experts, often appearing in press reports, that have gained some acceptance. In two notable cases—India and Indonesia—estimates for the entire country were scaled up from estimates originally articulated for major cities.

Reliance on any estimates involves an element of trust. Expert estimates are not without hidden bias; they must be used carefully (see Box 2.5). In lieu of an independent technique to measure civilian holdings, only the most patently absurd examples can be dismissed. Among the most egregious are claims that Switzerland has 12 million civilian guns (which would equal 1.5 guns for every Swiss man, woman, and child) or that Yemen has 60 or even 80 million (roughly 3–4 guns for every Yemeni). This leaves a total of 77 countries with usable, independent estimates of total civilian firearm ownership. Since there is no way to test their credibility, rival estimates have been averaged for each country to achieve a consensus (see Annexe 1).

Because these are estimates, cautious application is the rule. In this review, estimates have been used to establish likely ranges of civilian gun ownership, i.e. credible low and high boundaries. Where one extreme is more credible than the other, this is acknowledged in composite average data, presented in the annexes. Assembling all of these estimates and registration totals for these countries generates a cumulative total of 554–644 million civilian firearms. With a total of 3.7 billion people, these countries are home to roughly half the world's population. Among the countries not included here for lack of useful estimates are China, much of East Asia, and the Middle East.

Polls and focus groups surveys are the most promising tools for estimating civilian gun ownership.

Over time, additional countries will join the list of those with comprehensive estimates, and quality will improve, assuring greater statistical importance as progressively more monographic studies are completed. The most promising scientific tool for estimating civilian small arms ownership is surveys through polling and focus groups, which are sources of comprehensive and comparable data for every country where this is permitted. National surveys have been undertaken repeatedly in the United States, and intermittently in other countries such as the Russian Federation (NORC, 1999; Romir Monitoring, 2003). The technique has been used most extensively in South-East Europe, in a series of reports sponsored by SEESAC. Applications in sub-Saharan Africa show that firearm polling can be used in any circumstance, although not with equal reliability (Muchai and Jefferson, 2002).

To be sure, polling on civilian firearm ownership and its effects is an imprecise tool. A major problem is the typical confusion over a household's guns. Respondents often may not know whether there are guns in the household or how many there actually are. More fundamentally, there are often concerns that lead respondents to lie or refuse to cooperate (Kellermann et al., 1990; Wellford et al., 2005, pp. 35–36). In countries with mandatory registration, for example, there is an obvious incentive to avoid reporting unregistered guns, even in an anonymous survey. In legally unregulated environments, respondents still can feel inhibited about being forthright. And even in regions where armed violence is rare, asking about access to firearms is not a neutral act.

For want of comprehensive polling, research on gun ownership often relies on proxy indices. Firearm suicide has emerged as the most accepted of these substitute measures of gun ownership, but this tends to work best in circumstances where other data is already available. It is especially weak in societies where suicide is anathema and routinely concealed, disguised as a natural death or an accident, or just not reported at all (Wellford et al., 2005, ch. 7).

Box 2.5 Switzerland: public uncertainty and expert biases

Despite their cultural importance, the number of privately held Swiss firearms is extremely elusive. A recent survey found that 26 per cent (1.95 million) of Swiss own at least one firearm (Gasser, 2006; also see Becker, 2001, p. 14). Published estimates of total firearm ownership vary extraordinarily, ranging from 1.2 million to 12 million (see Table 2.6).

There is less room for disagreement over the nature of Swiss gun problems. This was poignantly demonstrated by the Zug massacre of 2001, and in 2006 by the murder of former Swiss ski champion Corinne Rey-Bellet (Foulkes, 2006). Firearm murders are only somewhat more common in Switzerland than most other European countries, but firearm suicide is significantly more prevalent (Ajdacic-Gross et al., 2006). Recent research concluded that greater availability of firearms has increased suicides by roughly 25 per cent in the last 20 years. Army-issued weapons are a major element in Switzerland's suicides. Although 60 per cent of Swiss firearm *murderers* use privately acquired weapons, 68 per cent of successful *suicides* use army-issued guns (Ajdacic-Gross et al., 2006). As a proxy variable for firearm accessibility, Swiss suicide data supports higher estimates of civilian ownership (Killias, 1993; Killias, Kesteren, and Rindlisbacher, 2001).

Traditionally, Swiss army reservists store their service weapons and sealed ammunition at home. The weapons can be kept after their service obligation ends, an option chosen by 57-75 per cent of former soldiers, after paying a fee (Papacella, 2004; Vonarburg, 2006). This process accelerated in 2004, when the army began reducing its ranks by over 300,000 reservists, a measure expected to release several hundred thousand additional high-powered rifles and pistols (Papacella, 2004).

One major area of disagreement is the number of modern military rifles in the hands of former reservists, their heirs, and clients. According to Peter Hug, roughly 100,000 Sturmgewehr 57 and Sturmgewehr 90 automatic and semi-automatic rifles have been released this way (Hug, 2006). Contrasting reports suggest that many more were released in 2004-06 alone (Mutter, 2006; Papacella, 2004). Even greater uncertainty surrounds privately purchased firearms. Hug (2006) estimates this category at some 450,000. Other estimates can be explained only by assuming that there are between one and three million privately acquired guns.

The lowest total estimates of 1.2-1.3 million private Swiss guns (Bachmann, 2002; SwissInfo, 2005) overlook major categories. The highest estimates of 5-12 million are hard to justify without a clear breakdown. The Small Arms Survey presents Swiss ownership at 2.3-4.5 million firearms, or 31-60 for every 100 residents.

The broad range of Swiss firearm estimates illuminates common biases of expert estimates. The perceptions of gun policy experts anywhere, regardless of their convictions, are vulnerable to classic problems of cognitive screening and selective attention, leading them to see what they expect to see (Bruner, 1957; Egeth, 1967). Higher numbers typically—but not always—come from gun owners and police; lower numbers usually are from gun control advocates. Whether they devote more time to shooting sports or responding to gun pathologies, owners tend to see more guns than non-owners. Because of their greater proximity to firearms, the estimates of law enforcement officials and gun advocates must be taken seriously. The perspectives of more distant observers can be equally valuable. Without comprehensive records or careful public polling, neither perspective is sufficient. Whenever possible, both methods must be applied together.

Table 2.6 Estimates of civilian firearms ownership in Switzerland

Estimate	Source
1.2	SwissInfo (2005)
1.3	Bachmann (2002)
1.0-3.0	Pescia (2006)
2.36	Hug (2006)
2.83-4.56	ProTell (2004)
5.0	Munday (1996, p. 12)
3.0-12.0	Hess (1995)
2.3-4.5	*2007 Small Arms Survey estimate*

EXTRAPOLATION FROM REGISTRATION DATA

When total civilian ownership cannot be calculated simply by adding together and evaluating official and published reports, statistical methods offer the most reliable method of estimation. The strongest basis for systematic estimation of civilian firearm ownership starts with official registration figures. There are 52 countries where both officially registered civilian firearms and independent estimates of unregistered civilian firearms are available. Used together, they form the strongest basis available for statistical modelling based on simple regression analysis of least squares trend line.[2] The registration figure offers certainty, while independent assessments give a sense of comprehensiveness. The sample is economically diverse, although it is skewed geographically by examples from the Caribbean, Latin America, and Europe. Asian and Middle Eastern examples are largely absent.[3]

This method is especially helpful when registration data is available, but not a comprehensive independent estimate. In these cases, registration data, in combination with per capita gross domestic product (GDP) and population, offers a basis for reliable correlation.[4] The resulting correlation, R + beta (registered total) = R^2, is extremely useful for estimating total unregistered civilian holdings in countries where the total number of registered weapons is known. Using the 52 cases with both reliable registration data and complete national estimates leads to an R^2 of 0.512. In other words, this coefficient of determination alone explains over half the variance among these countries.

In addition to these 52 cases, there are 25 countries that have released registration data, but lack a credible total country estimate that includes unregistered weapons. None are large countries, although they include several middle-sized states such as Belarus, the Czech Republic, and Venezuela (see Annexe 2). Averaging shows that unregistered holdings typically are 2.6 times larger than registered holdings, although the actual correlation appears to vary in relation to per capita GDP. The implication is that these 25 countries, with a known total of 4.2 million registered civilian firearms, also have a total of approximately 9.1 million unregistered civilian guns, averaging 350,000 guns for each society.[5] The sample subsumes several distinctive cases with notable divergence among them: it works better for a *set* of countries than any one in particular. In some cases, to be sure, there is no evidence of massive illegal parallel holdings. For example, in geographically or politically isolated countries such as Israel and Japan, unregistered holdings appear to be only one-quarter to one-half as large as registered holdings, and their entries have been adjusted.

Less credible are claims from countries with permeable borders and substantial internal trade that they too have minimal illegal accumulations. Officials in Finland, for example, state that unregistered weapons amount to two per cent of the country's total civilian holdings (50,000 unregistered compared to 2.1 million registered firearms), a claim that is suspiciously low compared to correlative expectations (Biting the Bullet, 2006, p. 94; Annexe 3). Balanced estimates must account for the rise of routine smuggling since 1989. Often, the qualitative changes are easier to spot. In Sweden, for example, a police spokesperson acknowledged that '[b]efore, there were a lot of shotguns—now it's all automatic weapons' (Tidningarnas Telegrambyrå, 2005). In recent decades this process appears to have inflated unregistered holdings on a scale comparable to other European countries.

Figure 2.2 **Correlation of registered to unregistered firearms in 52 countries**

EXPERT AVERAGE (MILLIONS)

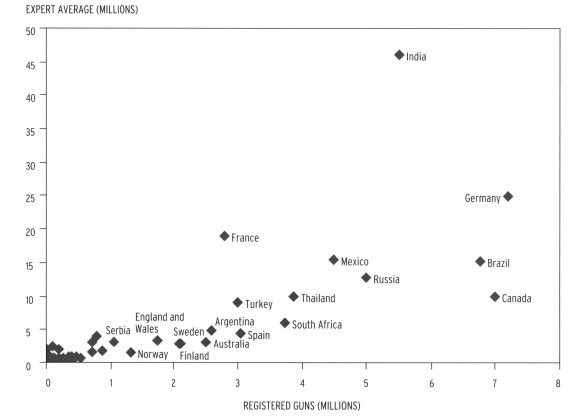

REGISTERED GUNS (MILLIONS)

Note: To make the figure legible, only the correlates for selected countries are labelled. The full list of 52 countries, including those for which the correlates are labelled, is: Albania, Argentina, Australia, Bangladesh, Belgium, Bosnia and Herzegovina, Brazil, Bulgaria, Canada, Chile, Colombia, Croatia, Ecuador, El Salvador, England and Wales, Finland, France, Germany, Greece, Guatemala, Haiti, Honduras, India, Indonesia, Israel, Jamaica, Jordan, Kyrgyzstan, Macedonia, Mexico, Montenegro, the Netherlands, New Zealand, Nicaragua, Norway, Panama, Paraguay, Peru, the Philippines, Poland, the Russian Federation, Serbia, South Africa, Spain, Sri Lanka, Sudan, Sweden, Tajikistan, Tanzania, Thailand, Turkey, and Uruguay.

Table 2.7 **Summary of registered to unregistered firearms correlation**

Model	R	R²	Adjusted R²	Standard error of the estimate
1	0.716[a]	0.512	0.502	3865058.943

a: Predictors: (Constant), registered guns

CORRELATING CIVILIAN GUN OWNERSHIP FROM BASIC NATIONAL INDICATORS

For countries where there is simply no suitable data on civilian gun ownership—either complete estimates or registration data—alternative indicators must be used instead. The model applied here is based on a hypothetical relationship between per capita GDP and civilian gun ownership. This model is refined by applying possession estimates from previously analysed countries to illuminate conditions in countries lacking comparable data. The approach is based on the theoretical assumption that civilian demand—a complex and varied phenomenon—is heavily influenced by macroeconomic forces, above all by a country's wealth and population figures. The approach treats firearms as an ordinary consumer good, ignoring distinctive factors such as personal insecurity or local gun culture.

Although actual country ownership will be strongly influenced by such vicissitudes as anxiety, law, institutions, and culture, this model permits crude prediction. The model relies on data from countries with complete civilian estimates, which are correlated with GDP and population figures to predict ownership elsewhere. From the sample of countries with comprehensive national estimates, the resulting correlation can be applied to most other countries for which we have only general indicators such as population and wealth data. This method has been applied here to 76 countries for which both complete estimates and registration totals are lacking. To enhance accuracy, regional correlations have been used when possible, and the global correlation when necessary.

This approach establishes the existence of approximately 76 million civilian-owned firearms, mostly in smaller countries, but with a few exceptions. More than 50 per cent of these guns are believed to be in China, which is estimated to have at least 40 million civilian firearms. The next largest to be estimated exclusively on the basis of regional or global correlations are Saudi Arabia, with an estimated 6 million civilian guns; Iran, with approximately 3.5 million; and Ukraine, with roughly 3.1 million. The remaining estimated 24 million firearms are distributed among 72 countries, suggesting an average civilian inventory among them of approximately 300,000 firearms each (see Annexe 4).

> Alternative indicators must be used to estimate civilian gun ownership for countries that lack suitable data.

With its R^2 of 0.287 for all countries, the model explains one-quarter of divergence from correlative expectations. The approach generates an estimated total civilian holding for any country when multiplied by per capita GDP and population. Although this is inferior to statistical predictions based on registration data, it still explains a major part of variance. The global correlation is especially robust. Eliminating extreme outliers—highest-ownership countries such as the United States and Yemen, and lowest-ownership countries such as Kyrgyzstan or the Solomon Islands—has a minimal effect on R^2, although such steps enhance statistical significance (gun possession in these last two countries is reviewed in MacFarlane and Torjesen [2004], and Muggah and Alpers [2003], respectively).

The one variant that produced better results was regional correlation, especially for sub-Saharan Africa, and Latin America and the Caribbean. Africa produced an R^2 of 0.359. Dropping Angola as a statistical outlier—probably the most heavily armed country on the continent in per capita terms—improved this to an impressive 0.838. For Latin America and the Caribbean, the comparable statistic was 0.436, still quite strong. Consequently, these regional correlations have been used preferentially where appropriate in Annexes 3 and 4.

This approach shows strengths and weaknesses (see Box 2.6). Tested against Brazil, for example, per capita GDP/population correlation suggests there are 14.4 million civilian small arms in that country, compared to expert estimates averaging 15 million (Fernandes et al., 2005, p. 120). Not all regions show consistent results. East Asia offers an especially weak statistical base, the result of poor information and limited official cooperation, as well as great national distinctiveness, which undermines estimates.[6]

No correlation coefficient fits all cases. The method used here is weakest at the highest levels of per capita GDP. For countries with annual per capita GDP of more than USD 20,000, this model tends to predict levels of civilian gun ownership higher than what is actually known or from independent estimates. The model expects countries such as England and Wales, Germany, and Japan to have much higher civilian holdings than they actually do. It appears that the continuous relationship between rising per capita GDP and rising gun ownership tapers off for high-income countries. Other factors outside the simple model used here, such as national laws and gun culture, become more influential than they were at lower income levels. Repeating the analysis using logarithmic transformation for wealth might reduce this distortion. The United States remains an exception, one of the few wealthy countries to follow the

Figure 2.3 Correlation of per capita GDP to civilian gun ownership in 76 countries

PER CAPITA GDP (2003 USD)

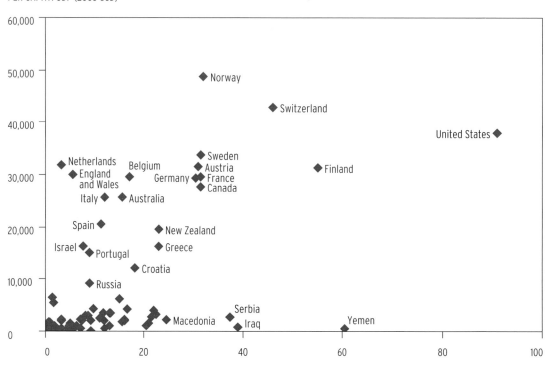

Note: To make the figure legible, only the correlates for selected countries are labelled. The full list of 76 countries, including those for which the correlates are labelled, is: Afghanistan, Albania, Angola, Argentina, Australia, Austria, Bangladesh, Belgium, Bosnia and Herzegovina, Brazil, Bulgaria, Burundi, Cambodia, Canada, Chile, Colombia, Croatia, Ecuador, El Salvador, England and Wales, Finland, France, Germany, Ghana, Greece, Guatemala, Guinea-Bissau, Haiti, Honduras, India, Indonesia, Iraq, Israel, Italy, Jamaica, Jordan, Kenya, Kazakhstan, Kosovo, Kyrgyzstan, Lebanon, Macedonia, Mexico, Montenegro, Morocco, Mozambique, the Netherlands, New Zealand, Nicaragua, Nigeria, Norway, Pakistan, Panama, Paraguay, Peru, the Philippines, Poland, Portugal, Russian Federation, Serbia, the Solomon Islands, Somalia, South Africa, Spain, Sri Lanka, Sudan, Sweden, Tajikistan, Tanzania, Thailand, Turkey, Uganda, the United States, Uruguay, Yemen, and Zimbabwe.

Table 2.8 Summary of per capita GDP to firearms correlation

Model	R	R²	Adjusted R²	Standard error of the estimate
1	0.536[a]	0.287	0.277	12.88236

a: Predictors: (Constant), GNP

Box 2.6 Testing the correlative civilian firearm ownership model

As this chapter notes, data for the global distribution of civilian-owned firearms is already available for a large number of countries. Comprehensive estimates were found for 81 countries. Another 25 countries supplied registration data, which provides a relatively high-confidence basis for estimating their total civilian ownership. GDP/population correlation is used for the remaining countries.

Although the latter is used as a residual technique to account for the final 10-16 per cent of civilian-owned firearms, it still must be evaluated for verisimilitude. Because all complete examples were used to construct the model, no truly independent test of its accuracy is possible. But comparing the results of this estimating method to a few relatively well-understood middle-income countries shows results close to low expert estimates (see Table 2.9). The low correlative results show that the approach must be used cautiously, since it tends to underestimate, reinforcing conservative conclusions.

The tendency for the model to underestimate does not apply everywhere. The extreme example is England and Wales, where it predicts much more than independent estimates show. This reflects a basic problem with applying the approach to high-income societies. When correlating civilian gun ownership primarily with national wealth, the model generates spurious results for high-income countries by failing to account for factors that suppress public access and demand, such as laws, regulations, and national gun culture.

In England and Wales, a strong anti-gun culture suppresses demand and regulative barriers inhibit buying, keeping ownership far below the levels that wealth alone would anticipate. The major exception to this trend for the wealthiest countries is the United States, where the model anticipates levels of civilian gun ownership slightly above the most widely accepted estimates, a match facilitated by the notoriously permissive gun laws and a generally positive gun culture.

Table 2.9 Comparing estimated and correlated civilian gun ownership

Country	Per capita GDP (USD)	Population	Low est. of total firearms	High est. of total firearms	Correlative total firearms estimate
Brazil	2,900	175,000,000	15,300,000	15,300,000	14,500,00
Colombia	1,900	43,000,000	2,300,000	3,900,000	2,300,000
England and Wales	29,900	60,400,000	2,000,000	5,700,000	50,600,000
Morocco	1,500	30,000,000	1,500,000	1,500,000	1,300,000
Turkey	3,400	71,000,000	7,000,000	11,000,000	6,800,000
United States	37,800	300,000,000	250,000,000	290,000,000	317,000,000

Sources: Brazil: Fernandes et al. (2005, p. 120); Colombia: Aguirre et al. (2006) and Small Arms Survey (2006); England and Wales: UK (2005), low est. from Cramb (2006), and high est. from Goodchild and Lashmar (2005); Morocco: Small Arms Survey (2005, pp. 87, 89); Turkey: UN (1998), BBC (2003), Braiden (2003), and Chiesa (2003); United States: based on Small Arms Survey (2003, p. 61) and US ATFE (2003; 2004; 2005), but the latter do not include military weapons sold to civilians or weapons imported as parts

model. The model predicts 317 million civilian firearms, whereas reliable estimates from other sources place the actual number at about 290 million (see Box 2.6). The absence of strong civilian gun laws—especially national registration—is the notable and relevant difference between the United States and other high-income countries, for which the model consistently under-predicts ownership.

The per capita GDP/population model is also weak in its predictions of ownership levels in the very poorest countries. As income declines, individual countries diverge from expectations. The problem is clearest as per capita GDP drops below USD 1,000 per person: R^2 drops to 0.081. For such poor countries, the model explains less than 10 per cent of the difference in civilian ownership; the rest (over 90 per cent) is explained by other factors.

Essentially, the model expects some poor countries, such as Ethiopia, Liberia, and Somalia, to have smaller holdings than appears to be the case. This probably reflects the role of armed conflict in inflating gun ownership.

The correlation also breaks down for the very smallest countries, with populations under 250,000. Most of the world's smallest countries are islands. With distinctive trading patterns, some can maintain very low gun ownership cultures, while others are vulnerable to rapid transformation with just a few shipments—sometimes just one such shipment (Alpers and Twyford, 2003, p. 8). With these problems in mind, this chapter estimates gun ownership only in countries with a population of at least 250,000.

THE CROSS-OVER EFFECT: THE MOVEMENT OF MILITARY FIREARMS TO CIVILIANS AND CIVILIAN FIREARMS TO COMBATANTS

Civilian holdings already far outnumber military small arms stocks. While military arms have historically differed significantly from civilian guns in terms of sophistication, this may be changing as well. There is widespread cross-over of military-style firearms into the civilian market. To a far lesser degree, civilian guns are also winding up in the hands of combatants.

The world's armed forces acquire no more than about one million *new* firearms annually, possibly considerably less. Although the number of military weapons in circulation in any year is much greater, most of these are second-hand. The number of newly manufactured military firearms is much smaller (Bevan, 2006). Civilians acquire approximately 7–8 million new small arms annually (Batchelor, 2002, pp. 9, 54), though, as noted above, the rate of attrition

A police chief holds a confiscated semi-automatic weapon at a police station in Montgomery, Alabama, in June 2004. The rifle is believed to have been used in the fatal shootings of three Birmingham police officers. © Haraz **Ghanbari/AP Photo**

is unknown (see Box 2.1). More fundamentally, the division between 'military' and 'civilian' weapons is no longer so clear cut.

In the first instance, the transfer of weapons from the armed forces to civilians is now common, as military weapons are given away, stolen, and sold. In some cases, the process is part of routine demobilization, as in Switzerland, where former reservists traditionally keep their military-issued weapons (see Box 2.5). Other countries sell surplus military weapons to civilian owners. In the United States, this takes the form of the Civilian Marksmanship Programme. Surplus military rifles can also be exported to private customers, as in 2006, when a Serbian firm transferred several thousand such rifles to private buyers in the United States (*VIP/Politika*, 2006). Elsewhere, the process is illegal, as weapons are stolen or illegally sold onto the civilian market. Iraq is the most extreme example of this.

There is movement from civilian to military holdings as well, as non-state guerrillas, insurgents, and terrorists initially arm themselves with any available weapons. In scale, though, this is relatively small—non-state actors are not that big as a portion of the global total of firearm owners, totalling fewer than a quarter of a million people in the late 1990s, and probably far fewer today (Small Arms Survey, 2001, p. 79).

Other indicators suggest that differences between military and civilian equipment may be declining. Civilians are gradually catching up with some of the technical developments armed services completed in the 1960s and 1970s (Kahaner, 2006). The steady transfer of automatic weapons from military arsenals into civilian hands, plus increasing legal sales of automatic weapons to civilians, means that they are drawing progressively closer in terms of firepower. In the United States alone, private ownership of automatic and semi-automatic rifles was estimated at four million in 1989 (IRSAS, 1989). Another million have subsequently been bought by American consumers (VPC, 2004). The total is almost four times the number owned by the US Army (Small Arms Survey, 2006, p. 53). Throughout much of Africa and the Middle East, civilian ownership of automatic rifles—typically AK-47s—is increasingly commonplace (Kahaner, 2006, chs. 8–9). Revolvers are rapidly becoming antiquated among civilians, who are replacing them with semi-automatic pistols.

> The transfer of weapons from the armed forces to civilians is now common.

The consequences of increasing civilian firepower are not hard to find. Already, civilians kill and maim many more of each other than do the armed forces. *Direct* combat fatalities were estimated at approximately 80,000–108,000 in 2003, of which 60–90 per cent were attributable to small arms and light weapons (Wille and Krause, 2005, pp. 230, 257). Non-conflict civilian violence appears to be far more destructive. As one analyst notes, 'while precise data are not available, murders, suicides, and accidents with firearms in areas not at war exceed 200,000 per year' (Cukier and Sidel, 2005, pp. 4, 14; also see Florquin and Wille, 2004, p. 174).

THE POST-MODERN ARMS RACE

For much of the 19th and 20th centuries, states competed in arms races for the largest, most destructive arsenals. In the post-modern world, though, conventional arms races have become increasingly rare (Mack, 2005). The term *arms race* is used today mostly as a metaphor for declining control over security (Tertrais, 2001; Sloss, 2001). Where it is gaining greater meaning, instead, is among individual civilians, for whom the see-saw pattern of self-conscious arming and counter-arming is becoming more and more real.

As described in the statistical model developed here, there is a strong connection among *per capita wealth, population,* and *guns.* In general, greater per capita wealth and population are positively associated with more civilian firearms. As per capita income rises, so does civilian gun ownership, unless there are strong legal barriers to public gun ownership and a cultural predisposition to view gun ownership negatively, as in Japan and Poland. Of course, further research is needed to disaggregate which segments of the civilian population are responsible for acquisition, and whether cross-national patterns can be identified.

Although the evidence is not conclusive, it appears that both restrictive national firearms laws and civilian gun culture inhibit normal trends. In countries with strong legal systems but weak cultural barriers, gun ownership can rapidly expand as income rises. China and India offer the clearest evidence of this tendency for wealth to outweigh law in countries with weak cultural barriers. All such countries show evidence of significant increases in civilian ownership, even though the legal regime remained unchanged or has even been tightened. The Russian Federation displays a more complicated picture. Estimated civilian ownership there increased from no more than 500,000 in 1989 to roughly 6–14 million today, based on household ownership rates (Keller, 1990, p. 1; Romir Monitoring, 2003). Greater gun ownership in the Russian Federation came despite falling incomes, helped instead by the erosion of legal barriers, loss of control over military stockpiles, and mounting personal insecurity. In England and Wales, restrictive ownership laws have also been overcome through higher illegal ownership (Hales, Lewis, and Silverstone, 2006, ch. 4).

Stronger correlations require longitudinal data, plotting changes in gun ownership over time from country to country. Currently, such data is available for only a handful of states, most notably the United States. Other countries, such as the Czech Republic and the United Kingdom, make time-series gun data available, but only for legally registered firearms.

Population size and national wealth are also basic forces shaping overall ownership. Regions with a permissive gun culture and rapidly rising income and population tend to witness sharp increases in civilian possession. Previous research has already substantiated the importance of greater wealth in small arms acquisition, noting, for example, that '[a]n important element of small arms demand . . . is the relative monetary value of firearms' (Glatz and Muggah, 2006, p. 153). But there are important exceptions, since 'low earned income does not prevent arms acquisition and possession if other demand factors are strong' (Glatz and Muggah, 2006, p. 158). A related consideration is the significance of gun ownership as a symbol of wealth in many societies (Bevan and Florquin, 2006, p. 306).

As wealth and population grow, civilian gun ownership tends to rise as well.

One region almost certain to be affected by these trends is the Middle East. Although several North African countries have restrictive gun laws, the legal environment is relatively permissive on the Arabian Peninsula. Independently of other forces such as the consequences of war in Lebanon in the 1970s and 1980s, the conflict in Iraq today, or sectarian violence in Gaza, gun buying is already common. In a permissive environment where firearm ownership is widely seen as a masculine necessity, population and wealth are key determinants of the growth of civilian ownership. The population of the Middle East doubled between 1970 and 2000. It is expected to increase at a slightly slower rate in the coming decades (PRC, 2004). In Arabic-speaking countries, population growth is even faster, and is predicted to grow by about 60 per cent between 2000 and 2020 (UNDP, 2002, pp. 35–38). Independent of changing security concerns and wealth, such trends seem likely to increase overall demand for firearms throughout the region (Bevan and Florquin, 2006).

These associations also illuminate the ongoing debate over small arms demand. A complicated phenomenon, gun demand can rarely be reduced to a single explanation. The connection here reinforces the conclusions of previous research emphasizing the role of non-security motives in acquiring small arms (Atwood, Muggah, and Widmer, 2005).

FROM HUNTING TO SECURITY: THE CHANGING NATURE OF CIVILIAN GUN OWNERSHIP

Crucial aspects of firearm ownership among civilians have been the urbanization of gun ownership and the switch to deadlier technologies.

Although exact data is lacking, there appears to be a steady increase in the number of civilian firearms in cities. This reflects the well-known global shift of populations from the countryside and villages to cities. Patterns of firearm ownership continue to change today, leading to a steady increase not only in the scale of civilian-owned weapons, but also their typical firepower.

Civilian firearm ownership used to be associated mostly with rural life. Through the 19th and early 20th centuries, the predominant firearms in civilian society were long guns—rifles and shotguns—for hunting or self-defence. This is best documented in the United States. As recently as 1899–1945, 75 per cent of all civilian firearms manufactured in the United States were long guns. Technological changes, especially the development of small and reliable hand-guns in the later 19th century, allowed greater firearm urbanization (US ATF, 2000). By the 1980s handguns averaged about 50 per cent of the American civilian market (US ATF, 2000, p. 7). Other countries witnessed similar trends. An extreme example is the Czech Republic, where the proportion of handguns rose from 3 per cent of all registered guns in 1991 to 37 per cent by 2000, due partially to legal reforms facilitating legal handgun ownership (Czech Republic, 2001, p. 42). The exceptions are countries such as the United Kingdom, where handgun ownership was prohibited in 1997–98 after the Dunblane massacre (Karp, 2003).

Long guns are poorly suited to urban environments, where they cannot be carried without attracting alarm. Firearms ceased to be a rarity in the city in the 1920s and 1930s as a result of the increase in the numbers of handguns. Regulation became more widespread or civilian ownership rose in response, leading to many of the pioneering licensing and registration laws of the mid-20th century. Pressure for greater gun control continued to grow in countries such as Australia, Canada, Jamaica, and the United Kingdom in direct response to easier civilian access to automatic rifles and, above all, semi-automatic pistols, often after major crimes involving these weapons (Greenwood, 1972; Malcolm, 2002, chs. 5 and 6).

> A major factor in patterns of civilian gun ownership is the decline of hunting.

Closely associated with changing patterns of civilian ownership is the decline of hunting. Economic development rapidly reduces the need for hunting, transforming it from a necessity for the poor into a luxury for those who can afford it (Herman, 2001). An increasingly urbanized global population also has few opportunities and less desire to hunt. The change is readily seen in Europe, where the number of licensed hunters shrank from ten million in the 1980s to six million in 2003.[7] In Italy the plunge was especially dramatic, as the total number of registered hunters shrank from 2.3 million in the mid-1970s to somewhat over 700,000 today (Hooper, 2005). By 1945 one-quarter of all American men hunted (Burbick, 2006, pp. 68, 198, fn. 1). By 2002 this had fallen to six per cent of all American adult men (Jonsson, 2003; Gamerman, 2005). Instead of countryside sports, civilian gun buyers are more likely to invest in weapons suited to urban life, especially sidearms (Rodengen, 2002, pp. 147–71).

The counterpart to growing markets for handguns in wealthy urban markets is greater interest in automatic rifles in poorer regions. Like revolvers, the bolt-action rifles that predominated among civilians are increasingly being supplanted with far more lethal semi- and fully automatic alternatives. In the 1980s, owners in Africa, the Middle East, and South Asia replaced their bolt-action rifles with AK-47s (Kahaner, 2006). The result is a poorly acknowledged revolution in civilian firepower. Easier access to high-powered firearms is a concern in a growing number of countries, including places previously all but immune to gun proliferation problems, such as Ireland and New Zealand

(*Dominion Post,* 2006; *Gun Policy News,* 2006). That said, major legal reforms have slowed or even reversed the proliferation of such weapons in Australia and the United Kingdom, accelerating the decline of firearm deaths and mass killings (Chapman et al., 2006).

A sign of the rising lethality of civilian holdings is a rising demand from law enforcement agencies for more potent weapons. Police officers around the world continue to trade revolvers for pistols, and pistols for sub-machine guns and automatic rifles (e.g. see Demarzo, 2005; Jahn, 2005; Murphy, 2006). In England, escalation has fuelled controversial demands to arm more police (BBC, 2006). Where social inhibitions against gun use are weak, the impact has been especially horrible, as illustrated by the waves of murders immediately following sudden access to automatic rifles in Papua New Guinea (Alpers, 2005). Elsewhere, this trend is associated with more civilian mass shootings, a phenomenon that declines when fully automatic and semi-automatic weapons are removed (Chapman et al., 2006).

FIREARM DESTRUCTION: REINFORCING CIVILIAN DOMINANCE

Although it is much slower than firearm acquisition, destruction continues to shape global holdings. Organized destruction projects have been responsible for the elimination of at least 8.5 million small arms since 1991 (see Annexe 5). This equals an average of at least 500,000 firearms annually. This figures only includes totals from projects that eliminated at least 10,000 weapons at a time; it does not include the numerous smaller undertakings. Although total destruction is not inconsequential, it is swamped by the annual production of roughly eight million new firearms annually (Batchelor, 2002, p. 54; Bevan, 2006, p. 26).

Destruction activity is concentrated among countries with the largest holdings. Just three countries—Germany, the Russian Federation, and the United States—were solely responsible for 64 per cent of confirmed military small arms units destroyed (see Table 2.10). Civilian firearm destruction was even more concentrated. Three countries—Australia, Brazil, and the United Kingdom—accounted for over 89 per cent of all known civilian firearm destruction activity.

More than 5.5 million military small arms were destroyed in the period 1991–2006, as were more than two million civilian firearms. The destruction of law enforcement and non-state armed group weapons rarely matches the scale of the most prominent civilian and military undertakings, despite the publicity that often surrounds them.

A large number of weapons taken by law enforcement authorities are not destroyed.

The destruction figures here do not include many of the small arms collected around the world through post-conflict disarmament and police seizures. Many highly publicized disarmament programmes, such as those in Mozambique in the early 1990s, or Sierra Leone in 2002, or Afghanistan in 2003–05, are not included (Caramés, Fisas, and Luz, 2006, p. 23), because they often collect the guns, but do not destroy them. Even weapons collected through post-conflict disarmament schemes may be reissued to state agencies or allowed back into black markets.[8] A large number of weapons taken by law enforcement authorities are not destroyed, but kept as criminal evidence and eventually sold. In the most extreme example—China's report of seizing 38 million illegal civilian firearms—their destruction can only be surmised (Xiao, 2006).[9]

Other important destruction programmes have not been listed here for want of actual destruction. In countries such as Kazakhstan and Ukraine, commitments have been finalized to eliminate large numbers of weapons, but none have actually been destroyed as of the time of writing. Nor do destruction programmes always end as planned. A prominent example was efforts by the Organization for Security and Co-operation in Europe (OSCE) to eliminate 300,000 surplus small arms in Belarus, which collapsed after all the preliminary studies had been completed.[10]

A side effect of destruction trends is to boost the dominance of civilian holdings. Not only are military-held guns being destroyed faster, there are fewer to begin with and they are not replaced as quickly. With an average of some 350,000 military guns destroyed annually, destruction may *surpass* average annual new procurement (Bevan, 2006). But civilian destruction, eliminating an average of 150,000 weapons annually, is offset by the roughly 7–8 million new firearms acquired by civilians every year.

Although local effects will vary widely, the net result of destruction trends is to reinforce civilian preponderance of global firearm possession. A comprehensive assessment of destruction would have to consider the effects of routine attrition on military stockpiles and civilian holdings through loss and breakage. Currently, neither the data nor analytical tools exist for such an assessment. Whether wastage affects civilian or military firearms more can only be guessed (see Box 2.1).

Table 2.10 The largest small arms destruction programmes, 1991–2006

Country	Source of weapons	Quantity destroyed	Years	Sources
Germany	Military	1,781,696	1991-2004	Germany (2005, p. 20)
Russian Federation	Military	1,110,000	1994-2002	Faltas and Chrobok (2004, p. 115)
United States	Military	830,000	1993-96	Small Arms Survey (2002, p. 75)
Australia	Civilian	643,726	1997-98	Small Arms Survey (2002, p. 75)
United Kingdom	Military	540,000	1992-2001	Faltas and Chrobok (2004, pp. 38-39)
Brazil	Civilian	443,719	2004-05	Mota (2006, p. 8)
South Africa	Military	262,667	1998-2001	Gould (2004, p. 155)
Bosnia	Military	250,000	2002-07	UK (2005, p. 15)
Albania	Civilian	222,918	1997-2005	Holtom et al. (2005, p. 7); OSCE (2002)
Cambodia	Military	198,000	1999-2006	EU ASAC (2006)
Romania	Military	195,510	2002-03	Romania (2003, p. 10)
United Kingdom	Civilian	185,000	1997-99	Small Arms Survey (2002, p. 75)
Australia	Civilian	150,000	1995-2004	Philip Alpers (private communication, 2006)
Netherlands	Military	143,632	1994-96	Small Arms Survey (2004, p. 58)
Nicaragua	Civilian	142,000	1991-93	Small Arms Survey (2002, p. 75)
Colombia	Various	141,719	2003-06	Kytömäki and Yankey-Wayne (2006, p. 77-78)
France	Military	140,000	1998-2000	France (2003, pp. 10-11)
Serbia	Military	117,269	2001-03	Small Arms Survey (2004, p. 58)
South Africa	Police	115,711	1999-2001	Small Arms Survey (2002, p. 75)
Brazil	Civilian	100,000	2001	Small Arms Survey (2002, p. 75)

Note: Programmes are ranked by magnitude, but all of them destroyed more than 10,000 small arms and light weapons. They do not include ammunition or planned destruction projects. The complete version of this table can be found in Annexe 5.

CONCLUSION

As illustrated here by countries as diverse as Ireland and Yemen, the proliferation of privately owned guns is a widespread, global phenomenon. In a world awash not just in arms, but also in fiery rhetoric, understanding the distribution of small arms and their effects is anything but easy. Confusion over firearm policy has often discouraged careful analysis of preconceived opinions and inhibited any questioning of the conventional wisdom. Yet the amount of information available is not small. As shown here, many countries have excellent statistics on the distribution of firearms within their borders. In other countries, it is possible to draw estimate sufficient to support basic conclusions.

It is increasingly possible to outline how many guns there are in existence, where they are, and who has them. There are approximately 875 million firearms in the world. Of these, the great majority—roughly 650 million—are in civilian hands. These findings support the conclusion of economist Steven Levitt and Stephen Dubner 'that the modern world, despite a surfeit of obfuscation, complication and downright deceit, is *not* impenetrable, is *not* unknowable, and—if the right questions are asked—is even more intriguing than we think' (Levitt and Dubner, 2006, p. xi).

The increasing atomization of global society has become something of a cliché; and more and more contemporary issues are too complicated for single solutions by single actors (Matthews, 1997). With the majority of the world's guns under civilian control, small arms issues are becoming much like everything else, displaying the same complexity affecting so many policy problems. The dominance of civilians as key players in the global small arms phenomena reminds us that there are no panaceas in gun policy: no one actor, no one programme can resolve small arms issues. Solutions to firearm-related problems rest in the hands of numerous actors, ranging from international organizations, to states and civilians themselves in their diverse manifestations.

Fortunately, we are learning more and getting better at managing these problems. As this chapter reveals, we know much more about the global diffusion of firearms than is commonly assumed. Even where official data is scarce, it is possible to make useful estimates of the scale of the distribution of firearms. While enduring solutions to gun problems may seem distant, our insights are improving rapidly. This chapter is not the final word on the subject; it should be seen, rather, as a stepping-stone, facilitating progress toward more effective small arms policy. Better understanding of gun ownership is necessary in every country. Vital steps include:

- many more country reports based on field research;
- time-series data on national small arms production, imports, and exports;
- time-series data on national registration;
- civilian ownership surveys; and
- detailed reports of military and law enforcement small arms inventories.

International small arms policy making is evolving from a broad instrument for raising awareness and dealing with general problems into a mechanism able to deal with more-specific problems. Continued progress will require better understanding of the problems themselves. Through better information, research will be able to better specify where the worst small arms problems are and which policy instruments are most promising. Vital steps toward clear insight, like those listed above, will facilitate sharper priorities and more effective action. ◼

LIST OF ABBREVIATIONS

GDP   gross domestic product

IRA   Irish Republican Army

OSCE   Organization for Security and
           Co-operation in Europe

SEESAC   South Eastern and Eastern Europe
           Clearinghouse for the Control of Small
           Arms and Light Weapons

ANNEXES (ONLINE AT <HTTP://WWW.SMALLARMSSURVEY.ORG/YEARB2007.HTML>)

Annexe 1. Seventy-seven countries with comprehensive civilian ownership data

This lists all countries for which meaningful independent estimates of total civilian gun ownership are available.

Annexe 2. Twenty-five countries with firearm registration data only

This lists countries for which official registration data is available, but not estimated total civilian gun ownership.

Annexe 3. Civilian firearm ownership for 178 countries, in alphabetical order

This shows all data sources used in Annexes 1 and 2, correlative estimates, and other estimates as noted.

Annexe 4. Civilian gun ownership for 178 countries, in descending order of averaged civilian firearms

This is identical to Annexe 3, except that entries are presented in descending order of magnitude of civilian firearm holdings, based on averaged values.

Annexe 5. Major small arms and light weapons destruction projects, 1991-2006

ENDNOTES

1   Owen Greene, private communication to the author, June 2003.

2   A correlation adjusted until the sums of the squares of y-axis deviations from the trend line are as small as possible.

3   As noted elsewhere, while most registration data is fully credible, four examples appeared suspiciously low and were not included. They were China, with a total of 680,000 registered guns, but there are regular reports of police seizures of millions of unregistered weapons; Mozambique, with 7,000 registered guns; Sudan, where the Ministry of the Interior claims to have registered a total of 6,724 guns in a war-ravaged country of 34 million people; and Tunisia, with 3,408 registered firearms. Otherwise, registration data was accepted as presented. In several cases, such as Ireland and South Korea, registration data came from rounded reports found in news accounts (O'Keeffe and Hogan, 2004; Bae, 2007).

4   The same correlation can be calculated on the basis of purchasing power parity (PPP) indexes to capture absolute differences in the buying power. In this case, PPP techniques appear unpromising due to the lack of domestic input into firearm production in many countries and the equalizing effect of widespread international trade.

5   For East Asian countries where gun ownership is believed to be exceptionally low, the 2.6 ratio of registered to total civilian guns was replaced by a multiplier of 1.72, based on Japanese data.

6   East Asia demonstrates the inability of any statistical model to fit all cases. Complete national civilian gun ownership estimates, the basis for regional correlation, are available for relatively few East Asian countries. The region also contrasts relatively high-ownership countries like Pakistan, the Philippines, and Thailand, and low-ownership countries like Cambodia, Indonesia, and Kyrgyzstan. With an R^2 of just 0.01, the region is simply too diverse and can be estimated only through global correlations.

7   Henri Heidebroek, secretary-general, Institut Européen des armes de chasse et de sport (Brussels), private communication to the author, 4 August 2003.

8   Well-documented post-conflict destruction efforts, such as those that occurred in Cambodia, are included in this analysis.

9   Of course, the number of illegal weapons reportedly seized by Chinese authorities cannot be confirmed or documented.

10 Author's conversations with OSCE officials, 2005–06.

BIBLIOGRAPHY

Aguirre, Katherine, et al. 2006. 'Colombia's Hydra: The Many Faces of Gun Violence.' In Small Arms Survey, ch. 9.

Ajdacic-Gross, Vladeta, et al. 2006. 'Changing Times: A Longitudinal Analysis of International Firearm Suicide Data.' *American Journal of Public Health,* Vol. 96. October, pp. 1752–55.

Al-Fawz, Dahir Fahad. 2002. 'The Phenomenon of Light Weapons Proliferation in Jordan.' In Gali Oda Tealakh, Atef Odibat, and Maha Al Shaer, eds. *Small Arms and Light Weapons in the Arab Region.* Amman: Jordanian Institute of Diplomacy.

Allen, Robin. 2000. 'President Fires a Warning Shot across Yemeni's Guns and Drugs Culture.' *Financial Times* (London). 12–13 September, p. 3.

Alpers, Philip. 2005. *Gun-running in Papua New Guinea: From Arrows to Assault Weapons in the Southern Highlands.* Special Report No. 5. Geneva: Small Arms Survey. June.

—— and Conor Twyford. 2003. *Small Arms in the Pacific.* Occasional Paper No. 8. Geneva: Small Arms Survey.

Al-Qadhi, Mohammed. 2005a. 'Drop Your Guns.' *Yemen Times,* 21 March. <http://yementimes.com/article.shtml?i=826&p=front&a=1>

——. 2005b. 'Demand for Law to Control Firearms as Crime Soars.' IRIN. 20 September.

Arab News (Jeddah). 2005. 'Yemeni Protestors Seek Weapons Ban.' 20 September.

Atwood, David, Robert Muggah, and Mireille Widmer. 2005. 'Motivations and Means: Addressing Demand for Small Arms.' In CHD, pp. 93–104.

Bachmann, Helena. 2002. 'Safety in Numbers.' *Time Europe,* Vol. 159, No. 19. 13 May.

Bae, Ji-sook. 2007. 'Concerns Mount on Weapons Control.' *Korea Times.* 17 January.

Batchelor, Peter. 2002. 'A Sick or Dying Industry?' In Small Arms Survey, ch. 1.

BBC (British Broadcasting Corporation). 2003. 'Father Seeks Tighter Gun Laws.' 21 August. <http://news.bbc.co.uk/1/hi/scotland/3168869.stm>

——. 2005. 'IRA "Has Destroyed All Its Arms".' 26 September. <http://news.bbc.co.uk/2/hi/uk_news/northern_ireland/4283444.stm>

——. 2006. 'Do We Need More Armed Police?' 16 May. <http://news.bbc.co.uk/2/hi/uk_news/4985634.stm>

Becker, Reinhard. 2001. *Zahlen und Fakten zum privaten Waffenbesitz in Deutschland.* Eisenach: Reinhard Becker. 6 September.

Bevan, James. 2004. 'Big Issue, Big Problem: MANPADS.' In Small Arms Survey, ch. 3.

——. 2006. 'Military Demand and Supply: Products and Producers.' In Small Arms Survey, ch. 1.

—— and Nicolas Florquin. 2006. 'Few Options but the Gun: Angry Young Men.' In Small Arms Survey, ch. 12.

Biting the Bullet. 2006. *Reviewing Action on Small Arms 2006: Assessing the First Five Years of the UN Programme of Action.* London and Bradford: International Alert, Saferworld, and the University of Bradford. June.

Braiden, Gerry. 2003. 'Time to End Turkish Gun Culture that Helped Kill Our Little Boy.' *Evening Times* (Glasgow). 14 August.

Brandon, James. 2006. 'Yemen Attempts to Rein in Outlaw Tribes.' *The Christian Science Monitor.* 24 January.

Breslin, John. 2004. 'Dramatic Increase in Firearms Offences.' *The Irish Examiner.* 2 January.

Bruner, Jerome. 1957. 'On Perceptual Readiness.' *Psychological Review,* Vol. 64, pp. 129–30.

Burbick, Joan. 2006. *Gun Show Nation: Gun Culture and American Democracy.* New York: New Press.

Burnham, Gilbert, et al. 2006. 'Mortality after the 2003 Invasion of Iraq: A Cross-sectional Cluster Sample Survey.' *The Lancet,* Vol. 368, No. 9545. 11 October, pp. 1421–28.

Caramés, Albert, Vicenç Fisas, and Daniel Luz. 2006 *Análisis de los programas de desarme, desmovilización y reintegración (DDR) existentes en el mundo durante 2005.* Barcelona: Escuela de Cultura de Paz. February. <http://www.colombiainternacional.org/Doc%20PDF/UE-AnalisisProgramasDesarme.pdf>

Castles, Francis G., ed. 2007. *The Disappearing State? Retrenchment Realities in an Age of Globalization.* Cheltenham: Edward Elgar.

Chapman, S., et al. 2006. 'Australia's 1996 Gun Law Reforms: Faster Falls in Firearm Deaths, Firearm Suicides, and a Decade without Mass Shootings.' *Injury Prevention,* No. 12, pp. 365–72.

CHD (Centre for Humanitarian Dialogue). 2005. *Missing Pieces: Directions for Reducing Gun Violence through the UN Process on Small Arms Control.* Geneva: CHD. July.

Chiesa, Alison. 2003. 'Picture of a Child Drives Anti-gun Campaign.' *The Herald* (Glasgow). 22 August.

China. 1996. Law of the People's Republic of China on the Control of Firearms. 5 July.

CIA (Central Intelligence Agency). 2006. *CIA World Factbook.* McLean: CIA. 24 January, ch. on Yemen. <https://www.cia.gov/cia/publications/factbook/>

Clonan, Tom. 2005. 'Huge Numbers of Lethal Firearms in the Hands of Young Criminals.' *The Irish Times.* 9 September, p. 3.

Connolly, Shaun. 2006. 'Gardai to Seize 3,000 Guns under Amnesty.' *The Irish Examiner.* 3 January.

Cooling, Benjamin Franklin, ed. 1981. *War, Business and World Military–Industrial Complexes.* New York: Kennikat.

Courrier international. 2005. 'Chine: Cinq millions d'armes dans la nature.' No. 770. 24 August, p. 22.

Cramb, Auslan. 2006. 'Children's Families still Waiting for Firearms Register.' *Daily Telegraph* (London). 13 March.

ČTK (Czech News Agency). 2002. 'Czech Fire Arms on Bavarian Black Market.' 25 February.

Cukier, Wendy and Victor W. Sidel. 2005. The Global Gun Epidemic. Westport: Praeger/Greenwood.

Cusack, Jim. 1996. 'Handguns Banned in Ireland since Early 1970s.' The Irish Times. 17 October, p. 10.

Czech Republic. Ministry of Foreign Affairs. 2001. The Czech Republic and Small Arms and Light Weapons. Prague: Ministry of Foreign Affairs.

DDP (Deutscher Depeschendienst Nachrichtenagentur). 2006. 'Polizeigewerkschaft fordert schärfere Waffengesetze.' 23 November.

Demarzo, Wanda J. 2005. 'Bad Guys still Have Firepower Edge on Some Cops.' Miami Herald. 19 December.

Dobler, Ernst Ulrich. 1994. *Schußwaffen und Schußwaffenkriminalität in der Bundesrepublik Deutschland (ohne Berücksichtigung der neuen Länder)*. Frankfurt: Peter Lang.

Dominion Post (Wellington). 2006. 'Kiwi Gun Collectors Hold Machine Guns, Rocket and Grenade Launchers.' 7 November.

The Economist. 2006. 'America's Population: Now We Are 300,000,000.' 12–19 October.

Egeth, Howard. 1967. 'Selective Attention.' *Psychological Bulletin*, Vol. 67, pp. 41–57.

Ellis, Tony and Kathryn Coleman. 2006. *Firearm Certificates England and Wales, 2004/05*. Home Office Statistical Bulletin. London: Home Office. 25 May.

Emigrant Online. 2006. 'Gun Crime Epidemic.' 24 July.

Der Enztäler (Neuenbürg). 2005. 'Fahnder entdecken Waffenlager.' 22 December.

EU ASAC (European Union Assistance on Curbing Small Arms and Light Weapons in the Kingdom of Cambodia). 2006. *An Overview of the EU ASAC Project*. Phnom Penh: EU ASAC. <http://www.eu-asac.org/>

Faltas, Sami and Vera Chrobok. 2004. *Disposal of Surplus Small Arms: A Survey of Policies and Practices in OSCE Countries*. Bonn, London, and Geneva: Bonn International Center for Conversion (BICC), British American Security Information Council, Saferworld, and Small Arms Survey.

Fernandes, Rubem César, et al. 2005. *Brazil: The Arms and the Victims*. Rio de Janeiro: Viva Rio. March.

Fetter, Gregory. 2001. 'Again I Say—Good Luck.' *Forecast International Weapons Group*. Newtown: Forecast International. 21 July.

Florini, Ann M. 2000. *The Third Force: The Rise of Transnational Civil Society*. Washington, DC: Carnegie Endowment for International Peace.

Florquin, Nicolas and Christina Wille. 2004. 'A Common Tool: Firearms, Violence, and Crime.' In Small Arms Survey, ch. 6.

Foulkes, Imogen. 2006. 'Domestic Killings Shock Swiss.' *BBC News*. 9 May. <http://news.bbc.co.uk/>

France. 2003. *Rapport national de la France sur la mise en oeuvre du programme d'action des Nations Unies, sur la lutte contre le commerce illicite des armes légères et de petit calibre, sous tous ses aspects, adopté lors de la conférence des Nations Unies à New York, le 20 juillet 2001*. Paris: Ministry of Foreign Affairs. April.

Gamerman, Ellen. 2005. 'Deer Hunting Caught in an Identify Crisis.' *The Wall Street Journal* (New York). 10 November.

Garda Síochána. 2006. *Annual Report of An Garda Síochána*. Dublin: Ministry of Justice, Equality and Law Reform.

Gasser, Richard. 2006. 'Schusswaffengebrauch: Zahlen und Fakten.' Berne: ProTell. 30 October. <http://www.protell.ch/Aktivbereich/19Archiv/de/2006/03.267d%20Schusswaffengebrauch%20061030.pdf >

Germany. 2005. *National Report on the Implementation of the United Nations Programme of Action to Prevent, Combat and Eradicate the Illicit Trade in Small Arms and Light Weapons in All Its Aspects, Submitted by the Federal Republic of Germany*. Berlin: Ministry of Foreign Affairs. 30 April.

Glatz, Anne-Katherin and Robert Muggah. 2006. 'The Other Side of the Coin: Demand for Small Arms.' In Small Arms Survey, ch. 6.

Goodchild, Sophie and Paul Lashmar. 2005. 'Up to 4m Guns in UK and Police are Losing the Battle.' *Independent on Sunday* (London). 4 September.

Gould, Chandré, et al. 2004. 'South Africa.' In Chandré Gould and Guy Lamb, eds. *Hide and Seek: Taking Account of Small Arms in Southern Africa*. Johannesburg: Gun Free South Africa. October.

Graff, James. 2002. 'Gunning for It.' *Time Europe*, Vol. 159, No. 19. 13 May.

Greenwood, Colin. 1972. *Firearms Control: A Study of Armed Crime and Firearms Control in England and Wales*. London: Routledge & Keagan Paul.

Grimmit, Richard F. 2006. *International Small Arms and Light Weapons Transfers: U.S. Policy*. Washington, DC: Congressional Research Service. 2 October.

Gun Policy News. 2006. 'Garda Demand More Firearms Training amid Rising Gun Crime.' 12 April.

Hales, Gavin, Chris Lewis, and Daniel Silverstone. 2006. *Gun Crime: The Market in and Use of Illegal Firearms*. Home Office Research Study No. 298. London: Home Office Research, Development and Statistics Directorate. December.

Hammond, Grant T. 1993. *Plowshares into Swords: Arms Races in International Politics, 1840–1991*. Columbia: University of South Carolina Press.

Herman, Daniel Justin. 2001. *Hunting and the American Imagination*. Washington, DC: Smithsonian Institution.

Hess, C. 1995. Correspondence from the Federal Police Office, Berne, Switzerland. Cited in Canada. Department of Justice. *Review of Firearms Statistics and Regulations in Selected Countries*. Ottawa: Research, Statistics and Evaluation Directorate, Department of Justice. 25 April. <http://www.cfc-cafc.gc.ca/pol-leg/res-eval/publications/reports/1990-95/siter_rpt_e.asp#4.0%20SWITZERLAND>

Hickisch, Kurt. 2000. 'James Bond's Dienstwaffe.' *Öffentliche Sicherheit: Das Magazin des Innenministeriums* (Vienna), No. 5. May, p. 26. <http://www.bmi.gv.at/oeffentlsicherheit/2000/05/artikel_11.asp>

Holtom, Paul, et al. 2005. *Turning the Page: Small Arms and Light Weapons in Albania*. London: Saferworld.

Hooper, John. 2005. 'Wedded to the Shotgun: Avian Flu is now Large in Europe but Berluscioni Government Appears Still to Support the Annual Italian Hunt of Migratory Birds.' *The Guardian* (London and Manchester). 20 October.

Hu, Xu. 2005. 'Statement of Mr Xu Hu, Ministry of Public Security, to the UN Workshop on Small Arms and Light Weapons.' Beijing. 19 April.

Hug, Peter. 2006. 'In der Schweiz zirkulierende Waffen.' Private communication with the Small Arms Survey. 21 September.

IICD (Independent International Commission on Decommissioning). 2005. *Report of the International Independent Commission on Decommissioning*. Belfast and Dublin: IICD. 26 September.

IMC (US Installation Management Command—Europe). 2006. 'Acquisition and Possession of Privately Owned Firearms in Germany.' 3 January.

Ireland. 2005. *Ireland's Report on Implementation of the United Nations Programme of Action to Prevent, Combat and Eradicate the Illicit Trade in Small Arms and Light Weapons in All Its Aspects*. Dublin: Department of Foreign Affairs.

IRIN (Integrated Regional Information Networks). 2005. 'Yemen: Population Grows to 19.7 million.' 21 March.

——. 2006a. 'When Cultural Norms Underpin Ownership.' 21 May.

——. 2006b. 'Yemen Weapons Proliferation Persists Despite Pressure on Government to Tackle Problem.' 10 June.

IRSAS (Institute for Research on Small Arms and Society). 1989. 'Assault Rifle Fact Sheet No. 1.' Alexandria: IRSAS.

Jahn, George. 2005. 'Iran Stockpiling High-Tech Small Arms.' Lexis-Nexis.

Jonsson, Patrik. 2003. 'Rural Tradition of Hunting Shows Signs of Decline.' *The Christian Science Monitor*. 9 January.

Jüttner, Judy. 2006. 'Armed to the Teeth and Crying for Help.' *Der Spiegel Online*. 21 November.

Kahaner, Larry. 2006. *AK-47: The Weapon that Changed the Face of War*. New York: John Wiley.

Karp, Aaron. 2003. 'Dunblane and the International Politics of Gun Control.' In Stuart Nagel, ed. *Policy and Peacemaking*. Lanham: Lexington Books, ch. 8.

——. 2006a. 'Escaping Reuterswärd's Shadow.' *Contemporary Security Policy*, Vol. 27, No. 1. April.

——. 2006b. *The Estimated Firearms Inventories of Sudan*. Geneva: Small Arms Survey, Human Security Sudan Baseline Project. 30 September.

Katzenstein, Peter J. 1996. *The Culture of National Security*. New York: Columbia University Press.

Keller, Bill. 1990. 'A Bad Soviet Mix: Guns and Grievances.' *International Herald Tribune*. 2 February.

Kellermann, A. L., et al. 1990. 'Confirming the Validity of Survey-based Measures of Firearm Prevalence: Gun Owners Tell the Truth.' *American Journal of Epidemiology*, Vol. 131, No. 6, pp. 1080–84.

Killias, Martin. 1993. 'International Correlations between Gun Ownership and Rates of Homicide and Suicide.' *Canadian Medical Association Journal*, Vol. 148, No. 10. October, pp. 1721–25.

——, John van Kesteren, and Martin Rindlisbacher. 2001. 'Guns, Violent Crime, and Suicide in 21 Countries.' *Canadian Journal of Criminology*, Vol. 43, No. 4, pp. 429–48.

Krott, Rob. 2007. 'Honor and Guns: The Guns of Yemen.' *The Small Arms Review*, Vol. 10, No. 1, pp. 31–32. October.

Lally, Conor. 2006. 'For Hiring and Firing, It Is not Hard to Get a Gun.' *The Irish Times*. 13 March, p. 4.

LaPierre, Wayne. 2006. *The Global War on Your Guns: Inside the U.N. Plan to Destroy the Bill of Rights*. Nashville: Nelson Current.

Laurance, Edward and Rachel Stohl. 2002. *Making Global Public Policy: The Case of Small Arms and Light Weapons*. Occasional Paper No. 7. Geneva: Small Arms Survey. December.

Levitt, Steven D. and Stephen J. Dubner. 2006. *Freakonomics: A Rogue Economist Explores the Hidden Side of Everything*, revised ed. London: Penguin.

MacFarlane, Neil and Stina Torjesen. 2004. *Kyrgyzstan: A Small Arms Anomaly in Central Asia?* Occasional Paper No. 12. Geneva: Small Arms Survey.

Mack, Andrew. 2005. 'Why the Dramatic Decline in Armed Conflict?' In Andrew Mack, ed. *Human Security Report 2005*. Oxford: Oxford University Press.

Madayash, Arafat. 2007. 'The Arms Trade in Yemen.' *Asharq Al-Awsat* (London). 9 January.

Malcolm, Joyce Lee. 2002. *Guns and Violence: The English Experience*. Cambridge, Mass.: Harvard University Press.

Matthews, Jessica Tuchman. 1997. 'Power Shift.' *Foreign Affairs*, Vol. 76, No. 1. January–February, pp. 51–66.

McDonald, Henry. 2006. 'Gardai Make Record Haul of Firearms in 2006.' *The Guardian* (London and Manchester). 30 December.

Miller, Derek. 2003. 'Living with Weapons: Small Arms in Yemen.' In Small Arms Survey, ch. 5.

Mota, Maria Aparencida Rezende. 2006. 'The October 2005 Referendum: From Many Conquests to Unexpected Defeat.' In Maria Aparencida Rezende Mota and Samyra Crespo, eds. *Referendum from Yes to No: A Brazilian Democracy Experience*. ISER Communication No. 62. Rio de Janeiro: Instituto de Estudos da Religião. <http://www.smallarmssurvey.org/files/portal/spotlight/country/americas.html#bra>

Muchai, Augusta and Clare Jefferson. 2002. *Kenya Crime Survey 2000*. Nairobi: Security Research and Information Centre. June.

Muggah, Robert and Philip Alpers. 2003. *Reconsidering Small Arms in the Solomon Islands*. Geneva: Small Arms Survey. August.

Mulqueen, Michael. 2007. 'National Security Agencies in the EU's Fight against Terrorism: An Institutional Investigation of the Irish Case.' *Contemporary Security Policy*, Vol. 28, No. 2.

Munday, Richard. 1996. *Most Armed and Most Free?* Brightlingsea: Piedmont.

Murphy, Mathew. 2006. 'Election Deal Could Arm Victoria Police with Semi-automatic Handguns.' *The Age* (Melbourne). 15 November.

Mutter, Bettina. 2006. 'Entscheid über Munition ausgesetzt.' *Tages-Anzeiger* (Zurich). 19 September.

NORC (National Opinion Research Center). 1999. Web site. University of Chicago. <http://www2.norc.org/online/gunrpt.pdf>

O'Keeffe, Cormac and Senan Hogan. 2004. 'Tough Laws to Tackle Soaring Gun Crime.' *The Irish Examiner*. 27 October.

OSCE (Organization for Security and Co-operation in Europe). 2002. *Essential Elements of Export Control: Germany's Point of View on SALW*, Workshop on Implementation of the OSCE Document on SALW. FSC.DEL/78/02. Vienna: OSCE. 5 February.

Papacella, Daniele. 2004. 'Sale of Army Weapons Triggers Heated Debate.' SwissInfo. 14 October.

Pearton, Maurice. 1982. *Diplomacy, War and Technology since 1830*. Lawrence: University of Kansas Press.

Pescia, Marzio. 2006. 'Senate Backs Revision of Weapons Law: There Are no Precise Figures on the Number of Firearms in Circulation.' SwissInfo. 8 June.

PRC (Population Resource Center). 2004. *The Middle East and North Africa*. <http://www.prcdc.org/summaries/middleeast/>

ProTell. 2004. 'Waffenregistrierung: ein Rohrkrepierer von Frau Bundesrätin R. Metzler.' 20 January. <http://www.protell.ch/>

Rodengen, Jeffrey L. 2002. *NRA: An American Legend*. Fort Lauderdale: Write Stuff Enterprises.

Romania. 2003. *Report on Implementation of the United Nations Programme of Action to Prevent, Combat and Eradicate the Illicit Trade in Small Arms and Light Weapons (SALW) in All Its Aspects*. Bucharest: Ministry of Foreign Affairs. June.

Romir Monitoring. 2003. Cited in *International Firearms Trade*. 1 August, p. 9.

Schwandner-Sievers, Stephanie. 2005. '"Gun culture" in Kosovo: Questioning the Origins of Conflict.' In Small Arms Survey, ch. 8.

Singh, Jasjit. 1995. *Light Weapons and International Security*. New Delhi: Institute for Defence Studies and Analyses. December.

Sloss, Leon. 2001. 'The New Arms Race.' *The Washington Quarterly*, Vol. 24, No. 4. Autumn, pp. 135–47. <http://www.twq.com/01autumn/sloss.pdf>

Small Arms Survey. 2001. *Small Arms Survey 2001: Profiling the Problem*. Oxford: Oxford University Press.

——. 2002. *Small Arms Survey 2002: Counting the Cost*. Oxford: Oxford University Press.

——. 2003. *Small Arms Survey 2003: Development Denied*. Oxford: Oxford University Press.

——. 2004. *Small Arms Survey 2004: Rights at Risk*. Oxford: Oxford University Press.

——. 2005. *Small Arms Survey 2005: Weapons at War*. Oxford: Oxford University Press.

——. 2006. *Small Arms Survey 2006: Unfinished Business*. Oxford University Press.

Statistisches Bundesamt. 2003. 'Fachserie 4: Produzierendes Gewerbe.' Xerox of a page from a report of the German Federal Statistical Office attached to a letter to Peter Batchelor, then project director at the Small Arms Survey, from Col. Gerhard Schepe of the German General Staff, then at the German Mission to the UN Conference on Disarmament in Geneva, dated 6 August.

SwissInfo. 2005. 'Troops to Pay to Keep Latest Assault Rifle at Home.' 11 March.

——. 2006. 'High Gun Suicide Rate Linked to Easy Access.' 29 August.

Tertrais, Bruno. 2001. 'Do Arms Races Matter?' *The Washington Quarterly*, Vol. 24, No. 4. Autumn, pp. 123–33.

Tiahrt, Todd. 2004. Consolidated Appropriations Act of 2004, HR 2673 (Public Law 108-199). 23 January.

Tidningarnas Telegrambyrå. 2005. 'Three Gun Crimes a Day in Sweden.' *The Local*. 6 September.
<http://www.thelocal.se/article.php?ID=2032&date=20050906>

UK (United Kingdom). 2005. *UK Implementation and Support for the UN Programme of Action on SALW*. London: Foreign and Commonwealth Office.

UN (United Nations). 1998. *United Nations International Study on Firearms Regulation*. New York: UN.

——. 1999. *United Nations International Study on Firearms Regulation*, revised ed. New York: UN.

UNDP (United Nations Development Programme). 2002. *Arab Human Development Report 2002*. New York: UN.

UNSC (United Nations Security Council). 2006. *Report of the Monitoring Group on Somalia Pursuant to Security Council Resolution 1676 (2006)*. S/2006/913 of 22 November. New York: UN.

US ATF (United States Bureau of Alcohol, Tobacco and Firearms). 2000. *Commerce in Firearms in the United States*. Washington, DC: Department of the Treasury, Bureau of Alcohol, Tobacco and Firearms. February.

US ATFE (United States Bureau of Alcohol, Tobacco, Firearms and Explosives). 2003. *Annual Firearms Manufacturing and Export Report, Year 2001*. Washington, DC: US ATFE.

——. 2004. *Annual Firearms Manufacturing and Export Report, Year 2002*. Washington, DC: US ATFE.

——. 2005. *Annual Firearms Manufacturing and Export Report, Year 2003*. Washington, DC: US ATFE. 31 March.

——. 2006. *Annual Firearms Manufacturing and Export Report, Year 2004*. Washington, DC: US ATFE. 18 January.

UTV (Belfast). 2006. '1,000 more police to tackle guns.' 20 December. <http://www.utvlive.com/newsroom/indepth.asp?id=78745&pt=n>

VIP/Politika (Belgrade). 2006. 'Serbian Gun Maker Sells 15,000 Assault Rifles to Unnamed US Client.' 2 March.

Vonarburg, Verena. 2006. 'Ein Gewehr für 100 Franken und ohne Waffenschein.' *Tages-Anzeiger* (Zurich). 9 November.

VPC (Violence Policy Center). 2004. 'Violence Policy Center Issues Statement on Expiration of Federal Assault Weapons Ban.' 13 September.
<http://www.vpc.org/press/0409aw.htm>

Wellford, Charles F., et al. 2005. *Firearms and Violence: A Critical Review*. Washington DC: National Research Council and National Academies Press.

Wille, Christina and Keith Krause. 2005. 'Behind the Numbers: Small Arms and Conflict Deaths.' In Small Arms Survey, ch. 9.

Willems, Peter. 2004. 'Curbing the Proliferation of Guns.' *Yemen Times*. 1 November.

WRI (World Resources Institute). 2007. *EarthTrends: Yemen*. Washington, DC: WRI. 24 January.

Xiao, Guo. 2006. 'Illegal Trade in Guns Problem for Poorer Regions.' *China Daily*. 13 June.

Yemen Observer. 2005. 'Anti-gun Law to Be Approved after Protests.' 21 September.

Yemen Times. 2005. 'Ruling Party Votes in Favour of Debating Arms Control Law.' 21 March.

ZDF (Zweites Deutsches Fernsehen, Germany). 2006. 'Täter kaufte Waffen im Internet.' *ZDF Heute.de*. 22 November.
<http://www.heute.de/ZDFheute/inhalt/26/0,3672,4078458,00.html>

Zimring, Franklin E. 2003. 'Continuity and Change in the American Gun Debate.' In Jens Ludwig and Philip J. Cook, eds. *Evaluating Gun Policy: Effects on Crime and Violence*. Washington, DC: Brookings Institution Press, pp. 446–47.

ACKNOWLEDGEMENTS

Principal author

Aaron Karp

Weapons for sale in the Bakaraaha market in Mogadishu, Somalia, in May 2004. © Ibrahim Hassan/Reuters

Probing the Grey Area

IRRESPONSIBLE SMALL ARMS TRANSFERS

3

INTRODUCTION

Between August 2004 and July 2005 the US Department of Defense (DOD) authorized the purchase and transfer of about 200,000 AK-47-type assault rifles and tens of millions of rounds of ammunition from Bosnia and Herzegovina as aid to Iraqi government forces. While not illegal, this transaction has the hallmarks of an irresponsible transfer: weapons were shipped via private arms brokers into a context where the human rights situation had been steadily deteriorating and where the likelihood of diversion was high due to poor oversight and generally weak stockpile security (see below). This chapter examines how even such duly authorized small arms transfers can be considered illicit.

Most international efforts concerned with small arms and light weapons have focused on stemming the illicit trade in such weapons, but usage of the term 'illicit' varies. It is often taken to refer to something that is clearly illegal, i.e. prohibited by law. However, in a more precise reading, 'illicit' also describes an action that contravenes widely accepted social or moral standards, even if not technically illegal.[1] In such terms, illicit arms transfers thus include those transfers that are irresponsible, even though authorized by a government, in addition to those that are demonstrably illegal.

While some recent multilateral small arms control initiatives have provided definitions of 'illicit', none has explicitly equated it with 'irresponsible'. In some of these undertakings (e.g. the *UN Firearms Protocol* [UNGA, 2001a] and the *Inter-American Convention* [OAS, 1997]) the definition of 'illicit trafficking' includes transfers that lack authorization by any of the states involved. However, in most instruments—and most notably in the *UN Programme of Action* (UNGA, 2001b)—the term is not defined at all, and governments have taken divergent positions on whether state-authorized transfers of small arms should be included within the scope of negotiations (TRANSFER CONTROLS).

The central argument of this chapter is that authorized transfers of small arms, light weapons, and their ammunition are not necessarily either legal or responsible. Authorized transfers may contravene agreed international law, rules, and customs—including legal norms relating to respect for human rights or to international conflict. Transfers may also be irresponsible because of a heightened risk of diversion to unauthorized recipients.

The chapter draws particular attention to the responsibility states have to refrain from transferring weapons that are at risk of being misused, e.g. to commit human rights abuses or to violate international humanitarian law. Building upon analysis in the *Small Arms Survey 2004,* this chapter provides numerous examples of government-authorized transfers that can be considered irresponsible because the governments authorizing them knew (or should have known) of circumstances creating a significant risk of misuse (TRANSFER CONTROLS). The chapter also updates and fine-tunes the annual Small Arms Trade Transparency Barometer. Transparency by governments is imperative to help clarify whether their exports are in fact 'legal' or 'illicit'. This year's Barometer underlines that transparency remains poor in many countries, and the chapter points to possible areas for improvement.

Box 3.1   Definitions of key terms

The global market for small arms, light weapons, and their ammunition can be represented as two overlapping circles (see Figure 3.1).

Authorized transfers are transfers that are authorized by at least one government.

Irresponsible transfers, also called *grey market transfers,* are transfers that are authorized by a government, but are nevertheless of doubtful legality, at least with reference to international law (significant risk of misuse), or irresponsible in some other sense (significant risk of diversion to unauthorized recipients).

Illegal transfers are synonymous with *black market transfers.* Both terms refer to transfers that are not authorized by any government.

Illicit transfers comprise both *irresponsible* and *illegal* transfers (grey/black market).

Covert transfers are those in which governments hide their involvement—often, though not always, because they are illicit.

Among the main findings of the chapter are the following:

- At least 60 states made what could reasonably be interpreted as irresponsible small arms shipments to 36 countries during the period 2002–04.

- The diversions of up to several hundred thousand small arms transferred by the United States to Iraq and tens of thousands of rounds of ammunition from South African peacekeeping troops in Burundi demonstrate a clear need for greater accountability and safeguards to ensure that efforts to resolve conflicts do not inadvertently fuel conflict.

- UN arms embargoes, legally binding for all UN members, are routinely broken on a large scale and with impunity, as government-authorized, but covert, arms transfers in 2006 to Lebanon, Somalia, and Sudan clearly illustrate.

- The top exporters of small arms and light weapons (those with an annual export value of at least USD 100 million), according to available data and estimates in 2004—the last year for which global data is available—were the United States, Italy, Germany, Brazil, Austria, Belgium, and China. The top importers (those with an annual import value of at least USD 100 million) were the United States, Germany, Saudi Arabia, Egypt, France, and the Netherlands.[2]

- According to the 2007 Small Arms Trade Transparency Barometer, the most transparent major small arms exporters are the United States, France, Italy, Norway, the United Kingdom, and Germany. The least transparent are Bulgaria, North Korea, and South Africa.

Figure 3.1   Locating irresponsible transfers

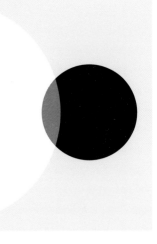

Large circle: authorized transfers

Small circle: illicit transfers

Overlap: irresponsible transfers/grey market

Black area: illegal transfers/black market

White area: legal transfers (authorized and responsible)

Note: This figure is not intended to express proportions.

IRRESPONSIBLE TRANSFERS I: HUMAN RIGHTS VIOLATIONS AND ARMED CONFLICT

The table in Annexe 1 lists small arms transfers reported for 61 exporting countries during the period 2002–04 to 36 countries where serious human rights violations and/or armed conflict were occurring (see also Annexe 2). In these contexts, there is a significant risk that transferred small arms, light weapons, and their ammunition will be misused. Using such criteria, one can therefore conclude that transfers to these countries during the specified years were not only ill-advised, but also illicit.

The rationale for using human rights and armed conflict criteria to assess responsible arms transfers is twofold. Firstly, serious human rights violations and armed conflict constitute the basis on which most UN arms sanctions are imposed. Mandatory UN sanctions legally bind all UN member states (UN, 1945, art. 25). Regional arms embargoes, and regional and international instruments—such as the European Union's (EU) *Code of Conduct* (EU, 1998) and the Wassenaar Arrangement's *Best Practice Guidelines* (WA, 2002)—employ similar criteria.[3] Moreover, key legal norms relating to human rights and the conduct of armed conflict have the status of customary international law, which is binding on all states (TRANSFER CONTROLS).

Secondly, small arms are often used to carry out or facilitate human rights violations. There is, in other words, a known risk that weapons transferred to countries with a record of serious human rights violations will be misused. Similarly, small arms play a central role in virtually all contemporary conflicts. Additional supplies of these weapons— along with their ammunition—often work against the goal of diminishing or ending armed conflict, instead fuelling, prolonging, or intensifying the fighting.

Available datasets, however, offer simplistic and imperfect proxies. Human rights conditions generally are not uniform across a country, and the existence of armed conflict is not necessarily an indication of misconduct. Moreover, small arms transfers can contribute to the ending of armed conflict and/or the self-defence of a threatened population. More specific information—including, for example, a dataset on violations of international humanitarian law—would improve the methodology employed here.[4]

Not all transfers to a country are equally risky. Information on the intended and actual recipient agency, as well as the intended and actual use of transferred weapons, would be necessary to fine-tune the risk analysis. However, when they have it, governments almost always withhold this information.[5] As a result, in many cases it is difficult to evaluate properly whether a government has in fact fulfilled its multilateral commitments. In order for governments to prove that they are *not* engaged in illicit small arms transfers when shipping to countries at higher than normal risk of misuse, they would have to publish more detailed information about such small arms transactions.

Given these caveats, this chapter uses a restrictive definition of 'serious human rights violations' and 'armed conflict' in an effort to exclude marginal cases from Annexe 1.

As in the *Small Arms Survey 2004* (pp. 127–33), the dataset used to determine serious human rights violations is the Political Terror Scale (PTS) (Gibney, 2006; Cornett and Gibney, 2003; Gibney and Dalton, 1996). The PTS examines reports published by Amnesty International and the US Department of State (DOS), both of which are widely acknowledged as credible sources on human rights.[6] These reports are coded and classified based on a scale from 1 to 5, with 5 corresponding to the most severe human rights violations. It is important to note that the PTS does not limit itself to human rights violations in the strict sense, i.e. those committed by governments, but generally assesses the human rights situation in a given country. Annexe 1 lists only small arms transfers to countries that appear in the PTS with a level of 4 or 5 for both Amnesty International and US DOS reports for the year preceding a particular transfer. Thus, only the two most severe levels of human rights violations are included here.[7]

Human rights violations and armed conflict bring forth most UN arms sanctions.

The chapter assigns the 'armed conflict' label to countries listed as involved in an 'active' conflict in the International Institute for Strategic Studies Armed Conflict Database (IISS, 2007) *and* at 'war' in the Uppsala Conflict Database (UCDP, 2007a) during the relevant period.[8] Therefore, some armed conflicts are not included because they did not reach this threshold.

Exporting governments are to explain how they aim to ensure that weapons will not be misused.

The small arms transfers data in Annexe 1 is based on small arms, light weapons, and ammunition categories in the United Nations Commodity Trade Statistics Database (UN Comtrade). UN Comtrade is the only existing global clearinghouse for this data, but it usually underestimates the actual scale of small arms transfers, since countries often under-report their transfers, and some do not report them at all.[9] (Covert transfers, by definition, do not appear in such sources.) For each country, Annexe 1 lists transfers for the year following one in which *either* serious human rights violations *or* active armed conflict was reported, ensuring that information on the human rights and/or armed conflict situation was widely available *before* a particular transfer was authorized. For both categories—human rights violations and armed conflict—only transfers during the years 2002–04 are included. 2004 is the most recent year for which global data from UN Comtrade was available at the time of writing.

Profiles of potentially irresponsible transfers

This section presents four brief case studies—drawn from Annexe 1—highlighting the well-known political, military, and human rights contexts into which governments introduced additional small arms, light weapons, and ammunition during the period 2002–04. All cases selected here appear in Annexe 1 because of their PTS (human rights) score. (Only a few countries appear in the table because of the armed conflict criterion alone.)

The four case studies presented here were chosen because they illuminate different aspects of the problems of illicit transfers, and because they raise questions that policy-makers and government officials must confront in considering whether to approve specific transfers. They are not the most egregious cases; rather, they are illustrative. They represent wide geographic distribution and different types of sociopolitical phenomena within which human rights violations are likely to worsen, including situations of prolonged insurgency and attempted coups.

In the case of Algeria, the use of civilian small arms such as shotguns and hunting rifles by armed groups in human rights violations has been documented for the mid-1990s, shortly before the period under consideration here. In Indonesia, armed conflict had begun to wane in the period 2002–04, while severe human rights violations by the government and the Free Aceh Movement (Gerakan Aceh Merdeka—GAM) continued. Israel appears in Annexe 1 not because of its conflict with Palestinian armed groups, but because of the human rights violations committed by both sides that are linked to that conflict.[10] Finally, the case study of Venezuela examines a situation of social unrest preceding and following the overthrow and reinstatement of the Chávez government in April 2002.

In each of these cases, there is not enough publicly available information to trace particular weapons shipments to particular end-using agencies (interior ministry, border control, military units). Therefore, these cases cannot conclusively demonstrate that the small arms transfers listed in Annexe 1 directly contributed to violations of the sort outlined in the case studies.

Rather, these cases invite policy-makers and the reader to consider whether such shipments are responsible, or whether they could or should in fact be considered to be irresponsible (i.e. authorized, but illicit). These cases also invite exporting governments to be more transparent in explaining the steps they have taken to ensure that weapons transferred into similar contexts are not misused.

Algeria

In 2001 Algeria was just emerging from a decade in which state security forces, state-armed militias, and Islamic militants killed well over 100,000 people. The violence was sparked by the government's decision in January 1992 to cancel Algeria's first multi-party election and ban the Islamic Salvation Front (Front Islamique du Salut—FIS), which was expected to win the election (US DOS, 2002). In the brutal fighting that ensued, the government security apparatus 'disappeared' as many as 7,000 people and engaged in widespread torture.[11] Militant Islamic groups brutalized both civilians and military targets. Through the end of 2004 there had been no independent or impartial investigation of the violence (AI, 2002a; 2005).

From 2001 to 2004, the state of emergency declared by the military in 1992 remained in effect (AI, 2005). During this period, according to the US DOS, Algerian security forces (army, national gendarmerie, national police, communal guards, and local self-defence forces) committed serious human rights abuses, including arbitrary arrests, long-term incommunicado detention, widespread torture, and unlawful killing. Almost 2,000 civilians, militants, and security force members died in 2001 during the ongoing turmoil (US DOS, 2002). Of these deaths, Amnesty International estimates that hundreds were civilians targeted or indiscriminately attacked by armed Islamic groups, hundreds were combatants killed in ambushes and armed confrontations, and dozens were civilians killed unlawfully by the security forces (AI, 2002a).

In the last of the categories, in 2001 security forces shot and killed more than 80 unarmed civilians and injured hundreds of others during demonstrations in Kabylia, a Berber-dominated region in the north-east of the country. The demonstrations—for greater cultural rights and economic opportunity—followed the death of a schoolboy held in custody by the gendarmerie in April 2001. According to accounts pieced together by Amnesty International, gendarmes 'fired on unarmed protesters standing more than 100 metres away from them and shot others in the back after dispersing them using tear gas. In several instances, protesters were pursued to their homes and shot dead inside' (AI, 2002a). A commission established by President Abdelaziz Bouteflika concluded that 'the gendarmerie and other security forces had repeatedly resorted to excessive use of lethal force' (AI, 2002a).[12] However, two years later there was no evidence that anyone had yet been brought to trial for these violations (AI, 2004b).

Despite such ongoing and openly acknowledged human rights violations, after the terrorist attacks in the United States of 11 September 2001 the United States and several EU members publicly endorsed Algeria's counter-terrorism policies and prepared to resume or increase weapons transfers to Algeria after several years of a 'de facto embargo' (AI, 2004b).[13]

Small arms shipments to Algeria recorded in Annexe 1 include mostly shotguns, hunting rifles, and associated ammunition (see Annexe 2). Amnesty International has documented the use of such weapons in attacks carried out by armed groups at the height of the terror in the mid-1990s (AI, 1997, p. 12). According to a journalistic account from the same time, it became very difficult for the Islamic militants to obtain firearms after Algerian authorities introduced strict regulations on villagers' possession of weapons, including those for hunting. Such guns had been one of the militants' main sources of firearms (Callies de Salies, 1997). Owing to their perceived security implications, as of 2003, the Ministry of Defence and National Security Directorate had to approve the importation of all hunting weapons (Wetzel, 2002).

Hunting rifles were used in attacks by armed groups in Algeria in the mid-1990s.

Indonesia

Since 1998 Indonesia has experienced armed uprisings in Timor-Leste, Papua, and Aceh. The situation in Aceh is examined here for the period 2001–03.[14]

The Aceh conflict began in the mid-1970s, when the Aceh/Sumatra National Liberation Front (ASNLF), also known as the GAM, declared independence. During the 1990s the Indonesian government made Aceh a 'Military Operations Zone'. This status ended in August 1998, but military operations resumed in January 1999 (Sukma, 2004, pp. 12–13).

Both the Indonesian security forces (military and police) and the armed pro-independence movement, the GAM, were responsible for grave human rights violations. In November and December 2000 members of the security forces carried out extrajudicial killings, torture, and cruel treatment of persons preparing a pro-independence rally in the province's capital, Banda Aceh. Human rights and political activists, humanitarian workers, and journalists were especially targeted by the Indonesian security forces. The GAM took hostages, burned public buildings, and carried out 'targeted killing[s] of suspected informers, government officials, civil servants and others with links to the Indonesian administration' (AI, 2004a, p. 6).[15]

In April 2001 large numbers of Indonesian security forces, including members of the paramilitary Police Mobile Brigade (Brimbo), were stationed in Aceh. Brimbo members had a reputation for having committed human rights violations in Aceh since 1999. Indonesian military were trained at the Kopassus (Special Forces Command) training centre in West Java before deployment to Aceh. Kopassus had been reported to have carried out grave human rights violations in Aceh, Papua (Irian Jaya), and East Timor (AI, 2001b, p. 1).

On 19 May 2003 a state of military emergency was declared in Aceh. Allegations of serious violations of human rights, 'including extrajudicial executions, "disappearances", arbitrary detention and torture' continued, but now

GAM (Free Aceh Movement) fighters patrol an area in Aceh Besar in Indonesia's Northern Sumatra province in January 2005. © Martin Adler/Panos Pictures

became much more difficult to confirm, since the province was practically closed to independent observers (AI, 2003a, p. 1).[16] In the following May (2004) a state of civil emergency was declared in Aceh, but 'military operations continued as before and human rights abuses [were] still being reported' (AI, 2004a, p. 3).

In 2002, 2003, and 2004, several countries, including some EU members and the United States, made significant sales of small arms to Indonesia, according to UN Comtrade. The weapons shipped included revolvers, pistols, and sporting and hunting weapons, as well as military weapons, including military firearms and small arms ammunition. From UN Comtrade data, it appears that in 2002 a smaller number of countries, including fewer Organization for Economic Co-operation and Development countries, exported small arms to Indonesia, but that in 2003 and 2004 the number of suppliers and the value of weapons increased, at a time when the human rights situation in Indonesia had not improved (see Annexe 2).

The overall context in Indonesia in 2001–2003 entailed a significant risk of misuse.

It is impossible to determine whether the weapons transfers reported to UN Comtrade were subsequently used to commit human rights violations. But the overall context entailed a significant risk of misuse, at least with regard to the weapons that were destined for the Indonesian military and police, i.e. military small arms and corresponding ammunition. This risk includes misuse by the Indonesian security forces, but also diversion from state stockpiles.

Israel

The second Palestinian Intifada (uprising) was under way when 22 governments listed in Annexe 1 decided to send Israel additional supplies of small arms and ammunition.

The current round of fighting began in September 2000. As in the 1987–91 Intifada, Palestinians threw stones and Molotov cocktails at Israeli soldiers, but this time Palestinian groups also used the arsenal of small arms they had acquired. In addition, Palestinian suicide bombers undertook dozens of attacks against civilian targets in Israel each year. The Israeli military responded with heavy weaponry (gun, rocket, and missile fire from helicopters and armoured vehicles) and also with rubber-coated metal bullets and regular ammunition. According to Amnesty International, Israeli security forces killed more than 460 Palestinians during 2001, among them many children. Palestinian armed groups killed 187 Israelis in 2001, nearly all of them civilians (AI, 2002b).

In 2002, many governments shipped small arms and ammunition to Israel even though civil society organizations, based in Israel and elsewhere, accused Israeli military forces of having committed serious violations of international humanitarian law during Operation Defensive Shield, conducted in the Palestinian territories in March–April 2002 (B'tselem, 2002; HRW, 2002).[17] In the same year, the Israel Defense Forces (IDF) killed at least 1,000 Palestinians, including at least 35 through targeted assassination. At the same time, Palestinian armed groups killed more than 420 Israelis, more than half of them civilians, and some 20 foreign nationals (AI, 2003b).

According to the US DOS, in 2003 'Israel's overall human rights record in the occupied territories remained poor and worsened in the treatment of foreign human rights activists as it continued to commit numerous, serious human rights abuses' (US DOS, 2004).[18] About 570 Palestinians were killed and about 3,000 injured by security forces in 2003, including innocent bystanders. Among the intended and unintended victims were 44 Palestinians targeted for assassination by Israel, 'many of whom were terrorists or suspected terrorists', and 47 bystanders. Moreover, '[t]he IDF did not regularly investigate the actions of security force members who killed and injured Palestinians under suspicious circumstances' (US DOS, 2004).

Throughout this period, both Amnesty International and the US DOS reported widespread police brutality, torture of Palestinians during interrogation, and collective punishment, including the closures of towns and villages, the demolition of homes, and prolonged curfews. The US DOS noted that in 2003 (as in 2002) the Government of Israel detained without charge thousands of persons in Israel, the West Bank, and Gaza (US DOS, 2004). Amnesty International found that in 2003 '[c]ertain abuses committed by the Israeli army constituted war crimes, including unlawful killings, obstruction of medical assistance and targeting of medical personnel, extensive and wanton destruction of property, torture and the use of "human shields"' (AI, 2004c).

Venezuela

Following the election of Hugo Chávez—a populist leftist—to Venezuela's presidency in 1998, opposition from business leaders mounted. On 9 April 2002 this animosity resulted in a call by leaders of the business-backed labour confederation for an indefinite national strike to demand that Chávez step down. Two days later, opposition demonstrators marched towards the presidential palace in Caracas and encountered pro-Chávez demonstrators. Unidentified persons fired into the crowd. In the ensuing melee, demonstrators, the Metropolitan Police, and the National Guard clashed, as a result of which 20 people were killed by firearms and more than 60 were injured (AI, 2003c; US DOS, 2003a).

On 12 April 2002 business leaders and elements of the military staged a coup, claiming that Chávez had voluntarily resigned (US DOS, 2003a). The coup government closed the National Assembly and dismissed the Supreme Court, the attorney general, and the human rights ombudsman. Police raided the homes of a number of Chávez's supporters and detained a minister and a National Assembly deputy (AI, 2003c).

Facing widespread condemnation when it became clear that Chávez had in fact been kidnapped and forcibly overthrown, the new government resigned two days later, on 14 April, and Chávez was reinstated. At least 50 people died and many more were injured in the civil unrest during those days (AI, 2003c).

In the aftermath, efforts to end the political crisis included an intervention by the secretary-general of the Organization of American States. A second general strike started by the opposition at the end of 2002 carried on into the new year. Grass-roots community groups threatening and carrying out attacks against journalists, and others close to the political opposition, were alleg-

Venezuelan police officers arrest a supporter of President Hugo Chávez during clashes in Caracas, in April 2002.
© Pedro Rey/AP Photo

edly armed by Chávez.[19] Deep social and political cleavages remained, and the potential for armed violence in 2003 was high (AI, 2003c; US DOS, 2003a).

It is into this context that a number of countries shipped revolvers, pistols, rifles, shotguns, and shotgun cartridges in 2003 (see Annexes 1 and 2). The largest suppliers of small arms and their ammunition to Venezuela were South Korea, Brazil, Italy, Spain, Austria, and—most curiously—the United States. Since entering office in January 2001, the Bush Administration had opposed Chávez's government, and the US DOS initially refused to condemn the 2002 coup (AP, 2002). But the US firearms shipments apparently went to agents of the government: in 1999, the Clinton Administration had stopped transfers of small arms to Venezuelan private companies due to concerns about possible diversion to combatants in neighbouring Colombia. The licensing of small arms exports to Venezuela resumed in 2002—but only to government buyers (Ceaser, 2005).

In an indication that at least some of the weapons shipments were not going to the central government, the minister of justice and the interior, Jesse Chacon, announced the establishment in July 2006 of a new firearms control plan. This initiative was necessitated, according to the Venezuelan Ministry of Justice, by the large influx of weaponry into Venezuela during the 2000–02 political crisis and the subsequent high level of armed violence in the country (Fox, 2006).[20]

IRRESPONSIBLE TRANSFERS II: STOCKPILE (IN)SECURITY AND RISK OF DIVERSION

It is irresponsible to transfer arms if there is a significant risk that they will be misused by the intended recipient, given the environment into which they are being sent. It is also irresponsible to transfer arms that are at risk of being diverted away from the intended recipient and misused by third parties. Presented here are two recent examples of states undertaking small arms transfers as part of peace-building or nation-building operations in which the transfers may have contributed to the armed violence they were intended to quell: US-sponsored small arms supply to Iraq and leakage from South African peacekeepers' stockpiles in Burundi.

US small arms to Iraq: missing in action

Following the fall of Saddam Hussein's government in April 2003, the Iraqi military lost most of the small arms it previously held, leading to at least seven to eight million firearms being in Iraqi hands (combined civilian holdings and military stockpile) (Small Arms Survey, 2004, pp. 44–47). At the same time, there was a dramatic rise in firearm violence, including abductions and murder by insurgents, militias, or criminal elements. According to a comprehensive survey in 2006, gunshots have been the leading cause of violent death in Iraq since the 2003 invasion (Burnham et al., 2006, p. 2).[21] Civilians now routinely arm themselves for protection, and prices for firearms are climbing, even as supplies increase (Chivers, 2006) (ECONOMICS).

Within this context, the United States has sought to train and equip with new weaponry approximately 325,500 Iraqi Security Forces (ISF) personnel in the Iraqi Ministries of Defence (MOD) and the Interior (MOI) by December 2006 (SIGIR, 2006a, p. i).[22] Two separate investigations have found serious deficiencies on the part of the United States in safeguarding weapons brought into Iraq. According to these investigations, thousands, if not tens of thousands, of imported small arms have been diverted from Iraqi police and military forces.

Table 3.1 **Number and % of violent deaths in surveyed households in Iraq attributable to gunshots, 2002–06**

	Pre-invasion (January 2002– March 2003)	March 2003– April 2004	May 2004– May 2005	June 2005– June 2006	Total post-invasion
Deaths from gunshots	0	36 (80%)	46 (51%)	87 (53%)	169 (56%)
Total violent deaths	2	45	90	165	300

Source: Burnham et al. (2006, p. 8, Table 2)

The Iraqi arms market

The US DOD invited bids for contracts to supply small arms to Iraq in late 2003 and again in late 2004. Given the familiarity of Iraqi personnel with the AK-47 and the weapon's durability, most US procurement has been of this weapon. Additionally, most of the US procurement calls for new (or unused) weapons (SIGIR, 2006a, pp. 4, 6). The bidders were primarily small logistics firms specializing in the procurement of non-standard (non-NATO) weapons or in transfers of arms to the Middle East. Among the companies winning US DOD contracts were Keisler Police Supply, Taos Industries,[23] Golden Wings, ANHAM Joint Venture, AEY, Inc., Defense Logistics Services, and Blane International (SIGIR, 2006b, Appendix D).

In addition, in February 2005 the US Army awarded a firm-fixed-price contract worth USD 174 million to International Trading Establishment (ITE) of Amman, Jordan for radios, heavy and light machine guns, AK-47 rifles, M4 shotguns, 9 mm handguns, and night vision goggles (US DOD, 2005).[24] Under a USD 29.3 million sub-contract, ITE hired the Beijing-based firm Poly Technologies to deliver 2,369 light and heavy machine guns, 14,653 AK-47 rifles, and 72 million rounds of ammunition by 30 April 2005 (Landay, 2005).

A significant portion of the funding for US-supplied small arms purchases has come from the Iraq Relief and Reconstruction Fund

An Iraqi gunsmith checks an imported gun at his shop in the central Iraqi city of Najaf in August 2006. On the table, imported assault rifles lie beside an Iraqi-made short assault rifle. © Ali Al-Saadi/AFP/Getty Images

Table 3.2 **ISF weapons purchased with IRRF funds, November 2003-April 2005, by type**			
Type of weapon	**Total**	**MOD**	**MOI**
Under-barrel grenade launcher	3,900	0	3,900
Rocket-propelled grenade launcher, RPG-7	1,528	100	1,428
Machine gun, M-2 .50 calibre	12	12	0
Machine gun, MP-5	518	0	518
Machine gun, PKM	5,221	1,170	4,051
Machine gun, RPK	14,982	6,310	8,672
Pistol 9 mm generic 9 mm Glock	 38,053 138,813	 15,329 13,650	 22,724 125,163
Assault rifle, AK-47	165,409	71,493	93,916
Assault rifle, M1-F	751	751	0
Assault rifle, M4	620	320	300
Shotgun	384	10	374
Sniper rifle	60	0	60
Total	**370,251**	**109,145**	**261,106**

Source: SIGIR (2006a, p. 4)

(IRRF), to which the US Congress assigned USD 18.4 billion (US Congress, 2003, pp. 1225–26).[25] In October 2006 the office of the Special Inspector General for Iraq Reconstruction (SIGIR) published an audit of US small arms procured with these funds, with special attention to the ISF's ability to safeguard and maintain the weapons. According to the report, since November 2003 the US DOS used about USD 133 million from the IRRF to acquire more than 370,000 weapons.[26] All of the weapons purchased for the ISF with these funds were small arms and light weapons, defined in the audit as 'man-portable, individual, and crew-served weapons systems used mainly against personnel and lightly armored or unarmored equipment.' Of the 12 types of weapon purchased, most prevalent were 9 mm semi-automatic pistols (nearly 80 per cent of these were Glocks) and AK-47 assault rifles (SIGIR, 2006a, pp. 2–4).

The audit revealed concerns about the Multi-National Security Transition Command-Iraq (MNSTC-I)—the military body responsible for recruiting, training, and equipping the ISF—in relation to small arms procurement and stockpile security practices. According to the report, the MNSTC-I exhibited 'questionable accuracy' regarding its arms inventories. In particular, the MNSTC-I was unable to account for 99 machine guns, more than 13,000 9 mm pistols, and 751 M1-F assault rifles.[27] Moreover, the command has systematically failed to comply with the requirement that it register the serial numbers of all weapons procured for the ISF in the DOD Small Arms Serialization Program (SASP) (SIGIR, 2006a, pp. 8–10).[28]

Only 2 of the 19 contracts for weapons funded by the IRRF specified that contractors provide serial numbers to the SASP. Overall, the MNSTC-I had recorded serial numbers for only 2 per cent of the more than 500,000 weapons provided from all funding sources to MOI or MOD personnel and/or warehoused (SIGIR, 2006a, pp. 9–10).

Box 3.2 **Coming soon: M16s for Iraq**

In late September 2006 the US Defense Security Cooperation Agency notified Congress of an intended sale of USD 750 million worth of weaponry to the Iraqi government, including more than 120,000 new small arms and light weapons (*Federal Register,* 2006, pp. 56501–07). The sales proposal included the following:

- 10,126 M17 9 mm Glock pistols
- 50,750 M16A2 rifles
- 50,750 M4A1 rifles
- 3,442 M24 sniper rifles
- 8,105 M249 machine guns
- 3,037 M240B machine guns
- more than 2 million rounds of 9 mm pistol ammunition
- more than 35 million rounds of 5.56 mm rifle ammunition
- more than 630 thousand rounds of 7.62 mm sniper rifle ammunition
- more than 1.6 million rounds of 5.56 mm machine gun ammunition
- more than 1.2 million rounds of M240 7.62 mm crew-served machine gun ammunition

Source: Federal Register (2006, p. 56503)

The failure of US forces to record serial numbers makes sense only as a hedge against public revelations that US-supplied weapons are falling into the hands of insurgents. Both the Iraqi military and police forces have been infiltrated by insurgents and suffer from high levels of corruption. The Iraq Police Service, in particular, lacks an effective equipment management system and an effective personnel management system (US DOD, 2006, p. 51).[29] Theft of pistols has been a particular problem (Chivers, 2006).

The Bosnian pipeline

Despite the US DOD's general requirement that newly manufactured AK rifles be procured for the ISF, at least one large exception was made.

In May 2006 Amnesty International reported US-funded shipments of more than 200,000 AK-variant assault rifles and tens of millions of rounds of ammunition from Bosnia and Herzegovina to Iraq during 2004–05. The report is based on information received from the EU Force in Bosnia and Herzegovina (better known as EUFOR), the Organisation for Security and Co-operation in Europe (OSCE), and the UN Office of the High Representative in Bosnia. According to these sources, the US military quietly negotiated with Bosnian government authorities for the purchase of surplus weapons that were stockpiled and slated to be destroyed. The deal undermined an ongoing British government-backed programme to destroy surplus weapons and ammunition remaining from the Bosnian civil war, because local citizens grew reluctant to give up their war weapons, believing that they might be able to sell them to the Americans (AI, 2006, pp. 104–17; Traynor, 2006).

The UN High Representative in Bosnia tried to stop the deal, and in late August 2005 a moratorium on further arms exports was finally put in place. According to Major Erwin Kauer, a NATO military officer who worked in Bosnia handling authorizations for arms transfers, up to 290,000 small arms and 64 million rounds of ammunition were shipped out before the moratorium was enacted. He said 60–70 per cent of these weapons were destined for Iraq (BBC, 2006a, pp. 6–7).

According to Amnesty International's research, a small US logistics firm—Taos Industries—was the party that was actually contracted to coordinate the shipping of the weapons, with diplomatic support from US officials (Taos had

Box 3.3 **Gun count: US-supplied small arms**	
Poly Technologies (AKs, machine guns)	17,000
Bosnia-Herzegovina pipeline (AKs)	200,000
IRRF-funded (AKs, Glocks, other)	370,000
Future deal announced in Sept. 2006 (M16s, Glocks, other)	126,000
Total	**713,000**

Sources: Landay (2005); Traynor (2006); SIGIR (2006a, p. 4); Federal Register (2006, p. 56503)

several contracts funded through the IRRF). The weapons were then moved via a chain of transport sub-contractors, at least one of which had been named in UN sanctions reports as having been involved in arms smuggling in the past. Although 'Coalition Forces in Iraq' were listed as the official end users on the Bosnian export documents for five shipments of arms, the MNSTC-I was unaware of any arms purchases from Bosnia. Amnesty International was unable to find any evidence that the weapons actually arrived in Iraq (AI, 2006, pp. 109–10).

Unintended consequences: South African peacekeepers and the leakage of weapons and ammunition in Burundi[30]

Public inquiry into the accounting of the South African National Defence Force (SANDF) and a recent journalistic investigation of the SANDF's lack of control over its military equipment while performing peacekeeping duties in Burundi have raised questions about the possible contribution of South Africa to small arms proliferation in a country that is emerging from a ten-year civil war.

The 2005/2006 report of the South African auditor-general found major irregularities in the accounting of the South African Defence Department. In particular, it established that the SANDF had not ensured proper storage, security, and accounting of its vehicles, weapons, and ammunition. Such statements were not without a precedent: the previous report (2004/2005) assessed the total cost of lost defence property at ZAR 48.7 million (USD 7.6 million). The South African Parliament requested some clarification from the Defence Department about the fate of the 70 army vehicles, over 110 weapons, and large quantities of other material reported to be missing. Most, if not all, of this missing material belonged to the South African contingent of the United Nations Operation in Burundi (ONUB) (Maughan, 2006a).[31]

A parallel investigation led by a South African newspaper, *The Star*, supports the results of the report. At the end of October 2006 it claimed that 'millions of rands worth of vehicles, guns, ammunition and bombs, and supplies worth over R27-million have vanished from the South African army base in Burundi over the last four years' (Maughan, 2006a).[32] The newspaper listed 40 mortar bombs, 54 R4 rifles, 4 R5 rifles, a sniper rifle, two 12-gauge shotguns, 8 machine guns, 8 pistols, and 27 grenade launchers, as well as ammunition, vehicles, and other matériel, as missing (Maughan, 2006a).

The South African minister of defence, Mosiuoa Lekota, admitted in September 2006 that some small arms and ammunition had been captured during ambushes and stolen in Burundi, including 22,000 rounds of ammunition seized in a single incident at the SANDF base (Maughan, 2006a; SAPA, 2006a; 2006b). He also admitted that South African peacekeeping missions in Burundi, Sudan, and the Democratic Republic of the Congo had since 2003 lost 97 mortar bombs, 46 assault rifles (R4s), 3 light machine guns, two 9 mm pistols, 2 grenades, 4 magazines for R4

Box 3.4   Missing in action: SANDF weapons in Burundi

The following weapons were reported missing:

- almost 50,000 rounds of ammunition
- 97 mortars
- 46 R4 rifles
- 4 R4 magazines
- 3 light machine guns
- 2 pistols (9 mm)
- 2 grenades

Source: South African Ministry of Defence, cited in Maughan (2006a)

---

rifles, and close to 50,000 rounds of 5.56 mm and 7.62 mm calibre ammunition. The minister vehemently contested *The Star*'s higher figures and denied allegations about missing vehicles (Maughan, 2006a; SAPA, 2006b).

As to the destination of this matériel, *The Star* claims that a number of the missing mortar rounds found their way into the arsenal of the Parti de libération du peuple hutu-Forces nationales de libération (Palipehutu-FNL), the only rebel group that did not take part in the ceasefire and peace process that led in 2005 to the democratic election of a new president, Pierre Nkurunziza (Maughan, 2006a) (BURUNDI).

Already in July 2004, the Burundian army had seized South African-made ammunition from Palipehutu-FNL rebels, and it identified some of the mortar rounds launched by the group on Kabezi as having been manufactured in South Africa. In November 2005 in Bujumbura the army arrested other Palipehutu-FNL members wearing uniforms from the South African contingent (IRIN, 2005).

The Palipehutu-FNL was not the only alleged recipient of the missing material: according to *The Star*, some of the missing South African ammunition was found in 2004 in the arsenal of the Burundian army (Maughan, 2006a). Burundian authorities forcefully denied these allegations. Serge Nizigama, communication adviser at the Burundian Ministry of Defence, noted that military material was procured through official channels, and that the alleged transfer of ammunition would have necessitated the knowledge and direct participation of the South African Defence Ministry (Burundi Réalités, 2006).

More recently, South African Defence Minister Lekota claimed that the missing material was not, in fact, missing, but instead the result of confusion in accounting during the rotation of contingents in Burundi (Dawes and Dibetle, 2006; SABC News, 2006).[33] A knowledgeable source, contacted by the Small Arms Survey, confirmed, however, that military equipment had been lost, adding that the report by *The Star* was broadly accurate.[34]

TRANSPARENCY

Past editions of the *Small Arms Survey* (Small Arms Survey, 2004; 2005; 2006) emphasized the importance of transparency on the part of governments exporting small arms, light weapons, and their ammunition. Transparency is a hallmark of responsible arms exporting; however, it is not the only one. As explored above, respect for norms concerning armed conflict and human rights, as well as basic precautions to secure transferred arms against diversion, are also necessary. When transferring arms or ammunition to a 'high risk' destination, governments need to be highly transparent about their actions, i.e. about whom they are authorizing to receive weapons, for what purpose, and under what conditions. Otherwise, exporting governments risk observers coming to the (perhaps erroneous) conclusion that such arms transfers are illicit.

In addition to providing a revision and update of the annual Small Arms Trade Transparency Barometer, this section profiles some of the ways in which governments can appear to be transparent while actually obfuscating small arms transfers.

For instance, as presented below, exporters might provide selective and, therefore, misleading data to UN Comtrade—perhaps to create an appearance that they are in compliance with export guidelines concerning human rights and armed conflict, when in fact they are not. Or governments might be quite transparent about *most* of their arms trade, except for that portion that is deliberately cloaked in secrecy.

In such cases, not only does the government in question withhold data about these covert transfers from UN Comtrade and other reporting mechanisms, but it also actively hides its involvement in the weapons shipments— usually by sourcing weapons abroad, using off-budget funding sources, and/or employing private brokers to move the weapons.

Small Arms Trade Transparency Barometer

The Small Arms Trade Transparency Barometer was introduced in *Small Arms Survey 2004*. It is a tool to assess countries' transparency in reporting on their small arms and light weapons exports, in particular with respect to aspects such as timeliness, accessibility, clarity, and comprehensiveness. It is based on governments' reports to UN Comtrade, as well as their annual national arms export reports.[35]

The 2007 Barometer includes transparency scores for all major exporters during the period 2001–04.[36] The maximum score is 25 points. The most transparent arms exporters are, in descending order, the United States, France, Italy, Norway, the United Kingdom, and Germany (all scoring more than 15 points). The least transparent are Bulgaria, North Korea, and South Africa, all scoring zero.

While the scores remain, in large part, comparable with those in the 2006 Barometer, this year's Barometer introduces a few modifications aimed at improving the methodology. Firstly, the scoring system was refined by including only those national arms export reports that have been published within the last 30 months.[37] As a result, the transparency of Canada and South Africa was assessed only on the basis of these countries' reporting to UN Comtrade, even if they did issue a national arms export report at some point previously. In addition, a new sub-category was added under the category 'Comprehensiveness' to account for information provided on re-exports. Only a very small number of states have provided such information to date.[38]

Governments can appear transparent while actually obfuscating small arms transfers.

It is also important to note that the Barometer does not assess the veracity of the information reported by governments. Doing so is difficult and better approached through case study research, as in the sections that follow. These case studies show that the Barometer captures only part of the picture, e.g. the United States is ranked as the most transparent country this year, even while it engaged in covert transfers (see below). Nevertheless, the Barometer remains useful for assessing the quality of states' public reporting in terms of specific categories such as accessibility and comprehensiveness. It shows that transparency is lacking in some of these categories even for the most transparent major exporters, and that their reporting needs to be improved. It also sets a reporting standard for smaller exporters.

Table 3.3 Small Arms Trade Transparency Barometer 2007, covering major exporters*

	TOTAL (25 max.)	Export report (year covered)	UN Comtrade	Timeliness (1.5 max.)	Access (2 max.)	Clarity (5 max.)	Comprehensiveness (6.5 max.)	Deliveries (4 max.)	Licences granted (4 max.)	Licences refused (2 max.)
United States	**20.5**	X (05)	X	1.5	2	4	5.5	3.5	4	0
France	**18.5**	X (04)	X	1	2	4	5.5	4	2	0
Italy	**17.5**	X (04)	X	1.5	1.5	4	6.5	3	1	0
Norway	**15.5**	X (05)	X	1.5	1.5	3.5	6	3	0	0
United Kingdom	**15.5**	X (05)	X	1	2	4	5.5	3	0	0
Germany	**15.25**	X (05)	X	1	1.5	4	4.75	2	2	0
Finland	**14**	X (03)	X	0.5	2	4	5.5	2	0	0
Netherlands	**14**	X (04)	X	1	2	2.5	5.5	3	0	0
Spain[1]	**13.75**	X (02–04)	X	1.5	2	2.5	4.75	3	0	0
Czech Republic	**13.5**	X (04)	X	1	2	3	5.5	2	0	0
Austria[2]	**13**	X (04)	X	0	1.5	2.5	5	2	2	0
Sweden	**12.75**	X (05)	X	1.5	2	3	4.25	2	0	0
Australia	**12.5**	X (02–04)	X	0.5	2	2.5	4.5	3	0	0
Switzerland	**12.5**	X (05)	X	1.5	2	2.5	4.5	2	0	0
Bosnia-Herzegovina	**12**	X (04)	X	1.5	1.5	2.5	4.5	2	0	0
Canada[3]	**11**	–	X	0	1	2.5	4.5	3	0	0
Croatia	**11**	–	X	0	1	2.5	4.5	3	0	0

Iran	10.5	–	X	0	1	2.5	4	3	0	0
Mexico	10.5	–	X	0	1	2.5	4	3	0	0
Portugal	10.25	X (04)	X	0.5	1.5	2.5	3.75	2	0	0
Serbia and Montenegro[4]	9.75	–	X	0	1	2.25	4.5	2	0	0
Brazil	9.5	–	X	0	1	2.5	3	3	0	0
China	9.5	–	X	0	1	2.5	3	3	0	0
South Korea	9.5	–	X	0	1	2.5	4	2	0	0
Turkey	9.5	–	X	0	1	2.5	4	2	0	0
Belgium[5]	9	–	X	0	1	2.5	3.5	2	0	0
Japan	8.5	–	X	0	1	2.5	3	2	0	0
Pakistan	8.5	–	X	0	1	2.5	2	3	0	0
Singapore	8	–	X	0	1	2.5	1.5	3	0	0
Thailand	8	–	X	0	1	2.5	2.5	2	0	0
Russian Federation	6.5	–	X	0	1	2	1.5	2	0	0
Saudi Arabia	6.5	–	X	0	1	1.5	2	2	0	0
Romania	5.5	X (02)	X	0.5	2	2	1	0	0	0
Israel	5	–	X	0	1	1	1	2	0	0
Bulgaria	0	–	–	0	0	0	0	0	0	0
North Korea	0	–	–	0	0	0	0	0	0	0
South Africa[6]	0	–	–	0	0	0	0	0	0	0

* Major exporters are those countries that export at least USD 10 million worth of small arms, light weapons, and their ammunition annually, according to UN Comtrade data. The 2007 Barometer includes all countries that were among the major exporters at least once in their reporting covering the years 2001–04. For major exporters in 2004, see Annexe 3 to the present chapter at <http://www.smallarmssurvey.org/yearb2007.html>; for those in 2003, see Small Arms Survey (2006, pp. 68–73); for those in 2002, see Small Arms Survey (2005, pp. 102–5); for those in 2001, see Small Arms Survey (2004, pp. 103–6).

Scoring system

(a) **Timeliness (1.5 points total, score based on national arms export reports data only):** A report has been published within the last 24 months (up to 31 January 2007) (0.5 points); information is available in a timely fashion (alternatively: 1 point if within 6 months of the end of the year in question, or 0.5 if within a year).

(b) **Access (2 points total):** Information is: available on Internet through UN Comtrade (1 point); available in a UN language (0.5 points); free of charge (0.5 points).

(c) **Clarity (5 points total):** The reporting includes source information (1 point); small arms and light weapons distinguishable from other types of weapons (1 point); small arms and light weapons ammunition distinguishable from other types of ammunition (1 point); detailed weapons description included (1 point); reporting includes information on types of end users (military, police, other security forces, civilians, civilian retailers) (1 point).

(d) **Comprehensiveness (6.5 points total):** The reporting covers: government-sourced as well as industry-sourced transactions (1 point); civilian and military small arms and light weapons (1.5 points); information on re-exports (1 point); information on small arms and light weapons parts (1 point); information on small arms and light weapons ammunition (1 point); summaries of export laws and regulations, and international commitments (1 point).

(e) **Information on deliveries (4 points total):** Data disaggregated by weapons type (value of weapons shipped [1 point], quantity of weapons shipped [1 point]), and by country and weapons type (value of weapons shipped [1 point], quantity of weapons shipped [1 point]).

(f) **Information on licences granted (4 points total):** Data disaggregated by weapons type (value of weapons licensed [1 point], quantity of weapons licensed [1 point]), and by country and weapons type (value of weapons licensed [1 point], quantity of weapons licensed [1 point]).

(g) **Information on licences refused (2 points total):** Data disaggregated by weapons type (value of licence refused [0.5 points], quantity of weapons under refused licence [0.5 points]), and by country and weapons type (value of licence refused [0.5 points], quantity of weapons under refused licence [0.5 points]).

Note 1: The Barometer is based on each country's most recent arms exports that were publicly available as of 31 January 2007 and/or on 2004 customs data from UN Comtrade.

Note 2: Under (e), (f), and (g) no points are granted for number of shipments or number of licences granted or denied, as such figures give little information about the magnitude of the trade. The data is disaggregated by weapons type if the share of small arms and light weapons in the country's total arms trade is delineated (x per cent of the total value of the arms exports consisted of small arms and light weapons; x number of small arms and light weapons were exported in total). The data is disaggregated both by country and by weapons type if there is information on the types of weapons that are transferred to individual recipient states (x numbers/x USD worth of small arms was delivered to country y).

Note 3: Under (e), (f), and (g), 'weapons type' means broader weapons categories (i.e. 'small arms' as opposed to 'armoured vehicles' or 'air-to-air missiles'), not specific weapons descriptions ('assault rifles' as opposed to 'hunting rifles').

Note 4: The fact that the Barometer is based on two sources—customs data (as reported to UN Comtrade) and national arms export reports—works to the advantage of states that publish data in both forms, since what they do not provide in one form of reporting they might provide in the other. Points achieved from each source of the two sources are added up. However, points are obviously not counted twice (e.g. if a country provides both customs data and export reports in a UN language, it gets 1 point for this under 'access', not more).

[1] Spain makes public its report on small arms and light weapons exports to the OSCE as an annexe to its arms export report. The report contains information both on licences granted (volumes by country and weapons type) and on actual deliveries (also volumes by country and weapons type). It covers only the OSCE states, and hence a very limited number of transactions. Spain is therefore granted only part of the points on licences and deliveries. Other states make their OSCE reports public, but separately from the arms export reports. These are therefore not taken into account in the Barometer.

[2] Austria's national arms export report (Austria, 2006) is a republication of the data it submitted for publication in the EU Annual Report covering 2004 exports (EU, 2005).

[3] Canada's most recent national arms export report (Canada, 2003) was published before the cut-off date for the 2007 Barometer.

[4] The 2007 Barometer covers reporting before Montenegro's independence in June 2006 (BBC, 2006b).

[5] Belgium has not published any national arms export reports since 2002, because export control was regionalized in September 2003 (for details, see Wallonia, 2004, pp. 3–12). The score is therefore based on customs data submissions only.

[6] South Africa's most recent national arms export report (South Africa, 2003) was published before the cut-off date for the 2007 Barometer.

Sources: Australia (2006); Austria (2006); Bosnia-Herzegovina (2005); Czech Republic (2005); Finland (2004); France (2005); Germany (2006); Italy (2005); Netherlands (2005); NISAT (2007a, 2007b); Norway (2006); Portugal (2006); Romania (2005); Spain (2006); Sweden (2006); Switzerland (2006); UK (2006); UN Comtrade (2007); US (2006)

Off the books: covert arms supplies

Countries considered highly transparent about their arms transfers in general may, at the same time, be providing military aid via covert operations, which, by definition, they do not report publicly. For instance, the United States—often described as a model of transparency in terms of its reporting on weapons authorizations and shipments (in the 2007 Barometer it receives the highest total score of 20.5)—has a long tradition of covert arms supply.[39] The US government (through the Central Intelligence Agency–CIA) has recently engaged in a covert arms supply operation in at least one country in furtherance of its global 'war on terrorism' (see below).[40]

The United States is by no means the only state to authorize covert arms supply operations. Such programmes have been a frequent component of the foreign policy of large countries and small, driven as often by short-term internal domestic political or economic pressures as by grand geopolitical goals. Most frequently, these goals include:

- the harassment, destabilization, or overthrow of the government in the recipient country by arming insurgent forces (usually, but not always, in a neighbouring country);[41]
- arms supply to an ally under a UN or regional embargo for political reasons; and
- arms supply to a state or non-state entity under a UN or regional embargo purely for commercial reasons (cash or natural resource concession).

Covert authorized arms transfers are in a legal limbo: they include fully legal shipments and legally questionable shipments, such as arms supply authorized by an exporting government, but against the wishes of the government where the weapons are being sent. Specific covert arms supply operations may also be illegal under either domestic or international law, or simply subject to domestic policy or public opinion constraints.

Whatever the case, governments go to great lengths to move weapons to combatants while masking their identity as suppliers. In so doing, they foster complex logistical, political, and economic networks—often including intelligence agencies in states bordering the destination of the weapons (if the supplier state is remote), as well as private arms brokers, financiers, and transport agents.[42] The secrecy cloaking covert arms supply breeds a lack of accountability, creating opportunities for corruption that can feed weapons directly into the (unauthorized) global black market. In addition, guerrilla forces (a principal recipient of covert authorized arms supply) often lack a chain of command or authority structure sufficient to ensure physical control of weapons, again resulting in weapons being siphoned off into the black market.

Secret government-authorized transfers of small arms often fuel armed conflict; they are generally intended to destabilize and topple governments through the force of arms. But they also tend to have several unintended consequences. Beyond serving as a proxy for the supplier state's goals, the local recipients have independent aspirations, which may coincide with the patron's short-term interest(s), but run counter to its medium- to long-term interest(s). A prime example is US covert arms supply via the Pakistani Directorate for Inter-Services Intelligence to the Afghan mujahideen in the 1980s; the operation succeeded in helping drive the Soviets out of Afghanistan (the short-term goal), but it strengthened the hand of radical Islamic forces, destabilizing Pakistan and secular elements in Afghanistan, and ultimately creating a direct threat to the United States (Mathiak and Lumpe, 2000, pp. 59–62).

> The secrecy cloaking covert arms supply breeds a lack of accountability.

During the period 2005–06, allegations of covert state-backed arms supply operations involving small arms were numerous. Proof—or even a detailed allegation—is more difficult to come by. Press reports provide indications of operations, but they rarely include specifics. Court documents—either domestic or international—and declassified government documents have been rich sources of information in the past, but only well after the fact. The reports of UN sanctions committees investigating violations of mandatory arms embargoes are becoming the primary source of highly vetted information on contemporary cases of covert government-backed arms supply.

One case of covert state-authorized arms supply that garnered a great deal of media attention in 2006 is that of Iran and Syria providing weapons to Hezbollah in Lebanon. During the war in Lebanon and northern Israel in August 2006, the UN Security Council passed Resolution 1701 (2006), which called on states to prevent arms transfers, military training, and assistance to any armed forces in Lebanon other than those of the UN or the Lebanese government (UNSC, 2006d, para. 15). Nevertheless, media reports in late 2006 cited Western, Israeli, and Saudi intelligence sources as saying that Iranian cargo planes continued to deliver rockets and small arms to Damascus, where the weapons were offloaded and trucked to Hezbollah camps in Lebanon (Shannon and McGirk, 2006; Leopold, 2006).

Another case involves ongoing transfers to armed groups in Darfur in violation of a UN embargo. The UN Panel of Experts monitoring the UN arms embargo of Sudan reported in January 2006 that the Sudanese Liberation Army and the Justice and Equality Movement—part of a new rebel alliance called the National Redemption Front, which declared renewed hostilities with the government—'have continued to receive arms, ammunition and/or equipment from Chad, Eritrea, the Libyan Arab Jamahiriya, non-governmental groups and other unknown sources' (UNSC, 2006a, para. 79). Reporting several months later, the panel reiterated that 'the Government of Chad, or elements within the Government of Chad, continues to actively support rebel groups in Darfur' (UNSC, 2006b, para. 13). The Sudanese government has also been implicated in breaking the embargo by transferring weapons to forces it supports in Darfur (UNSC, 2006b, p. 3). All small arms transfers to the Sudanese government, therefore, are at significant risk of diversion to Janjaweed and other Sudanese government-backed militias.

Perhaps the biggest covert arms supply news of the year, however, involves multiple states covertly arming warring factions in Somalia.

Small arms transfers to the Sudanese government risk diversion to Janjaweed and other militias.

Small arms supply to Somalia, 2005-06

Somalia has lacked a central government since it dissolved into armed chaos in 1991. In 1992 the UN Security Council passed Resolution 733, imposing a comprehensive arms embargo on Somalia (UNSC, 1992).[43] From 1992 through 2002, the Security Council took very little action to ensure implementation of the embargo.[44] However, following the attacks in the United States on 11 September 2001, Somalia gained international attention as a possible haven for terrorists, a concern that became the primary focus of US policy toward the country (US DOS, 2007). As a result, the Security Council increased its oversight of the embargo, establishing a Panel of Experts in 2002 and a Monitoring Group in January 2004 (UNSC, 2002; 2004).

At the same time, the international community redoubled its efforts to promote the establishment of a central government in Somalia. After a dozen failed previous attempts, a two-year reconciliation process led by the Inter-Governmental Authority on Development concluded in 2004, resulting in the formation of a Somali Transitional Federal Government (TFG) that was to hold office for five years. Abdullahi Yusuf was elected president in October of that year. The TFG was so weak, however, that it was not able to take up residence in Somalia until June 2005, and even then it failed to establish its authority throughout most of the country (De Temmerman, 2006).[45]

Yusuf's government was hobbled from the outset by armed opposition in Somalia—including from elements of his own government. Originally, Mogadishu-based businessmen and warlords were the main challengers to the TFG (De Temmerman, 2006).[46] In 2005, however, Islamic militants affiliated with the Union of the Islamic Courts came to the fore, spurred on by the entrance into Somalia of the TFG (which they opposed).[47] Within a year the Islamic militias controlled most of the country, having ousted the warlords from Mogadishu in early June 2006 and captured Kismayo (in the southern part of the country, which borders on Kenya) in September (Nzwili, 2006, pp. 5–6; Weinstein, 2006).

UN investigators responsible for monitoring implementation of the embargo reported that the inflow of weapons increased dramatically in 2005, in anticipation of the arrival of the TFG.[48] At that time the Monitoring Group cited multiple external sources of support for training camps and militias being formed by businessmen, warlords, and fundamentalists—but it did not identify the state sponsors (UNSC, 2005a). In a report issued the following May, the

Monitoring Group found that support by states to parties in the conflict had increased, and this time it named names—at least some of them. The report details the competing efforts of Ethiopia and Eritrea to provide the TFG and Islamic militias, respectively, with money and arms in violation of the embargo (UNSC, 2006c, paras. 15–24, 105–06).

The two countries—in effect—were arming Somali proxies to carry on their disastrous 1998–2000 war, which ended in a tenuous peace agreement following the death of an estimated 70,000 people (Reuters, 2006). Eritrean support of the Islamic militias is aimed primarily at destabilizing Ethiopia. One of the leaders of the Islamic Courts, Sheikh Hassan Dahir Aweys, was formerly a military colonel and vice-chairman of Al-Ittihad Al-Islami, an Islamic group that the US DOS placed on a terrorist group watch list. Aweys' militia battled with and was defeated by Ethiopian army forces in the mid-1990s (Nzwili, 2006).

Meanwhile, the Ethiopian government has been arming the TFG to stave off an unfriendly Islamist government, which it fears would wage a permanent destabilization campaign along the borders, block its access to the sea, and perhaps seek to recreate 'Greater Somalia'—incorporating eastern regions of Ethiopia and Kenya, historically and currently inhabited by ethnic Somalis (De Temmerman, 2006).

According to the UN Monitoring Group, the Government of Ethiopia provided at least three consignments of weapons to Mohamed Dheere, a warlord heading the Jowhar government (nominally part of the TFG) in January and March 2006. The first two of these, in January, included 2,000 AK-47 assault rifles, 100 PKM machine guns, 1,500 G3 rifles, 100 RPG launchers, 10 DShK anti-aircraft guns, 10 SKUs, landmines, spare parts, empty magazines and ammunition belts, and ammunition. This shipment was followed in late March by ten metric tons of arms, including mortars, machine guns, AK-47s, and RPG anti-tank weapons. In both cases, the weapons were trucked into Jowhar, Somalia from Ethiopia and brought to Dheere's storage facility or facilities (UNSC, 2006c, paras. 22–23).

The Monitoring Group also details at least four transfers of arms and ammunition from the Government of Eritrea to the Islamic fundamentalists in early 2006.[49] It records two flights in early March 2006 from Asmara, Eritrea to Baledogle airport in the Lower Shabelle region in Somalia, which conveyed 200 boxes of Zu-23 anti-aircraft ammunition, 200 boxes of B-10 anti-tank ammunition, 200 boxes of DShK anti-aircraft ammunition, 200 boxes of Browning M2 .50 heavy machine gun ammunition, ZP-39 anti-aircraft ammunition, 50 RPG anti-tank launchers and boxes of anti-tank ammunition, 50 light anti-armour weapons, 50 M-79 grenade launchers, communications equipment, 1,000 AK-47 rifles (short version), 1,000 remote-controlled bombs, 1,000 anti-personnel mines, and ammunition for 120 mm mortars (UNSC, 2006c, para. 19).

Despite the UN embargo, Eritrea and Ethiopia arm proxies in Somalia.

The Monitoring Group's 2006 report also makes careful reference to 'clandestine third-country involvement in Somalia'. During 2006 'financial support was being provided to help organize and structure a militia force created to counter the threat posed by the growing militant fundamentalist movement in central and southern Somalia.' This new Alliance for Peace Restoration and Combat against Terror (APRCT) consisted of Mogadishu businessmen, 'the militias of dissident TFG Ministers', and warlords (UNSC, 2006c, paras. 32–33).

The Monitoring Group did not specify the third country involved, which was widely reported to be the United States,[50] because it had not completed its investigation (UNSC, 2006c, para. 35). Around the same time, however, Somali interim President Yusuf publicly criticized US support for the warlords, 'arguing that the best way to hunt members of al Qaeda in Somalia was to strengthen the country's central government' (Mazzetti, 2006a).

In June 2006 *The New York Times* published details of the US covert aid programme, based on leaks from US officials. According to this source, warlords in Somalia received hundreds of thousands of dollars from the CIA over the year preceding the report, operating from its station in Nairobi. The goal was to capture or kill several suspected al Qaeda operatives (Mazzetti, 2006a). The news report alleges that 'the American activities in Somalia have been approved by top officials in Washington'—as is required under US law for covert operations—and that the National Security Council reaffirmed the government's support for the strategy in a March 2006 meeting (Mazzetti, 2006a). According to former US official John Roberts II, the CIA's operation in Somalia began in earnest in 2003 (Roberts, 2006b).[51] A Kenyan newspaper further alleges that the US government (i.e. the CIA) is working with and through the Ethiopian Secret Services (Amran, 2006).

The APRCT presumably purchased weapons from the Bakaraaha Arms Market, located in Irtogte in Mogadishu. This market sells to all comers and is routinely resupplied by Yemeni smuggling networks.[52] In January, February, and March 2006, the APRCT and militant Islamists engaged in several fierce battles in Mogadishu and Afgooye (north-west of Mogadishu). The UN reported that as a result of this fighting (which the Islamists won), practically all arms and ammunition available at the Bakaraaha Arms Market had been sold, causing a noticeable spike in prices (UNSC, 2006c, para. 11).

The Bakaraaha Arms Market in Mogadishu is routinely supplied by Yemeni smuggling networks.

Following the takeover by the Islamic Courts of much of the country by mid-2006—a result inadvertently encouraged by the United States' covert backing of the APRCT (Mazzetti, 2006a; 2006b)—news reports appeared of a new US government plan to work through an African-led peace operation (sanctioned by the UN Security Council, but opposed by the Islamic Courts) and a private military company to capture Mogadishu for the TFG (*Africa Confidential*, 2006b; Muhumuza, 2006).[53] The US government began pressing in late 2006 for the repeal of the UN comprehensive arms embargo to allow a peacekeeping force into Somalia (US DOS, 2006), and the UN Security Council subsequently passed Resolution 1725 (2006) exempting the TFG from the embargo (UNSC, 2006f, para. 5).

Around the same time (November 2006), the Somali embargo Monitoring Group published a report covering relevant events in the period May–October 2006 (UNSC, 2006b). This report dropped any reference to US involvement in arming the APRCT.[54] It highlights the role of Ethiopia and Eritrea, as well as other external actors—namely Djibouti, Egypt, Iran, Libya, Saudi Arabia, Syria, Uganda, and Yemen, as well as Hezbollah operating from Lebanon—in violating the arms embargo in the most recent period (UNSC, 2006e, paras. 9–145, 213–14).

In the last weeks of December 2006, thousands of Ethiopian soldiers invaded Somalia and quickly drove the Islamic Courts government out of Mogadishu and other strongholds (Albadri and Sanders, 2006; AP, 2006; Gettleman, Ibrahim, and Maxamuud, 2007). At the time of writing, the situation remains in flux, with the Islamic Courts militias waging an active insurgency against the TFG and its foreign allies in Somalia. In February 2007 the UN Security Council authorized the deployment of an African Union-led peacekeeping force (UNSC, 2007a).

Data issues: Austria, Brazil, and the curious case of the invisible pistols[55]

This section analyses how even seemingly transparent governments can be selective in their reporting to UN Comtrade—whether intentionally or accidentally. Although it profiles Austrian and Brazilian export data reporting, it is important to acknowledge that these countries are more transparent than most. The issues presented here highlight the weaknesses of UN Comtrade data, namely its reliance on the good faith and competence of national customs authorities. At the same time, since the dataset is universal (or as close to universal as exists), discrepancies can and do come to light, demonstrating the strength of the system.

Austria and Brazil rank among the world's leading small arms exporters.[56] The main firearm export product of each is handguns—pistols in the case of Austria, and revolvers and pistols in the case of Brazil.

Of Austria's handguns, Glock pistols are its leading export product. Government and civilian customers in more than 100 countries have bought more than 2.5 million Glock pistols since 1983. There are almost 40 different Glock pistol models in various calibres, and an estimated 90 per cent or more of its production is for export (Small Arms Survey, 2002, p. 30; Jones and Cutshaw, 2006, pp. 229–35).

However, according to the data reported to UN Comtrade by the Austrian government, Austria does not export pistols. Since 1992, with the exception of 1994, Austria has *not* reported on its exports of handguns to UN Comtrade. Information submitted by Austria's trade partners clearly shows, however, that they are receiving Austrian handguns: between 1992 and 2004 Austria exported USD 717 million worth of handguns, corresponding to 64 per cent of the country's total small arms exports, which totalled USD 1.1 billion during that period. The top five importers of Austrian handguns in 2004 were the United States, Mexico, Thailand, Poland, and Canada.[57]

In Brazil, small arms production and exports are concentrated among three large producers: Forjas Taurus, Companhia Brasileira de Cartuchos, and Indústria de Material Bélico. Taurus is a major player within this sector, producing around 40 revolver and around 20 pistol models, and has established itself in the US pistols market (Taurus, 2007; Dreyfus, Lessing, and Purcena, 2005, p. 61). From 1990 to 2005 Taurus exported on average 64 per cent of its production annually (CVM, 1990–2005).

Handguns comprised 35 per cent of all reported small arms exports from Brazil to the world between 1992 and 2004 (NISAT, 2006; UN Comtrade, 2006).[58] As in the Austrian case, however, Brazilian pistols are 'invisible' in terms of Brazil's own reporting of its exports. The value reported under the category 'revolvers and pistols' by Brazil in the period under study is zero (NISAT, 2006; UN Comtrade, 2006). In fact, Brazilian pistols and revolvers seem to

Figure 3.2 **Exports of Brazilian sporting and hunting rifles to the United States as reported by Brazil v. imports of Brazilian pistols and revolvers as reported by the United States, 1992-2004 (USD millions)**

USD (MILLIONS)

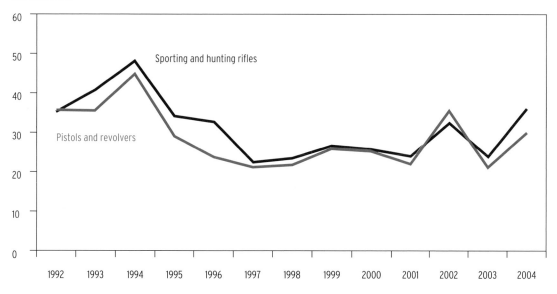

Note: Customs codes for items in this figure are 9302 (revolvers and pistols) and 930330 (sporting and hunting rifles).
Sources: calculations based on NISAT (2006) and UN Comtrade (2006). Data deflated to 2004.

have been embedded in the category of 'sporting and hunting rifles' in Brazil's customs data reported to UN Comtrade. Figure 3.2 contrasts exports of hunting/sporting rifles to the United States (the main destination of small arms from Brazil) as reported by Brazil with US-reported imports from Brazil of pistols and revolvers.

How can this practice be explained? It could simply be a mistake in the classification by government authorities. However, Brazilian officials have been aware of the discrepancy since at least 2003 and have not addressed it.[59]

Issues of commercial competitiveness might also drive these countries' choice to obscure handgun export data. When Taurus and Glock first launched their products on the international market, they faced fierce competition from European and US producers. By not revealing their export data, these countries might have intended to deprive competitors of information about their markets. However, the arrival of pistols would be clear to customs officials in the recipient country, and any 'commercial secret' would be revealed by mirroring data from the importing country, as demonstrated in Figure 3.2.

National security is almost certainly not the reason for the incomplete reporting. Countries do not win wars with pistols and revolvers. Pistols are short-range weapons and are used by the military as personal protection weapons. Moreover, and most curiously, the Brazilian army reports in its statistical yearbook on Brazil's global exports of handguns, in contrast to the non-reporting by Brazilian authorities to UN Comtrade (Brazil, 1976–2003, statistical annexe).[60]

Figure 3.3 **Paraguay: pistols and revolvers imported from Brazil (USD), 1992–2001**

USD (THOUSANDS)

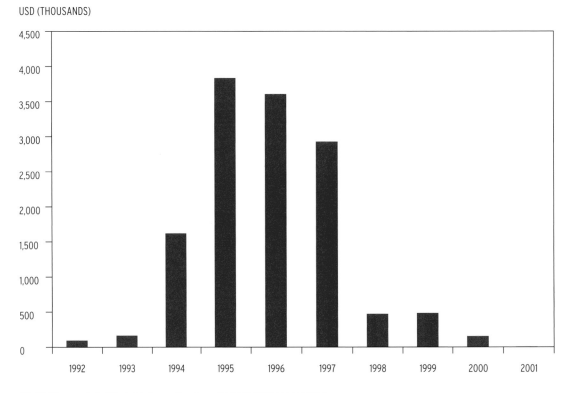

Note: This data was reported to UN Comtrade by Paraguay. The customs code included is 930200 (pistols/revolvers).
Source: calculations based on NISAT (2006) and UN Comtrade (2006). Data deflated to 2004.

Finally, it might be that Austria and Brazil are selectively reporting data in order to hide irresponsible exports to 'problematic countries', i.e. countries involved in conflict, with high levels of human rights violations, or which are regularly used as trans-shipment points to conflict or high-crime zones. Mirroring data uncovers such secrets, however. Data from Paraguay, a country that has been used as a trans-shipment point for the diversion of legally imported small arms and ammunition to conflict and high-crime areas (Dreyfus and Bandeira, 2006, pp. 14–32), shows a massive import of Brazilian pistols in the mid-1990s, according to UN Comtrade (see Figure 3.3).

The data discrepancies might simply be due to reporting errors: importing countries could be providing inaccurate data to UN Comtrade. However, Austria has 47 partner countries reporting imports of handguns in 2004 (the last year for which data is available under UN Comtrade), and Brazil has 27 partner countries doing so (NISAT, 2006; UN Comtrade, 2006). It is highly unlikely that all of these countries are misreporting their handgun imports. Moreover, Glock (Austria) and Taurus (Brazil) advertise their success as major exporters of handguns (Glock, n.d.; Taurus, 2007).

A comprehensive picture of irresponsible small arms transfers remains elusive.

CONCLUSION

Since 2001, UN conferences on small arms have focused on curbing the illicit trade in small arms and light weapons. While the *UN Programme of Action* does not include a definition of the term 'illicit', this chapter has argued that illicit transfers include government-authorized transfers to countries with a demonstrated record of human rights violations, to those engaged in armed conflict, and in situations posing a serious risk of diversion. The data presented here demonstrates that during the period 2002–04 many exports of small arms, light weapons, and their ammunition were undertaken in such circumstances. Of course, not all arms transferred to 'at risk' countries are eventually misused. Yet, as the chapter indicates, low levels of public disclosure typically prevent us from determining whether exporting states acted responsibly in authorizing arms shipments to countries presenting heightened risks.

The cases of small arms diversion profiled in this chapter underline a need for greater attention to the recording of serial numbers for all weapons procured on behalf of third parties. Similarly, improved stockpile security standards and practices would ensure that forces engaged in peace operations do not contribute—whether through individual corruption or negligence—to crises that they are supposed to help resolve or mitigate.

The Somalia case study describes the covert supply of arms by several states, including a permanent member of the UN Security Council (the United States), in contravention of a UN arms embargo. In the absence of any repercussions, one must conclude that the integrity of the UN sanctions process has been weakened.

Finally, the profiles of Austrian and Brazilian reporting of customs data to UN Comtrade show that false, partial, or misleading submissions by exporters can be brought to light by importers, underlining the incentive for all countries to submit accurate and complete information.

A comprehensive picture of irresponsible small arms transfers remains elusive. Improved transparency would help isolate those cases of greatest concern. At the same time, new international initiatives to encourage more responsible arms transfer practices (TRANSFER CONTROLS) indicate that states may be preparing to address the problem of the illicit trade in earnest, thus realizing one of the key promises of the *UN Programme of Action*. ◾

ANNEXES

Annexe 1. Known exports of small arms, light weapons, and their ammunition to countries where gross violations of human rights occur, and to countries involved in armed conflict (annual values in USD), 2002-04: summary table

Importing country	Year of reported serious human rights (HR) violations and/or armed conflict (2001–03)	Exporting country and year(s) of reported transfers (2002-04)	Value in USD (rounded) (UN Comtrade)
Afghanistan	2002 (HR violations), 2003 (HR violations)	Bosnia-Herzegovina (2003)	0.1 million
		Croatia (2003, 2004)	1.3 million
		Iran (2004)	27,000
		Italy (2003, 2004)	1.1 million
		Pakistan (2003, 2004)	45,000
		Poland (2003)	0.7 million
		Russian Federation (2003, 2004)	0.4 million
		South Korea (2003)	0.1 million
		Turkey (2003, 2004)	0.2 million
		US (2004)	0.5 million
Algeria	2001 (HR violations, armed conflict), 2002 (HR violations), 2003 (HR violations)	Brazil (2002, 2003, 2004)	8.6 million
		Canada (2004)	96,000
		France (2002, 2003, 2004)	1.3 million
		Italy (2002, 2003, 2004)	3.8 million
		Russian Federation (2003)	1.8 million
		Spain (2003)	37,000
Angola	2001 (HR violations, armed conflict), 2003 (HR violations)	Austria (2004)	16,000
		Namibia (2004)	35,000
		Portugal (2002, 2004)	0.3 million
		Serbia and Montenegro (2004)	0.5 million
		Spain (2002)	49,000
		US (2004)	26,000
Brazil	2001 (HR violations), 2002 (HR violations), 2003 (HR violations)	Argentina (2002)	33,000
		Austria (2002, 2003, 2004)	0.4 million
		Canada (2003)	0.3 million
		Chile (2002, 2004)	1.3 million
		China (2003, 2004)	40,000
		Finland (2003, 2004)	0.3 million

		France (2002, 2003)	0.9 million
		Germany (2002, 2003, 2004)	0.5 million
		Iran (2003)	78,000
		Israel (2003)	0.2 million
		Italy (2002, 2003, 2004)	0.6 million
		South Africa (2002, 2003, 2004)	1.5 million
		Spain (2002, 2003, 2004)	0.5 million
		UK (2002, 2003, 2004)	1 million
		US (2002, 2003, 2004)	4.5 million
Cameroon	2003 (HR violations)	Congo-Brazzaville (2004)	0.6 million
		Other Europe (2004)	26,000
		France (2004)	0.7 million
		Italy (2004)	74,000
		Spain (2004)	0.2 million
Central African Republic	2001 (HR violations)	Congo-Brazzaville (2002)	0.4 million
		France (2002)	87,000
		Portugal (2002)	13,000
		Spain (2002)	0.1 million
		Unspecified countries (2002)	33,000
Chad	2001 (HR violations)	France (2002)	26,000
China	2001 (HR violations), 2002 (HR violations), 2003 (HR violations)	Australia (2002, 2003, 2004)	0.5 million
		Austria (2002)	10,000
		Canada (2004)	14,000
		Finland (2003, 2004)	0.4 million
		Germany (2002, 2003, 2004)	1.4 million
		Hong Kong (2002, 2004)	71,000
		Indonesia (2003)	28,000
		Italy (2002, 2003, 2004)	1 million
		Spain (2002, 2003)	67,000
		Switzerland (2002, 2003, 2004)	0.6 million
		UK (2002, 2003, 2004)	1.4 million
		US (2002, 2003, 2004)	0.3 million
Colombia	2001 (HR violations, armed conflict), 2002 (HR violations, armed conflict), 2003 (HR violations)	Argentina (2002)	38,000
		Belgium (2004)	0.9 million
		Brazil (2002, 2003, 2004)	28 million
		Czech Republic (2002, 2003, 2004)	5.5 million

		Germany (2002, 2003, 2004)	1.7 million
		Israel (2002, 2003, 2004)	1.9 million
		Italy (2002, 2003, 2004)	0.8 million
		Netherlands (2004)	0.2 million
		Portugal (2002)	26,000
		Russian Federation (2002, 2003)	87,000
		South Africa (2002, 2003)	4.5 million
		UK (2002, 2003, 2004)	0.4 million
		US (2002, 2003, 2004)	19.4 million
		Unspecified countries (2004)	2.1 million
Congo-Brazzaville	2002 (HR violations), 2003 (HR violations)	Italy (2003, 2004)	0.8 million
		US (2004)	35,000
Côte d'Ivoire	2002 (HR violations), 2003 (HR violations)	France* (2003, 2004)	56 million
		Serbia and Montenegro (2004)	0.6 million
		Spain (2003)	90,000
Democratic Republic of the Congo	2001 (HR violations), 2003 (HR violations)	Germany (2002)	31,000
		Italy (2004)	95,000
Ethiopia	2002 (HR violations), 2003 (HR violations)	South Korea (2004)	83,000
		Ukraine (2003)	2.9 million
Guinea	2001 (HR violations)	France (2002)	0.4 million
		Iran (2002)	0.9 million
		Portugal (2002)	86,000
		Spain (2002)	0.7 million
		Switzerland (2002)	85,000
India	2001 (HR violations, armed conflict), 2002 (HR violations, armed conflict), 2003 (HR violations, armed conflict)	Australia (2002, 2003, 2004)	0.1 million
		Austria (2002, 2003, 2004)	1.5 million
		Belgium (2002)	23,000
		Canada (2002)	15,000
		Cyprus (2003, 2004)	87,000
		Czech Republic (2002, 2003, 2004)	0.2 million
		France (2002, 2003, 2004)	0.2 million
		Germany (2002, 2003, 2004)	1.4 million
		Israel (2003, 2004)	0.2 million
		Italy (2002, 2003, 2004)	0.5 million
		Poland (2003)	77,000
		Romania (2002)	50,000

		Russian Federation (2002)	27,000
		Slovenia (2002)	42,000
		Switzerland (2002, 2003)	94,000
		Turkey (2004)	0.2 million
		UK (2002, 2003, 2004)	0.3 million
		US (2002, 2004)	0.1 million
Indonesia	2001 (HR violations), 2002 (HR violations), 2003 (HR violations)	Asia (2003, 2004)	0.2 million
		Australia (2003)	0.2 million
		Austria (2002, 2003, 2004)	0.6 million
		Belgium (2003, 2004)	0.5 million
		Bosnia-Herzegovina (2004)	1.9 million
		Brazil (2002, 2003, 2004)	11.5 million
		Canada (2004)	34,000
		China (2002, 2003)	0.1 million
		Croatia (2004)	26,000
		Cyprus (2004)	0.2 million
		Czech Republic (2002, 2003, 2004)	0.7 million
		France (2003, 2004)	0.9 million
		Germany (2003, 2004)	0.1 million
		Hong Kong (2003, 2004)	0.2 million
		Hungary (2002)	11,000
		Italy (2002, 2003, 2004)	0.2 million
		Malaysia (2003)	24,000
		Philippines (2004)	12,000
		Russian Federation (2002)	17,000
		Serbia and Montenegro (2004)	0.5 million
		Seychelles (2003)	1.2 million
		Singapore (2002, 2003, 2004)	7.7 million
		South Africa (2002)	85,000
		South Korea (2002, 2003, 2004)	3.6 million
		Sri Lanka (2002)	13,000
		Sweden (2003)	17,000
		Switzerland (2003, 2004)	0.2 million
		Taiwan (2002, 2003, 2004)	0.4 million
		Turkey (2002, 2004)	0.2 million
		UK (2003, 2004)	2.8 million
		US (2003, 2004)	1.2 million
		Unspecified countries (2004)	0.8 million

Iraq	2002 (HR violations), 2003 (HR violations, armed conflict)	Austria (2003, 2004)	92,000
		Bosnia-Herzegovina (2004)	0.2 million
		Czech Republic (2004)	0.2 million
		Germany (2004)	1.7 million
		Poland (2004)	1.4 million
		Serbia and Montenegro (2004)	3.7 million
		Thailand (2003)	12,000
		UK (2004)	0.2 million
		US (2004)	3.1 million
Israel	2001 (HR violations), 2002 (HR violations), 2003 (HR violations)	Australia (2003)	30,000
		Austria (2003, 2004)	0.8 million
		Bosnia-Herzegovina (2004)	29,000
		Brazil (2002, 2003, 2004)	0.4 million
		Canada (2002, 2003, 2004)	0.1 million
		Croatia (2002, 2003)	0.1 million
		Czech Republic (2002, 2003, 2004)	2.8 million
		France (2002)	16,000
		Germany (2002, 2003, 2004)	0.3 million
		Italy (2002, 2003, 2004)	0.1 million
		Mexico (2004)	0.1 million
		Poland (2004)	0.3 million
		Serbia and Montenegro (2004)	8.3 million
		Slovakia (2004)	1.8 million
		South Korea (2002, 2003, 2004)	1.2 million
		Spain (2002, 2003, 2004)	0.6 million
		Sweden (2003)	23,000
		Switzerland (2002, 2003, 2004)	0.2 million
		Turkey (2002, 2003, 2004)	0.1 million
		UK (2002, 2004)	80,000
		US (2002, 2003, 2004)	66.5 million
Kenya	2002 (HR violations)	Brazil (2003)	0.4 million
		China (2003)	56,000
		Czech Republic (2003)	0.8 million
		Italy (2003)	75,000
		Norway (2003)	12,000
		Serbia and Montenegro (2003)	0.2 million
		UK (2003)	86,000
		US (2003)	27,000

Liberia	2003 (HR violations, armed conflict)	US (2004)	0.1 million
Macedonia (Former Yugoslav Republic)	2001 (HR violations)	Austria (2002)	15,000
		Croatia (2002)	0.4 million
		France (2002)	0.3 million
		Germany (2002)	98,000
		Greece (2002)	74,000
		Italy (2002)	16,000
		Russian Federation (2002)	30,000
		Serbia and Montenegro (2002)	0.2 million
		Spain (2002)	44,000
		US (2002)	19,000
Myanmar	2003 (HR violations)	Serbia and Montenegro (2004)	1.3 million
Nepal	2001 (HR violations), 2002 (HR violations, armed conflict), 2003 (HR violations, armed conflict)	Belgium (2003)	3 million
		Bosnia-Herzegovina (2003)	0.4 million
		China (2003)	38,000
		Hong Kong (2003)	0.1 million
		India (2002, 2003, 2004)	1.4 million
		Singapore (2003)	13,000
		UK (2002, 2003)	0.5 million
		US (2002, 2003, 2004)	7 million
Nigeria	2001 (HR violations), 2002 (HR violations)	Germany (2002)	1 million
		Greece (2002)	0.2 million
		Indonesia (2002)	62,000
		Israel (2002)	0.2 million
		Portugal (2003)	28,000
		South Africa (2002)	0.5 million
		UK (2002)	53,000
		US (2002, 2003)	0.4 million
North Korea	2003 (HR violations)	China (2004)	44,000
		France (2004)	40,000
Pakistan	2001 (HR violations), 2002 (HR violations), 2003 (HR violations)	Australia (2003, 2004)	74,000
		Austria (2003, 2004)	26,000
		Belgium (2004)	25,000
		Brazil (2002, 2004)	2.3 million
		China (2002, 2003, 2004)	1 million

		Czech Republic (2003, 2004)	0.8 million
		Germany (2003, 2004)	0.1 million
		Hong Kong (2003)	17,000
		Iran (2004)	2.2 million
		Italy (2002, 2003, 2004)	85,000
		Kenya (2003, 2004)	59,000
		Maldives (2003, 2004)	67,000
		Slovakia (2003, 2004)	0.1 million
		South Korea (2003)	87,000
		Switzerland (2004)	23,000
		UK (2002, 2003, 2004)	0.4 million
		US (2002, 2003, 2004)	0.2 million
Philippines	2003 (HR violations, armed conflict)	Argentina (2004)	24,000
		Australia (2004)	48,000
		Austria (2004)	0.4 million
		Bosnia-Herzegovina (2004)	0.3 million
		Brazil (2004)	1.3 million
		China (2004)	3.3 million
		Croatia (2004)	0.2 million
		Czech Republic (2004)	53,000
		Germany (2004)	0.3 million
		India (2004)	41,000
		Israel (2004)	0.2 million
		Italy (2004)	0.6 million
		Japan (2004)	21,000
		Poland (2004)	19,000
		South Korea (2004)	0.2 million
		Spain (2004)	0.2 million
		Taiwan (2004)	0.4 million
		Turkey (2004)	0.1 million
		US (2004)	2.1 million
		Vietnam (2004)	33,000
Russian Federation	2001 (HR violations, armed conflict), 2002 (HR violations), 2003 (HR violations)	Australia (2004)	24,000
		Austria (2002, 2003, 2004)	7 million
		Belgium (2002, 2003, 2004)	2.4 million
		Cyprus (2002, 2004)	30, 000
		Czech Republic (2002, 2003, 2004)	1.3 million
		Finland (2002, 2003, 2004)	1.2 million

		France (2002, 2003, 2004)	2.3 million
		Germany (2002, 2003, 2004)	21.3 million
		Greece (2002)	14,000
		Italy (2002, 2003, 2004)	13 million
		Japan (2002, 2003, 2004)	0.2 million
		Portugal (2002, 2003, 2004)	0.2 million
		Serbia and Montenegro (2004)	36,000
		South Korea (2002)	0.1 million
		Spain (2002, 2003, 2004)	0.5 million
		Sweden (2002)	38,000
		Switzerland (2002, 2003, 2004)	0.3 million
		Turkey (2002, 2003, 2004)	0.5 million
		Ukraine (2002)	32,000
		UK (2002, 2003, 2004)	0.6 million
		US (2002, 2003, 2004)	0.5 million
Rwanda	2001 (HR violations, armed conflict)	Saudi Arabia (2002)	11,000
		Turkey (2002)	38,000
Serbia and Montenegro	2001 (HR violations)	Austria (2002)	0.4 million
		Belgium (2002)	60,000
		Bosnia-Herzegovina (2002)	16,000
		Croatia (2002)	82,000
		Cyprus (2002)	0.1 million
		Czech Republic (2002)	0.1 million
		Finland (2002)	0.3 million
		Germany (2002)	57,000
		Greece (2002)	16,000
		Hungary (2002)	27,000
		Italy (2002)	0.4 million
		Russian Federation (2002)	26,000
		Switzerland (2002)	12,000
Sri Lanka	2001 (HR violations, armed conflict)	Australia (2002)	11,000
		Czech Republic (2002)	81,000
		Germany (2002)	61,000
		Slovakia (2002)	2.9 million

Sudan	2001 (HR violations, armed conflict), 2002 (HR violations), 2003 (HR violations)	China (2002, 2003, 2004)	4.7 million
		Cyprus (2004)	26,000
		Egypt (2002, 2004)	47,000
		Ethiopia (2004)	12,000
		Germany (2003)	59,000
		Hong Kong (2004)	1 million
		Iran (2002, 2003, 2004)	21 million
		Kuwait (2004)	31,000
		Russian Federation (2004)	0.2 million
		Saudi Arabia (2002)	58,000
		Turkey (2003, 2004)	53,000
Turkey	2001 (HR violations)	Belgium (2002)	1.3 million
		Bosnia-Herzegovina (2002)	10,000
		Cyprus (2002)	0.2 million
		France (2002)	27.6 million
		Germany (2002)	0.4 million
		Israel (2002)	0.2 million
		Italy (2002)	12.6 million
		Kyrgyzstan (2002)	58,000
		Lebanon (2002)	18,000
		Norway (2002)	22.1 million
		South Korea (2002)	0.2 million
		Spain (2002)	3.3 million
		Sweden (2002)	88,000
		Switzerland (2002)	0.2 million
		UK (2002)	51,000
		US (2002)	30.7 million
Uganda	2002 (HR violations, armed conflict), 2003 (HR violations)	China (2004)	64,000
		Czech Republic (2003)	32,000
		France (2003)	16,000
		Israel (2003)	10,000
		Kenya (2004)	0.5 million
		Slovakia (2003)	0.1 million
		South Africa (2002)	13,000
		Tanzania (2003)	0.2 million

		UK (2003, 2004)	32,000
		US (2004)	23,000
Venezuela	2002 (HR violations)	Argentina (2003)	89,000
		Austria (2003)	0.7 million
		Brazil (2003)	1.8 million
		Czech Republic (2003)	0.2 million
		Germany (2003)	40,000
		Italy (2003)	1 million
		Mexico (2003)	0.2 million
		Philippines (2003)	56,000
		Russian Federation (2003)	81,000
		South Korea (2003)	3.9 million
		Spain (2003)	1 million
		Turkey (2003)	15,000
		US (2003)	0.6 million
Zimbabwe	2003 (HR violations)	China (2004)	42,000
		South Africa (2004)	0.1 million

Note 1: A detailed version of this table, broken down by year of transfer and by weapon type, can be found in Annexe 2.

Note 2: 'HR violations' were assessed according to the Political Terror Scale (Gibney, 2006), and 'armed conflict' according to IISS (2007) and UCDP (2007a). For details on the methodology applied here, see section 'Irresponsible Transfers I' above.

Note 3: Only exports with a value equal to or greater than USD 10,000 per annum were included in the table.

Note 4: The table only lists years of reported serious HR violations and/or armed conflict where UN Comtrade data (transfers with a value equal to or greater than USD 10,000) was available for the year after. As a result, some years of reported serious HR violations and of armed conflict do not appear in the table.

Note 5: Some armed conflicts do not appear in the table because they are not classified as both 'active' in the Institute for Strategic Studies Armed Conflict Database (IISS, 2007) and 'war' in the Uppsala Conflict Database (UCDP, 2007a) during the relevant period.

* At least some of these SALW, which were reported as imports by Côte d'Ivoire, may have been destined for France's 'Operation Licorne' in that country (see Small Arms Survey, 2006, p. 74, note 4).

Sources: Calculations based on NISAT (2007b); UN Comtrade (2007)

Annexe 2. Known exports of small arms, light weapons, and their ammunition to countries where gross violations of human rights occur, and to countries involved in armed conflict (annual values in USD), 2002-04: Breakdown by year of transfer and weapon type

This annexe is available online at <http://www.smallarmssurvey.org/yearb2007.html>.

Annexe 3. Data and estimates on top and major exporters and importers

This annexe is available online at <http://www.smallarmssurvey.org/yearb2007.html>.

LIST OF ABBREVIATIONS

ASNLF	Aceh/Sumatra National Liberation Front	MOD	Ministry of Defence (Iraq)
APRCT	Alliance for Peace Restoration and	MOI	Ministry of the Interior (Iraq)
	Combat against Terrorism	NATO	North Atlantic Treaty Organisation
AU	African Union	ONUB	UN Operation in Burundi
Brimbo	Police Mobile Brigade (Indonesia)	OSCE	Organization for Security and
CIA	Central Intelligence Agency		Co-operation in Europe
DOD	Department of Defense (US)	PTS	Political Terror Scale
DOS	Department of State (US)	SANDF	South African National Defence Force
EU	European Union	SASP	Small Arms Serialization Program
FIS	Front Islamique du Salut (Islamic		(US DOD)
	Salvation Front)	SIGIR	Special Inspector General for Iraq
GAM	Gerakan Aceh Merdeka (Free Aceh		Reconstruction
	Movement)	TFG	Transitional Federal Government (Somalia)
ICRC	International Committee of the Red Cross	UK	United Kingdom
IDF	Israel Defense Forces	UN	United Nations Commodity Trade
ISF	Iraqi Security Forces	Comtrade	Statistics Database
IRRF	Iraq Relief and Reconstruction Fund	USD	US dollar
MNSTC-I	Multi-National Security Transition	ZAR	South African rand
	Command–Iraq		

ENDNOTES

1   According to *The Oxford English Dictionary*, 'illicit', from the Latin '*illicitus*', means 'not authorized or allowed; improper, irregular; esp. not sanctioned by law, rule, or custom; unlawful, forbidden'. 'Illegal', from the Latin '*illegalis*', on the other hand, means 'not legal or lawful; contrary to, or forbidden by, law' (OED, 2006). The term 'illicit' is thus broader than 'illegal'.

2   Data and estimates regarding top and major exporters and importers, following the methodology in Small Arms Survey (2006), are provided in Annexe 3 to the present chapter at <http://www.smallarmssurvey.org/yearb2007.html>. For detailed explanations of the methodology used to deal with UN Comtrade data and national arms export reports, see Small Arms Survey (2006, pp. 97–102), Glatz (2006, p. 72), and Marsh (2005).

3   For example, the *EU Code of Conduct* specifies in its Criterion Two that 'Member States will . . . not issue an export licence if there is a clear risk that the proposed export might be used for internal repression'. In addition, EU member states are to 'exercise special caution and vigilance in issuing licences, on a case-by-case basis and taking account of the nature of the equipment, to countries where serious violations of human rights have been established by the competent bodies of the UN, the Council of Europe or by the EU' (EU, 1998). Criterion Three states that 'Member States will not allow exports which would provoke or prolong armed conflicts or aggravate existing tensions or conflicts in the country of final destination' (EU, 1998). For an overview of sanctions and embargoes, as well as international and regional declarations and agreements relevant to small arms transfers, see SEESAC (2006) and Small Arms Survey (2004, pp. 263–71; 2005, p. 125, Table 5.1).

4   One effort to create such a dataset is at an early stage of development (see Morrow and Jo, 2006).

5   Officially released data rarely includes information on the intended end user, even though many governments require it when they license exports.

6   See, for example, Gibney and Dalton (1996, p. 83, fn. 1).

7   'Level 3: Imprisonment for political activity is more extensive. Politically-motivated executions or other political murders and brutality are common. Unlimited detention, with or without a trial, for political views is also commonplace. Level 4: The practices of level 3 affect a larger portion of the population and murders, disappearances, and torture are a common part of life. In spite of its pervasiveness, on this level political terror affects those who interest themselves in politics. Level 5: The terrors characteristic of level-4 countries, [*sic*] encompass the whole population at level 5. The leaders of these societies place no limits on the means or thoroughness with which they pursue personal or ideo-

logical goals' (Cornett and Gibney, 2003, pp. 2–3). The PTS attributes levels by year, based on the coding of Amnesty International and US DOS reports describing each country's situation during the previous year (Gibney and Dalton, 1996, p. 73). Levels are provided separately for Amnesty International and US DOS reports, and sometimes they differ between these sources for a given year and country. The framework applied in this chapter includes only countries with a level of either 4 or 5 for each source. If one source leads to classification of that country in that year in a lower level, it is not included here. For details on the coding procedure, see Gibney and Dalton (1996).

8   The IISS Armed Conflict Database includes 'current conflicts which may vary from low-intensity (or intermittent) encounters to high-intensity (or constant) combat' under the political status of 'active'. No further breakdown by intensity level is provided by this coding system (see IISS, 2007, 'Definitions'). In the Uppsala Conflict Database, 'war' is the highest intensity level of armed conflict, with at least 1,000 annual battle-related deaths (UCDP, 2007b, 'Intensity level').

9   For a detailed discussion of the advantages and limitations of UN Comtrade, see Small Arms Survey (2005, pp. 99–100, Box 4.1).

10   While small arms transfers can be justified in the context of legitimate self-defence, documented human rights violations committed by both sides in a conflict serve to undermine the argument of legitimate self-defence.

11   Amnesty International cites 4,000 disappearances (AI, 2002a), but in 2003 Human Rights Watch asserted that '[f]rom 1992 until 1998, Algeria's security forces and their accomplices made "disappear" more than 7,000 persons', a number exceeded in the same decade or since then only by wartime Bosnia (HRW, 2003, p. 13).

12   In its final report of December 2001 the commission expressed its concern with the 'excessive powers' of the military authorities and noted that it was unable to continue its investigations because of witnesses' fear to speak to representatives of the commission (AI, 2002a).

13   See also Escobar (2005).

14   It is important to note that Indonesia appears in Annexe 1 as a result of human rights violations (according to the PTS), not as a result of the conflict criterion. The documented human rights violations by the government and the GAM are linked to the ongoing conflict, but at the same time the 'Cessation of hostilities' agreement in December 2002 led to a significant decrease in armed conflict (Aspinall and Crouch, 2003, pp. ix–x).

15   See also AI (2001a, pp. 2, 5; 2001b, p. 2).

16   See also AI (2004a, p. 7).

17   In May 2002, after human rights organizations petitioned Israel's High Court of Justice to ban the use of human shields, the Israeli government announced the practice was being explicitly prohibited. See B'tselem (2002, p. 9).

18   The US DOS identified the units comprising the security forces (and responsible for abuses) in the West Bank and the Gaza Strip: the IDF, the Israel Security Agency (formerly the General Security Service), the Israeli National Police, and the paramilitary border police (US DOS, 2004).

19   There were no reports of political prisoners or political killings by the government in Venezuela in 2002 (US DOS, 2003a).

20   According to Minister Chacon, there are six million weapons in circulation in Venezuela. In 2003, 2004, and 2005 there were 11,643, 9,719, and 9,412 homicides, respectively, among a population of 27 million. In Venezuela, 98 per cent of homicides are committed with firearms. Venezuela's homicide rate in 2005 was six times higher than that of the United States (Fox, 2006).

21   As of July 2006 an estimated 650,000 more Iraqi people had died since the US–UK invasion than would have been expected under pre-war conditions. Among those were about 600,000 violent deaths (Burnham et al., 2006, p. 1).

22   This number was the planned target for December 2006; as of August 2006, 277,600 Iraqi police and military personnel had been trained and issued with weapons (US DOD, 2006, p. 41).

23   For a list of recent Iraq-related contracts by Taos Industries, see Taos Industries (2006).

24   This large procurement contract is not funded out of the IRRF (i.e. the weapons are in addition to those listed in the SIGIR (2006a) report).

25   The total sum appropriated amounts to USD 18.7 billion, of which two amounts of USD 100 million each are designated as assistance to Jordan and Liberia, respectively, and USD 10 million as assistance to Sudan (US Congress, 2003, pp. 1225–26).

26   The audit, carried out during the period July–September 2006, identified 19 contracts with 142 separate delivery orders from November 2003 to April 2005. The auditors found no small arms contracts funded by the IRRF after April 2005 (SIGIR, 2006a, pp. 2, 16).

27   Given that IRRF-funded weapons were mixed in inventories with weapons procured by other funds, and given that serial numbers were not recorded, complete accounting of other types of weapons cannot be assured. However, the SIGIR was not able to prove that they were missing (SIGIR, 2006a, pp. 8–10).

28   The SASP, run by the Defense Logistics Agency, is the US DOD's main stockpile security initiative. According to a US DOS fact sheet, '[t]he SASP is responsible for the control of, and accounting for, small arms' serial numbers from initial receipt to final disposition. All small arms are individually registered by serial number in the DOD Central Registry. Component units of the U.S. armed forces maintain individual registries and provide reports on holdings to the DOD Central Registry on a monthly basis. Small arms with missing, obliterated, mutilated or illegible serial numbers are assigned a serial number for registry purposes. This system allows accounting for all small arms, including those on hand, in transit, lost, stolen, demilitarized or shipped outside the control of DOD' (US DOS, 2003b).

29   Neither the US DOD nor the Iraqi MOI knows how many of the more than 29,000 National Police on the payroll are alive and have actually been trained and equipped (US DOD, 2006, p. 51).

30   This section is based on Pézard (2006).

31   The SANDF has served in Burundi since October 2001, first as part of a bilateral arrangement with Bujumbura in support of the Arusha peace process, later as part of the African Union (AU) peacekeeping mission, and then with ONUB. The SANDF remains in the country as part of the AU Special Task Force, which succeeded ONUB (Berman, 2007).

32   ZAR 27 million corresponded to USD 4.2 million at that time.

33   Specifically, the replacement of contingent number three by number four in August 2005 would explain why inaccurate amounts of equipment ended up being recorded in the auditor-general's report (Dawes and Dibetle, 2006; SABC News, 2006).

34   Email correspondence with former SANDF official, 3 April 2007. Two other sources, contacted by phone and email, noted that accounting problems were themselves indicative of poor stockpile management: phone interview with a South African journalist, 26 March 2007; email correspondence with a South African journalist, 8 April 2007.

35   The Barometer does not include countries' reporting to other mechanisms, such as the *EU Code of Conduct*, the Wassenaar Arrangement, or the UN Register of Conventional Arms. The *EU Code of Conduct* is a regional mechanism, and non-EU countries would be at a disadvantage if it were included in the Barometer. Furthermore, the information reported remains confidential among members, unless a country chooses to publish the information it submitted (this is the case for Austria, for example, whose report covering 2004 data was therefore included in the Barometer). The same is true for the Wassenaar Arrangement and the OSCE. The UN Register to date covers mainly larger conventional weapons (it does include some types of light weapons, and reporting on all small arms and light weapons has been optional since 2003; see UNGA [2006, para. 32]).

36   Major exporters are countries with an annual export value of at least USD 10 million reported to UN Comtrade.

37   The cut-off dates for the Barometer are 31 January 2007 for national arms export reports and 1 March 2007 for UN Comtrade data.

38   Countries systematically reporting re-exports under UN Comtrade include the United States and New Zealand (the latter is not a major exporter and therefore does not appear in the Barometer table).

39   During the 1970s, and particularly during the Reagan Administration (1980s), covert arms supply operations run by the Central Intelligence Agency (CIA) and the National Security Council were a major source of small arms, light weapons, and ammunition for insurgent groups around the world. At the same time, the Soviet Union and the Warsaw Pact ran clandestine arms supply operations to their allies in the developing world. In the late 1990s the CIA ran a covert train-and-equip operation for Kurdish factions in northern Iraq, in an effort to destabilize the regime of Saddam Hussein. Instead of overthrowing Hussein, the Kurdish recipients waged war against each other in 1996 (Mathiak and Lumpe, 2000, pp. 56–57, 68–70).

40   The US National Security Act of 1947 authorizes covert political and military operations, including secret arms supply. The president must first make a 'finding' that the operation is vital to US national security. Section 505 of the Act requires the CIA, or other government agencies engaging in such activities, to notify the Congressional committees responsible for oversight of US intelligence community activities of any arms supply operation undertaken valued at USD 1 million or more (US Congress, 1947, secs. 503, 505).

41   On the issue of arms supply to non-state armed groups, see TRANSFER CONTROLS.

42   States' use of middlemen in this way provides the latter with financial and political support that they might use in subsequent, completely free-lance and illegal arms supply activities. Most importantly, the connections that result from working with or for intelligence agencies in carrying out covert government-backed arms operations result in protection from prosecution for clearly illicit deals. Russian arms dealer Victor Bout is a case in point: despite having been named in several UN reports as being complicit in violating embargoes and being the subject of a Belgian warrant of arrest, as of 2003 he lived quite openly in Moscow (see Landesman, 2003).

43   This embargo was partially lifted in December 2006. UNSC Resolution 1725 (2006) eliminated the ban on arms supplies, military equipment, and military training for forces of the Transitional Federal Government (UNSC, 2006f).

44   See UNSC (2007b).

45   The TFG was only able to assert control in early 2007, following a large-scale military intervention by Ethiopia (AP, 2007), and this control is tentative at the time of writing.

46   According to one news report, 'the illicit small arms and light weapons in the hands of the ragtag armies of the warlords, most of whom are ministers in the new government, have been a source of enduring insecurity' (De Temmerman, 2006).

47   On 26 June 2006 this became known as the Supreme Council of the Islamic Courts. The name is shortened to 'Islamic Courts' in the discussion that follows.

48   The businessmen and warlords were interested in 'protect[ing] their unregulated commercial activities', and the fundamentalists sought to use military power against the TFG to impose Shariah law (UNSC, 2005a, paras. 19–22).

49   Eritrea denied the charge made by the Monitoring Group that it had supplied any weapons (UNSC, 2006c, para. 20).

50   See, for example, Amran (2006) and Roberts (2006a; 2006b).

51   In a critique of Ron Suskind's book *One Percent Doctrine*, John Roberts II, a former Reagan Administration White House official who writes fre-quently on US intelligence operations, says: 'Astoundingly, it contains no reference whatsoever to the CIA's covert action program against an active al Qaeda cell in Somalia, although the program was entering its third year when the book was published [in June 2006]' (Roberts, 2006b).

52   UNSC (2005a, paras. 46–48; 2005b, para. 9; 2006a, paras. 10–11; 2006b, paras. 138, 146–49).

53   A former Ugandan MP told a Ugandan newspaper that 'Washington is using Kampala, Addis Ababa [*sic*] and Nairobi to fight a silent counter-terrorism war in Somalia' (Muhumuza, 2006).

54   This omission is not surprising, given that the Islamic Courts militias drove the APRCT from Mogadishu during the first week of June 2006 (see UNSC, 2006b, para. 147).

55   This section is based on Dreyfus (2006), NISAT (2006), and UN Comtrade (2006).

56   See Annexe 3 to this chapter at <http://www.smallarmssurvey.org/yearb2007.html>.

57   Calculations based on NISAT (2006) and UN Comtrade (2006). The majority of this data is based on importers' reports, since Austria only partially reports to UN Comtrade on its exports of military firearms and of pistols/revolvers. Customs codes include 9301 (military weapons), 930120

(rocket and grenade launchers, etc.), 930190 (military firearms), 9302 (revolvers and pistols), 930320 (sporting and hunting shotguns), 930330 (sporting and hunting rifles), 930510 (parts and accessories of revolvers and pistols), 930521 (shotgun barrels), 930529 (parts and accessories of shotguns or rifles), 930621 (shotgun cartridges), and 930630 (small arms ammunition).

58   Brazil's total small arms exports in the period 1992–2004 were valued at USD 1.3 billion, of which an amount of USD 461 million corresponded to exports of revolvers/pistols. The top five importers of revolvers/pistols from Brazil in 2004 were the United States, Indonesia, Germany, the Philippines, and Argentina (calculations based on NISAT [2006] and UN Comtrade [2006]). This data is partly based on importers' reports, since Brazil does not report on its exports of pistols/revolvers to UN Comtrade. The total value for pistols/revolvers is therefore likely to be underestimated. Customs codes included 9301 (military weapons), 930120 (rocket and grenade launchers, etc.), 930190 (military firearms), 9302 (revolvers and pistols), 930320 (sporting and hunting shotguns), 930330 (sporting and hunting rifles), 930510 (parts and accessories of revolvers and pistols), 930521 (shotgun barrels), 930529 (parts and accessories of shotguns or rifles), 930621 (shotgun cartridges), and 930630 (small arms ammunition).

59   In a letter addressed to Viva Rio researchers in 2003, officials of the Ministry of Finance of Brazil acknowledged the discrepancy between exports to the United States and imports by the United States, but they could not explain it (Brazil, 2003).

60   The statistical yearbook of the Brazilian army is not made public, but Viva Rio was able to obtain the information cited here (email correspondence with Pablo Dreyfus, Viva Rio, 18 April 2007).

BIBLIOGRAPHY

Africa Confidential. 2006a. 'A Threat to the Horn and Beyond: Rising Tensions between the Regimes of President Yusuf and Chairman Aweys Could Escalate into a Regional War.' *Africa Confidential,* Vol. 47, No. 18, p. 1. 8 September.

——. 2006b. 'Mission Mogadishu.' *Africa Confidential,* Vol. 47, No. 18, p. 2. 8 September.

AI (Amnesty International). 1997. *Algeria: Civilian Population Caught in a Spiral of Violence.* AI Index: MDE 28/023/1997. London: AI. 18 November. <http://web.amnesty.org/library/Index/engMDE280231997>

——. 2001a. *Briefing on the Current Human Rights Situation in Indonesia.* AI Index: ASA 21/006/2001. London: AI. 31 January. <http://web.amnesty.org/library/Index/ENGASA210062001?open&of=ENG-IDN>

——. 2001b. *Amnesty International Briefing on the Deteriorating Human Rights Situation in Aceh for Participants in the ASEAN Regional Forum (ARF), July 2001.* AI Index: ASA 21/020/2001. London: AI. June. <http://web.amnesty.org/library/Index/ENGASA210202001?open&of=ENG-IDN>

——. 2002a. 'Algeria.' In AI. *Annual Report 2002.* London: AI. <http://web.amnesty.org/web/ar2002.nsf/mde/algeria!Open>

——. 2002b. 'Israel and the Occupied Territories.' In AI. *Annual Report 2002.* London: AI. <http://web.amnesty.org/web/ar2002.nsf/mde/israel+and+the+occupied+territories+!Open>

——. 2003a. *Indonesia: A Briefing for Members of the Consultative Group on Indonesia.* AI Index: ASA 21/042/2003. London: AI. <http://web.amnesty.org/library/pdf/ASA210422003ENGLISH/$File/ASA2104203.pdf>

——. 2003b. 'Israel and the Occupied Territories.' In AI. *Annual Report 2003.* London: AI. <http://web.amnesty.org/report2003/Isr-summary-eng>

——. 2003c. 'Venezuela.' In AI. *Annual Report 2003.* London: AI. <http://web.amnesty.org/report2003/Ven-summary-eng>

——. 2004a. *New Military Operations, Old Patterns of Human Rights Abuses in Aceh (Nanggroe Aceh Darussalam, NAD).* AI Index: ASA 21/033/2004. London: AI. 7 October. <http://web.amnesty.org/library/index/engasa210332004>

——. 2004b. 'Algeria.' In AI. *Annual Report 2004.* London: AI. <http://web.amnesty.org/report2004/dza-summary-eng>

——. 2004c. 'Israel and the Occupied Territories.' In AI. *Annual Report 2004.* London: AI. <http://web.amnesty.org/report2004/isr-summary-eng>

——. 2005. 'Algeria.' In AI. *Annual Report 2005.* London: AI. <http://web.amnesty.org/report2005/dza-summary-eng>

——. 2006. *Dead on Time: Arms Transportation, Brokering and the Threat to Human Rights.* AI Index: ACT 30/008/2006. London: AI. May. <http://web.amnesty.org/library/pdf/ACT300082006ENGLISH/$File/ACT3000806.pdf>

Albadri, Abukar and Edmund Sanders. 2006. 'Ethiopian Airstrikes Target Somalian Towns; Jets Hit Positions Held by Islamists, Including the Capital's Airport. Regional War is Feared.' *Los Angeles Times.* 25 December.

Amran, Athman. 2006. 'Unease as Islamists Take over Somalia.' *The Sunday Standard* (Nairobi). 1 October. <http://www.eastandard.net/archives/sunday/hm_news/news.php?articleid=1143958987&date=1/10/2006>

AP (Associated Press). 2002. 'Rice Says Chávez Undermined Democracy Long Before Coup.' 29 April.

——. 2006. 'Prospect of War with Somalia Raises Fears, Questions in Ethiopia.' 22 December. <http://www.iht.com/articles/ap/2006/12/22/africa/AF_GEN_Ethiopia_Somalia.php?page=1>

——. 2007. 'Somalia, Ethiopia, Eritrea Trade Accusations about Their Roles in Somalia.' 13 April.

Aspinall, Edward and Harold Crouch. 2003. *The Aceh Peace Process: Why It Failed.* Policy Studies No. 1. Washington, DC: East–West Center. http://www.eastwestcenter.org/stored/pdfs/PS001.pdf>

Australia. 2006. *Annual Report: Exports of Defence and Strategic Goods from Australia: Financial Years 2002–03 and 2003–04.* Canberra: Department of Defence, Defence Trade Control and Compliance, Strategy Group. February.

Austria. 2006. *Nationaler Bericht für konventionelle Waffenausfuhren 2004.* Vienna: Federal Ministry for Foreign Affairs. 24 March.

BBC (British Broadcasting Corporation). 2006a. 'Transcript of "File on 4"—"Iraqi Guns".' 23 May. <http://news.bbc.co.uk/2/shared/bsp/hi/pdfs/06_06_06_iraqi_guns.pdf>

——. 2006b. 'Montenegro Declares Independence.' 4 June. <http://news.bbc.co.uk/2/hi/europe/5043462.stm>

Berman, Eric. 2007. *Deployed African Regional Organizations' Peace Operations*. Unpublished background paper. Geneva: Small Arms Survey.

Bosnia-Herzegovina. 2005. *Informacija o izdatim dozvolama za izvoz/uvoz naoružanja i vojne opreme u 2004. godini (Information on Granted Authorizations of Exports and Imports of Armament and Military Matériel in 2004)*. Sarajevo: Ministry of Foreign Trade and Economic Relations, Foreign Trade and Investment Division. February.

Brazil. Ministério da Defesa. 1976–2003. *Anuário Estatístico do Exército*. Brasília: Estado-Maior do Exército Brasileiro.

——. 2003. 'Letter sent to Viva Rio by officials of the Secretariat of Economic Policy of the Ministry of Finance.' 10 December.

B'tselem. 2002. *Operation Defensive Shield: Soldiers' Testimonies, Palestinian Testimonies*. Journal. Jerusalem: B'tselem. September.
    <http://www.btselem.org/Download/200207_Defensive_Shield_Eng.pdf>

Burnham, Gilbert, et al. 2006. *The Human Cost of the War in Iraq: A Mortality Study, 2002–2006*. Baltimore: Bloomberg School of Public Health, Johns Hopkins University, and Baghdad: School of Medicine, Al Mustansiriya University.
    <http://www.jhsph.edu/refugee/research/iraq/Human_Cost_of_WarFORMATTED.pdf>

Burundi Réalités. 2006. 'Disparition du matériel militaire sud africain au Burundi: Mise au point du ministère de la défense nationale et des anciens combattants.' 10 November.

Canada. 2003. Exports of Military Goods from Canada: Annual Report 2002. Ottawa: Department of Foreign Affairs and International Trade/Export Controls Division of the Export and Import Controls Bureau. December.

Callies de Salies, Bruno. 1997. 'Algeria in the Grip of Terror.' *Le Monde Diplomatique*. October. <http://mondediplo.com/1997/10/alger1>

Ceaser, Mike. 2005. 'US Plays Both Venezuela Sides.' *Christian Science Monitor*. 10 August. <http://www.csmonitor.com/2005/0810/p01s04-woam.html>

Chivers, Chris J. 2006. 'Black-Market Weapon Prices Surge in Iraq Chaos.' *The New York Times*. 10 December. <http://www.nytimes.com/2006/12/10/world/middleeast/10weapons.html?ex=1323406800&en=d09a572021ade4b1&ei=5088&partner=rssnyt&emc=rss>

Cornett, Linda and Mark Gibney. 2003. *Tracking Terror: The Political Terror Scale 1980–2001*. Commissioned by the Human Security Centre. 3 August.
    <http://www.humansecurityreport.info/background/Cornett-Gibney_Political_Terror_Scale_1980-2001.pdf>

CVM (Securities and Exchange Commission of Brazil). 1990–2005. *Consulta de Documentos de Companhias Abertas*. Online database.
    <http://cvmweb.cvm.gov.br/SWB/Sistemas/SCW/CPublica/CiaAb/FormBuscaCiaAb.aspx?TipoConsult=c>

Czech Republic. 2005. *Annual Report on Export Control of Military Equipment and Small Arms for Civilian Use in the Czech Republic in 2004*. Prague: Ministry of Foreign Affairs of the Czech Republic.

Dawes, Nic and Monako Dibetle. 2006. 'SANDF: We Need Bean Counters.' *The Mail and Guardian Online*. 10 November.
    <http://www.mg.co.za/articlePage.aspx?articleid=289601&area=/insight/insight__national/>

De Temmerman, Els. 2006. 'Somalia Dragged into the War against Terror.' *New Vision* (Kampala). 23 September.

Dreyfus, Pablo. 2006. *Austria, Brazil, the Invisible Pistols and the Politics of Hiding Data*. Unpublished background paper. Geneva: Small Arms Survey.

—— and Antônio Rangel Bandeira. 2006. *Watching the Neighborhood: An Assessment of Small Arms and Ammunition 'Grey Transactions' on the Borders between Brazil and Paraguay, Bolivia, Uruguay and Argentina*. Working Document No. 2. Small Arms Control Project. Rio de Janeiro: Viva Rio. <http://www.smallarmssurvey.org/files/portal/spotlight/country/amer_pdf/americas_arg_bol_bra_para_uru_2006.pdf>

——, Benjamin Lessing, and Júlio César Purcena. 2005. 'The Brazilian Small Arms Industry: Legal Production and Trade.' In Rubem César Fernandes, ed. *Brazil: The Arms and the Victims*. Rio de Janeiro: 7 Letras/ISER, pp. 50–93. <http://www.vivario.org.br/publique/media/The_Brazilian_Small_Arms_Industry_Legal_production_and_Trade_By_Pablo_Dreyfus_Benjamin_Lessing_e_Julio_Cezar_Purcena.pdf>

Escobar, Pepe. 2005. 'The Algerian Connection.' *Asia Times* (Hong Kong). 29 July. <http://www.atimes.com/atimes/Middle_East/GG29Ak01.html>

EU (European Union). 1998. *European Union Code of Conduct on Arms Exports ('EU Code of Conduct')*. 8 June. Reproduced in UN doc. A/CONF.192/PC/3 of 13 March 2000. <http://www.smallarmssurvey.org/files/portal/issueareas/measures/reg.html#eu>

——. 2005. *Seventh Annual Report according to Operative Provision 8 of the European Union Code of Conduct on Arms Exports*. Official Journal of the European Union. Notice No. 2005/C 328/01. 23 December.
    <http://europa.eu.int/eur-lex/lex/LexUriServ/site/en/oj/2005/c_328/c_32820051223en00010288.pdf>

Federal Register. 2006. 'Transmittal No. 06-69: Notice of a Proposed Issuance of Letter of Offer Pursuant to Section 36(b)(1) of the Arms Export Control Act, as Amended.' Vol. 71, No. 187. 27, pp. 56501–07. September.
    <http://a257.g.akamaitech.net/7/257/2422/01jan20061800/edocket.access.gpo.gov/2006/pdf/06-8320.pdf>

Finland. 2004. *Annual Report according to the EU Code of Conduct on Arms Exports: National Report of Finland for 2003*. Helsinki: Ministry of Defence.

Fox, Michael. 2006. 'Venezuela Announces Gun Control Plan to Lower Crime.' Venezuelanalysis.com. 3 July.
    <http://www.venezuelanalysis.com/news.php?newsno=1999>

France. 2005. *Rapport au parlement sur les exportations d'armement de la France en 2004*. Paris: Ministry of Defence. December.

Germany. 2006. *Bericht der Bundesregierung über ihre Exportpolitik für konventionelle Rüstungsgüter im Jahre 2005 (Rüstungsexportbericht 2005)*. Berlin: Federal Ministry of Economics and Technology.

Gettleman, Jeffrey, Mohammed Ibrahim, and Yusuuf Maxamuud. 2007. 'American Diplomat to Visit Strife-torn Somali Capital.' *The New York Times*. 6 January.

Gibney, Mark. 2006. *Political Terror Scale 1980–2005*.
    <http://www.unca.edu/politicalscience/DOCS/Gibney/Political%20Terror%20Scale%201980-2005.pdf>

—— and Matthew Dalton. 1996. 'The Political Terror Scale.' *Policy Studies and Developing Nations*, Vol. 4, pp. 73–84.
    <http://www.unca.edu/politicalscience/DOCS/Gibney/Gibney%20and%20Dalton.pdf>

Glatz, Anne-Kathrin. 2006. 'Buying the Bullet: Authorized Small Arms Ammunition Transfers.' In Stéphanie Pézard and Holger Anders, eds. *Targeting Ammunition: A Primer.* Geneva: Small Arms Survey.

Glock. n.d. 'Perfection for Professionals.' Company brochure. Deutsch Wagram: Glock. Accessed 18 April 2007.
<http://www.glock.com/downloads/GLOCK_en.pdf>

HRW (Human Rights Watch). 2002. *Jenin: IDF Military Operations.* HRW Index No. E1403. New York: HRW. May.
<http://hrw.org/reports/2002/israel3/>

——. 2003. Time for Reckoning: Enforced Disappearances and Abductions in Algeria. HRW Index, Vol. 15, No. 2. New York: HRW. February.
<http://www.hrw.org/reports/2003/algeria0203/algeria0203.pdf>

IISS (International Institute for Strategic Studies). 2007. *Armed Conflict Database.* <http://www.iiss.org/publications/armed-conflict-database>

IRIN. 2005. 'Burundi: Army Probes Source of UN "Military Uniforms" in Rebel Hands.' 18 November.
<http://www.irinnews.org/report.asp?ReportID=50169>

——. 2006. 'Burundi: FNL Intensifies Attacks as Peace Talks Go On.' 2 June.
<http://www.irinnews.org/report.asp?ReportID=53665&SelectRegion=Great_Lakes&SelectCountry=BURUNDI>

Italy. 2005. *Relazione sulle operazioni autorizzate e svolte per il controllo dell'esportazione, importazione e transito dei materiali di armamento nonché dell'esportazione e del transito dei prodotti ad alta tecnologia (Anno 2004).* Rome: Camera dei Deputati. 30 March.

Jones, Richard D. and Charles Q. Cutshaw, eds. 2006. *Jane's Infantry Weapons 2004–2005.* Coulsdon: Jane's Information Group.

Landay, Jonathan S. 2005. 'Army Contract under Scrutiny: Chinese Company under Indictment.' *Tallahassee Democrat.* 28 April.

Landesman, Peter. 2003. 'Arms and the Man.' *The New York Times Magazine.* 17 August.

Leopold, Evelyn. 2006. 'Annan Finds 13 Incidents of Illicit Arms in Lebanon.' Reuters. 1 December.

Marsh, Nicholas. 2005. *Accounting Guns: The Methodology Used in Developing Data Tables for the Small Arms Survey.* Background paper. Oslo: PRIO/ NISAT. 14 November.

Mathiak, Lucy and Lora Lumpe. 2000. 'Government Gun-running to Guerrillas.' In Lora Lumpe, ed. *Running Guns: The Global Black Market in Small Arms.* London: Zed Books, pp. 55–80.

Maughan, Karyn. 2006a. 'Burundi Bungle Leaves SANDF Chiefs Red-faced.' *The Star* (Johannesburg). 31 October.
<http://www.int.iol.co.za/index.php?set_id=1&click_id=13&art_id=vn20061031034304313C570808>

——. 2006b. 'Get Your Facts Right, Mr Lekota.' *The Star* (Johannesburg). 2 November.
<http://www.int.iol.co.za/index.php?set_id=1&click_id=13&art_id=vn20061102035752728C658231>

Mazzetti, Mark. 2006a. 'Efforts by CIA Fail in Somalia, Officials Charge.' *The New York Times.* 8 June. <http://www.nytimes.com/2006/06/08/world/ africa/08intel.html?ex=1307419200&en=7b3e527023537e10&ei=5090&partner=rssuserland&emc=rss>

——. 2006b. 'US Signals Backing for Ethiopian Incursion into Somalia.' *The New York Times.* 27 December.

Morrow, James D. and Hyeran Jo. 2006. 'Compliance with the Laws of War: Dataset and Coding Rules.' *Conflict Management and Peace Science,* Vol. 23, No. 1, pp. 91–113. Spring.

Muhumuza, Rodney. 2006. 'Country Denies Smuggling Guns into Somalia.' *The Monitor* (Kampala). 30 September.

Netherlands. 2005. *Annual Report on The Netherlands Arms Export Policy in 2004.* The Hague: Ministry of Economic Affairs and Ministry of Foreign Affairs. September.

NISAT (Norwegian Initiative on Small Arms Transfers). 2006. *Data from the NISAT Database on Authorized Small Arms Transfers.* Unpublished background paper. Geneva: Small Arms Survey.

——. 2007a. *Data from the NISAT Database on Authorized Small Arms Transfers.* Unpublished background paper. Geneva: Small Arms Survey.

——. 2007b. *Calculations from the NISAT Database on Authorized Small Arms Transfers.* Unpublished background paper. Geneva: Small Arms Survey.

Norway. 2006. *Eksport av forsvarsmateriell frå Noreg i 2004, eksportkontroll og internasjonalt ikkje-spreiingsamarbeid.* Oslo: Ministry of Foreign Affairs.

Nzwili, Fredrick. 2006. 'Leadership Profile: Somalia's Islamic Courts Union.' *Terrorism Focus,* Vol. 3, No. 23, pp. 5–6. Washington, DC: The Jamestown Foundation. 13 June. <http://jamestown.org/terrorism/news/uploads/tf_003_023.pdf>

OAS (Organization of American States). 1997. *Inter-American Convention against the Illicit Manufacturing of and Trafficking in Firearms, Ammunition, Explosives, and Other Related Materials ('Inter-American Convention').* Adopted in Washington, DC on 14 November. Entered into force on 1 July 1998. Reproduced in UN doc. A/53/78 of 9 March 1998. <http://www.oas.org/juridico/english/treaties/a-63.html>

OED (*The Oxford English Dictionary*). 2006. *OED online.* Oxford: Oxford University Press. <http://www.oed.com/>

Pézard, Stéphanie. 2006. *Unintended Consequences: South African Peacekeepers and the Leakage of Weapons and Ammunition in Burundi.* Unpublished background paper. Geneva: Small Arms Survey.

Portugal. 2006. *Anuário estatístico da defesa nacional 2004.* Lisbon: Ministry of Defence. September.

Pyadushkin, Maxim. 2006. *Russia's SALW Transfers in 2003–2005.* Unpublished background paper. Geneva: Small Arms Survey.

Reuters. 2006. 'Factbox: Tensions in the Horn of Africa.' 25 December.
<http://www.reuters.com/article/worldNews/idUSL2523621320061225?pageNumber=1>

Roberts, John B, II. 2006a. 'Setback in Somalia: Covert CIA Operations and al Qaeda.' *The Washington Times.* 13 June.
<http://www.washingtontimes.com/op-ed/20060612-093253-7262r.htm>

——. 2006b. 'Suskind Gets It Wrong.' *The Washington Times.* 29 June. <http://www.washingtontimes.com/op-ed/20060628-094625-2795r.htm>

Romania. 2005. *Report on Arms Export Controls in 2002.* Bucharest: National Agency for Export Control.

SABC (South African Broadcasting Corporation) News. 2006. 'Lekota Acknowledges Problems in His Department.' 9 November.
<http://www.sabcnews.com/south_africa/general/0,2172,138139,00.html>

SAPA (South African Press Association). 2006a. 'Livid Lekota Denies Burundi Claims.' 1 November.
  <http://www.int.iol.co.za/index.php?set_id=1&click_id=13&art_id=qw1162375021152B253>

——. 2006b. 'No Vehicles in Burundi—Lekota.' 1 November.
  <http://www.int.iol.co.za/index.php?set_id=1&click_id=13&art_id=qw1162380063401B253>

SEESAC (South Eastern and Eastern Europe Clearinghouse for the Control of Small Arms and Light Weapons). 2006. *Countries under Weapons Sanctions/Arms Embargoes/Moratorium/Agreements: Summary Information.* Edition 5. Belgrade: UNDP/SEESAC. 22 November.

Shannon, Elaine and Tim McGirk. 2006. 'Iran and Syria Helping Hizballah Rearm.' *Time.* 24 November.
  <http://www.time.com/time/world/article/0,8599,1562890,00.html>

SIGIR (Special Inspector General for Iraq Reconstruction). 2006a. *Iraqi Security Forces: Weapons Provided by the US Department of Defense Using the Iraq Relief and Reconstruction Fund.* SIGIR-06-033. 28 October. <http://www.sigir.mil/reports/pdf/audits/06-033.pdf>

——. 2006b. *Quarterly Report to Congress.* 30 October. <http://www.sigir.mil/reports/quarterlyreports/Oct06/Default.aspx>

Small Arms Survey. 2002. *Small Arms Survey 2002: Counting the Human Cost.* Oxford: Oxford University Press.

——. 2004. *Small Arms Survey 2004: Rights at Risk.* Oxford: Oxford University Press.

——. 2005. *Small Arms Survey 2005: Weapons at War.* Oxford: Oxford University Press.

——. 2006. *Small Arms Survey 2006: Unfinished Business.* Oxford: Oxford University Press.

South Africa. 2003. South African Export Statistics for Conventional Arms 2000–2002. Pretoria: Directorate of Conventional Arms Control.

Spain. 2006. *Estadísticas españolas de exportación de material de defensa, de otro material y de productos y tecnologías de doble uso, año 2005.* Madrid: Ministerio de Industria, Turismo y Comercio/Secretaría de Estado de Turismo y Comercio. June.

Sukma, Rizal. 2004. *Security Operations in Aceh: Goals, Consequences and Lessons.* Policy Studies No. 3. Washington, DC: East–West Center.
  <http://www.eastwestcenter.org/stored/pdfs/PS003.pdf>

Sweden. 2006. *Strategic Export Controls in 2005: Military Equipment and Dual-Use Goods.* Government communication 2005/06: 114. Stockholm: Ministry of Foreign Affairs. 16 March.

Switzerland. 2006. *Exportations de matériel de guerre en 2005.* Berne: Secrétariat d'Etat à l'économie (SECO).

Taos Industries. 2006. Company Web site. Press releases. <http://www.taos-inc.com/press.htm>

Taurus. 2007. Company Web site. Accessed 17 April. <http://www.taurus.com.br>

Traynor, Ian. 2006. 'US in Secret Gun Deal: Small Arms Shipped from Bosnia to Iraq "Go Missing" as Pentagon Uses Dealers.' *The Guardian* (London and Manchester). 12 May. <http://www.guardian.co.uk/armstrade/story/0,,1773106,00.html>

UCDP (Uppsala Conflict Data Programme). 2007a. Uppsala Conflict Database. <http://www.pcr.uu.se/database/index.php>

——. 2007b. 'Definitions.' <http://www.pcr.uu.se/database/definitions_all.htm>

UK (United Kingdom). 2006. *United Kingdom Strategic Export Controls: Annual Report 2005.* London: Foreign and Commonwealth Office/Department for International Development/Department of Trade and Industry/Ministry of Defence. July.

UN (United Nations). 1945. *Charter of the United Nations and Statute of the International Court of Justice.* Adopted in San Francisco, 26 June. Entered into force on 24 October. <http://www.un.org/aboutun/charter/index.html>

UN Comtrade. 2006. *United Nations Commodity Trade Statistics Database.* Department of Economic and Social Affairs/Statistics Division. Accessed 6 September 2006. <http://unstats.un.org/unsd/comtrade/>

——. 2007. *United Nations Commodity Trade Statistics Database.* Department of Economic and Social Affairs/Statistics Division. Accessed 1 March 2007. <http://unstats.un.org/unsd/comtrade/>

UNGA (United Nations General Assembly). 2001a. *Protocol against the Illicit Manufacturing of and Trafficking in Firearms, Their Parts and Components and Ammunition, Supplementing the United Nations Convention against Transnational Organized Crime ('UN Firearms Protocol').* Adopted 31 May. Reproduced in UN doc. A/RES/55/255 of 8 June. <http://www.unodc.org/pdf/crime/a_res_55/255e.pdf>

——. 2001b. *Programme of Action to Prevent, Combat and Eradicate the Illicit Trade in Small Arms and Light Weapons in All Its Aspects ('UN Programme of Action').* 20 July. Reproduced in UN doc. A/CONF.192/15.
  <http://www.smallarmssurvey.org/files/portal/issueareas/measures/interun.html#unconf>

——. 2006. *Report on the Continuing Operation of the United Nations Register of Conventional Arms and Its further Development.* 15 August. Reproduced in UN doc. A/61/261.

UNSC (United Nations Security Council). 1992. Resolution 733 (1992). Adopted by the Security Council at its 3039th meeting. 23 January.

——. 2002. *Letter Dated 22 August 2002 from the Secretary-General Addressed to the President of the Security Council.* Reproduced in UN doc. S/2002/951 of 26 August.

——. 2004. *Letter dated 22 January 2004 from the Secretary-General Addressed to the President of the Security Council.* Reproduced in UN doc. S/2004/73 of 26 January.

——. 2005a. *Report of the Monitoring Group on Somalia pursuant to Security Council Resolution 1558 (2004).* Reproduced in UN doc. S/2005/153 of 9 March.

——. 2005b. *Report of the Monitoring Group on Somalia pursuant to Security Council Resolution 1587 (2005).* Reproduced in UN doc. S/2005/625 of 4 October.

——. 2006a. *Report of the Panel of Experts Established pursuant to Paragraph 3 of Resolution 1591 (2005) concerning the Sudan.* Reproduced in UN doc. S/2006/65 of 30 January.

——. 2006b. *Second Report of the Panel of Experts Established pursuant to Paragraph 3 of Resolution 1591 (2005) concerning the Sudan.* Reproduced in UN doc. S/2006/250 of 19 April.

——. 2006c. *Report of the Monitoring Group on Somalia pursuant to Security Council Resolution 1630 (2005)*. Reproduced in UN doc. S/2006/229 of 4 May.

——. 2006d. Resolution 1701 (2006). Adopted by the Security Council at its 5511th meeting on 11 August 2006. S/RES/1701 (2006) of 11 August.

——. 2006e. *Final Report of the Monitoring Group on Somalia pursuant to Security Council Resolution 1676 (2006)*. Reproduced in UN doc. S/2006/913 of 22 November.

——. 2006f. Resolution 1725 (2006). Adopted by the Security Council at its 5579th meeting on 6 December 2006. S/RES/1725 (2006) of 6 December.

——. 2007a. Resolution 1744 (2007). Adopted by the Security Council at its 5633rd meeting, on 20 February 2007. S/RES/1744 (2007) of 21 February.

——. 2007b. *Security Council Committee Established pursuant to Resolution 751 (1992) concerning Somalia*. Web site. Accessed 18 April. <http://www.un.org/sc/committees/751/index.shtml>

US (United States). 2006. *Fiscal Year 2005 'Section 655' Report*. Washington, DC: US DOS/US DOD. 14 March.

US Congress. 1947. National Security Act of 1947 (as Amended). Washington, DC: US Congress. 26 July. <http://www.intelligence.gov/0-natsecact_1947.shtml>

——. 2003. An Act Making Emergency Supplemental Appropriations for Defense and for the Reconstruction of Iraq and Afghanistan for the Fiscal Year Ending September 30, 2004, and for Other Purposes. Public Law 108–106. 108th Congress. 117 Stat. 1209–1239. H.R. 3289. 6 November. <http://frwebgate.access.gpo.gov/cgi-bin/getdoc.cgi?dbname=108_cong_public_laws&docid=f:publ106.108.pdf>

US DOD (United States Department of Defense). 2005. 'Contract No. 160-05.' 15 February. <http://www.defenselink.mil/contracts/2005/ct20050215.html>

——. 2006. *Measuring Stability and Security in Iraq: Report to Congress in Accordance with the Department of Defense Appropriations Act 2006 (Section 9010)*. August. <http://www.defenselink.mil/pubs/pdfs/Security-Stabilty-ReportAug29r1.pdf>

US DOS (United States Department of State). 2002. *Algeria (Country Reports on Human Rights Practices—2001)*. 4 March. <http://www.state.gov/g/drl/rls/hrrpt/2001/nea/8244.htm>

——. 2003a. *Venezuela (Country Reports on Human Rights Practices—2002)*. 31 March. <http://www.state.gov/g/drl/rls/hrrpt/2002/18348.htm>

——. 2003b. *United States Support for the United Nations Program of Action to Prevent, Combat and Eradicate the Illicit Trade in Small Arms and Light Weapons in All Its Aspects*. Washington, DC: Bureau of Political–Military Affairs, US DOS. 24 July. <http://www.state.gov/t/pm/rls/othr/misc/23105.htm>

——. 2004. *Israel and the Occupied Territories (Country Reports on Human Rights Practices—2003)*. 25 February. <http://www.state.gov/g/drl/rls/hrrpt/2003/27929.htm>

——. 2006. 'US Submits UN Resolution on Regional Force for Somalia.' 2 December. <http://usinfo.state.gov/xarchives/display.html?p=washfile-english&y=2006&m=December&x=20061202151620atiayduj0.0524866>

——. 2007. 'Background Note: Somalia.' Washington, DC: Bureau of African Affairs, US DOS. March. <http://www.state.gov/r/pa/ei/bgn/2863.htm>

WA (Wassenaar Arrangement on Export Controls for Conventional Arms and Dual-Use Goods and Technologies). 2002. *Best Practice Guidelines for Exports of Small Arms and Light Weapons (SALW)*. 12 December. <http://www.wassenaar.org/docs/best_practice_salw.htm>

Wallonia (Belgium). 2004. *Rapport au parlement wallon sur l'application de la loi du 05 août 1991, modifiée par les lois du 25 et du 26 mars 2003 relatives à l'importation, à l'exportation et au transit d'armes, de munitions et de matériel devant servir spécialement à un usage militaire, et de la technologie y afférente, du 1er septembre 2003 au 31 décembre 2003*. Government of Wallonia.

Weinstein, Michael A. 2006. 'Somalia's Islamists Resume Their Momentum and Embark on a Diplomatic Path.' *Power and Interest News Report*. 27 September. <http://www.pinr.com>

Wetzel, Hayden. 2002. *Algeria Country Commercial Guide FY 2003: Trade Regulations and Standards*. US & Foreign Commercial Service and US DOS. 29 November. Accessed through STAT-USA. <http://www.stat-usa.gov/>

ACKNOWLEDGEMENTS

Principal authors

Anne-Kathrin Glatz and Lora Lumpe

Contributors

Pablo Dreyfus and Júlio César Purcena (Viva Rio), Thomas Jackson and Nicholas Marsh (NISAT), Stéphanie Pézard, and Maxim Pyadushkin

Back to Basics

TRANSFER CONTROLS IN GLOBAL PERSPECTIVE

INTRODUCTION

In December 2006 a large majority of UN member states voted to begin a process that could lead to the adoption of a legally binding Arms Trade Treaty (ATT). This capped a year marked by other important achievements, notably the adoption of *The Geneva Declaration on Armed Violence and Development* (*Geneva Declaration,* 2006), and a major disappointment, the 2006 UN Programme of Action Review Conference (Review Conference).[1] Although their focus has narrowed following the failure of the Review Conference to reach a substantive outcome, UN member states are now attending to fundamentals.

Much of the illicit small arms trade depends, in fact, on the control—or lack of control—of legal transfers. As they grapple with the specifics of the transfer controls issue, states are moving towards a clearer understanding of their core commitments within the UN small arms framework. Key challenges include clarifying existing responsibilities, deciding whether and how to address the question of transfers to non-state actors, and developing means of effectively implementing transfer licensing criteria.

This chapter takes stock of the latest developments in the global small arms process, with a specific focus on new initiatives and continuing debates relating to transfer controls. Its principal conclusions include the following:

- The failure of the Review Conference to reach a substantive outcome derived from a broad range of factors, notably the inability of the UN small arms process to accommodate aspects of the issue falling outside of the traditional arms control/disarmament paradigm.

- The global small arms process is fragmenting. While not a problem as such, this does pose certain risks, such as inconsistency among measures and the possible neglect of the universal framework provided by the UN.

- States' existing obligations in relation to small arms transfers are extensive. Relevant, binding legal norms include direct limitations on certain transfers, as well as the rule holding states 'complicit' in violations of international law committed with arms that they transfer notwithstanding a known (or knowable) risk of misuse.

- While the question of banning arms transfers to non-state actors (NSAs) remains controversial, only NSAs that are *not authorized* to import arms by the state where they are located are, in fact, a major concern.

- Guidelines identifying factors to be considered as part of arms transfer licensing decisions can help states ensure that these are systematic, rigorous, and objective.

The chapter is divided into two parts. The first provides an overview of recent activity at the global level—in particular the 2006 Review Conference—while the second focuses on the issue of transfer controls. The transfer control sections include brief descriptions of the latest initiatives, as well as an exploration of key questions and challenges arising in this area.

GLOBAL UPDATE

This part of the chapter reviews key developments in global measures in 2006 and early 2007, focusing firstly on the 2006 Review Conference and then briefly recapping some of the other main initiatives. As we will see, the UN, long the leading standard setter at the global level, now has competition.

A collision of interests: the 2006 UN Review Conference

For the UN small arms process, the key event on the 2006 calendar was the first Review Conference for the *UN Programme of Action* (*Programme*). As specified in the *Programme* and repeated in the mandate conferred by the UN General Assembly, the Review Conference was 'to review progress made in the implementation of the Programme of Action' (UNGA, 2001b, para. IV.1.a; 2003, para. 1).

The two-week session of the Review Conference's Preparatory Committee (PrepCom), held from 9 to 20 January 2006, made clear that there was no consensus on how to interpret that mandate, nor on most of the specific issues states brought to the table. While the PrepCom, under the chairmanship of Ambassador Sylvester Rowe of Sierra Leone, adopted several decisions and recommendations of an organizational nature, it forwarded no substantive recommendations, let alone draft text, to the Review Conference.[2] During the period following the PrepCom, the conference president-designate, Ambassador Prasad Kariyawasam of Sri Lanka, held a series of informal consultations with UN member states and produced two versions of a draft Review Conference outcome document (Sri Lanka, 2006a; 2006b).

The Review Conference was held at UN headquarters in New York from 26 June to 7 July 2006. No meetings were held on 4 July, the US national holiday. Over half of the remaining nine days were devoted to organizational matters, high-level statements by and exchanges of views among states, and statements from civil society and international organizations. On one estimate, this left the conference only 20 hours to negotiate the outcome document (Prins, 2006, p. 117). In an effort to make up additional time, informal negotiating sessions were held until late in the evening on 5 and 6 July. During the two weeks, Conference President Kariyawasam issued several new versions of his draft outcome document (Sri Lanka, 2006c–g). In an effort to secure agreement on a limited number of points in the conference's last hours, he proposed adoption of the *Draft Declaration* (Sri Lanka, 2006h).

There were a few
silver linings to the
Review Conference.

At the end of the day, the Review Conference reached no substantive agreement of any kind. This included the question of post-conference follow-up, which was left dangling.[3] The failure of states to wrestle some minimum outcome from the Review Conference process was deeply disappointing to many. Nevertheless, there were a few silver linings.

States, international organizations, and civil society exchanged much information on *Programme* implementation at the Review Conference. Although this was far removed from the systematic review (and evaluation) of implementation that many wanted, it did constitute a small step in that direction.

Perhaps more importantly, the event sparked renewed national and international attention to the small arms issue. Civil society and, to some extent, the media were mobilized. Governments were also obliged to focus on the small arms issue as they prepared their ministers or other 'high-level' representatives for the event. At the beginning and end of the conference, states repeatedly expressed their renewed commitment to the *Programme*. They also seemed to agree that, while significant progress had been made in implementing the *Programme,* much more needed to be done.

Moreover, as disappointing as the non-result was, as Conference President Kariyawasam pointed out at the very end of the conference, it at least preserved the status quo.[4] Much of the language discussed during the last week of the conference represented a step back from existing provisions in the *Programme* (UNGA, 2001b) and *International Tracing Instrument* (UNGA, 2005a; 2005e),[5] underlining their 'extreme vulnerability'[6] to a process that seemed increasingly counter-productive. In an interesting twist of fate, the Review Conference, seen by many as a chance to 'fix' the *Programme,* 'renewed appreciation for this often maligned document' (Buchanan, 2006, p. 3). The Review Conference also steeled the resolve of many diplomats to achieve rather better results at the autumn 2006 session of the General Assembly's First Committee (see text below).

However one assesses the Review Conference, there can be little doubt that it represented a lost opportunity to advance the cause of effective *Programme* implementation and, however modestly, strengthen the UN's existing normative framework for small arms. Yet, given the forces at play, it is hard, in retrospect, to see how anything substantive could have emerged from the Review Conference process.

States came to that process with conflicting interpretations of the mandate, a broad and diverse set of interests, and, in many cases, an acute aversion to compromise. Any structure would have had difficulty coping with such tensions. The task was certainly beyond the means of the Review Conference, which relied on consensus for its decisions. The following sub-sections explore, in greater detail, the difficult mix of factors contributing to the failure of the Review Conference.[7]

Conflicting objectives. Up to the final stages of negotiations on the *Programme* in July 2001, the draft language concerning the review conference included a mandate to 'examine ways to strengthen and develop measures contained' in the *Programme* (Small Arms Survey, 2002, pp. 227–28). This text was not retained in the final version of the provision, which, like the General Assembly resolution that convened the 2006 Review Conference, simply indicated that states would 'review progress made in the implementation of the Programme of Action' (UNGA, 2001b, para. IV.1.a; 2003, para. 1).

In 2006, many states were eager to 'strengthen and develop' various aspects of the *Programme,* even championing issues that had been excluded from it due to a lack of consensus, such as transfers to NSAs, or others that had attracted relatively little attention in 2001, such as ammunition. Other states, however, insisted that there could be no discussion of any 'new issues', i.e. those not already explicitly included in the *Programme*. These states, moreover, tended to cling to a literal interpretation of the mandate. In their view, the Review Conference should concentrate on a review of *Programme* implementation, not the development of new norms. Whatever space for compromise that might have existed between these two camps was squeezed by the sheer number of issues the pro-norm group brought to the table.

A complex issue. Quite a few of the 'new issues' states promoted, such as development, human rights, or gender, are dealt with in other UN forums; many arms control diplomats have trouble grasping their relationship to small arms.[8] Although the *2005 World Summit Outcome* document underlines the 'interlinked and mutually reinforcing' nature of development, peace, security, and human rights (UNGA, 2005b, para. 9),[9] this understanding has yet to influence the mechanisms employed to address the small arms issue within the UN, which remains confined to the General Assembly's First Committee (Disarmament and International Security).

At the Review Conference, some countries, in particular European Union (EU) states, sought to break down such barriers, while others, such as the United States, insisted on maintaining them. In practical terms, the number of

Much of the language discussed during the last week represented a step back from the existing *Programme*.

issues being debated before and during the Review Conference became a problem, for the simple reason that time was relatively short and many states were in no mood to compromise.

Political will. Many observers singled out the United States as the main author of the Review Conference 'melt-down' (IANSA, 2006b). As discussed below, the United States made no secret of its willingness to block consensus on a number of issues it considered vital (its so-called 'redlines'). These included issues, such as global follow-up, that were crucial components of any minimally useful outcome document. This approach suited a number of states that had equally strong views on certain issues, but did not need to subvert or block the conference, so long as this was being done for them by the United States.

Yet, while some of this resistance was hidden, a good deal was apparent.[10] The Review Conference arguably set a new standard among small arms conferences for displays of diplomatic ill-will. The prevailing mood favoured pulling things apart, thwarting compromise, and sticking to established positions (or even hardening them). Many of the countries that suffer disproportionately from the small arms problem remained quiet, while some states took the opportunity to attack the United States. Overall, there was little or no substantive discussion. Politics prevailed and the search for compromise foundered. All of which was completely incompatible with a process based on consensus.[11]

> The prevailing mood favoured pulling things apart.

The consensus-based approach. From the beginning, UN small arms negotiators have preferred a consensus-based approach. This was important for many states because of the issue's (perceived) implications for national security. It also had the undeniable advantage of strengthening a process that, to date, has evolved within a political—as opposed to legal—framework.[12] This practice came under considerable strain during the UN tracing nego-tiations (Batchelor and McDonald, 2005). It had met with even rougher treatment at the 2005 and 2006 sessions of the General Assembly First Committee. At the Review Conference, an increasing number of states seemed prepared to use (and abuse) the rule to their advantage. As explained below, this led to its abandonment at the 2006 session of the First Committee.

Time. As noted earlier, states had very little time to negotiate a conference outcome document. The failure of the PrepCom to reach any substantive agreement made the task considerably more difficult, notwithstanding the infor-mal consultations Conference President Kariyawasam undertook during the period bridging the PrepCom and the Review Conference.

Much of the time initially set aside for negotiations at the Review Conference was gobbled up by the 'high-level segment', as 116 states took the floor to outline their policies and practices on small arms.[13] Relatively few of these statements, however, were designed to feed into the negotiations. When negotiations got under way in earnest, in the second (and last) week of the conference, some states had difficulty receiving timely instructions from their capitals on the issues under debate.

Process. The conference president, Prasad Kariyawasam, was 'in a difficult situation'.[14] Too much firmness, and he risked provoking a backlash; not enough, and states would run away with the process. Facilitators were appointed to broker consensus on the three main sections of the draft outcome document.[15] The range of outstanding issues was broad, however, and differences at the end of the first week, when the facilitators submitted their initial proposals to the conference president, remained deep.

A brief experiment with rolling text early in the second week proved disastrous, as states blanketed the provisions of the draft text with their preferred language. Conference President Kariyawasam then returned to his earlier practice of issuing new versions of his draft outcome document based on continuing discussions. Some conference participants, interviewed by the Small Arms Survey, felt that the conference president should have asserted more control and provided clearer guidance during the conference. Others noted that the extreme tensions in play rendered any form of 'direction' difficult.

Venue. Not for the first time, some stakeholders wondered if the result would have been different had Geneva (the home of many arms control processes), rather than New York, been the venue of the Review Conference. Geneva-based diplomats, by and large, tend to have a better understanding of small arms issues than their New York counterparts. The latter, in contrast, are well versed—arguably too well versed—in the hard political issues that tend to dominate the UN New York agenda. In fact, at the Review Conference it often appeared that the differences among countries were more political than substantive in nature.

In its immediate aftermath, many dismissed the Review Conference as a colossal waste of time and resources. Certainly, it appeared that the limits of UN norm-building had been reached. Yet, although it was difficult to find much of value in the Review Conference rubble, some of the debates undoubtedly helped to identify the most promising terrain for future normative work, within or outside the UN. The issue of transfer controls was prominent among these.

UN Secretary-General Kofi Annan speaks at the Small Arms Review Conference at UN headquarters in New York in June 2006. © Keith Bedford/Reuters

Good, bad, and ugly: Review Conference debates

In order to ascertain progress made at the Review Conference in various issue areas, including the question of obstacles to consensus, the Small Arms Survey solicited the views of key actors in the process. Unless otherwise noted, the following sections rely on this study.[16] The discussion begins with a consideration of transfer controls, including transfers to NSAs, before turning to some of the other issues debated at the conference. Since no outcome document was agreed, many states never indicated their final position on the subjects under discussion. The following analysis can therefore provide only a tentative account of the state of play in the areas under review.

Transfer controls

As described below, the United Kingdom has championed the cause of small arms transfer controls since early 2003. At the Review Conference it led efforts to secure agreement on some significant elaboration of the *Programme of Action*'s basic, national-level commitment, namely:

> *To assess applications for export authorizations according to strict national regulations and procedures that cover all small arms and light weapons and are consistent with the existing responsibilities of States under relevant international law, taking into account in particular the risk of diversion of these weapons into the illegal trade* (UNGA, 2001b, para. II.11).

Also under discussion were measures designed to enhance multilateral coordination on small arms transfers, including information exchange.

Many of the conference participants interviewed by the Small Arms Survey claimed that states reached consensus on such issues before the end of the meeting. A few others, however, questioned this. It is, in fact, impossible to know the truth of these claims. States that remained opposed to language on transfer controls could have concealed their opposition so long as there was no agreement on a text (a final outcome document) within which to anchor such language. Moreover, the Survey found some discrepancy in texts that members of different delegations claimed reflected final consensus.

One of these texts was a UK proposal discussed in the late-night negotiating session of 6–7 July and incorporated in the draft text that the conference president issued the following morning, on the last day of the conference. States would have agreed, at the national level:

The UK led efforts to secure some significant elaboration of the *Programme*'s basic transfer controls commitment.

> *To ensure effective control on the import, export, transfer and re-transfer of small arms and light weapons in accordance with national laws and practices and according to States' existing responsibilities under relevant international law including their obligations under the UN Charter and any other relevant international treaties to which they are party, as well as to apply an end user certificate and authentication process, with a view to avoiding their diversion into the illicit trade* (Sri Lanka, 2006g, para. II.6).[17]

While its references to the UN Charter and international treaty law helped clarify the phrase 'relevant international law', found in paragraph II.11 of the *Programme,* overall this text represented a step back from paragraph II.11. The phrase 'in accordance with national laws and practices' conflicts with the commitment states have made in the *Programme* to abide by 'relevant international law' when exporting small arms and light weapons. In essence, 'national laws and practices' would have trumped 'relevant international law'. This problem was noticed by some, though not all, delegations.[18]

Such language, if it had consensus support, at least meant the end of opposition to any discussion of legal transfers. In the months preceding, and again during, the Review Conference, some states argued that legal transfers were beyond the scope of the *Programme,* which, they claimed, covered only 'illicit' small arms and light weapons. In fact, the *Programme* regulates many legal activities, such as international arms transfers and brokering, in order to prevent legal weapons from becoming illicit. Paragraph II.11 is just one example of this approach.[19]

A more tangible gain of the Review Conference was consensus—or at least widespread agreement—on the need for further consideration of global measures. China had previously resisted this, preferring to keep all transfers-related initiatives at the regional or sub-regional levels. Paragraph II.25 of the conference president's 7 July draft text is modest, aiming only at an exchange of views at the global level; there is no commitment to develop global transfers guidelines, still anathema to several states. The draft also puts rather more emphasis on regional—as opposed to global—practices and measures (Sri Lanka, 2006g, para. II.21).

Those states that appeared most sceptical about international transfer controls at the Review Conference included China, Cuba, Egypt, India, Iran, Israel, Pakistan, the Russian Federation, and Venezuela. The US position was unclear.[20]

End-user certification

The issue of end-user certification was largely uncontroversial. States seemed to understand its importance in preventing weapons diversion. A US proposal to broaden the term 'end-user certificate', used in the *Programme* (UNGA, 2001b, para. II.12), to 'end-user certification process'[21] probably enjoyed consensus support. Yet, the establishment of a UN Group of Governmental Experts (GGE) on the subject met with opposition and was deleted from later draft outcome documents. Despite broad acceptance of the concept, there was little substantive discussion of end-user certification at the Review Conference. Without a structure, such as a GGE, that would allow states to develop the issue further, it may not progress much at the global level.

> States seemed to understand the importance of end-user certification in preventing weapons diversion.

Transfers to non-state actors

Along with the regulation of civilian possession, the issue of a ban on small arms transfers to NSAs nearly broke the back of the July 2001 UN Small Arms Conference (Small Arms Survey, 2002, p. 220). Before the 2006 Review Conference, many of the states that wanted strong language on the NSA issue hoped that the United States, which had adamantly opposed this in 2001, would soften its position, especially in the light of recent General Assembly resolutions that encourage UN member states 'to ban the transfer of man-portable air defence systems [MANPADS] to non-State end-users', excepting 'agents authorized by a Government' (UNGA, 2004, para. 5; 2005c, para. 5).

Yet, in 2006 the issue remained a 'redline' for the United States, and it firmly opposed any consideration of the NSA question by the Review Conference. A few other states also expressed opposition to the creation of a specific framework for such transfers, while, on the other side of the divide, sub-Saharan African states, joined by Israel and a few others, pushed for significant measures.

Conference President Kariyawasam offered language that sought to define a middle ground. States would have agreed:

> *To continue exchanging views on the policies, practices and considerations related to the transfer of small arms and light weapons to actors not authorized by the recipient State, with a view to developing common understandings or measures, taking into account the different contexts and approaches of States* (Sri Lanka, 2006e, para. II.26).

Yet, the United States and supporters maintained their opposition to any consideration of the issue, and there was little or no discussion of substance at the conference.

Other issues

Ammunition. Ammunition was one of the issues that bedevilled the UN tracing negotiations in 2004–05 (Small Arms Survey, 2006, pp. 102–03), and it remained contentious at the 2006 Review Conference. The EU and many other states sought to secure a place for ammunition in the conference outcome document, arguing, in some cases, that it was implicitly addressed in parts of the existing *Programme*. A few other states, most prominently the United States, indicated they would not accept any reference to ammunition in the conference outcome document.

In line with the recommendation agreed, by consensus, at the end of the UN tracing negotiations, Conference President Kariyawasam's final draft outcome document proposed dealing with ammunition as part of a separate UN process.[22] This too, however, was resisted by the United States.

Appropriate use/human rights. All references to human rights were purged from the *Programme* as a result of opposition from a number of states, including China, when the document was negotiated in July 2001 (Small Arms Survey, 2002, p. 221). Some states hoped to change this during the Review Conference process, pushing specifically for a reference to UN standards governing the use of force and firearms by law enforcement officials.[23] While included in Conference President Kariyawasam's pre-conference draft outcome documents,[24] the issue fell by the wayside soon after the Review Conference started. Those states that were opposed to human rights language expressed this indirectly, insisting, for example, on a narrow interpretation of *Programme* scope that would limit its application to the *trade* in *illicit* small arms and light weapons—not the use of legally procured weapons.[25] In this case, too, there was little or no discussion of substance.

> The regulation of civilian possession was another 2001 controversy that was revisited in 2006.

Civilian possession. The regulation of the civilian possession of small arms was another 2001 controversy[26] that was revisited in 2006. Some states, such as Mexico, as well as most civil society groups, pushed hard to get language in the final outcome document in 2006. Overall, it appeared that, since 2001, there was increased understanding of the importance of regulating civilian access in order to prevent the misuse of weapons and their diversion to the illicit market.

The issue, however, cuts quite close to the core of national sovereignty and, moreover, constitutes a red flag for the influential, US-based National Rifle Association (NRA).[27] True to 2001 form, the United States, with some support, insisted there could be no discussion of civilian weapons at the Review Conference. Attempts to find a compromise led nowhere, though attention was drawn to the use of the word 'possession' in the existing *Programme*. Arguably, the latter already applies, to a limited extent, to civilian possession.[28]

Demand. Although the document, as a whole, focuses on the supply of small arms, the *Programme* does mention the issue of demand in its preamble (UNGA, 2001b, para. I.7). The challenge, five years after its adoption, was to flesh out the concept and, above all, operationalize it. Yet the 2006 Review Conference made no progress towards this end. Conference participants and observers interviewed by the Small Arms Survey offered several explanations for this. Firstly, it appears that many diplomats, especially those based in New York, are unfamiliar with the issue and do not understand its policy implications. Recent research on demand issues[29] has yet to filter through. Secondly, the compartmentalized nature of the committee system within the UN General Assembly undoubtedly impairs consideration of an issue that exemplifies the cross-cutting, multi-dimensional nature of the small arms problem. Finally, many developing countries associate the demand question with state—as opposed to individual or community—demand, any discussion of which they oppose. These factors helped push the issue quickly and quietly off the Review Conference table.

Development. To the surprise of many, language linking small arms and development proved highly controversial at the Review Conference. While some developing countries supported proposals made by the EU along such lines, many others initially opposed them—whether because of concerns over conditionality, possible substitution, or a loss of control over national priority setting. Among the opponents, Barbados, representing Caribbean Community states, was especially vocal. The United States also resisted the linkage on the grounds that development was not an arms control issue and should therefore be addressed in other forums. Compromise text that mentioned plans or strategies[30] drawn up by recipient states themselves appeared to rally most—perhaps all[31]—of the sceptics by the end of the conference:

> *Noting the steps taken by the developed countries to provide development assistance towards efforts aimed at preventing, combating and eradicating the illicit trade in small arms and light weapons in all its aspects, States and appropriate international and regional organizations are encouraged to support such efforts, upon request and in accordance with overall national priorities and practices, and, where appropriate, to assist in their continued integration into relevant national and local plans and strategies.[32]*

Follow-up. At the end of the Review Conference, the United States stood alone in its opposition to any form of global follow-up to the *Programme*. This was a hardening of its position. In its high-level statement at the beginning of the conference, the United States indicated that it would 'not commit to another Review Conference', but left open the possibility of 'follow-on actions that are focused, practical, and intended to strengthen the implementation of the Program of Action' (US, 2006).[33]

No other state disputed, at least openly, the importance of global follow-up to *Programme* implementation.[34] Many states argued that the 2003 and 2005 Biennial Meetings of States (BMSs) had been unproductive and needed revamping, although there was some disagreement on this point. In his draft outcome documents, Conference President Kariyawasam rejected the term 'BMS' in favour of 'Action Implementation Meeting'. His 27 June text stated, moreover, that the chair's report of such meetings 'can serve as a basis for further recommendations by the General Assembly, if appropriate, on implementation of the Programme of Action' (Sri Lanka, 2006c, para. IV.3). Yet, the conference did not grapple with the details of a more practical, problem-solving approach to *Programme* follow-up.

> The conference did not grapple with the details of a more practical, problem-solving approach to *Programme* follow-up.

Gender/age considerations. In this area as well, the diplomatic community mostly failed to respond to the latest research—in this case, illustrating the differential impact of weapons on society. States were comfortable with the themes of child soldiers and the protection of women, but did not understand the practical implications gender and age distinctions have for small arms policy and programmes. The conference president's drafts reflected this, dropping, at an early stage, references to 'women and men' in favour of 'women' alone.[35] By the end of the Review Conference, gender and age had largely faded from view as states wrestled over other issues.

MANPADS. Israel, with support from the United States, pushed hard at the Review Conference for language on MANPADS. Somewhat surprisingly, given the existence of two General Assembly resolutions on the issue (UNGA, 2004; 2005c), this was resisted by several Non-Aligned Movement states, in particular Egypt and Iran. Officially, these countries opposed 'singling out' a particular weapon system for special treatment, yet most observers point to other factors. The common, US–Israeli front on MANPADS may have triggered the reflexive opposition of some states, while others could have been seeking a bargaining chip, especially vis-à-vis the United States. More fundamentally, some countries in the Muslim Middle East are reportedly concerned that the transfer of MANPADS—and eventually other light weapons—to governments could be restricted.

Victim assistance. The issue of victim assistance was discussed at the PrepCom and figured in the two draft texts Conference President Kariyawasam circulated during the period preceding the Review Conference (Sri Lanka, 2006a, para. I.16; 2006b, para. I.10). At the conference itself, however, it met with relative indifference and some suspicion. The issue was unfamiliar to most states, while others were wary of the potential financial implications of recognizing a new—and potentially very broad—category of victims.[36]

UN General Assembly First Committee 2006

The 2006 session of the UN General Assembly's First Committee[37] offered an opportunity to pick up some of the pieces left by the Review Conference, including the question of *Programme* follow-up. In the event, states seized the opportunity, and several important resolutions were adopted, providing, among other things, for a continuation of the *Programme* process. At the same time, however, the committee's 2006 session confirmed and amplified the recent trend away from consensus adoption of the small arms resolutions.

The 2006 session of the General Assembly's First Committee adopted several important resolutions.

The principal resolution on small arms, termed 'omnibus resolution', was adopted by a margin of 176 votes to 1 (the United States).[38] Most significantly, Resolution 61/66 provides for the continuation of the *Programme* process, with the convening of another BMS in 2008 (UNGA, 2006c, para. 4). Despite broad dissatisfaction with the 2003 and 2005 BMSs, the First Committee took no steps to ensure that the 2008 BMS will do more to bolster *Programme* implementation. Several states remain uncomfortable with new approaches to *Programme* follow-up.[39] It remains to be seen whether the committee can achieve more in this regard at its 2007 session.

A second resolution on the issue of 'conventional ammunition stockpiles in surplus' provided for a process of consultation and—'no later than 2008'—the establishment of a group of governmental experts (UNGA, 2006d, paras. 5, 7). It was adopted by 175 votes, with 1 state voting against (the United States) and 1 abstaining (Japan).[40] The 2006 resolution on the Arms Trade Treaty or ATT (UNGA, 2006e), like that on ammunition stockpiles, targeted not only small arms and light weapons, but all conventional weapons. It was adopted by 153 votes, with 1 vote against (the United States) and 24 abstentions,[41] and is discussed in more detail below. The First Committee also articulated next steps for the implementation of the *International Tracing Instrument* (UNGA, 2005a; 2005e), calling on states to provide the UN with critical information needed for weapons tracing and deciding that the first meeting on *Tracing Instrument* implementation would be held within the framework of the 2008 BMS (UNGA, 2006c, paras. 3, 5).

Overall, the 2006 session of the First Committee successfully put the UN small arms process back on track, yet this achievement was diminished somewhat by the loss of consensus support for critical elements of this process.

Other UN Initiatives

Independently of the 2006 First Committee, several other UN initiatives on small arms progressed in the latter part of 2006 and early 2007. These included the GGE on brokering, due to report to the UN Secretary-General in mid-2007 (UNGA, 2005d), as well as efforts by the UN Office on Drugs and Crime (UNODC) to advance implementation of the *UN Firearms Protocol* (UNGA, 2001a).[42] Several weeks after the 2006 Review Conference, the UN Sub-Commission on the Promotion and Protection of Human Rights endorsed the *Principles on the Prevention of Human Rights Violations Committed with Small Arms,* developed by Special Rapporteur Barbara Frey (UNGA HRC, 2006),[43] transmitting them to the Human Rights Council for consideration and possible adoption.

Non-UN initiatives[44]

For a time, the UN had a monopoly on the development of small arms norms at the global level. The *Programme of Action* (UNGA, 2001b) and *UN Firearms Protocol* (UNGA, 2001a) provided the key frameworks. Yet, UN pre-eminence in global standard setting, already eroding before 2006,[45] declined further in June 2006 with the adoption of *The Geneva Declaration on Armed Violence and Development* (*Geneva Declaration,* 2006).

A number of governments, international organizations, and NGOs had stressed the relationship between armed violence and development well before this.[46] Crucially, the links among development, peace, security, and human rights were spelled out in the *2005 World Summit Outcome* document (UNGA, 2005b, para. 9).[47] In the same year, the Development Assistance Committee of the Organization for Economic Co-operation and Development agreed that official development assistance could be used for conflict prevention and peace-building activities, including measures to tackle small arms proliferation.[48]

The Geneva Ministerial Summit, convened in June 2006 by Switzerland and the United Nations Development Programme, sought to generate international support for a set of practical commitments that would reduce the negative impact of armed violence on socioeconomic and human development. While the resulting *Geneva Declaration* (2006), adopted by 42 states[49] and 17 international organizations and NGOs, can hardly lay claim to universality, it is a global initiative, since participating states come from all regions of the world.

A core group of like-minded states[50] was established in November 2006 to promote the implementation of the *Geneva Declaration* and develop follow-up activities. The core group has drafted an Action Plan, which will be submitted to *Geneva Declaration* states later in 2007. Regional meetings are planned for South America and the Caribbean, Africa, and Asia in 2007–08. Progress made in the implementation of the *Geneva Declaration* is to be reviewed at a ministerial meeting, scheduled for June 2008.

> The global small arms process is fragmenting.

Variable geometry in global measures

The global small arms process, centred on the UN and the *Programme of Action,* is fragmenting. Some of the latest initiatives apply to the full UN membership, while others involve a narrower group of states. At the same time, not all UN initiatives have the support of all UN member states. The United States has broken ranks over the issue of *Programme* follow-up. The United States and other leading exporters, such as China and the Russian Federation, appear sceptical about the merits of an ATT.

While it makes sense for some states, such as those endorsing the *Geneva Declaration,* to move forward at a faster pace on issues of interest to them, the current cracks in the UN's universal framework for small arms are cause for concern. Consensus support lends important strength to the political norms contained in the *Programme* and *International Tracing Instrument.* US backing for the UN small arms process, while clearly useful, will not make or break the regime; yet there is a risk of it unravelling if other states follow the US example and opt out as well, whether wholly or partially.

Fragmentation also raises the prospect of inconsistency or incoherence among different initiatives. The problem is not that some states undertake measures that require more of them than the common minimum standards set out in the *Programme* and *International Tracing Instrument.* A problem arises, rather, where by complying with one norm, states breach a second.[51] In this regard, it is especially important that standards developed in relation to all conventional weapons—e.g. as part of the UN ATT or ammunition initiatives—do not conflict with those applicable to small arms and light weapons.

Last, but not least, even assuming the needs of consistency are met as states push forward on various fronts, it is crucial that the universal framework provided by the *Programme* not be left too far behind. Many of the common minimum standards found in the *Programme* are quite basic. Paragraph II.11 concerning transfer licensing has attracted attention for this reason. Moreover, even from a narrow arms control/disarmament perspective, critical gaps remain in the UN small arms framework, such as specific norms for ammunition.

SPOTLIGHT ON TRANSFER CONTROLS

While several multilateral instruments of the past decade regulate the licensing and conduct of weapons transfers, only the *UN Programme of Action,* specific to small arms, is of universal scope (UNGA, 2001b, sec. II, paras. 11–15).[52] There are few comparable standards covering the broader range of conventional weapons.[53] Yet, precisely because *Programme* norms in this area are relatively open-ended, the subject of arms transfer controls has risen to the top of the UN agenda. The question of a prohibition on arms transfers to non-state actors, first discussed at the 2001 UN Small Arms Conference, also remains important to many states. This part of the chapter will review recent initiatives in these areas and, above all, explore in some depth relevant concepts and debates.

The subject of arms transfer controls has risen to the top of the UN agenda.

While strengthened measures to prevent the diversion of weapons to unintended recipients, such as end-user certification, appear to have fairly broad support, the next steps at the global level are unclear. The latest initiatives on transfer controls focus on licensing decisions—specifically, the criteria and guidelines to be used in deciding whether to transfer arms to specific end users. This chapter also concentrates on these issues.

New initiatives[54]

Civil society has led efforts to develop global principles for arms transfers. Although some states, such as Costa Rica and Mali, were early converts, most governments have prioritized the issue only recently. Some of these initiatives have been developed with small arms and light weapons in mind, while others encompass the full range of conventional weapons.

Civil society initiatives

An important starting point for civil society initiatives was the formal launch, in May 1997, of the *International Code of Conduct on Arms Transfers* by Nobel Peace Prize laureates (*Nobel Laureate Code,* 1997). It was followed, in 2000, by the Framework Convention on International Arms Transfers (Framework Convention).[55] Modelled on components of the *Nobel Laureate Code* (1997) and the *EU Code of Conduct* (EU, 1998), it was drafted by a group of civil society organizations in collaboration with legal experts at Cambridge University. In contrast to the *Nobel Laureate Code,* which, in some areas, reached well beyond the status quo,[56] the Framework Convention sought to codify states' existing

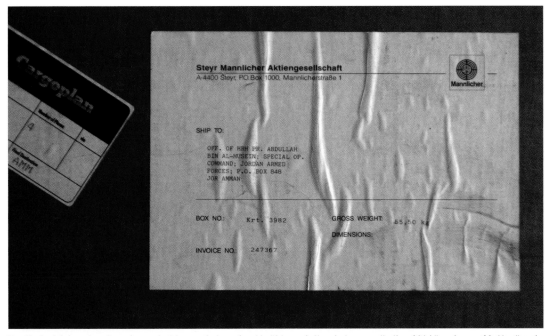

The shipping label on a box of guns from an Austrian manufacturer, found by US troops in the private arms collection of Odai Hussein, son of Saddam Hussein, in Baghdad in April 2003. © John Moore/AP Photo

obligations under international law, drawing on the UN Charter (UN, 1945) and other sources. The term 'framework' anticipated the development of related, but separate protocols covering various issues. Although the original draft applied to all conventional weapons, it was refined to focus on small arms and light weapons after the adoption of the *Programme* in July 2001.

A Steering Committee was established in 1999 to shape the initiative's strategic direction.[57] As of 2003, the Framework Convention became known as the Arms Trade Treaty (ATT).[58] The Control Arms Campaign[59] was launched in October 2003 in order to increase awareness and pressure governments on transfer control issues, in particular the ATT. After the UK government swung its support behind a legally binding treaty covering all conventional weapons in March 2005 (see below), the civil society initiative was again recast. The initial emphasis on a specific text gave way to the promotion of general principles designed to underpin an eventual instrument. The latest version of the *Global Principles,* issued by the ATT Steering Committee in March 2007, apply to all conventional arms, as well as their ammunition. They are equally applicable to the narrower category of small arms and light weapons (ATT SC, 2007).

In the period 2003–05, the Biting the Bullet Project[60] led a series of discussions involving governments, international organizations, and civil society designed to develop shared understandings in relation to small arms transfer guidelines, as well as restrictions on transfers to NSAs. The outcomes of the Small Arms Consultative Group Process include concrete proposals for transfer guidelines, which, reflecting the approach taken by the civil society ATT initiative, are addressed not only to exporting states, but also to importing and transit states (BtB, 2006b).

Government initiatives

Following the adoption of the *Programme* in July 2001, government initiatives on transfer controls targeted small arms and light weapons. More recently, they have also encompassed the full range of conventional arms. The UK government's Transfer Controls Initiative (TCI), launched at a conference at Lancaster House in London in January 2003 (UK, 2003), is situated within the *Programme*'s small arms framework. The Lancaster House conference, with participation from around the world, was followed by a series of meetings designed to build support for strengthened controls within different regions, as well as to ensure that regional perspectives were reflected in the initiative.

The TCI returned to the global stage in April 2006 when Kenya and the UK convened a meeting in Nairobi of nine other states from various regions, along with representatives of civil society. This meeting resulted in the adoption of *Suggested Common Guidelines* designed to elaborate upon the *Programme*'s basic commitments on transfer controls (*Nairobi Guidelines,* 2006). Participants hoped these would be used as the basis for further negotiations, but in the event, as noted earlier, relatively little progress was made on transfer controls at the 2006 Review Conference. There did, however, appear to be widespread agreement—even consensus—on the need for further consideration of global measures. An informal global meeting on *Programme*-related issues, including transfer controls, to be convened in Geneva by Canada and Switzerland at the end of August 2007, offers an initial opportunity to pursue these discussions.

As governments wrestle with the transfer controls issue, they confront some basic questions and challenges.

Since 2005, in parallel with the TCI, the UK has supported—indeed, promoted—an initiative covering all conventional arms. In contrast to the TCI, it aims at the negotiation of a legally binding treaty. Like the civil society initiative on transfer controls, it has been labelled the Arms Trade Treaty (ATT). In 2006, Argentina, Australia, Costa Rica, Finland, Japan, Kenya, and the United Kingdom joined forces to draft the UN General Assembly ATT resolution, mentioned earlier (UNGA, 2006e). It provides for the establishment of a group of governmental experts with a mandate 'to examine, commencing in 2008, the feasibility, scope and draft parameters for a comprehensive, legally binding instrument establishing common international standards for the import, export and transfer of conventional arms' (UNGA, 2006e, para. 2).

Resolution 61/89 also requests the UN Secretary-General 'to seek the views of Member States' on these issues (UNGA, 2006e, para. 1). A deadline of 30 April 2007 was set for written submissions by governments, with the Secretary-General then reporting to the General Assembly during its 62nd session (2007–08). The report of the planned group of governmental experts is to be prepared for the General Assembly's 63rd session (2008–09).

Key challenges

As governments wrestle with the transfer controls issue, they confront some basic questions and challenges: how to elaborate upon the *Programme of Action*'s basic norms; whether and how to address the question of transfers to non-state actors; and how to apply licensing criteria effectively.

'Existing responsibilities . . .'[61]

As outlined above, as of April 2007 the *Programme* is the only universal instrument that establishes standards for the transfer of small arms and light weapons. Paragraph II.11 of the *Programme* usefully points out that national export licensing decisions must be 'consistent with the existing responsibilities of States under relevant international law' (UNGA, 2001b). This, however, begs the question. What are these 'existing responsibilities'? What international law is 'relevant'? Government officials responsible for arms licensing decisions, along with their national legislatures, need more specific guidance than that provided by paragraph II.11. The *Nairobi Guidelines, Global Principles,* and other initiatives described previously in the chapter are designed to address this need. They are based on certain principles of international law, which, however translated, will be crucial to any common interpretation of paragraph II.11 that UN member states may, in future, agree upon.

The two principal sources of international law are treaty and custom. Treaties bind states that are party to them, whereas customary international law binds all states.[62] As we will see, many of the international legal norms that are most relevant to international arms transfers are customary in nature, applicable to all states. Others, including UN Security Council arms embargoes, derive from the UN Charter (UN, 1945)—a treaty, yet of near-universal application.

Box 4.1 Complicity in violations of international law

The relationship between arms exporting and importing states is not simply a matter of policy or ethics; it is, in fact, defined by law. Rules drafted by the International Law Commission (ILC)[63] specify when states incur legal responsibility as a result of assistance they give to a second state in its commission of an internationally wrongful act.[64]

Article 16
Aid or assistance in the commission of an internationally wrongful act
A State which aids or assists another State in the commission of an internationally wrongful act by the latter is internationally responsible for doing so if:

(a) That State does so with knowledge of the circumstances of the internationally wrongful act; and

(b) The act would be internationally wrongful if committed by that State (UNGA ILC, 2001).

While the UN General Assembly took note of the ILC articles and commended them to the attention of governments, it did not formally adopt them. Nor have they been incorporated in any legally binding instrument. In early 2007, however, in its judgement in the Bosnian genocide case, the International Court of Justice (ICJ) indicated that Article 16 reflects customary international law (ICJ, 2007, para. 420), meaning that it legally binds all states. This is an important development, since, before the ICJ ruling, the principle's status had been unclear.

Article 16(b) limits the scope of the rule to those cases where both assisting and assisted states are subject to the same primary rule of international law. This would exclude a treaty that the assisted–but not assisting–state is party to. It has little or no application to international arms transfers, as virtually all of the relevant primary rules form part of customary international law, binding on all states. There are many primary rules that apply to non-state actors as well as states, including international humanitarian and international human rights norms. It therefore seems reasonable also to apply the complicity rule where the assisted entity (i.e. the arms recipient) is a non-state actor.

The practical application of the rest of Article 16 raises more complex questions. What 'knowledge' must the assisting state have if it is to be considered complicit in the commission of an internationally wrongful act? What counts as 'aid or assistance'? At this relatively early stage in the interpretation and application of the rule, there are no definite answers. In his commentary on Article 16, the ILC's last Special Rapporteur on state responsibility asserted that 'the aid or assistance must be given with a view to facilitating the commission of that act, and must actually do so' (Crawford, 2002, p. 149). Yet, this interpretation is at odds with the text of Article 16 and would, moreover, render its application extremely difficult.

If one focuses on the text of Article 16, one must conclude that the assisting state does not have to *intend* to facilitate the commission of the internationally wrongful act. Under the terms of that Article 16, it must simply have 'knowledge of the circumstances' of the act (UNGA ILC, 2001, art. 16(a)). This would include, for example, knowledge that a state receiving transferred weapons has a poor human rights record. It is unclear whether the assisting state must actually know of such circumstances or could instead be presumed to know–specifically where a problem, though not actually known, could easily be ascertained by the exporting state. This latter interpretation would obviously enhance the effectiveness of the rule.

Article 16 provides little guidance on the question of what would qualify as 'aid or assistance'. More specifically, do transferred weapons need to be used in actual violations of international law before the transferring state becomes complicit in these? In discussing 'complicity in genocide', which it acknowledged was 'similar' to the concept of 'aid or assistance' mentioned in Article 16, the ICJ referred to 'the provision of means to enable or facilitate the commission of the crime' (ICJ, 2007, para. 419). This hints at a relatively accommodating standard: the assistance would not have to be essential to the commission of the wrongful act, but merely 'facilitate' it in some less direct sense.[65]

The ICJ has stated that the complicity rule is customary international law, applicable to all states. While its exact contours have yet to be defined, if exporting states wish to remain well beyond the reach of the rule, they would be well advised not to transfer arms if they know (or should know) of circumstances creating a significant risk that these weapons will be used for violations of international law.

Source: Hasan (2007)

Whether they take the form of custom or treaty, 'primary rules' of international law establish substantive obligations for states, while 'secondary rules' specify the conditions under which the primary rules are breached, as well as the legal consequences of such breaches (Cassese, 2005, p. 244). Secondary rules include those governing state responsibility—in particular the concept of complicity, relevant to all arms exporting states (Box 4.1).

Direct limitations on arms transfers. Many primary rules of international law limit or prohibit the transfer of arms in specific circumstances. Mandatory UN Security Council arms embargoes, legally binding on all UN member states (UN, 1945, art. 25),[66] offer one prominent example. Certain principles of the UN Charter—for example, that of non-intervention in the internal affairs of another state—also serve as direct restraints on international arms transfers.[67] Certain rules of international humanitarian law (IHL) also limit the right of states to transfer arms. These include the rule requiring parties to an armed conflict to distinguish between combatants and civilians, and, by extension, prohibiting the use of weapons intrinsically incapable of doing so (*Add. Protocol I*, 1977, arts. 48, 51(2), 52(2); *Add. Protocol II,* 1977, art. 13(2)); and the rule prohibiting the use of weapons that 'cause superfluous injury or unnecessary suffering' (*Add. Protocol I,* 1977, art. 35(2)). While both prohibitions concern weapons use, not transfer, they are clearly incompatible with a right of transfer. Both rules are customary in nature (ICJ, 1996, paras. 78–79).

Limitations based on likely use. Other restrictions on international arms transfers derive from the risk that such weapons will be used for violations of primary international rules. An arms exporting state would be considered 'complicit' in such violations if it knew (or ought to have known) of circumstances creating such a risk (Box 4.1).

The 'existing responsibilities of States under relevant international law' are, in fact, extensive.

Relevant primary rules include UN Charter and customary rules relating to the use of force and non-intervention; IHL;[68] international human rights law; as well as the crime of genocide, crimes against humanity, and war crimes. Focusing, purely for purposes of illustration, on international human rights law, the norms most relevant to international arms transfers (and possible misuse) are those enshrining the right to life (UNGA, 1948, art. 3; 1966, art. 6), and the right not to be subjected to torture or to cruel, inhuman, or degrading treatment or punishment (UNGA, 1948, art. 5; 1966, art. 7). These rules, too, are customary in nature, legally binding on all states.

This chapter will not offer a complete enumeration of international norms that are directly or indirectly applicable to international arms transfers, as this can be found elsewhere (Gillard, 2000; ATT SC, 2007). For our purposes, it is sufficient to note that the 'existing responsibilities of States under relevant international law' are, in fact, extensive. States commit an 'internationally wrongful act' if they transfer small arms in violation of a direct limitation on such transfers (e.g. an arms embargo). They are probably also in breach of their international obligations if they transfer arms even though they know (or should know) of circumstances creating a significant risk that these weapons will be used for violations of international law (e.g. human rights norms); they are 'complicit' in such violations. While the scope and application of the complicity rule is not yet settled, at a minimum one would have to conclude that transfers of this kind are of questionable legality and thus irresponsible (TRANSFERS).

Non-state actors[69]

Several regional instruments incorporate the principle of a ban on small arms transfers to NSAs (OAU, 2000, para. 4(i); EU, 2002, art. 3(b); ECOWAS, 2006, art. 3(2)). UN Security Council Resolution 1373, adopted just after the 11 September 2001 terrorist attacks on the United States, takes the same approach with respect to 'the supply of weapons to terrorists' (UNSC, 2001, para. 2(a)).[70] International concern about the potential for terrorist or insurgent use of

MANPADS has prompted a range of regional and global measures, including two UN General Assembly resolutions (UNGA 2004; 2005c), that similarly aim to curtail and control the supply of these weapons to NSAs.[71]

Nevertheless, as described earlier in the chapter, the question of banning the transfer of all small arms and light weapons to NSAs, deeply divisive when the *Programme of Action* was adopted in July 2001, remained so at the 2006 Review Conference. In part, this can be attributed to differences in the nature of the perceived threat. MANPADS concerns mostly stem from fears of diversion, while proposals to ban the transfer of all small arms and light weapons to NSAs are more often motivated by the prospect of their deliberate transfer to rebel groups.

The Small Arms Consultative Group Process (CGP), mentioned earlier, examined the NSA transfer issue in depth from 2003 to 2005. The following text is informed, to a large extent, by the CGP's discussions and conclusions.[72]

What are NSAs? This seemingly simple question accounts for much of the polarization of the NSAs issue. During the 2001 UN Small Arms Conference, some states feared that any commitments relating to NSAs would impinge upon legitimate civilian possession and trade in firearms. Yet, those states seeking strong language on NSAs had different actors in mind: rebel groups, and criminal and terrorist organizations.

> Only some non-state actors are a concern for states.

A wide variety of NSAs acquire, use, and misuse small arms and light weapons. Their relationships with states range from legally authorized extensions of the state security sector to insurgent forces seeking to overthrow the established government. They include:

- *Armed rebel groups, 'freedom fighters', paramilitaries, or warlords;*
- *Paramilitaries and other NSAs closely associated with state agencies;*
- *Civilian militia including communal groups and militias, civil defence forces, vigilante groups;*
- *Terrorists and terrorist organisations;*
- *Criminals and criminal groups, including black market arms traders;*
- *Political parties and associated political groups;*
- *Private military companies;*
- *Private security companies, and other private companies with their own security staff;*
- *Arms traders: domestic legal retail markets, traders and wholesalers, arms brokers, and front companies;*
- *Civil institutions, such as museums;*
- *Civilians: sports shooters, hunters, gun collectors, holders of guns for personal protection* (BtB, 2006a, p. 3).

Only some of these actors are a concern for states; they may or may not pose a significant risk of small arms diversion or misuse. National policy clearly needs to be sensitive to such differences, yet it is important to note that simple disaggregation of actor types, though useful, does not yield a neat separation of problematic and unproblematic NSAs. A more policy-relevant distinction is that between those NSAs authorized to import arms by the government on whose territory they are located and those who have no such authorization.

Within the CGP, transfers to authorized NSAs, including authorized civilians, were not seen as a major source of concern. By contrast, arms flows to unauthorized NSAs were associated with adverse impacts on internal and international security, and a relatively high risk of weapons misuse and diversion. Such transfers also raise concerns surrounding sovereignty.

These considerations explain why most governments support a ban on any transfer to an unauthorized NSA. Some governments, however, maintain that in certain exceptional cases, such a transfer would be justified. Discussions within the CGP consequently focused on two policy options: a total ban on transfers to unauthorized NSAs and a presumption of non-transfer with an international framework that would allow for 'hard case' exceptions. A third option is to address NSA transfer concerns through regular licensing systems and principles. Rigorous transfer licensing systems could, arguably, remove the need for separate measures on NSAs.

The CGP explored at some length the 'hard cases' that might offer grounds for an exceptional transfer of small arms to an unauthorized NSA (the second policy option). Four elements were identified that, in combination, could provide such justification. These relate to the context of the transfer, the motivations for it, the characteristics of the NSA, and the potential effectiveness of the transfer in achieving legitimate aims.

In the view of the CGP, only two contexts might yield a 'hard case', specifically where the territory to which arms were to be sent was:

- experiencing civil war or internal armed conflict; or
- experiencing large-scale oppression or genocide.

The only legitimate motivations would be to:

- protect vulnerable communities or populations from imminent or ongoing attack, violent oppression, or genocide;
- promote a relatively desirable peace settlement (e.g. by preventing an unjust victory by better-armed forces); or
- support international peace operations or humanitarian interventions (e.g. by providing small arms to NSAs working directly under instruction from the international operations/interventions).

Rebels of the Moro Islamic Liberation Front raise their weapons at their main base in Darapanan, Maguindanao, on the Philippine island of Mindanao, in June 2005. © Erik de Castro/Reuters

Only NSAs with certain characteristics would be considered potentially legitimate recipients of small arms. Such NSAs should:

- command substantial legitimacy and internal support among the population of the relevant state;
- have unselfish aims consistent with the motivations underlying the proposed transfer;
- have demonstrated commitment and capacity to use the supplied arms effectively and with appropriate restraint;
- be unlikely to misuse the arms supplied to them on a substantial scale; and
- have a credible commitment and capacity to control the transferred arms effectively, including relatively safe and secure storage, and low risk of re-export or diversion to unauthorized uses or users.

Even if these elements of a hard case were present, any decision to supply small arms would need to be informed by an assessment of the transfer's potential effectiveness. It would have to have a reasonable prospect of achieving its aims and would normally be part of a package of other measures, including efforts to reduce risks of diversion. Some CGP participants also argued that states transferring arms to NSAs should accept responsibility for their misuse and, moreover, take action to prevent such misuse. A final conclusion was that any transfer of arms to NSAs, even in hard cases, should not replace more robust and effective international responses (BtB, 2006a; Bourne, 2007).

The question of whether arms transfers to non-state actors are ever justified remains unresolved.

In practice, very few situations would satisfy this four-part test. The international community's response to the Rwandan genocide was largely ineffectual. A non-state actor, the Rwandan Patriotic Front (RPF), put an end to a genocide that was being perpetrated by the Rwandan government and allied militia. Yet, there is no evidence that the RPF needed additional supplies of arms or ammunition, or that such supplies would have enhanced its capacity or resolve to protect civilian populations (Bourne, 2007). While the Rwandan genocide offers a compelling example of a situation in which, one might think, a transfer of arms to an NSA would be justified, the facts of the case leave the question open.[73]

The fight against international terrorism would also seem to offer promising ground for hard case exceptions. In the weeks following the 11 September terrorist attacks, the United States and allied states gave the Northern Alliance arms and direct military support in its successful fight against Afghanistan's Taliban government. Nevertheless, it appears that it was the direct military support—not the (additional) weapons—that was the key to the Northern Alliance's success against the Taliban. It is debatable, moreover, whether this case belongs under the NSA rubric, as the international community had progressively withdrawn its recognition of the Taliban government as a result of its support for and protection of al Qaeda (Bourne, 2007).

Independent observers have also reported that both the RPF and Northern Alliance committed serious violations of international humanitarian law, including revenge killings of civilians and the summary execution of prisoners (HRW, 1999; 2002).

This brief consideration of two cases cannot settle the question of whether arms transfers to NSAs are ever justified. Yet it demonstrates the practical difficulty of meeting the criteria discussed by the CGP. Arguments favouring the exceptional transfer of weapons to NSAs tend to emphasize the context and motivation underlying such transfers. Often overlooked are the practical hurdles exporters face in ensuring that recipient NSAs act responsibly and that transferred weapons are effective in achieving their (legitimate) aims. Although the CGP has helped clarify some of the issues surrounding the NSA transfer question, the latter's complexity probably precludes an early end to the current diplomatic stalemate.

The challenge of implementation[74]

As indicated earlier, the 'existing responsibilities of States under relevant international law' are extensive. Despite the controversies that surround attempts to spell them out at the global level, there is, in reality, no escape. Key legal norms governing non-intervention, the non-use of force, the conduct of armed conflict, and human rights are customary in nature, applicable to all states. In the context of arms transfer licensing, these norms apply where the recipient is a state; many also apply where the recipient is an (unauthorized) NSA. Whatever the outcome of discussions on global criteria, arguably the critical challenge is the effective implementation of such principles.

The question of how to apply arms transfer criteria has received limited attention to date, even though they are increasingly part of national (and regional) control frameworks. In some cases, their application is relatively straightforward—as when determining, for example, whether a recipient is subject to an arms embargo. Yet, when the

---

Box 4.2 Applying IHL criteria

Whether within the framework of a regional instrument or independently, many states have agreed to take the recipient's respect for IHL into account in their arms transfer decisions. The specific wording used to formulate such criteria varies, but most stipulate that arms transfers should not be authorized if there is a 'serious', 'clear', or 'likely' risk that transferred weapons or material would be used to commit violations of IHL.

These terms raise difficult questions of interpretation. When does a risk become 'serious' or 'clear' or 'likely'? What time period is relevant to an assessment of potential future misconduct? Isolated examples of past violations may not provide sufficient grounds for concern. Yet, if there is evidence of a pattern of violations, or if no steps have been taken to prevent violations from recurring, there may well be a problem. The degree to which past behaviour is indicative of present or future conduct is also highly dependent on such developments as changes in government or to the country's political system.

Factors that are not directly related to a recipient's compliance with IHL may also be relevant when determining whether transferred weapons might be used for IHL violations. These include the security situation in the recipient state, the stability of its government, and its record of respect for human rights. Equally important is the possibility of diversion to other destinations where arms could be used for violations of IHL. Important considerations therefore include previous known or suspected cases of diversion involving the recipient, the quality of stockpile management and security for transferred arms, and control over re-exports.

The ICRC has distilled these and other factors in the form of nine key indicators (ICRC, 2007):

- Whether a recipient which is, or has been, engaged in an armed conflict has committed serious violations of IHL;
- Whether a recipient which is, or has been, engaged in an armed conflict has taken all feasible measures to prevent violations of IHL, or cause them to cease, including by punishing those responsible for serious violations;
- Whether the recipient has made a formal commitment to apply the rules of IHL and taken appropriate measures for their implementation;
- Whether the recipient state has in place the legal, judicial and administrative measures necessary for the repression of serious violations of IHL;
- Whether the recipient disseminates IHL, in particular to the armed forces and other arms bearers, and has integrated IHL into its military doctrine, manuals, and instructions;
- Whether the recipient has taken steps to prevent the recruitment of children into the armed forces or armed groups and their participation in hostilities;
- Whether accountable authority structures exist with the capacity and will to ensure respect for IHL;
- Whether the arms or military equipment requested are commensurate with the operational requirements and capacities of the stated end-user;
- Whether the recipient maintains strict and effective control over its arms and military equipment and their further transfer (ICRC, 2007).

Each indicator is accompanied by a checklist of questions for arms licensing officials (ICRC, 2007).

Sources: Waszink with ICRC (2007); ICRC (2007)

recipient's likely use of transferred arms is at issue, the assessment is more complex. By developing regulations or guidelines for the application of certain arms transfer criteria, states can facilitate licensing decisions.

Guidelines that identify specific factors to be considered when making assessments can contribute to more consistent implementation of arms transfer criteria adopted at the national, regional, or global level. They can also be a helpful tool for government officials involved in arms transfer decisions. With the increased number of criteria and instruments to be taken into account, the task of export-licensing officials has become more complex, yet it cannot be assumed that they will be experts in the range of areas they need to assess.

For this reason, in 2003 the EU Working Party on Conventional Arms Exports (COARM) began to develop best practice for the interpretation of the eight criteria in the *EU Code of Conduct* (EU, 1998). Of these criteria, best practices have so far been developed for the five criteria related to human rights, internal situation, regional stability, risk of diversion, and sustainable development (EU, 2006). As of early 2007, work on the last three was under way. The International Committee of the Red Cross (ICRC) has also produced a set of guidelines to assist states in their assessment of a recipient's compliance with the rules regulating the conduct of armed conflict, i.e. IHL (ICRC, 2007) (see Box 4.2).

While these evaluations will always involve an element of subjective judgement, guidelines such as those developed by COARM and the ICRC can help states to take a more systematic, rigorous, and objective approach to arms transfer licensing. They can also encourage decision-makers to articulate the risks they believe are associated (or not) with specific transfers.

CONCLUSION

Six years on from the adoption of the *UN Programme of Action,* the UN small arms process remains alive and relatively well—though somewhat resistant to those aspects of the issue falling outside of the traditional arms control/disarmament paradigm. A smaller group of states, from all parts of the world, are pushing ahead on the issue of armed violence and development (*Geneva Declaration,* 2006), putting a more intricate—and potentially more dynamic—stamp on global small arms activity. While the fragmentation of the global process is not a problem as such, it does carry certain risks. These include inconsistency among measures, as well as the possible neglect of the universal framework provided by the UN.

For the moment, despite the loss of consensus support for important elements of the process, UN member states are forging ahead on several fronts, including that of transfer controls. Championed by civil society at an early stage, governments are now prioritizing this issue. Key challenges include unpacking the *Programme*'s basic commitments on transfer controls, deciding whether and how to address the question of transfers to non-state actors, and developing means of effectively implementing transfer licensing criteria.

As the chapter describes, in the area of transfer controls states' 'existing responsibilities . . . under relevant international law' (UNGA, 2001b, para. II.11) are extensive. Relevant legally binding norms include direct limitations on certain arms transfers, as well as the rule holding states 'complicit' in violations of international law that are committed with arms they transfer to others, notwithstanding a known (or knowable) risk of misuse (see the section on 'Existing responsibilities . . .', above). Whatever the outcome of discussions on global criteria, arguably the critical challenge is the implementation of such principles. Guidelines identifying factors to be considered when deciding whether or not to authorize a particular transfer can help states take a more systematic, rigorous, and objective approach to these decisions.

In short, UN member states have much to consider as they attempt to come to terms, collectively, with their 'existing responsibilities . . . under relevant international law'. This includes the risk that the UN small arms process, recently revived, could again fade if the current focus on core transfer control commitments proves to be superficial. ▪

LIST OF ABBREVIATIONS

ATT	Arms Trade Treaty	ILC	International Law Commission
BMS	Biennial Meeting of States	MANPADS	man-portable air defence system
	(*UN Programme of Action*)	NRA	National Rifle Association
CGP	Small Arms Consultative Group Process	NSA	non-state actor
COARM	European Union Working Party on	PrepCom	Preparatory Committee (UN Programme
	Conventional Arms Exports		of Action Review Conference)
EU	European Union	*Programme*	*UN Programme of Action*
Framework	Framework Convention on International	Review	2006 UN Programme of Action Review
Convention	Arms Transfers	Conference	Conference
GGE	Group of Governmental Experts	RPF	Rwandan Patriotic Front
ICJ	International Court of Justice	TCI	Transfer Controls Initiative
ICRC	International Committee of the Red Cross	UNODC	United Nations Office on Drugs and
IHL	international humanitarian law		Crime

ENDNOTES

1   The full, official name of the conference was the United Nations Conference to Review Progress Made in the Implementation of the Programme of Action to Prevent, Combat and Eradicate the Illicit Trade in Small Arms and Light Weapons in All Its Aspects (UNGA, 2006b).

2   For more information on the PrepCom, see IANSA (2006a) and UNGA (2006a).

3   In the *Programme,* states recommended that the UN General Assembly convene a review conference in 2006, as well as biennial meetings to consider *Programme* implementation (no dates specified) (UNGA, 2001b, para. IV.1). Pursuant to these recommendations, the General Assembly convened Biennial Meetings of States in July 2003 and July 2005, along with the 2006 Review Conference. It made no provision for post-2006 follow-up, as the Review Conference was expected to decide this question.

4   'We haven't lost anything', Conference President Kariyawasam said in remarks made at the conference's closing session.

5   In relation to transfer controls, see the text below.

6   Remarks by a participant in a Geneva Forum meeting, held on the margins of the Review Conference on 6 July 2006.

7   This analysis draws on the Small Arms Survey study described in greater detail in the 'Review Conference Debates' section, below.

8   For more on these issues, see Small Arms Survey (2003, ch. 4; 2004, ch. 7; 2006, ch. 12).

9   See also UNGA (2005b, paras. 6, 12, 72).

10   See the 'Review Conference Debates' section, below, for more information on national positions.

11   Concerning the failure of (and opportunities for) disarmament diplomats to actively seek and develop compromise solutions in such negotiations, see Prins (2006).

12   Both the *Programme* (UNGA, 2001b) and the *International Tracing Instrument* (UNGA, 2005a; 2005e) are expressions of political commitment ('politically binding').

13   This number includes statements made by permanent observers to the UN. Some of the statements were given on behalf of regional or other groups of states. Text, and in some cases video, is available at <http://www.un.org/events/smallarms2006/mem-states.html>

14   Remarks of one conference participant, interviewed by the Small Arms Survey in December 2006.

15   Colombia acted as facilitator for section II (national, regional, and global measures), Switzerland for section III (international cooperation and assistance), and Japan for section IV (follow-up).

16   Eighteen participants in, or close observers of, the Review Conference process participated in the study (11 from government, 3 from international organizations, 4 from civil society). In relation to 12 different issue areas, they were asked to identify: (1) how close states came to reaching agreement on the issue; (2) the substance of any agreement or understanding; and (3) the main obstacles to progress. Participants were also asked for their general impressions of the conference, including those factors they thought had contributed to the failure to reach agreement on an outcome document. Participants responded in writing, or during in-person or phone interviews. Individual responses are confidential.

17   See also Sri Lanka (2006g, paras. II.5, II.21, II.25).

18   See Kidd (2006). Several participants in the Survey's study of the Review Conference also expressed concern about, or otherwise noted, this problem.

19   In relation to international transfers and brokering, see also UNGA (2001b, paras. II.2, 12–14).

20   See Kidd (2006).

21   This broader term would encompass other safeguards, such as delivery verification. For more on post-delivery controls applicable to man-portable air defence systems, see Small Arms Survey (2005, pp. 134–36).

22   See Sri Lanka (2006g, para. IV.4) and Small Arms Survey (2006, p. 102).

23   For more, see Small Arms Survey (2004, ch. 7).

24   See, for example, Sri Lanka (2006b, paras. I.3, II.22).

25   The phrase 'in All Its Aspects', included in the title of the *Programme,* was a key element of the bargain struck in July 2001 between those states that preferred a more comprehensive treatment of the small arms problem and those more comfortable with a narrower approach tied to the 'illicit trade'.

26   See Small Arms Survey (2002, pp. 223–24).

27   The influence of the NRA in Washington was reflected in the composition of the US delegation to the Review Conference; see Stohl (2006).

28   See UNGA (2001b, para. II.3).

29   See, for example, Centre for Humanitarian Dialogue (2005, theme 6) and Small Arms Survey (2006, ch. 6).

30   The word 'development' was omitted in the final version.

31   The US position, in particular, remained unclear.

32   One of two versions of substantially identical text retained at the end of the conference by key participants in the small arms–development debate.

33   Some conference participants interviewed by the Survey said that US diplomats had indicated, in advance of the conference, that the United States would not accept *any form* of global follow-up. This was not, however, the message that it relayed in its high-level statement at the beginning of the meeting.

34   Israel did, however, indicate that its support for follow-up would depend on the content of the conference outcome document.

35   See Sri Lanka (2006a, para. I.18; 2006b, para. II.25). Young men are the principal victims and perpetrators of small arms violence worldwide; see Small Arms Survey (2004, ch. 6; 2006, ch. 12).

36   Instruments relating to anti-personnel landmines and explosive remnants of war provide for victim assistance. For more information, see Brinkert (2006).

37   The First Committee on Disarmament and International Security meets annually, in October, for a 4–5 week session. It negotiates and drafts the resolutions that are formally adopted by the General Assembly as a whole in December. For more on the committee's 2006 session, see Parker (2007).

38   All voting results reported here were derived from the Reaching Critical Will Web site:
     <http://www.reachingcriticalwill.org/political/1com/1com06/res/resindex.html>

39   Interview with First Committee participant, 7 November 2006.

40   On the separate vote concerning para. 7 alone (the establishment of a GGE), both Japan and the United States voted no.

41   Those countries that abstained included major small arms exporters, such as China, Iran, Israel, and the Russian Federation (2004 data). For more information on these exporters, see Annexe 3 (TRANSFERS) at <http://www.smallarmssurvey.org/yearb2007.html>. Most Arab states also abstained on the ATT vote. Separate votes on paras. 2 and 3 followed these same trends. For more on the ATT vote, see <http://www.reaching criticalwill.org/political/1com/1com06/res/resindex.html>

42   In consultation with experts from states, inter-governmental organizations, and civil society, UNODC is developing guidelines designed to assist
      states parties in implementing the provisions of the *UN Firearms Protocol*. An initial expert working group meeting was held in November 2006,
      in Vienna. A draft of the guidelines is scheduled for completion by the end of 2007. Source: written correspondence with UNODC (16 March
      2007).

43   For the reports of Special Rapporteur Frey, see the University of Minnesota Web site: <http://www1.umn.edu/humanrts/demo/subcom.html>

44   This section is based on Dreyer (2007).

45   See, for example, WA (2002).

46   See, for example: Small Arms Survey (2003, ch. 4); <http://www.bradford.ac.uk/acad/cics/projects/arms/AVPI/>

47   See also paras. 6, 12, and 72.

48   For more information, see <http://www.hdcentre.org/OECD-DAC>

49   As of April 2007, 8 additional states have formally endorsed the *Geneva Declaration,* bringing the total number of participating countries to 50.

50   As of April 2007, the members of the core group were Canada, Finland, Guatemala, Kenya, Morocco, the Netherlands, Norway, Switzerland,
      Thailand, and the United Kingdom. The group is coordinated by Switzerland.

51   There would be inconsistency, for example, if (hypothetical) instrument A required states to paint all weapons for export red, while instrument
      B required them to paint the same weapons green. It would be impossible to comply with both commitments.

52   Regional instruments that establish criteria for transfer licensing decisions include EU (1998), OSCE (2000, sec. III.A), and SICA (2005). At the
      international level, the Wassenaar Arrangement has adopted a set of *Best Practice Guidelines* for small arms transfers (WA, 2002), yet member-
      ship in the organization is not universal.

53   See China et al. (1991); UNGA (1996).

54   This section is based on Stevenson (2007).

55   Since 2003, the original text of the Framework Convention (more recently called the ATT) has been redrafted several times. It is no longer cir-
      culating due to the new emphasis on the *Global Principles* (ATT SC, 2007).

56   See *Nobel Laureate Code* (1997, arts. 5, 7–10).

57   The current members of the ATT Steering Committee are listed at <http://www.armstradetreaty.com/att/aboutus.php>

58   This is distinct from the UN ATT initiative, discussed elsewhere in the chapter (UNGA, 2006e).

59   The Control Arms campaign is jointly run by Amnesty International, the International Action Network on Small Arms (better known as IANSA),
      and Oxfam.

60   International Alert, Saferworld, and the University of Bradford.

61   This section is based on Hasan (2007).

62   For more, see Small Arms Survey (2003, pp. 216–18).

63   In 1947, the UN General Assembly established the ILC with a mandate for the progressive development and codification of international law in
      accordance with Article 13(1)(a) of the UN Charter (UN, 1945). The ILC dealt with the topic of state responsibility from 1949 until 2001, when
      it adopted its articles on *Responsibility of States for Internationally Wrongful Acts* (UNGA ILC, 2001).

64   An 'internationally wrongful act' is an action or omission, attributable to a state, that '[c]onstitutes a breach of an international obligation' of that
      state (UNGA ILC, 2001, art. 2).

65   Clapham (2006, p. 263) comes to a similar conclusion in relation to corporations.

66   See also Small Arms Survey (2004, pp. 263–65).

67   The principle of non-intervention is expressed in Article 2(1) (as a corollary of the principle of the independence and equality of states) and in
      Article 2(7) (in relation to the UN itself) of the UN Charter (UN, 1945). It is part of customary international law, and is thus applicable to all
      states (ICJ, 1986, para. 202).

68   Note that under IHL, states also have an obligation 'to ensure respect' for IHL by the parties to an armed conflict. This means that third states
      have a responsibility not to encourage a party to an armed conflict to violate IHL, not to take action that would assist in such violations, and to
      take appropriate steps to cause such violations to cease; see ICRC (2003, pp. 48–52).

69   This section is based on Bourne (2007).

70   See also paras. 3(a) and 4. Pursuant to para. 6 of the resolution, the Security Council established a Counter-Terrorism Committee; see <http://
      www.un.org/sc/ctc>

71   See also Small Arms Survey (2005, ch. 5).

72   For more, see BtB (2006a) and Bourne (2007).

73   For more on the Rwandan case, see Bourne (2007).

74   This section is based on Waszink with ICRC (2007).

BIBLIOGRAPHY

Add. Protocol I (Protocol Additional to the Geneva Conventions of 12 August 1949, and relating to the Protection of Victims of International Armed Conflicts [Protocol I]). 1977. Adopted 8 June.
<http://icrc.org/ihl.nsf/7c4d08d9b287a42141256739003e636b/f6c8b9fee14a77fdc125641e0052b079>

Add. Protocol II (Protocol Additional to the Geneva Conventions of 12 August 1949, and relating to the Protection of Victims of Non-International Armed Conflicts [Protocol II]). 1977. Adopted 8 June.
<http://icrc.org/ihl.nsf/7c4d08d9b287a42141256739003e636b/d67c3971bcff1c10c125641e0052b545>

ATT SC (Arms Trade Treaty Steering Committee). 2007. *Compilation of Global Principles for Arms Transfers*. Revised and updated.
<http://web.amnesty.org/library/Index/ENGPOL340032007?open&of=ENG-366>

Batchelor, Peter and Glenn McDonald. 2005. 'Too Close for Comfort: An Analysis of the UN Tracing Negotiations.' *Disarmament Forum*, Vol. 4/2005–1/2006, pp. 39–47. Geneva: United Nations Institute for Disarmament Research. <http://www.unidir.org/pdf/articles/pdf-art2429.pdf>

Bourne, Mike. 2007. *Transfers to Non-State Actors*. Unpublished background paper. Geneva: Small Arms Survey.

Brinkert, Kerry. 2006. 'Successful Implementation of Protocol V.' *Journal of Mine Action*. Winter.
<http://maic.jmu.edu/journal/10.2/focus/brinkert/brinkert.htm>

BtB (Biting the Bullet Project). 2006a. *Developing International Norms to Restrict SALW Transfers to Non-State Actors*. January.
<http://www.smallarmssurvey.org/files/portal/issueareas/measures/t_control.html>

——. 2006b. *Developing International Guidelines for National Controls on SALW Transfers*. March.
<http://www.smallarmssurvey.org/files/portal/issueareas/measures/t_control.html>

Buchanan, Cate. 2006. 'The UN Review Conference on Small Arms Control: Two Steps Backwards?'
<http://www.hdcentre.org/datastore/Small%20arms/ISS_Article.pdf>

Cassese, Antonio. 2005. *International Law,* 2nd edn. Oxford: Oxford University Press.

Centre for Humanitarian Dialogue. 2005. *Missing Pieces: Directions for Reducing Gun Violence through the UN Process on Small Arms Control*. Geneva: Centre for Humanitarian Dialogue. <http://www.hdcentre.org/Missing%20Pieces>

China, France, Union of Soviet Socialist Republics, United Kingdom, and United States. 1991. *Guidelines for Conventional Arms Transfers*. London. 18 October. <http://www.sipri.org/contents/expcon/unp5_london91.html>

Clapham, Andrew. 2006. *Human Rights Obligations of Non-State Actors*. Oxford: Oxford University Press.

Crawford, James. 2002. *The International Law Commission's Articles on State Responsibility: Introduction, Text and Commentaries*. Cambridge: Cambridge University Press.

Dreyer, Ronald. 2007. *The Geneva Declaration on Armed Violence and Development*. Unpublished background paper. Geneva: Small Arms Survey.

ECOWAS (Economic Community of West African States). 2006. *ECOWAS Convention on Small Arms and Light Weapons, Their Ammunition and Other Related Materials*. Adopted in Abuja, Nigeria, 14 June. <http://www.iansa.org/regions/wafrica/documents/CONVENTION-CEDEAO-ENGLISH.PDF>

EU (European Union). 1998. *European Union Code of Conduct on Arms Exports ('EU Code of Conduct')*. 8 June. Reproduced in UN doc. A/CONF.192/PC/3 of 13 March 2000. <http://www.smallarmssurvey.org/files/portal/issueareas/measures/reg.html#eu>

——. 2002. *Council Joint Action of 12 July 2002 on the European Union's Contribution to Combating the Destabilising Accumulation and Spread of Small Arms and Light Weapons and Repealing Joint Action 1999/34/CFSP.*
<http://www.smallarmssurvey.org/files/portal/issueareas/measures/reg.html#eu>

——. 2006. *User's Guide to the EU Code of Conduct on Arms Exports*. 10713/06 of 20 June.
<http://register.consilium.europa.eu/pdf/en/06/st10/st10713.en06.pdf>

Geneva Declaration (The Geneva Declaration on Armed Violence and Development). 2006. Adopted in Geneva, 7 June.
<http://www.smallarmssurvey.org/files/portal/issueareas/measures/inter.html#oin>

Gillard, Emanuela. 2000. 'What's Legal? What's Illegal?' In Lora Lumpe, ed. *Running Guns: The Global Black Market in Small Arms*. London: Zed Books, pp. 27–52.

Hasan, Sahar. 2007. *Transfer Controls: Legal Aspects*. Unpublished background paper. Geneva: Small Arms Survey.

HRW (Human Rights Watch). 1999. *Leave None to Tell the Story: Genocide in Rwanda*. New York: Human Rights Watch. March.
<http://hrw.org/reports/1999/rwanda/>

——. 2002. *World Report 2002: Afghanistan*. <http://hrw.org/wr2k2/asia1.html>

IANSA (International Action Network on Small Arms). 2006a. *Global Action to Stop Gun Violence: PrepCom for the Review Conference, 9–20 January 2006. Report*. <http://www.iansa.org/un/review2006/documents/PrepCom-report.pdf>

——. 2006b. 'UN Arms Talks Meltdown: Conference Allows Global Gun Crisis to Continue.' Press release. New York. 7 July.

ICJ (International Court of Justice). 1986. *Military and Paramilitary Activities in and against Nicaragua (Nicaragua v. United States of America)*. Judgement of 27 June (Merits). *ICJ Reports (1986)*. <http://www.icj-cij.org/docket/index.php?p1=3>

——. 1996. *Legality of the Threat or Use of Nuclear Weapons*. Advisory Opinion of 8 July. *ICJ Reports (1996/I)*.
    <http://www.icj-cij.org/docket/index.php?p1=3>

——. 2007. *Case Concerning the Application of the Convention on the Prevention and Punishment of the Crime of Genocide (Bosnia and Herzegovina v. Serbia and Montenegro)*. Judgement of 26 February. <http://www.icj-cij.org/docket/files/91/13685.pdf>

ICRC (International Committee of the Red Cross). 2003. *International Humanitarian Law and the Challenges of Contemporary Armed Conflicts*. Report 03/IC/09. Geneva: ICRC. <http://www.icrc.org/Web/eng/siteeng0.nsf/htmlall/5XRDCC/$File/IHLcontemp_armedconflicts_FINAL_ANG.pdf>

——. 2007. *Arms Transfer Decisions: Applying International Humanitarian Law Criteria. A Practical Guide*. (This is a working title at time of writing.) Geneva: ICRC.

Kidd, Richard. 2006. Interview by *Arms Control Today*. 11 August. <http://www.armscontrol.org/interviews/20060811_Kidd.asp>

Nairobi Guidelines (Suggested Common Guidelines for National Controls Governing Transfers of Small Arms and Light Weapons). 2006. Nairobi, 21 April. Reproduced in UN doc. A/CONF.192/2006/RC/WP.2 of 22 June. <http://www.un.org/events/smallarms2006/documents.html>

Nobel Laureate Code (International Code of Conduct on Arms Transfers). 1997. Formally launched in New York, 29 May. Reproduced in UN doc. A/54/766–S/2000/146 of 24 February 2000.

OAU (Organization of African Unity). 2000. *Bamako Declaration on an African Common Position on the Illicit Proliferation, Circulation and Trafficking of Small Arms and Light Weapons*. Adopted in Bamako, Mali, 1 December. SALW/Decl. (I). <http://www.smallarmssurvey.org/files/portal/issueareas/measures/reg.html>

OSCE (Organization for Security and Co-operation in Europe). Forum for Security Co-operation. 2000. *OSCE Document on Small Arms and Light Weapons*. FSC.DOC/1/00. Adopted 24 November. <http://www.osce.org/documents/fsc/2000/11/1873_en.pdf>

Parker, Sarah. 2007. *Moving ahead on Small Arms Control: A Focus on the 2006 Session of the UN First Committee*. Geneva: Centre for Humanitarian Dialogue. January. <http://www.hdcentre.org/datastore/Small%20arms/UN%20Process/2006FirstCommittee.pdf>

Prins, Daniël. 2006. 'Engineering Progress: A Diplomat's Perspective on Multilateral Disarmament.' In J. Borrie and V. Martin Randin, eds. *Thinking outside the Box in Multilateral Disarmament and Arms Control Negotiations*. Geneva: United Nations Institute for Disarmament Research.

SICA (Central American Integration System). 2005. *Code of Conduct of Central American States on the Transfer of Arms, Ammunition, Explosives and Other Related Material*. Adopted in León, Nicaragua, 2 December. Reproduced in UN doc. A/CONF.192/2006/RC/WP.6 of 30 June 2006. <http://www.un.org/events/smallarms2006/pdf/rc.wp.6-e.pdf> Spanish original available at: <http://www.iansa.org/regions/camerica/documents/code-of-conduct-on-arms-transfers-dec05.pdf>

Small Arms Survey. 2002. *Small Arms Survey 2002: Counting the Human Cost*. Oxford: Oxford University Press.

——. 2003. *Small Arms Survey 2003: Development Denied*. Oxford: Oxford University Press.

——. 2004. *Small Arms Survey 2004: Rights at Risk*. Oxford: Oxford University Press.

——. 2005. *Small Arms Survey 2005: Weapons at War*. Oxford: Oxford University Press.

——. 2006. *Small Arms Survey 2006: Unfinished Business*. Oxford: Oxford University Press.

Sri Lanka. 2006a. *President's Non-Paper for Informal Consultation Purposes: The United Nations Programme of Action to Prevent, Combat and Eradicate the Illicit Trade in Small Arms and Light Weapons in All Its Aspects: A Strategy for Further Implementation*. Part I, 27 February; Part II, 21 March; Part III, 27 March.

——. 2006b. *President's Non-Paper for Informal Consultation Purposes: The United Nations Programme of Action to Prevent, Combat and Eradicate the Illicit Trade in Small Arms and Light Weapons in All Its Aspects: A Strategy for Further Implementation*. 18 May.

——. 2006c. *President's Non-Paper*. 27 June, 17h00.

——. 2006d. *President's Non-Paper*. 3 July, 12h00.

——. 2006e. *Informal Consultations*. 5 July, 19h44.

——. 2006f. *Informal Consultations*. 6 July, 19h12.

——. 2006g. *Informal Consultations*. 7 July, 08h41.

——. 2006h. *Draft Declaration*. 7 July (issued subsequent to Sri Lanka, 2006g).

Stevenson, Chris. 2007. *Transfer Controls: New Initiatives*. Unpublished background paper. Geneva: Small Arms Survey.

Stohl, Rachel. 2006. 'Power of NRA Showcased in U.S. Delegation to Small Arms Conference.' Press information. Center for Defense Information. 26 June. <http://www.cdi.org/friendlyversion/printversion.cfm?documentID=3562&from_page=../program/document.cfm>

UK (United Kingdom). 2003. *Implementing the UN Programme of Action: Strengthening Export Controls*. Chairman's Conference Summary. Lancaster House, London, 14–15 January.

UN (United Nations). 1945. *Charter of the United Nations and Statute of the International Court of Justice* ('UN Charter'). Adopted in San Francisco, 26 June. Entered into force on 24 October. <http://www.un.org/aboutun/charter/index.html>

UNGA (United Nations General Assembly). 1948. *Universal Declaration of Human Rights*. Adopted and proclaimed by Resolution 217A (III) of 10 December. <http://www.unhchr.ch/udhr/>

——. 1966. *International Covenant on Civil and Political Rights*. Adopted by Resolution 2200A (XXI) of 16 December. Entered into force on 23 March 1976. Reproduced in General Assembly Official Records, Twenty-first Session, Supplement No. 16 (A/6316). <http://www.unhchr.ch/html/menu3/b/a_ccpr.htm>

——. 1996. *Guidelines for International Arms Transfers in the Context of General Assembly Resolution 46/36 H of 6 December 1991*. A/51/182 of 1 July, pp. 64–70. <http://disarmament.un.org/undiscom.htm>

——. 2001a. *Protocol against the Illicit Manufacturing of and Trafficking in Firearms, Their Parts and Components and Ammunition, Supplementing the United Nations Convention against Transnational Organized Crime ('UN Firearms Protocol')*. Adopted 31 May. Entered into force 3 July 2005. A/RES/55/255 of 8 June. <http://www.undcp.org/pdf/crime/a_res_55/255e.pdf>

——. 2001b. *Programme of Action to Prevent, Combat and Eradicate the Illicit Trade in Small Arms and Light Weapons in All Its Aspects ('UN Programme of Action')*. 20 July. A/CONF.192/15. <http://www.smallarmssurvey.org/resources/2001_un_conf.htm>

——. 2003. *The Illicit Trade in Small Arms and Light Weapons in All Its Aspects*. Resolution 58/241 of 23 December. A/RES/58/241 of 9 January 2004.

——. 2004. *Prevention of the Illicit Transfer and Unauthorized Access to and Use of Man-Portable Air Defence Systems*. Resolution 59/90 of 3 December. A/RES/59/90 of 17 December.

——. 2005a. *International Instrument to Enable States to Identify and Trace, in a Timely and Reliable Manner, Illicit Small Arms and Light Weapons ('International Tracing Instrument')*. A/60/88 of 27 June (Annex). <http://disarmament2.un.org/cab/salw-oewg.html>

——. 2005b. *2005 World Summit Outcome*. Incorporated in Resolution 60/1 of 16 September. A/RES/60/1 of 24 October. <http://daccessdds.un.org/doc/UNDOC/GEN/N05/487/60/PDF/N0548760.pdf?OpenElement>

——. 2005c. *Prevention of the Illicit Transfer and Unauthorized Access to and Use of Man-Portable Air Defence Systems*. Resolution 60/77 of 8 December. A/RES/60/77 of 11 January 2006.

——. 2005d. *The Illicit Trade in Small Arms and Light Weapons in All Its Aspects*. Resolution 60/81 of 8 December. A/RES/60/81 of 11 January 2006.

——. 2005e. *International Instrument to Enable States to Identify and Trace, in a Timely and Reliable Manner, Illicit Small Arms and Light Weapons*. Decision No. 60/519 of 8 December. A/60/463, para. 95 (16 November 2005). A/60/PV.61, p. 41 (*Official Records*, 8 December 2005).

——. 2006a. *Report of the Preparatory Committee for the United Nations Conference to Review Progress Made in the Implementation of the Programme of Action to Prevent, Combat and Eradicate the Illicit Trade in Small Arms and Light Weapons in All Its Aspects*. A/CONF.192/2006/RC/1 of 26 January. <http://www.un.org/events/smallarms2006/pdf/RC-1%20(E).pdf>

——. 2006b. *Report of the United Nations Conference to Review Progress Made in the Implementation of the Programme of Action to Prevent, Combat and Eradicate the Illicit Trade in Small Arms and Light Weapons in All Its Aspects*. A/CONF.192/2006/RC/9 of 12 July. <http://www.un.org/events/smallarms2006/pdf/rc.9-e.pdf>

——. 2006c. *The Illicit Trade in Small Arms and Light Weapons in All Its Aspects*. Resolution 61/66 of 6 December. A/RES/61/66 of 3 January 2007.

——. 2006d. *Problems Arising from the Accumulation of Conventional Ammunition Stockpiles in Surplus*. Resolution 61/72 of 6 December. A/RES/61/72 of 3 January 2007.

——. 2006e. *Towards an Arms Trade Treaty: Establishing Common International Standards for the Import, Export and Transfer of Conventional Arms*. Resolution 61/89 of 6 December. A/RES/61/89 of 18 December.

——. HRC (Human Rights Council). Sub-Commission on the Promotion and Protection of Human Rights. 2006. *Principles on the Prevention of Human Rights Violations Committed with Small Arms*. Adopted 24 August. A/HRC/Sub.1/58/L.11/Add.1 of 24 August. <http://daccessdds.un.org/doc/UNDOC/LTD/G06/137/29/PDF/G0613729.pdf?OpenElement>

——. ILC (International Law Commission). 2001. *Responsibility of States for Internationally Wrongful Acts*. Adopted by the ILC at its 53rd session. Reproduced in UN doc. A/RES/56/83 of 28 January 2002 (Annex). <http://daccessdds.un.org/doc/UNDOC/GEN/N01/477/97/PDF/N0147797.pdf?OpenElement>

UNSC (United Nations Security Council). 2001. Resolution 1373 (2001) of 28 September. S/RES/1373 (2001) of 28 September.

US (United States of America). 2006. 'Remarks at UN Review Conference on the Illicit Trade in Small Arms and Light Weapons.' Statement by Robert G. Joseph, Under Secretary for Arms Control and International Security. USUN Press Release No. 137 (06). 27 June. <http://www.state.gov/t/us/rm/68537.htm> Video available at: <http://www.un.org/events/smallarms2006/mem-states060627.html>

WA (Wassenaar Arrangement on Export Controls for Conventional Arms and Dual-Use Goods and Technologies). 2002. *Best Practice Guidelines for Exports of Small Arms and Light Weapons (SALW)*. 12 December. <http://www.wassenaar.org/docs/best_practice_salw.htm>

Waszink, Camilla with ICRC (International Committee of the Red Cross). 2007. *Putting Arms Transfer Criteria into Practice: Assessing the Recipient's Compliance with International Humanitarian Law*. Unpublished background paper. Geneva: Small Arms Survey.

ACKNOWLEDGEMENTS

Principal authors

Glenn McDonald, Sahar Hasan, and Chris Stevenson

Contributors

Mike Bourne, Ronald Dreyer, and Camilla Waszink/ICRC

GUNS IN THE FRAME

Urban violence in the Philippines

Photos by Lucian Read, January–February 2007

Lucian Read's images of Basilan Island, Cotobato, Danao, Davao, and Manila in the Philippines capture a fast-growing population in overdrive, caught between sectarian conflict and abject poverty. With more than 10 million residents, Manila has one the world's highest population density rates. Oblivious to the rubble and tangled cables of her makeshift environment, a young girl wanders through Baseco, one of Manila's largest slums (Frame 1).

According to official police figures, civilians throughout the country own 1.1 million licensed firearms and 100,000 unlicensed weapons, probably a serious underestimate of actual holdings (CIVILIAN FIREARMS). A thriving craft weapon industry supports several thousand families in Danao, 550 kilometres south-east of Manila. Inside the grimy Danao workshops, a gunsmith scrutinizes a weapon he is crafting (Frame 2, left) and men who apply chrome to replica guns wear particle masks in a feeble attempt to shield their lungs from fumes (Frame 2, centre right).

High crime rates, political violence, and a protracted separatist war fuel demand for weapons. In conflict-ridden Mindanao province, a merchant displays part of the 50-strong gun collection he has amassed to protect his family and businesses in downtown Cotabato (Frame 3).

Neighbours of a murdered soldier prepare wreaths for the funeral on the island of Basilan, south-west Philippines (Frame 3, right). On a nearby bridge, his blood dries on the asphalt, the spot marked by white candles (Frame 4, left). At another funeral in Davao, Mindanao, mourners encircle the coffined body of a former gang member (Frame 5, left), the victim of a vigilante killing. The friend who carried him to hospital was murdered days later.

The Filipino justice system struggles to keep pace with escalating gun crime. In Quezon City Hall, Metro Manila, witnesses swear an oath (Frame 5, top right) before testifying against the man in the foreground, who is accused of shooting a petrol station attendant. In an adjacent room, a young man listens as he is charged with shooting a friend after a night of drinking (Frame 5, inset).

A tattered poster calls for a week of peace in Cotabato in the run-up to national elections, typically a period of heightened violence (Frame 6, top left). Elsewhere in the city an armed soldier studies the crowd at the site of a failed grenade attack on a police commander (Frame 6, top right).

Children from Maluso, a fishing village in Basilan, pass a police sign warning of a five-month, pre-election weapons ban (Frame 7, left), enforced in Manila (Frame 7, top and bottom right). Only the most obsolete of confiscated guns are reportedly stored at police warehouses in Manila (Frame 6, bottom left and centre); the more modern types are refurbished for use by security forces.

At least 25 journalists have been murdered since 2000, making the Philippines the most dangerous country after Iraq for those in the profession. Reporters who advocate carrying guns for self-defence practise at a police shooting range in Manila (Frame 8, left). At another range, a Catholic priest trains impoverished youths to become security guards (Frame 8, bottom right). ✉

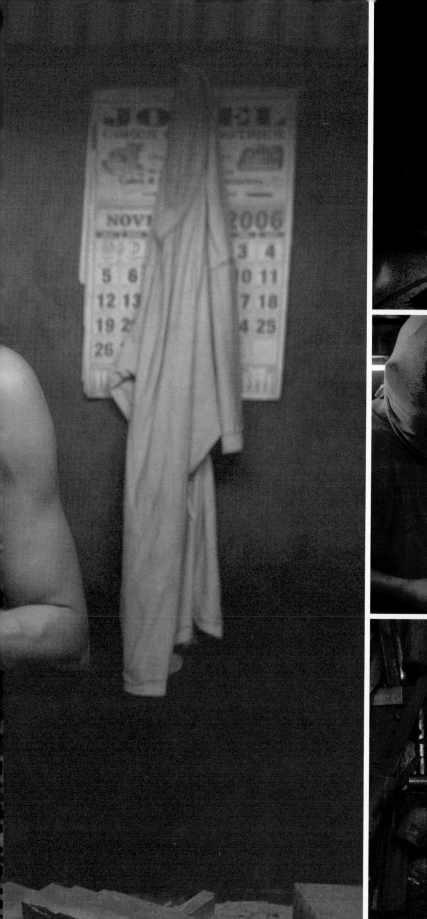

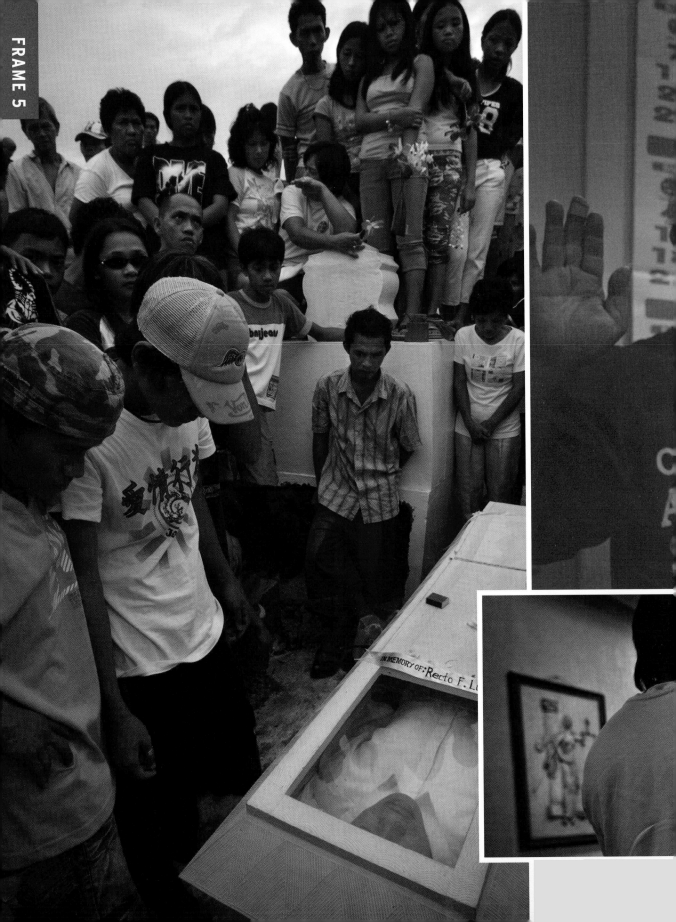

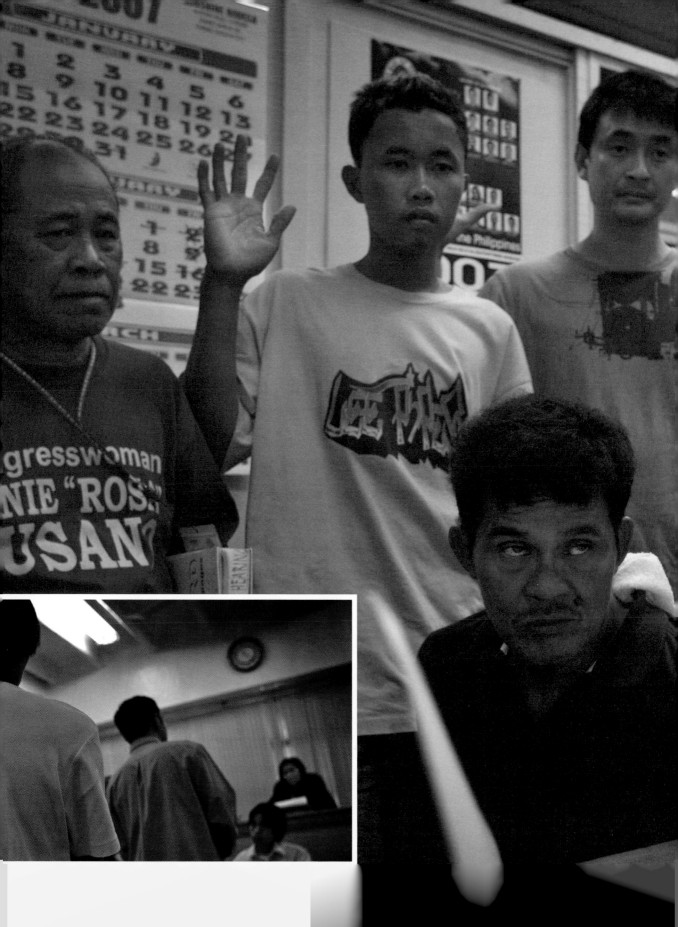

Soldiers patrol the streets of the Rocinha favela in March 2006 during a military operation to find ten FAL 7.62 rifles and one 9 mm pistol stolen from an army barracks in Rio de Janeiro. © Antonio Scorza /AFP/Getty Images

Guns in the City
URBAN LANDSCAPES OF ARMED VIOLENCE

INTRODUCTION

Urban armed violence forces us to rethink our mental geography of state, society, and governance—including the factors that lead to armed violence and the proliferation and misuse of small arms and light weapons. Previous editions of the *Small Arms Survey* have focused on the role of small arms in conflict and crime as well as on the consequences of proliferation and misuse on development and humanitarian activity. This theme chapter concentrates on the specific features of urban armed violence and insecurity, introducing evidence from a wide range of cities in Latin America and the Caribbean, North America, Europe, Africa, and South and East Asia.

For the first time in human history, cities are home to the majority of the world's population. More than one billion of these people, however, live in slums, and the number looks set to rise (UN-HABITAT, 2003). In 1950 there were 86 cities with a population greater than one million; today there are 400; and by 2015 there will be at least 550, according to UN estimates (Davis, 2006, p. 1). Most population growth will be concentrated in urban areas of the developing world, and the experience and consequences of urbanization will be especially dramatic in Africa, South and East Asia, and Latin America.

Cities will thus also be focal points for the development of effective violence prevention and reduction programmes and policies. In concentrating on urban armed violence, the *Small Arms Survey* is contributing to an expanding chorus of study by governments, analysts, and international agencies, including UN-HABITAT (and its Safer Cities programme), the Inter-American Development Bank (and its work on urban violence), the Brookings Institution, and the Canadian government. These and other stakeholders recognize that the issue of guns in cities is one that will continue to require direct intervention.

It should be noted that urban violence is strikingly heterogeneous and results from multiple causes (Brennan-Galvin, 2002). It is linked to factors such as the drug trade, the availability of weapons, and forms of social organization (gangs, militias). However, collected data reflects neither a simple nor a necessary causal link between urbanization and armed violence.

The evidence presented in this chapter points to the highly segmented and spatially concentrated dynamics of urban armed violence, highlighting key issues through a series of examples from around the world. The main findings reveal that:

- large-scale urbanization tends to be associated with increased rates of armed violence;
- rapid urbanization is often coupled with decreasing levels of public safety, posing serious challenges to the provision of security and justice;
- in the global South, urban violence is often political as much as criminal in nature, and criminal violence is usually structured and organized, both socially and geographically;

- real and perceived insecurities inform individual and collective responses to armed violence, which often involve strategies to contain violence or export it to the urban periphery;

- municipal interventions to reduce or prevent armed violence can be coercive, compliance-oriented, or voluntary, while successful programmes often combine these approaches;

- ultimately, any appraisal of or policy response to urban armed violence must be shaped by a multi-disciplinary understanding of the phenomenon.

The chapter is divided into three parts. First, it briefly examines urban–rural differences in patterns of armed violence, illustrating these through the cases of the United States, Canada, and Brazil. It then examines the emergence of new forms of urban order, including peri-urban, semi-urban, and inner-city forms of habitation. While slums, shanty-towns, and gated communities are becoming increasingly prominent in cities, the experience of violence and insecurity differs widely among them. This transformation of urban landscapes is often driven by individual or collective reactions to perceived (subjectively experienced) versus real (empirically observed) insecurities. The localization of armed violence to the periphery or the interior of urban spaces and the simultaneous creation of safe and secure places are contributing to the fragmentation of public space through processes of *isolation, exportation,* and *containment.*

The second part of the chapter presents an overview of the state of knowledge on urban armed violence, demonstrating the tremendous variation in the incidence and type of violence across cities and regions, and distinguishing between criminal and political armed violence. This survey is complemented by short sections that explore firearm ownership and use in African cities, the problem of armed violence in Port-au-Prince, Haiti, and the phenomenon of gated communities amid the 'violence of urbanization'.

There is neither a simple nor a necessary causal link between urbanization and armed violence.

The final section of the chapter introduces a three-fold approach to understanding, preventing, and reducing urban armed violence. It observes that effective municipal-level interventions must consider the different dimensions of the urban landscape, the importance of real and perceived violence, and the role of isolation, containment, and exportation in relation to violence reduction. The chapter also offers a typology for understanding local efforts to reduce armed violence and control small arms, highlighting potential entry-points for rethinking local interventions to improve human security and public safety. These interventions can be coercive, compliance-oriented, or voluntary. The most successful interventions, which appear to be planned and executed on the basis of robust evidence, carefully sequence elements of all three approaches.

UNDERSTANDING URBAN ARMED VIOLENCE IN THE 21ST CENTURY

The emergence of massive urban sprawls has blurred basic distinctions between urban and rural and has yielded a new vocabulary. Today, demographers and urban planners talk of 'megacities' of more than eight or ten million inhabitants, and even 'hypercities' or 'metacities' of more than 20 million, virtually all of which are located in the developing world. For example, by 2025, Dhaka will probably surpass 25 million inhabitants—up from 400,000 in 1950; Karachi will grow to 26.5 million—up from 1 million; Jakarta is set to attain 24.9 million—up from 1.5 million; and Mumbai is to reach 33 million people—up from 2.9 million (Davis, 2006, pp. 4–5). By 2005, these megacities (20 in total) already accounted for nine per cent of the world's urban population (UNDESA, 2005).

Twenty-first-century urbanization is about more than demographic changes, however, and the notion of the 'megacity' captures only part of the transformation. Indeed, the burgeoning literature on 'global cities' or 'world cities'

Figure 5.1 **The urban explosion**

POPULATION (BILLIONS)

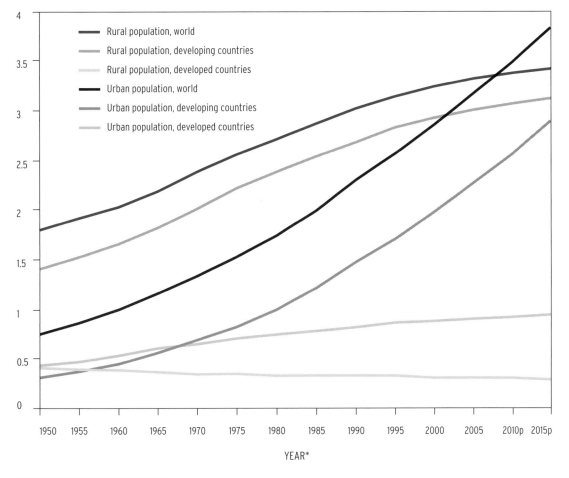

* A p after a year indicates projected population figures.
Source: United Nations (2005)

points to the ways in which globalization has dramatically altered the status of large urban centres in terms of eco-nomic, political, social, and ecological interaction and interdependence (Brenner and Keil, 2006). One of the features of the 'global city' is that it is more interconnected with similar cities than with its own hinterland (Sassen, 1994).

Yet not all of the world's cities are on the same playing field. Tokyo, London, and New York are financial and cultural nodes linking three continents, but their ties with Dhaka or Lagos are much less obvious. Between these two poles lie fragmented cities such as Manila and Shanghai, whose business districts are linked to global cities, but whose fringes are home to bleak and vast slums and squatter communities—with militant groups and gangs at times creat-ing their own transnational ties and networks. As will be elaborated below, urban growth and development do not necessarily go hand in hand.

Headlines of urban violence in Johannesburg, Nairobi, and Rio de Janeiro paint a picture (if occasionally exag-gerated) of these cities as rife with violence or riddled with no-go zones. In fact, there is some agreement among

Box 5.1 Definitions

The World Health Organization's *World Report on Violence and Health* defines *violence* as 'the intentional use of physical force or power, threatened or actual, against oneself, another person, or against a group or community, that either results in or has a high likelihood of resulting in injury, death, psychological harm, maldevelopment, or deprivation' (WHO, 2002, p. 30).

For the purposes of this chapter, and unless otherwise stated, *armed violence* thus refers to violence committed through the threatened or actual use of small arms and light weapons as defined by the *UN Report of the Panel of Governmental Experts on Small Arms* (UNGA, 1997).[1]

criminologists that the strongest risk factor for serious crimes (including armed robbery, car theft, and violence against women) across countries is urbanization. As an overview analysis of the entire range of International Crime Victims Surveys (ICVS) concludes, 'Victimization by more serious crime is strongly correlated with increases in the proportion of the population living in larger cities' (van Dijk, 1998, p. 69). Moreover, urban density 'is thought to be associated with crime as greater concentrations of people lead to competition for limited resources, greater stress, and increased conflict' (Naudé et al., 2006, p. 73).

This chapter, however, will show that understanding urban armed violence requires a more nuanced vision of this emerging urban landscape. Focusing on urban growth and population density is not enough. In addition, urban armed violence must be understood as being intricately linked to the structural dynamics of urban agglomeration, as well as to the competing interests of—and power relationships between—social groups. Armed violence is both a result of and a catalyst for transformations in urban governance and spatial organization (Moser and Rodgers, 2005).

Urban-rural divides and urban transformations

A key question guiding this study is whether armed violence in urban areas exceeds that encountered in rural areas. Historically, cities were among the first zones of security created in modern states. They were relatively easy to police and supervise (and possessed the first modern police and security forces); they also developed a dense infrastructure, were subject to urban planning policies, and benefited from the 'civilizing process' (Elias, 2000) of industrial development, rising literacy, and social interaction. As Europe became increasingly urban, rates of violent crime (measured by homicide rates) declined steadily from the 16th to the 20th centuries: in England they dropped from 4.3 homicides per 100,000 at the end of the 17th century to 0.8 per 100,000 by the 20th century; in Continental Europe they fell from 5.5–9.2 per 100,000 to 1.7–2.0 per 100,000 over the same time period (Eisner, 2001; Gurr, 1981). Although the exact timing and scope of the decline varies from country to country, it is systematically linked to urbanization and the Industrial Revolution, and to the expansion of state control and the provision of security and public order (Chenais, 1981).

Yet some general analyses of 20th-century figures—at least from the United States, Canada, and Brazil—seem to mark a reversal of this trend towards cities as safe places. One factor that appears to play a role is city size: as Buvinic and Morrison (2000, p. 62) point out, 'crime rates in Latin America are strongly correlated with city size. Crowding intensifies antisocial behaviour and facilitates anonymity and imitation of violent acts.'[2] Similarly, some of the World Bank's econometric modelling of crime rates suggests that, under certain conditions, rapid urbanization rates are associated with higher homicide rates (Fajnzylber et al., 1998, p. 32).[3] In particular, city size and rapid rates of growth are likely to influence levels of armed violence in that they represent serious challenges in terms of governance and the provision of security, especially in today's megacities.

Although a simple link between city size and violence may not hold everywhere, it is at least confirmed in the US case. Between 1985 and 2004 the average homicide rate in the United States was 7.57 per 100,000.[4] Available data also demonstrates a linear relationship between city population size and 20-year average homicide rates (see Table 5.1). Cities of more than one million residents had the highest 20-year average homicide rates at 19.04 per 100,000; the average for cities of 500,000–1 million population was 13.86 per 100,000; for populations of 250,000–500,000 the rate was 11.31 per 100,000; and for cities of 100,000–250,000 the rate of 7.21 per 100,000 was below the national 20-year average. This is also true for crime in general in the United States, where victimization rates in large cities (more than one million residents) have been more than double those of small cities and towns (Glaeser and Sacerdote, 1996, p. 20).

There are, however, huge variations in homicide rates within each category of city. As Table 5.1 shows, homicide rates reach their peak in smaller, not larger, cities. Gary, Indiana (which had the highest homicide rate of any US city during this period), and Richmond, Virginia, had overall homicide rates of 60.22 and 48.78, respectively, much higher than the 7.21 average for other small cities in their category. Among medium to large cities, New Orleans' 20-year average homicide rate of 53.87 is almost five times higher than the 11.31 average rate of other medium-size cities. Meanwhile, Washington, D.C., with an average of 55.18, and Detroit, with an average of 50.43, have rates that are about four times higher than the average homicide rate of 13.86 for cities in their category. And while murder rates have fallen in larger cities, they appear to be rising in middle-sized ones (FBI, 2005; *Economist,* 2006). This variation highlights the central role of contextual factors in levels of urban armed violence.

Although it almost certainly does not hold in all countries, a similar pattern, albeit at much lower levels, holds in Canadian cities and in Brazil. The average homicide rate in 1995–2004 for Canadian cities with a population greater than 500,000 was 1.96 per 100,000, compared to a rate of 1.52 for cities with a population of 100,000–500,000. The national rate was 1.88 per 100,000, again suggesting that smaller cities are less violent. Overall, firearm homicides represent about one-third of all homicides, a percentage that has increased in the past three years (Dauvergne and Li, 2006, p. 17). Perhaps somewhat exceptionally, however, the homicide rate in the largest Canadian city, Toronto, has been consistently below the national average (1.71 during the period under review).

Urbanization correlates with higher levels of armed violence in Brazil as well (BRAZIL). The average firearm homicide rate in urban municipalities (with more than 94 per cent 'urban' residents and a density of 840 persons per square kilometre) is 27.5 per 100,000, more than double that of peri-urban municipalities (where the density is 66 persons per square kilometre), and more than four times the rate of rural municipalities (6.8 per 100,000). In many

Table 5.1 **US homicide rates by city population, 1985–2004 (per 100,000)**			
City population	**20-year mean rate**	**Low**	**High**
1 million +	19.04	8.24	27.82
500,000-999,999	13.86	1.74	55.18
250,000-499,999	11.31	1.09	53.87
100,000-249,999	7.21	0.31	60.22
United States overall	**7.57**	**5.50**	**9.80**

Source: Wilkinson and Bell (2006)

Box 5.2   Homicide in US cities: all about the gun

Since the mid-1980s, homicide rates have fluctuated and dramatically declined in many US cities. When the data is disaggregated to separate firearm from non-firearm homicides for a city such as New York, the role of guns in the 'peaks' of criminal violence is clear.

Figure 5.2 below shows the growing importance of guns in homicides in each of the three homicide peaks in New York City in 1968-2004. Increases in both firearm and non-firearm homicides contributed to the tripling of homicide rates through 1972. In 1972, the ratio of firearm to non-firearm homicides was 1.23. By the next peak, in 1981, the 1,187 firearm deaths were nearly 1.76 times greater than the 673 non-firearm homicides. In 1991, the most recent peak, the 1,644 firearm homicides were 3.16 times greater than the 519 non-firearm homicides.

In addition to sharp increases in the number of firearm homicides, the gun v. non-gun ratio also rose because of a long-term decline in the number of non-gun homicides. Since 1980, the number and rate of non-gun homicides has declined by nearly 50 per cent, from 735 to 335 non-firearm killings in 1996. There are thus two dynamic and different patterns in the data on homicide by weapon. Firearm killings follow the rollercoaster pattern of steadily increasing peaks beginning in 1972. Non-firearm killings have declined since 1980—to rates unseen since 1960. This secular decline in non-firearm killings is substantial.

Source: Wilkinson and Bell (2006)

Figure 5.2   **Firearm v. non-firearm homicides in New York City, 1968-2004 (per 100,000)**

RATE PER 100,000

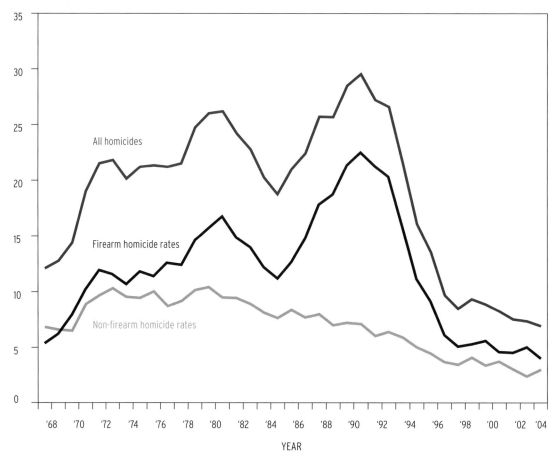

YEAR

Source: Wilkinson and Bell (2006)

Brazilian cities, the consequences are stark. Wealthy residents of São Paulo, for example, 'retreated to areas such as Alphaville, a walled city surrounded by high electrified fences and patrolled by a private army of 1,100 guards' (Brennan-Galvin, 2002, p. 136). Today's *favela* dwellers live in a climate of fear, and 'whereas, in the late 1960s, people were afraid of being forcibly relocated . . . today they are afraid of dying in the crossfire between police and dealers or between opposing gangs' (Brennan-Galvin, 2002, p. 138; Perlman, 2005).

Anecdotal evidence from major cities in Africa also seems to corroborate the relationship between city size and levels of violence. Pérouse de Montclos's study of three cities in Nigeria (Lagos, Kano, and Port Harcourt) demonstrates that violence in each city has specific causes and manifestations, but that overall, 'a city of 100,000 residents constitutes, it seems, the threshold below which "typical" urban violence cannot develop [authors' translation]' (Pérouse de Montclos, 2003, p. 6).[5]

As is the case elsewhere, these general trends conceal large variations within different categories, suggesting that other factors associated with particular cities are at work. Furthermore, these findings may fail to hold more generally in (or beyond) North and South America, although data has seldom been disaggregated in a way that would generate a clear picture of urban–rural differences. In Australia, for example, the average firearms homicide rate is higher in major urban areas than in outer and remote regions: with 66 per cent of Australia's population, major urban areas experienced 58 per cent of homicides between 1990 and 2004 (Mouzos, 2006). Victimization rates also varied widely among urban areas, from 0.04 per 100,000 in Canberra, to 0.15 per 100,000 in Western Australia (Perth), and 0.45 per 100,000 in areas around Sydney and Adelaide.

> Slums defy traditional models of municipal governance.

To provide a more nuanced picture of which factors render large cities more vulnerable to armed violence, it is useful to consider the four categories identified by criminologists and sociologists, some of which have been alluded to above:

- the social dislocation and anonymity of large cities;
- the opportunities for criminal gain;
- the relatively low risk of being caught; and
- the effects of social interaction, especially on vulnerable groups.[6]

These factors are not uniformly related to city size; they depend on such characteristics as the geography and design of the urban space, the demographics of the urban population (age, patterns of recent migration, origins), forms of social organization (segregation by wealth and ethnicity), legislative frameworks regulating firearms, and levels of inequality. To date, few studies have sought to compare systematically different cities according to these factors in order to identify any links to levels of armed violence.[7]

The new urban landscape: modern slums and megacities

Cities that experience rapid growth are almost always characterized by the uncontrolled establishment and expansion of slums, squatter communities, and shantytowns. These defy traditional models of municipal governance and conventional definitions of urbanity. As opposed to rural areas, cities have generally been understood to be tied to social functions such as industrial or commercial activity or transportation and communications infrastructures. In many parts of the world, however, this link between economics, infrastructure, and urbanization has been weakened or broken. Population growth is thus not necessarily accompanied by economic opportunity or welfare gains.

Such uncontrolled growth stands in contrast to urbanization in many European and North American countries, where the process was traditionally coupled with industrialization. In many 18th–20th-century cities, urban planners made attempts—the most well-known of which was Baron Haussmann's reshaping of 19th-century Paris—to ensure that physical and social infrastructures could deal with the social pathologies of rapid urbanization, including crime, disease, poverty, and filth. Economic growth allowed the governance capacities of states and cities to expand and keep in check the side effects of urbanization and industrial capitalism.

But one feature of contemporary urbanization in many developing countries is that city size is delinked from economic or infrastructure growth. Cities such as Johannesburg, Mumbai, Buenos Aires, and São Paulo have in fact been *deindustrialized* by the closure of their manufacturing sectors, or as businesses and economic actors flee the decaying urban core. Even so, population growth in these cities continues to soar. As the poor migrate from the countryside in search of employment, the city expands outwards, swallowing up the rural areas. Davis (2006, p. 9) notes that throughout the developing world 'rural people no longer have to migrate to the city: it migrates to them'.

A dearth of
employment
opportunities has
contributed to the
onset of some urban
conflicts.

The result of such uncontrolled and rapid urban expansion is almost inevitably the prevalence of slums, or even *megaslums,* consisting of massive squatter communities, often exceeding one million inhabitants, who live without secure land titles and with few or irregular public services such as electricity, water, sanitation, and sewers. Such areas are often sites of violence and coercion as masses of people are repeatedly evicted in city clean-up operations or to make way for urban renewal schemes. Though anthropologists, sociologists, and community workers have long recognized this phenomenon, the international and national policy-making community has generally lagged behind in developing robust policy responses (Muggah, 2003; Neuwirth, 2005). In one noteworthy step, the United Nations recently set as one of its Millennium Development Goals improving the livelihoods of at least 100 million slum dwellers by 2020 (of an estimated total of more than one billion). Yet given that slum populations worldwide seem to be growing by around 25 million each year, this is a monumental task (UN-HABITAT, 2005).

Alarmist authors claim that these megaslums constitute the new frontier of armed violence and sources of insecurity (Rapley, 2006). One argues that what he calls 'feral cities' are 'natural havens for a variety of hostile non-state actors' and that they may pose 'security threats on a scale hitherto not encountered' (Norton, 2003, p. 105).

The evidence, however, is thin, and many large slums, while suffering from a variety of deprivations, do not seem to be rife with armed violence or insecurity. Indeed, whether small arms violence is of greater concern in semi-urban or peripheral slums and shantytowns than in areas that are more developed and vigorously policed remains to be determined. As systematic evidence becomes available, it will serve to inform contemporary urban planning and security-building.

A more nuanced analysis of what has aptly been termed *cityspace* reveals the interdependence of highly heterogeneous urban populations and focuses on the linkages arising from 'the purposeful clustering and collective cohabitation of people in space, in a "home" habitat' (Soja, 2000, p. 12). In simple terms, a city such as Caracas, Venezuela, is utterly dependent on the informal labour force residing in the *barrios* or squatter settlements, which include more than half the entire population. Of course, the linkages within these spaces are not necessarily positive or symbiotic. Because the vast majority of residents in cities such as Lagos or Dhaka live in slums that, by definition, are poorly planned and thus acutely vulnerable, they are also in danger of suffering from ecological disaster. In addition, this vulnerability may exacerbate social unrest among alienated or excluded populations.

Moreover, a dearth of employment opportunities and resources in some cities has contributed to the onset of urban conflicts, from Brazil and Guatemala to South Africa and India. These conflicts can erupt over the unequal

Box 5.3 Distinguishing 'urban' from 'rural' spaces

The term *urban* used to be applied to free-standing built-up areas of at least 1,000–2,000 inhabitants, with an observable core fulfilling a range of social and civic functions of an administrative, commercial, cultural, or educational nature. Continuous growth and coalescence of towns and cities over time, however, meant the development of subsidiary spaces in the form of suburbs and satellite towns. In Britain, for instance, the General Register Office for England and Wales thus introduced the concept of 'conurbations' in 1951 to meet the demands of an increasingly complex scenario, but the problems of classification persisted. Recognizing that the lack of a consistent and comprehensive government definition of 'rurality' hindered effective rural policy-making, the Countryside Agency (2004) has now established a new definition of urban and rural areas of England and Wales, based on both morphological and contextual aspects of settlements.

Beyond the United Kingdom the patchwork of slums and gated communities that is fast becoming the norm in many of the world's megacities renders traditional concepts of *urban* and *rural* obsolete. An example would be what geographers now call the Rio-São Paulo Extended Metropolitan Region, a 500-kilometre-long urban-industrial megalopolis with a population nearing 40 million. The urban-rural divide is also increasingly blurred in the more confined spaces of Bangladesh, where 84.7 per cent of the country's urban population—more than 30 million people—live in slums (Davis, 2006, p. 24). Dhaka alone has around 10 million slum dwellers in a city of about 15 million inhabitants. This sea of squatter communities and shantytowns—alternately called *megaslums* or *shadow cities* (Neuwirth, 2005)—defies urban-rural classifications.

Such classifications, however, are a vital element of policing and violence reduction programmes, since authority is exercised through the organization of jurisdictional boundaries. A new vocabulary is thus emerging. Sieverts, for instance, has coined the term *Zwischenstadt*, 'cities without cities' that are no longer characterized by centrality and a threshold of density. Instead, today's urban environment features a series of development clusters linked by a network of transportation routes. The result is a 'city web' in which notions of public space and social cohesion are replaced by the prioritization of (elite) personal space and the competition for power among arbitrarily divided urban enclaves (Sieverts, 2003). Such is the daunting setting for 21st-century urban violence reduction programmes.

distribution of basic goods and services and land (DFAIT, 2006). In extreme cases, 'issues of rural–urban change can be both underlying causes and trigger factors for increasing violence and insecurity, or indeed consequences of the phenomenon itself' (Moser and Rodgers, 2005, p. v).

URBAN POLITICAL AND CRIMINAL VIOLENCE

Given the diverse geography and socio-economic situation of cities, urban violence is highly heterogeneous, and few cross-city or cross-regional generalizations can be made. This section examines different facets of urban armed violence, reviewing the limited research and evidence that has been collected concerning political and criminal armed violence in urban settings.

Urban criminal armed violence

Around the world, urban armed violence is linked to organized criminal activity, the availability of weapons, opportunities for criminal gain, weak or ineffective police and security, and stark patterns of inequality or a lack of alternative economic opportunities. Diverse studies have illustrated the overall impact of armed violence on urban populations and the broader climate of insecurity that is created.

The most systematic study of urban violence—the International Crime Victims Surveys—has been conducted under the auspices of the UN Interregional Crime and Justice Research Institute (UNICRI). Its study of criminal victimization in urban Europe (based on surveys carried out in the year 2000) examines victimization in 16 Eastern and Central European cities, and nine Western European urban areas. It found no major differences between Western and Eastern

European levels of victimization, with 27 per cent of all respondents being a victim of one of 11 crimes in the preceding year (Alvazzi del Frate and van Kesteren, 2004). Arms were used in about one-quarter of 'contact crimes' (robbery, assault, sexual offences). There were no significant differences in the prevalence of guns in these crimes, with the exception of assaults, where weapons were much less frequently present in Western European cities (only six per cent of the threat and assault incidents). Further work is needed to disaggregate these findings across different urban contexts, but the widespread availability and use of firearms in violent crimes is relatively clear. What is less well understood is how and by whom these weapons are used, and the specific role of weapons as enablers of/or catalysts for violence.

This issue is somewhat better understood in other contexts. Latin America, emerging from long periods of civil war, still has one of the highest rates of armed violence in the world, and criminal violence is intertwined with the phenomena of *pandillas* and *maras*—small- and large-scale organized gangs that engage in predatory behaviour, drug trafficking, protection rackets, and other forms of gang violence. Their impact on overall levels of armed violence cannot be overestimated. In Managua, Nicaragua, for example, one in four individuals surveyed in 1997 claimed to have been the victim of a crime in the *previous four months,* and 40 per cent of all crimes were reported in the capital city (with only around 20 per cent of the population) (Rodgers, 2004, p. 116). Even with significant under-reporting, armed violence appears to have risen steadily throughout the 1990s, and to have evolved 'from a form of collective social violence to a more individually and economically motivated type of brutality' (Rodgers, 2006, p. 267).

A similar pattern is evident throughout Central America. In 2006, more than 40 per cent of reported homicides in Guatemala occurred in Guatemala City, which has less than 20 per cent of the country's population. Even accounting for under-reporting in rural areas, Guatemala City's reported homicide rate of 110 per 100,000—higher than the Latin

Armed with a whipping cane and a sawn-off shotgun, a member of the Bakassi Boys vigilante group returns from patrolling the market in Onitsha, Nigeria, in June 2002. © Boris Heger/AP Photo

American average—suggests a high concentration of urban violence. Small arms were responsible for 85 per cent of homicide deaths (Matute and García, 2007).[8] Recent surveys systematically rank insecurity as the most important concern (above unemployment) in Guatemala, highlighting that 'armed violence is recognized as a major social problem . . . that seriously hinders the possibilities for progress' (Matute and García, 2007). In El Salvador, almost two-thirds of armed violence is gang-on-gang, which, given the urban concentration of the *maras,* means high levels of violence in the capital city (and a national level of armed violence that is among the world's highest as well) (Cruz, 2006, p. 129). Both cases illustrate that the long-term effects of violent conflict are dramatic.

Municipal governments have increasingly assumed security responsibilities in Guatemala, and although these initiatives are relatively new, they appear to have some impact on overall violence levels. But tackling armed criminal gang violence will be a longer-term effort, since the phenomena of *maras* and *pandillas* are continental in scale, and perhaps global in nature (Hagedorn, 2007). Gang violence in major US cities (Miami, Los Angeles) has been clearly linked to Central American cities, and one result is that, in the case of Los Angeles, African Americans and Latinos account for 85 per cent of homicide victims (Maxwell, 2006).

Armed violence and crime in major African cities are less clearly linked to large-scale gang activity, representing a mixture of criminal and 'political' (broadly defined) motives. They have been linked 'to the increased intensity and complexity of urbanization' (Gimode, 2001, p. 297), including land use and expropriation policies that systematically exclude marginal groups from land and public services. Armed vigilante groups such as the Bakassi Boys (active in Aba, Nigeria) have summarily executed alleged criminals, have enjoyed support from important political figures (local and state-level), and have often become tools of predation against competing groups (communal or economic rivals) (Harnischfeger, 2003; Smith, 2004).

Box 5.4 Firearm ownership and use in African cities

Over the past decade, crime victim surveys have produced a wealth of information on experiences of crime in Africa.[9] The standard International Crime Victims Survey (ICVS) questionnaire includes questions on ownership of firearms, the type of arm, and reasons for ownership.[10] The ICVS is also a general victimization survey addressing issues of safety.

On average, 9 per cent of the interviewed households in urban areas worldwide declared that they owned a firearm and 6 per cent (about two-thirds of gun owners) had a handgun. Among those owning handguns, the majority (60 per cent) said that the purpose of their keeping the weapon at home was to protect themselves from crime (see Figure 5.3).

The Small Arms Survey has conducted surveys in households in Burundi and the Democratic Republic of the Congo (DRC) in which respondents were asked a variety of questions about firearms. For a number of reasons, the results of these surveys are likely to show higher rates than those of the ICVS. Unlike the ICVS survey, this household questionnaire deals only with firearms as opposed to larger security issues (though it also asks for a respondent's lifetime experience and other background). The question on firearms ownership ('Have you ever had one of these arms in your possession?') is also more general than its ICVS equivalent. Furthermore, since both countries are experiencing post-conflict situations, access to weapons may be easier than elsewhere.

Indeed, more than half of the respondents in Burundi and approximately one-third in DRC admitted to owning a firearm. Among the reasons mentioned for detaining a weapon, belonging to a rebel group was mentioned by 42 per cent of the owners in Burundi and 8 per cent in the DRC. Self-protection was the main reason in Burundi (53 per cent), while it captured only 11 per cent of the responses in the DRC, where the main reason stated by respondents was being a member of the army (48 per cent).

According to available statistics for Africa, guns are used to commit on average one in four homicides and, apart from killings, violence is more often committed with firearms when gaining property is the object of the crime. An average of nine per cent of respondents who owned a car had been victims of a carjacking, and victimization rates were highest in Lusaka, Mbabane, and Johannesburg (see Figure 5.4). This crime has become a major issue of concern for car drivers in African cities, especially because of the frequent involvement of firearms in crime.

Source: Alvazzi del Frate (2007)

Figure 5.3   **Percentage of households owning firearms in African capital cities or large urban areas, per country**

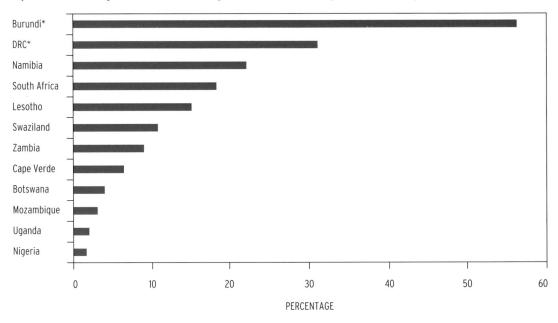

* UNODC analysis of data from results of surveys conducted by the Small Arms Survey in Burundi (Bubanza, Bujumbura, Bururi, and Cibitoke) and DRC (North Kivu and South Kivu) in 2004.
Sources: ICVS survey data; Alvazzi del Frate (2007)

Figure 5.4   **Percentage of respondents who were victims of carjackings at gunpoint or not involving firearms in African capital cities or urban areas (survey data)**

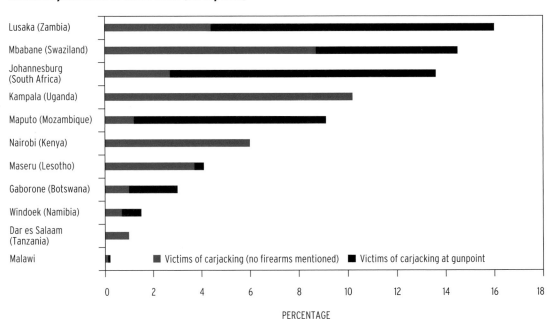

* Data for Nairobi from Stavrou (2002).
Source: Alvazzi del Frate (2007)

Levels of victimization in African cities do not generally reach the heights of some Latin American cities, although the pattern of victimization is similar (concentrated among particular groups and among young men). In Nairobi, 18 per cent of residents reported being a victim of physical assault in a 12-month period (2000–01). Guns were used in only around ten per cent of the assault cases (most of which involved robbery), but in two-thirds of the homicides (which were usually theft-related) (Stavrou, 2002, pp. 54, 118–19). In Cape Town, almost half the residents were victims of a crime in a five-year period (relatively long for such surveys), while Johannesburg reached 62 per cent. Only 20 per cent of violent crimes in Cape Town involved guns (although nearly half the murders were committed with a gun) (Camerer et al., 1998; Louw et al., 1998). Homicide rates were also highest in Johannesburg and Cape Town, reaching levels of 30 and 29 per 100,000, respectively (Isserow, 2001).

Urban political armed violence

In Western cities armed violence is associated predominantly with organized or small-scale criminality. In the global South, however, urban violence is often political as much as criminal in nature, and can be part of larger armed conflicts. Political armed violence includes clashes between rival political (or communal) groups and between state officials (police and other security forces); it can also represent the instrumental use of violence by the state against its population (Winton, 2004). In situations where local or national governments are unrepresentative or anti-democratic, politics can spill over into violence, or armed groups can be mobilized to enforce or maintain power.

The situation in Baghdad in 2006 and early 2007, which witnessed high levels of armed violence in the context of a civil war between heavily armed militias, is an extreme case. By early 2007, one in 160 of Baghdad's 6.5 million inhabitants had been violently killed since the beginning of the war in 2003, many (if not most) by small arms and light weapons (Iraq Body Count, 2007). Conflict and post-conflict urban armed violence also heavily affects cities ranging from Bujumbura (BURUNDI) to Mogadishu and Kabul. As one analyst has noted, 'war-related violence tends to quickly lead to the demise of city administrations, and the resultant power vacuum may be filled by military authorities or armed groups' (van Brabant, 2007, p. 20).

In the global South, urban violence is often political as much as criminal in nature.

Urban armed violence can also be high in non-war settings such as Colombia, where the line between political and criminal violence is often blurred. Here, criminal activity (assault, robbery) is often politicized in the sense that it is undertaken for political ends. Moreover, criminal organizations are intertwined in complex relations of competition and cooperation with state authorities (Gutiérrez Sanín and Jaramillo, 2004).

Although the absolute number of victims may not be high (relative to the population), urban political violence has consequences beyond the number of people killed, since it is usually associated with intimidation, threat, and a chilling effect on popular participation in politics. Several examples from around the world can illustrate how major cities are affected by this form of armed violence.

Caracas, for instance, was ranked by the Inter-American Development Bank (IADB) as the second most violent city in Latin America for death due to homicide (see Box 5.12). In recent years, many of these deaths have been political, as clashes between demonstrators and the police increased by nearly 800 per cent between 1999 and 2004. Violent deaths across Venezuela are increasingly being registered as 'resistance to authority' and 'other violent deaths' rather than as homicides.

Port-au-Prince, Haiti, presents another grim example (see Box 5.5). A study conducted in 2004–05 and published in the *Lancet* estimated the homicide rate for the city at 219 per 100,000, with an estimated 8,000 people having been murdered between February 2004 and December 2005, 65 per cent of them by firearms (Hutson and Kolbe, 2006). In

Box 5.5 Port-au-Prince, Haiti

In 2004, a violent insurrection by members of the disbanded Haitian army overthrew the elected government. Groups on all sides accused their political opponents of systematic human rights abuses. Neither the United Nations, which established a mission in Haiti in mid-2004, nor the Interim Haitian Government had a firm estimate of the numbers of human rights violations committed or the identity of the perpetrators (Dupuy, 2005). Qualitative studies from the US State Department (US DOS, 2005), Human Rights Watch (HRW, 2005), and others (AI, 2004; Griffin, 2005; Freedom House, 2005) indicated that gross human rights abuses including prolonged illegal detentions, politically motivated executions, and physical and sexual assaults had occurred.

Estimating human rights violations

Using household surveys, an estimate of the patterns of human rights violations in greater Port-au-Prince was established. The surveys covered murders, detentions, physical/sexual assaults, theft/vandalism, death threats, threats of physical violence, and threats of sexual violence. The study covered incidents that occurred between 29 February 2004 and December 2005.

Standard random sampling techniques for survey research, such as cluster and stratified samples, often cannot be used in developing countries because they require census data, address lists, or population density maps that are unavailable or unreliable. Instead, Random GPS (Global Positioning System) Coordinate Sampling (RGCS) was used for this study. RGCS differs from traditional techniques in that selection is based on randomly determined spatial locations. The geographic boundaries of the area examined are determined before selection and GPS locations within the boundaries are randomly generated.

Using RGCS, 1,500 locations within the Port-au-Prince area (estimated population 2,121,000) were identified and visited to determine if a household resided at the site. Of the 1,389 valid households, 1,260 participated in the study—a response rate of 90.7 per cent. The 1,260 households interviewed accounted for 5,720 residents with an average household size of 4.5 individuals. Nearly 40 per cent (38.4 per cent) of the household members were under 20. More than half (52.7 per cent) were female.

Twenty-three households reported that a homicide had taken place during the period under review. The resulting calculated crude murder rate was 219 per 100,000 per year. This means that an estimated 8,000 (95 per cent confidence interval 5,000-12,000) individuals were murdered. The most common cause of death was by gunfire (n=15; 65 per cent). Other causes were blunt force trauma, 'torture', sharp object wound, and asphyxiation. Findings suggest 5,200 individuals were murdered by firearms during the 22-month period examined. Criminals were the largest group of perpetrators in these murders (47.8 per cent), while police officers were named as responsible in 21.7 per cent, and members of the demobilized army and armed anti-Lavalas groups (e.g. Lame TiMachete) in 26 per cent. Of the firearm deaths, 40 per cent involved an unknown type of gun, 33 per cent involved a handgun, and 27 per cent were committed with a rifle.

The politics of information

This study generated significant controversy. Critics claimed to perceive bias because the study did not detect any Lavalas murders or sexual assaults; some argued that Lavalas partisans had thus been 'exonerated'. Others accused the authors of having a 'pro-Lavalas' bias, in part because one of the authors had volunteered ten years earlier at an orphanage founded by Jean-Bertrand Aristide, of the Lavalas party, and had covered Haiti as a journalist.

Given the statistical power of the sample size and the survey methodology employed, it is not possible to detect all cases in which a particular political actor may have been involved. The study did not detect UN killings either, though the UN has accepted responsibility for such deaths. Misunderstandings of the standard epidemiological methodologies and procedures used in this study—by both the press and parties with vested interests—appear to have contributed to the controversy. Individuals critical of the findings may also have had political motivations.

By Royce A. Hutson and Athena R. Kolbe

addition, up to 11,000 people were victims of kidnapping or extra-judicial detention by various paramilitary organizations. Violence increased during this period against the backdrop of a deteriorating political situation in the country. With external support, former soldiers had ousted President Jean-Bertrand Aristide in February 2004. Armed violence then increased in part as a result of the criminal banditry perpetrated by politicized armed militias or *chimères*. About 170,000–210,000 small arms were in circulation during this period—the vast majority of them illegal (Muggah, 2005a).

Karachi, a city of more than 10 million inhabitants, had the highest reported crime rate in Pakistan, with a reported homicide rate of 13 per 100,000 in the mid-1990s (Chotani et al., 2002, p. 58). While the order of magnitude may be lower than that of Caracas or Port-au-Prince, the city nonetheless reported more than 2,100 political murders in 1995. Detailed epidemiological studies of the pattern of victimization established that 83 per cent of the victims were killed by firearms, and that 46 per cent of the dead and injured were from only four neighbourhoods, popu-lated mostly by Mohajirs, Muslim immigrants from India. One neighbourhood, Korangi, which had only six per cent of the population, witnessed 22 per cent of the homicides (Chotani et al., 2002, pp. 58–59). Studies of more than 4,000 victims of intentional injury in 1993–96 demonstrate that opposition to political activity was a clear predictor of victimization, and that firearms were the overwhelming weapon (83 per cent) (Mian et al., 2002; Chotani et al., 2002; Esser, 2004).

Karachi is not the only South Asian city suffering from political violence. Mumbai was rocked by communal–political violence in 1993, with the Hindu Shiv Sena movement targeting Muslim minorities in riots and large-scale acts of violence that left more than 800 dead. Small arms were frequently used, particularly by the police to contain riots. A subsequent government inquiry established 'Shiv Sena's and other political parties' blatant involvement in the violence, and the abuse of authority by the police' (Hansen, 2001, p. 132).

A similar structure exists in Nigerian cities, which exhibit a tendency towards inter-communal conflict; in 2002, armed violence killed more than 100 people in Lagos, where links between armed gangs, local political elites, and the criminal underworld are strong (CNN, 2002; Harnischfeger, 2003). The same pattern of inter-linked criminal and political violence is manifest in Nairobi (Anderson, 2002). While not confined to urban areas, the political mobilization of communal groups and the creation of armed militias in urban areas have contributed to insecurity and violence in many Southern cities.

Real and perceived levels of violence are often linked to the fragmentation of public space.

Violent urbanization: containment in fragile and fragmented cities

There is no necessary causal relationship between urbanization and armed violence, and not all urban spaces are sites of violence and victimization. Tokyo is a case in point: with 35 million residents, it is by far the most populous urban agglomeration in the world, yet it is also one of the safest cities on the planet. Levels of violence and victim-ization are also dynamic across time: large cities such as New York and Atlanta experienced dramatic declines in armed violence during the 1990s, while others witnessed increases or no change. But decreasing levels of armed violence do not necessarily correlate with people's perceptions of their security.

As the IADB has noted, 'even where statistics on violence are accurate, tremendous gaps can exist between sub-jective perceptions of violence and objective fact'. A single violent incident in an upscale district can generate lasting impacts on attitudes and real-estate estimates, and 'it is not unusual for governments to take action . . . as a result of pressure from the public's perception of a lack of public safety, even when statistics suggest relatively low levels of crime and violence' (Guerrero Velazco, 2003). Briceño-León argues that 'fear is distributed on a more egalitarian basis than that of the population's real security . . . the role of the mass media, vicarious victimization and rumour lead to similar feelings in victimized and non-victimized groups' (Briceño-León, 2005, p. 1632).

In many parts of the developing world, real and perceived levels of violence are intricately linked to the fragmen-tation of public space, which in turn can be related to the speed at which urbanization is taking place. In this context, it is suitable to talk about the violence of urbanization rather than urban violence (Boisteau, 2006). In some cities, parts of slums and shantytowns have taken on the character of forbidden gang and crime zones beyond the control of public security forces. As a result, middle- and upper-class residents may feel the need to build walls to shield themselves, giving rise to a landscape of gated communities. Real and perceived violence mutually reinforce each other to create what Agbola (1997), describing conditions in contemporary Lagos, has aptly termed an 'architecture of fear'. In frantic efforts to protect themselves, the wealthy hide behind increasingly elaborate systems of security, supplied and maintained by private firms. The result is a fragmentation of public space, a breakdown of social cohesion through the generation of new forms of spatial segregation and social discrimination, and potentially more violence (see Box 5.6).

According to the Canadian Department of Foreign Affairs and International Trade (DFAIT, 2006), almost half of all Latin American and Caribbean cities have areas that are considered dangerous and inaccessible to state security services. In such spaces, gangs, vigilantes, militia groups, and organized crime syndicates prosper, reordering social networks and offering alternative forms of social cohesion. In the light of the extent of these new forms of socio-spatial organization and informal governance, some analysts have begun to talk about failed or fragile cities (Moreau and Hussain, 2002). Not unlike certain states, some cities are powerless as their authorities lose their monopoly over the legitimate use of force—powerful gangs are in control on one side of the wall, and private security forces on the other.

Police attempt to keep watch over Nairobi's Mathare slum following overnight clashes in November 2006. © Tony Karumba/AFP/Getty Images

Box 5.6 Undermining public space: the phenomenon of gated communities

'Residents from all social groups argue that they build walls and change their habits to protect themselves from crime. However, the effects of these security strategies go far beyond self-protection. By transforming the urban landscape, citizens' strategies of security also affect patterns of circulation, habits, gestures related to the use of streets, public transportation, parks, and all public spaces. How could the experience of walking on the streets not be transformed if one's environment consists of high fences, armed guards, closed streets, and video cameras instead of gardens and yards, neighbors talking, and the possibility of glancing at some family scene through the windows? The idea of going for a walk, of naturally passing among strangers, the act of strolling through the crowd that symbolizes the modern experience of the city, are all compromised in a city of walls. People feel restricted in their movements, afraid, and controlled; they go out less at night, walk less on the street, and avoid the "forbidden zones" that loom larger and larger in every resident's mental map of the city, especially among the elite. Encounters in public space become increasingly tense, even violent, because they are framed by people's fears and stereotypes. Tension, separation, discrimination, and suspicion are the new hallmarks of public life.'

—Teresa Caldeira, City of Walls (2000, p. 297)

A gated suburban community borders on the La Cava slum on the outskirts of Buenos Aires, underscoring the glaring divide between rich and poor in Argentina. © Natacha Pisarenko/AP Photo

These new circumstances have had profound effects on urban governance. The logic of spatial fragmentation clearly puts the focus on containment rather than prevention, exclusion rather than participation. As Moser and Rodgers write, the 'policing of urban order is increasingly concerned with the management of space rather than the disciplining of offenders' (2005, p. vii). Policies and programming designed to reduce urban violence must take into account this social and physical reorganization of urban space, and must understand that it is shaped as much by people's perceptions of armed violence and victimization, as by actual criminality. In much the same way as the 'war on terror', the architecture of fear requires continuous affirmation of threat in order to justify its continuation.

URBAN RESPONSES TO ARMED VIOLENCE

Multilateral donors and national policy-makers are becoming increasingly aware that the prevalence of urban armed violence constitutes a major constraint to achieving meaningful development and good governance.[11] Notwithstanding certain disagreements over the underlying causes, costs, and consequences of urban armed violence, rates of homicide and other forms of armed violence—and the attendant fear and insecurity—are a major preoccupation within the public and private sectors (Moser, 2006, p. 2). In some cases, the virulence of urban violence rivals that commonly found in armed conflicts. Mounting concern over 'urban warfare' has generated a corresponding policy discourse with responses seeking to 'combat' violent crime and win the 'war' against drug and arms trafficking.

As the impacts of armed violence are felt locally, pressure to reduce them is often brought to bear at the municipal level. Governors, mayors, elected councillors, and civil servants are on the front line of reducing gun violence. A vast assortment of non-governmental organizations, trade unions, private sector entities, and activists are responsible for advocating for and implementing initiatives to prevent and reduce armed violence. The growing international aware-

---

Box 5.7   The Armed Violence Prevention Programme: towards evidence-guided prevention of armed violence

The Armed Violence Prevention Programme (AVPP) is an inter-agency collaboration initiated by the UN Development Programme and the World Health Organization. Its overall objective is to promote effective inter-institutional synergies and partnerships to enhance strategies and policy frameworks designed to prevent armed violence. Global and national activities, including focused assessments in Brazil and El Salvador, have been undertaken since 2004.

Systematic inventories of violence prevention programmes documented information on more than 175 Brazilian and 145 Salvadoran municipal violence prevention programmes. In both countries, interventions tended to be urban-based, initiated with local political support, and combining a variety of violence prevention strategies. At the same time, the majority of documented interventions were constrained by funding and human resource limitations and weaknesses in coordination and systematic exchange and learning.

From the broader sample, a smaller selection of violence prevention and reduction activities was thoroughly evaluated. Three of these included activities targeting high-risk youth, another entailed a community-based programme to prohibit weapons-carrying. Despite a number of constraints, these efforts were deemed to have generated a broadly positive impact on reducing risk factors associated with armed violence or actual perpetration rates of armed violence.

Several international processes are raising the profile and relevance of the AVPP. The Geneva Declaration on Armed Violence and Development of 2006 and the work of the Organisation for Economic Co-operation and Development/Development Assistance Committee to develop guidance on armed violence reduction are two examples. Findings from the AVPP are feeding directly into both of these efforts and future activities at the global and national level will aim to increase programming effectiveness through more integrated and cooperative work at a national level, inclusive activities with civil society and international agency partners, and a commitment to enhancing measurement, monitoring, and evaluation.

By David R. Meddings and Peter Batchelor

ness of the scope and impact of urban armed violence has coincided with a trend towards the decentralization of government administration and services, and the delegation and reallocation of related functions and resources to local government structures. These forces have combined to generate mounting pressure on mayors and local authorities to craft responses, often without a commensurate reallocation of resources.

Tensions persist between national and municipal approaches to violence reduction and arms control. For example, multilateral and bilateral donors often privilege *national* programming when it comes to development and security-related priorities. Investment in legislative reform and good governance, enabling mechanisms for arms control and disarmament, demobilization, and reintegration (DDR) or security sector reform (SSR) are channelled through ministries and departments for foreign affairs, the interior, finance, justice, and defence of developing countries. In many cases, donors design and finance programmes in collaboration with national institutions of recipient governments—including parliaments and national commissions. Financing mechanisms are approved and accounted for within national executives and legislatures, thus assuring donors that programmes are 'nationally owned'. While the positive outcomes are expected to be felt locally, overall control remains a national prerogative. At best, as in Uganda, Sierra Leone, Liberia, and Ghana, armed violence prevention and reduction priorities are mainstreamed into national development planning frameworks, including Poverty Reduction Strategy Programmes and UN Development Assistance Frameworks.

Though national institutions may be essential for sustaining and expanding the reach and scale of discrete prevention and reduction projects, it is often the mayors, local officials, non-governmental agencies, and faith-based groups that are responsible for advancing the process. Precedents are emerging for bridging the international–national–municipal divides. For example, Colombia's efforts to promote municipal-based armed violence reduction and arms control offer a model for the Andean region. Specifically, Bogotá, Medellín, and Cali applied for and obtained loans from the IADB in the late 1990s to finance violence prevention and public safety programmes. Though loans were guaranteed by the national government, they were secured, managed, and repaid by the three cities. The IADB approved similar loan arrangements for Uruguay and other Latin American countries: as much as USD 150 million has been committed to six 'citizen security' loans and technical cooperation projects (Alda et al., 2006; Buvinic, Morrison, and Shifter, 2002; Buvinic and Morrison, 2000).

> Mayors, local officials, and civil society often advance violence reduction and prevention projects.

There is, of course, a range of established risk factors that contribute to the onset and virulence of urban armed violence. In addition to rapid urbanization, these factors may include inefficient and non-credible judicial and law enforcement sectors, the absence of employment opportunities for youth, the prevalence of alcohol and substance abuse, and unregulated small arms possession. The chapter on Brazil (BRAZIL) reveals that risks can vary widely from one city to another. Municipal authorities are aware that interventions must be tailored to the particular context in which they are planned and executed. There is no standard template or blueprint for local armed violence reduction. Rather, there are thousands of heterogeneous and variegated municipally based interventions to mitigate urban crime, armed violence, and arms availability.

Typology of municipal small arms control

Multilateral agencies and developed country governments are becoming increasingly committed to investing in human security and public safety in urban areas. Coupled with developmental objectives such as a significant reduction in the number of slum-dwellers by 2020, the relationships between urban spaces, organized crime, and post-conflict reconstruction and recovery are also intensifying security-oriented concerns (UNDP, 2006; UN-HABITAT, 2005; Brennan,

Box 5.8 Freedom from fear in urban areas

The Canadian Department of Foreign Affairs and International Trade (DFAIT) recently launched an initiative entitled 'Human Security–Cities: Freedom from Fear in Urban Spaces'. The adoption of an 'urban lens', they argue, 'allows for a better understanding of peace-building or conflict-generating trends that are unique to cities, so as to strengthen and improve upon human security policy and programming'.

The mushrooming of slums in many cities around the world, coupled with a lack of corresponding investment in public security, has led to a stark increase in the number of areas without an effective police presence. With the authorities often accused of social cleansing, the excessive use of force, and collusion with gangs, private security services are on the rise. The result is a 'bifurcated security structure' of gated communities on the one hand, and gangs selling security services to residents on the other.

A further consequence of the failure to provide public security is the potentially explosive combination of youth, arms, and gangs in urban areas, with well-armed, organized gangs controlling streets and neighbourhoods. The affordability and availability of small arms in cities means that these gangs are often better armed than the police. DFAIT's initiative thus emphasizes the need for effective security sector reform, explores the notion of 'conflict-resilient cities', and highlights the need to think about urban governance as one of the key tools in the promotion of human security.

Source: DFAIT (2007)

Figure 5.5 **Conceptual typology of municipal arms control strategies**

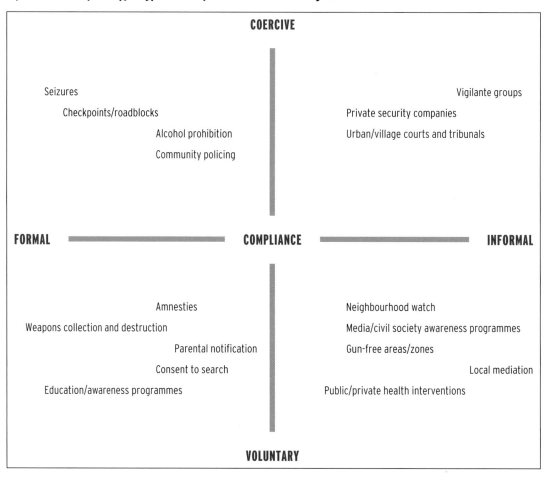

1999). Uncontrolled urban growth brings the social and economic segregation of the wealthy from the poor into sharp relief. As a result, certain donor governments have defined improvements in public and private security and demilitarization as foreign and national policy objectives (DFAIT, 2007; see Box 5.8). Many cities in developed and developing countries alike have themselves launched an array of interventions to rein in armed violence.

Though highly varied in form and content, municipal-level armed violence prevention and reduction activities can be mapped out as a conceptual typology (see Figure 5.5). These can be organized according to their form (coercive, compliance-based, or voluntary) and institutional structure (formal or informal). *Coercive* approaches encompass aggressive top-down strategies to deterring and reducing violence such as forcible disarmament, cordon, and search activities and intelligence-led interventions. They often target high-risk groups including would-be perpetrators, repeat offenders, ex-combatants, and young men. *Compliance-based* activities seek to encourage changes in behaviour through the threat and enforcement of selective penalties. They often include decentralized and community-centred approaches to policing and promoting the rule of law.

Meanwhile, *voluntary* interventions are designed to encourage participation in armed violence prevention and reduction. As such they often include temporary amnesties, educational and awareness-building initiatives, and community-led arms collection activities. All three forms of interventions can be formal—that is, mandated and organized by the state—or informal, organized and implemented outside the remit of the state.

Effective urban violence prevention and reduction interventions apply a combination of coercive, compliance-oriented, and voluntary approaches. 'Effectiveness' here implies sustained improvements in objective and subjective indicators of security (McCord, 2003). For example, the widely lauded Boston Gun Project and the St. Louis 'consent-to-search' programme piloted a carefully sequenced package of activities to enhance real and perceived safety (US NIJ, 2004). Coercive approaches—including swift and selective arrests, pedestrian and traffic stops, and search warrants—together with compliance-promotion (e.g. consent searches, parent notification) and voluntary initiatives (e.g. gun buybacks, turn-in campaigns, and town hall meetings) were pursued via a partnership between federal, state, and local security providers. In selected catchment areas in Boston, fatal and non-fatal firearm injuries decreased while perceived security increased: between 1990 and 1998, homicides dropped threefold and non-fatal gunshot injuries decreased by 65 per cent (Cook and Ludwig, 2004; Mogul, 1999). Analogous problem-oriented policing approaches have been consciously exported to and adopted in Manchester (Bullock and Tilley, 2002).

Box 5.9 Bottom-up and top-down approaches to violence prevention and reduction

Participatory urban appraisals of armed violence intervention programmes in Colombia and Guatemala identified several approaches to designing, implementing, and measuring the impact of armed violence prevention and reduction interventions. They emphasize criminal justice; public health; human rights; citizen security; environmental design; and community empowerment (Moser, 2006, p. 6).

The *criminal justice* perspective privileges deterrence through arrest, conviction, and punishment by the police, courts, and prison system. The *public health* approach emphasizes 'risk triggers' and promotes case-by-case interventions by isolating causal pathways—alcoholism, single-headed households, and firearms availability. The *rights-based* approach draws from existing human rights principles and norms and promotes basic entitlements of freedom from armed violence. The *citizen security* approach combines both criminal and health-related interventions to promote peace and co-existence by strengthening juvenile violence prevention, community–police relations, and rehabilitation at the local level. The *environmental* approach is spatially focused on dangerous or high-risk areas and aims to restore and enhance physical structures through urban renewal. Finally, *community organizations* emphasize the restoration of social capital—namely trust and unity—through informal and formal institution-building (Lederman et al., 2002).

Effective urban violence prevention and reduction programmes often build on a solid evidence base and robust public–private partnerships. Collaborative arrangements can be formally institutionalized, while in other cases they remain informal and ad hoc. For example, certain cities in the European Union and Latin America established multi-stakeholder 'crime prevention councils' to act as a forum to enhance the sustainability of armed violence reduction (Shropshire and McFarquhar, 2002; Bullock and Tilley, 2002). During the early 1990s, the Dutch government negotiated a USD 19 million security contract with 'problem municipalities' in order to undertake community policing, anti-hooligan programmes, the recruitment of mediators, and the development of a network of communal substance abuse centres to reduce armed violence (Vourc'h and Marcus, 1993). In other cases, municipal programmes are combined with larger-scale SSR initiatives.[12]

Coercive approaches

Urban armed violence prevention and reduction interventions traditionally advanced coercive deterrence-based approaches to affect changes in real and perceived victimization. High-profile national programmes emphasizing repression and police deployment were more likely to secure greater public sympathy and assuage popular anxieties —particularly among elite segments of the population—than low-key voluntary initiatives. As noted by Buvinic and Morrison, 'prevention . . . is a long-term proposition and one that does not buy many votes' (2000, p. 69). An expectation was that muscular police-led operations to 'crack down' on high-risk groups—from paramilitaries, militia, gangs, and 'terrorist cells' to unemployed youth, 'delinquents', and others—could generate visible improvements in safety.

The results of coercive violence reduction and prevention interventions are mixed.

Coercive strategies to reduce armed violence typically emphasized heightened police presence as well as increases in arrests and long-term incarceration. Such approaches persist over time in different states: the United States and the Russian Federation reported incarceration rates of 5 per 1,000 during the mid-1990s as compared to 1.7 per 1,000 in the rest of the world during this period (Vanderschueren, 1996, p. 103). Potential acts of armed violence were expected to be pre-empted through the credible threat and use of force, the rapid dispensing of justice, and the broadcasting of severe penalties and incarceration rates. The 'demonstration effects' of successfully executed coercive approaches were expected to discourage would-be violators and repeat offenders.

The results of coercive approaches, however, are mixed. Across time and space coercive interventions alone do not appear to deter successfully or measurably reduce armed violence. There were also rising concerns that high-profile coercive initiatives diverted resources away from more effective, low-visibility preventive programmes and served to stigmatize the 'targets', thereby further contributing to criminality. Although in most cases such approaches are supported by the electorate owing to the enhanced sense of security they engender, the statistical evidence is limited. In the UK, the 2001 Halliday Report estimated that a 15 per cent increase in prison populations would be required to generate a mere one per cent drop in crime (Home Office, 2001, p. 9).

Coercive approaches to preventing and reducing armed violence also tend to focus on seizing weapons from illegal traffickers, brokers, and owners. Weapons seizures and confiscations, together with enhanced police and private security presence, are expected to send a message to high-risk groups. Targeted interventions designed to gather assault rifles, sub-machine guns, and even grenades, mortars, and light weapons are not uncommon in North and Latin American, Balkan, and African cities. For example, more than 53,500 handguns were forcefully collected by police between 1990 and 2001 from Rio de Janeiro's 700 *favelas*—though the casualty rates of such operations were tremendously high. This should be compared to the 250,000 firearms collected voluntarily through weapons

Box 5.10 Guns and gang violence in Los Angeles

Although levels of crime in Los Angeles have dropped over the past five years, the city has experienced a surge in gang violence. Gang membership has actually fallen in the past decade from more than 60,000 in the mid-1990s to fewer than 40,000
in 2006. But urban violence is highly concentrated among gangs: according to municipal police statistics, about half of all
reported homicides are gang-related. Beyond firearms-related deaths and injuries, the widespread use of arms also takes a
daily toll on residents living in low-income neighbourhoods, in particular in South Central and East Los Angeles.

Gun violence related to gang activity is the result of fights over turf, status, and revenge (VPC, 2001). It can be described
as a neighbourhood 'ecology of danger' in which racial discrimination and geographic isolation contribute to an inner-city
environment devoid of resources and opportunities and access to adequate housing, schools, grocery markets, and neighbourhoods that are available in mainstream society. African American and Latino youth in South Central and East Los Angeles
succumb to alternate methods of attaining status and wealth—whether by joining gangs, selling narcotics, theft, or engaging
in gun violence.

Successive interventions have been launched to reduce this urban armed violence. As recently as late 2006, a joint LAPD-
FBI task force was established to deal with gang violence and attempt to increase transnational cooperation among police
departments across North and Central America. Other interventions have focused on joint patrols, greater focus on intelligence collection, the prioritization of interventions on high-risk gangs, cooperation with neighbouring cities (within the
state, across state lines, and across international borders), crackdowns on graffiti, increased surveillance and investigations
of narcotics and firearm-related violations by federal agents, and the application of stiffer federal penalties (FBI, 2007).

Source: Maxwell (2006)

collection programmes between 2003 and 2005, during which time no civilians were killed or injured (WHO, PAHO,
and Small Arms Survey, 2005).

Declining public confidence in governance and formal police and judicial systems in certain contexts has led to
a growth in informal and privatized responses to urban insecurity. In the context of limited employment opportunities, vigilantes, gangs, militia, and for-hire private security groups have emerged to fill the gaps left by under-
resourced police forces. These privatized security groups are becoming increasingly transnational in character: mayors
and police authorities in the United States have described armed violence by gangs as 'a problem of international
scope, [to be faced] on an international scale' (BBC, 2007; Tita et al., 2003b).

The strategies employed vary in the level of coercion applied. For example, in Los Angeles, inter-agency interventions focus on the arrest and deportation of members of the estimated 463 gangs (Tita et al., 2003a; see Box 5.10).
Meanwhile, in several northern Nigerian cities, militant Muslim groups supplanted police functions by vigorously
enforcing *sharia* law (Florquin and Berman, 2005). In Medellín and Bogotá, both guerrilla and paramilitary groups
impose 'taxes' on local business as a form of protection, while in Cape Town vigilante groups such as People Against
Gangsterism and Drugs regularly execute gang leaders to 'cleanse' the streets. As noted above, militant groups and
gangs in inner cities and shantytowns of the world's major cities are becoming increasingly institutionalized and
internationally connected (Hagedorn, 2005, p. 159; Moser and Rodgers, 2005, p. 23).

Compliance-based approaches

The police and criminal justice systems serve as the fundamental pillars of law and order in a society. For a variety
of reasons, their administration, management, and financing are normally centralized at the national and federal
levels, thereby circumventing or overriding the control of municipal authorities. In most countries, national, military,
and municipal policing and justice entities may experience overlapping jurisdictions within a single municipality or
city. In certain instances, institutional relationships can become highly politicized and adversarial, while in others

they may be complementary and reinforcing. Compliance-based interventions thus occur at the interface of these internally competing agendas and tend to reinforce even greater decentralized community-based responses with an emphasis on enhanced judicial functions.

An array of compliance-based approaches to managing armed violence—including community-based policing—have emerged in a wide variety of contexts. Community policing emphasizes community-centred awareness and solutions, proactive rather than reactive interventions, more on-the-ground engagement of police in the everyday affairs of neighbourhoods, enhanced visibility and active patrolling on foot or bicycle, and a participatory approach with increased delegation and discretion. The expectation is that local governments are in a better position to successfully apply and monitor police and the dispensation of justice. In some cases, community policing is formally institutionalized in existing security structures. In Japan, for example, policing services are highly decentralized and focused on enhancing visibility at the local level: 15,000 neighbourhood police stations are spread out across the country with some 9,000 also serving as permanent residences for police in rural areas. Japanese police officers have wide discretion in managing offenders, thus allowing them to cut through bureaucracy and reserve the shame of trial for more serious offences.[13] In other cases, community policing is introduced in a targeted fashion to enhance outreach and support devolved services—as in Brazil, Malawi, and Tanzania (UNODC, 2007).

Compliance-based approaches rely on the decentralization of justice services. As opposed to sanctioning interventions from above, compliance-based approaches aim to enhance local-level resilience in relation to preventing and reducing urban violence. One approach—described as the 'broken-window theory'—advocates decentralization and delegation of policing functions to the precinct and community level, enhanced local monitoring and surveillance, and a practical problem-solving approach to visible petty offences in order to encourage reductions in violent crime. The theory, itself heavily contested among urban sociologists, is that there is an iterative relationship between improvements in perceived and real security as well as between different types of criminality (Kelling and Coles, 1996). Broken-window strategies were consciously employed in New York, and later in Los Angeles and Mexico City, in a bid to contain and reduce firearm-related homicide. Over a five-year period in the mid-1990s, then New York City Police Commissioner William Bratton was credited with overseeing a drop in firearm-related homicide by almost 70 per cent, with general violations of the law cut in half. Interventions focused on mitigating petty crime, but there were also simultaneous efforts to control firearms and interrogate suspects to uncover the origins of seized weapons.[14] Strategies encouraged the visible dismantling of gangs on a neighbourhood-by-neighbourhood basis and targeted efforts to rein in non-violent crime, such as prostitution and drug trafficking (Harnett and Andrews, 1999; Kelling and Coles, 1996).

A governing assumption of compliance-based approaches is that the decentralization of justice services will overcome the inertia of overburdened and inefficient judicial systems. Such reforms are expected to restore public confidence in the rule of law and the tendency to take justice into one's own hands and settle grievances through recourse to weapons rather than the courts. Conventional reforms focus on national-level improvements to the administration of justice, increases in the quality and quantity of judicial services, enhanced prison and incarceration systems, and even alternative methods for conflict mediation. But there are also innovative decentralized approaches focused on improving local service delivery. Especially effective pilots introduced in certain countries include the *Maisons de Justice* (France) and neighbourhood tribunals such as *people's reconciliation* in China, the *barangay* in the Philippines, and *barrio courts* in Latin America.

Municipal authorities frequently experiment with innovative approaches to improving the efficiency and public perception of the justice system, especially in relation to armed violence prevention and reduction. For example, in

Colombia, the *casas de justicia* (houses of justice) are an experiment in the decentralization of the courts and increased local processing. From the mid-1990s onwards, several *casas* were established in both Cali and Bogotá, then considered among the most violent cities in the country (Muggah et al., 2006). These entailed the involvement of the office of the District Attorney, Family Violence Intake Centres, Victim Assistance Offices, Forensic Medicine and Prosecution, as well as police oversight and legal aid services to on-site locations in acutely affected areas. Although no comprehensive evaluation has been undertaken, early results relating to processing claims and public perception suggest dramatic reductions in armed violence and gun use (Buvinić et al., 2005).

Other, more informal approaches to enhancing the delivery of justice services have emerged in Africa. Following the Ugandan civil war in the 1980s, for example, a series of 'resistance councils' emerged with responsibilities delegated to cities and rural areas. Legalized in 1988 and with democratically elected leaders, the councils sought to guarantee security and respect for the law in their areas of jurisdiction, to interface with government initiatives, and to promote development according to participatory processes. They played a pivotal role by intervening in civil cases—whether for debt, contracts, damage to property, land disputes, or in certain criminal cases. In contrast to the formal courts, they delivered justice quickly, free of charge, and in a locally appropriate fashion (Nsibambi, 1991).

Voluntary approaches

The bulk of contemporary urban armed violence and arms control activities emphasize primarily voluntary approaches—albeit often in combination with other types of interventions. Indeed, the UN and other multilateral organizations tend to discourage coercive interventions, or at least avoid undertaking such activities outside of mandated peace-enforcement operations. Voluntary interventions range from firearm amnesties and weapons collection programmes to urban sensitization and awareness-raising campaigns (see Box 5.11). In 2002, Kuhn et al. (2002)

Box 5.11 Philadelphia students campaign against gun violence

In January 2004, we, the students of Philadelphia's Jubilee School had a discussion about an epidemic that was destroying our neighbourhood: gun violence. A former Jubilee student had been shot and killed-he was 18. We decided to do something about guns by starting the Children's Campaign against Gun Violence.

As part of our campaign, we wrote a petition that says: 'We, the children of Pennsylvania, are asking you to let kids live their future. We want neighborhoods to be gun-free. Please change the laws so we can experience life in a safe environment. You should make the right choice and help us get rid of guns and drugs. We want to grow up with dignity and power instead of being scared.'

We went to schools and discussed gun violence with other children. The teenagers we met said: 'We need guns to protect us.' The children in elementary school were more willing to accept the fact that guns are killing, not protecting. We got almost 300 signatures on our petition by students from eight different schools. We presented the petitions to the Philadelphia City Council, the governor of Pennsylvania, and a state representative.

We organized and participated in a Children's March against Gun Violence. Overall, our campaign went beyond what we thought it would. We were invited to a small arms conference held by the United Nations to share our experience with gun violence and how the laws should be changed. Representatives from other countries listened to us and treated us seriously and with respect.

Although we are children, we want to do our part to make the world a safer place. We want to have another children's march, speak in more schools, and collect more signatures for our petition. We also plan to work on a documentary film about gun violence and its effects. We would like to interview activist groups, so they can give us the knowledge we need to succeed in ending this epidemic.

By the students of the Jubilee School, Philadelphia

A Guacaipuro gang member holds on to his gun as he takes a swig in the
Petare slum of Caracas, October 2006. © Fabio Cuttica/Contrasto/eyevine

Box 5.12   Addressing armed violence in Caracas[15]

While publicly committed to addressing longstanding social injustices in one of Latin America's most unequal societies, the administration of President Hugo Chávez has ushered in the most violent period in Venezuela's recent history. Demonstrations and clashes between government and opposition groups have left a polarized and intolerant climate that led citizens to rank insecurity over unemployment as the principal problem facing the country today. Though increasingly unreliable and inconsistent, official statistics confirm these perceptions. At 65 deaths per 100,000 inhabitants in 2004, the annual homicide rate in Venezuela more than doubled since 1998, surpassing even neighbouring Colombia in 2003.[16]

The Inter-American Development Bank ranked Caracas the second most violent city in Latin America in terms of death due to homicide during the period 1999-2003, with an estimated 133 homicides per 100,000 inhabitants. More than half of Caracas's 3.5 million residents lack access to basic services and infrastructure. Unchecked violence in the city's barrios, such as Petare, is accompanied with a weak justice system and ineffective public security institutions. This is due in part to Caracas' fragmented administrative base; the city's five municipalities share territory with different states and have their own distinctly uniformed police forces. Popular militias, or *Círculos Bolivarianos,* have taken up arms in self-defence and wage urban warfare with opposition groups. One result has been that the percentage of homicides associated with firearms rose from 64 per cent in 1998 to 87 per cent in 2004.[17]

In Caracas deaths occurring in clashes between demonstrators and the police increased by nearly 800 per cent between 1999 and 2004, and violent deaths are increasingly registered as 'resistance to authority' and 'other violent deaths' rather than as homicides. Such extra-judicial killings are reflected in a ratio of civil to police victims of 39:1 nationally, much higher than that observed in Brazil (10:1) and far above the international average (5:1). Moreover, these violations are rarely investigated; of 9,719 known homicides in 2004, 62 per cent were referred to prosecutors, 14 per cent led to arrests, and only 7 per cent resulted in sentences.

Public and community-based security initiatives have had little impact so far on the escalating violence. In September 2006, the Chávez administration proposed a USD 4.6 million gun buyback programme that would offer USD 140-230 to people who turn in revolvers and pistols (San Francisco Chronicle, 2006). Such disarmament programmes are likely to have little lasting impact without significant reform of the police, justice, and penitentiary systems. Leopoldo López, mayor of the municipality of Chacao in Caracas, has proposed a comprehensive plan that includes institutional reforms as well as a range of strategies for violence monitoring and prevention.[18] Initiatives such as better street lighting, reclaiming public space, and the construction of 'vertical' gymnasiums have also had positive impacts.[19] In 2006, however, the proposed budget for the Ministry of Defence was some 80 times greater than that of the Ministries of Interior and Justice, implying that municipal safety and security in Venezuela's urban centres is not a high priority (Venezuela National Budget Law, 2006).

reported that there had been more than 100 separate firearm buy-back programmes in the United States alone in the past decade.[20] Previous editions of the *Small Arms Survey* reviewed national and community-based arms collection initiatives ranging from conventional DDR to discrete arms control interventions focused on national regulation, export and import controls, enhanced registration, improved border and customs control, and stockpile inventory security.[21]

Various types of amnesties are frequently administered by a national or municipal authority to encourage voluntary reductions in armed violence. Though often voluntary and time-bound, they are usually preceded and followed by a series of penalties and are thus implicitly linked to the compliance and coercive-based approaches reviewed above. Amnesties were successfully introduced in several urban contexts to encourage the voluntary surrendering of illegal or legal arms for public destruction, as in Albania, Mali, Cambodia, Brazil, and Colombia (Muggah, 2006). They are also frequently legislated to encourage the surrender and destruction of replicas and toy weapons, and thus serve a useful educational function.

Awareness and sensitization programmes are credited with successfully influencing access and resort to armed violence and small arms. Because prevailing social norms structure the motivations for acquiring firearms, an appreciation of and response to relevant risk factors as well as associated means (real and relative prices and resources) constitute important entry points for altering behavior. Education—particularly at the primary, secondary, and vocational levels—can play a major role in shaping the motivations and means of weapons acquisition and misuse (Brauer and Muggah, 2006; Atwood et al., 2006).

Many examples of community-based education programmes exist to reinforce tolerance and anti-violence norms among male and female youth in urban environments. For example, in Jamaica, the PALS programme adopted the Foundation for Peace Education model and aims to educate children about conflict resolution and alternatives to gun violence.[22] In Colombia, voluntary disarmament programmes were bolstered by a deliberate strategy of enhancing a *cultura ciudadana* (citizen culture) and distributing textbooks in exchange for toy handguns. As a result of these and other interventions, firearm-related homicide and unintentional injury rates reportedly declined among youth segments of the population (Aguirre et al., 2006, p. 232).

Changing demographics and priorities in rapidly urbanizing contexts are forcing classical approaches to violence prevention and reduction—including disarmament—to adapt. At a minimum, interventions are accommodating a more multidisciplinary approach (Cuesta et al., 2007). There is awareness that no single disciplinary perspective—whether sociology, demography, public health, or economics—adequately captures the inherent complexities of urban violence. A growing number of urban planners and policy-makers are conscious that bringing to bear the whole range of policy-relevant research—including criminology, epidemiology, and human geography—with evidence-based analysis is essential to identifying the dynamics of and effective solutions to urban armed violence.

> Classical approaches to violence prevention and reduction are being forced to adapt.

CONCLUSION

Cities are remarkably vibrant and resilient and, given their diversity, few global generalizations can be made about the phenomenon of urban armed violence. This chapter has provided an overview of the wide variation in the level and scope of urban armed violence: from its near-total absence in such megacities as Tokyo, to near-epidemic levels in places such as Guatemala City or Cali—and from its links to conflict and post-conflict dynamics (Baghdad) to large-scale criminal activity in Latin American cities.

Despite this diversity, at least three major conclusions can be drawn to supplement the more specific observations made above. First, large-scale and rapid urbanization places enormous stress on the governance capacity of states and municipal authorities while also providing new opportunities for criminal and violent activity. Whether this potential becomes actual violence, however, depends on contextual factors, such as the availability of weapons and the strength of community and public security institutions.

Second, the changing nature of urban architecture (in its broadest sense) is often driven by individuals' real and perceived sense of insecurity, and violence is often contained or exported to peripheral urban zones characterized by poverty, poor infrastructure and services, and at times rampant insecurity.

Finally, and perhaps most significantly, municipal interventions to reduce or prevent armed violence represent an important—and potentially the most important—policy instruments available to governments and international agencies and donors seeking to reduce the scope and scale of armed violence. Cities will thus be the object of an increasing focus of policy attention in the 'urban century'. ■

LIST OF ABBREVIATIONS

AVPP	Armed Violence Prevention Programme	ICVS	International Crime Victims Survey
DDR	disarmament, demobilization, and reintegration	RGCS	Random GPS Coordinate Sampling
		SSR	security sector reform
GPS	Global Positioning System	UNICRI	UN Interregional Crime and Justice
IADB	Inter-Agency Development Bank		Research Institute

ENDNOTES

1   See p. 3 of the Introduction to this volume for the *UN Report* definition.

2   Further support for this theory is provided by research in the United States and Latin America, although for crime as a whole, and not specifically armed violence. See Fajnzylber et al. (2002) and Gaviria and Pagés (2000). On violent crime in the United States, see Shaw-Taylor (2002), which notes that violent crime rates in smaller cities (average population around 200,000) were much lower than in the largest cities.

3   A correlation was found when the model controlled for country-specific effects, but not in the model without country-specific effects. This highlights the need for a contextual analysis of urban armed violence.

4   Material in this section is drawn directly from Wilkinson and Bell (2006). Moreover, Wintemute (1999) has shown that half of all US homicides occurred in 63 cities with 16 percent of the population.

5   See also Pérouse de Montclos (1997).

6   Glaeser and Sacerdote (1996); Campbell and Ormerod (n.d.); Vanderschueren (1996); and Sampson et al. (1997).

7   One notable exception is Blau and Blau (1982).

8   See also Rodriguez and León Wantland (2001, p. 207) and León and Sagone (2006, pp. 195–96).

9   Since 1989 the International Crime Victims Survey (ICVS) has been conducted in approximately 80 countries and large cities across the world. Data here refers to capital cities and urban areas (more than 100,000 population) that took part in different editions of the survey. Data presented in this box also includes victim surveys carried out in African capital cities and urban areas by UNODC (Cape Verde); UN-HABITAT–Safer Cities Programme (Nairobi, Dar es Salaam); the Institute for Security Studies (ISS) (Malawi); and the Small Arms Survey (Burundi, Republic of Congo, DRC).

10   The main question asks, 'Do you or someone else in your household own a handgun, shotgun, rifle, or air rifle?' Then the respondent is
      requested to specify which type and for what purpose. The purpose categories are the following: hunting, target shooting as a sport, as a
      collector's item, for crime prevention/protection, as duty because the respondent is in armed forces or the police, or because it has always been
      in the family/home.

11   See, for instance, UNODC and World Bank (2007) on crime and violence in the Caribbean.

12   Justice and security sector reform, security system reform, and security sector reform are here treated as synonymous. See the OECD-DAC (2007)
      IF–SSR Guidelines.

13   In 1989, for example, police were responsible for 73 per cent of all arrests (and 96 per cent of arrests for homicide) and 76 per cent of thefts
      were solved (Brennan, 1999).

14   Specifically, an offensive was mounted against violators of weapons possession laws who, after being arrested, were interrogated to locate the
      source of small arms. People arrested for other minor offences were also interrogated.

15   Unless otherwise indicated, data in this box is drawn from information provided by the Cuerpo de Investigaciones Científicas Penales y
      Criminalísticas, Venezuela, and the Center for Peace and Human Rights of the Central University of Venezuela.

16   Data provided by the National Institute of Legal Medicine and Forensic Sciences, Colombia; Security and Democracy Foundation, Balance de
      Seguridad; and the National Institute of Statistics, Venezuela.

17   Data from annual mortality reports (1998–2004) of the Ministry of Health and Social Development, Venezuela.

18   See Alcaldía de Chacao (<http://www.chacao.gov.ve/plan180/presentacion.htm>)

19   See the Caracas Urban Think Tank (<http://www.ccstt.org/>)

20   These programmes range from individual activities such as interventions in Boston, Wisconsin, or Los Angeles, to a national buyback programme,
      co-funded by the US Department of Housing and Urban Development and implemented in approximately 90 cities in 1999. The programme
      was discontinued in 2001. See <http://usgovinfo.about.com/library/weekly/aa073101b.htm>

21   See also Faltas et al. (2001).

22   See, for example, <http://www.peace-ed.org/curricula/>

BIBLIOGRAPHY

Agbola, Tunde. 1997. *Architecture of Fear: Urban Design and Construction Response to Urban Violence in Lagos, Nigeria.* Ibadan: African Book
      Publishers.

Aguirre, Katherine, et al. 2006. 'Colombia's Hydra: The Many Faces of Gun Violence.' In Small Arms Survey, 2006.

Alda, Erik, Mayra Buvinic, and Jorge Lamas. 2006. 'Neighbourhood Peacekeeping: The Inter-American Development Bank's Violence Reduction
      Programs in Colombia and Uruguay.' *Civil Wars.* Vol. 8, Iss. 2, pp. 197–214.

AI (Amnesty International). 2004. 'Haiti: Perpetrators of past abuses threaten human rights and the reestablishment of the rule of law.' 3 March.
      <http://web.amnesty.org/library/Index/ENGAMR360132004?open&of=ENG-HTI>

Alvazzi del Frate, Anna. 2007. *Firearm-related Violence in Africa.* Unpublished background paper. Geneva: Small Arms Survey.

— and John van Kesteren. 2004. *Criminal Victimization in Urban Europe: Key Findings of the 2000 International Crime Victim Surveys.* Turin:
      UNICRI.

Anderson, David. 2002. 'Vigilantes, Violence and the Politics of Public Order in Kenya.' *African Affairs.* No. 101, pp. 531–55.

Atwood, David, Anne-Kathrin Glatz, and Robert Muggah. 2006. *Demanding Attention: Addressing the Dynamics of Small Arms Demand.* Occasional
      Paper 18. Geneva: Small Arms Survey.

BBC. 2007. 'Plea for gang violence crackdown.' 8 February. <http://news.bbc.co.uk/2/hi/americas/6338609.htm>

Blau, Judith and Peter Blau. 1982. 'The Cost of Inequality: Metropolitan Structure and Violent Crime.' *American Sociological Review.* Vol. 47, No. 1,
      pp. 114–29.

Boisteau, Charlotte. 2006. 'Violences et transformations urbaines: un rideau de fer est tombé sur les villes?' Unpublished background paper. Geneva:
      Small Arms Survey.

van Brabant, Koenraad. 2007. 'Human Insecurity in Six Post-conflict Cities.' *Human Security for an Urban Century.* Vol. 4, No. 3. Ottawa: DFAIT, pp.
      20–21.

Brauer, Jürgen and Robert Muggah. 2006. 'Completing the Circle: Building a Theory of Small Arms Demand.' *Contemporary Security Policy*. Vol. 27, No. 1. April, pp. 138–54.

Brennan, Ellen. 1999. 'Population, Urbanisation, Environment and Security: A Summary of the Issues.' *Environmental Change and Security Project Report*. Issue 5.

Brennan-Galvin, Ellen. 2002. 'Crime and Violence in an Urbanizing World.' *Journal of International Affairs*. Vol. 56, No. 1 (Fall), pp. 123–46.

Brenner, Neil and Roger Keil (eds.). 2006. *The Global Cities Reader*. London and New York: Routledge.

Briceño-León, Roberto. 2005. 'Urban Violence and Public Health in Latin America: A Sociological Explanatory Framework.' *Cad. Saúde Pública*. Vol. 21, No. 6, pp. 1629–64.

Bullock, Karen and Nick Tilley. 2002. *Shootings, Gangs and Violent Incidents in Manchester: Developing a Crime Reduction Strategy*. Crime Reduction Research Series Paper 13. London: Home Office.

Buvinić, Mayra, Erik Alda, and Jorge Lamas. 2005. *Emphasizing Prevention in Citizen Security: The Inter-American Development Bank's Contribution to Reducing Violence in Latin America and the Caribbean*. IADB Sustainable Development Department Best Practices Series. Washington, D.C.: IADB. <http://idbdocs.iadb.org/wsdocs/getdocument.aspx?docnum=647713>

Buvinić, Mayra and Andrew Morrison. 2000. 'Living in a More Violent World.' *Foreign Policy*. Vol. 118 (Spring), pp. 58–72.

— and M. Shifter 2002. 'La violencia en América Latina y el Caribe.' In Fernando Carrión (ed.), *Seguridad ciudadana, ¿espejismo o realidad?* Quito: FLACSO/PAHO.

Caldeira, Teresa. 2000. *City of Walls: Crime, Segregation, and Citizenship in São Paulo*. Berkeley and Los Angeles: University of California Press.

Camerer, Lala et al. 1998. *Crime in Cape Town: Results of a Victim Survey*. Monograph 23. Johannesburg: Institute for Security Studies.

Campbell, Michael and Paul Ormerod. n.d. 'Social Interaction and the Dynamics of Crime.' Unpublished paper.
   <http://www.volterra.co.uk/Docs/crime.pdf>

Chenais, Jean-Claude. 1981. *Histoire de la violence en Occident de 1800 à nos jours*. Paris: Robert Laffont.

Chotani, H.A., J.A. Razzak, S.P. Luby. 2002. 'Patterns of Violence in Karachi, Pakistan.' *Injury Prevention*. Vol. 8, pp. 57–59.

CICS–Bradford. 2005. *The impact of armed violence on poverty and development*. Bradford: Armed Violence and Poverty Initiative.

CNN. 2002. 'Lagos Violence Death Toll Mounts.' 5 February. <http://archives.cnn.com/2002/WORLD/africa/02/05/nigeria.killings/>

Cook, Philip and Jens Ludwig. 2004. 'Principles for Effective Gun Policy.' Unpublished paper.
   <http://www.pubpol.duke.edu/people/faculty/cook/gunpolicy.pdf>

Countryside Agency. 2004. 'The new definition of urban and rural areas of England and Wales.' *CRN*. Vol. 86. 1 August.
   <http://www.ruralcommunities.gov.uk/publications/thenewdefinitionofurbanandruralareasofenglandandwales>

Cruz, José Miguel. 2006. 'El Salvador.' In *La cara de la violencia urbana en América Central*. San José, Costa Rica: Arias Foundation, pp. 105–61.

Cuesta, José, Erik Alda, and Jorge Lamas. *Social Capital, Violence and Public Intervention: The Case of Cali*. IADB Economic and Sector Study Series. Washington, D.C.: IDAB. <http://idbdocs.iadb.org/wsdocs/getdocument.aspx?docnum=973008>

Dauvergne, Mia and Geoffrey Li. 2006. 'Homicide in Canada, 2005.' *Juristat*. Vol. 26, No. 6, pp. 1–25.

Davis, Mike. 2006. *Planet of Slums*. London: Verso.

DFAIT (Department of Foreign Affairs and International Trade), Canada. 2006. 'Freedom from Fear in Urban Spaces: Discussion Paper.' Ottawa: DFAIT.

—. 2007. *Human Security for an Urban Century*. Ottawa: DFAIT. <http://www.humansecurity-cities.org>

van Dijk, Jan. 1998. 'Criminal Victimisation: A Global View.' In *Surveying Crime: A Global Perspective*. Proceedings of the International Conference, 19–21 November. Rome: UNICRI.

Dupuy, Alex. 2005. 'From Jean-Bertrand Aristide to Gérard Latortue: The Unending Crisis of Democratization in Haiti.' *Journal of Latin American Anthropology*. Vol. 10, No. 1, pp. 186–205.

Economist. 2006. 'Murder Most Common.' 17 August, pp. 35–36.

Eisner, Manuel. 2001. 'Modernization, Self-Control and Lethal Violence: The Long-term Dynamics of European Homicide Rates in Theoretical Perspective.' *British Journal of Criminology*. Vol. 41, No. 4, pp. 618–38.

Elias, Norbert. 2000 [1939]. *The Civilizing Process*. Oxford: Blackwell.

Esser, Daniel. 2004. 'The City as Arena, Hub and Prey: Patterns of Violence in Kabul and Karachi.' *Environment and Urbanization*. Vol. 16, No. 2. October, pp. 31–38.

Fagan, Jeffrey, Deanna Wilkinson, and Garth Davies. 2007. 'Social Contagion of Violence.' In Daniel Flannery, Alexander Vazsonyi, Irwin Waldman (eds.), *The Cambridge Handbook of Violent Behavior and Aggression*. Cambridge: Cambridge University Press, pp. 688–723.

Fajnzylber, Pablo, Daniel Lederman, and Norman Loayza. 1998. *Determinants of Crime Rates in Latin America and the World: An Empirical Assessment.* Washington, D.C.: World Bank.

—. 2002. 'Inequality and Violent Crime.' *Journal of Law and Economics.* Vol. 45, No. 1. April, pp. 1–39.

Faltas, Sami, Glenn McDonald, and Camilla Waszink. 2001. *Removing Small Arms from Society: A Review of Weapons Collection and Destruction Programmes.* Occasional Paper No. 2. Geneva: Small Arms Survey.

FBI (US Federal Bureau of Investigation). 2005. *Crime in the United States 2005.* Table 12. <http://www.fbi.gov/ucr/05cius/data/table_12.html>

—. 2007. *Headline Archives: the Gangs of LA – the City Fights Back.* <http://www.fbi.gov/page2/jan07/lagangs012407.htm>

Ferguson, Brodie. 2007. 'Urban Security in Caracas.' Unpublished background paper. Geneva. Small Arms Survey

Florquin, Nicolas and Eric G. Berman, eds. 2005. *Armed and Aimless: Armed Groups, Guns, and Human Security in the ECOWAS Region.* Geneva: Small Arms Survey.

Freedom House. 2005. Press release. 31 March. <http://www.freedomhouse.org/template.cfm?page=70&release=255>

Gaviria, Alejandro and Carmen Pagés. 2000. *Patterns of Crime Victimization in Latin America.* Washington, D.C.: IADB. <http://www.iadb.org/res/publications/pubfiles/pubWP-408.pdf>

Gimode, Edwin. 2001. 'An Anatomy of Violent Crime and Insecurity in Kenya: The Case of Nairobi, 1985–1999.' *Africa Development.* Vol. 26, Nos. 1 and 2, pp. 295–335.

Glaeser, Edward and Bruce Sacerdote. 1996. *Why Is There More Crime in Cities?* NBER Working Paper W5430. Cambridge, Mass.: National Bureau of Economic Research. January. <http://papers.ssrn.com/sol3/papers.cfm?abstract_id=10167>

Griffin, Thomas. 2005. *Haiti human rights investigation: November 11–21, 2004.* Miami, FL: University of Miami School of Law and Center for the Study of Human Rights. <http://www.law.miami.edu/news/368.html>

Guerrero Velazco, Rodrigo. 2003. 'Violence Control at the Municipal Level.' IADB Technical Note 8. Washington, D.C.: IADB. <http://www.iadb.org/IDBDocs.cfm?docnum=362968>

Gurr, Ted Robert. 1981. 'Historical Trends in Violent Crime: A Critical Review of the Evidence.' *Crime and Justice.* Vol. 3, pp. 295–353.

Gutiérrez Sanín, Francisco and Ana María Jaramillo. 2004. 'Crime, (counter-)insurgency and the privatization of security: the case of Medellín, Colombia.' *Environment and Urbanization.* Vol. 16, No. 2, pp. 17–30.

Hagedorn, John. 2005. 'The Global Impact of Gangs.' *Journal of Contemporary Criminal Justice.* Vol. 21, No. 2, pp. 153–69.

—, ed. 2007. *Gangs in the Global City: Alternatives to Traditional Criminology.* Chicago: University of Illinois Press.

Hansen, Thomas Blom. 2001. *Wages of Violence: Naming and Identity in Post-Colonial Bombay.* Princeton: Princeton University Press.

Harnett, Patrick and William Andrews. 1999. 'How New York Is Winning the War on Drugs.' *City Journal.* Vol. 9, No. 3. <http://www.city-journal.org/html/9_3_a2.html>

Harnischfeger, Johannes. 2003. 'The Bakassi Boys: Fighting Crime in Nigeria.' *Journal of Modern African Studies.* Vol. 41, No. 1, pp. 23–49.

Home Office, United Kingdom. 2001. *Making Punishments Work: Report of a Review of the Sentencing Framework for England and Wales* (the Halliday Report). London: Home Office Communications Directorate.

HRW (Human Rights Watch). 2005. *Human Rights Watch World Report 2005.* Available from: <http://hrw.org/wr2k5>.

Hutson, Royce and Athena Kolbe. 2006. *Urban Armed Violence in Haiti.* Unpublished background paper. Geneva: Small Arms Survey.

IADB (Inter-American Development Bank). 2002. *Violence as an obstacle to development.* IADB Technical Note 4. Washington, D.C.: IADB.

—. n.d. *Guidelines for the Design of Violence Reduction Projects.* Washington D.C.: IADB.

ICVS (International Crime Victims Survey). <http://www.unicri.it/icvs>

IHSI (Institut haïtien de statistique et d'informatique). 2003. Recensement Général de la Population et de l'Habitat. Port-au-Prince: IHSI. August.

Iraq Body Count. 2007. 'Year Four: Simply the Worst.' Press release 15. 18 March. <http://www.iraqbodycount.org/press/pr15.php>

Isserow, Mark. 2001. 'Crime in South Africa's Metropolitan Areas, 2001.' Unpublished paper. Johannesburg: Centre for the Study of Violence and Reconciliation. <http://www.csvr.org.za/papers/papstats.htm>

Kelling, George and Catherine Coles. 1996. *Fixing Broken Windows: Restoring Order and Reducing Crime in Our Communities.* New York: Free Press.

Kuhn, Evelyn et al. 2002. 'Missing the target: a comparison of buyback and fatality-related guns.' *Injury Prevention.* Vol. 8, pp. 143–46.

Lederman, Daniel, Norman Loayza, and Ana María Menéndez. 2002. *Violent Crime: Does Social Capital Matter?* Chicago: University of Chicago Press.

de Léon, Carmen Rosa, and Itzair Sagone. 2006. 'Guatemala.' In *La cara de la violencia urbana en América Central.* San José: Arias Foundation, pp. 163–200.

Louw, Antoinette et al. 1998. *Crime in Johannesburg: Results of a City Victim Survey*. Monograph 18. Johannesburg: Institute for Security Studies.

Matute, Arturo and Iván García. 2007. 'Guatemala.' Unpublished background paper. Geneva: Small Arms Survey.

Maxwell, Tanya. 2006. *Guns, Gangs, and Armed Violence in Los Angeles*. Unpublished background paper. Geneva: Small Arms Survey.

McCord, Joan. 2003. 'Cures that Harm: Unanticipated Outcomes of Crime Prevention Programs.' *AAPSS Annals*. Vol. 587, No. 1, pp. 16–30.

Mian, A. et al. 2002. 'Vulnerability to Homicide in Karachi: Political Activity as a Risk Factor.' *International Journal of Epidemiology*. Vol. 31, No. 3, pp. 581–85.

Mogul, J. 1999. 'Boston: una ciudad que tuvo éxito.' Seminar paper. Rio de Janeiro/Washington, D.C.: IADB.
   <http://www.iadb.org/IDBDocs.cfm?docnum=362968>

Moreau, Ron and Zahid Hussain. 2002. 'Failed cities: terror's urban jungle.' *Newsweek International*. 14 October, p. 39.

Moser, Caroline. 2004. 'Urban Violence and Insecurity: An Introductory Roadmap.' *Environment and Urbanization*. Vol. 16, No. 2. October, pp. 3–16.

—. 2006. 'Reducing Urban Violence in Developing Countries.' Policy Brief No. 1. Washington, D.C.: Brookings Institution.
   <http://www.brookings.edu/views/papers/20061121moser.htm>

— and Cathy McIlwaine. 2004. *Encounters with Violence in Latin America: Urban Poor Perceptions from Colombia and Guatemala*. London and New York: Routledge.

— and Dennis Rodgers. 2005. 'Change, Violence and Insecurity in Non-Conflict Situations.' Working Paper No. 245. London: Overseas Development Institute. March. <http://www.odi.org.uk/publications/working_papers/wp245.pdf>

— and Alisa Winton. 2002. 'Violence in the Central American Region: Towards an Integrated Framework for Violence Reduction.' Working Paper No. 171. London: Overseas Development Institute.

Mouzos, Jenny. 2006. 'Firearm-related violence in Australian states and territories.' Unpublished background paper. Geneva: Small Arms Survey.

Muggah, Robert. 2003. 'A Tale of Two Solitudes: Comparing Conflict and Development-induced Internal Displacement and Involuntary Resettlement.' *International Migration*. Vol. 41, No. 5. December, pp. 5–31.

—. 2005a. *Securing Haiti's Transition*. Occasional Paper 14. Geneva: Small Arms Survey. October.

—. 2005b. 'Managing "Post-conflict" Zones: DDR and Weapons Reduction.' In Small Arms Survey, 2005, pp. 267–301.

— et al. 2006. 'Colombia's Hydra: The Many Faces of Gun Violence.' In Small Arms Survey, 2006, pp. 214–45.

Naudé, Beaty, Johan Prinsloo, and Anastasios Ladikos. 2006. *Experiences of Crime in Thirteen African Countries: Results from the International Crime Victim Survey*. Turin: UNICRI–UNODC.

Neuwirth, Robert. 2005. *Shadow Cities: A Billion Squatters, A New Urban World*. London: Routledge.

Norton, Richard. 2003. 'Feral Cities.' *Naval War College Review*. Vol. 66, No. 4, pp. 97–106.

Nsibambi, Apolo. 1991. 'Resistance Councils and Committees: A Case Study from Makerere.' In Holger Hansen and Michael Twaddle (eds.), *Changing Uganda: The Dilemmas of Structural Adjustment and Revolutionary Change*. London: James Currey, pp. 286–89.

OECD–DAC (Organisation for Economic Co-operation and Development– Development Co-operation Directorate). 2005. 'Small Arms and Light Weapons.' Issue Brief. <http://www.oecd.org/dataoecd/13/27/35034375.pdf>

—. 2007. IF-SSR Guidelines (The OECD–DAC Handbook on SSR: Supporting Security and Justice). Paris: OECD. <www.oecd.org/dac/conflict/if-ssr>

Perlman, Janice. 2005. 'The Myth of Marginality Revisited: The Case of *Favelas* in Rio de Janeiro, 1969–2003.' Unpublished paper.
   <http://www.worldbank.org/urban/symposium2005/papers/perlman.pdf>

Pérouse de Montclos, Marc-Antoine. 1997. *Violence et sécurité urbaines en Afrique du Sud et au Nigeria : Un essai de privatisation*. Paris: l'Harmattan. Vols. 1 and 2.

—. 2003. *Villes et violence en Afrique noire*. Paris: Karthala.

Rapley, John. 2006. 'The New Middle Ages.' *Foreign Affairs*. Vol. 85, No. 3. May/June, pp. 95–103.

Rice, Susan, Corinne Graff, and Janet Lewis. 2006. *Poverty and Civil War: What Policymakers Need to Know*. Global Economy and Development Working Paper 2. Washington, D.C.: Brookings Institution.

Richmond, Therese, Rose Cheney, and C. William Schwab. 2005. 'The global burden of non-conflict-related firearm injury.' *Injury Prevention*. Vol. 11, No. 6. December, pp. 348–52.

Rodgers, Dennis. 2004. '"Disembedding" the City: Crime, Insecurity and Spatial Organization in Managua, Nicaragua.' *Environment and Urbanization*. Vol. 16, No. 2. October, pp. 113–23.

—. 2006. 'Living in the Shadow of Death: Gangs, Violence and Social Orer in Urban Nicaragua, 1996–2002.' *Journal of Latin American Studies*. Vol. 38, No. 2. May, pp. 267–92.

Rodriguez, Mario and Mayda de Léon Wantland. 2001. 'Armas ligeras y violencia en Guatemala.' In *El Arsenal Invisible*. San José, Costa Rica: Arias Foundation.

Sampson, Robert, Stephen Raudenbush, and Felton Earls. 1997. 'Neighborhoods and Violent Crime: A Multilevel Study of Collective Efficacy.' *Science*. Vol. 277. 15 August, pp. 918–24.

San Francisco Chronicle. 2006. 'Wave of Violent Crime Sweeps Venezuela.' 21 April.
<http://sfgate.com/cgi-bin/article.cgi?f=/n/a/2006/04/21/international/i045413D52.DTL>

Sassen, Saskia. 1994. 'The urban complex in a world economy.' *International Social Science Journal*. Vol. 46, pp. 43–62.

Shropshire, Steve and Michael McFarquhar. 2002. 'Developing Multi-Agency Strategies to Address the Street Gang Culture and Reduce Gun Violence Among Young People.' Briefing No. 4. <http://www.iansa.org/documents/2002/index.htm>

Shaw-Taylor, Yoku. 2002. 'Data Watch: Change in Violent Crime in the 100 Largest Cities of the US: 1980–2000.' *Cities*. Vol. 19, No. 2. April, pp. 123–28.

Sieverts, Thomas. 2003. *Cities without Cities. An Interpretation of the Zwischenstadt*. London and New York: Spon Press.

Small Arms Survey. 2005. *Small Arms Survey 2005: Weapons at War*. Oxford: Oxford University Press.

—. 2006. *Small Arms Survey 2006: Unfinished Business*. Oxford: Oxford University Press.

Smith, Daniel J. 2004. 'The Bakassi Boys: Vigilantism, Violence, and Political Imagination in Nigeria.' *Cultural Anthropology*. Vol. 19, No. 3. August, pp. 429–55.

Soja, Edward. 2000. *Postmetropolis: Critical Studies of Cities and Regions*. Oxford: Blackwell.

Stavrou, Aki. 2002. *Crime in Nairobi: Results of a Citywide Victim Survey*. Nairobi: UN-HABITAT and UNDP.

Tita, George, et al. 2003a. 'Unruly Turf: the Role of Interagency Collaborations in Reducing Gun Violence.' *Rand Review*. Fall.

— et al. 2003b. *Reducing Gun Violence: Results from an Intervention in East Los Angeles*. Santa Monica: RAND.

United Nations. 2005. *World Urbanization Prospects: The 2005 Revision*. <http://esa.un.org/unup/>

UNDESA (UN Department of Economic and Social Affairs). 2005. *Urban and Rural Areas 2005*.
<http://www.un.org/esa/population/publications/wup2005/2005urban_rural.htm>

UNDP (UN Development Programme). 2006. *Practice Note: Disarmament, Demobilization and Reintegration of Ex-Combatants*. New York: UNDP.
<http://www.undp.org/bcpr/whats_new/ddr_practice_note.pdf>

UNGA (UN General Assembly). 1997. *Report of the Panel of Governmental Experts on Small Arms*. A/52/298 of 27 August.
<http://www.un.org/sc/committees/sanctions/a52298.pdf>

UN-HABITAT. 2003. *The Challenge of Slums: Global Report on Human Settlements 2003*. New York: UN-HABITAT.

—. 2005. 'Sounding the Alarm on Forced Evictions.' Press Release. 7 April.
<http://www.unhabitat.org/content.asp?cid=1744&catid=441&typeid=6&subMenuId=0>

—. 2006. *State of the World's Cities 2006/7*. New York: United Nations.

UNODC (UN Office on Drugs and Crime). 2007. South–South Crime Prevention Project.
<http://www.southsouthcrime.org/Projects/cp_saferStreets.asp>

— and World Bank. 2007. Crime, Violence, and Development: Trends, Costs, and Policy Options for the Caribbean. March.
<http://www.unodc.org/pdf/world%20bank%20C&V%20Report.pdf>

US DOS (Department of State). 2005. *Country Report on Human Rights Practices in 2005: Haiti*.
<http://www.state.gov/g/drl/rls/hrrpt/2005/61731.htm>

US NIJ (National Institute of Justice). 2004. *Reducing Gun Violence: The St. Louis Consent-to-Search Program*. Washington, D.C.: US Department of Justice. <http://www.ncjrs.gov/pdffiles1/nij/191332.pdf>

Vanderschueren, Franz. 1996. 'From Violence to Justice and Security in Cities.' *Environment and Urbanization*. Vol. 8, No. 1. April, pp. 93–111.

Villaveces, Andres. 2007. *Urban Armed Violence in Cambodia*. Unpublished background paper. Geneva: Small Arms Survey.

VPC (Violence Prevention Coalition of Greater Los Angeles). 2001. Gang Fact Sheet. <http://www.vpcla.org/factGang.htm>

Vourc'h, Catherine and Michel Marcus. 1993. 'Security and Democracy.' Paper for the European Forum for Urban Safety. Paris: Analytical College on Urban Safety.

Wilkinson, Deanna and Kerryn Bell. 2006. *Urban Gun Homicide and Youth Violence: Perspectives from Trends in the United States and Violent NYC Youth*. Unpublished background paper. Geneva: Small Arms Survey.

Wintemute, Garen. 1999. 'The Future of Firearm Violence Prevention: Building on Success.' *Journal of the American Medical Association*. Vol. 282, No. 2. August, pp. 475–78.

Winton, Ailsa. 2004. 'Urban Violence: A Guide to the Literature.' *Environment and Urbanization*. Vol. 16, No. 2. October, pp. 165–84.

World Bank. 2003a. *Development Cooperation and Conflict: Operational Policies 2.30.* World Bank Operational Manual.

—. 2003b. *World Bank Group Work in Low-Income Countries Under Stress: A Task Force Report.* Washington, D.C.: World Bank.

WHO (World Health Organization). 2002. *World Report on Violence and Health.*
    <http://www.who.int/violence_injury_prevention/violence/world_report/en/full_en.pdf>

—. 2004. *The Economic Dimensions of Inter-Personal Violence.* Geneva: WHO.

— PAHO, and Small Arms Survey. 2005. *Firearm-related Violence in Brazil.*
    <http://www.smallarmssurvey.org/files/sas/publications/co_publi_pdf/2004/2004-brasil-full_text_eng.pdf>

ACKNOWLEDGEMENTS

Principal authors

Oliver Jütersonke, Keith Krause, and Robert Muggah

Contributors

Anna Alvazzi del Frate, Peter Batchelor, Kerryn Bell, Brodie Ferguson, Ivan García, Royce A. Hutson, Athena R. Kolbe, Arturo Matute, Tanya Maxwell, David R. Meddings, Jenny Mouzos, and Deanna Wilkinson

Armed Violence in Burundi

CONFLICT AND POST-CONFLICT BUJUMBURA

6

INTRODUCTION

On 24 July 2006 the remaining rebel group in Burundi, the Parti de libération du peuple hutu-Forces nationales de libération (Palipehutu-FNL), launched a mortar attack on the capital, Bujumbura, injuring one person (Reuters, 2006a).[1] A week later, a particularly brutal attack was carried out with small arms and hand grenades in two bars in Bujumbura, killing 4 people and injuring 17 (Reuters, 2006b). These incidents are among the latest in a series of attacks that have targeted the capital since the beginning of the civil war in 1993 and continued after the November 2003 ceasefire agreement signed between the transitional government of Burundi and the main rebel group, the Conseil national pour la défense de la démocratie-Forces pour la défense de la démocratie (CNDD-FDD). In spite of the adoption of a new constitution, the reform of the armed forces, the demobilization of combatants, and the holding of relatively peaceful elections, armed violence still plagues the daily life of Bujumbura's inhabitants.

Through the specific example of Bujumbura, this chapter tackles the issue of armed violence in cities, and in particular capital cities, during and after war. The chapter hypothesizes that the war period poses certain challenges to capital cities, which are home to most state institutions and represent, in this regard, a target of choice for rebel movements. Even after the guns have been silenced, wars leave a legacy of arms proliferation and residual armed violence that seem to particularly affect urban settings. This chapter examines the case of Burundi, which has recently emerged from a long and bloody civil war. The questions examined in the chapter include:

- How did violence during the civil war affect Bujumbura compared with the rest of the country?
- How has insecurity changed since the end of the conflict, both in the country as a whole and in the capital?
- What is the role of small arms and light weapons in post-conflict insecurity in the country?
- Who are the main perpetrators of armed violence in the post-conflict period?

The chapter draws on research carried out by the Small Arms Survey between September 2005 and June 2006 in Burundi. The study was commissioned by the United Nations Development Programme (UNDP) and NOVIB/Oxfam International, and was undertaken in partnership with Ligue Iteka, a Burundian human rights NGO. It relied on the following research methods and sources: a survey of 3,060 households covering 6 out of the 17 provinces, a two-day workshop with ex-combatants representing 6 different former rebel movements, key informant interviews, and analysis of data gathered from national institutions and international organizations present in Burundi.[2]

The chapter first examines how the civil war that raged in Burundi between 1993 and 2006 affected its main centre, Bujumbura, and then provides a quick demographic overview of the country. It then assesses levels of armed violence in Bujumbura and the rest of the country in order to understand who commits acts of violence and with what means. The main conclusions include:

Map 6.1 Percentage of respondents whose households include at least one victim of an act of violence between May and November 2005, by district

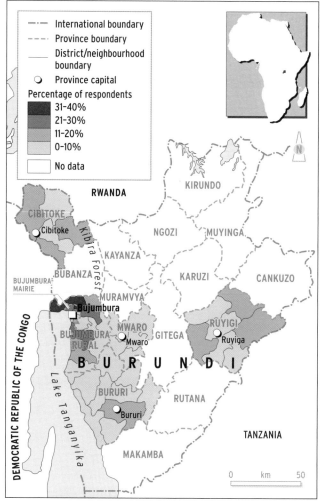

- During the war, Bujumbura was the theatre of armed violence among increasingly segregated—and armed—neighbourhoods, which caused many residents to flee the city.

- Rebel attacks on Bujumbura continued after the 2003 ceasefire and became a means for the last active rebel group to assert its bargaining power.

- Although the security situation in the country has improved markedly since 2003, this progress has been weaker in Bujumbura than in most other regions of Burundi.

- Small arms left over from the conflict—particularly grenades and assault rifles—are weapons of choice for those perpetrating post-conflict violence in Burundi, including in the capital city.

- The disarmament, demobilization, and reintegration (DDR) process and civilian disarmament initiatives have produced mixed results. An estimated 100,000 small arms and grenades are still at large in the country.

- Ex-combatants, few of whom decided to settle in Bujumbura, are generally not identified by the population as a source of insecurity.

- Post-conflict urban violence leads many residents of Bujumbura to keep defensive types of small arms—i.e. handguns—for self-protection.

ARMED VIOLENCE IN BURUNDI: THE SOCIAL AND HISTORICAL CONTEXT

A historical account of conflict in Burundi

Burundi is a small country (about two-thirds the size of Switzerland) in the Great Lakes region, on the shores of Lake Tanganyika. It borders on the Democratic Republic of the Congo (DRC), Rwanda, and Tanzania. A German protectorate as of 1903, Burundi fell under Belgian influence during World War I and became a League of Nations (later UN) trusteeship administered by Belgium in 1926. It gained independence in 1962 (UNHCHR, 1999).

Burundi's population is composed of a large Hutu majority (85 per cent) and a Tutsi minority (14 per cent); the remaining 1 per cent are Twas.[3] Ethnicity—though to a large extent socially constructed—underpins the country's 'rigid . . . stratification and unequal distribution of power' (Ndikumana, 1998, p. 30).[4] In the past, Tutsis largely dominated the army and police, as well as the political institutions and the economy. In addition to the ethnic factor, social hierarchy depends on an individual's region of origin: military and political actors (the former having often dominated the latter) usually come from Bururi and Makamba provinces, in the south of the country (Ndikumana, 1998, pp. 36–37).[5] This differential treatment of Burundian citizens has been particularly flagrant in the area of access to education (Ndikumana, 1998, pp. 38–39; Ngaruko and Nkurunziza, 2000, p. 382).

This power and economic imbalance explains in part why Burundi's history since independence has been marked by numerous episodes of violence and political instability (Ndikumana, 1998, pp. 30–31). The country experienced five successful military coups between 1966 and 1996, and a large number of failed ones (BBC, 2007). In 1972, a Hutu rebellion and its ensuing repression resulted in 200,000 deaths and a flow of 300,000 Hutu refugees leaving the country—a particularly bloody and traumatic episode that is still present in most Burundians' memories (Ndikumana, 2000, pp. 433–34; Ngaruko and Nkurunziza, 2000, p. 375; ICG, 2003, p. 2). According to Ngaruko and

---

Box 6.1 The civil war in Burundi: a chronology of key events, 1993–2006

June 1993: Melchior Ndadaye wins the elections, ending the military regime of Pierre Buyoya. Ndadaye is the first Hutu president in the history of Burundi.

21 October 1993: President Ndadaye is killed in a coup led by Tutsi army officers, which is followed by massacres of Hutu and Tutsi civilians. This marks the beginning of a civil war between the Burundian army (the majority of the personnel of which at the time are Tutsi) and Hutu armed groups.

5 February 1994: Cyprien Ntaryamira, a Hutu, is named interim president by the parliament.

6 April 1994: President Ntaryamira and Rwandan President Juvenal Habyarimana die when their aircraft is shot down near Kigali, Rwanda. This event causes more ethnic violence in Burundi and ignites the Rwandan genocide (April-July 1994).

July 1996: Buyoya leads a successful coup against President Sylvestre Ntibantunganya (who had succeeded Ntaryamira).

1999: Peace talks begin under the mediation of the former Tanzanian president, Julius Nyerere.

28 August 2000: The government and several armed groups sign the Arusha Peace and Reconciliation Agreement. The two main Hutu-dominated rebel groups, CNDD-FDD and Palipehutu-FNL, refuse to sign.

October 2001: Under the auspices of South Africa's Nelson Mandela, who replaced Nyerere after the latter's death in 1999, further talks lead to the setting up of a transitional government in which Hutus and Tutsis share power. Non-signatory rebel groups intensify their fighting.

16 November 2003: Signing of the Global Ceasefire Agreement between the Government of Burundi and the Hutu rebel group CNDD-FDD in Dar es Salaam (Tanzania). Only the Palipehutu-FNL remains outside the peace process.

June 2004: Beginning of the United Nations Operation in Burundi (ONUB), succeeding the African Union mission.

December 2004: Beginning of the DDR process.

March 2005: Voters approve a power-sharing constitution by referendum.

August 2005: Pierre Nkurunziza, leader of the CNDD-FDD, is elected president.

April 2006: The curfew that had been enforced in the whole country since the early 1970s is lifted.

8 September 2006: The government and the Palipehutu-FNL sign a ceasefire agreement in Dar es Salaam (Tanzania).

Sources: La documentation française (2005); BBC (2007); ONUB (2006a)

Figure 6.1 **Number of displaced Burundians by province, September 2002**

PROVINCE

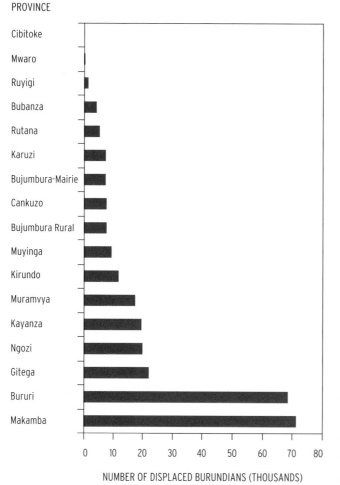

NUMBER OF DISPLACED BURUNDIANS (THOUSANDS)

Note: See endnote 1 for an explanation of the name 'Bujumbura-Mairie'.
Source: ICG (2003, p. 3, using 2002 UN Population Fund figures)

Nkurunziza, '[t]he 1972 events have crystallized ethnic tension in Burundi in such a way that all subsequent crises have been, in one way or another, their consequence' (Ngaruko and Nkurunziza, 2000, p. 375).

In 1993 violence flared up again. It led to a fully fledged civil war between the army and Hutu-dominated rebel groups that resulted in large-scale massacres on both sides (Ndikumana, 1998, p. 36).[6] Ndikumana notes that '[u]nlike earlier ethnic conflicts (in 1965, 1969, 1972, 1988, and 1991), the crisis that followed the October 1993 military coup has been longer, bloodier, and has affected the entire country' (Ndikumana, 1998, p. 36). A first peace agreement brokered by regional leaders with the international community was reached in 2000, but the main rebel groups refused to sign it and fighting continued until 2003 (see Box 6.1).

In late 2005, when the Small Arms Survey– Ligue Iteka survey was conducted, only one armed group, the Palipehutu-FNL, remained active. It operated mainly from the province of Bujumbura Rural, which surrounds the capital Bujumbura, and allegedly launched mortar attacks until the September 2006 ceasefire with the Burundian government.

Political violence has caused the displacement of a large number of Burundians since the early 1970s. In 2003 it was estimated that 300,000 Burundians were internally displaced, while Tanzania was home to another 800,000 refugees (ICG, 2003, p. 1). Burundians principally fled from the south (Bururi and Makamba), centre (Gitega and Muramvya), north (Ngozi, Kayanza, Kirundo, and Muyinga), and west (Bujumbura Rural) of the country, which were generally the areas most affected by the conflict (ICG, 2003, p. 3). In comparison with other provinces, relatively few displaced people relocated to Bujumbura (see Figure 6.1).[7] This can possibly be explained by the fact that acts of ethnic cleansing were widespread in Bujumbura, a fact that did not make it a very attractive destination for displaced people, but instead pushed a number of residents of the city to seek refuge in other provinces (Barahinduka, 2006).

Burundi itself is home to a large number of refugees, mainly from the DRC. About 30,000 Congolese refugees live in Burundi, the majority (18,000) of whom live in urban areas, where they often survive in precarious conditions.

In May 2006 a first group of 67 refugees was relocated by the Office of the United Nations High Commissioner for Refugees (UNHCR) from Bujumbura to a refugee camp where they would receive more assistance. More urban refugees were expected to follow (UNHCR, 2006).[8]

Map 6.2 The pre- and post-war ethnic composition of Bujumbura neighbourhoods

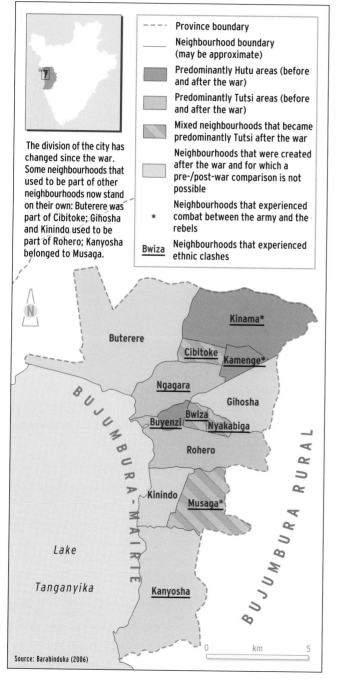

The division of the city has changed since the war. Some neighbourhoods that used to be part of other neighbourhoods now stand on their own: Buterere was part of Cibitoke; Gihosha and Kinindo used to be part of Rohero; Kanyosha belonged to Musaga.

Legend:
- – – – Province boundary
- ——— Neighbourhood boundary (may be approximate)
- Predominantly Hutu areas (before and after the war)
- Predominantly Tutsi areas (before and after the war)
- Mixed neighbourhoods that became predominantly Tutsi after the war
- Neighbourhoods that were created after the war and for which a pre-/post-war comparison is not possible
- * Neighbourhoods that experienced combat between the army and the rebels
- _Bwiza_ Neighbourhoods that experienced ethnic clashes

Source: Barahinduka (2006)

Bujumbura: a city at war[9]

Bujumbura played an important role during the war. The government, the parliament, the army and police headquarters, the national radio and television, the international airport, and many other national institutions are located in the city, which represented a very attractive target for the rebels, as seizing Bujumbura would be synonymous with victory. However, it is curious to note that the crises that preceded the 1990s never took place in Bujumbura. The first attack against the capital occurred in 1991, and this also represented a shift from the use of traditional weapons to the use of small arms and light weapons:

> This marked a change from previous attacks where rebels had struck in remote areas of the country using mainly traditional weapons such as machetes, arrows and spears. Combat casualties were limited but the rebels had sent the message that they could strike anywhere (Ngaruko and Nkurunziza, 2000, p. 380).

During the civil war, rebels tried to blockade Bujumbura by cutting the surrounding roads, and launched isolated attacks against its peripheral neighbourhoods. The neighbourhood[10] of Kamenge was the theatre of fierce combat between the army and the rebels between December 1993 and April 1994.[11]

Bujumbura was also the target of smaller, sporadic attacks or reprisals: Hutu individuals

Box 6.2   Bujumbura: a segregated city

Even before the war, some neighbourhoods of Bujumbura were mainly 'Tutsi' or 'Hutu'. Between 1993 and 2003, however, the massacres carried out in most areas of the city intensified this separation (see Map 6.2).

In 1993–94 Hutus were driven out of the predominantly Tutsi neighbourhoods of Musaga, Nyakabiga, Ngagara, and Cibitoke, while Tutsis were driven out of the predominantly Hutu areas of Kamenge and Kinama in the north of the city, as well as part of Kanyosha in the south.

Expelled Hutus and Tutsis found shelter in improvised refugee camps within neighbourhoods of their ethnicity, or in 'neutral' places, such as churches. Some Hutus also moved into neighbourhoods of relatively mixed ethnicity, such as Bwiza, or in which ethnic groups cohabited peacefully, such as Buyenzi. Others left for the surrounding province of Bujumbura Rural or crossed the border into the DRC, settling mainly in Uvira (South Kivu province). Some Hutus even commuted between Bujumbura, where they still worked, and Uvira, to where they returned at night.

In 1994–95 the 'mixed' neighbourhoods of Bwiza and Buyenzi were the theatre of combat between Hutu and Tutsi militias. In March 1995 Tutsi militias, with the support of the military, eventually prevailed, causing the Hutu population to flee towards Gatumba (on the DRC border) and into the DRC.

With Buyoya's return to power in 1996, and increasingly after 2003, some displaced persons came back to their areas of origin. Some were relocated by the government to sites on the northern outskirts of the city, in Buterere and Carama. As of 15 July 2006, 506 (out of an expected total of 519) Gardiens de la paix and 13 (out of an expected total of 35) Militants combattants had been demobilized in Bujumbura-Mairie. Many sources indicate, however, that a number of both militias and ordinary citizens have kept the weapons they had obtained during the war, and that there are considerable holdings of assault rifles, pistols, and grenades hidden in Bujumbura's households. It also seems that the areas where there was the most fighting and where the presence of militias was strongest remain among the most heavily armed today.[12]

Ex-combatants who settled in Bujumbura after the war chose neighbourhoods based on their ethnicity. Demobilized (mainly Tutsi) military personnel went to Ngagara, Nyakabiga, Musaga, or Cibitoke. Former members of rebel groups (mainly Hutus) went to Kamenge, Kinama, Buterere, Buyenzi, or Kanyosha. Hutu neighbourhoods are also attractive for ex-combatants because they are poorer, which means that they have cheap rents and offer the possibility of engaging in small jobs, such as bike- or moto-taxi drivers, welders, carpenters, or street vendors.

Sources: Barahinduka (2006); CNDRR (2006a)

or families were killed or abducted as early as November 1993 in Bujumbura, mainly in the central market area. Peripheral areas were also particularly at risk from mortar attacks launched from the nearby hills. In this regard, it is worth noting that the Kibira forest, which served as a base for rebel groups during most of the war, is only 30 km away from Bujumbura (Ngaruko and Nkurunziza, 2000, p. 379). Rebels occupied the heights around the city and sent in spies or recruiters, who blended with the urban population. The capital turned out to be a place of recruitment for both sides. Newly enrolled combatants were rapidly trained and sent to the battlefields outside the city.

In spite of this, it seems that rebel groups never considered the capital to be a realistic target for an attempt to take over the city. The lack of faith in their ability to take control of Bujumbura can be explained in part by the fact that the city was well defended by the army and the population, some of whom were armed by the government to form a loose (mainly Tutsi) militia known as the Gardiens de la paix (Peace Guardians). On the rebel side, the CNDD-FDD formed its own militia, the Militants combattants. Both militias recruited heavily in Bujumbura, where the existing segregation dramatically worsened during the war (see Box 6.2).

The level of violence in Bujumbura varied over time. It decreased in 1996 after Buyoya's coup, before increasing again in 1998–99, with rebels launching attacks not just in Bujumbura, but across the whole country. A rebel attack on Bujumbura's international airport on 1 January 1998 caused more than 200 civilian deaths (UNHCR, 2005, p. 37). In 2001 rebels attacked the Kinama area, probably because they expected to find a lot of support within the population in that particular location. Located in the northern outskirts of Bujumbura, this neighbourhood was mainly populated by Hutus, and the war only amplified this situation. This did not, however, prove sufficient to guarantee the rebels military victory.

Areas mainly populated by Tutsis were as exposed to violence as those mainly populated by Hutus. In July 2003 the predominantly Tutsi neighbourhood of Musaga, located in the southern periphery of the capital, found itself under heavy attack, causing the displacement of large numbers of people towards more central areas of the city. The location of the prison, as well as a number of military installations, among which were the headquarters of the army's logistics unit (the Brigade logistique) and the training centre for army officers (Institut supérieur des cadres militaires), in Musaga may explain why rebels chose this neighbourhood as a target. Another likely reason is the fact that Musaga is a peripheral neighbourhood of Bujumbura, located close to the hills that served as a refuge for the rebels, who may have seen it as an 'easy' target.

ARMED ACTORS IN BURUNDI

Armament and disarmament of armed groups: armed parties and political movements

The Hutu-dominated rebel groups who attempted to seize power during the civil war experienced a number of divisions and rivalries. Six groups eventually took part in the 2001 peace process: the Conseil national pour la défense de la démocratie (CNDD, also called the CNDD-Nyangoma), the CNDD-FDD, the Front national de libération Icanzo (FNL-Icanzo), the Front pour la libération nationale (FROLINA), the Kaze-Forces pour la défense de la démocratie (Kaze-FDD), and the Palipe-Agakiza. They are known under the generic name of armed parties and political movements (PMPAs).

Members of PMPAs were demobilized within a DDR programme carried out by the Commission nationale chargée de la démobilisation, de la réinsertion et de la réintégration (CNDRR) and financed by the World Bank's Multi-Country Demobilization and Reintegration Programme (MDRP). Members of the PMPAs could choose between integration into the new army and police or demobilization. Demobilized combatants received a benefit equivalent to 18 months' salary, calculated on the basis of the pay given by the Force de défense nationale (FDN), the new army that replaced the old, Tutsi-dominated Forces armées burundaises (FAB), for the corresponding army rank. They also received in-kind support for their socioeconomic reintegration (CNDRR, 2004).

As of July 2006, 10,134 former combatants from the PMPAs had been demobilized, 4.75 per cent of whom were women and a little more than 7 per cent children (CNDRR, 2006a). The distribution of these combatants according to their PMPA provides a good indication of the groups' relative strengths, with the CNDD-FDD being the largest by far (see Figure 6.2).

A specific programme was put into place by the MDRP and the United Nations Children's Fund for the demobilization of child soldiers. For a year and a half, demobilized children received the equivalent of USD 20 each month in various goods, as

Figure 6.2 **Group membership of demobilized PMPAs**

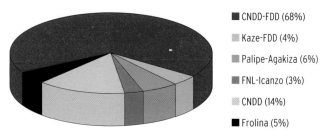

- CNDD-FDD (68%)
- Kaze-FDD (4%)
- Palipe-Agakiza (6%)
- FNL-Icanzo (3%)
- CNDD (14%)
- Frolina (5%)

Source: CNDRR (2006a)

Table 6.1 Small arms and light weapons used by Burundian rebel groups during the war

Type of small arm	Model and country of manufacture
Pistols	Browning 1903 (Belgium); Glock 17 (Austria); Makarov, Tokarev (Russian Federation); Mauser HSc (Germany)
Automatic rifles	AKSU-74, Dragunov SVD, Kalashnikov AK-47, Kalashnikov AK-74, Simonov SKS (Russian Federation); Type 56 (China); CZ58 (Czechoslovakia); FN FAL (Belgium); G3 (Germany); M4, M16 (United States); R1, R4, R5 (South Africa)
Sub-machine guns	Ruger Mp-9, M3 (United States); Uzi (Israel)
Machine guns	Browning (model unspecified, United States); FN MAG, FN Minimi (Belgium); Goryunov SG43, PK, RPK, 7.62 mm RPD (Russian Federation)
Mortars	60 mm, 81 mm, 82 mm, 120 mm
Rocket-propelled grenade launcher	RPG-7

Note: Table 6.1 lists some of the weapons that were held by the PMPAs, but does not pretend to be exhaustive.

Sources: Interviews between the authors and ex-combatants from the CNDD, CNDD-FDD, FNL-Icanzo, FROLINA, and Kaze-FDD, Bujumbura, 1–2 February 2006; interviews between Eric Niragira of the Centre d'encadrement et de développement des anciens combattants (CEDAC) and ex-combatants, Bujumbura, Muramvya, and Cibitoke, July–August 2006; confidential document, March 2006

well as food assistance from the World Food Programme. In addition, children willing to receive professional training received a 'starter kit'. A total of 3,015 children benefitted from this programme, which was completed in June 2006 (MDRP, 2006).

The number of weapons held by each group was taken into account to assess how many of their members would be integrated into the new Burundi army. A total of 5,404 weapons were handed in during the process (Info-Burundi. net, 2005) and went into army stockpiles.[13] ONUB collected 326 weapons and 45,433 rounds of ammunition.[14] Weapons collected by ONUB include mainly AK-47s, G3s, and South African R1s and R4s, but it seems that many more types of weapons were in the hands of rebel groups (see Table 6.1). Also, combatants used some craft weapons known as *mugobore* (see Box 6.3).

As the DDR process continued, the initial requirement of one weapon handed in per demobilized combatant was less and less strictly enforced. This explains why relatively few weapons were collected in comparison with the number of individuals demobilized. This was justified, to some extent, by the fact that not all combatants carried a weapon: interviews conducted among ex-combatants tend to indicate that the CNDD-FDD had an average of one weapon for one or two fighters, and that the CNDD had only one weapon for three fighters.[15] These different ratios of weapons per combatant show that rebel groups were unequally successful in their arms procurement. In addition, not all members of the groups were combatants. Former CNDD-FDD members interviewed estimated that only 50–70 per cent of the group members were fighters.[16]

A large number of the weapons handed in were in bad condition: it is estimated that about a third of the weapons collected by the army were unusable.[17] Understandably, most unusable weapons seem to have been handed in at the beginning of the disarmament process, when it had yet to gain the participants' trust. For instance, up to 80 per cent of the weapons handed in during the first phase of integration in Bururi turned out to be unusable.[18] This figure seems to have decreased over time, since only one-fifth of the weapons collected by ONUB over the whole disarmament period were classified as unserviceable.

Box 6.3 Craft production of weapons in Burundi

Some craft weapons are produced in Burundi, where they are known under the generic name of *mugobore*. These locally made rifles consist of a metal barrel inserted in a piece of wood. The design is particularly crude, with a metal stick held by a rubber band that serves as a firing pin, and another metal stick used to eject the spent cartridge. The effective range of such rifles, which are usually heavy and cumbersome, does not exceed ten metres. They can function with cartridges for automatic rifles, such as Kalashnikovs. The main areas of production are the provinces of Bujumbura Rural, Bubanza, and Cibitoke, in the north-western corner of the country.

The number of such weapons currently in circulation is difficult to assess. *Mugobore* seem to have been widely used during the war, and they tend to be over-represented in arms collection ceremonies, such as those organized by ex-combatants. This is not, however, indicative of the actual proportion of *mugobore* in the armed groups' arsenals, since former combatants are more inclined to give these poorly performing weapons away than more efficient and expensive industrial models. No conclusion can therefore be drawn as to the ratio between craft and industrial weapons possessed by ex-combatants or the general population.

The number of *mugobore* in circulation is likely to be relatively high, however, since their fabrication is quite easy: almost anyone who can find a metal barrel can put one together. Particular attention should therefore be given to the processes by which collected or surplus weapons are destroyed in Burundi, for they must ensure the complete destruction of the weapons' barrels. At the moment, such weapons are simply burnt, running the risk that some elements of the weapons will survive the destruction process and be used to make *mugobore*.

Sources: Interviews between the authors and ex-combatants from the CNDD, CNDD-FDD, FNL-Icanzo, FROLINA, and Kaze-FDD, Bujumbura, 1–2 February 2006; interviews between the authors and the director of a private security company based in Bujumbura, 31 January 2006; interview between the authors and an official FDN source, Bujumbura, 2 February 2006

Examples of mugobore handed in during a weapons collection ceremony, Muramvya province, May 2006.© Pézard and Florquin

Armament and disarmament of armed groups: militias

During the conflict, the warring parties armed a number of civilian supporters. The FAB issued weapons to the Gardiens de la paix, who were of several different types. Some were young men recruited, under the army's advice, by local administrators for personal protection against rebel attacks. At first, they were unarmed, and two soldiers supervised them. Increasingly, however, they armed themselves with supplies from army stockpiles, with apparently little oversight from the army. Other Gardiens de la paix were youth who provided logistical assistance to the army; after the war, a number kept the weapons that the military had given them for their personal protection.[19] A smaller group of armed civilians were the 'Groupes pour l'autodéfense civile', which consisted of civil servants armed by the government in order to defend their neighbourhoods from potential attacks.

Another militia provided assistance to the main rebel group, the CNDD-FDD. These civilians were known as the Militants combattants. According to several sources, they were generally not armed, since the CNDD-FDD kept the available weapons—which were in short supply—for its combatants. Militants combattants assisted the CNDD-FDD by providing intelligence about military positions, supplying the combatants with food, or carrying wounded combatants.[20]

Figure 6.3 **Numbers of Gardiens de la paix and Militants combattants expected to be demobilized, by province, 2006**

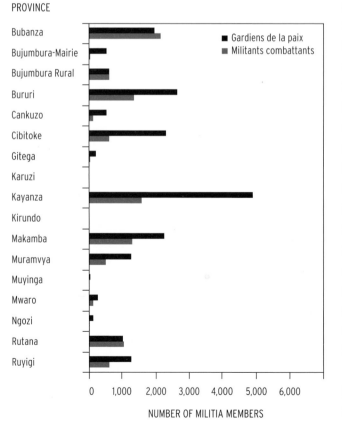

PROVINCE

- Gardiens de la paix
- Militants combattants

NUMBER OF MILITIA MEMBERS

Source: CNDRR (2006a)

The disarmament of Gardiens de la paix and Militants combattants was completed in June 2006. Each demobilized individual received FBU 100,000 (approximately USD 100) to assist with reintegration into civilian life. A number of difficulties arose, however, when the lists of Gardiens de la paix and Militants combattants who could claim these benefits turned out to be inaccurate. Some names were forgotten; others were falsely added: a list with 500 names of supposed Gardiens de la paix was published in the Kirundo province, in spite of the fact that this region apparently never had a single Gardien de la paix during the war (ONUB, 2005a, p. 1). In October 2005, 176 persons claiming to be Gardiens de la paix found out that they were not on the lists; they protested through demonstrations and the erection of barricades in Bujumbura (IRIN, 2005a; 2005b).

A total of 18,709 Gardiens de la paix and 9,674 Militants combattants were demobilized.[21] This represents, overall, 95 per cent of the total number of militia members who were meant to go through the process (CNDRR, 2006a). Militias do not appear to have been particularly strong in Bujumbura in comparison with the rest of the country; some provinces, such as Kayanza, Bururi, Cibitoke, Makamba, and Bubanza, had a much higher number of militia members on their territory (see Figure 6.3).[22]

The total number of arms collected from the militias was 1,255 rifles—mainly AK-47s and Simonovs (ONUB, 2006b, p. 2)—245 grenades, 2 mines, and 68 *mugobore*.[23] This gives the very low ratio of 1 weapon (or grenade or mine) for 18 combatants. It is difficult to assess how closely this ratio conforms to actual armament levels. Clearly, not all Gardiens de la paix and Militants combattants were armed: some were only providing logistical support or information, especially among the ranks of the Militants combattants (see above). Even those who were fighting sometimes had to share their weapon with one or more other combatants. Sources interviewed on this question range from an estimation of anywhere from 1 firearm for 1–15 combatants, and show major differences among provinces.[24] The disarmament process shows some anomalies, such as, for instance, 2,006 Gardiens de la paix and Militants combattants being demobilized in November 2005 without handing in a single weapon (ONUB, 2005b, p. 1).

Restructuring the army and police

Adopted in August 2000, the Arusha Peace and Reconciliation Agreement for Burundi defined the principles for reforming the Burundian national army and police (Arusha Agreement, 2000, Protocol III, ch. II). The FDN, the new army, replaced the old FAB in order to incorporate members of both the FAB and PMPAs. The main purpose of this reform was to ensure a balanced composition of state forces, which had previously been dominated by Tutsis.

The FDN was officially created in December 2004 (UNHCR, 2005, p. 50). It integrated former members of the FAB and of the PMPAs in order to reach a total of 30,000 members (15,000 Hutus and 15,000 Tutsis). Each PMPA was assigned a certain number of positions in the FDN, calculated on the basis of the number of combatants and weapons each group had declared. The main rebel group, the CNDD-FDD, received the largest share of positions among all the PMPAs (Info-Burundi.net, 2005). The integration of former combatants into the new army is complete, but the restructuring of this institution is still ongoing. Not all former combatants joined the FDN: 9,605 former FAB soldiers and 10,134 members of the PMPAs were demobilized (CNDRR, 2006a).

The new police force—the Police nationale du Burundi or National Police of Burundi—follows the opposite trend and will grow from previously 3,000 to 18,000–20,000 members. Here again, former members of the PMPAs will join former police members, with special attention being given to ethnic balance (Arusha Agreement, 2000, Protocol III, ch. II, art. 14). Since all police personnel are equipped with a weapon (usually a Kalashnikov rifle), except for officers, who have two (a Kalashnikov and a handgun), such an increase in the size of the police suggests that there may not be sufficient stocks of weapons for the new recruits, and purchase orders have been placed.[25] Weapons for both army and police are stockpiled at the Brigade logistique in Bujumbura.[26] During the war, weapons were taken from government stockpiles to be distributed to Gardiens de la paix. As mentioned above, it is still unclear how many of these weapons were distributed and what proportion was returned after the war during the militia demobilization process.

BURUNDI'S URBAN LANDSCAPE

Urban centres are generally not particularly attractive to the Burundian population. The urban population is growing, but is still at low levels. In 2000 it was estimated that only nine per cent of the total population was living in urban

Figure 6.4 **Urban population in Burundi and neighbouring countries as a percentage of total population, 1975, 2003, and 2015**

PROVINCE

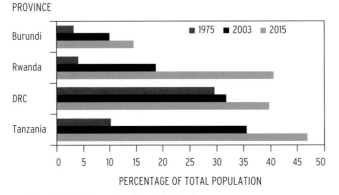

Note: Figures for 2003 and 2015 are medium-variant projections by UNDP.
Source: UNDP (2005, pp. 234–35)[27]

Figure 6.5 **Comparison between Bujumbura-Mairie and the other provinces' most populated provincial districts, 2003**

PROVINCE

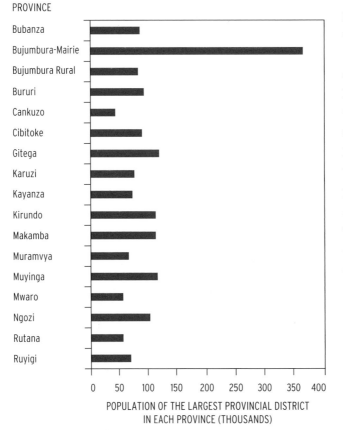

Note: The largest provincial districts represented here are the most populated in each province, not necessarily the provincial capitals.
Source: Burundi (2004)

areas (the proportion was seven per cent in 1993) (UNHCHR, 1999; WRI, 2006). This figure is extremely small if compared with the sub-Saharan Africa average of 34 per cent, or the world average of 47 per cent (WRI, 2006). Based on projections over the next ten years, it appears that, as for most other countries worldwide, the urban population can be expected to grow in Burundi, but less sharply than in Burundi's three neighbouring countries (see Figure 6.4).

This low rate of urban population in Burundi also applies at the provincial level. Provincial districts hosting the provincial capitals rarely host significantly more people than other, less-urban districts. Overall, there seems to be no strong phenomenon of population concentration around provincial capitals.

In terms of the services that can be offered in these cities, it appears that only Bujumbura and Gitega can be referred to as 'urban'. Others lack means of communication and have only their main roads tarred. In terms of population, there is a large gap between the capital and other cities. Bujumbura is by far the most populated, and is home to slightly more than 350,000 people. The second most populated city in the country, Gitega, has a population one-third of the size (Burundi, 2004). Most urban centres in Burundi have a population of fewer than 100,000 inhabitants (see Figure 6.5). This fact makes certain types of urban violence in Burundian cities less likely, since size appears to be one factor leading to such violence. According to Pérouse de Montclos, '[a] city of 100,000 inhabitants seems to constitute the minimal threshold below which "typical" urban violence can not develop'

(Pérouse de Montclos, 2002, p. 6)—which is not to say, of course, that small cities are entirely devoid of violence. Population density is another factor that seems conducive to urban violence (Aguirre and Restrepo, 2005, pp. 33–34). However, population density is rather low in Bujumbura, with 3,292 inhabitants per km^2 (UNHCHR, 1999).[28]

ARMED VIOLENCE IN POST-CONFLICT BURUNDI

As one could expect from the many positive developments in Burundi since 2003 that this chapter has outlined—including the ceasefire agreement, the demobilization of combatants, and the reform of state institutions—various sources point to a relative return to security in the country in the post-conflict period. This section will show, however, that this overall improvement extends only partially to the capital city, Bujumbura-Mairie, and to Bujumbura Rural, a province that experienced conflict up to mid-2006.[29]

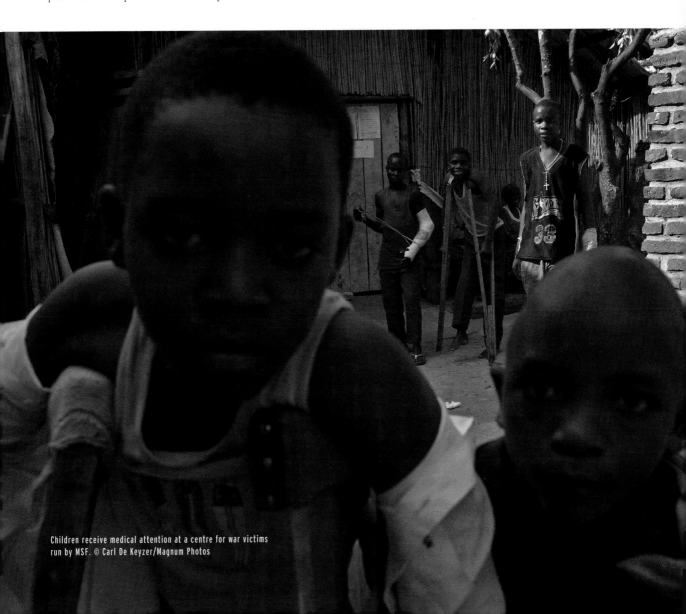

Children receive medical attention at a centre for war victims run by MSF. © Carl De Keyzer/Magnum Photos

Figure 6.6 **Variations in levels of violence by source, 2001–05**

VIOLENT INCIDENTS

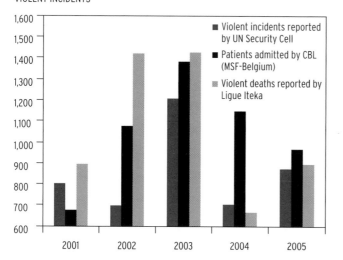

Note: The CBL figures for 2001 and 2002 should be treated with caution: because the CBL had to operate clandestinely for security reasons, it became known and used by the population only after 2002, according to an interview with an international source, Bujumbura, February 2006.
Sources: MSF-Belgium (2001–05); Ligue Iteka (2005; 2006); authors' calculations based on the UN Security Cell's weekly insecurity reports (2001–05)

Figure 6.7 **Number of violent incidents recorded by the UN Security Cell, by province, 2005**

PROVINCE

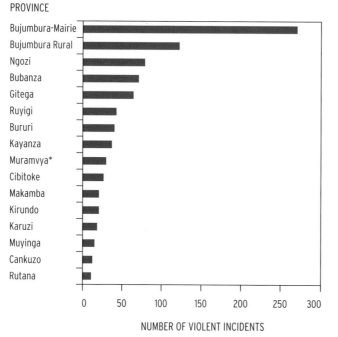

NUMBER OF VIOLENT INCIDENTS

* Including Mwaro
Source: Authors' calculations based on the UN Security Cell's weekly security reports for 2005

Figure 6.6 compares levels of insecurity from 2001 to 2005 as measured through three indicators: the number of admissions registered at Médecins sans frontières (MSF)-Belgium's clinic, Centre des Blessés Légers (CBL), in Kamenge neighbourhood in Bujumbura, violent deaths recorded in human rights NGO Ligue Iteka's annual reports, and incidents of insecurity and criminality recorded by the UN Security Cell.[30] All three sources point to lower levels of insecurity in 2005 when compared with 2003, which stands out as the peak of insecurity over the five years under consideration.

Findings from the Small Arms Survey–Ligue Iteka household survey conducted between 23 November and 21 December 2005 tend to confirm this overall improvement in the security situation. In the six provinces covered by the study, perceptions of security have clearly improved over the last two years. In Bururi, Mwaro, Cibitoke, and Ruyigi, more than 90 per cent of respondents declared that security levels had increased in the previous two years. Bujumbura Rural stands out as the province where improved security was a less widespread feeling, with only 63 per cent of respondents noting an improvement—a finding explained by the fact that this province was still experiencing conflict between government forces and the last active rebel movement at the time the survey was administered. More than 12 per cent of the Bujumbura Rural respondents interviewed thought the security situation had actually deteriorated.

Despite overall progress, the situation remained difficult in several provinces as of late 2005. The UN Security Cell recorded high numbers of incidents, particularly in the capital (267 incidents) as well as in Bujumbura Rural (122). Other provinces that remained affected by insecurity included Ngozi (78 incidents), Bubanza (71), and Gitega (64) (see Figure 6.7). While the number of incidents across the country generally declined after 2003, it remained stable or even increased in Bujumbura Rural and Bujumbura-Mairie.

Household survey results confirm these regional variations in levels of security. In Bujumbura Rural, for instance, a greater proportion of respondents (31.5 per cent) did not feel safe 'at all', while less than 15 per cent felt 'totally safe'. The situation in Bujumbura-Mairie was almost as worrying: the proportion of respondents who felt 'not at all' or 'only a little' secure also exceeded that of people who felt 'very' or 'totally' secure (41.6 v. 34.7 per cent) (Figure 6.8). Perceptions of security were rather better in the other provinces surveyed (Cibitoke, 4.8 per cent; Bururi, 7.1 per cent; Ruyigi, 2.9 per cent; and Mwaro, 2.5 per cent). In Mwaro, more than 50 per cent of respondents stated that they felt totally safe.

Bujumbura-Mairie and Bujumbura Rural were also the provinces where a greater proportion of respondents declared knowing at least one household member who had been a victim of violence over the previous six months. The household survey found that, throughout Burundi, almost one out of ten households consulted was home to a victim of violence. Again, victimization rates were much higher in Bujumbura-Mairie and Bujumbura Rural than in the other four provinces covered in the study (Figure 6.9). One should note, however, that some of these victims may have sought shelter in

Figure 6.8 **Percentage of respondents claiming not to feel safe at all, by province, November–December 2005**

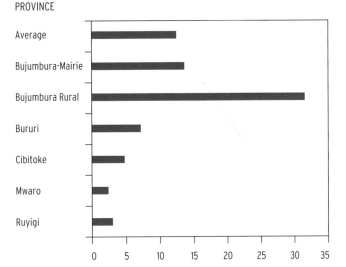

Note: The average reflects the percentage of the total number of respondents who fall into this category. Since population size, and therefore the number of respondents, varies per province, the average provided here is not the average of the percentages shown per province.
Source: Nindagiye (2006)

Figure 6.9 **Percentage of respondents who declared that at least one person in their household had been the victim of acts of violence over the six months preceding November–December 2005, by province**

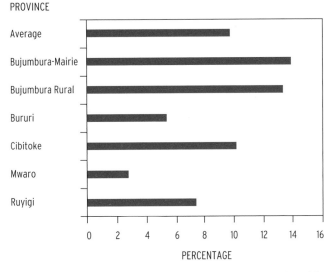

Note: The average reflects the percentage of the total number of respondents who fall into this category. Since population size, and therefore the number of respondents, varies per province, the average provided here is not the average of the percentages shown per province.
Source: Nindagiye (2006)

Map 6.3 **Percentage of Bujumbura respondents whose household include at least one victim of an act of violence between May and November 2005, by neighbourhood**

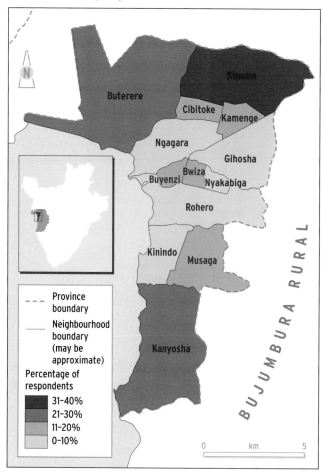

relatives' households in Bujumbura-Mairie after fleeing violence from other provinces, which could explain the higher victimization rates in the capital city when compared with other provinces. Map 6.3 reflects violence levels in Bujumbura.

The types of violence most frequently cited by respondents included, in decreasing order and for all six provinces, armed robberies, gang violence, fights due to alcohol, other fights, and assassinations. Armed robberies were commonly reported in Bujumbura-Mairie, while assassinations were frequently cited in Bujumbura Rural, which may reflect the different types of threat (criminal v. conflict-related, respectively) that affected the two provinces at the time of the interviews. Gang violence was most frequently cited in the provinces of Bururi, Mwaro, and Ruyigi.

The two provinces identified above as experiencing the highest rates of insecurity in 2005—Bujumbura-Mairie and Bujumbura Rural—also stand out as the provinces where small arms were most frequently used and misused. As Figure 6.10 illustrates, gunshots were most frequently heard in Bujumbura-Mairie and Bujumbura Rural. It is also in these two provinces that most respondents declared that the majority of violent acts were carried out using firearms: 32.4 per cent of people interviewed in the capital and 40.3 per cent in Bujumbura Rural answered that violent acts often or always involved small arms, as opposed to just 18.6 per cent for the overall sample.

Data obtained from public health actors, such as MSF's CBL, also point to the primary role played by small arms in post-conflict violence in Burundi (see Figure 6.11).[31] CBL data on the cause of injury, including by weapon type, is available for 2004 and 2005.[32] During these two 'post-conflict' years, the CBL treated 1,298 violence-related injuries. Almost 60 per cent of these wounds were inflicted by firearms, while grenades were responsible for 22 per cent of admissions for violent injuries. When adding injuries from mortar shells, 83 per cent of all violent injuries treated by the centre were caused by small arms and light weapons. Given that a number of victims of small arms violence—whose wounds are usually more serious than those inflicted by other types of weapons (Small Arms Survey, 2006, ch. 8)—died before reaching the CBL, the proportion of violent injuries attributable to small arms and light weapons

Figure 6.10 **Percentage of respondents who declared hearing gunshots in their neighbourhood at least once a week, November–December 2005, by province**

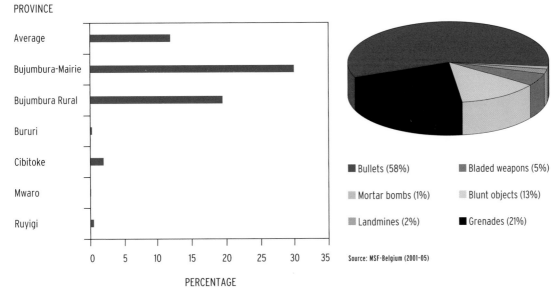

Note: The average reflects the percentage of the total number of respondents who fall into this category. Since population size, and therefore the number of respondents, varies per province, the average provided here is not the average of the percentages shown per province.
Source: Nindagiye (2006)

Figure 6.11 **Violent injuries treated at the CBL by weapon type, 2004–05 (n = 1,298)**

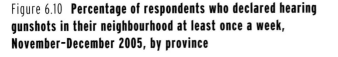

- Bullets (58%)
- Mortar bombs (1%)
- Landmines (2%)
- Bladed weapons (5%)
- Blunt objects (13%)
- Grenades (21%)

Source: MSF-Belgium (2001–05)

Figure 6.12 **Monthly distribution of CBL admissions, by weapon type, 2004–05**

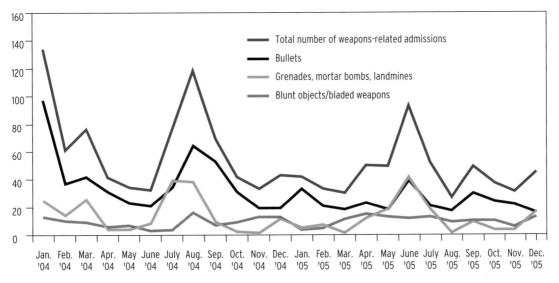

WEAPONS-RELATED ADMISSIONS

- Total number of weapons-related admissions
- Bullets
- Grenades, mortar bombs, landmines
- Blunt objects/bladed weapons

Source: MSF-Belgium (2001–05)

was probably even higher.[33] Blunt objects and bladed weapons were responsible for only 15 per cent of treated injuries. Interestingly, officials at the Kamenge Military Hospital, which treats wounded army soldiers, note that while landmine injuries were common during the conflict period (i.e. until 2003), they became much scarcer after the war. The proportion of patients treated for bullet wounds in the military hospital therefore increased after the war when compared with landmine injuries.[34]

The CBL data also shows how small arms and light weapons played an important role during peaks of violence. Monthly admissions of blunt object and bladed weapon injuries remained relatively stable during 2004 and 2005. On the other hand, admissions due to firearm violence varied greatly and accounted for the variations in the overall number of patients treated for violent injuries (Figure 6.12).

Box 6.4 Survivors of armed violence in Burundi

Although overall levels of armed violence in Burundi appear to have declined since 2003, small arms continue to wound people. Armed violence has particularly dramatic consequences for Burundian victims in a context of widespread poverty, as many of them cannot afford proper treatment. While the government and international organizations recognize the problem, it seems highly unlikely that specific measures will be put in place to care for the victims of armed violence, given the other public health emergencies the country is facing.

The Burundian public health infrastructure is seriously under-funded. In 2005 only 2.5 per cent of the national budget was allocated to the public health sector, which is an allocation of USD 0.70 per person per year (MOH, 2005, p. 12). The number of inhabitants per facility is below World Health Organization standards (1 facility for every 10,000 people) in 13 out of Burundi's 17 provinces (MOH, 2005, p. 21). The public health system also faces significant medical supply and personnel shortages (MOH, 2005, pp. 23-26). Burundi lacks more than half of the required doctors and specialists, a consequence of low pay, the emigration of qualified personnel, and insufficient national training capacities.[35] In addition, qualified staff are concentrated in Bujumbura-Mairie, which is host to 80 per cent of the country's doctors and more than 50 per cent of paramedics, and this leaves the rest of the country with only the most basic services (MOH, 2005, p. 24).

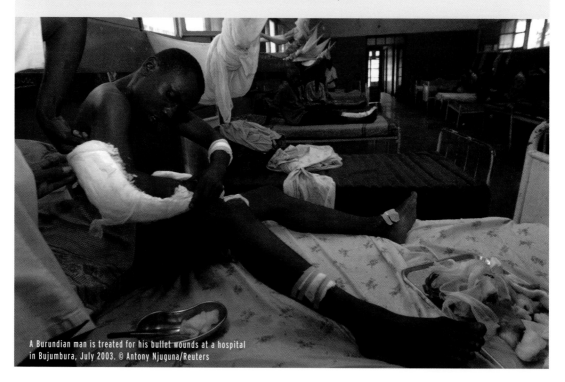

A Burundian man is treated for his bullet wounds at a hospital in Bujumbura, July 2003. © Antony Njuguna/Reuters

As a result of this lack of infrastructure and other important factors, the government estimates that between only 0.2 and 3 per cent of the people who require hospital admission every year actually use hospitals (MOH, 2005, p. 21). A key reason for many Burundians not using the public health infrastructure lies in the prohibitive cost of health care for the great majority of the population (MSF-Belgium, 2004, p. 6). According to a 2004 MSF survey, almost three out of four Burundians who had used public health facilities needed to go into debt or sell their belongings to pay their medical bills. The study found that Burundi's health care reimbursement schemes were insufficient to provide health care to about one million people (out of a total population of seven million) (MSF-Belgium, 2004, p. 6). As a result, 17.4 per cent of people needing treatment had no access to health care, primarily due to financial considerations (in more than 80 per cent of cases) (MSF-Belgium, 2004, p. 6). When patients are unable to pay their bills, they can be effectively 'imprisoned' within health facilities until their relatives can collect enough money to get them out (FIACAT, 2005; MSF-Belgium, 2004, pp. 46, 53). National Solidarity Minister Françoise Ngendahayo acknowledged the issue on 23 December 2005 when she ordered the release of all such 'imprisoned' patients and settled their bills (Netpress, 2005). Despite growing government recognition of the problem, the situation remains difficult even today (HRW, 2006).

However limited access to health care is for the general Burundian population, it can only be even more restricted for victims of armed violence, who, in addition to financial constraints, are also faced with the fear of being seen by the authorities as criminals because of the nature of their wounds.

Small arms wounds also require far more complex (and expensive) treatment than other types of injuries (Small Arms Survey, 2006, pp. 199-200, 204-5). Indeed, the lack of specialists and medical equipment forces even the country's only–and relatively well-equipped–military hospital in Bujumbura to transfer its most serious cases to Kenya or South Africa.[36] With the closing of the free MSF facility in February 2006, and despite the periodic assistance provided by international NGOs such as Handicap International Belgium, other MSF facilities, and the International Committee of the Red Cross, victims of post-conflict armed violence have little hope of finding the appropriate treatment.[37] Lastly, owing to the seriousness and long-term impact of small arms injuries, their cumulative burden on the health system and state after years of conflict is significant.

As the Burundian government strives to tackle the issue of small arms and light weapons control as part of its reconstruction and peace-building efforts, it remains unclear to what extent victims of armed violence will feature in its small arms policies. Early versions of the national strategy against small arms do call on society to 'continue caring for the victims of armed conflict at both the physical and psychological levels' (Burundi, 2006, art. 14), but the Ministry of Health's national health plan for 2006-10 does not mention armed violence among the major causes of death and injury in the country–a long list topped by malaria, HIV/AIDS, and other diseases (MOH, 2005, pp. 15-19). As armed violence is unlikely to figure as a specific public health concern in the years to come, it is becoming urgent to find ways of caring for the victims of armed violence.

Source: Centre for Humanitarian Dialogue (2007)

CIVILIAN GUN POSSESSION: A CITY TRADEMARK?

Household survey results make it possible to compare general weapons availability patterns among the six provinces studied. Answers to the question 'How many households in your neighbourhood possess firearms?' show extreme differences among provinces. Bujumbura-Mairie stands out as the province where civilians possess the most weapons: 16.1 per cent of respondents stated that many or most households owned guns. Provinces close to the DRC (Bujumbura Rural with 9.8 per cent and Cibitoke with 8.2 per cent) also appear to experience relatively high rates of civilian small arms ownership.[38] Bururi, which has historically experienced political tensions, rates high as well (11.6 per cent). Firearm availability seems to be less of an issue in the central and eastern provinces of the country, such as Mwaro (2.3 per cent) and Ruyigi (1 per cent). These results clearly demonstrate that the western part of the country, and in particular the city of Bujumbura, experiences the highest rates of small arms ownership (Figure 6.13).

Given the sensitive nature of the issue and the low response rate to such questions, household survey results do not make it possible to appraise the exact proportion of households possessing weapons. Qualitative interviews with key informants suggest that, depending on the province, between 5 and 25 per cent of households possess at least

Figure 6.13 **Percentage of respondents stating that many or most households in their neighbourhood/district own at least one firearm, November–December 2005, by province**

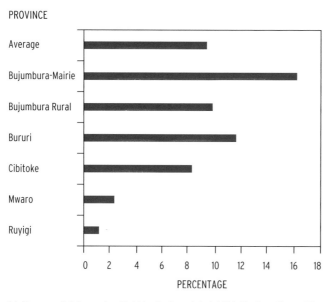

Note: The average reflects the percentage of the total number of respondents who fall into this category. Since population size, and therefore the number of respondents, varies per province, the average provided here is not the average of the percentages shown per province.

Source: Nindagiye (2006)

one small arm.[39] It is important to note here that such estimates include all small arms and light weapons, as defined by the UN (UNGA, 1997), as well as grenades, which appear to be particularly common in Burundi. Key informants also confirm the trend suggested by the household survey: small arms owner- ship levels are higher in Bujumbura, as well as in provinces bordering the DRC and those particularly affected by the conflict.[40]

Based on this admittedly limited data, one can assign a rough small arms ownership multiplier at the provincial level to produce small arms availability estimates. The rate of one weapon for four households is applied to Bujumbura-Mairie, which both survey results and informants indicate is by far the most armed province. The intermediary rate of one firearm for every ten households is applied to the five provinces in the west and south of the country: Bubanza, Bujumbura

Rural, Bururi, Cibitoke, and Makamba. The lowest rate of 1 out of 20 is used for the remaining provinces in the central, northern, and eastern parts of the country (see Table 6.2).

Multiplying these small arms ownership rates by the number of households per province suggests that close to 100,000 Burundian households possess at least one small arm, which is a significantly higher number than the esti- mated 3,500 to 4,000 Burundians who have legally registered their guns since 1960.[41] These figures tend to confirm some previous estimates.[42]

The types of weapons held by civilians in Bujumbura-Mairie are different from those in other provinces. Household survey results (Nindagiye, 2006) and key informant interviews[43] show that while Kalashnikovs and grenades are the weapons types most present in Bujumbura, the capital city stands out as the only province where handguns (pistols and revolvers) are held. In other provinces, Kalashnikovs and grenades are the main types of weapons available. This difference may be explained by the fact that many weapons owners in Bujumbura may hold handguns—which are typical defensive weapons—for self-defence purposes, given the ongoing post-conflict insecurity, while the weapons in other provinces appear to be essentially left over from the conflict period.

Survey results indicate that civilians own weapons primarily for reasons of personal protection (33.7 per cent of respondents in all 6 provinces), and particularly so in the city of Bujumbura (48.7 per cent). Bujumbura-Mairie also stands out as the province where the most respondents declared that protecting family was a key motivation for owning firearms (34 per cent v. less than 10 per cent in the other 5 provinces), while fewer than 1 per cent of respon- dents mentioned tradition, peer pressure, and prestige as motivating factors for owning a gun.[44]

Table 6.2 Small arms and light weapons used by Burundian rebel groups during the war

Province	Number of households	Weapons multiplier	Minimum number of small arms
Bubanza	57,738	1/10	5,774
Bujumbura-Mairie	62,728	1/4	15,682
Bujumbura Rural	109,662	1/10	10,966
Bururi	84,017	1/10	8,402
Cankuzo	35,683	1/20	1,784
Cibitoke	75,102	1/10	7,510
Gitega	133,398	1/20	6,670
Karuzi	73,471	1/20	3,674
Kayanza	109,421	1/20	5,471
Kirundo	116,635	1/20	5,832
Makamba	49,447	1/10	4,945
Muramvya	55,109	1/20	2,756
Muyinga	110,180	1/20	5,509
Mwaro	51,445	1/20	2,572
Ngozi	125,001	1/20	6,250
Rutana	52,778	1/20	2,639
Ruyigi	65,260	1/20	3,263
Total	**1,367,165**	**1/14**	**99,699**

Sources: Number of households : ISTEEBU, 2004; weapons multipliers : interviews with ex-combatants, Bujumbura, 1 February 2006; interview with international source; interview with high-ranking Burundian official, Bujumbura, February 2006

The Burundian population in general appears to have a rather negative perception of small arms. When asked whether small arms 'serves to protect' or are 'dangerous', more than two-thirds of respondents typically selected the second answer. Interestingly, Bujumbura-Mairie again stands out, this time as the province where the lowest proportion of respondents thought small arms were dangerous (58.8 per cent), while in Bujumbura Rural the overwhelming majority of respondents had a negative perception of guns (more than 80 per cent) (see Figure 6.14). These important differences between urban and rural provinces most affected by armed violence at the time of the survey confirm the previous observation that motivations for weapons ownership and the types of weapons owned are different in the capital from those in other provinces. Residents of Bujumbura-Mairie were more inclined to arm themselves for personal protection, while those of Bujumbura Rural felt threatened by the ongoing conflict and placed little hope in using weapons for individual protection. Similarly, the types of weapons present in the capital—handguns—were typically perceived as self-defence weapons, as opposed to the more offensive nature of the grenades and assault rifles found in the rest of the country.

Figure 6.14 **Respondents' perceptions on firearm ownership (%), by province, November–December 2005**

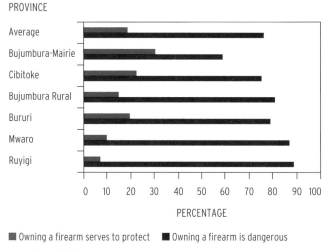

PROVINCE

PERCENTAGE

■ Owning a firearm serves to protect   ■ Owning a firearm is dangerous

Source: Nindagiye (2006)

Figure 6.15 **Province of destination of demobilized ex-combatants, 2006**

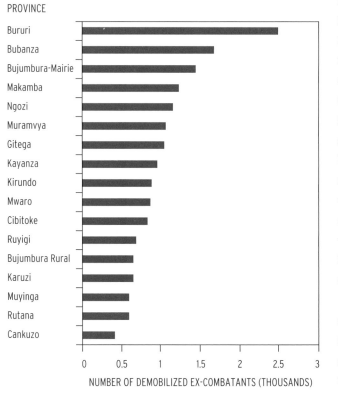

PROVINCE

NUMBER OF DEMOBILIZED EX-COMBATANTS (THOUSANDS)

Source: CNDRR (2006b)

EX-COMBATANTS IN THE CITY

In terms of post-conflict criminality, ex-combatants usually represent a population at risk.[45] Some of them may have failed to reintegrate into society, or they may feel strongly disillusioned with the political and social aftermath of the conflict. This latter issue is particularly salient in Burundi: after a war that lasted more than ten years, a large number of young men and women have been deprived of basic education and may find it even more difficult than their older peers to find some sort of employment.

Destination of ex-combatants

An analysis of the province of destination of demobilized ex-combatants shows that Bujumbura ranks only third, after Bururi and Bubanza (see Figure 6.15). The large number of ex-combatants going to Bururi and Bubanza can be explained by the fact that these were, to a large extent, their provinces of origin. The same logic applies for the Gardiens de la paix. The CNDD-FDD was founded in 1994 in Kamenge (a predominantly Hutu neighbourhood of Bujumbura), but was soon driven out of the capital by the military, and found refuge in Bubanza, where it recruited many combatants. The organization also recruited heavily in Bururi, which was the home province of its leader, Léonard Nyangoma, and his chief of staff, Colonel Jean-Bosco Ndayikengurukiye.[46]

An ex-combatant's decision to relocate to an urban or a rural area depends on several factors that include his/her personal background, the armed group he/she belonged to, and the length of time he/she spent in the group (Colletta, Kostner, and Wieder-

Figure 6.16 Expected reintegration activity of ex-combatants, 2006

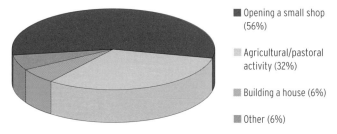

■ Opening a small shop (56%)

■ Agricultural/pastoral activity (32%)

■ Building a house (6%)

■ Other (6%)

Notes: These figures do not include former child soldiers. The category 'Other' includes professional training, handcraft activities, going back to school, and other types of assistance.
Source: CNDRR (2006b)

hofer, 1996, p. 33). In the case of Burundi, there has not been a massive settling of ex-combatants in Bujumbura, with only eight per cent of ex-combatants choosing to settle there rather than in another province (CNDRR, 2006b).[47] This choice is also reflected in the types of activities elected by ex-combatants for their reintegration: almost one-third chose an agricultural/pastoral activity (CNDRR, 2006b), drawing them towards rural areas (see Figure 6.16).

Ex-combatants and insecurity

How did the ex-combatants who decided to settle down in Bujumbura (either because they were originally from the capital or because they found that they had more economic opportunities there) manage to blend into society? One way to approach this question is to look at how they are perceived by the rest of the population: are they treated as any other category of the population or are they stigmatized as a potentially threatening group?

On this issue, the household survey's results allow for some optimism. A first question enquired about the odds that some ex-combatants would have retained some of their weapons after the war. When asked who, in their province, holds one or more firearms, less than four per cent of the population in all six provinces surveyed cited ex-combatants

Figure 6.17 Categories of the population holding one or more firearms (%), November–December 2005

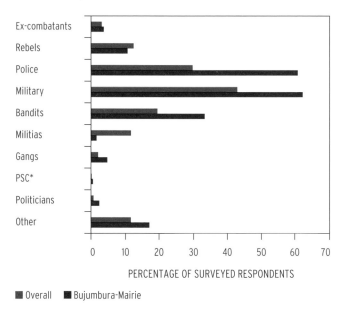

PERCENTAGE OF SURVEYED RESPONDENTS

■ Overall ■ Bujumbura-Mairie

* Private security companies
Source: Nindagiye (2006)

(Nindagiye, 2006). Ex-combatants do not, therefore, seem to be considered as more heavily armed than the rest of the population (see Figure 6.17).[48]

Another question on the main sources of insecurity identified by respondents resulted in bandits and rebels being overwhelmingly cited, whereas ex-combatants ranked only eighth. Ex-combatants do appear to be more feared in Bujumbura than in the rest of the country, but even in this specific case, only 6.6 per cent of the population identified them as a source of insecurity (Nindagiye, 2006). Ex-combatants do not, in general, seem to be perceived as a threat by the population (see Figure 6.18).

Although it is likely that ex-combatants kept a number of weapons after the war, a fact that some of them acknowledge, it is difficult to assess the extent of this phenomenon.[49] Grenades, because of their small

Figure 6.18 **Sources of insecurity cited by respondents in Bujumbura-Mairie and the six provinces overall (%), November-December 2005**

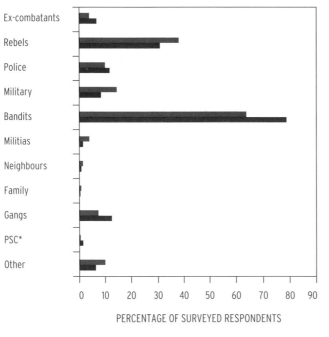

PERCENTAGE OF SURVEYED RESPONDENTS

■ Overall   ■ Bujumbura-Mairie

Note: These figures represent the percentage of respondents who chose the answer mentioned. The total is higher than 100, because respondents were allowed to give more than one answer.
* Private security companies
Source: Nindagiye (2006)

size, seem to have been the easiest weapon to conceal from the group; combatants could pretend to have used them during combat and hide them instead. Grenades too are among the weapons most used in post-conflict violence in Burundi, and in Bujumbura specifically. A common practice is for burglars to throw grenades behind them to cover their escape.[50] According to data from CBL MSF-Belgium in Bujumbura, 21 per cent of violence-related injuries among patients in 2004–05 were due to grenades (MSF-Belgium, 2001–05, note 'CBL statistics'; see also Figure 6.11).

The answers given by respondents to the survey show that firearms are predominantly perceived as dangerous, and that in this context ex-combatants are not perceived as particularly armed or dangerous (unless one tacitly considers them as part of the 'Bandits' or 'Militias' categories). Although Bujumbura-Mairie experiences more criminality than the other provinces surveyed, the population usually does not blame ex-combatants for it.

CONCLUSION

As of early 2007, Burundi has taken most of the steps that should allow for a return to the normal functioning of its institutions. It adopted a new Constitution, held peaceful elections, restructured the army and police, and completed most DDR activities. The country has not yet, however, emerged from its transitional period. Although attacks by the last active rebel group—the Palipehutu-FNL—appear to have ceased since the signing of a ceasefire agreement in September 2006, the road to peace remains long and a comprehensive agreement has yet to be signed.

During the conflict, Bujumbura was the target of numerous attacks on its peripheral neighbourhoods. It was never, however, really at risk of being seized by the rebels. The war effectively strengthened the ethnic polarization of certain areas of Bujumbura, with previously 'mixed' areas gradually disappearing. A few displaced people have returned to their areas of origin, but, overall, Bujumbura now seems more ethnically divided than it was prior to the war.

Most demobilized ex-combatants have not settled in Bujumbura, preferring instead to go back to their provinces of origin. The rest of the population does not perceive those who chose to relocate to Bujumbura as a threat to security, however.

Demobilization of former combatants and militias, and the restructuring of the army have enabled the government to seize a number of weapons that would otherwise still be beyond its control. This number, however, has proved disappointing in relation to the quantity of small arms and light weapons that were used during the conflict and those that are now in the possession of private citizens. Overall, an estimated 100,000 small arms, light weapons, and grenades are unaccounted for, and are most likely in circulation in the country.

Burundi must now tackle the issue of 'residual' violence in the post-conflict period. This violence appears to involve mainly small arms and grenades. It is true that armed violence has decreased in the whole country and that current levels are far lower than they were during the war. This should not, however, hide important differences between Bujumbura and the other provinces, with post-conflict violence apparently concentrated in the capital. This violence may be of a criminal nature: 'conflict weapons' such as assault rifles and grenades have now made their way into the hands of criminal elements, and 'bandits' are identified by the population as the main source of insecurity. In response, worried civilians have turned to handguns for self-protection. However, some of this violence may still be political. Political, sociological, and ethnic tensions inherited from the civil war—and from the political troubles and massacres that preceded it—are unlikely to have disappeared with the signing of the peace agreement in 2003. In both cases, the persistence of armed violence in Bujumbura shows that the causes of violence, whatever they are, have not been completely addressed by the new authorities. While the government has made visible efforts in early 2007 towards resolving dangerous political tensions,[51] the durable restoration of security will require constant attention and efforts, all the more so as ONUB peacekeeping troops withdrew in February 2007 (BBC, 2007).

If it wants to restore security in its capital city, the government will need to design strategies that not only recognize urban specificities (see Burundi, 2006, art. 42), but also help remedy the long-standing heritage of ethnic segregation and suspicion in Bujumbura. The city, in fact, reflects the ethnic and regional fault lines that run through the country as a whole. These tensions are especially visible in Bujumbura, given the city's concentration of political, economic, and military power. Measures targeting small arms proliferation in Bujumbura therefore need to be underpinned by broader efforts to consolidate recent security gains and achieve lasting reconciliation—in the capital city and nationwide. ✒

LIST OF ABBREVIATIONS

CBL	Centre des blessés légers (MSF)	DDR	disarmament, demobilization, and reintegration
CEDAC	Centre d'encadrement et de développement des anciens combattants	DRC	Democratic Republic of the Congo
CNDD	Conseil national pour la défense de la démocratie	FAB	Forces armées burundaises (Burundian Armed Forces)
CNDD-FDD	Conseil national pour la défense de la démocratie–Forces de défense de la démocratie	FBU	Burundian franc
		FDN	Force de défense nationale
		FNL-Icanzo	Front national de libération Icanzo
CNDRR	Commission nationale chargée de la démobilisation, de la réinsertion et de la réintégration	FROLINA	Front pour la libération nationale
		Kaze-FDD	Kaze-Forces pour la défense de la démocratie

MDRP	Multi-Country Demobilization and	PMPA	armed parties and political movements
	Reintegration Programme (World Bank)	UNDP	United Nations Development Programme
MSF	Médecins sans frontières	UNHCR	Office of the United Nations High
ONUB	United Nations Operation in Burundi		Commissioner for Refugees
Palipehutu–	Parti de libération du peuple hutu–	USD	US dollar
FNL	Forces nationales de libération		

ENDNOTES

1   In this chapter, the names 'Bujumbura' and 'Bujumbura-Mairie' are used interchangeably. Bujumbura-Mairie is a province name, but physically the province Bujumbura-Mairie and the city of Bujumbura overlap. The areas around the city of Bujumbura belong to another province, Bujumbura Rural.

2   See Pézard and Florquin (2007) for more details about methodology and full results. The household survey was carried out between 23 November and 21 December 2005, and covered 3,060 randomly selected households in 6 provinces representative of the different dynamics of violence affecting the country. Bujumbura-Mairie (see endnote 1) was selected because of its strategic position as capital city and as the main—if not only—urban centre in the country; Bujumbura Rural was at the time of the survey one of the last provinces still affected by conflict; Bururi was not particularly affected by violence throughout the conflict, but has long been at the centre of political and ethnic tensions, and is therefore more likely to experience high rates of small arms availability; Cibitoke is also affected by residual armed violence in the aftermath of the conflict; Ruyigi is a province bordering on Tanzania, a country that has hosted many refugees during and after the war and saw movements of armed groups across its border; and Mwaro was selected as a province that has been spared armed violence and was expected not to experience a small arms problem.

3   Twas are a minority whose members are marginalized politically, economically, and socially, and are the victims of discrimination (Jackson, 2004, p. 7).

4   See, for example, Ngaruko and Nkurunziza (2000, p. 371, n. 2).

5   Ndikumana notes that 'Muramvya comprises a large proportion of the national intelligentsia. The South has dominated the political scene after the independence and has always considered Muramvya as a political rival. However, ethnic cohesion always takes precedence over regional differences when Hutu–Tutsi antagonism threatens the Tutsi supremacy' (Ndikumana, 1998, p. 37).

6   Another difference is the fact that the crisis initated in 1993 '[was] a genuine war in the sense that it opposed armed factions' (Ndikumana, 2000, p. 435).

7   A caveat here is that it is possible that a larger number of displaced people did relocate to Bujumbura, but do not appear in the statistics, because they were housed by friends and family members.

8   UNHCR already runs two camps, Gasorwe in Muyinga province and Gihinga in Mwaro province; it is developing a third camp in Giharo (Rutana province) with a capacity of up to 30,000 people (UNHCR, 2006).

9   This section is based on Barahinduka (2006).

10 Neighbourhoods of the capital city are called 'communes' in Burundi, but 'neighbourhood' is used throughout the chapter, for clarity. In the rest of the country, communes are the equivalent of provincial districts.

11 Bujumbura also experienced episodes of civil unrest, such as the so-called 'operation dead city' (*opération ville morte*) in early 1994. Two politicians who had not obtained seats in the new government organized barricades all over the city. These barricades were organized by young Tutsis, who violently attacked people attempting to go through the barriers. This operation ultimately ended with the inclusion of the two politicians in the government.

12 Various authors' interviews with Burundian officials, international organizations, and NGO representatives, Bujumbura, February and May 2006.

13 Interview with a Burundian official source, Bujumbura, February 2006.

14 According to a confidential ONUB document, March 2006.

15 Interview with ex-combatants, Bujumbura, 1–2 February 2006.

16 Interview with two CNDD-FDD ex-combatants, Bujumbura, 1 February 2006.

17 Interview with a Burundian official source, Bujumbura, February 2006.

18 Interview with a Burundian official source, Bujumbura, February 2006.

19 Interview between the UNDP technical adviser on small arms and armed violence reduction and an official Burundian source, Bujumbura, 28 September 2005.

20 Correspondence with a Burundian source, 14 and 15 January 2007.

21 Correspondence with official Burundian sources, 17 April 2007.

22 The large presence of Gardiens de la paix in Kayanza can be explained by the fact that the Kibira forest, which borders Kayanza, was a major rebel stronghold. The army therefore recruited many young civilians from Kayanza province to fight the rebels. A similar explanation holds for

Cibitoke, where the army confronted the rebel groups in many instances. The Bubanza case results from the establishment of a CNDD-FDD base in this province (after it was driven out of Kamenge neighbourhood in Bujumbura-Mairie), where it recruited a large number of Militants combattants (phone interview with Eric Niragira, CEDAC, 23 August 2006; correspondence with a Burundian source, 26 January 2007). Bururi and Makamba are the two provinces from where most Tutsi politicians and army officers came, which may explain why the Gardiens de la Paix movement was particularly strong there.

23   It should be noted, however, that the numbers of arms cited here come from observations made by UNOB, which was not directly involved in the demobilization or disarmament of the militias.

24   Correspondence with the UNDP technical adviser on small arms and armed violence reduction, 12 March 2006; correspondence with a former CNDD-FDD combatant, 12 March 2006.

25   Authors' interview with an official Burundian source, Bujumbura, February 2006.

26   Correspondence between the authors and an international source, April 2006.

27   This source notes that '[b]ecause data are based on national definitions of what constitutes a city or metropolitan area, cross-country comparisons should be made with caution' (UNDP, 2005, p. 235).

28   The figure of 3,292 is for 1993. As means of comparison, Nairobi has a density of 4,412 inhabitants per km^2 (Boisteau, 2006, p. 98).

29   Trends since 2003 do not mean that the situation in these two provinces is worse than during the peak of conflict in the mid-1990s, when curfews had to be put in place due to the dramatic insecurity discussed in the above sections. Owing to the limited coverage of existing data sources, however, quantitative comparisons can be made only between the very last stages of the war (after 2001) and the aftermath of the 2003 ceasefire.

30   This is the UN office in Burundi responsible for UN staff security, which also monitored incidents of violence as reported by the local media and key informants from 2001 onwards.

31   The CBL was located in Kamenge, on the outskirts of Bujumbura-Mairie. Opened by MSF in 1995, it treated the war wounded free of charge and with almost no interruption until it closed in February 2006. Having no operating theatre, it could treat only 'light' wounds and had to refer more serious cases requiring surgery to hospitals, most often covering the associated costs. The CBL maintained statistics on its patients from August 2000 to December 2005, although data gathered in 2000 and 2001 is not representative. Because the CBL had to operate semi-clandestinely for security reasons, it became known and used by the population only after 2002. Most patients treated were originally from Bujumbura Rural, a major conflict zone deprived of a public hospital, with others coming from Bujumbura-Mairie, Bubanza, and Cibitoke (interview with an international source, Bujumbura, February 2006).

32   Interview with an international source, Bujumbura, February 2006.

33   Although the magnitude of the phenomenon is impossible to estimate from the available data, for security reasons many wounded do not report to health centres.

34   Interview with a Burundian public health official, Bujumbura, 31 March 2006.

35   Interview with an international public health official, Bujumbura, 31 May 2006.

36   Interview with a Burundian public health official, Bujumbura, 31 March 2006.

37   Interview with an international public health official, Bujumbura, 31 May 2006.

38   These numbers are likely to be artificially low because of respondents' bias against full disclosure. The numbers do, however, provide insights into relative weapons availability levels at the provincial level (e.g. which provinces are the most armed).

39   Interviews with ex-combatants, Bujumbura, 1 February 2006; interview with an international source; interview with a high-ranking Burundian official, Bujumbura, February 2006. See Pezard and Florquin (2007) for more information.

40   Interviews with ex-combatants, Bujumbura, 1 February 2006.

41   Interviews with the UNDP technical adviser on small arms and armed violence reduction, and Burundian officials, January 2006; written correspondence with an international source, March 2006.

42   Existing estimates of the number, type, origin, and use of civilian-held weapons in Burundi have little scientific basis. The transitional government put forward the number of 100,000 illegal weapons (including assault rifles, grenades, and RPGs) in May 2005, at the time the decree on civilian disarmament was adopted (Niyoyita, 2005). The UN Group of Experts on the DRC quoted a higher figure of 300,000 in its 25 January 2005 report, which was subsequently quoted in reports by the UN Secretary-General (UNSC, 2005, para. 30) and the UN Economic and Social Council (UNECOSOC, 2005, para. 5).

43   Various interviews, Bujumbura, February and May 2006.

44   These results confirm those of a study published in 2006 by the Groupe de recherche et d'information sur la paix et la sécurité (GRIP), which covered about 300 inhabitants of Bujumbura Rural, Cibitoke, and Bubanza, and found that personal protection (85 per cent of respondents), as well as protection of goods (51 per cent) and family (57 per cent), were the key motivating factors cited by the 138 people who admitted owning a firearm in 2004 (Ntibarikure, 2006, p. 24).

45   This risk should, however, not be overstated, and ex-combatants should not be identified altogether as potential delinquents. It is worth remembering that in Uganda, for instance, '[u]p until mid-1995, only 159 veterans had been found guilty of some criminal act, that is, 0.5 percent of all veterans discharged . . . this is a far lower percentage than the normal crime rate in an equivalent civilian population and allays fears that veterans are undisciplined troublemakers, drug abusers, or thieves' (Colletta, Kostner, and Wiederhofer, 1996, pp. 277–78).

46   Telephone interview with Eric Niragira of CEDAC, 23 August 2006.

47   A potential caveat here is that this group does not include those who chose to join the police and the army rather than be demobilized, many of whom are now in Bujumbura.

48   A potential caveat here is the fact that some ex-combatants may be among the bandits or militias that are seen by the population as heavily armed.

49 Interview with ex-combatants, Bujumbura, 1–2 February 2006. There is no general agreement, however, on the likely ratio of combatants who have kept their weapons, with tentative answers ranging from 10 to 99 per cent on this question.

50 Interview with an international source, Bujumbura, January 2006.

51 A major development was the dismissal of Hussein Rajabu as president of the ruling CNDD-FDD at the party's congress on 6 February 2007. Rajabu had been criticized by civil society, government officials, and international observers as corrupt and the source of many of the government's controversial actions (ICG, 2006, pp. 10–11, p. 17, fn. 84).

BIBLIOGRAPHY

Aguirre, Katherine and Jorge Restrepo. 2005. *Aproximación a la situación de violencia e inseguridad en Bogotá D.C.* VUPS (Violences urbaines et politiques de sécurité) and CERAC (Centro de Recursos para el Análisis de Conflictos) research report.
<http://www.cerac.org.co/pdf/LASUR-Baja.pdf>

Arusha Agreement (Arusha Peace and Reconciliation Agreement for Burundi). 2000. Arusha, Tanzania. 28 August.
<http://www.usip.org/library/pa/burundi/pa_burundi_08282000_toc.html>

Baehler, Claudio. 2006. 'Burundi: Does Lasting Peace Require Army Reform?' *The East African* (Nairobi). 3 July.
<http://www.afrika.no/Detailed/12474.html>

Barahinduka, Celcius. 2006. *Etude sur le rôle joué par la ville de Bujumbura dans la guerre civile (1993–2006)*. Unpublished background paper. Geneva: Small Arms Survey.

BBC (British Broadcasting Corporation). 2007. 'Timeline: Burundi.' 13 May. <http://news.bbc.co.uk/2/hi/africa/country_profiles/1068991.stm>

Boisteau, Charlotte. 2006. 'Aménagements urbains et politiques de sécurité.' In Charlotte Boisteau, ed. *Construire le vivre-ensemble: aménagements urbains et politiques de sécurité*. Cahier du LaSUR No. 9, pp. 97–118. <http://www.cifalbarcelona.org/IMG/pdf/UNITAR_CIFAL_final_fr.pdf>

Burundi. 2004. Ministry of Development and National Reconstruction. *Population Burundaise en 2003*. Bujumbura. September.

——. 2006. *Stratégie nationale de lutte contre la prolifération des armes légères et de petit calibre et de désarmement des civils (projet)*. Bujumbura. May.

Centre for Humanitarian Dialogue. 2007. *Surviving armed violence in Burundi*. Background paper for the Centre's project on victims and survivors. June. <http://www.hdcentre.org/Survivors+of+armed+violence>

CNDRR (Commission nationale chargée de la démobilisation, de la réinsertion et de la réintégration). 2004. 'Executive Secretariat press release.' September.

——. 2006a. *Sommaire du rapport statistique sur les activités de démobilisation*. Bujumbura : CNDRR. 15 July.

——. 2006b. *Répartition des démobilisés selon leurs attentes par province et commune de destination*. Bujumbura: CNDRR. 25 July.

Colletta, Nat J., Markus Kostner, and Ingo Wiederhofer. 1996. *Case Studies in War-to-Peace Transition: The Demobilization and Reintegration of Ex-Combatants in Ethiopia, Namibia, and Uganda*. World Bank Discussion Paper No. 331. Washington, D.C.: World Bank.

FIACAT (Fédération internationale de l'action des chrétiens pour l'abolition de la torture). 2005. *BURUNDI: A Bujumbura, des hôpitaux transformés en prison*. November. <http://www2.fiacat.org/fr/article.php3?id_article=207>

HRW (Human Rights Watch). 2006. *A High Price to Pay: Detention of Poor Patients in Hospitals*. Vol. 18, No. 8(A). September.
<http://hrw.org/reports/2006/burundi0906/burundi0906webwcover.pdf>

ICG (International Crisis Group). 2003. *Réfugiés et déplacés burundais: construire d'urgence un consensus sur le rapatriement et la réinstallation*. Nairobi/Brussels: ICG. 2 December. <http://www.crisisgroup.org/library/documents/africa/31202_refugies_et_deplaces_burundais.pdf>

——. 2006. *Burundi : Democracy and Peace at Risk*. Africa Report No. 120. Nairobi/Brussels: ICG. 30 November.
<http://www.crisisgroup.org/home/index.cfm?id=4553&l=1>

Info-Burundi.net. 2005. 'Vers la formation de la FDN: progrès significatifs, lueurs d'espoir . . . .' 16 February.
<http://www.info-burundi.net/modules.php?name=News&file=print&sid=1195>

IRIN (Integrated Regional Information Networks). 2005a. 'Burundi: Youth Stage Protests over Demobilisation Pay.' 12 October.

——. 2005b. 'Burundi: New Demobilisation Team Picked, List of Ex-combatants Being Reviewed.' 20 October.

ISTEEBU (Institut de statistiques et d'études économiques du Burundi). 2004. *Actualisation de la base de sondage*. Bujumbura: ISTEEBU. December.

Jackson, Dorothy. 2004. *Femmes twas et droits des Twas dans la région africaine des Grands Lacs*. Report. Minority Rights Group International.
<http://minorityrights.org/admin/Download/pdf/TwaWomenFr2004.pdf>

La documentation française. 2005. 'Le conflit des grands lacs en Afrique, chronologie.'
<http://www.ladocumentationfrancaise.fr/dossiers/conflit-grands-lacs/chronologie.shtml>

Ligue Iteka. 2005. *De la logique de guerre aux vicissitudes d'application des accords: Rapport annuel sur la situation des droits de l'homme au Burundi, édition 2004*. Bujumbura: Ligue Iteka. March.

——. 2006. *Rapport annuel sur la situation des droits de l'homme*. Preliminary version (April 2006). Bujumbura: Ligue Iteka.

MDRP (Multi-Country Demobilization and Reintegration Programme). 2006. *Countries: Burundi*. Web site. <http://www.mdrp.org/burundi.htm>

MOH (Burundi Ministry of Health). 2005. *Plan National de Développement Sanitaire*. Bujumbura: Ministry of Public Health. 13 December.

MSF (Médecins sans frontières)-Belgium. 2001–05. *Statistiques des admissions au Centre des blessés légers (CBL) de Kamenge.* Bujumbura: MSF-Belgium.

——. 2004. *Accès aux soins de santé au Burundi: résultats de trois enquêtes épidémiologiques.* Bujumbura: MSF-Belgium. March.
<http://www.grandslacs.net/doc/3037.pdf>

Ndikumana, Léonce. 1998. 'Institutional Failure and Ethnic Conflicts in Burundi.' *African Studies Review,* Vol. 41, No. 1, pp. 29–47. April.

——. 2000. 'Towards a Solution to Violence in Burundi: A Case for Political and Economic Liberalisation.' *Journal of Modern African Studies,* Vol. 38, No. 3, pp. 431–59.

Netpress. 2005 'Le ministère ayant en charge la solidarité nationale fait libérer tous les convalescents indigents détenus dans les hôpitaux.' Bujumbura. 23 December. <http://www.tutsi.org/Act241205.htm>

Ngaruko, Floribert and Janvier D. Nkurunziza. 2000. 'An Economic Interpretation of Conflict in Burundi.' *Journal of African Economies,* Vol. 9, No. 3, pp. 370–409.

Nindagiye, Emmanuel. 2006. *Résultats de l'enquête auprès des ménages sur la prolifération des ALPC au Burundi.* Report commissioned by the Small Arms Survey and Ligue Iteka. Bujumbura: Small Arms Survey and Ligue Iteka. February.

Niragira, Eric. 2006. 'Complément du rapport de la consultation sur les groupes armés burundais.' Unpublished paper.

Niyoyita, Aloys. 2005. 'Burundi Attempts Disarmarmament Drive.' SAPA-AP. 5 May.

Ntibarikure, Jacques. 2006. 'Trafic d'armes : enquête sur les armes légères dans la plaine de la Ruzizi (RDC-Burundi).' GRIP Report. Brussels: Groupe de recherche et d'information sur la paix et la sécurité. October. <http://www.grip.org/pub/rapports/rg06-1_ruzizi.pdf>

ONUB (United Nations Operation in Burundi). 2005a. *DDR-SSR Newsletter,* Issue 22/2005. 1–7 October.

——. 2005b. *DDR-SSR Newsletter,* Issue 24/2005. 19–25 November.

——. 2006a. 'Chronologie.' <http://www.un.org/french/peace/peace/cu_mission/onub/chrono_F.pdf>

——. 2006b. *DDR Related Information: Monthly Report from 01 February till 28 February.* Bujumbura. 1 March.

Pérouse de Montclos, Marc-Antoine. 2002. *Villes et violence en Afrique noire.* Paris: IRD–Karthala.

Pézard, Stéphanie and Nicolas Florquin. 2007. *Small Arms in Burundi: Disarming the Civilian Population in Peace Time.* Special Report. Geneva: Ligue Iteka and Small Arms Survey.

Reuters. 2005. 'Chronology—Key Events in Burundi's Civil War.' 17 August.

——. 2006a. 'Burundi Rebels Fire on Capital Despite Peace Talks.' 24 July. <http://www.alertnet.org/thenews/newsdesk/L24783669.htm>

——. 2006b. 'Grenade Attack Kills Four in Burundi, Wounds 17.' 31 July. <http://www.alertnet.org/thenews/newsdesk/L31432685.htm>

Small Arms Survey. 2006. *Small Arms Survey 2006: Unfinished Business.* Oxford: Oxford University Press.

Sunday Times (Johannesburg). 2005. 'Burundi Campaign to Disarm Civilians.' 6 May.

UNDP (United Nations Development Programme). 2005. *Human Development Report 2005: International Cooperation at a Crossroads: Aid, Trade and Security in an Unequal World.* <http://hdr.undp.org/reports/global/2005/pdf/HDR05_HDI.pdf>

UNECOSOC (United Nations Economic and Social Council). 2005. *Report of the Economic and Social Council Ad Hoc Advisory Group on Burundi.* E/2005/82 of 27 June.

UNGA (United Nations General Assembly). 1997. *Report of the Panel of Governmental Experts on Small Arms.* A/52/298 of 5 November.

UNHCHR (United Nations High Commissioner for Human Rights). 1999. *Core Document Forming the Initial Part of the State Party Reports: Burundi, 16/06/99. HRI/CORE/1/Add.16/Rev.1 ('Core Document').* International Human Rights Instruments. 16 June.
<http://www.unhchr.ch/tbs/doc.nsf/0/f16eb57823ca2f4580256825005cf2f7?Opendocument>

UNHCR (Office of the United Nations High Commissioner for Refugees). 2005. *Fiche pays Burundi.* January. <http://www.unhcr.org/cgi-bin/texis/vtx/home/opendoc.pdf?tbl=RSDCOI&id=3ae6a5c10#search=%22attaque%20aeroport%20bujumbura%20janvier%201999%22>

——. 2006. 'Congolese Refugees Quit the Burundian Capital and Head for a Camp.' *UNHCR News Stories.* 4 May.
<http://www.unhcr.org/cgi-bin/texis/vtx/news/opendoc.htm?tbl=NEWS&page=home&id=445a12a84>

UNSC (United Nations Security Council). 2003. 'Letter Dated 19 November from the Chargé d'affaires a.i. of the Permanent Mission of Burundi to the United Nations Addressed to the President of the Security Council.' S/2003/1105.

——. 2005. *Third Report of the Secretary-General on the United Nations Operation in Burundi.* S/2005/149 of 8 March.

WRI (World Resources Institute). 2006. *EarthTrends: The Environmental Information Portal.* Washington, D.C.: WRI.
<http://earthtrends.wri.org/pdf_library/country_profiles/pop_cou_108.pdf>

ACKNOWLEDGEMENTS

Principal authors

Stéphanie Pézard and Nicolas Florquin

Contributors

Celcius Barahinduka and Eric Niragira

A member of the 'Amigo dos Amigos' drug gang patrols the streets of the Morro do Macaco favela in Rio de Janeiro, August 2003. © Mimi Mollica/Corbis

Mapping the Divide

FIREARM VIOLENCE AND URBANIZATION IN BRAZIL

7

INTRODUCTION

Tourists consider Brazil to be a friendly and inviting destination.[1] Sociologists speak of it as a 'cordial culture' and a 'racial democracy' (Owensby, 2005), while historians describe a gradual and peaceful transformation in politics from pre-independence times onward[2] and the country as having almost no record of violent conflict in its recent history (Skidmore, 1976). Yet, Brazilian society stands out today for its high levels of firearm violence. Firearm victimization has increased steadily from the 1970s to 2004, when the first signs of a tapering off were publicized.[3] The firearm death rate grew threefold from 7 to 21 deaths per 100,000 in the period 1982–2002 (Phebo, 2005, p. 11).

The news media have covered the country's escalating gun violence extensively, but simplistically. News accounts focus on spectacular actions by organized criminal organizations—such as the 12 simultaneous attacks on random people and on police in particular on 29 December 2006 that left 19 people dead and 12 seriously wounded across Rio de Janeiro (Astor, 2006). Focusing on such events overshadows the deadlier effects of common, routine firearm violence, which is, furthermore, not only an urban phenomenon, but also a rural one. Map 7.1 shows the changes

Map 7.1 **Brazilian firearm death rates per 100,000 people, 1980, 1991, and 2000**

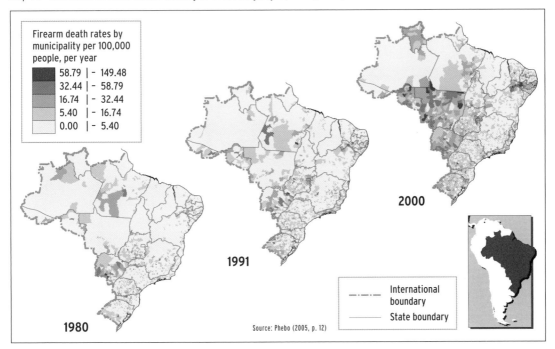

Firearm death rates by municipality per 100,000 people, per year

58.79	– 149.48
32.44	– 58.79
16.74	– 32.44
5.40	– 16.74
0.00	– 5.40

2000

1991

1980

Source: Phebo (2005, p. 12)

International boundary

State boundary

in firearm death rates in Brazil by municipality for a 20-year period, indicating the dramatic increase in such rates across the country.

Brazil is a society with rates of firearm victimization that surpass some countries at war. In the absence of major political conflicts, explaining this phenomenon requires examining other causes; it also means focusing on 'micro' contexts where individuals and small groups interact and act against each other. In the language of public health, it requires focusing on the risk and protection factors at work in firearm violence in Brazilian society.[4]

This chapter reviews the incidence of firearm violence in Brazil's municipalities and rural areas, with special attention to social risk and protection factors. Among its main findings are the following:

Brazil's firearm victimization rates surpass those of some countries at war.

- Firearm homicide is correlated to urbanization, but firearm suicide is not.
- Males are 17 times more likely to be victimized by firearm violence in urban areas than women, but that difference diminishes in rural areas.
- Handguns and automatic weapons are more common in urban than in rural areas, where shotguns predominate. Particular types of firearm are highly associated with particular kinds of uses and users.
- Social inequality is correlated with firearm violence, while poverty as such is not.
- The most significant risk factors for firearm violence are being young (aged 15–29 years), out of school, and out of work.
- The variable 'single-parent families headed by women with children under the age of 21 years not working' is clearly associated with firearm violence.
- Risk for firearm homicide victimization varies according to ethnic group, with blacks and those of mixed race more likely to be victims than whites, while whites are more likely to commit suicide than black or mixed race people.[5]
- The lower the income, the higher the chances of being a victim of firearm homicide. However, the opposite is true for suicides: higher income is associated with self-inflicted injury and death.
- Participation in religion (the Catholic and Protestant churches) is a protection factor against firearm violence.
- Although the presence of firearms in the household is a risk factor in all circumstances, both for homicide and suicide, in urban and rural contexts it should not be considered alone. There is a higher prevalence of firearm ownership in rural than in urban contexts, but a lower incidence of firearm deaths in rural areas.

This chapter proceeds by discussing the data sources and methodologies used to analyse firearm violence in Brazil. It then describes the patterns of homicides and suicides by municipality and age, gender, and ethnic group. Thereafter it presents the results of multiple regression analysis applied to a range of key social determinants of urban and rural firearm violence for both firearm homicide and firearm suicide. The chapter ends with a set of conclusions and policy-relevant observations based on the findings.

FIREARM VIOLENCE BY MUNICIPALITY TYPE: GATHERING THE DATA

Municipal data

In Brazil, municipal governments deliver annual reports on the number of rural and urban inhabitants in their respective municipalities. This is the official source used by the Brazilian government when it requires information on the divide between urban and rural populations in the country. The official municipal records, however, may be biased

A boy with the word 'peace' written on his back participates in an anti-violence campaign in Rio de Janeiro, December 2004. © Kita Pedroza/Viva Rio

by local interests, such as the property tax value for property and public services, which vary between urban and rural settings. Therefore, to improve on this resource, this chapter has added two other variables widely recognized as essential criteria when differentiating rural areas from urban ones. They are the size of the population in a given municipality and the density of the population per km². By weighting and combining these three criteria (the official classification, population size, and density), municipalities can be divided into three categories: urban, rural, and an intermediary group of urban municipalities with significant rural characteristics, which are called 'medium urban' areas in the chapter (see Table 7.1).[6]

Box 7.1 Study methodology

The database used for this study integrates information from three different sources. The Unified Database of the Ministry of Health (Datasus) is the dataset of the Brazilian Ministry of Health, which includes data on firearm deaths (Brazil, n.d.). Data from the Instituto Brasileiro de Geografia e Estatística, the official Brazilian Department of Statistics, includes demographic information from the most recent census in 2000 (IBGE, n.d.). The research report *Brazil: The Arms and the Victims* (Fernandes, 2005a) is a study produced by ISER (the Instituto de Estudos da Religião), Viva Rio, and the Small Arms Survey reporting on firearm availability. Data from these three sources was consolidated by municipality, the smallest unit in the Brazilian system of government. By cross-referencing these datasets, the authors of this chapter were able to explore the relationships between numerous social factors, small arms availability, and firearm victimization within the 5,507 municipalities of Brazil.[7] Urban and rural differences in firearm mortality and the influence of social factors were estimated by multiple regression models. Deviations from the identified patterns were submitted to a rapid qualitative assessment.

Table 7.1 Municipalities in Brazil: urban, medium urban, and rural			
Urban: 455 municipalities			
	Population	**Population density per km²**	**Official percentage of urban population**
Mean	202,103	840	94%
Medium urban: 996 municipalities			
	Population	**Population density per km²**	**Official percentage of urban population**
Mean	28,448	66	78%
Rural: 4,056 municipalities			
	Population	**Population density per km²**	**Official percentage of urban population**
Mean	12,206	22	50%

Figure 7.1 Firearm deaths in Brazil by cause (%), 2000

PER CENT

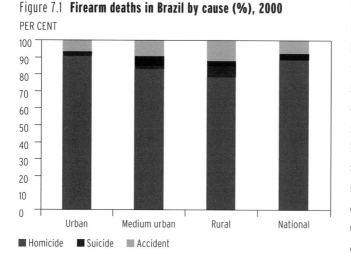

■ Homicide   ■ Suicide   ■ Accident

Figure 7.2 Homicide and firearm homicide rates per 100,000 inhabitants in urban, medium urban, and rural municipalities

DEATHS PER 100,000 INHABITANTS

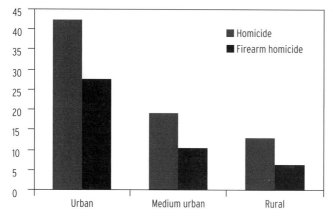

Firearm mortality rates for municipalities

Having assigned the 5,507 municipalities into urban, medium urban, and rural categories, firearm mortality rates by municipality type can be compared (see Figure 7.1). Homicide is at the core of the problem in Brazil, which has one of the highest rates in the world. Suicide, on the other hand, remains at a relatively low level compared to other countries, even within Latin America.[8] Unintended firearm deaths (accidents) are more common among children and in rural municipalities (Phebo, 2005). This chapter focuses on firearm homicides and suicides only.

HOMICIDES AND FIREARM HOMICIDES: URBAN V. RURAL

The pattern for the distribution of homicides across the urban/rural divide is fairly consistent throughout Brazil. Figure 7.2 indicates that urbanization in this country has a strong correlation with homicides of all kinds. The average homicide rate in the urban municipalities of Brazil is more than double the

Box 7.2 Urban and rural firearms

Previous studies have indicated a higher prevalence of firearms in rural than in urban areas in Brazil (Dreyfus and de Sousa Nascimento, 2005). However, the types of weapons vary according to municipality. In Brazil, hunting shotguns are more common in rural settings, whereas handguns are more prevalent in cities. Inhabitants of some areas of the larger cities favour automatic weapons, often used in turf wars by gangs and organized crime actors.

The type of weapons predominating has a powerful effect on mortality rates. Handguns and automatic weapons are more often associated with lethal events than shotguns, and partly explain why urban homicide rates outpace rural ones, even when firearm ownership is higher in rural areas.[9]

rate found in the medium urban municipalities and more than triple the average rate for rural municipalities. Firearms are an important factor of that equation, as they aggravate the disparities. As shown in Figure 7.2, the use of firearms in homicides increases as one moves from rural to medium urban to urban areas. Thus, the role played by firearms in homicides is larger in the urban municipalities (65 per cent) than in the medium urban municipalities (55 per cent), which in turn is larger than that in the rural municipalities (53 per cent). Urbanization in Brazil is therefore associated with higher rates of lethal violence and also with increased use of firearms.

Gender is one clear, relevant factor. The lethal use of firearms is dominated by males, whether as victims or as perpetrators. The role of men in firearm violence increases with urbanization level in Brazil, as shown in Figure 7.3. Men are ten times more likely than women to be killed by a firearm in rural settings. This huge disparity widens to 17 times at the highest level of urbanization. Similarly, the magnitude of difference in firearm death rates among rural men compared to urban men (4.4 times greater) also far exceeds the difference in death rates among rural women compared to urban women (2.5 times greater).[10]

Ethnic group proves to be another powerful indicator for small arms victimization in Brazil, as shown in Figure 7.4. The figures are clear: the chances of being killed with a firearm in Brazil change according to ethnic group, with whites least likely to die by firearm, mixed race people more likely to die than whites, and black people the most likely to die by firearms.[11] The pattern is well established in the rural context: black people have the highest victimization rates, followed by people of mixed race, and finally by white people. Overall death rates increase dramatically from rural to urban settings, with one important variation: the disparities among ethnic groups change dramatically as one moves from rural to urban settings. For example, in rural settings, the death rate for people of mixed race is 19 per cent higher than the rate for whites. In the medium-urban setting, the difference in rates for these two groups jumps to 47 per cent, then to 108 per cent in an urban setting. Urbanization somehow protects whites while increasing risks for people of mixed race and blacks.

Figure 7.3 **Firearm homicides by gender and area, 2000**

FIREARM HOMICIDES PER 100,000 INHABITANTS

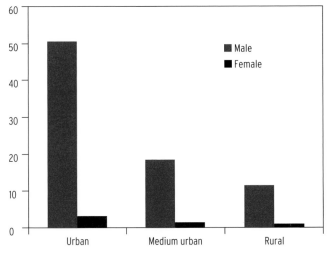

Figure 7.4 **Firearm homicide by ethnic group, 2000**

FIREARM HOMICIDES PER 100,000 INHABITANTS

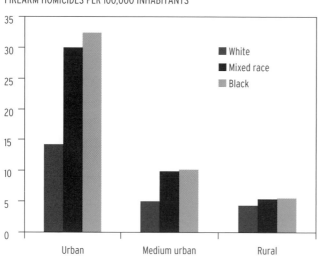

Thus, where firearm violence increases, Brazilian society appears to move from the traditional triad model of ethnic classification (black, mixed race, white) towards a bipolar division between whites, and mixed race people and blacks grouped together. 'Mixed race' as a category, which often indicates a midway point between 'black' and 'white' in terms of social indicators, here no longer can support such a position and gives way to a radical polarization between black and mixed race people combined, and white people, where white signifies protection and black/mixed race signifies risk.

Firearm mortality rates are often sensitive to age variation (WHO, 2002). But separating Brazilian rates by age *and municipality type* produces a different picture, as shown in Figure 7.5. The firearm homicide rates are relatively low for the 10–14 years age group, then grow and separate significantly to varying degrees. Most noticeably, the urban rate rockets to 70 deaths per 100,000 inhabitants in the 20–24 years age bracket, more than 5 times the rate for the same rural segment. The curve shapes are even more revealing. In rural settings, firearm homicides reach their peak for young males aged 20–24 and then slowly decline through adulthood. In urban settings,

Figure 7.5 **Firearm homicides by age group, 2000**

FIREARM HOMICIDES PER 100,000 INHABITANTS

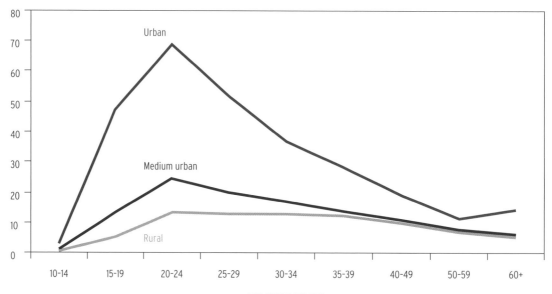

AGE GROUP (YEARS)

conversely, the decline is sharper with the onset of adulthood. The intermediate curve has a consistent intermediary shape between the rural slope and the urban peak.[12]

SOCIAL DETERMINANTS OF URBAN AND RURAL FIREARM HOMICIDES

To explore the various social factors that, together, may substantially affect firearm violence in Brazil, the technique known as *multiple regression model (the OLS method)* was applied.[13] The variables tested were narrowed down from about 100 indicators. Most were excluded because of redundancy or for lack of significance. More details on the modelling exercise for firearm homicides are found in Annexe 3.

In this case, multiple regression analysis was conducted on data for the nation as a whole, and for urban, medium urban, and rural settings. The results are summarized in Table 7.2 and discussed below.

The coefficients of determination by urbanization decline from urban (55 per cent), to medium urban (33 per cent), and to rural (24 per cent) settings. In all cases, however, an acceptable level of evidence was obtained, though the results are better adjusted for urban than for rural municipalities. In other words, these causal factors seem to be more concentrated—i.e. have more explanatory power—in urban settings, where the diversity of experience is limited, than in rural ones, where circumstances are more open. This would suggest that a wider range of variables is needed to explain rural firearm violence. At the same time, it points to the highly concentrated nature of urban

Table 7.2 **Social determinants of firearm homicide in Brazil**				
	National	**Urban**	**Medium urban**	**Rural**
Coefficient of determination (R²)	33%	55%	33%	24%
Risk factors				
Demographic density				
Inequality				
Percentage of youth (15-29 years) in the population				
Youth (15-29 years) out of school and out of work, with less than 8 years of study				
Average number of years of study				
Vulnerable families (single-parent, headed by women, with children under 21 not working)				
Percentage of migrants in the population				
Firearms per residence				
Protection factors				
Percentage of Catholics				
Percentage of Protestants				
Dependent variable: Firearm homicide rate per 100,000 inhabitants				

firearm violence: geographically, demographically, and sociologically, a smaller number of variables can account for it. Despite these differences, the factors identified in this model are associated with variations in firearm violence across all settings. A number of the factors that were retained in the model, and some that were excluded, are discussed below.

- **Demographic density** turned out to be the best indicator in the model across all levels of urbanization, and nationwide: as a rule, the higher the number of inhabitants per km^2, the higher the rate of firearm homicides in a given municipality. Population size, which in many cases is a significant indicator, is not as strong. For this reason, and because density and population share common characteristics, the former was retained and the latter excluded. The official definition of 'urban' and 'rural' populations in Brazil was the weakest indicator concerning the impact of urbanization in the model.

- **Inequality** is also significant in explaining variations in firearm homicides across municipalities. It holds the test for the nation as a whole and for the variations in the urban/rural gradient. The hypothesis that the sharper the inequality, the higher the level of firearm homicides was checked with two well-known techniques, Theill-L and Gini, which are used to compare observed income distributions and their deviation from a standard distribution. Both tests suggested that inequality is indeed a relevant factor for firearm homicide in Brazil.[14]

Figure 7.6 **Firearm homicide rate by percentage of people living in poverty in Brazilian municipalities***

FIREARM HOMICIDE RATE PER 100,000 INHABITANTS

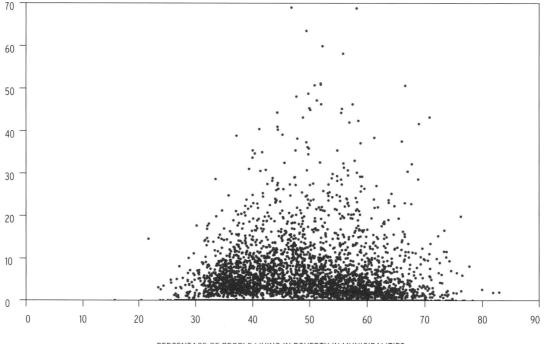

PERCENTAGE OF PEOPLE LIVING IN POVERTY IN MUNICIPALITIES

* The definition of the term 'people living in poverty' is the 'percentage of persons with a mean per capita family income of less than 50 per cent of the minimum wage (about USD 41.00 in 2000) per month'.

- **Income variation** was significant in some contexts, but quickly lost explanatory value when combined with other variables indicative of social hierarchy, such as years of study. For this reason, income was excluded from the model. Inequality, in turn, proved to have a stronger hold over the data, surviving most combinations.

- The percentage of people living in **poverty**, like income, was not a robust predictor of firearm homicide. Defined as the 'percentage of persons with a mean per capita family income of less than 50 per cent of the minimum wage (about USD 41.00 in 2000) per month', it did not alone appear to predict firearm homicide in any setting. Poverty, defined in this way, was therefore excluded from the model. Figure 7.6 illustrates this point.

    In Figure 7.6, the horizontal axis describes the percentage of people living in poverty in all 5,507 municipalities. The vertical axis captures the rates of homicide by firearms per 100,000 inhabitants in the same context. The figure shows that even though the percentage of people living in poverty varies widely (25–75 per cent), many municipalities have low firearm homicide rates (below 10 per 100,000 inhabitants). In other words, poverty, as such, shows little association with firearm homicide.

- **The proportion of youth within the population** is another significant factor in all types of municipality. When focusing on the 'percentage of individuals between 15 and 29 years of age in the population', the proportion of youth and the firearm homicide rate are positively and consistently associated in Brazil. This was true not only for the nation as a whole, but also for urban, medium urban, and rural municipalities.

- **Youth out of school and out of work** is another significant indicator, even when compared with associated variables such as the proportion of youth or years of study. The specific variable, 'individuals of 15–29 years of age who have not finished elementary education (8th grade) and who are neither studying nor working' could even serve as a practical guide for defining the group of risk factors in situations of firearm violence in Brazil. It has a clear institutional profile ('out of school and out of work') that can be useful for the definition of corrective public policies.

- The **vulnerable families** variable passed the empirical test for predicting firearm violence in all settings. The variable was defined as 'single-parent households headed by women, with children below 21 years of age who are not working'. The results were unequivocal, indicating a family structure that is likely to reproduce the conditions of inequality and to generate children and youth most exposed to firearm violence.

- Together with urbanization, the **presence of firearms in the home** stands out as a significant factor in the model. In rural municipalities, firearm availability among ten different variables shows the highest coefficients in explaining firearm mortality. In medium urban environments, it is the second-strongest factor, and in urban settings it is the third-strongest. Small arms availability alone cannot explain the variations in firearm homicides. However, combined with other key variables, such as population density, vulnerable families, or youth out of school and out of work, small arms availability does stand out consistently as an aggravating condition. Following the patterns revealed by the model, an increase of 1 per cent in arms availability per household implies, on average, increased firearm homicide rates of 2.2 per cent in urban areas, 0.9 per cent in medium urban, and 0.7 per cent in rural contexts.

- The presence of **migrants** appears to be associated with firearm homicide in rural settings, but not in urban municipalities. The variable measured here is the proportion of inhabitants who were not born in that particular municipality, but who have come to be an integral part of its population. When measured in terms of recent migration (less than one year) or a longer time (ten years), the proportion of migrants in the population was

Urbanization and small arms availability contribute to firearm mortality.

A blood-stained blanket shields the body of a 14-year-old boy shot in the head with a rifle, allegedly the victim of a police shooting in the community of Morro do Alemão, Rio de Janeiro. © Rodrigues Moura/Viva Rio

consistently associated with firearm homicide in the rural context, but was not as significant in the urban settings. A history of massive migration into the larger cities in Brazil seems to have diluted the explanatory power of this variable.

- **Religion** is a protection factor for firearm violence in Brazil, specifically participation in either Catholic or Protestant churches. The same holds true when 'Protestants' and 'Pentecostals' are disaggregated. Each is a protection value in every setting. In other words, the results tell us that participation in a Christian church is associated with lower levels of firearm violence in Brazil. The two church traditions might even be said to play complementary protection roles, since the Catholics hold a larger majority in rural settings, while Protestantism is growing faster in urban neighbourhoods generally, and in the poorer urban areas most rapidly of all.[15]

Inequality within cities

The social factors of risk—including population density, income inequality, youth out of school without a job, and vulnerable families—tend to concentrate and reinforce one another in some urban neighbourhoods. Inequality is thus materialized in the human geography of the city. The standard rate measure (X events per 100,000 inhabitants) effectively hides the internal differences that make big cities so much more vulnerable to the expressions of violence. Map 7.2 and Table 7.3 illustrate the point in the case of Rio de Janeiro. The southern portion of the city concentrates resources and protection against the threats of firearm violence. There lies 'the Marvellous Rio', situated between the mountains and the ocean, in contrast to the northern and the western zones of the city, beyond the mountains and on the low plains, seldom seen by foreigners. The homicide rate in São Conrado, a beautiful neighbourhood in the southern region, can be 50 times lower than that found in Bonsucesso, in the northern part of the same city.

Map 7.2 **Human Development Index* per neighbourhood, city of Rio de Janeiro, 2000**

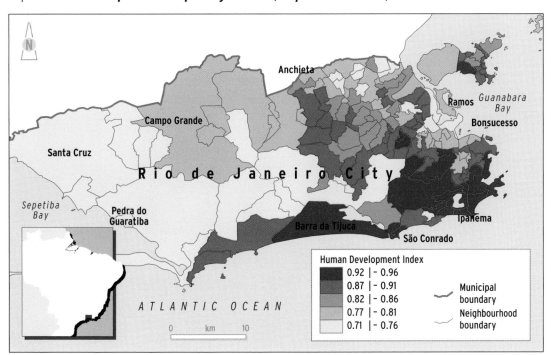

* The Human Development Index is a comparative measure of life expectancy, literacy, education, and standard of living for countries worldwide. It is a standard means of measuring well-being, especially child welfare. It is used to determine and indicate whether a country is developed, developing, or underdeveloped, and also to measure the impact of economic policies on quality of life. The index was developed in 1990 by Pakistani economist Mahbub ul Haq and has been used since 1993 by the United Nations Development Programme in its annual Human Development Report. The closer to 1, the more developed the area/country according to three criteria: a long and healthy life, level of knowledge, and a decent standard of living.

Table 7.3 **Rio de Janeiro: homicide in a city's geography**						
Neighbourhood	**Homicides**		**Population**		**Homicide rate per 100,000 inhabitants**	
	2003	**2004**	**2003**	**2004**	**2003**	**2004**
South						
Ipanema	8	5	47,106	47,739	17	11
São Conrado	1	1	11,226	11,377	8	8
Barra da Tijuca	23	15	92,819	94,068	25	16
North						
Anchieta	58	62	54,150	54,879	107	112
Ramos	54	47	37,776	38,284	142	123
Bonsucesso	79	93	19,421	19,682	406	471
West						
Campo Grande	218	232	299,385	303,414	73	76
Santa Cruz	145	159	193,055	195,653	75	81
Pedra de Guaratiba	26	24	9,755	9,886	267	246

Prosperous Rio de Janeiro viewed from a favela on a hillside. © Jon Spaull/Panos

Comparative studies across neighbourhoods of Rio de Janeiro show remarkable differences in human development. Growing at current rates, 'Alemão Complex' in Bonsucesso would take almost one hundred years to arrive at São Conrado's present human development level. Within the same city, neighbourhoods can be decades apart in terms of income, health, and education.[16]

YOUTH AND FIREARM VIOLENCE IN BRAZIL

Figure 7.7 indicates the paramount importance of the age factor for evaluating firearm mortality in Brazil. A seminal essay by Marcos Lisboa and Mônica Viegas Andrade (2000) proposes that age be the basic reference for the calculation of the social causes of urban violence. As these authors note, youth can be sensitive to indicators whose significance is weakened when distributed through the population in general. Taken for the population as a whole, the indicator 'per 100,000 inhabitants' hides the variation of impact of a given social factor over the various age groups. In particular, the behaviour of children, at the one extreme, and of adults and elders, at the other, often dilutes the impact of some social factors on youth. For this reason, calculating rates and respective explanatory models by age groups is a promising approach.

For instance, as noted above, when plotted against the population in general, the percentage of people living in poverty is not significantly associated with firearm violence in Brazil. Aggregating the data by age, however, produces a different result. Poverty does correlate with firearm violence in Brazil for youth. This is an important difference from the previous findings, where this fact was hidden by the 'per 100,000 inhabitants' denominator.

Figure 7.7 **Causes of death in Brazil by age group, 2000**

PER CENT

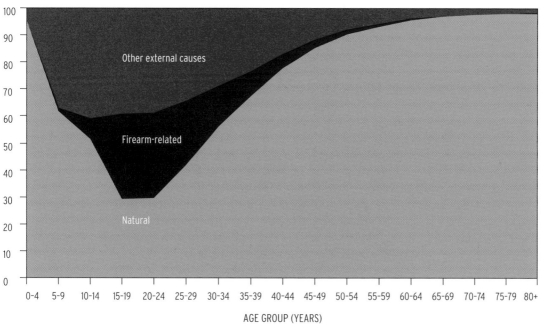

Figure 7.8 **Poverty per age group and firearm homicides**

POVERTY COEFFICIENT

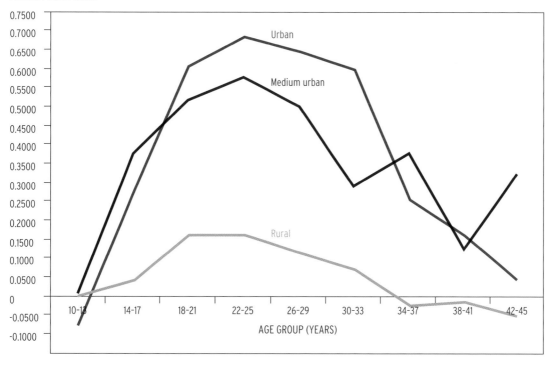

In Figure 7.8, the *coefficient* at stake is a measure of the impact of the percentage of people living in poverty on the firearm homicide rate. As the figure shows, the coefficient value varies from -1 to +1, where -1 signifies a negative impact (implying a protection effect) and +1 signifies a positive impact (or risk). Zero, in this scale, means no recognizable impact. Testing the correlation by each age group reveals that poverty is a significant factor for firearm homicide among youth and less so or not at all among adults. Furthermore, this finding is more robust in urban settings; the impact of poverty on youth firearm homicide rates is less pronounced in medium urban settings and much less in rural ones.[17] In subjective terms, one might say that young people are more sensitive than their elders to the social failings in city life.

In short, strong correlations can be found between firearm homicides and the impact of social deficiencies on young people. Differences that seem to be disregarded in the opinion of adults are of critical importance to adolescents and young men. Juvenile violence does not translate into an ideological discourse in Brazil, but it is certainly expressive of severe social inequities, which are perceived as such by youth.

The significance of youth in firearm violence in Brazil is further heightened by a particular historical fact. The demographic pyramid of Brazil (see Figure 7.9) reveals a populous generation coming of age. Researchers speak of a 'demographic bonus' in contemporary Brazil: a larger class of teenagers and young adults will soon become economically active, in contrast to gradually reduced numbers of children and elders. The effect of firearm violence on young people has not been factored into this 'bonus', however.

Two young men, one holding a gun, protect their identities as they are filmed about their lives in a favela. © Viva Rio

Figure 7.9 **Brazil's demographic pyramid: population distribution according to age group and gender, 2000**

AGE GROUP (YEARS)

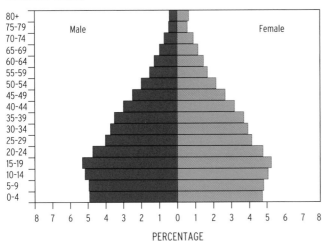

PERCENTAGE

OUTLYING CASES

A number of municipalities deviated from the patterns described above. Their actual firearm homicide rates were either much higher or much lower than the model would have predicted. These special outlying cases comprised about 4 per cent of the total sample, or 237 out of 5,507 municipalities. Table 7.4 describes how many urban (75), medium urban (41), and rural (105) municipalities had real rates much higher than those estimated by the model, as well as the number of municipalities with rates of firearm homicides much lower than expected for each type of municipality (8, 2, and 6, respectively).

Many of the municipalities with higher than expected rates of firearm homicides are grouped in two states of the federation. Together, Pernambuco state in the north-east and Parana state in the south account for almost half of the special cases on the higher side of the scale. They are also typically located along roads that lead to and from areas with high levels of illicit activities. In Pernambuco, the 'Marijuana Roads' leading from the inland areas, where the drug is cultivated, to the coastal centres, where consumption occurs, leaves a trail of unusually violent medium urban and rural municipalities. Turf wars over the opportunities created by the illicit trade, in an otherwise stable, traditional society, are likely to account for the increase in fatal violence.[18] In Parana state, a concentration of more violent than expected municipalities is found along the BR277 road, which leads from Iguaçu, in the Triple Frontier, to Curitiba, the state capital. Besides drugs and arms, various kinds of illicit goods are transported along the same route. From Curitiba, the merchandise follows the flows of the market, mostly towards São Paulo and beyond, with other municipalities being singled out by higher levels of violence along the way. A similar pattern holds for Rio Grande do Sul, the southernmost state in Brazil, whose borders with Uruguay and Argentina seem to account for a number of 'special cases'.

Table 7.4 **Firearm homicide rates: cities out of the pattern**

Estimation error: standardized residual				
Level of urbanization	Less than -2 SD*	Between -2 and 2 SD	More than 2 SD	Total
Urban	8	372	75	455
Medium urban	2	953	41	996
Rural	6	3,945	105	4,056
Total	16	5,270	221	5,507

* SD = standard deviation

Map 7.3 **Municipalities with firearm homicide rates far above or below expectations**

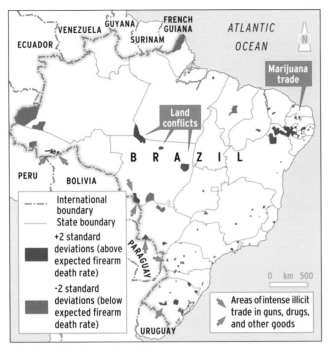

Source: Research by ISER for this chapter

Besides the transit of illicit business along strategic roads, land disputes are another likely explanation for higher than expected levels of firearm violence. They are often expressions of chronically unresolved property and power issues (Alston, Libecap, and Mueller, 1999).

Taken together, these outliers reveal particular aspects of the general history of violence in contemporary Brazil. They are more exposed to the externalities that aggravate and multiply firearm violence, such as the drugs and arms trade or the property conflicts over land and mineral riches. These cases are plotted in Map 7.3, where a -2 standard deviation is marked in black and a +2 standard deviation is marked in red.

On the positive side of the deviation, a broader set of explanations is needed. Successful public administration and human development achievements are part of the puzzle, and help explain the good experiences of Atalaia do Norte in the Amazonas, São Caetano do Sul and Santana de Parnaíba in São Paulo, and Timóteo and Coronel Fabriciano in Minas Gerais. Municipalities that have grown around religious or ecological tourism also seem to do better than expected. There are a good number of those, scattered through various regions in Brazil. Cities with religious tourism include Anchieta in Espírito Santo, Barra do Garças in Goiás, and Camutanga in Pernambuco. Ecological tourism destinations appear in every region: a representative location is Navegantes in Santa Catarina, which has grown as one of the most prosperous and peaceful municipalities in the region, thanks to a radical and young kind of tourism. There is yet another category of municipalities distinguished by very low levels of violence: fairly isolated places, subsisting by fishing along the seashore or along the rivers in the Amazon region, which have not yet been touched by the wider circles of social tensions and firearm violence.

URBAN AND RURAL FIREARM SUICIDE RATES

Self-inflicted injury and death rates in Brazil are among the lowest in the world. The suicide rates for the urban/rural gradient form neither a progressive nor a regressive linear pattern (see Figure 7.10). In contrast to the homicide findings, there is no clear nexus between urbanization and suicide in Brazil. In 2000 the rates for both suicide and firearm suicide were lowest for urban settings, highest for the medium urban areas, and in between for the rural.

Figure 7.10   **Suicide and firearm suicide rates by municipality type, 2000**

SUICIDES PER 100,000 INHABITANTS

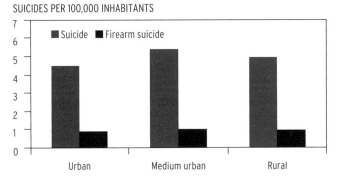

Figure 7.11   **Suicide rates by gender and municipality type, 2000**

SUICIDES PER 100,000 INHABITANTS

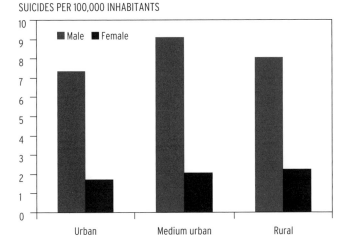

Figure 7.12   **Firearm suicide rates by gender and municipality type, 2000**

SUICIDES PER 100,000 INHABITANTS

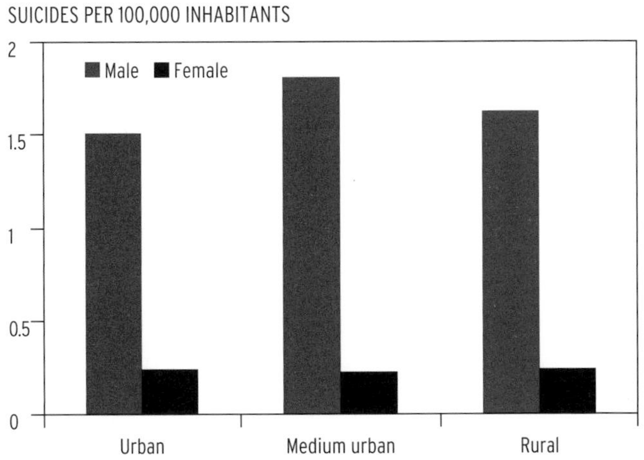

Across all municipality types in Brazil, men are more prone to committing suicide than women. As with firearm violence generally, men are also more prone than women to committing suicide with a firearm (see Figures 7.11 and 7.12). In considering the social conditions of firearm violence, the gender association of firearms is unmistakable.

By combining gender and age groups for firearm suicides, a subtle and interesting contrast emerges. The rates for men remain stable throughout adulthood and tend to increase at old age, past the age of 60. This holds true for men in all municipality types, as shown in Figure 7.13. Among women, the opposite trend prevails. Suicide rates diminish with age across all settings, after peaking in adolescence and young adulthood (Figure 7.14). Cultural values associated with gender differences may account for such discrepancies. In contemporary Brazilian culture, and in contrast to men, who tend to be associated with weakening social bonds in old age, the responsibilities of motherhood may reinforce women's commitment to life as their age increases.

Social determinants of firearm suicide in Brazil

In the absence of a pattern distinguishing the rates of suicide in the urban/rural scale, this chapter closes with an overview of social factors that may determine risk of suicide in the country as a whole. Results are consistent with foundational insights from sociology, articulated by Durkheim (1951). Specifically, the indicators of individual isolation and of weakening social bonds were found to be significant in Brazil. They are summarized in Table 7.5 and are discussed below.[19]

Figure 7.13 **Male firearm suicide rate by age group, 2000**

SUICIDES PER 100,000 INHABITANTS

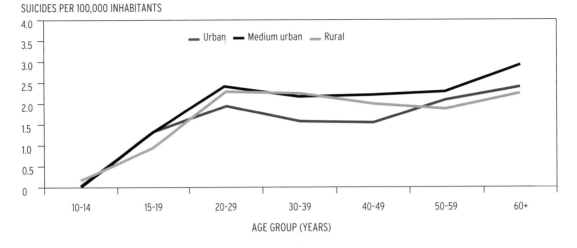

AGE GROUP (YEARS)

Figure 7.14 **Female firearm suicide rate by age group, 2000**

SUICIDES PER 100,000 INHABITANTS

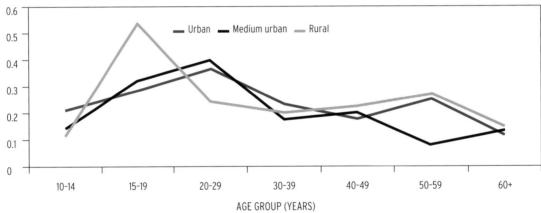

AGE GROUP (YEARS)

Variables in this model not previously discussed above include the following:

- **Persons living alone** involves an array of situations, including, for instance, single people and widows.

- As described in the firearm homicide analysis, **vulnerable families** are defined as the 'single-parent households headed by women, with children below 21 years of age who are not working'. Any particular marital status alone (single, married, separated, divorced, widowed) is not a significant variable in this model. The informal and unstable nature of gender relations in Brazil seems to make marital status a poor reference for the realities of family life. However, families headed by young women, a growing phenomenon in poor communities in Brazil, do form a relevant indicator of risk, not only for homicides, but for suicides as well.

- **'White'** is the ethnic category with the highest coefficient regarding firearm suicide. It contrasts with 'black' and 'mixed race', as noted above. In a reversal of the situation found in firearm homicide, 'black' and 'mixed race' correlate with *protection* from the risks of suicide in contemporary Brazil—'white', instead, is associated with

Table 7.5 **Social conditions of firearm suicide in Brazil**
According to the Multivariate Linear Model, the coefficient of determination (R^2) = 31%
Risk factors
Persons living alone, over population in general
Vulnerable families ('single-parent households headed by women, with children below 21 years of age who are not working')
White people, over population in general
Inequality
Households with firearms, over total of households
Protection factors
Poverty ('percentage of persons with a mean per capita family income of less than 50 per cent of the minimum wage (about USD 41.00 in 2000) per month')
Women aged 40 or older, over population in general
Pentecostals, over population in general
Protestants, over population in general
Dependent variable: Firearm suicide rate

higher suicide rates. It was decided to keep the category 'white' in the model because of other interesting con-
notations. Omitting it from tests gives the Human Development Index greater significance as a risk factor. The
more developed a municipality is (in terms of income, education and health conditions), the higher the suicide
rate becomes. When the category 'white' is brought back into the equation, the Human Development Index fades
out of the picture. These two factors overlap too much to co-exist in the same model. The explanation may be
found in the growing individualistic culture in Brazil. If you are white, richer, and more educated, you are more
likely to bear the marks of an 'autonomous individual' and hence, according to received sociological ideas, run
a higher risk of suicide.

- Interestingly, **inequality** is also a risk factor for firearm suicide. Here the effect is mostly felt in the higher
classes. Inequality in Brazil is consistent with enhanced modernization and individualism among the middle class
and upwards.

- **Households with firearms** is similarly an important risk factor. This variable holds solid coefficients in every
combination of factors it is run with, which confirms observations on the subject held in other cultural contexts,
such as in Kellermann and Mercy (1992) and Lester (1995).

- Conceptually, **poverty**, as previously defined, stands out as a protection: the poorer the municipality, the lower
the suicide rate. Unfortunately, it was not possible to combine poverty with the categories of 'black' and 'mixed
race' people, also protection variables, because the overlap is too high. In the opinion of the chapter's authors, the
explanation lies in the fact that the poor in Brazil socialize in complex relational and hierarchical forms, around the
family and the immediate community. Although affected by individualism, much like anyone else, the poor are often
imbedded in solidarity and loyalty ties and are therefore less exposed to the isolationist side of individualization.

- **Women over 40 years of age** is a significant category of protection. This is not so with women in general, but only in adulthood, when responsibilities associated with motherhood in Brazilian culture make them key agents of social solidarity.

- A large segment of people self-identifying as **Pentacostals** in Brazil have the second-strongest coefficient, just after the category 'white', but now as a protective indicator. The numbers of Pentecostals grow most quickly among the poor, and these people form strong community ties. 'Healing,' often a weekly ritual practice, deals with the psyche and its interventions in group interactions and in the internal processes of body and self. Pentacostals have a language to address the uncertainties of life and death.

- The **Protestant or Reformed faiths** are also significant as a protection factor. These so-called 'historical' Protestant churches in Latin America were introduced by missionaries in the 19th century, before the Pentecostal revival, and include Lutherans, Episcopalians, Methodists, Baptists, Presbyterians, and Congregationalists. These churches are closer to the individualistic culture of modern society. However, in the Brazilian context, their strong **congregational** aspect, which contrasts with the traditional devotions of popular Catholicism, may create a difference that can count as protection in regard to troubled individuals. The **Catholic** faith did not work as a significant component of this ensemble. The authors were forced to leave it out of this particular exercise and thus to suspend judgement on its impact in suicidal practices in Brazil.

CONCLUSION

This chapter suggests that it is possible at the outset to understand the primary risk factors underlying firearm violence in the country. Urbanization is an important variable in the constellation of factors, along with ethnic group, age, and gender differences. In terms of firearm homicides, the contrasts conditioned by those variables are severely aggravated in urban society. The tensions underlying lethal aggression grow with cities and do so in a selective manner. Risks are concentrated among young males who are black or of mixed race.

Inequality, rather than poverty, increases the likelihood of firearm violence, which is reinforced and reproduced by the growing presence of vulnerable families, headed by single mothers with unemployed children. Teenagers and young adults are the main risk groups, particularly those who have dropped out of school before finishing elementary education and have not found a stable position in the labour market. Protection from those risks, on a wide societal scale, is found mainly in religious participation, whether in Catholic or Protestant churches.

Given those conditions and the epidemic proportions of small arms violence in Brazil, the availability of firearms has proven to be a severe risk factor for homicides.

A rapid assessment of outlying cases in the model led to a number of hypotheses. Municipalities that had higher than expected rates of firearm homicides included those on roads leading to and from international borders loaded with illicit practices; roads leading from the 'Marijuana Polygon' in the state of Pernambuco and the coast; and those near or on the site of chronic land conflicts. Municipalities that had lower than expected rates of firearm homicides suggest special protective circumstances such as best practices in human development and religious or environmentally oriented tourism.

Conversely, firearm suicides produced no clear pattern of association with the urbanization process. The main sociological finding here was the correlation of suicide rates with an 'individualistic culture', which is more expressive among the middle class and the wealthy in Brazil, people distinguished by higher income and education, in all municipality types. Individual isolation, as signified by the variable 'living alone', stands out as a risk factor. On the other hand, 'poverty' and being 'black' or of 'mixed race' count as protection factors, indicative of more complex primary relations in the family and in the community. Here again, the availability of firearms proved to be a significant factor in increasing the risk of self-inflicted death.

In addition to these findings, the study has a number of policy implications:

- Firstly, firearm violence in Brazil, while a complex phenomenon, is broadly explicable using social science and public health methodologies. These findings, and the findings of similar studies, are worthy of being raised, addressed, and debated by policy-makers at all levels who have a stake in reducing firearm violence.

- Secondly, it is clear that no single factor is responsible for firearm violence in Brazil, but rather several significant factors are at work. Accordingly, interventions and public policy will clearly benefit from integrating several approaches, agencies, and specialties in a multisector and multilevel effort.

- Thirdly, young people are at highest risk in Brazil, particularly unemployed school drop-outs. Fresh approaches are needed for educational inclusion, geared specifically to drop-outs, which take their experience, language, and social networks into account. Income generation, work opportunities, and cultural activities for young people are also promising components of a well-rounded approach to protecting young people from firearm violence.

- Fourthly, certain realities of family life in Brazil, including early pregnancy and single parenthood, need to be faced squarely. Health-based prevention strategies for addressing these crucial issues in schools and through civil society efforts can have positive 'ripple' effects in the area of firearm violence reduction.

- Fifthly, at the macro level, this study confirms that inequality is a core factor that brings all the other variables into play. No firearm violence-prevention and -reduction approach can long ignore the centrality that this deep, societal phenomenon plays. Similarly, policy initiatives to reverse—or at least manage—urban sprawl should acknowledge the potential positive changes that could accrue in the area of violence prevention.

- Sixthly, reducing both the supply of and the demand for firearms—both legal and illicit—should remain an essential policy goal.

- Finally, maintaining focus on populations at highest risk requires law enforcement capacity that is well integrated with all of the social and development efforts discussed above. ◢

ANNEXES

Annexe 1. Estimating mortality rates for small municipalities

In 2000 the population of 4,018 municipalities in Brazil was less than 20,000 inhabitants, a condition that exposes death rates to great variations: small oscillations in the number of deaths cause great variation in the death rates. The example in Figure 7.15 illustrates the problem.

This pattern of deaths (a variation between 0 and 4 deaths) for a city of 100,000 inhabitants would give us a rate variation of 0–4 deaths per 100,000 people. However, in a township of 16,000 inhabitants, the same numbers (0–4 deaths) would lead to a rate variation of 0–25 per 100,000 people. To reduce such extreme results and to have a more robust estimate than a mean of the nine points in Figure 7.15, the researchers chose to adjust a simple linear regression for the nine years in question. The model thus obtained was the source for an estimated value for the year 2000. This methodology was applied to all 5,507 Brazilian municipalities. This exercise was carried out with different time spans. In this particular case, however, where the year of interest (2000) happens to be at the symmetrical centre of the time range, the result is equal to the arithmetical average.

Figure 7.15 **Hypothetical death rate for a city of 100,000 inhabitants**

DEATHS PER 100,000 INHABITANTS

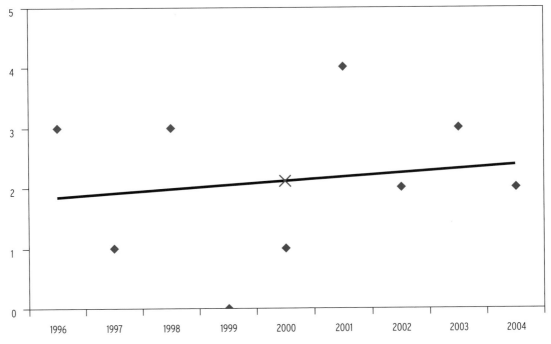

Annexe 2. The distinction between 'urban' and 'rural'

The criteria

Several criteria can be used to distinguish urban and rural areas: population size, occupied area, dominant economic activity, infrastructure, access to public facilities and services, etc. In Brazil, as in other Latin American countries, an administrative distinction is applied. Diversity in these criteria poses comparative problems. In this chapter a combination of three indicators is applied: (i) the official administrative division; (ii) population size; and (iii) population density (inhabitants per km²); each of which, on its own, produces different results.

(i) The *official administrative division* of the country is produced for administrative purposes every year based on reports by all municipalities in the country. It gives the following result in Brazil:

% of population living in urban areas	Number of municipalities	% of municipalities (rounded)
Less than 60%	2,811	51.0
60-80%	1,464	26.6
More than 80%	1,232	22.4
Total	**5,507**	**100.0**

(ii) *Population size*

Population size is the sole criterion for distinguishing between 'urban' and 'rural' areas for several countries, such as Spain, Portugal, Italy, and Greece. In this chapter, the following three categories are distinguished: (a) up to 19,999 inhabitants; (b) from 20,000 to 99,999 inhabitants; and (c) 100,000 or more inhabitants. This indicator presents extreme variation. In 2000 the municipality with the smallest population had 795 inhabitants, while the biggest (São Paulo) had 10.4 million. The tripartite division per size of population is the following:

Population	Number of municipalities	% of municipalities (rounded)
Up to 19,999 inhabitants	4,018	73.0
From 20,000 to 99,999 inhabitants	1,265	23.0
100,000 inhabitants or more	224	4.1
Total	**5,507**	**100.0***

* The individual percentages do not exactly total 100, due to rounding.

(iii) *Density: inhabitants per km²*

This is another interesting indicator, with great variation. In 2000 the most densely populated municipality in Brazil had 12,900 inhabitants per km², while the least dense had less than one inhabitant per km². The result is the following:

Demographic density	Number of municipalities	% of municipalities (rounded)
Less than 30 inhabitants/km²	3,263	59.3
30-100 inhabitants/km²	1,605	29.1
Over 100 inhabitants/km²	639	11.6
Total	**5,507**	**100.0**

Combining the criteria

Each category received a value of 1 to 3 on an ascending scale. After classifying all municipalities according to each criterion and weighting them accordingly, final classification comes from the formula:

Rank = Class official division + Class population size + Class population density

The results indicate the category of each municipality. These are the categories used in this study.

Categories	Rank
Urban	7-9 points
Medium urban	4-6 points
Rural	3 points or less

Thus the final classification adopted by this chapter has the following breakdown:

Urbanization	Number of municipalities	% of municipalities (rounded)
Rural	4,056	74.0
Medium urban	996	18.0
Urban	455	8.0
Total	**5,507**	**100.0**

Annexe 3. Modelling social conditions for firearm homicides in Brazil

Modelling firearm homicides in Brazil	National		Urban		Medium urban		Rural	
R^2 =	0.325		0.551		0.325		0.239	
Coefficients	St. beta	Sig.	St. beta	Sig.	St. beta	Sig.	St. beta	Sig.
Demographic density	0,276	0.000	0.280	0.000	0.171	0.000	0.082	0.000
Inequality (Theill-L)	0.092	0.000	0.048	0.146	0.120	0.000	0.153	0.000
% of population aged 15-29 years	0.124	0.000	0.099	0.014	0.178	0.000	0.051	0.002
% of youth (15-29 years) out of school and out of work	0.075	0.000	0.104	0.023	0.058	0.110	0.068	0.001
% of vulnerable families	0.043	0.005	0.085	0.010	0.056	0.038	0.020	0.147
% of firearms per household	0.253	0.000	0.244	0.000	0.316	0.000	0.317	0.000
% of Catholics	-0.321	0.000	-0.595	0.000	-0.393	0.000	-0.154	0.000
% of Protestants	-0.175	0.000	-0.233	0.000	-0.225	0.000	-0.081	0.000
% of migrants	0.061	0.014			-0.085	0.005	0.206	0.000
Average years of study	0.074	0.000					-0.030	0.163
Dependent variable: Rate of death by firearms								

Significance: Student's T-test

The parameters of regression were estimated in accordance with the OLS (multiple regression model) methodology. Other methods, using weights for proximity, level, or similarity, were tested against OLS, but did not show different results.

Annexe 4. Modelling social conditions for firearm suicides in Brazil

Modelling firearm suicides in Brazil	National		Urban		Medium urban		Rural	
$R^2 =$	0.160		0.375		0.152		0.172	
Coefficients	St. beta	Sig.	St. beta	Sig.	St. beta	Sig.	St. beta	Sig.
(Constant)		0.108		0.025		0.461		0.661
Prevalence of firearms in household	0.167	0.000	0.259	0.000	0.152	0.000	0.146	0.000
Life expectancy at birth	-0.143	0.000			-0.365	0.000	-0.207	0.000
% of population aged 15-29 years	-0.123	0.000			-0.129	0.000	-0.167	0.000
Human Development Index	0.520	0.000			0.971	0.000	0.551	
Index of informal labour in labour force	-0.037	0.031	-0.189	0.000	-0.125	0.000		
Inequality (Theil-L)	0.077	0.000	0.106	0.008				
% of economically active persons in total population	0.083	0.002					0.086	0.003
% persons not working	-0.031	0.098	-0.295	0.000				
Family income per capita in minimum salaries in year 2000	-0.094	0.008			-0.146	0.081		
% of households headed by women, without a partner, with children younger than 24 years who do not work	0.043	0.003	0.290	0.000				
Average years of study	-0.187	0.000			-0.319	0.003		
% of undetermined religion	0.025	0.078					0.032	0.057
Total population in year 2000					0.114	0.001	0.085	0.000
Demographic density	-0.035	0.021					-0.063	0.000

ENDNOTES

1   Market research by the tourism industry has identified 'joy' ('*alegria*') as the most important characteristic of Brazil for foreigners; see Bignami (2002).

2   Brazil became independent in 1822.

3   After a two-decade rise in firearm deaths in Brazil, from 2003 to 2004 the number dropped from 39,325 to 36,091. The reduction was sustained in 2005, and results from some key populous states, such as São Paulo, Minas Gerais, and Rio de Janeiro, suggest that numbers should continue to fall in 2006. Together with other factors, the new firearm legislation, the December 2003 Disarmament Statute, has probably contributed to these results; see Ministério da Saúde (2005) and Fernandes (2005b).

4   Ramos and Lemgruber (2004); Cano and Santos (2001); Beato Filho (2000); Luiz Soares (1996); Soares (2006).

5   See endnote 11.

6   A description of criteria and methods applied when establishing the distinction between urban and rural areas is found in Annexe 2. A discussion of the urban–rural distinctions in Brazil is found in IPEA, IBGE, and UNICAMP (2002).

7   On the methodological problems of estimating the death rate in small municipalities, see Annexe 1.

8   WHO (2002, pp. 186–87) reports the following suicide rates for Latin American and Caribbean countries per 100,000 inhabitants: Argentina, 8.7; Brazil, 6.3; Chile, 8.1; Colombia, 4.5; Costa Rica, 8.8; Cuba, 23.0; Ecuador, 7.2; El Salvador, 11.2; Mexico, 5.1; Nicaragua, 7.6; Paraguay, 4.2; Puerto Rico, 10.8; Uruguay, 12.8; Venezuela, 8.1.

9   Carrying a gun is common practice among men in some rural sub-regions of Brazil, such as the 'Gaucho' country in the south, the savanna in the mid-west, or the forest in the Amazon. Hunting is a regular activity in these regions, which explains the preference for long-barrelled hunting arms. Most handguns and even shotguns used in Brazil are Brazilian-made, while automatic weapons found among civilians are typically foreign-made—and in principle illegal. For a detailed discussion of small arms supply, stocks, and demand in Brazil, see Dreyfus and de Sousa Nascimento (2005), Lessing (2005), Phebo (2005), and Rivero (2005).

10   On gender and violence in Brazil, see Barbara Soares (1996), Jordão (2006), and Moura (2007).

11   Terminology for ethnic groups varies throughout the world. Official Brazilian statistics use categories such as 'black', 'brown', 'white', and 'yellow' (see <http://www.ibge.gov.br/home/estatistica/populacao/censo2000/metodologia/metodologiacenso2000.pdf>, and especially pp. 213–14). This chapter applies the categories used by the UK Office of National Statistics, namely 'black', 'mixed race', and 'white' (see <http://www.statistics.gov.uk/CCI/nugget.asp?ID=467&Pos=&ColRank=2&Rank=1000>). On race and violence in Brazil see Batista, Escuder, and Pereira (2004) and Ramos and Musumeci (2006).

12   On youth and violence in Brazil, see Novaes and Vannuchi (2004), Waiselfisz (2006), and Dowdney (2003).

13   Multiple regression analysis measures the relationship between a dependent (or criterion) variable (here, the firearm homicide rate) and several independent (or predictor) variables. The R^2 (the *coefficient of determination*) value is an indicator of how well the model fits the data.

14   A thorough discussion of social inequalities in Brazil is found in Hasenbalg and Silva (2003).

15   Other religious traditions are not well enough represented in the census across the municipalities to be included in the discussion here. Afro-American beliefs (Candomblé, Umbanda, etc.) in particular, widespread as they are, tend to be under-notified in the census. Most people will simply respond 'Catholic', not bothering to register their double or even multiple religious practices. However, the protective aspect found here suggests that further research should be carried out concerning the relationships between religion and armed violence in Brazil. Children under ten years of age were attributed with the religion of their parents. To follow research on religions and the social facts in Brazil, see the journal *Religião e Sociedade,* published by ISER since 1977.

16   See the report on human development for the city of Rio de Janeiro, 2001, data from which is available at <http://www.pnud.org.br/pdf/Tabela%206.2.22%20IDH%20bairro%2091_00-15_12_03.xls>. On the uneven distribution of crime within the city of Belo Horizonte, see also Beato et al. (2001).

17   Figure 7.8 follows a different modelling procedure: (i) rates of firearm homicides were calculated for each age group; and (ii) social and economic indicators were equally established for each age group; so that (iii) the numbers shown in Figure 7.8 are the standardized coefficients for the multivariated models adjusted for each age group.

18   The Federal Police have made progress in reducing illicit drug production in the interior of Pernambuco, the so called 'Marijuana Polygon'. The impact of these actions for the rates of violence in the region should become clearer in the coming years.

19   On the modelling of the social conditions of firearm suicides, see Annexe 4.

BIBLIOGRAPHY

Alston, L. J., G. D. Libecap, and B. Mueller. 1999. 'A Model of Rural Conflict: Violence and Land Reform Policy in Brazil.' *Environment and Development Economics*, Vol. 4, No. 2, pp. 135–60. Cambridge: Cambridge University Press.

Astor, M. 2006. '19 Killed as Gangs Attack Buses, Police Posts around Rio de Janeiro.' *The Washington Post*. 29 December.
<http://www.washingtonpost.com/wp-dyn/content/article/2006/12/28/AR2006122801301.html>

Batista, Luís Eduardo, Maria Mercedes Loureiro Escuder, and Julio Cesar Rodrigues Pereira. 2004. 'The Color of Death: Causes of Death according to Race in the State of São Paulo. 1999 to 2001.' *Revista Saúde Pública*, Vol. 38, No. 5, pp. 630–36. October. Portuguese version at <http://www.scielo.br/scielo.php?pid=S0034-89102004000500003&script=sci_arttext&tlng=pt> English version at <http://www.scielosp.org/pdf/rsp/v38n5/en_21749.pdf>

Beato Filho, Claudio Chaves. 2000. 'Determining Factors of Criminality in Minas Gerais.' *Revista Brasileira de Ciências Sociais*.
<http://www.scielo.br/pdf/rbcsoc/nspe1/a10nesp1.pdf>

—— et al. 2001. 'Conglomerados de homicídios e o tráfico de drogas em Belo Horizonte, Minas Gerais, Brasil, de 1995 a 1999.' *Caderno de Saúde Pública*, Vol. 17, No. 5, pp. 1163–71. <http://www.scielo.br/pdf/csp/v17n5/6324.pdf>

Bignami, Rosana. 2002. *A imagen do Brasil no turismo: Construção, Desafios e Vantagen Competitiva*. São Paulo: Aleph.

Brazil. Ministry of Health. n.d. Unified Database. <http://www.datasus.gov.br>

Brent, D. A. et al. 1993. 'Firearms and Adolescent Suicide: A Community Case-Control Study.' *American Journal of Diseases of Children*, Vol. 147, p. 1066.

Cano, Ignácio and Nilton Santos. 2001. *Violência letal, renda e desigualdade social no Brasil*. Rio de Janeiro: 7 Letras.

Dowdney, Luke T. 2003. *Children of the Drug Trade: A Case Study of Organised Armed Violence in Rio de Janeiro*. Rio de Janeiro: Viva Rio/ISER, 7 Letras.
<http://www.smallarmssurvey.org/files/portal/issueareas/perpetrators/perpet_pdf/2003_Dowdney.pdf>

Dreyfus, Pablo and Marcelo de Sousa Nascimento. 2005. 'Small Arms Holdings in Brazil: Toward a Comprehensive Mapping of Guns and Their Owners.' In Fernandes, 2005a, pp. 94–145. <http://www.vivario.org.br/publique/media/Small_Arms_Holding_in_Brazil_Toward_a_comprehensive_mapping_of_guns_and_their_owners_By_Pablo_Dreyfus_e_Marcelo_de_Souza_Nascimento.pdf>

Durkheim, Emile. 1951 (first published 1897). *Suicide: A Study in Sociology*. Translated by John A. Sapulding and George Simpson. New York: Free Press.

Fernandes, Rubem César, ed. 2005a. *Brazil: The Arms and the Victims*. Rio de Janeiro: ISER, Viva Rio, and Small Arms Survey.
<http://www.vivario.org.br/publique/cgi/cgilua.exe/sys/start.htm?UserActiveTemplate=_vivario_en&sid=28&infoid=962>

——. 2005b. Dados para uma Avaliação do Programa de Entrega Voluntária de Armas no Brasil. ISER.
<http://www.comunidadesegura.org/?q=pt/node/32175>

Hasenbalg, Carlos and Nelson do Valle Silva. 2003. *Origens e Destinos: Desigualdades sociais ao longo da vida*. Rio de Janeiro: Topbooks.

IBGE (Instituto Brasileiro de Geografica e Estatistica). n.d. Web site. <http://www.ibge.gov.br>

IPEA (Instituto de Pesquisa Econômica Aplicada, Ministério do Planejamento, Orçamento e Gestão), IBGE (Instituto Brasileiro de Geografia e Estatística, Ministério do Planejamento, Orçamento e Gestão), and UNICAMP (Universidade Estadual de Campinas, Autarquia, autônoma em política educacional, mas subordinada ao Governo do Estado de São Paulo). 2002. 'Configuração Atual e Tendências Da Rede Urbana.' In *Caracterização e Tendências da Rede Urbana do Brasil*, Vol. 1. Brasília: IPEA, IBGE, and UNICAMP, 2002.

ISER (Instituto de Estudos da Religião). 1977 onwards. *Religião e Sociedade*. Rio de Janeiro: ISER.

Jordão, Fátima Pacheco. 2006. *Percepção e Reações da Sociedade sobre a Violência Contra a Mulher, Pesquisa*. São Paulo: IBOPE/Instituto Patrícia Galvão.
<http://www.patriciagalvao.org.br/apc-aa-patriciagalvao/home/pesquisa_ibope_2006_versao_site.pdf>

Kellermann, A. L. and J. A. Mercy. 1992. 'Men, Women, and Murder: Gender-Specific Differences in Rates of Fatal Violence and Victimization.' *Journal of Trauma*, Vol. 33, pp. 1–5.

Lessing, Benjamin. 2005. 'Demand for Firearms in Rio de Janeiro.' In Fernandes, 2005a, pp. 202–21.
<http://www.vivario.org.br/publique/media/The_demand_for_firearms_in_Rio_de_Janeiro_by_Benjamin_Lessing.pdf>

Lester, D. 1995. 'Preventing Suicide by Restricting Access to Methods for Suicide.' In R. F. W. Diekstra et al., eds. *Preventive Strategies on Suicide*. Leiden: Brill, pp. 163–72.

Lisboa, Marcos de Barros and Mônica Viegas Andrade. 2000. 'Desesperança de Vida: Homicídio em Minas Gerais, Rio De Janeiro e São Paulo: 1981 a 1997.' *Ensaios Econômicos Da EPGE*, No. 383, pp. 3–4. <http://epge.fgv.br/portal/arquivo/1232.pdf>

Ministério da Saúde. 2005. *Vidas Poupadas*. Brasília: UNESCO. <http://unesdoc.unesco.org/images/0014/001408/140846por.pdf>

Moura, Tatiana. 2007. *Rostos Invisíveis da Violência Armada*. Rio de Janeiro: Viva Rio, Universidade de Coimbra, and 7 Letras.
<http://www.ces.uc.pt/publicacoes/outras/200313/rostos_invisiveis.pdf>

Novaes, Regina and Paulo Vannuchi, eds. 2004. *Juventude e sociedade: trabalho, educação, cultura e participação*. São Paulo: Instituto Cidadania, Editora Fundação Perseu Abramo.

Owensby, B. 2005. 'Toward a History of Brazil´s "Cordial Racism": Race beyond Liberalism.' *Comparative Studies in Society and History,* Vol. 47, No. 2, pp. 318–47. Cambridge University Press.
<http://journals.cambridge.org/download.php?file=%2FCSS%2FCSS47_02%2FS0010417505000150a.pdf&code=a550941418e433703f42f347c677729f>

Phebo, Luciana. 2005. 'The Impact of Firearms on Public Health in Brazil.' In Fernandes, 2005a, pp. 4–25.
<http://www.vivario.org.br/publique/media/The_Impact_of_Firearms_on_Public_Health_in_Brazil_By_Luciana_Phebo.pdf>

Ramos, Silvia and Julita Lemgruber. 2004. *Urban Violence, Public Safety Policies and Responses from Civil Society*. Social Watch Report.
<http://www.socialwatch.org/en/informesNacionales/408.html>

Ramos, Silvia and Leonarda Musumeci. 2006. *Elemento Suspeito: Abordagem political e discriminação na cidade do Rio de Janeiro*. Rio de Janeiro: Civilização Brasileira.

Reuters. 2006. 'Sao Paulo Gang Violence Death Toll Put at 187.' 27 May. <http://www.chinadaily.com.cn/world/2006-05/27/content_601750.htm>

Rivero, Patrícia S. 2005. 'The Value of the Illegal Firearms Market in the City of Rio de Janeiro.' In Fernandes, 2005a, pp. 146–201.
<http://www.vivario.org.br/publique/media/The_Value_of_the_Ilegal_Firearms_Market_in_the_City_os_Rio_de_Janeiro_by_Patricia_Rivero.pdf>

Skidmore, Thomas E. 1976. 'The Historiography of Brazil, 1889–1964, Part II.' *Hispanic American Historical Review,* Vol. 56, pp. 81–109.

Soares, Barbara Musumeci. 1996. 'Delegacia de atendimento à mulher: questão de gênero, número e grau.' In Luiz Eduardo Soares, 1996, pp. 107–23.

Soares, Gláucio A. Dilon. 2006. 'Whose Death Is It Anyway?' *Ciência & Saúde Coletiva,* Vol. 11, No. 2, pp. 273–75. April–June. Rio de Janeiro: Associação Brasileira de Pós-Graduação em Saúde Coletiva. <http://redalyc.uaemex.mx/redalyc/pdf/630/63011206.pdf>

Soares, Luiz Eduardo, ed. 1996. Violência e Política no Rio de Janeiro. Rio de Janeiro: ISER/Relume Dumará.

Waiselfisz, Julio Jacobo. 2006. *Mapa da Violência 2006: Os Jovens no Brasil*. Brasília: Organização dos Estados Ibero-americanos.

WHO (World Health Organization). 2002. *World Report on Violence and Health*. Geneva: WHO.
<http://whqlibdoc.who.int/hq/2002/9241545615.pdf>

Zaluar, Alba. 2000. 'Exclusion and Public Policies: Theoretical Dilemmas and Political Alternatives.' *Revista Brasileira de Ciências Socias,* No. 1.
<http://www.scielo.br/pdf/rbcsoc/nspe1/a03nesp1.pdf>

ACKNOWLEDGEMENTS

Principal authors

Rubem César Fernandes and Marcelo de Sousa Nascimento

Contributors

Jaison Cervi, Leonardo Costa, Miriam Costa, Pablo Dreyfus, Keila Lola, Julio Purcena, Patricia Rivero, Diego Solares, Alexis Teixeira, Nelson do Valle, and Christina Vital da Cunha

A Yemeni man sells AK-47 assault rifles outside his shop in a village in the Haraz Mountains, 2004. © Christian Gahre

What Price the Kalashnikov? 8

THE ECONOMICS OF SMALL ARMS

INTRODUCTION

Since its inception, the Small Arms Survey has compiled information on various aspects of small arms and light weapons, including total weapons numbers, the value of overall trade, and the specific impacts of weapons misuse. There is one indicator, however, that has not yet been systematically collected—price. Prices communicate information: they contain detail on valuation and scarcity. Since weapons are generally durable goods, there is an active secondary market that makes weapons prices observable. Documenting and analysing global price variations of a representative class of weapon (the Kalashnikov) can help identify key drivers of changes in the small arms market. By identifying factors that influence the market, policy-makers can better determine which policy instruments may be used to curb small arms proliferation.

Researchers and journalists have produced a significant amount of survey and case study work on the small arms trade. Insight can be provided by compiling this wealth of survey data—along with that garnered from close investigation of single cases—into a format suitable for statistical analysis. Drawing on archives of journalistic accounts and field reports, a dataset has been constructed that allows for a preliminary statistical analysis of a representative segment of the small arms market—that for Kalashnikov assault rifles.

Collecting and coding data on weapons prices across countries is not a simple task. Which exact weapon should be observed? What condition was the weapon in? Where was the weapon bought? Who was buying the weapon? These are some of the many issues involved with collecting price data. This chapter does not provide an exhaustive or definitive record of global weapons prices. Instead, it represents a first attempt at documenting Kalashnikov prices and offers a basis for further efforts to deepen our understanding of the small arms market.

In order to understand this market, it is necessary to view it as a function of the incentives and constraints faced by buyers, suppliers, and regulators. This chapter introduces a basic demand-and-supply model of the small arms market and then, using the model, applies statistical analysis to the newly compiled price data. As with other commodities, the trade in weapons responds to the forces of demand and supply. Although the trade in weapons is generally subject to official restrictions, trade on illicit markets is nevertheless flourishing. The demand side of the market is modelled by adapting the means and motivation framework of Brauer and Muggah (2006). On the supply side, the two key components are conceived as intrinsic supply costs and the regulatory costs of restricting trade.

In addition to using price data to examine the properties of the small arms market, the data can also be used to investigate the relationship between weapons and civil war. This chapter summarizes the results of including weapons price as a variable in models of civil war risk. The key findings of the chapter are:

- The more effective a country's regulations are, the higher weapons prices will be.
- Countries with more porous borders tend to have lower weapons prices. This is especially the case in Africa, where porous borders allow the supply of weapons to meet potential demand more readily.

- Contrary to popular perception, when controlling for other factors, the collapse of the Soviet Union does not appear to have had a significant impact on weapons prices.
- Increases in the military spending of neighbouring countries tend to reduce weapons prices in a particular country, apparently because of resulting proliferation.
- Weapons prices do not appear to be associated with homicide rates, economic downturns, or young male demographics.
- Cheaper weapons prices lead to an increased risk of civil war, independently of other conflict risk factors.
- Excess weapons in post-conflict environments keep prices low and contribute to the risk of conflict throughout the region for some time after the conflict has ended.

Cheaper weapons prices lead to an increased risk of civil war.

This initial compilation and analysis of price data is intended to provide a stimulus and framework for further quantitative research on small arms issues. Albeit imperfect, the existing dataset serves as a useful starting point for such efforts. The chapter begins by presenting this dataset, then introduces and applies a demand-and-supply model designed to tease out salient features of the small arms market. The chapter's last section explores the relationship of this market to the risk of conflict.

COLLECTING WEAPONS PRICE DATA

The subject of analysis: the Kalashnikov

Collecting price data across different countries and across time requires a consistent subject of analysis. In the case of small arms, there is a clear choice: the Kalashnikov assault rifle.[1] Of the estimated 875 million firearms worldwide (CIVILIAN FIREARMS), approximately 50–100 million belong to the Kalashnikov family (Small Arms Survey, 2004; Shilin and Cutshaw, 2000). The popularity of the Kalashnikov is accentuated by the view that it was often used to remove colonial rulers in Africa and Asia. Indeed, an image of the rifle still appears on the Mozambique national flag, and 'Kalash', an abbreviation of Kalashnikov, is a common boys' name in some African countries (Burrows, 2006, p. 11). The Kalashnikov as a weapon has been the subject of a number of book-length treatments by enthusiasts and critical observers, e.g. Long (1988) and Kahaner (2006).

The pervasiveness of this weapon may be explained in large part by its simplicity. The AK-47 was initially designed for ease of operation and repair by glove-wearing Soviet soldiers in arctic conditions. Its relatively small size and simplicity means that it can also be operated by child soldiers in the African desert. Kalashnikovs are a weapon of choice for armed forces and non-state actors alike. They are to be found in the arsenals of armed and special forces of more than 80 countries (Jane's Information Group, 2003). In practically every theatre of insurgency or guerrilla combat, a Kalashnikov will be found.

The Kalashnikov's ubiquity is generally attributed to its functional characteristics, ease of operation, robustness (i.e. ability to endure mistreatment), and negligible failure rate (Burrows, 2006, p. 3). The weapon's weaknesses—it is less accurate, less safe for users, and has a smaller range than equivalently calibrated weapons—are usually overlooked, or considered to be less important than the benefits of its simplicity and efficiency in other areas. Other assault rifles are almost as simple to manage, yet they have not experienced the soaring popularity of the Kalashnikov.

Figure 8.1 **Key members of the Kalashnikov family**

Illustration: Daly Design

Economic historians may answer this puzzle of popularity with reference to a concept called *path dependence,* which says that an equivalent or even inferior product can persist when a small but early advantage becomes large over time and builds up a legacy that makes switching costly (David, 1985). In the case of the AK-47, that early advantage was arguably that, as a Soviet innovation, it was not subject to copyright (LICENSED PRODUCTION). Furthermore, large caches of these weapons were readily distributed to regimes and rebels sympathetic to the Soviet Union, thereby giving the Kalashnikov a foothold advantage in the emerging post-Second World War market for assault rifles.

Whatever the exact causes, it remains a fact that for the last half-century the Kalashnikov has enjoyed a dominant role in the market for assault rifles. Since the essential characteristics of the original AK-47 are similar to the subsequent variants of the Kalashnikov, one can be reasonably confident that the prices observed across time and countries are determined predominantly by market conditions rather than fundamental changes in the nature of the product itself. The assumption of homogeneity in Kalashnikov derivatives for the purposes of statistical analysis may, of course, be challenged and is discussed in Box 8.1.

Data collection and sources

The Kalashnikov price data has been compiled from a range of field research, journalistic reports, and industry interviews. Prices are calculated in US dollars for Kalashnikov purchases made by non-governmental entities. Five-year intervals are used to track price variations over time: 1986–90, 1991–95, 1996–2000, and 2001–05. The coding of price observations for such things as location, weapon type, and source of observation reflects at least some of the large variation in the nature of the reported transactions and price quotes. There are, however, some important aspects that have not been coded, e.g. whether the observed transaction or price quote was between groups or individuals; or whether the status of the transaction was legal, covert, or illicit. A future, more complete dataset would account for these additional factors.

Box 8.1 Kalashnikov varieties: similarities and differences

There are in excess of 30 varieties of Kalashnikov assault rifle built around the original specification designed by Mikhail Kalashnikov in 1947.[2] The basic similarity among Kalashnikov-derived weapons is that they have a similar basic shape, as shown in Figure 8.1, with the distinctive banana-shaped clip for the ammunition. Other key characteristics of Kalashnikovs are that, within the assault rifle class, they are generally more compact in size, and have full capability for selective fire, smaller cartridges, and commensurately shorter ranges of fire (Poyer, 2004, p. 1).

The term AK-47 is often mistakenly used to describe Kalashnikovs in general, when in fact it is only one specific type. Even the AK-47 itself has a number of sub-types that reflect different production methods and weapons weights based on the types of materials used (Shilin and Cutshaw, 2000). Despite a series of modifications over the last 60 years, the basic AK-47 is still a popular weapon in its own right. A new Romanian-made AK-47 can be purchased online from Atlantic Firearms (2006) for USD 439.[3] A bulk contract of 1,000 or more Russian-made weapons can be purchased for approximately USD 180 each (Agentsvo Voyenkykh Novostey, 2005). Norinco Chinese-made Kalashnikov replicas sell from USD 600 online in the United States, while the estimated cost of producing an AK-47 replica in China stands at approximately USD 40 per unit.[4]

One misconception in explaining the popularity of Kalashnikovs is that it uses a common type of ammunition. In fact, Kalashnikov derivatives use different types of ammunition. The AK-47 and AKM fire the 7.62 x 39 mm cartridge, while the AK-74 fires the 5.45 x 39 mm cartridge. Subsequent AK versions (e.g. AK-101, AK-103) are chambered for various calibres, depending on which type of ammunition the purchaser can most readily access (Shilin and Cutshaw, 2000).

The dataset makes extensive use of the *Small Arms Black Market File Archive,* maintained by the Norwegian Initiative on Small Arms Transfers (NISAT, 2006). The *Archive* contains over 9,000 documents relating to illicit small arms trade. Articles with references to quoted prices or reported transactions involving AK-47 or equivalent Kalashnikov derivative assault rifles were extracted and the information converted into the data format using the coding rules outlined in Annexe 1.

References to assault rifle prices were also extracted from previous Small Arms Survey working papers, field reports, and yearbook chapters. In addition, the dataset benefitted from interviews with arms industry experts and regulators who have had considerable experience with arms markets throughout Africa and Asia. Of particular note is Brian Johnson Thomas, an investigative journalist with Amnesty International. Johnson Thomas has been following the illicit arms trade from factory to fight for the last 15 years and has recorded the going prices for assault rifles in a range of locations at different times. The frequency distribution of data sources for price observations is as follows: NISAT *Small Arms Black Market File Archive* (58 per cent); Small Arms Survey (17 per cent); US Bureau of Alcohol, Tobacco, Firearms and Explosives (16 per cent); Johnson Thomas (6 per cent); and other sources (3 per cent).

Summary of Kalashnikov price data

The full table of price data used in the statistical analysis is shown in Annexe 2. Table 8.1 summarizes the key features of this data. Country coverage is reasonably broad: 115 out of a possible 208 countries have at least one observation, and there are a total of 326 independent country-period observations (out of a possible 742[5]). Table 8.2 indicates that there are relatively more observations for more recent periods. For the first period, 1986–90, there are only 45 unique country observations, whereas for the fourth period, 2001–05, there are 100. This is probably due to more thorough information dissemination facilitated by the Internet, and the recent increase in attention given to the small arms trade by the media, activists, and policy-makers. There is also an uneven distribution of price observations across countries: there are relatively more weapons price observations for countries that have experienced civil war and countries situated in areas where a war has occurred.

Table 8.1 Descriptive statistics for Kalashnikov prices, 1986–2005

Region	Min. (USD)	Max. (USD)	Average (USD)	Std. dev. (USD)	No. of obs.	Unique countries	Total possible countries
Asia	40	6,000	631	810	81	27	48
Africa	12	500	156	95	80	24	47
Middle East	150	3,000	869	1,030	29	27	31
Former Soviet Union & Eastern Europe	50	1,200	303	189	55	20	42
Americas	25	2,400	520	367	47	6	26
Western Europe	225	1,500	927	960	34	11	14
	Lowest price = 12	Highest price = 6,000	Overall avg. = 471*	Overall std. dev. = 605	Total = 326	Total = 115	Grand total = 208

Notes:

Std. dev. = standard deviation.

obs. = observations.

* This is a weighted average: a region is weighted according to how many observations it has, and the figure given is the average for all the observations in the sample.

Table 8.2 Global average Kalashnikov price and number of observations, 1986–2005

Five-year period	1986–90	1991–95	1996–2000	2001–05
All countries	USD 402	USD 393	USD 538	USD 495
Observations per period	45	78	103	100

Figure 8.2 Regional Kalashnikov prices (USD), 1986–2005*

REGIONAL PRICES

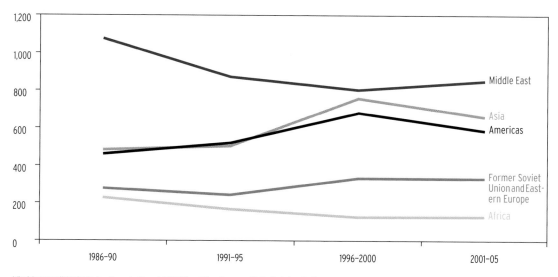

* No data was available for Western Europe for the period 1986-90, so this region was omitted entirely from the figure.

DEMAND AND SUPPLY IN THE SMALL ARMS MARKET

Constructing a model of the small arms market

Despite being a key component in violence and conflict, small arms have only recently begun to receive rigorous analytical attention. So far, research has been mostly case study-driven, making it difficult to draw general empirical lessons. By collecting cross-country time-series data on assault rifle prices and constructing an economic model to represent small arms demand and supply, it is possible to expose some of the quantitative features of the Kalashnikov market.

Since price in a market is modelled as a function of demand and supply, it is necessary to identify the key components of both these factors, and then evaluate how they can be measured with available data.[6] The key components of demand in the small arms market are conceived as income and preferences. Brauer and Muggah (2006) describe this in terms of *means* (income, or the ability to buy weapons) and *motivation* (the preference or desire to purchase weapons). It is possible that an individual or group may have the motivation to buy a weapon, but lacks the means with which to do so because either the available income is too low or weapons prices are too high. Conversely, one may have sufficient income to buy a weapon, but have no interest in owning one.

Map 8.1   **A selection of world Kalashnikov prices (USD), 2001–05**

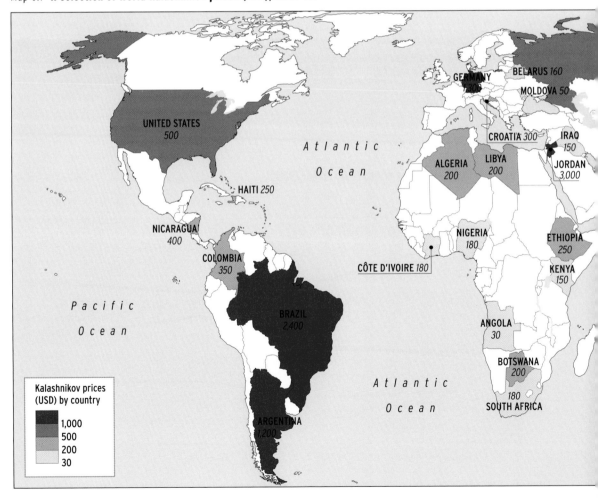

Box 8.2 Economic models and proxy variables

One of economists' main activities is to construct models that represent human choice and interaction. They do this by identifying key variables for a particular situation and hypothesizing a set of logical and quantitative relationships. The most popular economic model is that of demand and supply, which for the present study provides a useful 'off-the-shelf' toolkit to investigate empirically the key determinants of prices for Kalashnikov assault rifles.

Once an economic model is constructed, it needs to be brought to life and tested with data. Often the variables that the model would most likely include cannot be measured directly. In such cases, it may be helpful to use a proxy variable. A proxy variable is a substitute for an underlying reality that cannot be accessed directly. These are legitimate and commonly used modelling tools, provided they map onto the underlying reality in some significant sense. Among other things, this means that any 'errors' (deviations of the proxy from reality) are randomly, not systematically, distributed. Although proxy variables will not be an exact match for the underlying concept, it is usually better to attempt some approximate measure of the concept than omit it from the analysis. Examples found in the chapter include negative income growth as a proxy for the motivation to buy weapons, and the distance from Moscow as a proxy for transport costs.

Glatz and Muggah (2006, p. 150) conceptually unpack weapons demand in considerable detail and propose policy responses to address each sub-component of demand, identifying factors such as personal, social, and economic security, as well as individual and group status. While it is not possible to statistically test each of the concepts individually, certain variables can be used to proxy the major components of the weapons demand model. Table 8.3 notes the observable variables used to proxy each component. The concept of means is proxied by per capita income, and possible proxies for motivation to buy weapons include the average homicide rate, the proportion of young men in the population, lagged income growth, and a civil conflict onset.

On the supply side of the small arms market, the key elements are considered intrinsic supply costs and regulatory costs. Proxy variables intended to capture the height of the regulatory barriers to weapons trade include quantitative measures of government effectiveness, degree of law and order, democratic accountability, and border porousness. Indicators to capture the intrinsic costs involved with supplying weapons include levels of military expenditure and the distance from Moscow to proxy transport costs.

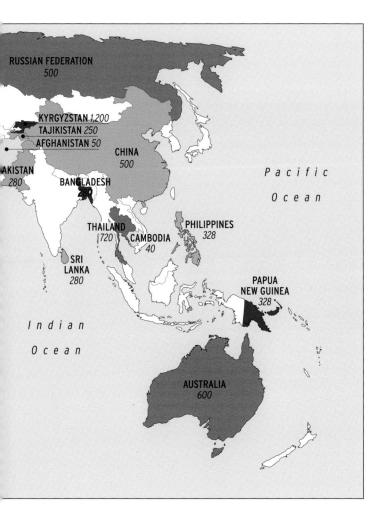

Box 8.3 A single market or many?

Analysing the small-arms market is more complicated than studying conventional, legal markets. Unlike markets for commodities such as oil or gold, where headline market-clearing global prices are available, the market for weapons is considerably more segmented. Does it make any sense therefore to refer to a single small-arms market? Even though a market may be separated by geography or legislative systems, it is seldom possible for a single country's market to be completely isolated from the rest of the world. Trucks, ships, and planes can transport weapons from one country to another and readily overcome geographic boundaries. In the case of illicitly traded weapons, legislation prohibiting weapons trade may simply be viewed as a hurdle to be cleared rather than an impassable obstruction that prevents trade entirely. For these reasons, the singular use of the term 'small-arms market' is generally used, even though on the face of it trade in small arms appears to be made up of hundreds of local markets. In empirically analysing the trade in small arms, one of the key features of interest is what connects these sub-markets. The price data in Annexe 2 shows how localized and variable these sub-markets are, while the statistical analysis (the results of which are given in Annexe 4) aids in identifying which factors drive changes in these local sub-markets and which factors facilitate or impede interaction among them.

Using this basic demand-and-supply model of weapons price determination, it is possible to ascertain which factors are relatively more important in explaining changes in the small arms market. The variables used in the statistical analysis, their expected signs, and statistical significance are summarized in Table 8.3. Annexe 4 outlines the formal results, and Annexe 3 presents the descriptive statistics for all the variables used in the analysis.

The statistical method used to analyse the data is panel regression.[7] Panel regression uses data over time and across countries to explain variation in an observed variable, in this case weapons prices. In the small arms market

Table 8.3 Variables for estimating weapons price determinants

Component	Observable proxy measure	Expected sign	Significance
Income/means	GDP per capita	+	*
Motivation	Lagged income growth	–	
	Prop. of young men in pop.	+	
	Civil war onset	+	
	Homicide rate	+	
Regulatory	Government effectiveness	+	***
	Democratic accountability	+	*
	Law and order	+	
	Border porousness	–	***
Supply costs	Military expenditure–neighbours'	–	***
	Military expenditure–own	–	
	Civil war legacy	–	**
	Post-Soviet collapse	–	
	Transport costs	+	**

Notes:
GDP = gross domestic product.
* Statistically significant at 90 per cent. ** Statistically significant at 95 per cent. *** Statistically significant at 99 per cent.
Those factors unmarked in the 'Significance' column are not statistically significant.

model, it is hypothesized that weapons prices are associated with certain empirical variables reflecting demand and supply factors. If a variable is good at explaining a variation in weapons prices, it is said to be significant. A statistical significance of 90 per cent, for example, means that there is a 90 per cent probability of the weapons price being affected by a change in the explanatory variable, and a 10 per cent chance that there will be no effect at all. The expected sign refers to whether it is initially believed that the weapons prices are positively or negatively associated with a particular variable.[8]

Results for each component

Income

One would expect that the higher income is in terms of per capita GDP, the higher weapons prices will be. This is due to two factors: firstly, that higher income implies a higher ability, or means, to pay for a weapon; and secondly, because official trade barriers lead to the partial non-tradability of weapons. According to international trade models, free trade will tend to equalize commodity prices (Markusen et al., 1995, pp. 36–44). However, non-government weapons trade between countries is subject to considerable regulatory hurdles. It is much more difficult to buy a Kalashnikov from overseas than it is to order a shipment of television sets, for example. To the extent that laws controlling weapons trading are enforced, weapons will take on the attributes of non-tradable goods. In economics, it has been found that the prices of non-tradable goods are determined by domestic factor prices, which are driven by income. In the same way that non-tradable goods such as haircuts are more expensive in London than Nairobi, the level of income reflects a wealth mark-up (or mark-down) on weapons prices.

Motivation

Obtaining a satisfactory proxy for the motivation to purchase assault rifles is a difficult task. None of the proxy variables for motivation used in the regression analysis demonstrate a statistically significant relationship with weapons prices. In the first instance, income growth was tested as an indirect measure of the desire to buy weapons. Negative income growth has been found to increase the risk that a country will face an outbreak of civil war (Collier and Hoeffler, 2004; Miguel, Satyanath, and Sergenti, 2004). It has also been found to increase the incidence of violent crime (Fajnzylber, Lederman, and Loayza, 2002). One would expect negative income shocks to lead to an increased motivation to purchase weapons for the purpose of crime or conflict, since weapons are instrumental in undertaking these activities, which have been shown to be more likely to occur in economic downturns.

The fact that there appears to be no relationship between income shocks and weapons prices may be the result of competing effects in the small arms market during economic downturns. While the increased demand for weapons for crime and conflict would tend to drive weapons prices up, there is also an offsetting supply-side effect. Agents on the margin of the legal labour market become unemployed in an economic downturn, and a fraction of those unemployed take on employment in the black market, including the arms trade, which is profitable compared with no work at all. The extra (illicit) employment in the arms trade creates a more competitive arms market and the increase in supply appears to offset the increase in demand. On the basis of these statistical results, it may be hypothesized that the illicit weapons market adapts extremely well to changes in economic conditions, so that the effect of economic shocks on weapons prices is neutralized.

Other variables were tested in an effort to capture the motivation to purchase weapons, such as the proportion of young men in the population, and the average homicide rate as an approximate measure for a country's underlying proclivity towards violence.[9]

Negative income growth can increase the risk of civil war and violent crime.

Another hypothesized driver of the motivation to purchase assault rifles is civil conflict, which is the setting where such weapons are most likely to be used for their intended purpose. A variable for civil war is included to proxy demand for weapons.[10] The civil war variable was not significant, so it is not possible to identify a clear demand effect on weapons prices during a period of civil conflict,[11] even though one would expect a civil conflict to increase the demand for weapons. As in the case of income shocks, there is the problem that in trying to identify the demand-side effect of civil conflict, there are countervailing supply-side effects that reduce the price, offsetting the upward pressure of demand.

In this preliminary analysis, all proxy measures for motivation proved insignificant for explaining weapons prices. This is not to conclude that motivation is unimportant in determining weapons prices. Rather, it indicates that more refined measures of the preferences for purchasing weapons are required.

Regulatory costs

Most countries have at least some laws designed to control the trade in and possession of small arms. What differs systematically is the ability of countries to enforce these laws. One would expect that the more effective a government is at upholding its laws, the greater will be the cost of traded weapons, legal or otherwise. Regulatory variables are used to capture the effective height of the trade barriers that must be overcome in order to sell a weapon.

Better enforcement of laws and regulations raises the price of weapons.

A number of measures of regulatory effectiveness are employed, and all indicate with varying degrees of significance that better enforcement of laws and regulations raises the price of weapons. The World Bank's government effectiveness variable, which measures the competence of each country's bureaucracy, is positive and significantly correlated with weapons prices.[12] Data from the *International Country Risk Guide* (ICRG) (Political Risk Services Group, 2005) confirms the importance of regulatory capacity as a determinant of weapons price. Democratic accountability measures from the ICRG are statistically significant, suggesting that checks on different levels of government and public services are important in enforcing legislation relating to illicit weapons.

The ICRG's law and order variable is intended to proxy the on-the-ground ability of the police to enforce the law and prosecute weapons violations. This variable was correlated positively with weapons prices, but not as strongly as expected. This may be explained by an offsetting demand effect at very low levels of law and order. Households and groups are acutely aware of internal security forces being ineffective and may attempt to fill a security vacuum with their own weapons acquisition.

The regulatory costs variables are principally concerned with the effective height of the trade barriers that need to be overcome in order to trade a Kalashnikov. The regulatory variables considered so far account for the relative ease of *within*-country trade for weapons. Arguably, though, *between*-country trade barriers are at least as important. The ideal measure of between-country barriers would be some measure of the porousness of a country's borders. Since no data on border porousness currently exists, it is proposed to use a control variable for African countries. Africa provides a natural reference point, because its countries possess more neighbours on average than the rest of the world (3.4 per country versus 2.1), and its borders are generally perceived as being more porous than the rest of the world (CIA, 2005).[13]

Even controlling for income, regulatory effectiveness, war legacy, and supply cost variables, being located in an African country makes purchasing an assault rifle around USD 200 cheaper than the world average. It is postulated that this staggering Africa discount on top of the variables already mentioned is driven predominantly by porous borders. Since its borders are more porous than elsewhere, the trade in assault rifles across the African continent approaches a deregulated market in which prices converge, and there are only negligible trade barriers that arms supply must overcome to meet demand. The demand profile for weapons across the African continent changes over time with changes in military/insurgency activity, as localized tensions rise and recede. Relatively more porous borders enable larger supplies of weapons to meet whichever countries currently have high weapons demand, thereby tending to smooth and lower prices.

Intrinsic supply costs

The intrinsic supply costs variable in the model of the small arms market is designed to capture the non-regulatory costs associated with the supply of arms. A range of proxy variables are used to represent the key factors that affect supply costs.

The supply cost variable that proves most robust is neighbours' average military expenditure. This variable measures the average of neighbouring countries' annual government military expenditure as a share of GDP. It is intended to capture the relative availability of foreign sources of weapons. The statistical analysis indicates a strong negative correlation between neighbours' average military expenditure and weapons prices. This effect is theorized to be caused by weapons finding their way into circulation via spillovers and leakages.

Spillovers arise where some fraction of a country's military expenditure is allocated (covertly or otherwise) to supplying arms directly to anti-government forces in rival neighbouring countries. The exact reasons for governments supplying foreign rebel forces are not considered here, but one may conjecture that such supply involves strategic decisions designed to destabilize or divert the attention of a threatening neighbour's regime. The leakage effect arises not from a conscious effort by neighbours, but from misappropriation of official weapons stocks by arms dealers and rebels. Such acquisition is typically facilitated by unauthorized sales by defence force personnel (corruption) or the forcible seizure of weapons stocks during combat or raids on government arsenals.

Own-country military expenditure was not a satisfactory explanator of weapons price. This is surprising, as some governments deliberately distribute weapons to their own people to defend the country against hostile neighbours. Governments sometimes also provide weapons to loyal militias to ward off domestic anti-government rebels, as did the Sri Lankan government during the Indian Peace Keeping Force's conflict with the main Tamil rebel group, the Liberation Tigers of Tamil Eelam, from 1987 to 1989 (Narayan Swamy, 2002). Furthermore, there are numerous instances of forcible seizures and looting of domestic inventories, including the notorious cases of Albania in March 1997 (*Economist*, 1997a) and more recently in Iraq (Small Arms Survey, 2004, pp. 44–50; Human Rights Watch, 2004).

> A country's civil war legacy is strongly correlated with weapons prices.

The supply cost variable, which seeks to proxy the stock of weapons in circulation, is a country's civil war legacy. The legacy variable is constructed using population-weighted cumulative civil war battle deaths since 1960 (Gleditsch et al., 2002). Since small arms cause a significant proportion of battle deaths, their number may be considered a suitable proxy for the quantity of functioning weapons in a country. A discount rate of 5 per cent is applied to reflect the fact that a war 30 years ago, for example, matters proportionately less for the stock of Kalashnikovs on the ground than an equivalent-sized battle last year. This discount rate captures the depreciation of Kalashnikovs over time and is consistent with a weapon's life expectancy of up to 50 years. The civil war legacy variable is population-weighted to account for the residual stock of conflict weapons relative to the population size.

As an approximation of the number of active weapons in circulation, the civil war legacy variable is reasonably robust. The analysis indicates that civil war legacy is strongly correlated with weapons prices. This conforms with basic price theory, which predicts that, all else being equal, the relatively more plentiful a commodity is, the cheaper it will be.

The arms dealer Yuri Orlov (Nicolas Cage) presents an assault rifle to a client in Lord of War.
© Lions Gate Films/ZUMA Press/supplied by eyevine

It is commonly believed that the collapse of the Soviet Union released enormous stocks of weapons, especially Kalashnikovs, onto the world market. This view has been popularized in a recent Hollywood film, *Lord of War*, in which Nicholas Cage plays a Ukrainian arms dealer who profitably liquidates the former Soviet state's military arsenal. Was the collapse of the Soviet Union a significant supply shock for price levels in the illicit weapons market? Statistical analysis suggests that it was not; or, at the very least, that it was not as important as previously believed (e.g. Musah and Castle, 1998). When controlling for other factors (such as changes in government effectiveness, income, etc.), correlation with the post-Soviet collapse period (1991–95) is not significant.[14]

An explanation for this finding is to be found in the role of secondary markets. Since weapons are durable goods, they can, like shares in a firm, be repeatedly sold from agent to agent. During the cold war, even though the superpowers thought they were giving or selling weapons to their political allies, their weapons were regularly—and profitably—sold on to secondary markets that had no regard for the political affiliation of the initial source of the weapon. There is no reason, in other words, to assume that the end of the cold war yielded a sudden change in

patterns of weapons diffusion and proliferation. Two caveats to the finding of insignificance in relation to the Soviet collapse must be acknowledged. Firstly, there is only one observation period (1986–90) before the Soviet collapse. Secondly, there are only 45 observations for this pre-collapse period, whereas there are more than 78 for each of the three subsequent periods.

While the collapse of the Soviet Union did not in itself appear to generate a significant supply shock for the small arms market, the supply of weapons by the Soviet Union

Harbingers of the end of the cold war: Berliners sing and dance on top of the Berlin Wall to celebrate the opening of East–West German border in November 1989.
© Thomas Kienzle/AP Photo

and its successor states, throughout the period under examination, does appear influential. The distance a country is from Moscow is adopted as a proxy for the transport costs of getting weapons (in this case the Kalashnikov) from their initial sources in Russia and the Soviet satellite states to the secondary markets on which they are traded.[15] The distance from Moscow variable (Gleditsch and Ward, 2001) is positively correlated with weapons prices, indicating that transport costs do indeed matter in determining the price of weapons.[16]

CHEAP GUNS, MORE WAR?

In low- to medium-intensity modern civil conflict, assault rifles are an indispensable piece of military equipment. Kalashnikov assault rifle prices may therefore be considered a proxy for the costs of acquiring weapons linked to civil war.

An important empirical question, then, is whether the availability of small arms, as proxied by Kalashnikov prices, increases the probability of civil war. Existing quantitative approaches to explain conflict risk (Collier and Hoeffler, 2004; Fearon and Laitin, 2003) have adopted proxies for labour (the level and growth of work-related income, which measure the opportunity cost of belonging to a rebel group) and capital (lootable resources and diaspora funding, which provide operating finance). Adding a measure of the conflict-specific capital input (Kalashnikov prices) may aid the explanatory power of statistical conflict models.

Including weapons price in a modified Collier-Hoeffler (2004) conflict risk model[17] indicates that lower weapons prices are associated with a higher risk of civil war, independently of other known quantitative determinants of civil conflict.[18] A natural question that arises with this result is whether cheap weapons are a cause or consequence of civil conflict; i.e. are weapons cheaper in war-affected countries because of the war, or was conflict made more feasible in part due to relatively cheaper weapons? Various statistical techniques have been used to isolate the specific effect of weapons prices on conflict risk. The application of these methods is outlined in detail in Killicoat (2006). They do not alter the finding outlined above. In as far as it is possible to demonstrate statistically, holding all else constant, the relatively lower weapons prices are, the relatively more at risk a country is of engaging in civil conflict.[19]

The general robustness of the result permits evaluation of the average marginal effects of weapons prices on conflict. Controlling for other factors, if the average world price of weapons were to rise by 10 per cent, the risk of civil conflict would fall by approximately 0.5 per cent.[20] Of course, this effect is not equally distributed across all countries. In some regions, the marginal effect of cheaper weapons will be more likely to influence the susceptibility of a country to civil conflict, depending on the prevailing conditions and other risk factors.

Box 8.5   The market for Kalashnikovs in Iraq

As explained above, lower Kalashnikov prices result in a higher risk of civil war, independently of other risk factors. Once a war has begun, however, the relationship between weapons prices and the intensity and duration of conflict takes on a different dynamic. In African conflicts, weapons prices have tended to rise in the early stages of a civil conflict and then fall over time as supply chains are established (Austin, 1999, pp. 29–48). In Iraq, Kalashnikov prices have been consistently rising over the last three years (Chivers, 2006).

Prior to the coalition offensive in 2003, Kalashnikovs were trading for between USD 80 and USD 150. After the Baathist defence forces were routed in 2003, prices fell to USD 50–80. This is largely because stockpiles of weapons were seized by enterprising would-be arms traders. Caches of Kalashnikovs had been left around the country to give citizens something with which to challenge the incoming coalition forces. These weapons were not used for their intended purpose, but rather were hoarded and then sold. Since 2003, weapons prices have been steadily rising to quite extraordinary levels. A basic wooden stock AK-47 was selling in 2006 for USD 400–800. Short-barrelled folding-stock Kalashnikovs (the preferred model of Osama bin Laden[21]) are attracting premium prices of USD 700–1,500 (Chivers, 2006).[22]

The high and rising prices of Kalashnikovs indicate that demand is exceeding supply. Generally, people want to buy Kalashnikovs for security, crime, or conflict. In Iraq, they are being bought for all three reasons, and so prices are at atypically high levels, even for a war zone. If and when the coalition forces leave, prices are likely to fall. Foreign military control is the only thing currently keeping supply by neighbouring countries from fully meeting the Iraqis' strong demand for assault rifles.

The price of a Kalashnikov has similar properties to stock/shares in a company—the price says a lot about expectations of future value. That prices are high and rising in Iraq indicates that Iraqis on the ground are preparing for a long period of conflict and uncertainty.

Phillip Killicoat and C. J. Chivers

An interesting result from the statistical analysis of weapons price determination is that a war in a country does not appear to affect significantly the price of weapons in that particular period. In fact, weapons prices on average rise in the first period of conflict onset. Once the conflict episode is over, however, weapons prices on average fall. Weapons in the post-conflict period have both a temporal and a spatial effect. The surplus of weapons in circulation keeps prices low and availability high throughout the neighbouring region for some time after the end of conflict.

CONCLUSIONS AND FUTURE DIRECTIONS

Tracking Kalashnikov prices has the potential to provide a useful step towards better understanding the small arms market. By documenting prices of a representative class of weapon across countries and time, it is possible to investigate which factors are significant in determining weapons price variation. Price data is difficult to collect, and a number of caveats to the consistency of the observed prices must be recognized. While it would be desirable to observe exactly the same weapon type, in the same condition, transacted between similar individuals, such detailed price reports remain elusive. While acknowledging the limitations of the sample data, it is nevertheless possible to undertake preliminary statistical analysis of this first effort to document cross-country time-series Kalashnikov price data.

A basic demand-and-supply model of the small arms market was developed above and was theorized to be determined by four main factors: income (means), motivation, regulation, and supply costs. Estimating this model using the new price data and proxies for the relevant concepts yielded results that suggest that supply-side factors such as regulatory effectiveness, transport costs, and border porousness are most important in the determination of weapons prices. Since the analysis is at the aggregate macro level, the policy implications of these findings are necessarily general in nature, for example:

- Increasing regulatory effectiveness raises the barriers to trading weapons. It may also reduce the motivation to purchase weapons for purposes of personal or group security.
- Securing national borders is a generally desirable policy objective for governments, and is especially compelling in the case of illicit small arms trade.
- Neighbours' military expenditure was found strongly to reduce weapons prices; therefore, where mutual disarmament is feasible, it will diminish at least one channel of weapons supply.

Economic development and government effectiveness reduce the risk of civil war directly.

Although motivational variables on the demand side of the model did not prove statistically significant, this does not necessarily mean that they are unimportant for weapons price determination. This is more likely due to the absence of suitable proxy measures to capture appropriately the motivational component of demand for small arms.

Including weapons prices in statistical conflict models indicated that cheaper weapons are independently associated with an increased risk of civil conflict. To this end, there are a number of general policy measures that would increase the price of weapons and thereby mitigate the effect of weapons availability on conflict outbreak. In particular, economic development and government effectiveness reduce the risk of civil war directly, and also indirectly, by raising the regulatory barriers to illicit trade in small arms.

The statistical analysis of the small arms market and conflict risk described in this chapter relies on the sample data collected being broadly representative of underlying 'true' prices. While every effort has been made to adopt a consistent measure of Kalashnikov prices across countries and time, there are a number of factors that are difficult to account for explicitly. Such factors include the exact Kalashnikov type, the precise location of the transaction, the nature of the trading parties, and their financing methods.

This initial price data collection effort and statistical analysis are intended to provide a stimulus and framework for quantitative and rational choice approaches to small arms issues. The field of small arms research has produced a sizeable quantity of case-specific data. Compiling this growing wealth of information into a format amenable to statistical analysis has the potential to provide insights in addition to those garnered from close investigation of single cases.

Collecting data on small arms is a slow, ongoing process, but the cumulative effect will be to provide a more robust understanding of the relative importance of different factors in the small arms market. The information that will be of most benefit for understanding the small arms market are weapons prices, ammunition prices, trading quantities, stockpile quantities, and production quantities. The Small Arms Survey has begun to compile some of this information. Quantitative analysis of such data can enhance the effectiveness of national and multilateral small arms policy, identifying with greater precision the most effective means of preventing unnecessary suffering from these weapons. ◾

ANNEXE 1. DATA COLLECTION METHODOLOGY

In order to maintain consistency, the exact variable of interest is the quoted or transacted price in US dollars (USD) for a non-government entity to take possession of an AK-47 assault rifle. Each price observation was coded with:

- country;
- USD price;
- time period (1986–90, 1991–95, 1996–2000, 2001–05);
- exact assault rifle type observed (e.g. AK-47, AK-74, craft replica);
- location where price was quoted (city, province, border, international transaction);
- quality of the weapon: new, used, or in need of repair; and
- source of the price observation.

Sufficiently reliable indicators for the last four of these factors were not available to justify their inclusion in the statistical analysis, so only the first three points were included (see Annexe 2). Where there are multiple price observations for the same country-period, a set of coding rules is employed to determine which observation appears in the dataset for analysis. All observations are nevertheless kept in a master dataset. The coding rule dictates that a quote or transaction involving an AK-47 in good condition observed in a city will take precedence over other observations.

The majority of prices were originally reported in USD. Where prices were observed in the local currency, the price was converted to USD at the prevailing exchange rate at the time of the quoted price or transaction (World Bank, n.d.). To control for inflation in the statistical analysis, weapons prices are deflated using the US consumer price index (World Bank, n.d.).

Region coding:

1 = Asia

2 = Africa

3 = Former Soviet Union and Eastern Europe

4 = Americas

5 = Western Europe

6 = Middle East

ANNEXE 2. AVAILABLE KALASHNIKOV PRICES FOR SPECIFIC COUNTRIES AND PERIODS

For region codes, see Annexe 1. Figures for the four periods are in USD.

Country	Region	1986–90	1991–95	1996–2000	2001–05
Afghanistan	1	80	100	100	150
Albania	3	300	50	150	180
Algeria	2	400	400	300	200
American Samoa	1				
Andorra	5				
Angola	2	150	12	30	30
Antigua and Barbuda	4	609			
Argentina	4	800	700	1,000	1,200
Armenia	3				
Aruba	4				
Australia	1	500	500	550	600
Austria	5				
Azerbaijan	3				
Bahamas, The	4				
Bahrain	6				
Bangladesh	1		982	1,080	1,200
Barbados	4				
Belarus	3	150	250	140	160
Belgium	5			1,200	1,500
Belize	4				
Benin	2				
Bermuda	4				
Bhutan	1				
Bolivia	4			1,000	
Bosnia and Herzegovina	3		350	400	500
Botswana	2	200	250	200	200
Brazil	4		1,350	2,000	2,400
Brunei	1	1,200	1,200	1,500	1,500
Bulgaria	3		200	300	

Burkina Faso	2			
Burundi	2			
Cambodia	1	200	250	40
Cameroon	2			
Canada	4		800	880
Cape Verde	2			
Cayman Islands	4			
Central African Republic	2		35	150
Chad	2			
Channel Islands	5			
Chile	4		1,000	
China	1	450	400	350
Colombia	4	609	800	350	400
Comoros	2			
Congo, Democratic Republic of	2	200	215	120	50
Congo, Republic of the	2	200	180	120	50
Costa Rica	3		400	400
Côte d'Ivoire	2	180	100	100	120
Croatia	3	330	180	250	300
Cuba	4	120	100	150	180
Cyprus	3	200	300	320
Czech Republic	3	200	300	360
Denmark	5			
Djibouti	2			
Dominica	4			
Dominican Republic	4			
Ecuador	4	600		
Egypt	1	400	400	300	300
El Salvador	4		400	400
Equatorial Guinea	2			
Eritrea	1		220	250
Estonia	3	300	150	180

Ethiopia	1			220	250
Faeroe Islands	5				
Fiji	1				
Finland	5				
France	5				
French Polynesia	1				
Gabon	1				
Gambia, The	1				
Georgia	3	150	135		250
Germany	5			1,400	1,300
Ghana	1			100	120
Greece	1		180	260	400
Greenland	5				
Grenada	4	120	100	150	180
Guam	1				
Guatemala	4				
Guinea	2				
Guinea-Bissau	2				
Guyana	4				
Haiti	4		250	250	250
Honduras	4		25	200	200
Hong Kong, China	1	400	400	450	
Hungary	3		200	300	
Iceland	5				
India	1		982	1,080	1,200
Indonesia	1			228	250
Iran	6		225	250	200
Iraq	6	300	250	250	150
Ireland	5				
Isle of Man	5				
Israel	6	2,500	3,000	2,800	3,000
Italy	5				

Jamaica	4				
Japan	1			6,000	
Jordan	6	1,000	1,000	2,500	3,000
Kazakhstan	3				
Kenya	2	500	100	200	150
Kiribati	1				
Korea, North	1		250	300	320
Korea, South	1		600	400	400
Kuwait	6				
Kyrgyz Republic	3	400	500	1,000	1,200
Lao PDR	1		200	250	300
Latvia	3		150	150	180
Lebanon	6	500	500	500	700
Lesotho	2	100	100	100	100
Liberia	2	100	100	100	45
Libya	2				250
Liechtenstein	5				
Lithuania	3		150	150	180
Luxembourg	5				
Macao, China	3				
Macedonia, FYR	3		300	250	350
Madagascar	2				
Malawi	2		50	60	60
Malaysia	1				
Maldives	1				
Mali	2				
Malta	5				
Marshall Islands	4				
Mauritania	2				
Mauritius	2				
Mayotte	2				
Mexico	4	400	400	400	450

Micronesia, Federated States of	1				
Moldova	3				50
Monaco	5				
Mongolia	1				
Morocco	2				
Mozambique	2	160	60	15	30
Myanmar	1		200	250	
Namibia	2				250
Nepal	1				
Netherlands	5			1,200	1,500
Netherlands Antilles	4				
New Caledonia	1				
New Zealand	1				
Nicaragua	4		700	350	400
Niger	2				150
Nigeria	2			150	180
Northern Mariana Islands	1				
Norway	5				
Oman	6			185	320
Pakistan	1	120	200	200	280
Palau	1				
Panama	4	609	700	400	400
Papua New Guinea	1		1,600	1,800	2,400
Paraguay	4			1,000	
Peru	4		600	1,000	
Philippines	1	250	300	300	328
Poland	3		248	436	
Portugal	5		600		
Puerto Rico	4				
Qatar	6				
Romania	3	120	180	260	300
Russian Federation	3		300	450	500

Rwanda	2				
Samoa	1				
San Marino	5				
São Tomé and Principe	4				
Saudi Arabia	6			220	280
Senegal	2				
Serbia and Montenegro	3		180	250	300
Seychelles	2				
Sierra Leone	2	270	150	120	100
Singapore	1	1,200	1,200	1,500	1,500
Slovak Republic	3			400	500
Slovenia	3		180	250	300
Solomon Islands	1			1,800	2,400
Somalia	2	165	200	120	160
South Africa	2	160	200	195	180
Spain	5		600	225	
Sri Lanka	1		200	250	280
St. Kitts and Nevis	4				
St. Lucia	4				
St. Vincent and the Grenadines	4				
Sudan	2	150	150	100	86
Suriname	4				
Swaziland	2				
Sweden	5				
Switzerland	5				
Syrian Arab Republic	6				200
Tajikistan	3	500	600	300	250
Tanzania	2			200	200
Thailand	1		200	400	720
Timor-Leste	1				
Togo	2				
Tonga	1				

Trinidad and Tobago	4			
Tunisia	2			
Turkey	3		900	
Turkmenistan	3			250
Uganda	2	500	200	100	86
Ukraine	3		250	300	350
United Arab Emirates	6		250	300	320
United Kingdom	5			1,200	1,500
United States	4	420	450	480	500
Uruguay	4			1,000	
Uzbekistan	3			250	250
Vanuatu	1				
Venezuela, RB	4			1,000	360
Vietnam	1	180	200	250	300
Virgin Islands (US)	4				
Yemen	6			185	320
Zambia	2	200	250	80	80
Zimbabwe	2	200	250	200	150

Source: World Bank (2005)

ANNEXE 3. DESCRIPTIVE SUMMARY STATISTICS

Variable	No. of obs.	Mean	Std. dev.	Min.	Max.
Weapon price (current USD)	334	511.36	660.84	12	6,000
Weapon price (current USD)$_{t-1}$	234	494.57	651.07	12	6,000
Weapon price (constant 2000 USD)	334	515.3	662.37	12.38	6,000
War start (UCDP/PRIO)	770	0.06	0.24	0	1
GDP per capita (PPP 2000 USD)	668	8,360.66	8,646.46	499.82	60,536
GDP per capita (constant 2000 USD)	711	5,492.38	8,143.59	80.32	46,191
GDP per capita growth	706	1.41	5.28	-43.7	32.9
Military expenditure (% of GDP)	547	3.24	3.94	0	44.66
Neighbours' avg. mil. exp.	536	3.48	3.21	0	22.61
Post-Soviet collapse period	824	0.25	0.43	0	1
Ln population*	785	15.21	2.12	9.9	20.97
Africa	824	0.22	0.41	0	1
Civil war legacy	785	538.6	1,836.66	0	20,672
Government effectiveness	808	0.03	0.97	-2.32	2.43
Ln distance from Moscow*	692	8.44	0.8	4.3	9.71
Law and order	522	3.75	1.46	0.57	6
Democratic accountability	522	3.6	1.61	0	6
Young men (15–29% of population)	744	0.13	0.02	0.09	0.23
Homicide rate (per 100,000 deaths)	504	8.11	10.72	0.3	63.36

Notes:

* Ln = natural log: a tool to scale down magnitudes without losing data relativity.

UCDP = Uppsala Conflict Data Project.

PRIO = International Peace Research Institute of Oslo.

PPP = purchasing power parity.

ANNEXE 4. RESULTS OF WEAPONS PRICE REGRESSION

Annexe 4 considers a variety of model specifications, with each column corresponding to a different version of the model. Variables are included according to their significance.

Part 1

	1	2	3	4	5	6	7	8
GDP per capita (PPP 2000 USD)	0.003	0.004	0.004	0.01		0.01	0.01	0.01
	[0.01]	[0.01]	[0.01]	[0.01]		[0.01]	[0.01]*	[0.01]*
Neighbours' avg. mil. exp.	-36.55	-29.71	-30.24	-31.87	-29.55	-28.32	-27.28	-31.75
	[12.35]***	[12.54]**	[10.81]***	[10.93]***	[9.01]***	[10.89]***	[12.98]**	[13.55]**
Government effectiveness	215.83	176.17	173.12		135.59	173.4		
	[59.62]***	[61.89]***	[60.67]***		[56.08]**	[60.66]***		
GDP per capita growth, t-1	0.25	0.74						
	[2.86]	[2.97]						
Civil war legacy		-0.03	-0.02	-0.03	-0.03	-0.03	-0.05	-0.05
		[0.02]*	[0.01]*	[0.01]**	[0.01]**	[0.01]**	[0.02]*	[0.02]*
Africa (dummy)		-292.5	-293.87	-394.04	-356.95	-302.34	-332.79	-364.85
		[122.54]**	[120.93]**	[120.78]***	[113.85]***	[121.06]**	[136.46]**	[139.41]***
Ln distance from Moscow[a]		124.05	125.45	129.76	112.53	125.16	134.17	130.08
		[62.66]**	[61.54]**	[64.20]**	[53.57]**	[61.52]**	[68.80]*	[71.45]*
Law and order								2.98
								[25.88]
Democratic accountability							33.9	
							[19.32]*	
Post-Soviet collapse period						-41.42		
						[30.15]		
No. of observations	222	212	228	228	265	228	187	187
No. of countries	85	81	81	81	94	81	69	69
R^2	0.08	0.18	0.17	0.18	0.10	0.17	0.18	0.11

Notes:
Standard errors appear in square brackets. All regressions contain a constant.
* Statistically significant at 90 per cent. ** Statistically significant at 95 per cent. *** Statistically significant at 99 per cent.
[a] Ln = natural log: a tool to scale down magnitudes without losing data relativity.

Part 2

	9	10	11	12	13	14	15	16
GDP per capita (PPP 2000 USD)	0.01	0.01	0.01	0.01	0.01	0.01	0.01	0.01
	[0.01]	[0.01]	[0.01]	[0.01]*	[0.01]	[0.01]	[0.01]	[0.01]
Neighbours' avg. mil. exp.	-33.16	-30.1	-34.78	-35.25	-35.46	-32.04	-32.16	-32.16
	[12.56]***	[12.45]**	[11.37]***	[10.96]***	[10.97]***	[10.90]***	[10.91]***	[10.91]***
Government effectiveness	175.05							
	[66.64]***							
Civil war legacy	-0.03	-0.03	-0.03	-0.03	-0.03	-0.03	-0.03	-0.03
	[0.02]*	[0.02]	[0.01]**	[0.01]**	[0.01]**	[0.01]**	[0.01]**	[0.01]**
Africa (dummy)	-325.54	-378.19	-390.35			-331.24	-337.8	-337.8
	[126.03]***	[126.94]***	[125.89]***			[126.47]***	[126.95]***	[126.95]***
Ln distance from Moscow[a]	132.02	125.18	90.47	70.81	72.3	120.79	123.66	123.66
	[62.89]**	[67.57]*	[72.46]	[64.19]	[64.50]	[64.06]*	[64.27]*	[64.27]*
Gov. effectiveness, 33rd–66th percentile					224.1		-105.61	125.22
					[120.90]*		[130.42]	[120.88]
Gov. effectiveness, 66th–100th percentile					307.48			230.83
					[134.81]**			[131.67]*
Gov. effectiveness, 33rd percentile				-257.91		-169.57	-230.83	
				[107.03]**		[107.58]	[131.67]*	
Young men (15–29% of population)			26.66					
			[32.06]					
War start		1.5						
		[70.47]						
Military expenditure	14.55							
	[9.40]							
No. of observations	201	196	215	228	228	228	228	228
No. of countries	77	78	76	81	81	81	81	81
R^2	0.13	0.17	0.18	0.07	0.08	0.08	0.13	0.14

Notes:

Standard errors appear in square brackets. All regressions contain a constant.

* Statistically significant at 90 per cent. ** Statistically significant at 95 per cent. *** Statistically significant at 99 per cent.

[a] Ln = natural log: a tool to scale down magnitudes without losing data relativity.

LIST OF ABBREVIATIONS

AK-47	Avtomat Kalashnikova, 1947	NISAT	Norwegian Initiative on Small Arms
GDP	gross domestic product		Transfers
ICRG	*International Country Risk Guide*	USD	US dollar

ENDNOTES

1   The AK-47—Avtomat Kalashnikova, 1947—is named after its designer, Mikhail Kalashnikov, and the year it first went into production.

2   The AK-47 was not the first effective personal automatic weapon (or assault rifle); indeed, it was not much of an invention at all. It has been claimed that the weapon was nothing more than a rough copy of the German StG44 (Long, 1988). While the two weapons look very similar, and Kalashnikov undoubtedly drew on the StG44 and US M1 carbine, the bolt carrier mechanism and the design of the receiver of the AK do mark a significant innovation that sets it apart.

3   Purchasing a weapon online in the United States requires the purchaser to do so through a recognized federal firearms licence dealer.

4   Author's interviews with Alan Offringa, former assault rifle monitor, US Bureau of Alcohol, Tobacco, Firearms and Explosives (ATF) in Boston, Massachusetts, November–December 2005; correspondence by phone between Offringa and the author.

5   There were not 208 countries for every period, as some were created in the last 15 years (e.g. ex-Soviet republics that became independent states), hence 742 and not $208 \times 4 = 832$.

6   The model of the small arms market is based on a simultaneous equations model of demand and supply. Demand for small arms depends on three factors: relative price (P), income (I), and the motivation for acquiring a weapon (M). The supply side of the small arms market is determined by price (P), the prevailing regulations in relation to small arms (R), and intrinsic supply costs (S). The structural demand (Qd) and supply (Qs) equations of this simultaneous equations system are given by:

$$Qd = -a + bP + cI + dM$$
$$Qs = e + fP - gR - hS$$

Price is determined by the meeting of demand and supply. Setting these equations equal to each other:

$$Qs = Qd$$
$$e + fP - gR - hS = -a - bP + cI + dM$$

Solving the equilibrium conditions for the dependent variables price (P) and quantity traded (Q) gives the following reduced-form equations:

$$P = -\left\{\frac{e+a}{b+f}\right\} + \left\{\frac{c}{b+f}\right\}I + \left\{\frac{d}{b+f}\right\}M + \left\{\frac{g}{b+f}\right\}R + \left\{\frac{h}{b+f}\right\}S$$

$$Q = -\left\{\frac{be-af}{b+f}\right\} + \left\{\frac{cf}{b+f}\right\}I + \left\{\frac{df}{b+f}\right\}M + \left\{\frac{gb}{b+f}\right\}R + \left\{\frac{hb}{b+f}\right\}S$$

Since there are currently no country estimates for the quantity of Kalashnikov trades (Q), it is not possible to estimate both reduced-form equations. As a result, the structural parameters from the initial demand and supply equations cannot be directly estimated. With the benefit of the collected price data, however, it is possible to estimate the reduced-form equation for weapons price. While the magnitude of the estimated coefficients should not be interpreted in the normal linear fashion, their signs and significance can nevertheless provide meaningful insights into the nature of the small arms market. A 20-year cross-country panel is used to estimate the reduced-form model for weapons price determinants:

$$P_{it} = \beta_0 + \beta_1 I_{it} + \beta_2 M_{it} + \beta_3 R_{it} + \beta_4 S_{it} + e_{it}$$

What we are looking for is whether the coefficient estimates (β_1, β_2, etc.) are statistically significant. This indicates whether the variation in a particular explanatory variable is significant in explaining changes in Kalashnikov prices.

7   The estimation method is random effects generalized least squares. Further details on panel data methods employed in this analysis are given in Killicoat (2006).

8   A variable that is statistically significant but has the opposite sign to that which was expected would suggest a problem with the choice of variables included in the model of the market.

9   It may be argued that weapons price determination is partly endogenous to the homicide rate; i.e. one may suspect that when prices fall, homicide rates may rise. This effect is ignored in the current analysis, given the weak result. It may be addressed in future with appropriate use of instrumental variables.

10   The civil war variable is coded as one if, in a five-year period, a civil conflict claims at least 25 battle deaths in a given year and is based on the Uppsala Conflict Data Project/International Peace Research Institute of Oslo Armed Conflicts Dataset (Gleditsch et al., 2002).

11   The result was similar for a threshold of 1,000 battle deaths.

12   See Kaufmann, Kraay, and Mastruzzi (2005, pp. 37–8) for a full description of how government effectiveness is calculated by the World Bank.

13   This data fact regarding neighbouring countries was obtained from the World Bank's World Development Indicators (World Bank, n.d.).

14   The Soviet collapse is deemed not to be significantly correlated with weapons prices because there is less than a 90 per cent chance of the Soviet collapse being statistically associated with weapons prices. In statistics, 90 per cent is the lowest band for accepting a hypothesis.

15   Although dozens of other countries—in particular, China, Egypt, and Iraq—produce large quantities of Kalashnikovs, the majority of Kalashnikov derivative weapons over the last 20 years are believed to be sourced from the former Soviet Union (Kahaner, 2006, pp. 55–71).

16   It is important to understand that the distance from Moscow proxy variable does not literally measure transport costs. Rather, it represents the approximate transport costs of countries relative to one another.

17   The specification of each model type is a trimmed version of the Collier-Hoeffler (2004) conflict regression model. Since the sample for this study contains only four time-series observations (price data is for a 20-year period) compared with the conventional eight five-year periods (the 40 years since 1960), a greater degree of parsimoniousness is required when determining which regressors to include. The period of each observation is the same as for the estimation of the small arms market (1986–90, 1991–95, 1996–2000, and 2001–05). Small sample problems from weapons price coverage would be exacerbated by including all ten significant regressors from Collier and Hoeffler (2004). With all ten variables in a Collier-Hoeffler model included, listwise (i.e. in turn) deletion of observations with missing data would reduce the sample to only 106 panel observations.

18   The quantitative conflict research community has come to some degree of convergence on the factors that seem most important in explaining civil conflict onset, namely, population size, the level and growth of income, dependence on lootable natural resources, and geographic features that reduce the cost of incubating an insurgency. For reviews of the quantitative literature on civil war, see Sambanis (2004) and Lacina (2004).

19   In economics, it is necessary to define the causal mechanism by which cheap weapons are hypothesized to lead to an increased probability of civil conflict. Cheap weapons imply that the cost of conflict-specific capital is low, thus increasing the feasibility of rebellion. Weapons prices are, in effect, a signal to would-be insurgents about the extent to which conflict-specific capital will be a constraint in the decision to rebel violently.

20   This is roughly equivalent to the effect that a 0.5 per cent increase in per capita income would have on reducing the risk of conflict. For details on marginal probabilities of different factors in conflict risk, see Collier and Hoeffler (2004, pp. 580–92).

21   As Chris Chivers found when talking to small-time arms sellers in Iraq over the last few years.

22   Also confirmed in the author's interview with Chris Chivers, *New York Times* correspondent in Iraq, 6 December 2006.

BIBLIOGRAPHY

Achen, Christopher. 1986. *The Statistical Analysis of Quasi-Experiments.* Berkeley: University of California Press.

Agentsvo Voyenkykh Novostey. 2005. 'Russian Izhmash Weapons Applauded at Venezuelan Arms Show.' 27 August. Accessed from NISAT (2006).

Alvarez, R. Michael and Garrett Glasgow. 2000. 'Two-Stage Estimation of Non-Recursive Choice Models.' *Political Analysis,* Vol. 8, No. 2. Spring, pp. 147–66.

Amnesty International, Oxfam, and IANSA Control Arms Campaign. 2003. 'Media Briefing: Key Facts and Figures.' Amnesty International. 9 October. Accessed 30 August 2006. <http://web.amnesty.org/library/index/ENGPOL300182003>

Angrist, Joshua D. and Alan B. Krueger. 2001. 'Instrumental Variables and the Search for Identification: From Supply and Demand to Natural Experiments.' *Journal of Economic Perspectives,* Vol. 15, No. 4. Fall, pp. 69–85.

Atlantic Firearms. 2006. Web site. Accessed 11 November 2006. <http://www.atlanticfirearms.com/programming/listview.asp?CatId=2>

Austin, Kathi. 1999. 'Light Weapons and Conflict in the Great Lakes Region of Africa.' In Boutwell and Klare, pp. 29–48.

Boutwell, Jeffrey and Michael Klare, eds. 1999. *Light Weapons and Civil Conflict.* Lanham: Rowman and Littlefield.

Brauer, Jurgen. 2007. 'Arms Industries, Arms Trade, and Developing Countries.' In Keith Hartley and Todd Sandler, eds. *Handbook of Defense Economics,* Vol. 2. Amsterdam: Elsevier, ch. 11.

—— and Robert Muggah. 2006. 'Completing the Circle: Building a Theory of Small Arms Demand.' *Contemporary Security Policy,* Vol. 27, No. 1. April, pp. 138–54.

Burrows, Gideon. 2006. *The Kalashnikov AK47.* Oxford: New Internationalist Publications.

Chivers, Chris J. 2006. 'Black-Market Weapon Prices Surge in Iraq Chaos.' *New York Times,* 10 December.

CIA (Central Intelligence Agency). 2005. *The CIA World Factbook 2005.* Washington, DC: CIA.

Collier, Paul. 2000. 'Rebellion as a Quasi-Criminal Activity.' *Journal of Conflict Resolution,* Vol. 44, No. 2, pp. 839–53.

—— and Anke Hoeffler. 2004. 'Greed and Grievance in Civil War.' *Oxford Economic Papers,* Vol. 56, No. 4. August. pp. 563–95.

——. 2005. 'Resource Rents, Governance, and Conflict.' *Journal of Conflict Resolution,* Vol. 49, No. 4, pp. 625–33.

——. 2006. 'Military Expenditure in Post-Conflict Societies.' *Economics of Governance,* Vol. 7, No. 1, pp. 89–107.

David, Paul. 1985. 'Clio and the Economics of QWERTY.' *American Economic Review (Papers and Proceedings),* Vol. 75, No. 2. May, pp. 332–37.

Economist, The. 1997a. 'Albania: Bad to Worse.' 13 March, p. 35.

——. 1997b. 'Hold Your Breath'. 20 March, p. 33.

Fajnzylber, Pablo, Daniel Lederman, and Norman Loayza. 2002. 'What Causes Violent Crime?' *European Economic Review,* Vol. 46, pp. 1323–57.

Fearon, James D. and David D. Laitin. 2003, 'Ethnicity, Insurgency, and Civil War.' *American Political Science Review,* Vol. 97, No. 1. February, pp. 75–90.

Glatz, Anne-Kathrin and Robert Muggah. 2006. 'The Other Side of the Coin: Demand for Small Arms.' In Small Arms Survey, *Small Arms Survey 2006: Unfinished Business.* Oxford: Oxford University Press, pp. 141–63.

Gleditsch, Kristian Skrede. 2004. 'A Revised List of Wars between and within Independent States, 1816–2002.' *International Interactions,* Vol. 30, No. 3. July–September, pp. 231–62.

—— and Michael D. Ward. 2001. 'Measuring Space: A Minimum-Distance Database and Applications to International Studies.' *Journal of Peace Research,* Vol. 38, pp. 739–58.

Gleditsch, Nils Petter, Peter Wallensteen, Mikael Eriksson, Margareta Sollenberg, and Harvard Strand. 2002. 'Armed Conflict 1946–2001: A New Dataset.' *Journal of Peace Research,* Vol. 39, No. 5, pp. 615–37.

Grossman, Herschel I. 1991. 'A General Equilibrium Model of Insurrections.' *American Economic Review,* Vol. 81, No. 4. September, pp. 912–21.

Hayek, Frederick. 1945. 'The Use of Knowledge in Society.' *American Economic Review,* Vol. 35, No. 4. September, pp. 519–30.

Hirshleifer, Jack. 1995. 'Theorizing about Conflict.' In Keith Hartley and Todd Sandler, eds. *Handbook of Defense Economics,* Vol. 1. Amsterdam: Elsevier, ch. 7, pp. 165–89.

Human Rights Watch. 2004. 'Iraq: Coalition Ignored Warnings on Weapons Stocks.' 29 October. <http://hrw.org/english/docs/2004/10/29/iraq9575.htm>

IISS (International Institute for Strategic Studies). 2006. *The Armed Conflict Database.* Accessed August 2006. <http://www.iiss.org/databases.php>

Jane's Information Group. 2003. *Jane's Infantry Weapons: Yearbook 2002–2003.* Coulsdon: Jane's Information Group.

Kahaner, Larry. 2006. *AK-47: The Weapon that Changed the Face of War.* New Jersey: John Wiley.

Kaufmann, Daniel, Aart Kraay, and Massimo Mastruzzi. 2005. *Governance Matters IV: Governance Indicators for 1996–2004.* World Bank Policy Research Working Paper No. 3630. Washington, DC: World Bank.
<http://www.worldbank.org/wbi/governance/pdf/Synthesis_GovMatters_IV.pdf>

Killicoat, Phillip. 2006. 'Cheap Guns, More War? The Economics of Small Arms.' Dissertation for MPhil in Economics, Oxford University.
<http://pkillicoat.googlepages.com/Thesis060320.pdf>

Kopel, David, Paul Gallant, and Joanne Eisen. 2004. 'Global Deaths from Firearms: Searching for Plausible Estimates.' *Texas Review of Law and Politics,* Vol. 8, No. 1, pp. 113–41.

Lacina, Bethany. 2004. 'From Side Show to Centre Stage: Civil Conflict after the Cold War.' *Security Dialogue,* Vol. 35, pp. 191–205.

Laurance, Edward J. 2005. *Small Arms and Light Weapons: A Call for Research.* New York: Harry Frank Guggenheim Foundation.

Levitt, Steven D. and Stephen J. Dubner. 2005. *Freakonomics: A Rogue Economist Explores the Hidden Side of Everything.* Chicago: William Morrow.

Long, Duncan. 1988. *AK47: The Complete Kalashnikov Family of Assault Rifles.* Boulder: Paladin Press.

Lott, John R., Jr. 2000. *More Guns, Less Crime: Understanding Crime and Gun-Control Laws,* 2nd edn. Chicago: University of Chicago Press.

Lumpe, Lora, ed. 2000. *Running Guns: The Global Black Market in Small Arms.* London: Zed Books.

Mack, Andrew, Macartan Humphreys, and Jeremy Weinstein. 2004. 'Understanding Civil War: Quantity versus Quality?' Paper presented at the conference on Toward More Effective Collaboration between the Quantitative and Qualitative Conflict Research Communities, Bellagio, Italy, 5–7 April.

Manski, Charles F. 1993. 'Identification of Endogenous Social Effects: The Reflection Problem.' *Review of Economic Studies,* Vol. 60, No. 3. July, pp. 531–42.

——. 2000. 'Economic Analysis of Social Interactions.' *Journal of Economic Perspectives,* Vol. 14, No. 3. Summer, pp. 115–36.

Markusen, James, James Melvin, William Kaempfer, and Keith Maskus. 1995. *International Trade: Theory and Evidence.* Boston: McGraw-Hill.

Marsh, Nicholas. 2007. 'Conflict Specific Capital: The Role of Weapons Acquisition in Civil War.' *International Studies Perspectives,* Vol. 8, No. 1, pp. 54–72.

Marshall, Monty G. and Ted Robert Gurr. 2003. *Peace and Conflict 2003: A Global Survey of Armed Conflicts, Self Determination Movements, and Democracy.* College Park: Center for International Development and Conflict Management.

Miguel, Edward, Shanker Satyanath, and Ernest Sergenti. 2004. 'Economic Shocks and Civil Conflict: An Instrumental Variables Approach.' *Journal of Political Economy,* Vol. 112, No. 4, pp. 725–53.

Musah, Abdel Fatau and Robert Castle. 1998. *Eastern Europe's Arsenal on the Loose: Managing Light Weapons Flows to Conflict Zones.* BASIC Papers: Occasional Papers on International Security Policy No. 26. May.

Narayan Swamy, M. R. 2002. *Tigers of Lanka: From Boys to Guerrillas,* 2nd edn. Dehli: Konark.

Nicchol, Andrew, dir. 2005. *Lord of War.* Endgame Entertainment. Distributed in the United States by Lions Gate Films.

NISAT (Norwegian Initiative on Small Arms Transfers). 2006. *NISAT Black Market File Archives.* Accessed September 2005–January 2006. <http://www.nisat.org>

Political Risk Services Group. 2005. *International Country Risk Guide.* Chicago: Political Risk Services Group.

Poyer, Joe. 2004. *The AK-47 and AK-74 Kalashnikov Rifles and Their Variations.* Tustin: North Cape.

Sambanis, Nicholas. 2002. 'A Review of Recent Advances and Future Directions in the Quantitative Literature on Civil War.' *Defence and Peace Economics,* Vol. 13, No. 3, pp. 215–43.

——. 2004. 'What Is Civil War? Conceptual and Empirical Complexities of an Operational Definition.' *Journal of Conflict Resolution,* Vol. 48, No. 6, pp. 814–58.

Sandler, Todd and Keith Hartley, eds. 2007. *Handbook of Defense Economics: Defense in a Globalized World,* Vol. 2. Amsterdam: Elsevier.

Shilin, Val and Charlie Cutshaw. 2000. *Legends and Reality of the AK: A Behind-the-Scenes Look at the History, Design, and Impact of the Kalashnikov Family of Weapons.* Boulder: Paladin Press.

Singer, J. David and Melvin Small. 1992. *Correlates of War Project: International and Civil War Data 1816–1992.* Technical report. Ann Arbor: Inter-University Consortium for Political and Social Research.

Small Arms Survey. 2001. *Small Arms Survey 2001: Profiling the Problem.* Oxford: Oxford University Press.

——. 2004. *Small Arms Survey 2004: Rights at Risk.* Oxford: Oxford University Press.

——. 2005. *Small Arms Survey 2005: Weapons at War.* Oxford: Oxford University Press.

——. 2006. *Small Arms Survey 2006: Unfinished Business.* Oxford: Oxford University Press.

Varian, Hal. 1992. *Microeconomic Analysis,* 3rd edn. New York: Norton.

Wooldridge, Jeffrey M. 2002. *Econometric Analysis of Cross Section and Panel Data.* Boston: MIT Press.

World Bank. 2005. *World Bank World Development Indicators.* <http://www.worldbank.org/data/wdi2000>, follow links to 'wdi data 2005'.

——. n.d. *World Bank World Development Indicators.* Accessed March 2006. <http://www.esds.ac.uk/International/access/dataset_overview.asp#desc_WBWDI>

ACKNOWLEDGEMENTS

Principal author

Phillip Killicoat

Contributors

C. J. Chivers, Paul Collier, and Anke Hoeffler

Karimojong cattle herders display their weapons near Moroto, Uganda. © Crispin Hughes/Panos Pictures

Enemy Within

AMMUNITION DIVERSION IN UGANDA AND BRAZIL

INTRODUCTION

In October 2006 warriors in the Karamoja region of northern Uganda shot dead 16 Ugandan soldiers who were conducting forcible disarmament operations in the region (*New Vision,* 2006). The findings in this chapter suggest that some of those soldiers may have been killed by bullets that were destined for their own use. In Rio de Janeiro, Brazil, 52 police officers were killed on duty in 2004 (AI, 2005). The evidence presented in this study indicates that some of them may have been killed by bullets originally issued to their own forces.

Ammunition has recently gained prominence on the international agenda. This chapter investigates the mechanics of its proliferation at the local level in Karamoja and Rio de Janeiro. Most notably, it looks at the problem of ammunition diversion from the stocks of state security forces to non-state actors.[1]

Karamoja is home to several pastoralist groups whose warring and cattle raiding have escalated in recent years with the proliferation of modern assault rifles. The study finds that ammunition that should have been manufactured exclusively for state security forces is in the hands of Karimojong warriors.

Brazil is a well-documented example of very high small arms-related crime and homicide rates. The intricacies of the ammunition trade that fuels this dynamic are less-well documented. The study finds that a significant quantity of ammunition seized by the police from criminals is of the same type used by the police of Rio de Janeiro.

Findings in the studies presented in this chapter were generated by taking samples of ammunition from non-state actors. Importantly, the two studies use slightly different data collection and analysis methods. In the Karamoja case, a Small Arms Survey researcher collected ammunition directly from the private stocks of warriors in the region.[2] This data was then compared with data about ammunition stocks of state security forces, which was recorded in the same way. In Rio de Janeiro, police had seized the ammunition from criminals.

In both cases, a selection of the sampled ammunition was compared with trends in security force ammunition of the same calibre and origin. Each study uses the markings on individual rounds of ammunition to determine the year of manufacture and the factory in which the ammunition was produced. The data on this 'headstamp' is then used to create profiles of the ammunition in the hands of various groups of actors and to compare among them. The results of these analyses are then reviewed in light of qualitative research findings, including field research, interviews, government documents, and press reports.

In Karamoja and Rio de Janeiro, the similarity between state and non-state stocks of assault rifle ammunition suggests that cross-border traffic of this type of ammunition may not be the main conduit for illicit trade. The specific findings of the chapter are as follows:

- In Karamoja and Rio de Janeiro, non-state actors possess ammunition that is produced almost exclusively for the state security forces of each country.

- In both cases, these types of ammunition in the hands of non-state actors correspond in volume and origin to types used by state security forces.
- In each case study, state and non-state actors exhibit very 'young' stocks of ammunition, suggesting a short chain of supply.
- Other sources of information corroborate the findings from the ammunition data. These sources include reports of diversion and other evidence of trade between state and non-state groups.

The chapter concludes that the ammunition-tracing methodologies presented here are vital research tools for understanding illicit flows of ammunition. The cases of Karamoja and Rio de Janeiro re-emphasize the role of state security forces in the acquisition of ammunition by non-state armed groups. There is a clear need to address this problem if the forces that are employed to curtail armed violence are not to contribute to it.

THE USUAL SUSPECTS? THE CASE FOR LEAKAGE FROM STATE STOCKS IN KARAMOJA, NORTHERN UGANDA

As its title suggests, the first part of this chapter presents a strong case for the leakage of ammunition from Ugandan security forces to non-state actors in Karamoja. The Karimojong are semi-nomadic pastoralist groups who have fought what is essentially a low-intensity, inter-clan conflict with small arms since the 1970s. Despite numerous state-led initiatives to disarm the Karimojong warriors, such attempts appear to be in part undermined by flows of domestic ammunition to these non-state actors. Governments in the region claim illicit cross-border trade is a major reason for sustained insurgency, crime, and general violence in their countries. But in the case of Karamoja, and indeed elsewhere, the roots of the problem may well lie at home rather than abroad.

The roots of the problem may well lie at home rather than abroad.

This part of the chapter finds that stocks of ammunition in the hands of Karimojong warriors match closely those of state armed forces in Karamoja. From the evidence of ammunition data collected in August 2006, press reports, military statements, and key informant interviews it presents clear evidence of the illicit transfer of ammunition from members of Uganda's military and auxiliary forces to the Karimojong.

Aims and methodology

This study was designed to compare the stocks of ammunition in the hands of various state and non-state groups in Karamoja. Underpinning the analysis is the following hypothesis: groups that display very similar ammunition profiles may do so because they trade or capture ammunition from the same sources, or from one another.

The study involved noting the markings on individual live (unfired) rounds of ammunition. These rounds were taken directly from the magazines of the Karimojong and from state security forces, including the Uganda Wildlife Authority (UWA), the Local Administration Police (LAP), and, indirectly, Uganda People's Defence Forces (UPDF) stocks.[3] All the actors who contributed ammunition to the study were located within 40 kilometres of one another.

Table 9.1 lists the number of rounds recorded from each group of actors in the sample. It shows clearly that there were significant variations in the numbers of rounds recorded from each group. This variation was due to a number of factors—most notably security—that made some groups less willing or able to share information. In each case, it was only possible to record ammunition information because of sustained contact and dialogue between the researcher

Table 9.1 Numbers and percentage of 7.62 x 39 mm rounds sampled from groups in Karamoja, August 2006			
Group		**Number of rounds**	**Percentage of total**
Non-state:	Karimojong 1	8	1.8
	Karimojong 2	69	15.8
	Karimojong 3	89	20.3
	Karimojong 4	66	15.1
	Karimojong 5	61	13.9
State:	LAP	82	18.7
	UWA	28	6.4
	UPDF	35	8.0
Total		**438**	**100.0**

and the parties concerned. Despite variations in sample size, the objective of the study was to compare state and non-state forces (the Karimojong and state groups listed in Table 9.1),[4] and, when aggregated into two groups, the samples are sufficiently large to permit such a comparison.

From the markings or headstamps, the Small Arms Survey was able to trace the majority of rounds in the sample to a manufacturer and to identify the year in which they were produced.

Figure 9.1 shows the headstamp of a spent (used) 7.62 x 39 mm cartridge case that was retrieved from the scene of a shooting in Karamoja. This round was not in the sample, but it is illustrative of the types of ammunition prolif-erating in Karamoja. The upper marking (61) indicates the factory in which the round was produced. In the case of 7.62 x 39 mm ammunition, this mark is usually numerical, although other types of ammunition display various con-figurations of characters, numerals, and symbols.

This particular mark is specific to Factory Number 61 in China—a state-owned manufacturing facility of China North Industries Corporation. Its origin was identified using the *Cartwin Professional Edition* identification soft-ware for small-calibre cartridges (Cartwin, 2006), in con-junction with the comprehensive *Culots de Munitions* reference books (Jorion and Regenstreif, 1995a; 1995b). These sources permit cross-referencing of ammunition calibres, headstamps, and dates of production runs, as well as general factory information.

Figure 9.2 gives a hypothetical example of how this kind of data can be used to create the ammunition pro-file of an armed group.

Figure 9.1 **Head-stamp of a spent 7.62 x 39 mm cartridge, Karamoja, 2006**

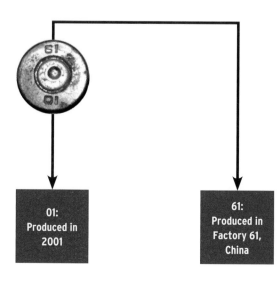

01:
Produced in
2001

61:
Produced in
Factory 61,
China

Figure 9.2 **Hypothetical ammunition profile of an armed group created using data from the headstamps of single rounds of ammunition**

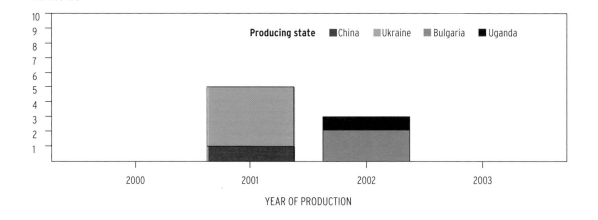

NO. ROUNDS

YEAR OF PRODUCTION

The lower marking on the cartridge in Figure 9.1 indicates the date of manufacture: in this case, 01 means the round was produced in 2001. Together with information about the current 'owner' of the ammunition, data from several such cartridges can be combined to create an 'ammunition profile' for that owner. As Figure 9.2 illustrates, this is a chronological profile of a particular actor's ammunition stocks—indicating the date and origin of the rounds stocked. This does not mean that the actor in question acquired these rounds on the date indicated, nor does it mean that the actor obtained them directly from the country in which they were produced.

Given the numerous ages and origins of ammunition available in most markets, a profile such as Figure 9.2 should be fairly unique for any individual or group. It is highly improbable that any two actors or groups would display exactly the same ammunition profile—i.e. we would expect variations in combinations of ammunition age or origin.

It is important to note that, for reasons of clarity, the ammunition in Figure 9.2 (and in subsequent figures) is not displayed by headstamp or manufacturer, but by country of origin. The sheer number of different headstamps and manufacturers involved would make the task of plotting manufacturer data in a chapter such as this impossible.[5] The ammunition recorded in Karamoja displayed 49 different headstamps—i.e. 49 variations of manufacturer code and year. Sixteen different factories around the world were represented (excluding unmarked rounds). But despite such a multitude of manufacturers, ammunition in the sample was produced in only eight different countries (excluding unknown cases). Table 9.2 lists the producer states and factories, along with the number of rounds each contributed to the sample.

The study recorded a total of 438 rounds of 7.62 x 39 mm ammunition (Table 9.2). Of these, 396 could be traced to a specific factory and date of manufacture; 36 rounds were unmarked (i.e. they were unstamped and bore no identifying marks whatsoever); and 6 rounds carried factory marks that could not be traced to a specific producer, but nevertheless could be identified by year of manufacture. The latter rounds were included in the study under the category 'unknown' in Table 9.2 and 'other' elsewhere. In addition, some of the countries listed in Table 9.2 comprise only a tiny fraction[6] of the overall sample and are also condensed into 'other' in Figures 9.3 and 9.4. The working sample of Karamoja ammunition was therefore 402 rounds of 7.62 x 39 mm ammunition (i.e. the original 438 rounds, excluding the 36 unmarked rounds).

Table 9.2 Manufacturers of 7.62 x 39 mm rounds in the sample

Producer state and factory	No. of rounds	Percentage of total*
China, Factory Number 72	1	0
China, Factory Number 811	1	0
Bulgaria, Dirjavna Voenna Fabrika, Kazanlak	2	0
China, Factory Number 311	2	0
East Germany (GDR), VEB Spreewerk	3	1
China, Factory Number 312	4	1
China, Factory Number 31 (Jing An Factory)	5	1
China, Factory Number 51	5	1
Czechoslovakia, Sellier and Bellot/Zbrojovka Vlásim	7	2
Ukraine (USSR), Factory Number 270, Lugansk	9	2
Yugoslavia, Igman Zavod, Konjic	15	3
Russia (USSR), Ulyanovsk Machinery Plant	20	4
Russia (USSR), Tulski Patronny Zavod	28	6
China, Factory Number 71	41	9
Unknown (unmarked or unidentifiable)	42	10
Uganda, Luwero Industries	59	13
China, Factory Number 61	194	44
Total	**438**	**100**

* Figures are rounded, so the figures in this column do not total precisely 100.

Comparing ammunition profiles

Overall, there is a great deal of similarity between stocks of ammunition in the hands of the five Karimojong groups and Ugandan security forces. Figure 9.3 presents ammunition profiles of the five Karimojong groups and the three security forces sampled.

Perhaps the most striking aspect of the Ugandan samples is the volume of relatively new ammunition. While most Karimojong weapons are old, more than 65 per cent of ammunition in the hands of the Karimojong groups was produced between 2000 and 2005. Similarly, state security forces stock just under 50 per cent of ammunition of this age. Overall, around 60 per cent of ammunition in the entire sample was produced during or after 2000.

The profiles displayed in Figure 9.3 illustrate the traces of procurement decisions, the legacy of alliances and supply networks, and the inheritance patterns whereby groups of actors acquire ammunition from other groups. Quite plausibly, the profiles of the state and non-state groups in Figure 9.3, when combined, yield a broad history of Uganda's arms and ammunition acquisition (addressed below). But why should the Karimojong, who have no history

More than 65% of ammunition in the hands of the Karimojong was produced in 2000–05.

of direct trade with foreign powers such as China and Russia, display such similar profiles to those of state forces? If their ammunition is sourced elsewhere—for instance, in Kenya, Sudan, or Ethiopia—their profiles could differ greatly.

Such observations suggest that state and non-state actors in Karamoja, who have very similar ammunition profiles, may have sourced their ammunition from the same or similar channels. Before investigating whether this is likely to be the case in Karamoja, it is necessary to first investigate the ammunition characteristics of the actors concerned and what these mean.

Profiling Ugandan state forces

Uganda People's Defence Forces: The sample of UPDF ammunition displayed in Figure 9.3 is for the most part very new, produced in China by Factory Number 61 of China North Industries Corporation and dated 2004. That it originates in China is not unexpected. Uganda entered into a trade agreement with China in 1996, and in that year its defence staff also exchanged visits with high-ranking Chinese military figures (China. Ministry of Foreign Affairs, 2003; Xinhua, 1996a; 1996b). Comtrade data and secondary sources suggest considerable defence cooperation and military trade between Uganda and China beginning around that date and continuing to this day (AI, 2006; UN Comtrade, 2006). Despite the fact that China consistently under-reports its defence exports to Comtrade, it has reported large exports of small arms ammunition to Uganda.

Figure 9.3 **Origin and year of manufacture of 7.62 x 39 mm ammunition stocked by groups in Karamoja, Uganda (n = 402)**

NO. ROUNDS

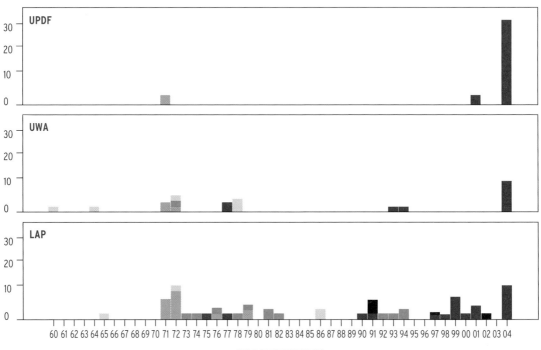

YEAR OF PRODUCTION

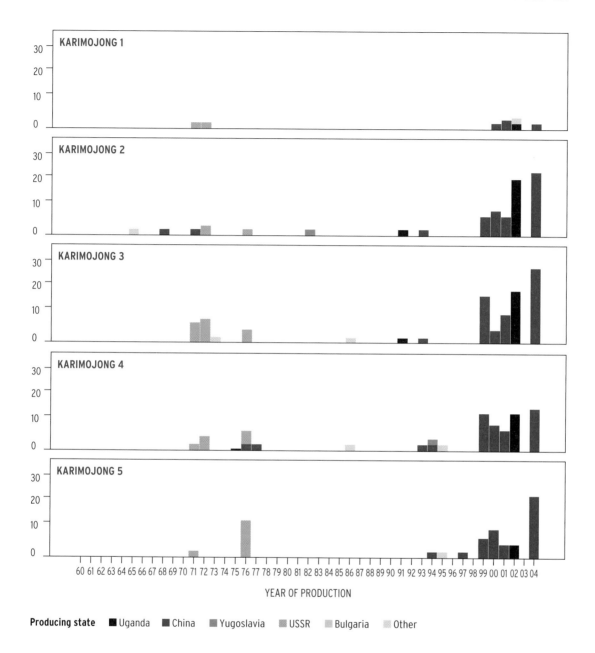

KARIMOJONG 1

KARIMOJONG 2

KARIMOJONG 3

KARIMOJONG 4

KARIMOJONG 5

YEAR OF PRODUCTION

Producing state   ■ Uganda   ■ China   ■ Yugoslavia   ▨ USSR   ▨ Bulgaria   ▨ Other

The UPDF undoubtedly retains older stocks of ammunition. Interviews conducted by the Small Arms Survey in August 2006 indicate that the UPDF supplies a number of Ugandan actors with ammunition, including district officials, LAPs, local defence units (LDUs), and the UWA. Much of this ammunition is old, indicating that the UPDF itself stockpiles older types, but may well prefer to issue its active forces with newer ammunition, leaving the remaining, older stocks to auxiliary forces. These stocks are largely the legacy of former defence agreements between Uganda and foreign powers—notably the former Union of Soviet Socialist Republics (USSR) in the early to mid-1970s (Byrnes, 1990)—but also of recent, albeit relatively low-scale, domestic production (Figure 9.4).

Figure 9.4 **Ammunition stocked by state forces and Karimojong: a history of Uganda's military alignment and arms imports (n = 402)**

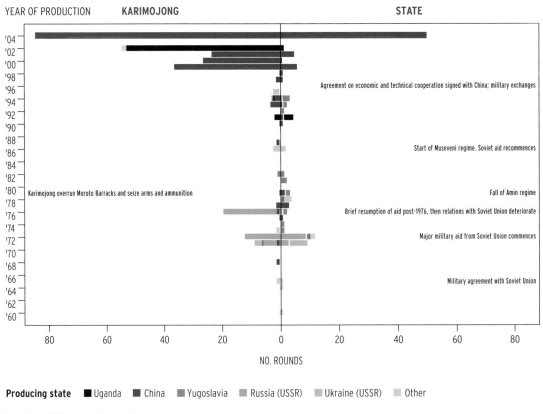

Source: Byrnes (1990); interviews in Uganda, various dates

Uganda Wildlife Authority: The UPDF supplies ammunition to the UWA.[7] The UWA ammunition profile (Figure 9.3) is commensurate with this. It stocks old ammunition, but like the UPDF that supplies it, also possesses Chinese ammunition produced in 2004. The UWA, when interviewed, appeared smarter in appearance and generally better equipped than the LAP or the similar LDUs, although less-well equipped than the UPDF. Its ammunition supplies appear to reflect this 'mid-range' position in the logistical hierarchy.

Local Administration Police: LAP stocks are generally older than those of the other state forces in the sample. As in the case of the UWA, LAP stocks include 2004 Chinese ammunition, but LAP members are open about the fact that they are primarily equipped with poor-quality arms and ammunition, and concede that the UPDF retain the newest stocks.[8] The similar LDUs (not in the sample) also note the same poor-quality ammunition.[9] Both forces are auxiliary troops, poorly paid, often shabby in appearance, and use arms and equipment that are surplus to regular forces. Perhaps because of this, the LAP ammunition profile in this sample contains the most variation of ammunition origins and ages of all eight groups in the study (Figure 9.3).

The varied ammunition profile of the LAP includes Ugandan-produced ammunition, which is notably absent in the profiles of either the UPDF or the UWA. This ammunition, produced by Luwero Industries, Nakasongola, was

Four 7.62 x 39 mm rounds in the possession of the Karimojong's neighbours, the Turkana of Kenya. On the Uganda-Kenya border, December 2006. © James Bevan

marked '91' and '02'.[10] The probable reason why it only appears in LAP stocks is its reportedly poor quality. The ammunition was heavily criticized by the inspector general of police. For this reason, the police chose to equip their forces with foreign-made ammunition rather than use the Ugandan-manufactured rounds (*Monitor,* 2002b; *Red Pepper,* 2004, pp. 1–2). LAP personnel report that the ammunition is unreliable and fouls the barrels of their weapons.[11] It is plausible that the UPDF shun the ammunition, given its questionable reliability, and instead issue it to secondary defence forces, such as LAPs and LDUs.

Taken together, the ammunition profiles of the three state security forces illustrate broadly what one would expect to find. The UPDF, as better-equipped, frontline troops, possess the most recent ammunition. Their stocks are illustrative of Uganda's newest acquisitions of defence material—from China. The UWA and LAP forces reveal a more holistic profile of the Ugandan state's ammunition stocks. Unlike the UPDF, they are issued with older varieties of ammunition from Ugandan state arsenals. These stocks include ammunition that may have been transferred from the Soviet Union in the 1970s and also ammunition from recent, albeit relatively low-scale, domestic production (Figure 9.4).

Profiling the Karimojong

Broadly speaking, the combined ammunition profile of the five Karimojong groups is very similar to that of the Ugandan state forces (Figure 9.4). This suggests that the state and non-state groups might share similar sources of ammunition, but what are these?

A brief review of the history of arms proliferation among the Karimojong reveals that they first came into possession of large quantities of arms and ammunition during the fall of the Amin regime in 1979. After troops loyal to Amin abandoned the barracks in Moroto, the Matheniko Karimojong overran the armouries, taking large quantities of arms and ammunition. In a second wave of mass acquisition in 1986, demobilized Karimojong from the defeated Uganda National Liberation Army returned to their communities with their weapons and ammunition (Mkutu, 2006, pp. 9–10). One would expect, therefore, to see this reflected in the ammunition profiles of the five Karimojong groups studied, and it is indeed the case. Karimojong stocks reflect Soviet transfers of the 1970s that are also present in the ammunition profiles of the Ugandan state forces (Figure 9.4). This may account for some of the 1970s stocks, but what of newer ammunition?

There is no record of a single, major capture of state stocks by the Karimojong since 1986, so why do the Karimojong hold a high number of Ugandan-produced rounds, manufactured after 1991? State forces do not appear to stock this ammunition in such high numbers, and it is highly unlikely that the Karimojong groups are in a position to procure it directly from the manufacturer. These stocks provide a particularly strong reason to suspect the Ugandan armed forces of 'losing' ammunition (through trade or capture) or distributing ammunition to other parties who subsequently 'lose' it, through trade or capture, to the Karimojong.

As noted above, a high level of trade or capture between groups should yield similar profiles. But this is not always the case. For example, if a group, (a), were to consistently trade only its old ammunition with another group, (b), then we would expect group (a) to have a considerably younger ammunition profile than group (b). The same kind of differences would appear if group (a) discriminated according to ammunition type or origin.

State forces have criticized Ugandan-produced ammunition. If trade does occur, members of the Ugandan state forces may well discriminate, according to quality, as to which rounds they distribute to other actors. Such actors could include local civilian officials, civilians armed by the military in the regions to the west of Karamoja, or the Karimojong (who would acquire ammunition through unofficial trade between themselves and security forces). Whichever source is more prolific (and all may be so), the offloading of poorer-quality ammunition is a plausible explanation for a high number of Ugandan-produced rounds in the hands of the Karimojong, but comparatively lower numbers in the hands of the state forces they were intended for (Figure 9.5).

What of the other newer stocks? The prime means of Karimojong acquisition are trade or capture, or a mixture of the two. In the first instance, the Karimojong certainly trade with neighbouring clans, including those on the Sudanese and Kenyan sides of the border. They also trade with members of the Lord's Resistance Army (LRA) on

Figure 9.5 **Luwero Industries (Uganda) 7.62 x 39 mm ammunition stocked by groups in Karamoja (proportion of each group's stock) (n = 402)**

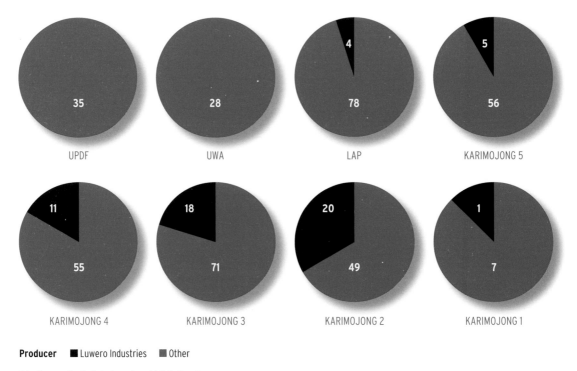

Producer ■ Luwero Industries ■ Other

Note: Figures on the pie charts give numbers of individual rounds.

occasions and with other Ugandan non-state actors to the west of Karamoja. In terms of capture, the Karimojong report that they have captured ammunition from the LRA, the Turkana and Pokot in Kenya, and in isolated incidents from UPDF soldiers.[12] Both trade and capture are therefore likely to be responsible for a portion of the rounds in the sample.

One feature of the sample, however, suggests that these sources cannot account for all acquisitions by the Karimojong. The prevalence of relatively new ammunition in the sample suggests a short chain of supply from place of manufacture to Karamoja. The most-recent ammunition in the sample originates predominantly in China, with a particular concentration of rounds manufactured in 2004 (Figure 9.4). It is highly improbable that China trades directly with any of the non-state armed groups in the region. This means that, in less than two years, ammunition has been manufactured in China; transported to one or more state parties in the region; and lost, captured by, or sold to the Karimojong. The time period between manufacture and acquisition by the Karimojong is very brief, and briefer still if one considers that the ammunition may have been stored in China before shipment, or stored in the arsenal of a state in the region prior to diversion or retransfer.

Is it possible that the trade and capture noted above could transfer this ammunition to the Karimojong in such a short space of time? The answer is yes, but probably not in such quantities.

There are a number of potential sources of the newer Chinese- and Ugandan-manufactured Karimojong ammunition, and all of them are plausible. Firstly, the Ugandan government long supported the Sudan People's Liberation Army (SPLA) in southern Sudan, which is (in arms trade terms) only a stone's throw from Karamoja. If Uganda no longer supplies the SPLA, this source is doubtful, but without conducting similar studies of ammunition in the regions of Kenya and Sudan proximate to Karamoja, it is difficult to ascertain whether this is the case and whether these stocks are available to the Karimojong.[13] Secondly, the Karimojong could acquire ammunition from the civilian population of Acholiland in Uganda, where the arming of civilians by the government has been pervasive in the past decade. A third option is that Ugandan state forces in Karamoja trade ammunition to the Karimojong. The data presented here, alone, cannot determine which explanation is more likely, and all may well be the case. However, when viewed together with interviews and reports by the Ugandan military and local press, the third explanation appears most valid.

Karimojong warriors interviewed in August 2006 were adamant that their main supply of ammunition was from individuals in the UPDF. The warriors reported how they would be approached by troops in town, who would later arrange a transfer of arms and/or ammunition at a discrete location in exchange for money or produce.[14] Other visual indicators of trade lend credence to such reports. Karimojong warriors have traditionally worn items of military apparel, such as combat jackets and military insignia, as symbols of victory over the soldiers they have killed in combat. There are simply too many such items in circulation today in Karamoja—and too few reports of hostile exchanges between the UPDF and Karimojong—for trade not to be a factor.[15]

Interviewed warriors did not implicate LDUs or LAPs in the trade in arms and ammunition, and mentioned only the UPDF, but this does not mean that only the UPDF may be involved.[16] Members of the UPDF have claimed that LDU units, formed during the 2001–02 disarmament initiative and composed of local Karimojong, have supplied fellow warriors with ammunition. As one UPDF commander claimed to the mainstream Ugandan press: 'The racket is very common whenever we despatch the LDUs to carry out operations in areas where they hail from' (*New Vision*, 2002). Warriors may be unwilling to implicate LDUs because of these family/clan ties—hence their implicating the UPDF. But the fact that the Karimojong profiles appear to be a good deal less varied than those of auxiliary forces

(Figure 9.3) and that their ammunition is a good deal younger could be evidence that, if they trade with a number of state forces, they may trade to a greater extent with the UPDF.

Implicated state forces

Despite a number of caveats, the evidence presented in this chapter suggests that Ugandan regular and auxiliary forces are a source of ammunition for the Karimojong. These findings do not, it should be stressed, implicate the Ugandan armed forces at the institutional level: there is no plausible reason to suggest any official policy of transfer to the Karimojong. The process is likely to be attributable to the actions of individuals within those forces. But the trade nevertheless appears to exist.

There are five mutually supporting reasons for this conclusion. Firstly, although ammunition profiles are not mirror images of one another, they are sufficiently similar to conclude that state and non-state actors have very similar sources of ammunition. Secondly, statements by the military, made in the Ugandan press, admit to trade between LDU members and their brethren Karimojong warriors. Thirdly, poor-quality, Ugandan-manufactured ammunition— which has been publicly criticized by members of the security forces—circulates among the Karimojong in relatively high numbers. Importantly, it is far less frequent in the hands of state armed forces, suggesting an 'off-loading' phenomenon on the part of state forces. Fourthly, there is considerable evidence of trade in military commodities other than arms and ammunition. Finally, and by no means least, Karimojong warriors are emphatic that their primary source of arms and ammunition is the UPDF and are angered at having been disarmed—in some cases a number of times—and then having to buy back arms and ammunition.[17]

These findings have a number of important, policy-relevant implications. Of particular significance is the illicit cross-border trade. The results suggest that it could be over-emphasized as a source of illegal arms acquisition in the region. More than likely, some of the ammunition in the hands of the Karimojong analysed in this study has been traded with non-state actors in other states. But the findings in this chapter—particularly the proliferation of recently manufactured Chinese and Ugandan ammunition—suggest domestic sources are also a component of the problem.

Fundamentally linked to this is the question of due diligence for the supplier states to the region. If states supply to other states that have little control over their stocks of arms and ammunition, then the former may indirectly perpetuate protracted internal conflicts. This study, and other research highlighting poor stock controls, may help to provide evidence to the supplier states concerned so that they may adapt their arms and ammunition transfer policies accordingly (TRANSFERS).

Also linked to these questions is the perennial issue of security sector reform and its absence in many states in the region and elsewhere. If troops are so poorly paid that it makes financial sense to sell relatively inexpensive munitions to non-state actors, there is a clear need to invest more heavily in salaries (or at least ensure regularity in payments) and to institute greater accountability over ammunition expenditure. One considerable problem in this regard, which is particularly acute in the case of Uganda, is the creation of non-state armed groups over which the state has little control. The profusion of quasi-state groups, such as LDUs and militias, in the region opens yet another avenue for loss of ammunition from state stocks. Little oversight, and even less pay than their regular counterparts, conspires to make these groups a high-risk factor in small arms leakage from state stocks.

At present this study contains too small a sample to give accurate weights to the volume of cross-border and domestically sourced ammunition, but it makes a clear case for the presence of Ugandan state forces' ammunition in the hands of the Karimojong. This trade undermines successive disarmament initiatives and contributes to the high levels of armed violence that characterize the region. It would take a wider sampling frame—and one that extends to the proximate regions of Kenya and Sudan[18]—to assess more accurately the role of cross-border trade into Karamoja. Future study requires increased attention to the trading habits of states, combined with data on how that ammunition is marked. The findings of this study are the first publicly available outcome of efforts to trace ammunition, systematically and comparatively, at the regional level.

WHOLESALING DEATH: THE CYCLE OF AMMUNITION DIVERSION FROM STATE ACTORS TO ORGANIZED CRIME IN RIO DE JANEIRO, BRAZIL

The setting and the problem: drugs; violence; corruption; and many, many bullets

The problem of armed violence is particularly serious in the Brazilian city of Rio de Janeiro. Since the mid-1980s, criminal organizations have gained territorial control of several poor neighbourhoods (*favelas*) of the city. These factions wage armed competition for control of profitable cocaine and marijuana retailing points and also confront public security forces.[19] Ammunition plays a fundamental role in fuelling this violence, but it seems that its origins are not solely the international illicit trade or diversion from legal civilian stocks. Much of this ammunition appears to have been diverted from state security forces.

This study focuses on ammunition that was seized by police from predominantly criminal organizations annually, between 2003 and 2006, and sent to the Forensic Institute Carlos Éboli (Instituto de Criminalística Carlos Éboli, or ICCE) for analysis. It profiles this ammunition by date, year of production, and manufacturer and compares it with trends in ammunition acquisition by state security forces. Together with qualitative research, including interviews and analysis of official documentation, the data shows a strong convergence between the types and volumes of state stocks and those in the hands of criminals in Rio de Janeiro.

Ammunition circulating in Rio de Janeiro

The diversion of small arms and ammunition from official stockpiles and inventories to criminal organizations and illegal armed groups in Latin America has been documented in several works.[20] However, this study is the first attempt to trace ammunition in Rio de Janeiro using ammunition headstamp data.

The study was designed to determine whether diversion from state security force stocks was the most likely reason for the high numbers of assault rifle rounds found to be circulating among criminal factions in Rio de Janeiro.

As with the case of Karamoja, discussed above, it compares the ammunition of state security forces with that of non-state armed groups. The analysis was designed to assess three possibilities regarding where the illicit ammunition could have been sourced. These were: (1) the ammunition was sourced abroad; (2) it was stolen or traded from legal civilian stocks; and (3) it was diverted from the security forces.

Data collection and analysis

This study adopts a similar methodology to the analysis of the situation in northern Uganda. It profiles ammunition that was seized from criminals and aggregates this into a single 'criminal ammunition profile'. However, unlike the Uganda case, it was not possible to record data directly from the stocks of state security forces. Instead, trends in state forces' acquisition of ammunition were compared with the criminal ammunition profile to identify similar trends.

Criminal ammunition data: This data was collected from ammunition stocks that were seized by the police in the city of Rio de Janeiro.

The study accumulated 2,860 rounds of live ammunition that had been collected in 2004, 2005, and 2006 by forensic experts of the Scientific and Technical Department (DPTC) of the police of Rio de Janeiro. Pending analysis, the ammunition had been stored at the ICCE,[21] which is the usual procedure for handling ammunition seized by the military and civilian police in the northern, southern, and eastern districts of the city.[22]

The DPTC records only the manufacturer and calibre of each round of ammunition. Rarely is more detail noted than the characteristics of the bullets (i.e. whether full-metal jacketed or not). For that reason, it was necessary to reinvestigate the ammunition to yield the information required for this kind of analysis. Personnel from the DPTC, working with Viva Rio and the Small Arms Survey, compiled the following data for the ammunition:

- the police station where the seized ammunition was received;
- the police file case number (indicating in which police operation the ammunition was seized);
- the quantity of seized ammunition in each police operation;
- the calibre;
- the model;
- the make and/or manufacturer;
- the year of manufacture (if available);
- the date of seizure;
- the lot number (if available);
- whether it was original or reloaded ammunition;
- the place of seizure (street, *favela,* etc.);
- the neighbourhood in which the ammunition was seized; and
- the related crime (the crime the seizure was related to).

While the sample in this study is far from statistically representative of all the ammunition seized in Rio de Janeiro,[23] it is nevertheless a strong indicator of the possible paths that ammunition follows from manufacturer to crime.

CBC cartridge with engraved lot number. © DPTC

State security forces ammunition data: The study did not retrieve stocks of ammunition directly from the security forces. Instead, it used reports and interviews to build up a broad outline of the types of ammunition used by them, when this ammunition was adopted, and in what quantities. These sources included the statistical yearbook of the Brazilian Army (Ministério da Defesa, 1998–2003), official small arms acquisition information provided by the Government of the State of Rio de Janeiro, information provided by the ammunition manufacturer Companhia Brasileira de Cartuchos (CBC) to the Brazilian Securities and Exchange Commission on ammunition sales, and information on exports and imports of Brazilian-manufactured ammunition.[24] Additional information was obtained through interviews.

In some countries, manufacturers are required by law to mark each round with a lot number, which is a code that identifies the recipient of the ammunition—such as a specific battalion of the police or army. By using this information it would have been easy to determine whether any of the ammunition found in criminal hands had been diverted from state security forces stocks.

However, the seized ammunition in the sample was not lot-marked. While Brazil is one of few states to do so, Brazilian legislation has only governed the lot-marking of ammunition since January 2005. At the time of writing, the State of Rio de Janeiro had not purchased ammunition from CBC in the previous 12 months (i.e. since lot-marking began), because of a surplus of ammunition purchased in previous years (*En la Mira,* 2006).[25] None of the seized ammunition was manufactured after 2004.

It is very important to mention that this chapter was finished almost at the same time that a Congressional Hearing Commission of the Lower House of the Brazilian Congress (CPI) that was investigating small arms trafficking activities closed its work and published its final report. The commission was set in place in March 2005 and published the report in November 2006. The members of the CPI listened to the declaration of government officials, protected witnesses, and imprisoned criminals (including policemen indicted under corruption charges). Viva Rio collaborated with members of the CPI particularly with the analysis of data of more than 10,500 small arms seized from 1998 to 2003 by the police of the State of Rio de Janeiro and traced back by the producers following a request by the CPI. Although the report does not particularly focus on ammunition, its information does not contradict the results of this chapter and also supports the chapter's findings, since the report finds evidence of small arms diversion from Brazilian state security institutions, particularly police forces, to criminal outfits (Câmara dos Deputados, 2006, pp. 358–72).

Identifying potential state stocks: restricted-use ammunition

As the study of Uganda in this chapter illustrates, comparing ammunition profiles of groups can give insights into whether groups' stocks are linked through trade or capture (including theft). In the Ugandan case, this was made easier because all of the groups sampled used the same ammunition. In the case of Brazil, the study retrieved many types of ammunition. The most practical way of assessing whether ammunition has been diverted from state security forces, therefore, was to focus on the specific types of ammunition used by those services and whether those types were present in the sample of 2,860 rounds seized by the police.

For this reason, the present study analyses a sub-sample of 'restricted-use' rifle ammunition. Restricted-use ammunition is distinguishable from unrestricted-use ammunition in Brazil. Although it can also be used by a small number

---

Box 9.1 Restricted-use ammunition

Restricted-use ammunition is defined by Brazilian legislation as ammunition for handguns with a muzzle energy superior to 407 joules, and ammunition for long barrel small arms with a muzzle energy superior to 1,355 joules, such as 357 Magnum, 9 Luger, .38 Super Auto, .40 S&W, .44 SPL, .44 Magnum, .45 Colt, .45 Auto, .22-250, .223 Remington (or 5.56 x 45 mm), .243 Winchester, .270 Winchester, 7 Mauser, .30-06, .308 Winchester (or 7.62 x 51 mm), 7.62 x 39, .357 Magnum, .375 Winchester, and .44 Magnum (Presidência da República, 2000, arts. 16, 17, chs. VIII and IX of Title V; 2004, art. 19).

Figure 9.6   **Remaining 2004 and 2005 ammunition stored at ICCE by calibre, 22% unrestricted use and 78% restricted use (n = 2,860)**

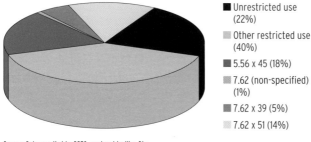

- Unrestricted use (22%)
- Other restricted use (40%)
- 5.56 x 45 (18%)
- 7.62 (non-specified) (1%)
- 7.62 x 39 (5%)
- 7.62 x 51 (14%)

Source: Data supplied by DPTC, analysed by Viva Rio
Note: 'Other restricted use' includes mainly 9mm; .45; and .40 cartridges

of civilian users, such as sporting shooters, hunters, and collectors, state security forces are, by far, the primary recipients of restricted use rifle ammunition.[26] In short, it is used predominantly by state security forces.

Interestingly, the sample as a whole is composed predominantly of restricted-use calibres, particularly calibres used in assault rifles and light machine guns—5.56 x 45 mm and 7.62 x 51 mm, respectively (Figure 9.6). This can be explained (Map 9.1) by the fact that most of the ammunition was seized in areas of the city were there is a strong presence of one of the four criminal organizations that dominate the cocaine trade—Comando Vermelho, Comando Vermelho Jovem, Amigos dos Amigos, and Terceiro Comando—or in areas with high crime rates (Dowdney, 2003, pp. 265–69). Numerous studies report that Rio de Janeiro's criminal factions favour assault rifles. This is linked not only to these weapons' firepower and potential to cause damage, but to their

Map 9.1   **Selected ammunition seizures in Rio de Janeiro, 2003–06**

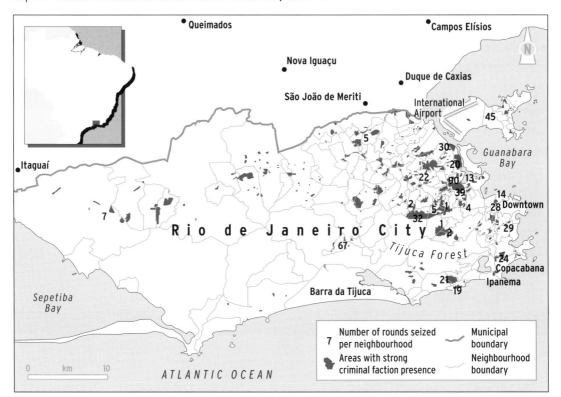

Notes: n=520. The ammunition seized was CBC restricted-use 7.62 (non-specified), 7.62 x 51 mm, and 5.56 x 45 mm rifle rounds. This map only shows cases in which the place of seizure was specified.
Sources: DPTC for the number of rounds; Dowdney (2003, p. 265) for the distribution of areas with strong presence of criminal factions

Figure 9.7 **Date-marked ammunition by manufacturer (n = 1,045; CBC n = 882)**

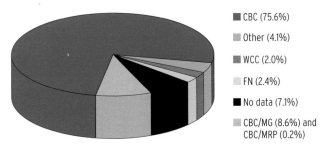

- CBC (75.6%)
- Other (4.1%)
- WCC (2.0%)
- FN (2.4%)
- No data (7.1%)
- CBC/MG (8.6%) and CBC/MRP (0.2%)

Notes: CBC-manufactured rounds were marked variously. They included ammunition marked CBC/MRP (Magtech Recreation Products) and CBC/MG. Magtech is the trade name used by CBC for its commercial exports and CBC/MG denotes production for the Brazilian Ministério da Guerra – ammunition produced exclusively for the armed forces before 1969 (Munición.org, 2006). WCC stands for Western Cartridge Co., Illinois, United States. FN is the mark of Fabrique Nationale d'Armes de Guerre, Belgium.
Source: Data supplied by DPTC, analysed by Viva Rio

symbolic significance vis-à-vis rivals and the police. Assault rifles are the weapons of choice of the 'soldiers' of the organizations. They are used to defend strategic drug retailing points, as well as arms and ammunition caches (Dowdney, 2003, pp. 39–117; Rivero, 2005; Small Arms Survey, 2006, pp. 84–86).

Is most of this ammunition in criminal hands therefore sourced from state security forces? The two predominant calibres—5.56 x 45 mm and 7.62 x 51 mm—are certainly the two used in the assault weapons of the Brazilian armed forces and the police of Rio de Janeiro.[27] Rio de Janeiro is one of the few states in which the police use automatic weapons routinely (Dreyfus and de Sousa Nascimento, 2005, p. 132). This does not, however, mean that ammunition used in crime is necessarily sourced from state security forces.

To further investigate paths of possible diversion, the data had to be filtered in two ways. Firstly, the study retained only rounds marked with the year of manufacture. This was needed to determine whether the ammunition seized from criminals matched the dates when state security forces acquired ammunition of that same type. Secondly, it retained ammunition manufactured by the same factories as those used by state security forces.

Of the 2,860 rounds in the entire sample, 1,045 were marked with year of production. Of these, 882 rounds were manufactured by CBC—the exclusive national supplier to the Brazilian state security forces (Figure 9.7).[28] For even greater specificity, only assault rifle calibres manufactured by CBC were chosen for further analysis. This sub-sample of 612 CBC rounds comprised both 7.62 x 51 mm and 5.56 x 45 mm assault rifle rounds—which became the working sample for this study. It is important to note that from this sample (612 rounds) only one round was identified by ICCE forensic experts as reloaded ammunition, and only three cases show no data on that particular field. Therefore 99.3 per cent of the sample is composed of non-reloaded ammunition.[29] This fact would exclude the possibility of these cartridges being the result of the collection of empty cases and illegal reloading by criminals.

> Domestically manufactured ammunition is in the hands of Rio de Janeiro's criminal gangs.

Potential sources of CBC ammunition in the hands of criminal organizations

The presence of 612 assault rifle rounds in the sample means that domestically manufactured ammunition, destined for use by security forces, is in the hands of Rio de Janeiro's criminal gangs. Does this therefore imply diversion from the stocks of Brazilian state security forces?

There is a particularly high concentration of security force users of CBC's restricted-use ammunition in the State of Rio de Janeiro—22% of total active duty and retired military personnel in the country and over 60,000 policemen (Dreyfus and de Sousa Nascimento, 2005, pp. 124–29). But this alone does not necessarily implicate state security forces as a source. There are two plausible alternatives.

Firstly, CBC exports military-calibre ammunition to a number of neighbouring countries. It is possible that this ammunition could re-enter Brazil via illicit channels to fuel Rio de Janeiro's violent crime. Secondly, since restricted-use ammunition can be acquired by (an albeit small number of) civilian users, such as sporting shooters, hunters, and collectors, these could be further sources of illicit ammunition. No single option can be excluded entirely, but the following sections give some idea of the probable magnitude of each source of ammunition in the hands of criminals.

Possible transfer from neighbouring countries

CBC is one of the region's largest exporters of ammunition. Could the ammunition in the hands of Rio's criminal gangs have been transferred illicitly from CBC clients in one of Brazil's neighbouring states?

A review of Brazil's arms exports suggests that its top ten export partners between 1980 and 2004 numbered several South American countries—most of them bordering on Brazil. Of particular note is Paraguay, which is known to be a major diversion point for state forces' ammunition into the illicit market, and hence a possible source of illicit re-entries of CBC ammunition (Dreyfus and Bandeira, 2006; Dreyfus, Lessing, and Purcena, 2005, pp. 75, 77–78).

However, while Paraguay was among the top ten importers of Brazilian ammunition during the mid-1990s, Brazilian small arms and ammunition commercial exports to that country were halted after 1999 (Dreyfus and Bandeira, 2006). Much of the ammunition in the sample post-dates 1999. In addition, since 2001, and with the exception of Mexico, Ecuador, Chile, and Argentina, commercial exports to Latin American and Caribbean countries have been virtually eliminated by a 150 per cent export tax on commercial exports of arms ammunition to the latter countries (Dreyfus and Bandeira, 2006, p. 12).

Colombia, Argentina, Chile, Peru, Bolivia, Venezuela, and Uruguay have also been important export destinations for Brazilian ammunition since the mid-1990s. However, there are several reasons why these states are very unlikely to be the source of Rio de Janeiro's illicit ammunition (Dreyfus and Bandeira, 2006; Dreyfus, Lessing, and Purcena, 2005, pp. 75, 77, 78).

Colombia is an unlikely source. Most of CBC exports to Colombia are of 5.56 x 45 mm ammunition and cases of the same calibre. However, these items, produced for the Colombian armed forces, are marked IM (the logo of INDUMIL—the Colombian state arms factory) prior to export.[30] There are no rounds marked IM in the sample seized by police in Rio de Janeiro.

This would leave the possibility of CBC restricted-use rifle ammunition exported for the armed forces (which are the state armed institutions that predominantly use that kind of ammunition) of other neighbouring countries, particularly Bolivia (which has domestic, although not significant, ammunition production), and Uruguay, Suriname, and Guyana (which do not have domestic ammunition production at all) (Dreyfus and Lessing, 2003; Small Arms Survey, 2004, pp. 17–27).[31] However, according to CBC sources, the company has not exported rifle and machine gun ammunition to the military of these countries 'for a long while'.[32]

Regarding civilian users in the remaining countries in the region, CBC ammunition is marked differently to the majority of the assault rifle ammunition in the sample. Ammunition produced by CBC for the civilian market (sporting shooters and hunters) is marked in inches instead of millimetres.[33] The percentage of .223 inch (5.56 x 45 mm) and .308 inch (7.62 x 51 mm) ammunition is insignificant (1.2%) in the sample seized in Rio de Janeiro. There are only 23 .223 calibre cartridges in the overall sample, of which only 6 were manufactured by CBC, and 12 .308 calibre cartridges, none of which were manufactured by CBC.

Figure 9.8 **Length of time (years) between date of manufacture and date of seizure by Rio de Janeiro police of restricted-use CBC assault rifle ammunition (n = 612)**

NO. ROUNDS

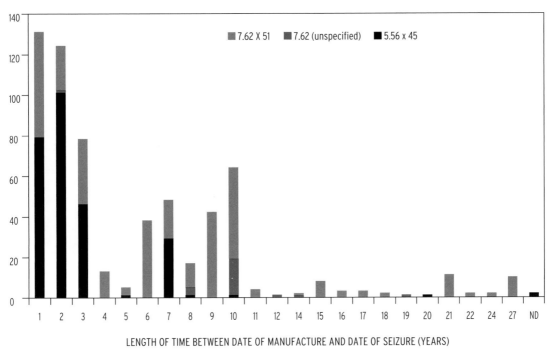

LENGTH OF TIME BETWEEN DATE OF MANUFACTURE AND DATE OF SEIZURE (YEARS)

ND = no date
Source: Data supplied by DPTC, analysed by Viva Rio

If ammunition has been diverted from the Brazilian-supplied armed forces of proximate states, it is likely to constitute a relatively small fraction of the sample seized from criminals. Given the fact that Brazilian security forces are equipped with the most common varieties of assault rifle ammunition in the sample, are they the source?

As in the case of Uganda, analysis of the period between date of production and the date on which the ammunition was seized, by its sheer brevity, may suggest domestic sources. Figure 9.8 indicates that, for the majority of rounds, time spans between production and seizure are between one and ten years, but rounds aged between one and three years at the date of seizure clearly predominate. Older ammunition stocks are likely to have a longer chain of supply. As noted in the Ugandan study, this is simply a function of 'being around longer'. The reverse is true of newer stocks of ammunition: there is a potentially shorter chain of supply. Given the age of the rounds seized by the police in Rio de Janeiro, a greater proportion of this illicit ammunition is likely to have been diverted from domestic security force stocks than from abroad. However, it could also have been diverted from the limited number of civilian users who are allowed to use restricted-use ammunition.

Possible loss from legally held civilian stocks

Diversion from civilian stocks within Brazil—and particularly within Rio de Janeiro—is another plausible source of illicit ammunition, but civilian stocks are likely to contain only a small volume of the assault rifle calibres found in

Figure 9.9 **CBC's gross ammunition sales by market segment, 1996–2005**

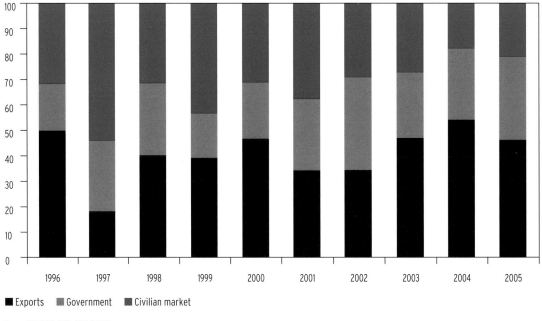

PER CENT

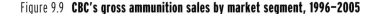

■ Exports ■ Government ■ Civilian market

Source: CVM (1996–2005a; 1996–2005b)

the sample. As mentioned before, ammunition produced for the civilian market is marked in inches, and ammunition marked that way is insignificant in the analysed sample.

As Figure 9.9 illustrates, in the last ten years the bulk of CBC ammunition sales have been to foreign markets and to Brazilian government institutions (CVM, 1996–2005a; 1996–2005b). Of its total sales, 46 per cent were derived from exports and 33 per cent from supplying the Brazilian police and military. The civilian market comprises 21 per cent of total sales—a contender for a source of illicit restricted-use rifle ammunition, but not a large one.

Moreover, the 21 per cent civilian market segment consists of many different types of ammunition, and it is possible that restricted-use rifle ammunition comprises a very small percentage of this share as it cannot legally be sold to most civilian users. It cannot be sold at gun shops, but may only be purchased directly from the factory or imported by the armed forces, with authorization from the Ministry of Defence and by law enforcement agencies, collectors, shooters, and hunters with special authorization from the Brazilian Army. Small arms collectors may only store inert ammunition of this type. Its only other legal civilian users are registered sporting shooters and hunters who have authorization from the Directorate of Controlled Products of the Brazilian Army.[34] Therefore, the majority of legal civilian users of restricted-use ammunition are unlikely to use assault rifle calibres.[35] Given the small civilian share of the restricted-use ammunition market and the large proportion of restricted-use ammunition in the seized sample, legal civilian users are unlikely to be a significant source of the assault rifle ammunition found in the hands of Rio de Janeiro's criminals.

Possible loss or diversion from state forces

Several features of the profile of assault rifle ammunition seized in Rio de Janeiro make it likely that much of it comprises rounds that have been diverted from state security forces.

Figure 9.10 **Quantity of seized restricted-use CBC assault rifle ammunition by calibre and year of manufacture (n = 612)**

QUANTITY

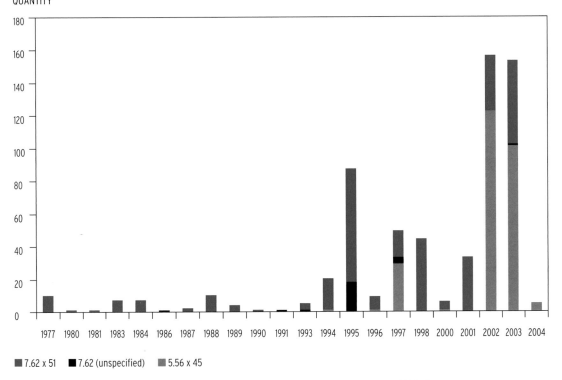

■ 7.62 x 51   ■ 7.62 (unspecified)   ■ 5.56 x 45

Note: No cartridges manufactured in 1978, 1979, 1982, 1985, 1992, and 1999 were found in the sample, which is why these years are not represented in the figure.
Source: Data supplied by DPTC, analysed by Viva Rio

Firstly, as Figure 9.10 illustrates, there is a high concentration of 7.62 x 51 mm manufactured in the mid- and late 1990s—most notably from 1995 onwards. The calibre has been used by the Brazilian Army since the 1960s, but in the mid-1990s (especially in 1995, 1996, and 1997) the army donated 7.62 x 51 mm FAL rifles to the police of Rio de Janeiro.[36] The police began adopting assault rifles in order to match the rising firepower of the drug-trafficking organizations (Câmara dos Deputados, 2005c, p. 7; Dreyfus and de Sousa Nascimento, 2005, p. 132; Lessing, 2005, p. 218). We must assume that this also necessitated the transfer—and continued supply—of the appropriate 7.62 x 51 mm ammunition. Figure 9.10 shows higher concentrations of 7.62 x 51 mm ammunition in the sample after 1995.

However, the Brazilian Marines (Fuzileiros Navais), a 14,600-strong force, maintains bases near Rio de Janeiro. These troops replaced their 7.62 x 51 mm FAL rifles with US-made M16A2 5.56 x 45 mm calibre rifles at around the same time as the police (1997 and 1998). Surplus FAL rifles were kept for training (Dreyfus and de Sousa Nascimento, 2005, p. 114). The possibility of a diversion of 7.62 x 51 mm surplus ammunition resulting from that shift in the type of weaponry should also not be discarded.

The 5.56 x 45 mm ammunition in the sample is more recent, having been manufactured primarily in 2002 and 2003 (Figure 9.10). This relative youth suggests a very rapid migration from legal manufacture to illicit use—0 to 4 years.

Again, there are some interesting parallels between the profile of the seized ammunition and the procurement policies of Rio de Janeiro police. The police first acquired 5.56 x 45 mm weapons in 1999 and 2000, when the

Table 9.3 **Ammunition purchased by the law enforcement agencies of the State of Rio de Janeiro, 2001-05**	
Year	**Purchased ammunition (rounds)**
2001	2,900,000
2002	–
2003	1,210,000
2004	7,400,000
2005	552,000

Note: Information for 2002 was provided in only in values (totalling USD 1.8 million) rather than quantities.

Source: Governo do Estado do Rio de Janeiro (2001)

Secretariat of Public Security purchased 1,500 Colt M-16 assault rifles (Partido Socialista Brasileiro, 2006).[37] The police forces of the State of Rio de Janeiro also purchased large quantities of ammunition from 2001 to 2005 (Table 9.3). Figure 9.10 shows a high concentration of 5.56 x 45 mm ammunition in 2002 and 2003.

Both 7.62 x 51 mm and 5.56 x 45 mm ammunition could plausibly have been diverted from police stocks into the hands of Rio de Janeiro's criminal factions. Between 2001 and 2004, over seven million rounds were purchased for the military police (preventive uniformed police) of Rio de Janeiro and over five million for the civilian police (investigative police) of Rio de Janeiro (Secretaría de Segurança Pública do Estado do Rio de Janeiro, 2004, p. 4). Both police forces (military police and civilian police) could potentially have been the source of the rounds in the sample.

The police of Rio de Janeiro are a strong candidate for diversion.

The data suggests that the police of Rio de Janeiro are a strong candidate for diversion. Recent disclosures of police involvement in the diversion of ammunition support this observation. In July 2005 the man who had for 16 years been the head of the ammunition depot of the civilian police of Rio de Janeiro was arrested together with nine other policemen on charges of diversion of at least 10,000 rounds to drug-trafficking organizations (Secretaría de Segurança Pública do Estado do Rio de Janeiro, 2005; Dreyfus, 2006).

According to Under Secretary of Public Security of Rio de Janeiro Cesar Campos, the number of rounds used in shootings in the *favelas* decreased after the arrest (*En la Mira,* 2006). Decreasing ammunition consumption may have been directly linked to a reduction in supply.

The case for leakage from state stocks in Rio de Janeiro

A combination of several factors suggests that state security forces—most notably the police—are the source of much of the assault rifle ammunition identified in this study as leaking to criminal gangs. No single indicator is sufficient to point the finger with any degree of certainty, but taken together these findings are mutually supportive.

Firstly, the ammunition is restricted-use, assault rifle ammunition used by the police of Rio de Janeiro. Its civilian customers are limited in number. Secondly, the prevalence of 5.56 x 45 mm ammunition in the sample manufactured in 2002 and 2003 coincides with the years in which the police forces of Rio de Janeiro purchased large quantities of 5.56 x 45 mm ammunition. There is a similar parallel between increases in 7.62 x 51 mm ammunition and the adoption by the police of weapons of that calibre in the mid-1990s. Thirdly, the July 2005 revelation of police involvement in large-scale diversion of ammunition implicates the police as a source of ammunition entering the illicit market. Fourthly, the time period between the ammunition's date of manufacture and its seizure on the illicit market is short, indicating a short supply chain and a source proximate to the place of seizure.

Some of the illicit ammunition may also re-enter Brazil from abroad, but little of this ammunition is marked in the same way as the ammunition destined for Brazil's security forces. The domestically manufactured assault rifle ammunition in the sample is mostly very young, and the factors listed above suggest that leakage from the security forces may play a part in facilitating Rio de Janeiro's high crime and mortality rates.

The Brazilian state has recognized that combating theft from these institutions is a priority. Lot-marking of ammunition sold to state institutions has already commenced. The observations made in this study suggest that such measures are required to ensure security force accountability for ammunition stocks in Brazil, and particularly in Rio de Janeiro. Its implications for illicit ammunition proliferation are clear—cleaning up the illicit market begins at home.

One by-product of this study, conducted by Viva Rio in conjunction with the DPTC, is that it may well improve the data collection methods of the latter. This is especially so with regard to statistical methods for the identification and detection of diversion patterns.

CONCLUSION

Karamoja in Uganda and the city of Rio de Janeiro in Brazil experience high levels of armed violence: levels that are well in excess of their country or regional averages. In both instances, ammunition is a vital ingredient in the armed violence that claims hundreds, if not thousands, of lives each year.

The two studies in this chapter have used different data collection and analysis methods. In the Karamoja case, the data was collected directly from the private stocks of warriors in the region. In Rio de Janeiro, the ammunition had been seized by the police prior to the study taking place. Both studies, however, reveal a worrying trend. Each can make a strong claim that a considerable quantity of ammunition used by non-state actors was sourced from state security forces.

In the Ugandan case, the evidence points firmly to members of the security forces transferring ammunition to the Karimojong. This is in direct opposition to successive and ongoing disarmament initiatives aimed at halting the conflict in this part of Uganda. In the case of Rio de Janeiro, there is insufficient evidence to suggest this kind of trade. There is, nevertheless, evidence that, whether through trade, loss, or theft, security forces' ammunition is fuelling some of the city's extreme armed violence.

Both Uganda and Brazil display a further trend of concern. The ammunition found in the hands of warring non-state actors is, for the most part, new. In Brazil, much of the ammunition was seized from criminals between one and three years after manufacture. Similarly, much of the Karimojong ammunition is dated 2004. Both findings indicate a short chain of supply—ammunition has been manufactured, issued to state forces, and 'lost' to non-state actors within the space of two or three years at most.

The findings of this chapter suggest that, in some countries, the principal supply of illicit ammunition may not be the international illicit market, but a flourishing domestic market with its origins in the state security forces. The issue of stockpile security has long been on the small arms policy radar. Research of this kind re-emphasizes just how important a focus on stockpile security is.

What happens when the very forces that are supposed to be diffusing conflicts actually fuel them? The outcome, in the absence of interventions in the form of security sector reform and efforts to introduce accountability over ammunition stocks, is a self-perpetuating dynamic. Security forces, with associated heavy firepower, are stationed in a region for the purposes of preventing or resolving armed violence. But by being there, they add to that very conflict or criminal violence, sustaining or even escalating it.

These findings should send a clear message to all governments: controlling small arms begins at home. It is extremely likely that time and again, the domestic security sector is a source of arms and ammunition to non-state actors. ■

LIST OF ABBREVIATIONS

CBC	Companhia Brasileira de Cartuchos	LDU	Local Defence Unit
CPI	Congressional Hearing Commission, Brazil	LRA	Lord's Resistance Army
DPTC	Departamento da Polícia Técnico-Científica	SPLA	Sudan People's Liberation Army
		UPDF	Uganda People's Defence Forces
ICCE	Instituto de Criminalística Carlos Éboli	USSR	Union of Soviet Socialist Republics
LAP	Local Administration Police	UWA	Uganda Wildlife Authority

ENDNOTES

1   The term 'state security forces' is used in this chapter to denote state-controlled armed forces and law enforcement forces.

2   The researcher was James Bevan, who also conducted all the interviews in Karamoja.

3   Some standard issue UPDF ammunition was supplied by the UPDF to an intermediary, who cannot be identified here for security reasons, two weeks prior to its being recorded in this study.

4   For purposes of anonymous identification, the five Karimojong groups from which ammunition was sourced were labelled Karimojong 1–5.

5   Theoretically, plotting ammunition this way could seriously affect assumptions made about whether any two sets of ammunition of the same year and country of origin are indeed the same. For example, ammunition in the hands of the Karimojong dated 2004 and originating from China and marked with a hypothetical 71 04 would differ from ammunition in the hands of the UPDF, for instance, marked 61 04—each having been produced in a different factory, albeit in the same year and country. In practice, cross-tabulating actor, headstamp, producing state, and year of manufacture revealed that cases of ammunition produced in only one country but by two different factories in a single year occurred only 5 times in 438 rounds sampled.

6   The category 'other' includes unknown producers (9.5 per cent), Czechoslovakia (1.6 per cent), and the former East Germany (0.7 per cent). They are omitted from the graphs presented in the chapter for reasons of clarity.

7   Interviews with UWA personnel. Karamoja, northern Uganda, August 2006.

8   Interviews with LAP personnel, Karamoja, northern Uganda, August 2006.

9   Interviews with a knowledgeable source, Karamoja, northern Uganda, June and August 2006.

10   Just prior to publication, the Small Arms Survey received a report that some Luwero Industries ammunition marked '02' (assumed 2002) is likely to have been produced in years other than 2002. Institutional marking practices are sometimes inconsistent and should thus be taken into consideration in any study of this kind.

11   Interviews with LAP personnel, Karamoja, northern Uganda, August 2006.

12   Interviews with Karimojong members, Karamoja, northern Uganda, May and August 2006.

13   Initial results from an expanded Small Arms Survey ammunition tracing project in Kenya, Uganda, and Sudan suggest that little of the ammunition circulating among the Karimojong is sourced in Kenya or Sudan. Results of the study will be published in late 2007.

14   Interviews with five separate groups of Karimojong warriors, Karamoja, northern Uganda, August 2006.

15   The November 2006 clash between Karimojong warriors and the UPDF mentioned in the introduction to this chapter indicates increasing hostilities in the region. Such attacks have been uncommon in the past, and it is important to stress that escalating hostilities occurred after the research for this chapter had been completed.

16   Interviews with five separate groups of Karimojong warriors, Karamoja, northern Uganda, August 2006.

17   Interviews with Karimojong members, Karamoja, northern Uganda, May and August 2006.

18 This study is already underway. See note 12 above.

19 Dowdney (2003); Misse (1999); Lessing (2005); Rivero (2005); Stefanini (2005).

20 Schroeder (2004, pp. 21–26); Small Arms Survey (2004, pp. 50–60); Câmara dos Deputados (2006); Dreyfus (2006, pp. 186–89); Small Arms Survey (2006, pp. 83–87).

21 Once at the ICCE, the seized material is analysed and studied by forensic experts. Details about the ammunition are written up, and the ammunition is sent to the vault of the Firearms and Explosives Control Division. These 2,860 rounds had not been analysed and were the remainder of stocks that had been collected by the ICCE for analysis. Since no accurate records had been kept, it was impossible to determine how many thousands of other rounds passed through the ICCE during that period.

22 Excluding the metropolitan area, the State of Rio de Janeiro, and the western districts of the city.

23 According to police sources, between 2002 and 2004 the firearms enforcement unit of the civilian police of Rio de Janeiro seized a total of over 440,000 rounds of ammunition of various calibres (Câmara dos Deputados, 2005b, p. 33; Dreyfus, 2006, p. 179).

24 This included information on ammunition exports by Brazil and imports of Brazilian ammunition by neighbouring countries, particularly Paraguay. As mentioned in other works (Dreyfus, 2006; Dreyfus and Bandeira, 2006), the illicit trafficking of ammunition legally exported to neighbouring countries is a source of supply for criminal organizations in Brazil. However, it is worth noting that since 1999 Brazil no longer exports ammunition for the civilian market in Paraguay. In addition, since 2001, and with the exception of Ecuador, Chile, and Argentina, commercial exports to South American, Central American, and Caribbean countries have been virtually eliminated by a 150% export tax on commercial exports of arms ammunition to these areas (Dreyfus and Bandeira, 2006). This information was compiled using the NISAT database and a private foreign trade consultant company in Paraguay (OCIT Trade).

25 In Brazil, marking by lot is relatively easy to implement, since only one company—CBC—produces ammunition for the civilian, police, and military markets.

26 According to Brazilian regulations, collectors can only hold disabled (inert) ammunition (Ministério da Defesa, 2000, art. 6).

27 With the exception of specialized units of the civilian police of Rio de Janeiro, which occasionally use Kalashnikov rifles, the standard calibres of the Brazilian armed forces and police forces are 5.56 x 45 mm and 7.62 x 51 mm. This is also the case for all the armed forces in South America, with the exception of Venezuela since 2005, when the country adopted the AK-103 as it standard assault rifle (Small Arms Survey, 2006, p. 87). In the sample used in this study there is a small quantity (26) of restricted-use rifle ammunition marked as just 7.62 without specifying the length of the case.

28 CBC is the only small arms ammunition producer in Brazil and the largest ammunition-manufacturing company in Latin America. Seventy-seven per cent of its sales derive from ammunition (CVM, 1996–2005a; 1996–2005b).

29 As explained in previous works, illicit ammunition reloading is considered to be only a minor problem by Rio de Janeiro's forensic analysts. CBC original primers are marked with a letter 'V' (Dreyfus, 2006, p. 193). This is not, however, the only method of identifying this feature used by the forensic experts, who have special techniques and observations in order to determine whether or not a cartridge has been reloaded.

30 Interview with INDUMIL officials and Colombian intelligence officials, Bogotá, October 2004.

31 All the other South American countries have domestic production of ammunition for their armed forces (Dreyfus and Lessing, 2003).

32 Inteview with a CBC official, Riberão Pires, São Paulo, October 2006.

33 Interview with a CBC official, Riberão Pires, São Paulo, October 2006.

34 Ministério da Defesa (2000, art. 6); Presidência da República do Brasil (2000, arts. 16, 17, 196, and 197, chs. VIII and IX of Title V); Presidência da República do Brasil (2004, arts. 19, 51. and 53); Dreyfus (2006, p. 180). According to a regulation from the Ministry of Defence, since 2001 sporting shooters cannot purchase and/or use .223 (5.56 x 45 mm) ammunition (Ministério da Defesa, 2001, art. 8).

35 In 2004 there were an estimated 15,091 hunters and sporting shooters in Brazil holding 60,364 small arms (not all of them restricted-use rifles), in a country were it is estimated that civilians (excluding hunters, collectors, and sporting shooters) hold about 4.4 million unrestricted-use small arms (Ministério da Defesa, 1998–2003; Dreyfus and de Sousa Nascimento, 2005, pp. 107, 120).

36 Interview with a high-ranking officer of the military police of Rio de Janeiro, Rio de Janeiro, December 2006.

37 Interview with a small arms importer and broker, Rio de Janeiro, July 2006.

BIBLIOGRAPHY

AI (Amnesty International). 2005. 'Brazil: "They Come in Shooting": Policing Socially Excluded Communities.' AI press release. AMR 19/033/2005. 2 December. Accessed 2 January 2007. <http://web.amnesty.org/library/index/ENGAMR190252005>

——. 2006. 'People's Republic of China Sustaining Conflict and Human Rights Abuses: The Flow of Arms Accelerates.' AI Index: ASA 17/030/2006. 11 June. Accessed 2 January 2007. <http://web.amnesty.org/library/index/engasa170302006>

Byrnes, Rita, ed. 1990. *Uganda: A Country Study*. DT433.222.U351992. Washington, DC: Federal Research Division, Library of Congress. <http://lcweb2.loc.gov/frd/cs/ugtoc.html>

Câmara dos Deputados. 2005a. CPI-Tráfico de Armas, Transcrição IPSIS VERBIS, Audiência Pública, Nº 0345/05, Brasília, Câmara dos Deputados, Comissão Parlamentar de Inquérito destinada a Investigar as Organizações Criminosas do Tráfico de Armas (CPI-TRÁFICO DE ARMAS Departamento de Taquigrafia, Revisão e Redação). 12 April. Accessed 20 December 2006.
<http://www2.camara.gov.br/comissoes/temporarias/cpi/cpiarmas/notas.html>

——. 2005b. CPI-Tráfico de Armas, Transcrição IPSIS VERBIS, Audiência Pública, Nº 0620/05, Brasília, Câmara dos Deputados, Comissão Parlamentar de Inquérito destinada a Investigar as Organizações Criminosas do Tráfico de Armas (CPI-TRÁFICO DE ARMAS Departamento de Taquigrafia, Revisão e Redação). 18 May. Accessed 20 December 2006.
<http://www2.camara.gov.br/comissoes/temporarias/cpi/cpiarmas/notas.html>

——. 2005c. CPI-Tráfico de Armas, Transcrição IPSIS VERBIS, Audiência Pública, Nº 0324/05, Brasília, Câmara dos Deputados, Comissão Parlamentar de Inquérito destinada a Investigar as Organizações Criminosas do Tráfico de Armas (CPI-TRÁFICO DE ARMAS Departamento de Taquigrafia, Revisão e Redação). 7 April. Accessed 20 December 2006.
<http://www2.camara.gov.br/comissoes/temporarias/cpi/cpiarmas/notas.html>

——. 2006. Relatório da Comissão Parlamentar de Inquérito destinada a Investigar as Organizações Criminosas do Tráfico de Armas (CPI-TRÁFICO DE ARMAS), Brasília, Câmara dos Deputados, Comissão Parlamentar de Inquérito destinada a Investigar as Organizações Criminosas do Tráfico de Armas (CPI-TRÁFICO DE ARMAS). November. Accessed 20 December 2006.
<http://www2.camara.gov.br/comissoes/temporarias/cpi/cpiarmas/RelatorioFinalAprovado.html>

Cartwin. 2006. *Cartwin Professional Edition Version 3: Identification Software for Small Caliber Cartridges*. Gytsjerk: Knap Visuals.

China. Ministry of Foreign Affairs. 2003. 'China and Uganda.' <http://www.fmprc.gov.cn/eng/wjb/zzjg/fzs/gjlb/3109/t16595.htm>

CVM (Comissão de Valores Mobiliários). 1996–2005a. *Informações Anuais (IAN) Companhia Brasileira de Cartuchos*. Brasília: Serviço Público Federal, CVM. < http://siteempresas.bovespa.com.br/consbov/ExibeTodosDocumentosCVM.asp?CCVM=13315&CNPJ=57.494.031/0001-63&TipoDoc=C>

——. 1996–2005b. *Demonstrações Financeiras Padronizadas (DFP) Companhia Brasileira de Cartuchos*. Brasília: Serviço Público Federal, CVM. <http://siteempresas.bovespa.com.br/consbov/ExibeTodosDocumentosCVM.asp?CCVM=13315&CNPJ=57.494.031/0001-63&TipoDoc=C>

Dowdney, Luke. 2003. *Children of the Drug Trade: A Case Study of Children in Organised Armed Violence in Rio de Janeiro*. Rio de Janeiro: 7Letras.
<http://www.coav.org.br/publique/media/livroluke_eng.pdf>

Dreyfus, Pablo. 2006. 'Crime and Ammunition Procurement: The Case of Brazil.' In Stéphanie Pézard and Holger Anders. *Targeting Ammunition: A Primer*. Geneva: Small Arms Survey, pp. 173–94.

—— and Antônio Rangel Bandeira. 2006. 'Watching the Neighborhood: An Assessment of Small Arms and Ammunition "Grey Transactions" on the Borders between Brazil and Paraguay, Bolivia, Uruguay and Argentina.' Working document No. 2, Small Arms Control Project, Viva Rio. Accessed 20 December 2006. <http://www.ploughshares.ca/libraries/Control/GlobalPrinciplesVivaRioEng.pdf>

Dreyfus, Pablo and Marcelo de Sousa Nascimento. 2005. 'Small Arms Holdings in Brazil: Toward a Comprehensive Mapping of Guns and Their Owners.' In Rubem Cesar Fernandes. *Brazil: The Guns and the Victims*. Rio de Janeiro: ISER, pp. 94–145. Accessed 2 January 2007.
<http://www.vivario.org.br/publique/media/Small_Arms_Holding_in_Brazil_Toward_a_comprehensive_mapping_of_guns_and_their_owners_By_Pablo_Dreyfus_e_Marcelo_de_Souza_Nascimento.pdf>

—— and Benjamin Lessing. 2003. *Production and Exports of Small Arms and Light Weapons and Ammunition in South America and Mexico*. Unpublished background paper. Geneva: Small Arms Survey.

—— Benjamin Lessing, and Julio Cesar Purcena. 2005. 'The Brazilian Small Arms Industry: Legal Production and Trade.' In Rubem Cesar Fernandes. *Brazil: The Guns and the Victims*. Rio de Janeiro: ISER, pp. 50–93. Accessed 2 January 2007. <http://www.vivario.org.br/publique/media/The_Brazilian_Small_Arms_Industry_Legal_production_and_Trade_By_Pablo_Dreyfus_Benjamin_Lessing_e_Julio_Cezar_Purcena.pdf>

En la Mira (Rio de Janeiro). 2006. 'A Quemarropa: Entrevista sobre control de munición con César Campos, Subsecretario Administrativo de Seguridad Pública del Estado de Rio de Janeiro.' Nº 0. Accessed 31 December 2006. <http://www.comunidadesegura.org/files/active/0/Entrevista%20Pablo%20Dreyfus.pdf>

Governo do Estado do Rio de Janeiro. Secretaria de Estado de Controle e Gestao. CONTROLE. 2001. *Relatório dos Produtos das Ações Realizadas em 2001*. Rio de Janeiro: CONTROLE. Accessed 23 January 2007. <http://www.controle.rj.gov.br/inst_gestao/rel_acomp/2001/relatorio_2001.pdf>

Jorion, Serge and Philippe Regenstreif. 1995a. *Culots de munitions atlas: Tome I, caractères alphabétiques latins*. Toulouse: Cépaduès-Éditions.

——. 1995b. *Culots de munitions atlas: Tome II, codes non-latins, chiffres et symboles*. Toulouse: Cépaduès-Éditions.

Lessing, Benjamin. 2005. 'The Demand for Firearms in Rio de Janeiro.' In Rubem Cesar Fernandes. *Brazil: The Guns and the Victims*. Rio de Janeiro: ISER, pp. 202–21. Accessed 2 January 2007.
<http://www.vivario.org.br/publique/media/The_demand_for_firearms_in_Rio_de_Janeiro_by_Benjamin_Lessing.pdf>

Ministério da Defesa. 1998–2003. *Anuário Estatístico do Exército*. Brasília: Estado-Maior do Exército Brasileiro.

——. 2000. *Portaria Nº 024-DMB de 25 de outubro de 2000. Aprova as Normas que Regulam as Atividades dos Colecionadores de Armas, Munição, Armamento Pesado e Viaturas Militares*. Brasília: Ministério da Defesa, Exército Brasileiro, Departamento de Material Bélico (Dir G de MB/1952).

——. 2001. *PORTARIA No 004-D Log, DE 08 DE MARÇO DE 2001. Aprova as Normas que Regulam as Atividades dos Atiradores*. Brasília: Ministério da Defesa Exército Brasileiro, Departamento Logístico.

Misse, Michel. 1999. *Malandros, Marginais e Vagabundos & a acumulação social da violência no Rio de Janeiro.* Ph.D. thesis, Instituto Universitário de Pesquisas do Rio de Janeiro.

Mkutu, Kennedy. 2006. 'Small Arms and Light Weapons among Pastoral Groups in the Kenya-Uganda Border Area.' *African Affairs,* Vol. 106, No. 422, pp. 47–70. 28 July.

Munición.org. 2006. *Apuntes sobre las Fábricas Brasileiras de Munición.* Accessed 23 January 2007. <http://www.municion.org/identificacion/Brasil.htm>

Monitor, The (Kampala). 2002a. 'Bullets, not Guns Are the Problem in Karamoja.' 20 February.

——. 2002b. 'UPDF Makes Fake Bombs and Bullets Sabotage Suspected.' 12 May.

New Vision, The (Kampala). 2002. 'UPDF Conned of Bullets.' 28 May.

——. 2006. 'Karimojong Warriors Kill UPDF Major.' 30 October.

Partido Socialista Brasileiro. 2006. *Deputado Josías Quintal, Deputado Federal, Partido Socialista Brasileiro.* Web site, now no longer online after October 2006 elections. <http://www.josiasquintal4010.can.br/>

Presidência da República do Brasil. 2000. Decreto N° 3665 de 20 de Novembro de 2000. Dá Nova Redação ao Regulamento para a Fiscalização de Protudos Controlados (R-105). Brasília: Casa Civil, Subchefia para Assuntos Jurídicos. Accessed 31 December 2006. <http://www.planalto.gov.br/ccivil_03/decreto/D3665.htm>

——. 2004. Decreto N° 5123 de 1 de Julho de 2004. Regulamenta a Lei N° 10826, de 22 de dezembro de 2003, que dispõe sobre registro, posse e comercialização de armas de fogo e munição, sobre os Sistema Nacional de Armas—SINARM e define crimes. Brasília: Casa Civil, Subchefia para Assuntos Jurídicos. Accessed 31 December 2006. <http://www.planalto.gov.br/ccivil_03/_Ato2004-2006/2004/Decreto/D5123.htm>

Rivero, Patricia. 2005. 'The Value of the Illegal Firearms Market in the City of Rio de Janeiro.' In Rubem Cesar Fernandes. *Brazil: The Guns and the Victims.* Rio de Janeiro: ISER, pp. 146–201. Accessed 2 January 2007.
<http://www.vivario.org.br/publique/media/The_Value_of_the_Ilegal_Firearms_Market_in_the_City_os_Rio_de_Janeiro_by_Patricia_Rivero.pdf>

Red Pepper, The (Kampala). 2004. 'Why did U Buy Israeli Bullets?' Vol. 4, No. 61. 30 September.

Schroeder, Matt. 2004. *Small Arms, Terrorism and the OAS Firearms Convention.* Federation of American Scientists, Occasional Paper No. 1. Washington, DC: Federation of American Scientists. Accessed 20 December.
<http://www.fas.org/asmp/campaigns/smallarms/OAS_Firearms_Convention.html#report>

Secretaria de Segurança Pública do Estado do Rio de Janeiro. 2004. 'Segurança para os policiais: R$ 287,5 milhões investidos em equipamentos e tecnologia.' *Jornal da Policia do Estado do Rio de Janeiro,* N° 17. Novembro.

——. 2005. *Operação Navalha na Carne: Navalha na Carne Prende Policiais que Vendiam Munição para Traficantes.* Rio de Janeiro: Secretaria de Segurança Pública. 20 July. Accessed 23 January 2007. <http://www.ssp.rj.gov.br/noticia.asp?id=1521>

Small Arms Survey. 2004. *Small Arms Survey 2004: Rights at Risk.* Oxford: Oxford University Press.

——. 2006. *Small Arms Survey 2006: Unfinished Business.* Oxford: Oxford University Press.

Stefanini, Roberto. 2005. *Mafie o Criminalità Dis-Organizzatta? I Fenomeni Criminali di Rio de Janeiro e le Politiche Pubbliche di Contrasto, una Comparazione con il Caso Italiano di Lotta Alla Máfia.* MA dissertation, Università degli Studi di Bologna, Sede di Buenos Aires. October.

UN Comtrade (UN Commodity Trade). Department of Economic and Social Affairs/Statistics Division. 2006. UN Comtrade database. <http://unstats.un.org/unsd/comtrade/>

Xinhua. 1996a. 'State-owned Enterprises: Economic Cooperation Agreement Signed with China.' 4 April. Reported in BBC Summary of World Broadcasts. 15 April 1996.

——. 1996b. 'Year-ender. Item No. 1219001.' Beijing: Xinhua News Agency. 19 December.

ACKNOWLEDGEMENTS

Principal authors

James Bevan and Pablo Dreyfus

Contributors

Walter Barros, Marcelo de Sousa Nascimento, and Júlio Cesar Purcena

A woman armed with a Kalashnikov prepares an evening meal with her child in a homestead in Rumbek, 900 km south of Khartoum, in September 2003. © Patrick Olum/Reuters

Persistent Instability

ARMED VIOLENCE AND INSECURITY IN SOUTH SUDAN

INTRODUCTION

Since January 2005 Sudan has been implementing a fragile peace deal. After 37 years of conflict in two North–South civil wars (1956–72 and 1983–2005), the signing of the Comprehensive Peace Agreement (CPA) marked the official beginning of a transition to peace and sustainable development. Yet the 'post-conflict' environment in the south of the country remains inherently unstable: small arms and light weapons are ubiquitous.

South Sudan remains a highly militarized society with few employment opportunities, a large number of armed groups, a heavily armed civilian population, and intractable local conflicts. Many sources of instability lie outside the framework of the two civil wars (and therefore beyond the influence of the CPA), particularly those related to access to scarce natural resources. All the actors—including the Sudan People's Liberation Movement/Army (SPLM/A), government security forces, militias, Other Armed Groups, paramilitaries, and civilians—have access to and (mis)use small arms and light weapons.

Given its porous borders with five other countries and the proximity to war-torn Darfur, South Sudan must become stable if the region as a whole is to achieve stability. Sudan is at the epicentre of one of the most vibrant arms markets in the world, resulting from decades of insurgencies, civil wars, proxy wars, communal clashes, weak governance, and criminal violence in the region. The Central African Republic, Chad, the Democratic Republic of the Congo (DRC), Eritrea, Ethiopia, Somalia, and Uganda have all been scenes of recent intra-state or inter-state wars. Most other countries in the greater Horn of Africa, such as Kenya, have also hosted lethal communal clashes. UN arms embargoes have been imposed on several states, including Sudan, but remain extremely difficult to enforce. Their enforcement is of increasing importance to international peace and security. The UN Refugee Agency (UNHCR) estimates that Sudan, DRC, and Somalia are among the top ten refugee-producing states in the world.[1] The US State Department also unofficially refers to the Horn as a second front in the war on terror.[2]

This chapter analyses some of the threats facing South Sudan in the wake of the signing of the CPA. It examines the political transition, the proliferation of armed groups, the role and effects of armed violence on its communities, and the emerging framework for making it more secure. In so doing, it draws on research by the Small Arms Survey's Human Security Baseline Assessment (HSBA) research project on Sudan.[3]

These are the chapter's main findings:

- The official end of the second civil war has failed to improve security for much of South Sudan's population.
- Inter-personal armed violence and criminality remain pervasive.
- Small arms are highly accessible and (mis)used by all sectors of society.
- Armed violence frequently involves inter-ethnic or intra-clan hostility over access to natural resources.
- Endemic poverty and a lack of educational and employment opportunities sustain armed violence.

- A robust demand for small arms is driven by the perceived need for protection in the absence of functioning security institutions.

- Disarmament of civilians must be transparent, reciprocal, and civilian-led to avoid igniting conflict.

- Counter-productive elements in the National Congress Party (NCP) continue to undermine the CPA.

- Sudan's natural resources are likely to be the cause of future North–South conflict.

- 'Post-conflict' South Sudan needs sustained international attention to prevent the CPA from breaking down.

The chapter concludes that the CPA and the Government of South Sudan (GoSS) have yet to deliver many of the expected peace dividends. It maintains that greater international focus and funding[4] are required if the region is to implement the peace agreement and undertake crucial disarmament, demobilization, and reintegration (DDR), civilian disarmament, and security sector reform (SSR). Almost half of all countries emerging from armed conflict have a tendency to suffer a relapse within five years of signing a peace agreement (Small Arms Survey, 2005, p. 267). South Sudan is in danger of becoming one of them.

'POST-CONFLICT' POLITICAL TRANSITION

On 9 January 2005, the SPLM/A signed a peace agreement with the Government of Sudan (GoS), officially ending the country's second North–South civil war. At the heart of the country's longest conflict—which was responsible for the death of some two million people (Lacina and Gleditsch, 2005, p. 159)[5] and the displacement of more than five million others[6]—was a struggle for political, economic, religious, and cultural autonomy for the southern region, and its resistance to exclusionary government policies and repression that had lasted decades.

Sudan's natural resources are likely to be the cause of future North–South conflict.

Differences of religion and ethnicity were manipulated and politicized on all sides to produce the clichéd paradigm of an Arab–Muslim north fighting an African–Christian/animist south. In fact, large numbers of Muslims also fought against the government, which in turn struck tactical agreements with many non-Muslim groups in the south in a divide-and-rule strategy. The GoS 'outsourced' the conflict to numerous militias and paramilitary outfits. Traditional rivalries over cattle, water, and grazing were exploited, with the ensuing struggles dividing along ethnic lines. Following a 1991 split in the SPLM/A, intra-south factional fighting produced a patchwork of territories under the control of different militias, which at various times had been aligned with the GoS (Young, 2006c, p. 19).

The CPA,[7] signed by the ruling NCP and the SPLM/A, was the fruit of a decade of negotiations. The deal included a historic compromise: the 'Islamist' government in Khartoum was granted *sharia* law in the north, while the south obtained the pledge of a referendum on independence after a transitional period of six years. With further provisions on an internationally monitored ceasefire, participation in central government, access to oil wealth, the separation of religion and state, autonomy in the interim period, and a southern army to act as guarantor should the agreement break down, the CPA addressed a number of key southern grievances. The agreement was designed to be implemented over a six-and-a-half-year period, consisting of a pre-interim period of six months (January–July 2005) and a six-year transitional period (July 2005–July 2011), culminating in the referendum on secession.

The use of the word 'comprehensive' in the name of the peace agreement is misleading. In reality, the CPA is an agreement between two dominant military elites, the NCP and the SPLM/A. The SPLM/A controls most, but not all, of South Sudan. The many other militias operating in the region, termed Other Armed Groups (OAGs) in the CPA,

Women celebrate after the signing of the Comprehensive Peace Agreement between the SPLM/A and the Government of Sudan, Malakal, South Sudan, 11 January 2005. © Reuters

were excluded from negotiations, giving rise to further internecine conflict. This approach was carefully incorporated into the peace agreement, which stipulates that no groups allied to either the SPLA or the Sudanese Armed Forces (SAF) shall be allowed to operate in the post-CPA environment.[8]

Since the death of the former vice-president of Sudan and GoSS president John Garang in a helicopter crash in July 2005, his successor, Salva Kiir, has introduced a more conciliatory tone (Young, 2006c, p. 25). The 8 January 2006 Juba Declaration on Unity and Integration between the SPLM/A and the South Sudan Defence Forces (SSDF),[9] a loose umbrella of government-aligned armed groups, was the culmination of this rapprochement. Since then a ceasefire has been in place between the SPLM and the SSDF and many—but not all—OAGs have aligned themselves with the SPLA.[10] Yet the risk of outbreaks of fighting involving 'rump' SSDF members remains. November 2006 saw two days of heavy clashes among SPLA forces (largely comprising former SSDF members), SAF, and the SAF-aligned militia of Gabriel Tang-Ginya in Malakal, the capital of the oil-rich Upper Nile region, in which an estimated 150 people were killed. This fighting, which led to a decisive victory for the SPLA, remains the most serious violation of the ceasefire to date.

Meanwhile, the Government of National Unity (GNU), in which the SPLM is a minority partner, has had to face armed conflict on two other fronts. The CPA's exclusivist nature and widespread grievances in other marginalized areas of Sudan have inspired groups in the west and east to challenge Khartoum through armed insurgencies. The bitter conflict in the western region of Darfur simmered for years, and then exploded in early 2003. A scorched-earth policy by government security forces and Khartoum-backed militia groups from Sudan and Chad has displaced more than two million people in Darfur and 230,000 in Chad[11] and resulted in the deaths of several hundred thousand.[12] The signing of the CPA, several cessation of hostilities agreements,[13] UN Security Council resolutions,[14] and arms embargoes coupled with the deployment of an African Union peacekeeping mission, have failed to bring peace to the region. The Darfur Peace Agreement, signed by the GoS and just one of several rebel factions on 5 May 2006, was widely rejected by the Darfurians themselves and is now considered a failure.[15] Far from bringing peace to the region, it splintered the anti-agreement bloc and resulted in a further surge of violence,[16] internecine fighting, and diminished humanitarian access[17] as the signatories tried to implement it by brute force. A proxy war with Chad has further exacerbated the situation, with both countries aiding the other's respective rebel groups[18] and increased fighting on Chadian soil. Flows of weapons to dozens of militias and armed groups in Darfur, Chad, and Central African Republic[19] risk further expanding the conflict, including to South Sudan.

Simmering resentment in eastern Sudan resulted in the Beja Congress political group taking up arms in 1995 and launching its first anti-government attacks the following year. In February 2005 the Beja Congress merged with the smaller Rashaida Free Lions rebel group to form the Eastern Front. In June 2006 the Eastern Front signed a declaration of principles for the resolution of the conflict, culminating in the signing of the Eastern Sudan Peace Agreement of 14 October 2006, which is deemed largely a deal between the governments of Sudan and Eritrea and offers little hope for the people of the region (Young, 2007a, p. 1).[20] Since then implementation of the agreement has stagnated (UNSC, 2007c, para. 21).

South Sudan's armed groups can be broken down into Khartoum-aligned, foreign, and community-based.

Against this background of widespread violence, the SPLM faces the challenge of transforming itself from a guerrilla movement into a functioning member of the GNU and a senior partner in the GoSS.[21] The GoSS was established on 22 October 2005, but its acute lack of experience in governance, institutional incapacity, administrative weakness, and the near-total absence of educated personnel hamper its ability to formulate and implement policy, and to professionalize itself. Allegations of corruption are rife (UNSC, 2007c, para. 16). Military costs continue to consume substantial resources[22] and sufficient priority is not being given to setting up viable systems of local government. Donors are keen to support the fragile government but are still failing to exert the necessary pressure on Khartoum to honour the CPA fully.

ARMED GROUPS IN SOUTH SUDAN

South Sudan has long been a particularly fluid political, military, and security environment. One of its most striking features is the array of armed groups operating within its borders, or transiting through them. Another is the blurred distinction that exists between civilians and combatants, most of whom are equipped with small arms. Outside the core SPLA forces, the majority of OAGs and community-based armed groups are 'harvest guerillas' who are not permanently engaged in military operations and can be mobilized as required. Many civilians who fall outside the ambit of these groups are also armed and operate either as part of or in conjunction with the formal armed groups.

Despite their overlapping roles, South Sudan's armed groups can be broken down into the following categories: Khartoum-aligned militias; foreign armed groups; and community-based armed groups. Small arms and light weapons have circulated freely to these groups from a combination of sources, foreign and domestic. For decades the principal source of weapons entering Sudan has been neighbouring states. Within Sudan sources of weapons include: the SPLA, SAF, and militia groups who distribute weapons in parallel system of patronage; pooled community arms for 'self-defence' forces; local militias; theft, desertion, purchases, and barter; cross-border trafficking and raiding; and abandoned stockpiles and battlefield losses (IDDRP, 2005, p. 9). In addition, arms distributions by the GoS have spiked since oil revenues began to flow in 2001. GoS channelling of weapons to local proxies has facilitated proliferation, which is further eased by the almost total absence of transparency in stockpile management. In recent years a booming private arms market operated by international traffickers has also thrived in the region (Small Arms Survey, 2007b).

As in other parts of Africa, multiple motivations drive the use of small arms and membership of armed groups, including forcible conscription into these groups, the dearth of employment and educational opportunities, poverty, and opportunities for pillage (Small Arms Survey, 2006a, p. 252). Ideological convictions are frequently absent, or evaporate in the face of opportunities for self-aggrandizement (Florquin and Berman, 2005, p. 386).

Khartoum-aligned militias[23] (see Annexe 1)

Throughout the CPA negotiations the SPLM/A maintained an inflexible approach to the way in which OAGs were addressed and, despite resistance from the Khartoum delegation and some concerns expressed by international advisers and observers, this position is reflected in the final wording of the peace agreement. Firstly, the SPLM insisted that the SPLA alone would be the lawful armed force of the GoSS. Secondly, OAGs could choose only between joining the SPLA or the SAF: no third-party armed groups would be accepted or recognized following the signature of the agreement. Finally, no framework for integrating OAGs into the lawful armed forces of the GoSS was considered—other than direct integration into the SPLA.

Despite this hard-line posture during negotiations, differences existed within the SPLM/A between Garang and his military commanders, notably the then chief of staff, Salva Kiir, on how to handle the OAGs. Garang's position reflected a belief that they should effectively surrender to the SPLA. Kiir and the majority of SPLA commanders favoured a more flexible approach. Subsequently, and despite Garang's replacement by Kiir, the absence of a clearly defined process of integration for the OAGs has undermined efforts to neutralize the threat they still pose in South Sudan. The piecemeal integration of various groups has been based largely on political inducements to OAG leaders, leaving some individual members resistant to, and fearful of, integration.

> Formed in 1997, the SSDF became the umbrella for the majority of South Sudan's government-aligned armed groups.

The SSDF—the most significant component of the OAGs—has a long history of causing disruption to civilian life in South Sudan. The SSDF derives its origins from two sources: local, tribal armed groups that formed to protect their communities from the SPLA; and the forces that followed commanders Riek Machar and Lam Akol when they split from Garang in 1991 (Young, 2006c, p. 13). The first was composed of militias from Equatoria with no articulate political programme. The second was made up of Nuer from Upper Nile who broke with Garang because of his authoritarianism and his commitment to a united Sudan, while Machar and his followers favoured southern self-determination.

Formed in 1997 after the signing of the Khartoum Peace Agreement between the GoS, the South Sudan Independence Movement, and five other southern factions, the SSDF became the umbrella for the majority of South Sudan's government-aligned armed groups. These groups shared a commitment to the Khartoum agreement, which held the GoS to a vote on self-determination for the south,[24] and an opposition to the SPLM/A and Garang. It gave its southern signatories a sense of identity, a rationale for tactical alliance with the GoS, and a measure of confidence that others would come to their aid if they were attacked. It also served as a rallying point for the large group of southerners who were left outside the peace process that led to the CPA but wanted their interests recognized. In return for their allegiance, the NCP rewarded SSDF officers, particularly those it favoured, with high ranks, generous salaries, houses, cars, and other material benefits. Rank-and-file soldiers, on the other hand, were provided with little more than guns and ammunition, forcing them to resort to looting to survive (Young, 2006c, p. 28).

Map 10.1 Other Armed Groups in South Sudan: main areas of operation as of September 2006

From the NCP's perspective, the SSDF was an effective ally because it could challenge the SPLA militarily; was successful in defending government assets, notably the oilfields; was economical (most of its members received limited training and weapons); and because it deepened divisions in the south, weakening the SPLA politically (Young, 2006c, p. 23).

The signing of the CPA effectively killed the Khartoum agreement and precluded the continued existence of the OAGs. The CPA stipulates that all OAGs in Sudan are required to declare their alignment to either the SPLA or the SAF within one year of the signing of the agreement.[25] Those remaining aligned with Khartoum were then expected to redeploy to northern Sudan to be integrated into the SAF, form part of the SAF component of the Joint Integrated Units (JIUs) which will serve as combined SPLA–SAF units until the 2011 referendum, or be demobilized.[26] This forced alignment led to much resentment and many analysts believed that Garang was laying the groundwork for another civil war in the south. When Kiir became president of South Sudan, he adopted a diametrically opposed approach

Paulino Matieb and Salva Kiir clasp hands during a ceremony in Juba, January 2006. © AFP/Getty Images

to the issue (Young, 2006c, p. 25). During his inauguration visit to Khartoum in August 2005, he held a number of informal meetings with the SSDF leadership, followed by a decision to appoint some 20 SSDF cadres as commissioners, and to assign an unspecified number to state legislatures. The 8 January 2006 Juba Declaration, which formally merged the SSDF and the SPLM, followed. Since then an alignment process has occurred with most commanders and soldiers within the formal SSDF ranks declaring their allegiance to the SPLA (see Map 10.1). As part of this process, former SSDF leader Paulino Matieb was appointed Kiir's deputy in the military structure of the GoSS, and therefore nominally the second most powerful figure in the SPLA. Since then there has been a consolidation of power within the SPLM/A between both men (Young, 2007a, p. 6).

While the Juba Declaration can be considered a success, a number of difficulties could trigger future insecurity in South Sudan: first, reaching agreement in the SPLA on the ranks that SSDF officers will hold—made difficult because the latter were promoted too rapidly by SAF to gain their allegiance; second, reaching agreement (and implementing it) on whether absorbed officers will be retired, placed on non-active lists, or given active commands; third, providing provisions and salaries to a large number of new members; and, finally, integrating high-ranking SSDF members into the SPLA, thereby bringing former enemies into positions of leadership.

Box 10.1 Pitfalls to accurate estimates of SSDF force size

There is no doubt that the SSDF comprised a significant number of fighters at the peak of its activity. During the latter stages of the second civil war, components of the SSDF (of which there were more than 30) controlled large parts of western, central, and eastern Upper Nile; parts of northern and western Bahr El Ghazal; and areas of Eastern Equatoria, where they provided security for GoS garrisons and the country's emergent oil industry. These achievements required large numbers of men in different places simultaneously.

But arriving at an accurate count of SSDF forces remains problematic. First, the numbers change constantly as recruitment in some groups is ongoing. Secondly, the SSDF is made up largely of irregular forces. Thirdly, some individuals may identify themselves as affiliated at one moment, but reject the label once a specific objective has been achieved.

Before the SPLA–SSDF merger, the latter's number was estimated to range from 10,000 to 30,000 (Small Arms Survey, 2006c, p. 3), but all such figures must be treated with caution.

Source: Small Arms Survey (2006c, p. 4)

As of March 2007 groups of former SSDF leaders and their followers, including Gordon Kong, Gabriel Tang-Ginya, Thomas Maboir, and Atom al-Nour, remained allied to Khartoum and based in South Sudan. In return, some of them were promised posts in the JIUs. Recent alignments with the SPLA include remnants of the Equatoria Defence Force (EDF) under John Belgium and some of al-Nour's Fertit militia in Wau (Young, 2007a, p. 12). Others have not yet declared their allegiance, or continue to change alignment. Most of those who have switched sides have done so from the SAF to the SPLA to avoid having to move to northern Sudan (UNMIS, 2007, p. 58). Indeed, more than 7,700 troops have been 'voluntarily discharged' by the SAF because of their unwillingness to redeploy to the north (UNMIS, 2007, p. 53).

Ongoing GoS support for these groups[27] is widely interpreted as part of an effort to foster insecurity and desta- bilize the fledgling GoSS. Following the violence that erupted in Malakal in November 2006, which involved Tang- Ginya's forces, there are fears of a repetition in other cities, such as Wau and possibly the southern capital, Juba.[28]

Box 10.2 Alignment with Khartoum in the aftermath of the Juba Declaration

Gordon Kong, who is one of the more formidable holdouts to the SPLA–SSDF merger, controls areas of particular significance to South Sudan's overall peace. Kong assumed leadership of the SSDF after Paulino Matieb aligned with the SPLA. His forces are based north of Nasir in Upper Nile State. As of August 2006 he claimed approximately 75–85 'active' forces, though he could also count on about 300 'reserve' forces in the surrounding area. Most of the weapons used by his militia are small arms, though there appear to be light machine guns and mortars scattered throughout militia camps.[29] Kong's core faction, the Nasir Peace Force, is based in Ketbek, a village a few kilometres north of Nasir.

Kong has publicly rejected alignment with the SPLM/A and denounced the Juba Declaration, although his motives are hard to discern. As with other militias who have not aligned themselves with the SPLM/A, his primary objective appears to be to retain his power base until the 2011 referendum on secession. By staying out of the SPLA, he expects to gain more leverage and authority. For this reason, it is likely that Kong's forces will resist all DDR efforts before the referendum.

A contingent of Kong's forces is located near Adar in northern Upper Nile State, as well as other small towns in the vicinity. These include two groups of some 200 fighters. Until spring 2006, the Adar unit also maintained a base in Guelguk, to the west of Adar. The proximity of these forces to one another, to local oilfields, and to the border with northern Sudan makes the area potentially incendiary. Particularly important is the Adar oilfield, which is currently operational.[30] According to SPLM/A sources, Adar will be a key strategic location for the GoS should hostilities between SAF and the SPLM/A reignite.[31] Logistical support to and command of these SAF-aligned forces comes from its bases in Kosti and Adar[32] (an assembly point for SAF forces in the south, under the CPA). Estimates vary, but in August 2006 there were reportedly 300–400 active SSDF forces in and around the area.[33] These included the arrival in July 2006 of four busloads of SSDF recruits previously based in Khartoum.[34]

Source: Small Arms Survey (2006c, p. 5)

After these clashes, GoS Defence Minister Abdelrahim Mohamed made a statement ordering militias in South Sudan to either choose the SPLA or move to North Sudan to join the SAF (*Sudan Tribune,* 2006). In so doing, he effectively acknowledged ongoing support from Khartoum for the militia (Young 2007a, p. 11). Since then security in South Sudan, and in particular greater Upper Nile, has improved (Young, 2007a, p. 20) apart from civil disturbances related to the non-payment of salaries. But the political wing of the SSDF, the South Sudan United Democratic Alliance (SSUDA), has issued a clear warning about possible future clashes. 'The SPLM/A cannot possibly claim, and misleads the world, that they are the only people who have fought in South Sudan liberation,' said a spokesman for the group in March 2007.[35] 'We could have a messy situation in the South because no members of the SSUDA/SSDF will move to the north against their free will,' he warned.

Foreign armed groups[36]

A number of foreign armed groups operate within, or transit through, South Sudan en route to neighbouring states. Among the best known is the Ugandan Lord's Resistance Army (LRA),[37] which has had bases in Sudan since 1994. During the 1990s, Khartoum supplied the LRA with arms, provisions, and shelter in its stronghold of Juba in return for weakening SPLA control of areas in Eastern Equatoria. Since 1994 the LRA has been a major source of regional insecurity, although some of its reported attacks against civilians may have been committed by members of the SPLA, the Ugandan People's Defence Forces (UPDF), bandits, or SAF-aligned components of the (EDF) militia. For the GoSS, neutralizing the group is a precondition to restoring security in Eastern and Western Equatoria, and implementing the CPA. Furthermore, the UPDF has had an unpopular official presence on Sudanese soil since 2002, when Khartoum issued a military protocol allowing it to operate against the LRA.

Although Khartoum officially stopped equipping the LRA in 1999, following another agreement with the Government of Uganda (GoU), sources say that it continued to send supplies for a long time after (Schomerus, 2006, p. 1). Local people reported seeing air drops as late as 2006, but these may have been directed at other GoS-backed militias, some of them EDF splinter groups. While the LRA says its relationship with Khartoum was severed in 2005, the SPLA reported an airdrop near an LRA base in March 2006, just before the LRA leader, Joseph Kony, moved his base into the DRC.[38] UN troops subsequently moved to Juba and this supply line was cut. The LRA has ensured the continuation of its weapons supply by seizing arms in battles with the UPDF, the SPLA, and even the SAF. Even without external support, however, it is certain that LRA weapons caches in Uganda and Sudan are sufficient for it to sustain an armed insurrection (Schomerus, 2006, p. 2).

> Arms are readily available through the porous borders between Uganda, DRC, and Ethiopia.

Arms are readily available through the porous borders between the DRC, Ethiopia, Kenya, and Uganda. Most small arms in Western Equatoria are traded across the Ugandan border, with Torit and Nimule acting as the main trading centres. Some of the newer weapons carried by the LRA bear Arabic inscriptions. At various stages in the Ugandan conflict, the group used a collection of Russian landmines and rocket-propelled grenades (RPGs), with the larger weapons usually acquired in combat. The main emphasis, however, has been on small arms, which enable the group to maintain the high level of mobility it needs to survive. Soviet-designed recoilless guns are commonly used, with the majority being standard 7.62 mm/short M43s (M-1943), AK-47s, and AKMs, but also FNs, Heckler & Koch firearms (mainly G3s, 7.62 mm), and a number of Browning pistols. Better-equipped LRA units at times carried general-purpose machine guns, most commonly the 7.62 mm RPK, single-barrel M79 40 mm grenade launchers or 40 mm grenade launchers. More expensive guns, such as new Dragunov SVDs and M60s with ample ammunition, were on display when the LRA attended peace talks in Juba in 2006.

The GoSS initiated these talks in 2006 after repeated attempts to establish contact with the LRA high command to offer it three options: withdraw from Sudan; declare war on the SPLA; or negotiate. The LRA chose to talk, leading to the first meeting between Joseph Kony and GoSS Vice-President Riek Machar near the border with the DRC on 3 May 2006. Peace talks between the GoU and the LRA began in July, leading to the signing of a cessation of hostilities agreement on 26 August 2006.

Since then both sides have violated the agreement; on 30 November the UPDF launched a helicopter gunship attack against the group after moving more troops into Sudan. In early 2007, the peace process remained extremely volatile after the LRA demanded a change of venue outside South Sudan and the cessation of hostilities agreement expired on 28 February. Peace talks resumed in Juba on 26 April.

Community-based armed groups: the white army[39]

Not all armed activity in South Sudan has been a source of insecurity. As in West Africa, research has shown that some armed groups evolved as, or continue to be, a source of security in the absence of functioning security institutions (Small Arms Survey, 2006a, p. 250). Local militias and tribal 'self-defence' organizations were common throughout the second civil war in South Sudan, particularly in Nuer areas. Their members were mostly young men aged 14–25 (Young, 2006a).

In eastern and central Upper Nile State, young men in cattle camps developed greater capabilities than elsewhere because of the martial values of pastoralist life, limited government authority, and the weapons supplied by the GoS through Riek Machar. Anxious to win local support, he distributed thousands of guns in the camps after his split with the SPLA in 1991. Initially the weapons were regarded as a collective resource to protect the community's cattle and were controlled by the tribal elders, but local chiefs soon lost their ability to monitor the use and whereabouts of these guns.

The dissolution of the white army produced a large number of armed, disaffected youths.

In 1991 the so-called white army self-defence units launched an attack against the Bor Dinka, precipitating long-lasting enmity between the two ethnic groups. Although the white army had no central leadership, structure, or guiding ideology, it was drawn into the civil war, albeit on its own terms. From the beginning, it acquired its weapons piecemeal from Machar's SAF suppliers, traders (particularly from those who had moved across the Ethiopian border), SPLA soldiers who sold their guns for food, or as loot acquired in battle. The army was never a standing body, but at times it could mobilize more fighters than either the SSDF or the SPLA, making it a formidable force.

Generally, competition between the SSDF and the SPLA for white army support resulted in the former winning because it provided weapons. The best examples of such 'bargaining' were in Mading, Upper Nile, and Akobo, Jonglei, which changed hands about six times in the three years prior to the CPA. More recently, the SPLM/A's refusal to permit the existence of OAGs and the SPLM's new focus on civilian disarmament have signalled the death knell for the white army.

While it unlikely to rise again as an armed force, its dissolution has produced a large number of armed and disaffected youths who are in danger of resorting to further violence. Research shows that young men who engage in armed violence tend to emerge in contexts of social and economic marginalization (Small Arms Survey, 2006a, p. 298; Hagedorn, 2001, pp. 42–45). When high unemployment, poverty, and relatively high levels of community violence come together, as they do in South Sudan, they produce environments in which youth find armed violence a rational, attractive, and even necessary course of action (Small Arms Survey, 2006a, pp. 302–07).

HUMAN INSECURITY IN SOUTH SUDAN[40]

While it is recognized that the proliferation of armed groups and accompanying firearms continues to contribute to widespread insecurity in South Sudan, quantitative and qualitative information on the extent and frequency of armed violence remains elusive, as does reliable information on the prevalence of civilian gun ownership. Despite these lacunae, the GoSS is actively engaging in civilian disarmament and laying the groundwork for formal DDR. To support their efforts, the Small Arms Survey has begun to conduct a series of household surveys to gather data on the effects and prevalence of both armed violence and small arms. These provide a baseline of information against which future security assessments can be measured. They will measure changes over time, and help assess the impact of both the CPA in general and specific initiatives aimed at reducing violence. Obtaining a baseline of reliable data is particularly important as a means of measuring the success rate of disarmament efforts.

The first survey—the first to address security perceptions and levels of firearm-related crime and victimization since the CPA and prior to post-war disarmament efforts—was undertaken in Lakes State in April 2006. Worryingly, and contrary to expectations, it found that security is widely perceived to have deteriorated in the post-CPA period, mostly due to the misuse of small arms. This follows an established pattern in 'post-conflict' settings in which levels of violence remain surprisingly high, often presenting more threats to civilians than the armed conflict itself (Small Arms Survey, 2005, p. 267).

The Lakes State survey focused on six counties: Rumbek East and Centre, Yirol East and West, Cueibet, and Wulu (see Map 10.2). The state was selected because pre-survey interviews indicated that firearms and explosives were often used in disputes and cattle-rustling episodes. Residents indicated that the police—whose presence was growing—and local authorities were working together to reduce lawlessness in towns, but violent outbreaks were still frequent and preventive police work minimal. This combination of lawlessness and the desire to create order made Lakes a suitable location for an initial survey.

Map 10.2 **Surveyed clusters in Lakes State, Sudan**

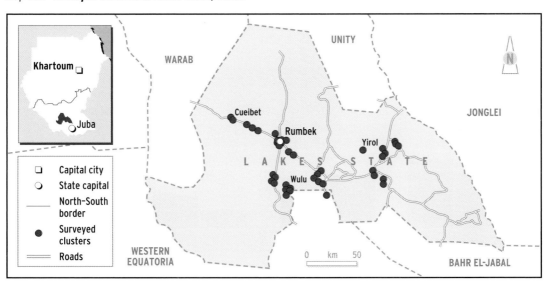

Box 10.3 Survey demographics

Eighty-five per cent of respondents interviewed for the Lakes State household survey were between the ages of 21 and 59; their average age was 35. The following pie charts reveal further demographic details.

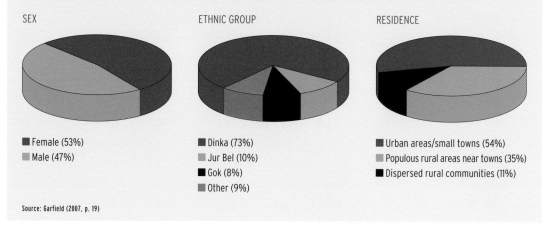

SEX

ETHNIC GROUP

RESIDENCE

■ Female (53%)
■ Male (47%)

■ Dinka (73%)
■ Jur Bel (10%)
■ Gok (8%)
■ Other (9%)

■ Urban areas/small towns (54%)
■ Populous rural areas near towns (35%)
■ Dispersed rural communities (11%)

Source: Garfield (2007, p. 19)

The survey instrument, developed with a group of experts from academic and aid organizations, draws on established epidemiological techniques to review mortality, morbidity, and victimization trends in affected communities. The survey contains more than 140 questions divided into a number of general areas, including: perceptions of security since the CPA; individual and family victimization; sexual assault and access to health services; weapons carrying and use (including small arms and light weapons); and perceived ways of reducing armed violence.

Twelve two-person teams were recruited, each of which was asked to administer 60 interviews with heads of households in a preselected area. In the absence of national or regional census data to construct a representative sample, a semi-representative selection of rural, semi-urban, and urban areas in six of the eight counties of the state was established. The average duration of each interview was slightly more than 30 minutes. More than 670 surveys were administered out of the initial target of 740, producing an overall response rate of 94 per cent, although not all questions were answered all of the time.

Figure 10.1 Safety and security since the CPA (N=579, 621)

PER CENT

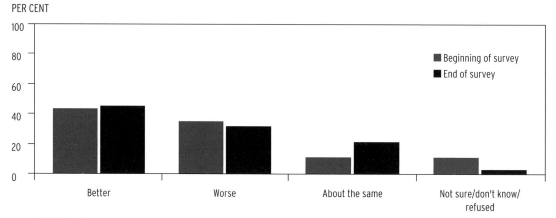

■ Beginning of survey
■ End of survey

Better   Worse   About the same   Not sure/don't know/refused

Source: Garfield (2007, p. 23)

The key findings of the survey include the following (Garfield, 2007, pp. 22–37):

- Respondents were asked twice whether security had improved since the CPA. In both cases, fewer than half reported that security had improved, with about one-third (35 per cent) claiming security had deteriorated since early 2005 (see Figure 10.1). Well under half of respondents claimed to feel safe walking alone at night or to another village (see Table 10.1). Even more dramatically, one-third reported feeling unsafe walking alone during the day.

- More than one-third (35 per cent) of respondents admitted that they or someone in their compound possessed a firearm. Among respondents reporting weapons ownership, the most commonly held arms included AK-47 automatic rifles (31 per cent), revolvers and pistols (26 per cent), shotguns (10 per cent), air guns (4 per cent), and RPG launchers (1 per cent). Firearm carrying outside family compounds was found to have decreased from 30 per cent before the CPA to approximately 15 per cent thereafter, although the reasons for this are unclear.

- Sixty-three per cent of respondents said there were too many guns in the community. The primary group perceived as over-armed was civilians (31 per cent), followed by youths (19 per cent), criminals (16 per cent), and ex-combatants (13 per cent). Civilians, youths, criminals, and private security companies—in addition to ex-combatants— were identified as important target groups of future disarmament programmes.

- More than half of all households reported that members had been robbed and involved in a physical fight with someone from outside their compound since the CPA (see Figure 10.2). More than one in 10 households experienced a sexual assault during the same period—one-third of which were committed by an armed assailant. Almost half of respondents claimed that armed robbery was the most common violent crime they had experienced since the CPA. On average, households were found to have experienced at least one robbery, nearly two fights, and close to one armed attack since the CPA (see Figure 10.3).

- The majority of both victims and perpetrators of all victimization events were found to be men in their twenties. Robberies, armed attacks, and intentional fatal injuries were most commonly attributed to conflicts over livestock. Violent deaths were also frequently linked to 'fights with enemies', usually over cattle, grazing, and water. Within compounds, such fights were most commonly associated with 'disobedience'.

- Guns were the predominant weapon used in each type of violent event (28–72 per cent). Guns were most frequently used in robberies, attacks with a weapon, and deaths from injuries or accidents. Although the use of RPGs or machine guns was reported less frequently, they were more frequently associated with deadly events (14 per cent) than any other weapon after firearms (68 per cent). Sticks, spears, and attacks with hands were more commonly reported in cases of sexual assault (see Table 10.2).

Table 10.1 Perceptions of public safety in daytime and at night

	Daytime	Nighttime	Walking to another village
Very safe	42	26	21
Fairly safe	25	12	18
Somewhat unsafe	12	12	17
Very unsafe	21	50	44

Source: Garfield (2007, p. 34)

Figure 10.2 **Relative frequency of victimization events**

PERCENTAGE OF HOUSEHOLDS
REPORTING AN EVENT

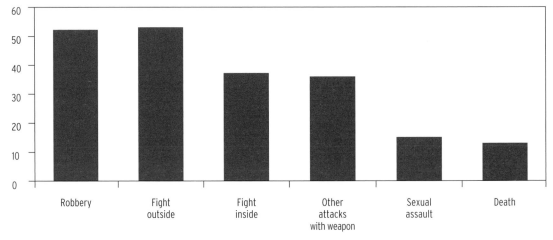

Source: Garfield (2007, p. 23)

Figure 10.3 **Average number of violent events reported in total sample**

AVERAGE NUMBER OF EVENTS
IN TOTAL SAMPLE

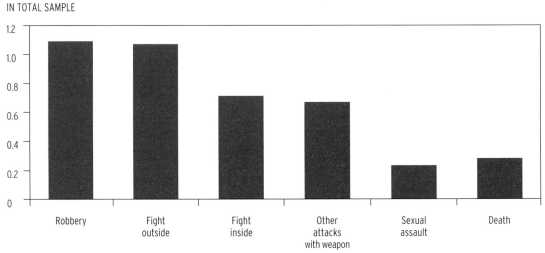

Source: Garfield (2007, p. 24)

- Two-thirds of respondents said reducing the numbers of firearms would make people feel safer, while 20 per cent said it would make people less safe.
- Disarmament and gun control, coupled with SSR and police training, were viewed as the highest priorities for the authorities. More than one-fifth of respondents contended that firearms were South Sudan's *most pressing concern*—outranking even improving access to education (20 per cent), improving health facilities (7 per cent), and reducing unemployment (4 per cent) as the region's most urgent priorities. Almost two-thirds of respondents reported that improvements to the security sector (police and/or military) were needed.

Table 10.2 **Weapons used**						
	Stick	**Gun or rifle**	**RPG or machine gun**	**Explosive**	**Hands**	**Other/none**
Fight outside compound	33	43	0	0	9	15
Fight within compound	42	28	2	0	11	17
Robbery	6	72	3	6	4	9
Sexual assault	23	34	1	6	15	21
Attack with weapon	18	57	2	2	4	17
Death from injury or accident	5	68	14	7	2	4

Source: Garfield (2007, p. 29)

FUTURE CHALLENGES IN SOUTH SUDAN: AN EMERGING FRAMEWORK FOR IMPROVING HUMAN SECURITY

Despite its shortcomings, the CPA is hailed as the only vehicle for the restoration of peace and the reduction of armed violence in South Sudan. It contains detailed provisions on security during the six-year interim period, including a ceasefire, the redeployment and downsizing of the SPLA and SAF, and the dissolution of the OAGs. Under the terms of the agreement, both the GoS and the GoSS are to maintain separate armed forces, with both sides gradually withdrawing behind the North–South border of 1 January 1956. The SAF is required to withdraw all its troops from South Sudan—except for those in the JIUs—in accordance with an agreed schedule, completing 72 per cent by January 2007 and 100 per cent by 9 July 2007.[41] The SPLM/A was required to have fully withdrawn from eastern Sudan by January 2006 and from South Kordofan and Blue Nile states (disputed border areas) within six months of the full deployment of the JIUs to these areas.[42]

The pace of implementation of the CPA, which is being monitored by the UN Mission in Sudan (UNMIS),[43] has been slow, however. The SPLA withdrew from the east in July 2006, some six months late, while the formation of the JIUs has suffered 'inordinate delays' (UNMIS, 2007, p. 53). The units are still not operational, integrated or trained and reportedly contain large numbers of unruly former OAG members.[44] Delays in formation have also prevented the SPLA from redeploying from border areas (UNMIS, 2007, p. 53), which was to have been completed by 9 April 2006. SAF deployment from southern Sudan has made progress but by March 2007 there were still no reliable figures available for the respective force sizes (including the aligned OAGs), complicating verification.[45]

Despite the uncertainty surrounding the numbers of combatants in South Sudan and the sizes of their stockpiles, DDR is clearly mandated by the CPA and recognized as a key step towards obtaining a more peaceful environment.[46] All combatants (and their dependants) affected by the dissolution of the OAGs and subsequent proportional down-sizing of the SPLA, SAF, and Popular Defence Force (PDF) paramilitaries are to be targeted. Long-term reintegration[47] is supposed to strike a balance between the needs of the ex-combatants and those of the communities from which they come, although how this will be implemented remains unclear. The question of whether individual compensation will be on offer has yet to be resolved, as well as what will be done with the weapons collected. Two commissions are scheduled to lead the implementation process—the North Sudan DDR Commission and the South Sudan DDR Commission (SSDDRC), with an overarching National DDR Coordination Council formulating and overseeing policy. State-level DDR Commissions are scheduled to implement the programme at the local level. Identifying exactly how many individuals are candidates for DDR has now become a key political issue as people hope to take advantage of DDR and anticipated accompanying material benefits.

Planning for DDR has been problematic. By January 2007, the SSDDRC had not been formally established and neither the GNU nor the GoSS legislatures had passed relevant legislation. State-level representation had not begun due to delays in recruiting staff (UNMIS, 2007, p. 62). Both parties had started preregistration, however, and preliminary target groups of some 60,000 SAF personnel (including SAF, PDF, and SAF-aligned OAGs) and 30,000 SPLA-personnel (including aligned OAGs) have been identified. However, the UN DDR Unit, mandated by the CPA to support[48] Sudanese institutions leading the process, has struggled to build a positive relationship with national authorities and to define its role in the process.

Notably, the CPA makes specific reference to the requirement that the parties engage in direct negotiations on force reduction in advance of DDR after the complete withdrawal of the SAF from South Sudan, and some 30 months following the signing of the agreement.[49] This provision reflects the reality that neither party was likely to undertake significant demobilization in the first two years of the interim period. On this basis the Sudan DDR programme (as outlined in the CPA) was specifically designed to focus on preparatory work, capacity building of the northern and

SPLA soldiers train in the Mestre area of western Sudan near to the border with Chad in August 2004. © Luc Gnago/Reuters

southern commissions, community arms issues, and the removal of children, women associated with armed groups, and the disabled from the armed forces for the first two years. It specifically excluded substantial demobilization until the completion of force reduction negotiations. A recent review of programme implementation strongly criticizes UNMIS's failure to follow through on the original programme strategy, however, and points out that the necessary preparatory work with the Sudanese authorities has not been undertaken (DFID, 2006). These shortcomings have resulted in a serious loss of momentum and confidence among the parties involved, alongside a reluctance to disarm in anticipation of possible future hostilities.

Indeed, as the focus of GoSS attention moves to the next phase of the peace process, which will see border demarcation, a census, elections in 2009, and the crucial referendum on secession in 2011, fears of a possible break-down of the CPA are growing (Young, 2007a). Both the elections and the referendum are dependent on the census which, in turn, is dependent on border demarcation—a process that will determine where crucial natural resources lie.[50] It is now widely expected that the entire North–South border area may become a focus of disagreement between the SPLM/A and the NCP and there is a build-up of armed forces in border areas as a result.[51] Areas of particular concern include oil-producing regions,[52] Hoffra near Raja, which is believed to have large deposits of copper and uranium, and Kaka, north of Melut, which has gum Arabic (Young, 2007a, pp. 19–25). Special petroleum police have reportedly replaced the SAF in the Polach and Adar oil production areas and similar units have been reported in Difra and other oilfields in Abyei.[53] In Bentiu SPLA officials report that these police have their origins in the intelligence forces and are well trained and equipped with heavy weapons (Young, 2007a, p. 22).[54]

> Community-based weapons-reduction initiatives are emerging frameworks for violence reduction.

Despite these ongoing security threats and what some see as preparation for future conflict, the GoSS and other actors are simultaneously making efforts to work to reverse insecurity and the widespread misuse of small arms at the local level. Community-based weapons-reduction initiatives and the informal harnessing of local security arrangements are two emerging frameworks for violence reduction.

Disarming civilians: the case of northern Jonglei State[55]

Initiatives aimed at reducing private weapons possession and associated violence are increasingly understood as a fundamental part of post-conflict recovery, alongside DDR (Small Arms Survey, 2005, pp. 279–80). They involve activities such as public awareness campaigns, the tightening of regulatory frameworks, and civilian disarmament pro-grammes. Increasingly, they are linked with DDR as follow-on activities or aim to address gaps in DDR programmes.

Well aware of the high levels of gun ownership among civilians (see above), the GoSS began an ad hoc programme of civilian disarmament ahead of formal DDR[56] but as of March 2007 had yet to develop a comprehensive plan that the international community could legitimately support. Research shows that disarmament initiatives are especially complex in environments such as South Sudan, where there is no tradition of civilian oversight or transparency (Small Arms Survey, 2005, p. 283). Added to this is the lack of protection from armed attack by a viable police service. Lessons learned from an SPLA-led disarmament campaign in 2006 in Jonglei State, which led to considerable blood-shed and ethnic tension, include the complex nature of the required approaches. The current challenge is to learn from recent mistakes and to continue the disarmament process without further heightening local insecurity.

In late 2005, the SPLA decided to disarm the Lou Nuer in northern Jonglei State. This programme was to serve a number of purposes: to end disputes between local ethnic groups; to reinforce recognition that the SPLA was the only force with the right to bear arms; to quash fears that the SAF was supporting Jonglei dissidents to undermine the peace process; and to respond to UN pressure to carry out disarmament and ensure the security necessary for

Map 10.3   Selected civilian disarmament sites, Jonglei State, 2006

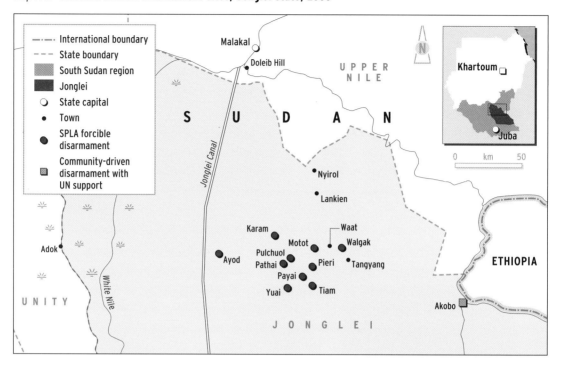

development (young, 2006b, p. 1). The disarmament task (see Map 10.3) was assigned to a Lou Nuer, Gen. Peter Bol Kong, whose force was ethnically mixed, to reduce the risk that the Lou would view the exercise as a means of weakening them.

Problems began in December 2005, when Lou and Gawaar Nuer pastoralists requested permission from the Dinka Hol and Nyarweng in Duk county to graze cattle on their land. The Dinka civil authorities asked the Nuer first to surrender their weapons, which they refused to do. In response, two conferences were held to resolve the dispute, but local white army members argued that they needed their weapons to protect themselves from neighbouring Murle, who had been allowed to retain their arms. During these meetings it was stressed that a forcible campaign would take place if weapons were not surrendered voluntarily. Against this background, the first skirmishes broke out between the white army and the SPLA. Wutnyang Gatkek, a Nuer spiritual leader and a former white army member, was killed in January 2006 when he went to Yuai on behalf of the SPLA to sell the disarmament programme, threatening an intensified inter-clan conflict. His death and the killing of a growing number of other SPLA soldiers stimulated demands from within the SPLA for a more aggressive response.

Skirmishing in January 2006 gave way to major battles pitting elements of the white army, the SSDF forces of Thomas Maboir, and those of Simon Gatwitch under his deputy Simon Wojong against the 'disarmament forces' of Gen. Bol Kong. A helicopter seen visiting Wojong's camp near Yuai was believed to be ferrying SAF supplies to his forces, which were assisting the white army.[57] The conflict ended on 18 May 2006, when the latter lost 113 fighters in a battle with the SPLA in the Motot area, against the loss of one SPLA soldier.[58] Between December 2005 and May 2006, some 1,200 white army members, 400 SPLA soldiers, and an undetermined number of civilians were reportedly killed.[59] The number of weapons collected during the disarmament campaign remains uncertain. According to the UN, the exercise resulted in 3,300 weapons being obtained from Lou Nuer, while local SPLM officials claimed that 3,701 weapons were acquired in the Nyirol area alone (Small Arms Survey, 2006d, p. 4). Some of these were taken to unknown destinations while others were held locally.

One significant impact of the disarmament exercise and the resulting fighting was a serious food shortage in the area. SPLA and white army units stole cattle and other livestock, impoverishing local communities, while the Lou Nuer were unable to plant. A further impact was the effective destruction of the white army in the region, as many members lost their weapons.[60] These developments also had a negative effect on other planned disarmament exercises, particularly in Akobo, another Lou Nuer community. In response to the violence, Commissioner Doyak Choal of Akobo hurriedly moved to carry out a disarmament process using traditional authorities and youth leaders, and without direct SPLA involvement. With the grudging approval of Bol Kong and the assurance of neighbouring Murle leaders that they would not attack, disarmament was peacefully carried out in Akobo in July 2006. Some 1,400 weapons were retrieved relatively peacefully (Small Arms Survey, 2006d, p. 5).

Most of the tribal leaders taking part in the Akobo exercise were anxious to demonstrate to the SPLA that an effective, peaceful, and voluntary disarmament process could take place in Jonglei. They were also seeking to regain authority in their communities and to reduce white army influence. A UN engagement[61] was added to improve legitimacy and to ensure the safe transportation of surrendered weapons. From a UN perspective, the Akobo cam-

Nuer men armed with Kalashnikovs guard their cattle against raiders, December 2005. © Sven Torfinn/Panos Pictures

paign offered UNMIS a pilot for other civilian disarmament programmes, although there were concerns that most agencies and state entities were unprepared.

Local security arrangements– 'governance without government'– comprise South Sudan's main source of community security.

The SPLM/A has said it is committed to the disarmament of all South Sudan's ethnic groups, and campaigns are ongoing, including in Jonglei and Lakes states. The above case study illustrates, however, that its capacity to undertake this without violence, and in the absence of a coherent and transparent strategy, remains in question. The civilian disarmament was led, planned, and implemented by the military with little sign of accountability. Many in the SPLM/A leadership do not think sufficient efforts were made to mobilize local authorities and chiefs to support the exercise. Questions were also raised as to whether the campaigns in Jonglei State retrieved most of the weapons in the area and what has been done with them since.[62] In addition doubts have also been expressed as to whether the SPLM/A wants to disarm these groups to improve security, or simply to reinforce its power base.

The UN role was deemed controversial for having encouraged the SPLA/M to disarm civilians before the outbreak of violence, and for failing to denounce it after the violence erupted. Significantly, the exercise was not truly voluntary[63] since the forces of Bol Kong had threatened intervention if the disarmament did not take place. Recognition of this has led to a fierce debate within the UN about whether it can support similar efforts in future.[64]

Finally, the initiative illustrated the importance of adopting a reciprocal and regional approach to disarmament grounded in a thorough knowledge of local politics and the root causes of local conflicts. This has major implications for future disarmament efforts, since any initiative that fails to address these issues will expose communities to attack by their neighbours.

Harnessing local security arrangements to reduce armed violence: the Kapoeta case[65]

The term 'local security arrangements' (LSAs) encompasses systems of 'governance without government' that currently comprise South Sudan's main source of community security. These arrangements emerged during years of warfare and provided communities with modest levels of security and conflict management in the absence of any effective state presence (Menkhaus, 2006). Such coping mechanisms are the product of extensive negotiation, and usually focus on the provision of basic communal and household security, law and order, conflict management and prevention, routinized sharing of common resources, and predictable market access. They are highly valued by local communities, but are typically illiberal in their application of law and order, and often incompatible with national constitutions.

Central governments have variable and fluid relations with LSAs. States can attempt to suppress, ignore, co-opt, co-exist, or partner with them, depending on their interests, needs, and circumstances. Traditionally, externally funded state-building and DDR initiatives in post-conflict settings have tended to view them as inconsequential, devoting resources exclusively to strengthening the capacity of central government. But recent evidence suggests that more post-conflict governments and donors are adopting a more proactive approach by seeking opportunities to forge partnerships in which LSAs can play a central role in delivering basic governance to communities beyond state reach. This includes the SPLM, which has enshrined in its guiding principles a commitment to 'acknowledge and incorporate the role of traditional elders and customary law in local administration' (Mullen, 2005, p. 3), and key external donors, which are actively exploring models to harmonize traditional authorities with emerging state structures. However, LSAs vary considerably in capacity, legitimacy, and composition: many are hybrid arrangements, blending customary law with contemporary actors and practices. Some may have an important role to play in DDR and state-building initiatives in South Sudan, whereas others may be only transitional coping mechanisms.

Map 10.4 **Selected ethnic groups in Eastern Equatoria**

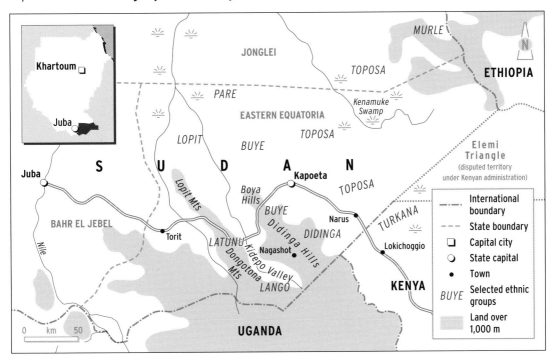

Research in Kapoeta, Eastern Equatoria, reveals that security has improved considerably at both local and regional levels in the past four years, although some residents express concern that peace remains incomplete and vulnerable to setback. Much of the improvement can be attributed to the harnessing of LSAs, in this case 'people-to-people' peace-building efforts that have facilitated the work of tribal chiefs in brokering and maintaining peace.

Greater Kapoeta, comprising the newly established counties of North, East, and South Kapoeta, is a remote, poor, very rural, agro-pastoral zone in the eastern third of Eastern Equatoria State, bordering Ethiopia, Kenya, and Uganda (see Map 10.4). During the second civil war, the town of Kapoeta changed hands several times between the SPLA and the SAF. Relations between the SPLM/A and the Toposa, the dominant ethnic group, were often strained in the 1980s and 1990s: the Toposa were periodically allied with, and armed by, the SAF, which sought to exploit ethnic tensions between the Toposa and the Dinka. Kapoeta has long been a transit point in regional small arms trafficking in and out of Sudan. Agro-pastoral communities in Greater Kapoeta are heavily armed, mainly with semi-automatic weaponry. Some local traders engage in cross-border small arms trafficking, conducting transactions in remote locations.

Armed conflict in Kapoeta over the past five years has mainly involved communal clashes over cattle raiding, and control of land and water, which have produced growing fatalities and increased levels of food insecurity. This is partly attributable to the great importance attached to cattle raiding, both as a rite of passage and as the main source of bride-wealth for young men wishing to marry. The clashes can be grouped in three conflict zones: (1) eastern Kapoeta (toward the Ethiopian border), where gang-driven cattle rustling produces intermittent conflict between Toposa and Turkana, as well as Toposa and Murle; (2) southern Kapoeta (toward the Kenyan border), where Toposa and Turkana clash over cattle and the control of grazing; and (3) western/northern Kapoeta, where Toposa and

Box 10.4 Factors influencing demand for weapons in Kapoeta

Disaggregating the motivations that shape demand for weapons is complex in any context, because demand is conditioned by a range of factors that are geographically, ecologically, culturally, socially, and economically tied. Yet a more sophisticated understanding of demand is crucial to identifying incentives for disarmament in any given context.[66]

In Greater Kapoeta, community members reported the following key drivers of demand:

- Protection of livestock from raiding
- Protection of communal access to, and control over, pasture and wells
- Self-defence in the context of clashes between ethnic groups in the region
- Deterrence against incursion and attack by rival groups
- Use of small arms by young men to engage in cattle raiding
- Prestige and status linked to gun ownership
- Use of small arms by local posses to arrest criminals
- Protection of urban property from break-ins
- Commercial sale in cross-border arms markets, and
- Stockpiling of weapons in anticipation of disarmament programmes.

Most of the population is subsistence agro-pastoralist and, with the exception of Kapoeta town's modest market, the economy is generally non-monetized. Semi-automatic weapons are one of the few manufactured goods that local households possess. Though the price of a semi-automatic is low, at times dipping to as little as USD 20, acquisition of a weapon is one of the biggest purchases most households make. That such poor people are willing, or feel compelled, to acquire a small arm is testimony to the power of demand as a driver of domestic weapons flows.

Residents cite the ubiquity of weaponry and ammunition as both the chief source of insecurity and a valued source of deterrence against crime and attack. There is clear recognition of the need for some form of gun control, but in current circumstances there is also strong opposition to disarmament, which would render local communities vulnerable to cross-border raiding from Kenya, Uganda, and Ethiopia. Because the border area is a crossroads for the regional small arms market, demand and supply of small arms in Kapoeta are likely to remain robust for years to come.

Source: Menkhaus (2006)

Buye, and Toposa and Didinga clash over cattle and grass. Recent research highlights the fact that the major sources of insecurity in Greater Kapoeta occur along fault lines between its main ethnic groups—the Toposa, Turkana, Buye, Didinga, and Murle.

Two of Kapoeta's larger conflicts—the Toposa–Turkana and Toposa–Didinga clashes—have been the target of successful peace negotiations led by local chiefs, local NGOs, churches, and local government. The use of such hybrid, ad hoc peace committees is not new: at the height of SPLM/A clashes with tribal militias in Greater Kapoeta in 1992, the SPLM/A formed a committee of militia, civil, and church leaders to investigate and end the fighting. More recently, external aid agencies have actively supported local NGOs and church groups engaged in peace processes, with positive results. This engagement has involved cross-border diplomacy and mediation by the GoSS and the Government of Kenya in the case of the Toposa–Turkana peace talks (Menkhaus, 2006, p. 3).

Women, especially war widows, played a critical, initial role in the Toposa–Buye and Toposa–Turkana peace negotiations by unilaterally walking across conflict lines to make contact with ethnic rivals and to request peace talks. Women's roles as lines of communication and catalysts of conflict resolution—known locally as the 'women's crusade'—is new and significant in this area. Women are also making efforts to dismantle the culture of cattle rustling by refusing to recite praise poetry in support of raiding or killing. An important deterrent to local crime and instability in Toposa areas is the strong taboo against cattle raiding and fighting, a taboo reinforced by the fear of the curse, or *lam-lam*.

Though government capacity to consolidate tribal peace accords has been weak, an important dimension of improved security in Greater Kapoeta is the increased commitment by GoSS officials in Eastern Equatoria. Recent peace talks between the Buye and Toposa were brokered by a coalition of senior GoSS officials and local chiefs. This commitment is threatened by growing government impatience with cattle raiding, and an inclination to pursue arrests rather than rely on customary mechanisms to arrange the return of stolen cattle. Nevertheless, the emerging actors who are taking an increasingly active role in conflict resolution constitute a hybrid coalition with the potential to develop into a more sustained partnership. Carefully targeted external support could allow them to enhance their effectiveness (Menkhaus, 2006, p. 4). Designers of effective DDR strategies must be fully cognizant of these LSAs so as not inadvertently to undermine them as sources of protection and governance.

CONCLUSION

If the CPA is implemented, South Sudan will continue its long process of recovery. Post-conflict orthodoxy points to a number of phases in this recovery: political reconstruction to build up a legitimate and capable state; economic reconstruction to rebuild infrastructure and institutions; social reconstruction to renew civil society and limit the excesses of the state; and the provision of general security to establish a safer environment (Diamond, 2004, p. 2).

Most of the region's current problems can be attributed to the inability of the fledgling GoSS to mould itself into a functioning and transparent government. To date it has demonstrated little success in the areas of conflict mediation (with some exceptions at the local level, as noted above), the provision of basic services such as water, education, and health, the institution of the rule of law, and the protection of citizens and their property. Such an uncertain climate offers ordinary people little incentive to renounce their weapons voluntarily.

However, a framework for reducing armed violence is now beginning to emerge and it is essential that the GoSS establish and implement a formal SSR strategy, as part of which DDR, civilian disarmament, and the harnessing of LSAs can be implemented. To date competition between SPLM/A factions, inter-ethnic rivalries, the absence of an effective framework for the integration of OAGs, and ongoing insecurity have effectively undermined efforts to build a consensus on this. Yet SSR constitutes one of the essential pillars of post-conflict recovery (Small Arms Survey, 2005, p. 276). Indeed, any action to prevent the proliferation of small arms and light weapons and the establishment of effective and regulated security forces will be dependent on effective SSR.

After extensive consultation within the SPLM/A in late 2006, a National Security Council (NSC) was established within the GoSS, headed by Salva Kiir and incorporating most of the key actors in the SPLM/A. The establishment of this key policy and planning organ represents a major step forward, and provides the necessary platform from which small arms and other security-related issues can be addressed. It remains to be seen, however, whether the establishment of the NSC will enable the diverse views on security issues in South Sudan to be reconciled in effective policy and programme implementation.

In sum, South Sudan may have signed a high-level peace accord, but it remains highly unstable in numerous respects and may yet return to war. The challenge of addressing its many security concerns and preventing further conflict is only just beginning. ◾

ANNEXE 1. STATUS OF ALIGNED OTHER ARMED GROUPS IN SOUTH SUDAN AS OF APRIL 2007*

No.	Group	Associated commander/ leader	Area(s) of operations	Comments
Merged with SPLA prior to the signing of the CPA				
1	SSIM (SPLA)	James Leah	Nimni	Reunited/merged with SPLA prior to the signing of the CPA.
2	SPLM/A-U Main	Lam Akol	Tonga, Warjok, Wau, Shilluk, Wadokana, Dhor	Reunited/merged with SPLA prior to the signing of the CPA.
3	EDF Main	Col. Martin Kenyi	Magwe County	Reunited/merged with SPLA prior to the signing of the CPA.
OAGs aligned with SPLA after the Juba Declaration				
4	SSUM	Lt.-Gen. Paulino Matieb	Bentiu, Rubkona, Majom, Mankien, Wankay, Nhialdiu, Heglig, Kharasana	Aligned with SPLA after the Juba Declaration, but integration process not yet finalized.
5	SSIM (SAF)	Maj.-Gen. Peter Dor	K-7 (HQ, 7 km south of Rubkona), Rubkona, Mirmir, Kaj El Sherika, along the Rubkona-Leer oil road	Aligned with SPLA after the Juba Declaration, but integration process not yet finalized.
6	Pariang National Forces (GUM)	Maj.-Gen. Samuel Mayiek	Pariang, Mankwa, Beo El Madarasa, El Gor	Aligned with SPLA after the Juba Declaration, but integration process not yet finalized.
7	Peter Gatdet's Forces	Maj.-Gen. Peter Gatdet	Wankay, Bentiu, Rubkona	Aligned with SPLA after the Juba Declaration, but integration process not yet finalized.
8	Fangak Forces (Jebel Forces II)	Brig. John Both	Kaldak, Doleib Hill, Canal Mouth	Aligned with SPLA after the Juba Declaration.
9	SPLM/A-U II	Maj.-Gen. James Othow	Tonga, Warjok, Wau, Shilluk, Wadokana, Dhor	Aligned with SPLA after the Juba Declaration.
10	Sobat Force	Simon Yei	Khor Flus	Aligned with SPLA after the Juba Declaration.
11	Saddam Shayot's Faction	Maj.-Gen. Saddam Shayot	Adar, Balkok, Langshem, Ghor, Machar, Malual Gauth, Renk, Shomdi, Longchuck	Aligned with SPLA after the Juba Declaration.
12	Mading Forces/ Chol Gagak Group	Col. Chol Gagak	Nasir, Ketbek, Mading, Malual, with an area of operations overlapping with Gordon Kong's Thor Jikany	Aligned with SPLA after the Juba Declaration.
13	Simon Gatwitch's Group	Maj.-Gen. Simon Gatwitch	Yuai, Malut, Waat	Aligned with SPLA after the Juba Declaration, but integration process not yet finalized. A small splinter group went to Doleib Hill after the SPLA disarmament in Jonglei.

14	Peace and Reconstruction Brigade (Aweil Group I)	Sultan Abdel Bagi	El Miram, Bahr El Arab, Agok, Malual, Tadama, Um Driesi, Futa, Bringi	Aligned with SPLA after the Juba Declaration, but integration process not yet finalized. Two of Abdel Bagi's sons and their adherents are aligned with Khartoum.
15	Peace and Reconstruction Brigade (Aweil Group II)	Maj.-Gen. Abdel Aki Akol	Unknown or unavailable at the time of writing	After a violent struggle with Abdel Bagi's forces after the Juba Declaration, aligned with the SPLA in October 2006.
16	Mundari Forces I	Maj.-Gen Clement Wani Konga	Terekaka, Juba, Gemmaiza, Tali, Rejaf East and West	Officially aligned with SPLA in July 2006 but integration process not yet finalized. A sub-component of this group aligned with the SAF.
17	Bahr El Jebel Peace Forces (Bari Forces)	Mohamed El Laj/ Col. Paulino Tombe (Lonyombe)	Juba, Mongalia, Gadokoro Island, around Juba, Rajaf West	Some of the Bari Forces have joined the SPLA after the Juba Declaration, but SAF claims that one component of BPF is aligned with them.
18	SSLA	Brig.-Gen. Gabriel Yoal Doc	Akobo	SSLA has been divided into two components since a failed integration process in 2005. One component is aligned with SPLA and the other one (Akobo Force SSLM) is aligned with SAF.
19	SSDF First Division	Maj.-Gen. Tahib Ghathluak	Bentiu	It is unclear whether this group is incorporated into the SPLA or aligned and separate.
20	A Brigade	Brig.-Gen. Adhong Kuol	Pariang	It is unclear whether this group is incorporated into the SPLA or aligned and separate.
21	B Brigade	Brig.-Gen. Keribino Rual	Mayom	It is unclear whether this group is incorporated into the SPLA or aligned and separate.
22	C Brigade	Brig.-Gen. Nyial Gatduel	Rupkona	It is unclear whether this group is incorporated into the SPLA or aligned and separate.
23	D Brigade	Brig.-Gen. Gatewheel Yeal Roam	Malualkon	It is unclear whether this group is incorporated into the SPLA or aligned and separate.
24	Mobile Forces	Brig.-Gen. Samuel Both Tap	Tunga	It is unclear whether this group is incorporated into the SPLA or aligned and separate.
25	Longchuk Guelgook	Brig.-Gen. John Kang Rek	Longchuk	It is unclear whether this group is incorporated into the SPLA or aligned and separate.
26	Kaldak	Brig.-Gen. Peter Tor Nyuel	Kaldak	It is unclear whether this group is incorporated into the SPLA or aligned and separate.

27	Tiger Battalion	Brig.-Gen. Lueth Akol	Jalhag	It is unclear whether this group is incorporated into the SPLA or aligned and separate.
28	Jamam Maban Battalion	Brig.-Gen. Deng Many	Jamam Maban	It is unclear whether this group is incorporated into the SPLA or aligned and separate.
29	Jamus Brigade	Brig.-Gen. Chuol Gaga	Nasser	It is unclear whether this group is incorporated into the SPLA or aligned and separate.
30	Jamus Second Battalion	Col. Joseph Lual	Akobo	It is unclear whether this group is incorporated into the SPLA or aligned and separate.
31	Watt Battalion	Brig.-Gen. Joseph Bilieu	Waat	It is unclear whether this group is incorporated into the SPLA or aligned and separate.
32	Pibor Faction	Maj.-Gen. Ismael Konyi	Pibor, Fertit, Gamrok, Loyikwangali	
33	Popular Defence Forces	Col. Luciano Pasquel Ulaw	Tonj	
34	Al Fursan (Fursan Forces)	Al-Haj Basheer Mawein	Raja	
Not on recent SAF/SPLA lists: probably absorbed or disintegrated				
35	Adong Peace Forces II	Unknown or unavailable at the time of writing	Adong, Baiet, Olang	Has previously been reported by SPLA as aligned group. However, does not appear on the recent SAF/SPLA lists. Possibly absorbed or disintegrated.
OAGs aligned with SAF after the Juba Declaration comprising some SSDF groups and several splinter groups				
36	James Gai's faction	Col. James Gai	Bentiu, Rubkona	Small splinter group after SSUM and SSIM (SAF) when they decided to join SPLA after the Juba Declaration.
37	Tut Galuak's faction	Col. Tut Galuak	Mayom, Wankay	Small splinter group.
38	Bafanj Mantuel's faction	Col. Bafanj Mantuel	Fariang, Mankien, Kwach	Small splinter group.
39	Fariang faction	Col. Denis Kor	Fariang, El Tor, Fanshien, Biu, Mankwao	Small splinter group.
40	Abyei Forces (SSDF Abyei)	Thomas Thiel	Fariang, El Tor, Fanshien, Biu, Mankwao	Thomas Thiel was recalled to Khartoum when his harassment of the UN became an embarrassment for SAF, but his group is still located in Abyei.

41	Nasir Group (Thor Jikany)	Maj.-Gen. Gordon Kong	Ketbek (HQ, 3 km south of Nasir), Nasir, Mading, Ulang, Kadbit, El Desin	As reported by SAF to the OAG Collaborative Committee.
42	Fangak Forces (Jebel Forces)	Maj.-Gen. Gabriel Tang-Ginya	Bashlakon, Fangak, Deil, Kwerkan, Kwerdaf, Faguer, Fag, Kaldak, Dor	As reported by SAF to the OAG Collaborative Committee.
43	Sabri Achol's Forces	Col. Sabri Achol	Akoka, Fanmadid, Rom	As reported by SAF to the OAG Collaborative Committee.
44	Akobo Faction (Akobo Force SSLM)	Brig. Koith Simon	Akobo, El Nasser, Denjok, Wallak, Alalli, Achuil, Bormad, Yakwach	As reported by SAF to the OAG Collaborative Committee.
45	Dinni Forces	Brig. Hassan Doyak	Dinni, Glashiel	As reported by SAF to the OAG Collaborative Committee.
46	The United Faction (SPLM/A-U II)	Brig. Ashuang Arop	Tonga, Warjok, Wau, Shilluk, Wadokana, Dhor	As reported by SAF to the OAG Collaborative Committee. A splinter group from James Othow's group when he decided to join SPLA after the Juba Declaration.
47	Doleib Forces	Maj.-Gen. Thomas Maboir	Doleib, Waj Mabor, Khor Flus, Wat	As reported by SAF to the OAG Collaborative Committee.
48	Yuai Faction	Col. David Hoth Lual	Doleib, Waj Mabor, Khor Flus, Wat	As reported by SAF to the OAG Collaborative Committee. A splinter group from Simon Gatwitch's group when he decided to join SPLA after the Juba Declaration.
49	Bor Salvation Forces (Bor Group)	Col. Kelia Deng Kelly	Bor	As reported by SAF to the OAG Collaborative Committee. However, sources within SPLA also claim that the Bor Group has decided to join SPLA.
50	Balkok Forces	Maj.-Gen. John Duet	Balkok, Langshek, Ruam, Khor Machar, Malual Gauth, Luak, Adar	As reported by SAF to the OAG Collaborative Committee.
51	Renk Faction	Brig. Mohamed Chol Al Ahmar	Renk, Shomdi, Al Mansura, Goy Fammi, Wadakona, Al Tuba, Madimar, Kaka	As reported by SAF to the OAG Collaborative Committee.
52	Mellut Faction	Col. William Deng	Melut, Kom, Falloj, Deltima, Fariak	As reported by SAF to the OAG Collaborative Committee.
53	Maban Forces	Lt. Col. Musa Doula	El Jamam, Kajuri, El Bonj	As reported by SAF to the OAG Collaborative Committee.
54	Allak Deng Faction (Northern Upper Nile Group)	Lt. Col. Allak Deng	Melut, Falloj, Fariak	As reported by SAF to the OAG Collaborative Committee.

55	Mading Forces	Lt. Col. Peter Tuaj	Nasir, Ketbek, Mading, Malual, with an area of operations overlapping with Gordon Kong's Thor Jikany, Baljok, Mayor, Forinang	As reported by SAF to the OAG Collaborative Committee.
56	El Nasser Forces	John Jok	Dit, El Deshin, Kech, Abiech, Ram Kiir	As reported by SAF to the OAG Collaborative Committee.
57	National Peace Forces (Fertit)	Maj.-Gen. El Tom El Nur Daldom	Bazia, Geitan, Taban, Buseri, Halima, Baggara, Angessa, Farajalla, Ambor, Boro El Medina, Katta Manaba, Khor Ghana, Dem Zuber, Ayabello, Sabo, Mangayat, Raja, Tumsah, Abu Shoka, Ghatena	As reported by SAF to the OAG Collaborative Committee.
58	Kaltok Forces	Lt. Col. Gabriel Mading Fon	Kaltok	As reported by SAF to the OAG Collaborative Committee.
59	Mundari Forces II	Unknown	Terekeka, Juba Road, Tali, Rejaf East, Kaltok, Jemeiza, Sudan Safari, Jebel Lado, Tali Road	As reported by SAF to the OAG Collaborative Committee.
60	EDF II	Brig. Fabiano Odongi	Torit, Juba, Torit Road, mountains around Torit	As reported by SAF to the OAG Collaborative Committee.
61	Toposa Forces	Chief Lokipapa/ Brig. Justin Akodo	Juba, Jabur, Lafon	As reported by SAF to the OAG Collaborative Committee.
62	Bahr El Jebel Peace Forces (Bari Forces) II	Mohamed El Laj/ Col. Paulino Tombe (Lonyombe)	Juba, Mongalia, Gadokoro Island, around Juba, Rajaf West	As reported by SAF to the OAG Collaborative Committee.
63	Boya Forces	Lt. Col. Mohamed Losek	Torit, Chukudum, Nokchok	As reported by SAF to the OAG Collaborative Committee.
64	Didinga Forces	Brig. Peter Lorot	Didinga hills, Chukudum hills, Chukudum, Nokchok	As reported by SAF to the OAG Collaborative Committee.
65	Lafon Forces	Col. Kamal Ramadan Balento	Lakoro/Lafon	As reported by SAF to the OAG Collaborative Committee.
66	West Equatoria Forces (Western EDF)	Maj. Samuel Steward	Juba, Coda	As reported by SAF to the OAG Collaborative Committee.
67	Akoka Peace Forces	Brig. Thon Amum	Akoka, Fanmadid, Rom	As reported by SAF to the OAG Collaborative Committee.
68	Saddam Shayot's Faction II	Unknown or unavailable at the time of writing	Adar, Balkok, Langshem, Ghor, Machar, Malual Gauth, Renk, Shomdi, Longchuck	As reported by SAF to the OAG Collaborative Committee.

* This list is not exhaustive.

Source: Young (2006b, pp. 42-48), updated

LIST OF ABBREVIATIONS

CPA	Comprehensive Peace Agreement	NSC	National Security Council
DDR	disarmament, demobilization, and reintegration	OAG	Other Armed Group
		PDF	Popular Defence Forces
DRC	Democratic Republic of the Congo	RPG	rocket-propelled grenade (launcher)
EDF	Equatoria Defence Force	SAF	Sudanese Armed Forces
GNU	Government of National Unity	SPLM/A	Sudan People's Liberation Movement/ Army
GoS	Government of Sudan		
GoSS	Government of South Sudan	SSDDRC	South Sudan Disarmament, Demobiliza- tion, and Reintegration Commission
GoU	Government of Uganda		
HSBA	Human Security Baseline Assessment	SSDF	South Sudan Defence Forces
JIU	Joint Integrated Unit	SSR	security sector reform
LRA	Lord's Resistance Army	SSUDA	South Sudan United Democratic Alliance
LSA	local security arrangement	UNMIS	UN Mission in Sudan
NCP	National Congress Party	UPDF	Ugandan People's Defence Forces

ENDNOTES

1   As of 1 January 2006 the top five recipients of Sudan's refugees were neighbouring Central African Republic, Chad, Ethiopia, Kenya, and Uganda. See <http://www.unhcr.org/basics/BASICS/3b028097c.html#Numbers>

2   Correspondence with US government officials, November 2006.

3   For more on the HSBA research project, see <http://www.smallarmssurvey.org/sudan>

4   For 2007 alone, nearly USD 1.3 billion is required for humanitarian activities and USD 560 million for recovery and development in Sudan. Of those totals, USD 279 million and USD 349 million, respectively, are for the south. See UNOCHA (2006b, pp. 6–10).

5   Lacina and Gleditsch (2005) estimate that the conflict claimed these lives between 1983 and 2002. The overwhelming majority (97 per cent) died from indirect causes, such as disease and malnutrition.

6   See UNHCR (2006).

7   The CPA is a collection of separate agreements negotiated up to 31 December 2004 and signed in a formal ceremony on 9 January 2005. They are: the Machakos Protocol (20 July 2002); Agreement on Security Arrangements (25 September 2003); Agreement on Wealth Sharing (7 January 2004); Protocol on Power Sharing (26 May 2004); Protocol on the Resolution of Conflict in Southern Kordofan/Nuba Mountains and Blue Nile States (26 May 2004); Protocol on the Resolution of Abyei Conflict (26 May 2004); Implementation Modalities of the Protocol on Power Sharing (31 December 2004); and Permanent Ceasefire and Security Arrangements Implementation Modalities (31 December 2004). See the full text of the agreement at <http://www.reliefweb.int/rw/RWB.NSF/db900SID/EVIU-6AZBDB?OpenDocument>

8   CPA (Agreement on Security Arrangements, para. 7(a)). Members of OAGs may either be incorporated into the respective armies, police, prisons, or wildlife forces of the signatories or reintegrated into society.

9   The full text of the Juba Declaration is available at <http://www.issafrica.org/AF/profiles/sudan/darfur/jubadecljan06.pdf>

10 Recent HSBA field research has found that new SSDF members are now being recruited to replace those who have joined the SPLA. For more information on the SSDF see Young (2006c).

11 For the latest figures on regional displacement see UN Human Rights Council (2007, p. 13) and UNSC (2007b, p. 3).

12 See USGAO (2006) for details on the debate surrounding the numbers of dead in Darfur. See also Tanner and Tubiana (2007) on armed groups operating in Darfur.

13 The following agreements have been signed: Humanitarian Ceasefire Agreement, 8 April 2004, N'Djamena, Chad; Protocol on the Establishment of Humanitarian Assistance in Darfur, 8 April 2004, N'Djamena, Chad; Agreement on the Modalities for the Establishment of the Ceasefire Commission and the Deployment of Observers, 28 May 2004, Addis Ababa, Ethiopia; Protocol on the Improvement of the Humanitarian Situation in Darfur, 9 November 2004, Abuja, Nigeria; Protocol of the Enhancement of the Security Situation in Darfur, 9 November 2004, Abuja, Nigeria;

Declaration of Principles for the Resolution of the Sudanese Conflict in Darfur, 5 July 2005, Abuja, Nigeria; and Darfur Peace Agreement, 5 May 2006. All are available at <http://www.unmis.org/english/2006Docs/DPA_ABUJA-5-05-06-withSignatures.pdf>

14   UN Security Council resolutions include resolution 1556 (30 July 2004), which paves the way for action against the GoS; resolution 1564 (18 September 2004), which states that sanctions will be considered; resolution 1591 (29 March 2005), which approves a travel ban and asset freeze for individuals accused of international crimes in Darfur; and resolution 1672 (25 April 2006), which imposes sanctions on four Sudanese individuals accused of human rights violations.

15   See Small Arms Survey (2006e) for background information on the Darfur Peace Agreement.

16   See report of the UN International Commission of Inquiry on Darfur (2005) and UN Human Rights Council (2007) for details on widespread abuses of human rights and humanitarian law committed by GoS-aligned and rebel forces in Darfur. UN Security Council Resolution 1593 (31 March 2005) has permitted the International Criminal Court to examine and act on alleged violations of international criminal law.

17   By November 2006 approximately four million people, or two-thirds of the entire population of Darfur, were in need of humanitarian assistance. During the last six months of 2006, more relief workers were killed than in the previous two years combined. In December 2006 alone, 29 humanitarian vehicles were hijacked in Darfur and 430 relief workers relocated. See UNSC (2007a, p. 5) and UN Human Rights Council (2007, p. 16).

18   For information on the regional impact of the conflict, in particular on the Central African Republic, see Small Arms Survey (2007a).

19   See UN Panel of Experts on Sudan (2006) at <http://www.un.org/Docs/journal/asp/ws.asp?m=s/2006/795>

20   See ESPA (2006). See also Young (2007b) for more on the Eastern Front.

21   Under the terms of the CPA, the SPLM controls 70 per cent of positions in the GoSS; the other southern parties 15 per cent; and the NCP 15 per cent.

22   The GoSS Assembly is currently demanding accountability for the defence budget, which consumes more than one-third of the government's entire budget. See Young (2007a, p. 13).

23   This sections draws upon information and analysis from Young (2006c).

24   Critically, it did not specify when that referendum would take place.

25   See CPA (Agreement on Permanent Ceasefire and Security Arrangements Implementation Modalities, para. 11.9). This date was subsequently extended to 9 March 2006, after which alignments were considered illegal.

26   The JIUs were designed as a symbol of national unity during the interim period and will form the nucleus of a national army in the event of a united Sudan. They are to contain equal numbers of SAF and SPLA and to be based in the following areas: South Sudan (24,000); Nuba Mountains (6,000); southern Blue Nile (6,000); and Khartoum (3,000). See CPA (Agreement on Security Arrangements, paras. 4 and 4.1).

27   Young (2007a) examines the uncertainty surrounding the numbers of SSDF, who remain aligned with Khartoum.

28   While precise numbers remain unclear, by April 2007 OAG members aligned with Khartoum were estimated to number fewer than 10,000.

29   Observations on field visit to Ketbec, August 2006.

30   See <http://www.ecosonline.org/> for general information on Sudan's oil industry.

31   See <http://www.sudantribune.com/IMG/pdf/oilfieldmap_Sudan_ECOS.pdf> to view Sudan's oil concessions.

32   Interview with county commissioner in Adar, August 2006.

33   Interviews with senior GoSS officials in Malakal, August 2006.

34   Interviews with senior SPLA officials in Malakal, August 2006.

35   Email correspondence with Peter Chuol Gatluak, SSDF Secretary General and spokesman, March 2007.

36   This section is from Schomerus (2006).

37   For more information on the LRA, see Small Arms Survey (2006a, ch. 11).

38   Interview with SPLA officer, Maridi, June–September 2006. This may have been a last attempt by Khartoum to maintain relations with the group.

39   This section is based on Young (2006a).

40   This section is based upon Garfield (2007).

41   CPA (Agreement on Security Arrangements, para. 3(b), and Permanent Ceasefire and Security Arrangements Implementation Modalities, para. 18.2).

42   CPA (Agreement on Security Arrangements, paras. 4(c) and 3(c), and Permanent Ceasefire and Security Arrangements Implementation Modalities, para. 18.5).

43   Having determined that the situation in Sudan constituted a threat to international peace and security, the UN Security Council established UNMIS (Resolution 1590 of 24 March 2005). Its mandate includes monitoring and verifying the implementation of the ceasefire, investigating violations, observing movements of armed groups, and assisting with DDR. As of 28 February 2007 the Mission's strength was 9,978 uniformed personnel, supported by more than three thousand civilian personnel.

44   Both sides are said to be reluctant to commit their best men and equipment to the JIUs for fear of an outbreak of future hostilities.

45   Relations between the SPLA and the SAF are characterized by mutual distrust and a general lack of transparency. The SPLA, in particular, has a history of inflating its figures to ensure respect from the SAF, which has always been superior in terms of access to technology and air power.

46   CPA (Agreement on Security Arrangements, para. 3(e)).

47   CPA (Agreement on Permanent Ceasefire and Security Arrangements Implementation Modalities, para. 24.6).

48   CPA (Agreement on Permanent Ceasefire and Security Arrangements Implementation Modalities, para. 24.3).

49   CPA (Agreement on Permanent Ceasefire and Security Arrangements Implementation Modalities, para. 19).

50   Notably, the GoS has already rejected the findings of the Abyei Boundary Commission, which placed oil-producing areas in South Sudan.

51   Young (2007a) contains a detailed examination of this thesis.

52   Since 1999 areas of Unity, Upper Nile, and Western Kordofan States have been producing oil. Both the GoSS and oil-producing states in the South maintain they are not receiving their fair share of oil revenues from Khartoum, in violation of the CPA (UNSC, 2007c, para. 19).

53   Interviews with UN officials, Abyei, February 2007.

54   The CPA stipulates that the JIUs are to monitor oil fields that are to be 'demilitarized', but this has yet to be implemented.

55   This section is based on Young (2006b). For a review of civilian disarmament, see Small Arms Survey 2006(d).

56   Notably, while the CPA calls for DDR of armed groups, it provides comparatively little guidance on the question of disarming civilians. The CPA's only reference to civilian disarmament is in section 14.6.5.15 of the Agreement on Permanent Ceasefire and Security Arrangements Implementation Modalities, which empowers the Ceasefire Joint Military Committee to 'monitor and verify the disarmament of all Sudanese civilians who are illegally armed'. This clause gives rise to two problems: first, there is a lack of clarity about what constitutes 'illegal' in this context since gun laws have not yet been enacted in South Sudan; second, the distinction between civilians and combatants is far from clear.

57   Interview with UN official in Malakal, 23 August 2006.

58   Interview with SPLM official in Motot, 25 August 2006.

59   These figures are very rough estimates.

60   In January 2007 local residents said in interviews that it was impossible to buy guns locally since the disarmament and that they feared being caught with them by local authorities. Punishments being meted out include fines, being beaten and having guns confiscated.

61   The UN did not participate in, or actively support, the forcible disarmament in northern Jonglei State.

62   At a February 2007 workshop on civilian disarmament Vice-President of South Sudan Riek Machar indicated that collected weapons may be recycled for police forces in South Sudan.

63   A 22 August 2006 UNMIS press release greatly overemphasized the voluntary nature of the process. See <http://www.unmis.org/English/2006 Docs/PR36.pdf>

64   Communications with senior UN DDR officials, November 2006.

65   This section is from Menkhaus (2006).

66   See Small Arms Survey (2006a, pp. 141–63).

BIBLIOGRAPHY

ASAP (African Security Analysis Programme). 2004a. *The South Sudan Defence Force: A Challenge to the Sudan Peace Process.* Pretoria: Institute for Security Studies. 8 April. <http://www.iss.co.za/AF/current/2004/sudanapr04.pdf>

——. 2004b. *The Sudan IGAD Peace Process: Signposts for the Way Forward.* Occasional Paper 86. Pretoria: Institute for Security Studies. March. <http://www.iss.org.za/pubs/papers/86/Paper86.htm>

Babiker, Mohammed and Alpaslan Ozerdem. 2003. 'A Future Disarmament, Demobilization and Reintegration Process in Sudan: Lessons Learned from Ethiopia, Mozambique, and Uganda.' *Conflict, Security and Development.* Vol. 3, No. 2. August, pp. 211–32.

Bechtold, Peter K. 1990. 'More Turbulence in Sudan: A New Politics This Time?' In John O. Voll, ed. *Sudan: State and Society in Crisis.* 1991. Washington, DC: Middle East Institute. Ch. 1, pp. 1–23.

CPA (Comprehensive Peace Agreement). 2005. Signed between the Government of Sudan and the Sudan People's Liberation Movement/Army, Nairobi. 9 January. <http://www.reliefweb.int/library/documents/2005/sud-sud-09janPart%20II.pdf>

Darfur Peace Agreement. 2006. Signed between the Government of Sudan and the Sudan Liberation Movement/Army (Minni Arkou Minawi), Abuja. 5 May. <http://allafrica.com/peaceafrica/resources/view/00010926.pdf>

Decaillet, Francois, Patrick Mullen, and Moncef Guen. 2003. *Sudan Health Status Report.* Draft version 1. Washington, DC: World Bank/AFTH3. 20 August. <http://www.emro.who.int/sudan/media/pdf/Sudan%20Health%20Status%20Report%20August%202003.pdf>

DFID (Department for International Development). 2006. *Every DDR is Unique: A Review of DFID Support to the Interim Disarmament, Demobilization and Reintegration Programme in Sudan.* Unpublished. 6 November.

Diamond, Larry. 2004. 'What Went Wrong in Iraq.' *Foreign Affairs.* Vol. 83, No. 5. September/October.

ESPA (Eastern Sudan Peace Agreement). 2006. Signed between the Government of Sudan and the Eastern Front, Asmara. 14 October. <http://www.sudantribune.com/IMG/pdf/Eastern_Sudan_Peace_Agreement.pdf>

Florquin, Nicolas and Eric G. Berman. 2005. *Armed and Aimless: Armed Groups, Guns, and Human Security in the ECOWAS Region.* Geneva: Small Arms Survey.

Gakmar, Chol Gidion. *Disarmament, Demobilization, Reintegration, and the Rights of Former Combatants*. Committee of the Civil Project in Sudan. Issue Paper E-4. London: Justice Africa. <http://www.justiceafrica.org/wp-content/uploads/2006/07/CivilProject_IssuePaperE4_Demobilization.pdf>

Garfield, Richard. 2007. *Violence and Victimization in South Sudan: Lakes State in the Post-CPA period*. HSBA Working Paper No. 2. Geneva: Small Arms Survey. February. <http://www.smallarmssurvey.org/files/portal/spotlight/sudan/Sudan_pdf/SWP%202%20Lakes%20State.pdf>

Hagan, John and Alberto Palloni. 2006. 'Death in Darfur.' *Science*. Vol. 313, No. 5793, pp. 1578–79. 15 September.

Hagedorn, John. 2001. 'Globalization, Gangs, and Collaborative Research.' In Klein et al., eds. *The Eurogang Paradox: Street Gangs and Youth Groups in the U.S. and Europe*. Dordrecht: Kluwer Academic Publishers, pp. 41–58.

Hartzell, Caroline, Matthew Hoddie, and Donald Rothchild. 2001. 'Stabilizing the Peace after Civil War: An Investigation of Some Key Variables.' *International Organization*. Vol. 55, No. 1, pp. 183–208.

Hutchinson, Sharon E. 2001. 'A Curse from God? Religious and Political Dimensions of the Post-1991 Rise of Ethnic Violence in South Sudan.' *Journal of Modern African Studies*. Vol. 39, No. 2, pp. 307–31.

ICG (International Crisis Group). 2006. *Sudan's Comprehensive Peace Agreement: The Long Road Ahead*. Africa Report No. 106. Nairobi/Brussels: ICG. 31 March. <http://www.crisisgroup.org/home/index.cfm?l=1&id=4055>

IDDRP (Interim Disarmament, Demobilization and Reintegration Programme) for Sudan. 2005. Khartoum: Government of Sudan Interim DDR Authorities, SPLM/A Interim DDR Authorities, and UN DDR Unit. Unpublished. December.

Johnson, Douglas H. 2003. *The Root Causes of Sudan's Civil Wars*. Oxford: James Currey.

Jooma, Mariam. 2005. *Feeding the Peace: Challenges Facing Human Security in Post-Garang South Sudan*. Pretoria: Institute for Security Studies. 23 August. <http://www.reliefweb.int/library/documents/2005/iss-sdn-23aug.pdf>

Juba Declaration on Unity and Integration between the Sudan People's Liberation Army and the South Sudan Defence Force. 2006. Juba, 8 January. <http://www.issafrica.org/AF/profiles/sudan/darfur/jubadecljan06.pdf>

Lacina, Bethany and Nils Petter Gleditsch. 2005. 'Monitoring Trends in Global Combat: A New Dataset of Battle Deaths.' *European Journal of Population*. Vol. 21, Nos. 2–3, pp. 145–66. June.

MENAANSA (Middle East North Africa Action Network on Small Arms). 2006. *Public Perceptions of Small Arms and Light Weapons and Community Security in the Middle East*. Amman: MENAANSA. February.
  <http://www.smallarmssurvey.org/files/portal/spotlight/country/nafr_pdf/mideast-leb-pales-sudan-2006_en.pdf>

Menkhaus, Kenneth. 2006. *Local Security Arrangements: Greater Kapoeta Case Study*. Unpublished background paper. Small Arms Survey: Geneva. January.

Millennium Project. 2004. *Investing in Development: A Practical Plan to Achieve the Millennium Development Goals*. New York: United Nations.

Mullen, Joseph. 2005. *Traditional Authorities and Local Governance in Post-CPA Southern Sudan*. Rumbek: UN Development Programme. June.

NSCSE (New Sudan Centre for Statistics and Evaluation)/UNICEF. 2004. *Towards a Baseline: Best Estimates of Social Indicators for Southern Sudan*. Series Paper No. 1. Khartoum: NSCSE. May.

Pronk, Jan. 2006. Blog of Jan Pronk, Special Representative of the UN Secretary-General in Sudan 2004–06. Accessed in December.
  <http://www.janpronk.nl/index2.html>

Richer, Michaleen. 2002. *Overview of the Health Situation in Southern Sudan*. Nairobi: UNICEF.
  <http://info.worldbank.org/etools/docs/library/33440/UNICEF%20OLS%20Health%20Overview%20%20-%20Narrative.pdf>

Rogier, Emeric. 2005. *Designing an Integrated Strategy for Peace, Security, and Development in Post-agreement Sudan*. Occasional Paper. The Hague: Clingendael Institute. April. <http://www.clingendael.nl/publications/2005/20050400_cru_paper_rogier.pdf>

Schomerus, Mareike. 2006. *The LRA in Sudan*. Unpublished background paper. Geneva: Small Arms Survey. September.

Scott, Philippa. 1985. 'The Sudan People's Liberation Movement and Liberation Army.' *Review of African Political Economy*. Vol. 12, No. 33, pp. 69–82.

Small Arms Survey. 2005. *Small Arms Survey 2005: Weapons at War*. Oxford: Oxford University Press.

——. 2006a. *Small Arms Survey 2006: Unfinished Business*. Oxford: Oxford University Press.

——. 2006b. *Persistent Threats: Widespread Human Insecurity in Lakes State, South Sudan, Since the CPA*. Sudan Issue Brief No.1. Geneva: Small Arms Survey. September.

——. 2006c. *Armed Groups in Sudan: The South Sudan Defence Forces in the Aftermath of the Juba Declaration*. Sudan Issue Brief No. 2. Geneva: Small Arms Survey. October.

——. 2006d. *Anatomy of Civilian Disarmament in Jonglei State: Recent Experiences and Implications*. Sudan Issue Brief No. 3, 2nd ed. Geneva: Small Arms Survey. November 2006–February 2007.

——. 2006e. *No Dialogue, No Commitment: The Perils of Deadline Diplomacy for Darfur*. Sudan Issue Brief No. 4. Geneva: Small Arms Survey. December.

——. 2007a. *A Widening of War around Sudan: The Proliferation of Armed Groups in the Central African Republic*. Sudan Issue Brief No. 5. January.

——. 2007b. *The Militarization of Sudan: A Preliminary Review of Arms Flows and Stockpiles*. Sudan Issue Brief No. 6. Geneva: Small Arms Survey. April. <http//:www.smallarmssurvey.org/sudan>

Sudan Tribune. 2006. 'Sudan Defence Minister Directs Southern Militia to Go to the North.' 6 December.
<http://sudantribune.com/spip.php?page=imprimable&id_article=19097>

Tanner, Victor and Jérôme Tubiana. 2007. *Divisions and Continuity: The Rebel Movements of Darfur*. Unpublished background paper. Geneva: Small Arms Survey. January. <http://www.smallarmssurvey.org/files/portal/spotlight/sudan/sudan.html>

Tealakh, Gali Oda, Atef Odibat, and Maha Al Shaer. 2002. *Small Arms and Light Weapons in the Arab Region: National and Regional Measures*. Proceedings of the regional workshop on 6–7 May, 2001. Amman: Regional Human Security Center at the Jordan Institute of Diplomacy. <http://www.mena-small-arms.org/SALW_in_the_Arab_Region-RHSC.pdf>

UNHCR (UN High Commissioner for Refugees). 2006. *Measuring Protection by Numbers*. November. <http://www.unhcr.org/publ/PUBL/4579701b2.pdf>

UN Human Rights Council. 2007. *Report of the High-Level Mission on the situation of human rights in Darfur persuant to Human Rights Council decision S-4/101*. A/HRC/4/80 of 7 March. Advance unedited version. <http://www.ohchr.org/english/index.htm>

UN International Commission of Inquiry on Darfur. 2005. *Report of International Commission of Inquiry on Darfur*. S/2005/60 of 1 February. <http://www.unmis.org/English/documents/SG-ReportsOnSudan/s2005-60.pdf>

UNMIS (UN Mission in Sudan). 2006a. *The CPA Monitor*. November.

——. 2006b. 'The UN Hails the Successful Completion of Community-Driven Disarmament in Akobo, Jonglei State.' Press release No. 36/06 of 22 August. <http://www.unmis.org/English/2006Docs/PR36.pdf>

——. 2007. *The CPA Monitor*. February. <http://www.unmis.org/english/cpaMonitor.htm>

UNOCHA (UN Office for the Coordination of Humanitarian Affairs). 2006a. 'Sudan: Calm after Heavy Fighting in Southern Town.' *IRIN News*. 30 November. <http://www.irinnews.org/report.asp?ReportID=56576&SelectRegion=East_Africa&SelectCountry=SUDAN>

——. 2006b. *United Nations and Partners 2007 Workplan for Sudan*. Vol. 1. <http://www.reliefweb.int/rw/rwb.nsf/db900SID/EGUA-6WGTW9?OpenDocument&rc=1&emid=ACOS-635PJQ>

UN Panel of Experts Established Pursuant to Security Council Resolution 1591 (2005) Concerning the Sudan. 2006. *Report of the Panel of Experts*. S/2006/795 of 30 October. <http://daccessdds.un.org/doc/UNDOC/GEN/N06/490/87/PDF/N0649087.pdf?OpenElement>

UNSC (UN Security Council). 2007a. *Monthly Report of the Secretary-General on Darfur*. S/2007/104 of 23 February. <http://daccessdds.un.org/doc/UNDOC/GEN/N07/245/97/PDF/N0724597.pdf?OpenElement>

——. 2007b. *Monthly Report of the Secretary-General on Chad and the Central African Republic*. S/2007/97of 23 February. <http://daccessdds.un.org/doc/UNDOC/GEN/N07/242/07/PDF/N0724207.pdf?OpenElement>

——. 2007c. Report of the Secretary-General on the Sudan. S/2007/213 of 17 April. <http://www.reliefweb.int/rw/RWFiles2007.nsf/FilesByRWDocUnid Filename/C321D14780DE7DC0492572C30003E8F8-Full_Report.pdf/$File/Full_Report.pdf>

UN Sudan Joint Assessment Mission. 2005. *Synthesis: Framework for Sustained Peace, Development, and Poverty Eradication*. Vol. 1. 18 March. <http://www.unsudanig.org/JAM/drafts/final/JAM-report-volume-I.pdf>

USGAO (United States Government Accountability Office). 2006. *Darfur Crisis: Death Estimates Demonstrate Severity of Crisis, but Their Accuracy and Credibility Could Be Enhanced*. GAO-07-24 of 9 November. <http://www.gao.gov/new.items/d0724.pdf>

Young, John. 2006a. *White Army: A Briefing*. Unpublished background paper. Geneva: Small Arms Survey. September.

——. 2006b. *The South Sudan Defence Forces in the Wake of the Juba Declaration*. HSBA Working Paper No. 1. Geneva: Small Arms Survey. November.

——. 2006c. *SPLA Civilian Disarmament: A Briefing*. Unpublished background paper. Geneva: Small Arms Survey. September.

——. 2007a. *Conflict Scenarios: Emerging Tensions on the North–South Border*. Unpublished background paper. Geneva: Small Arms Survey. March.

——. 2007b. *The Eastern Front and the Struggle against Marginalization*. HSBA Working Paper No. 3. Geneva: Small Arms Survey. May.

——. 2007c. *The Origins and Development of the White Army*. HSBA Working Paper No. 5. Geneva: Small Arms Survey. June.

ACKNOWLEDGEMENTS

Principal author

Claire Mc Evoy

Contributors

Matthew Arnold, Jeremy Brickhill, Richard Garfield, Anders Haugland, Matthew LeRiche, Ken Menkhaus, Mareike Schomerus, and John Young

INDEX